4th Watch Books™

Forward

Our purpose for publishing the documents issued by the National Institute of Standards and Technology (NIST) is twofold. First of all, each NIST title in and of itself is very informative, however I am of the opinion that they should be looked at from the standpoint that each title is an integral part of a holistic cybersecurity strategy. Rather than look at each title just by itself, we need to look at them in groups based on how they are interrelated and designed to work together to improve cybersecurity.

For example, this particular group on PRIVACY SECURITY includes the following titles:

NIST SP 800-53 R 4	Security and Privacy Controls for Federal Information Systems and Organizations
NIST SP 800-53A R 4	Assessing Security and Privacy Controls
NIST SP 800-122	Guide to Protecting the Confidentiality of Personally Identifiable Information (PII)
NIST SP 800-188	De-Identifying Government Datasets - (2nd DRAFT)
NISTIR 8053	De-Identification of Personal Information
NISTIR 8062	Introduction to Privacy Engineering and Risk Management in Federal Systems

In order to assemble the entire picture of privacy security – from what it is, how it works, what the vulnerabilities are, and how to mitigate them, one must assemble all of these documents. Only by going through all of them can a person understand the complete picture. Leave one of them out and you would be missing a valuable piece of the privacy security puzzle.

Why buy a book you can download for free?

That brings me to the second reason to publish the NIST standards and that is the logistics of it all. These 7 publications consist of 771 pages. That's enough paper to fill two large three-ring binders. Nobody has a secretary anymore, so an engineer that is paid $75 an hour has to do this. The amount of time it would take an engineer to print all 7 publications (using a network printer shared with 100 other people – and it's out of paper, and the toner is low), punch holes in 771 pages and assemble the binders would easily take half a day.

Our ability to deliver any NIST document quickly and efficiently is unmatched because we are printing books on demand and we are backed up by Amazon, so the titles are easy to find and simple to order. Just search Amazon.com by NIST number and you can have a copy shipped to you in a matter of days. We print all books a full 8 ½ inches by 11 inches, with large text. If there are color images in the publication, the book is probably in color, unless the color is merely decorative, in which case we print in black and white to keep the cost to you as low as possible.

Luis Ayala,
My email is cybah@webplus.net   Our website is: cybah.webplus.net
4th Watch Books is a Service Disabled Veteran Owned Small Business (SDVOSB).

Copyright © 2017 – 4th Watch Books Co.

NIST Special Publication 800-53
Revision 4

Security and Privacy Controls for Federal Information Systems and Organizations

JOINT TASK FORCE
TRANSFORMATION INITIATIVE

This publication is available free of charge from:
http://dx.doi.org/10.6028/NIST.SP.800-53r4

NIST Special Publication 800-53
Revision 4

Security and Privacy Controls for Federal Information Systems and Organizations

JOINT TASK FORCE
TRANSFORMATION INITIATIVE

This publication is available free of charge from:
http://dx.doi.org/10.6028/NIST.SP.800-53r4

April 2013
INCLUDES UPDATES AS OF 01-22-2015

U.S. Department of Commerce
Rebecca M. Blank, Acting Secretary

National Institute of Standards and Technology
Patrick D. Gallagher, Under Secretary of Commerce for Standards and Technology and Director

Authority

This publication has been developed by NIST to further its statutory responsibilities under the Federal Information Security Management Act (FISMA), Public Law (P.L.) 107-347. NIST is responsible for developing information security standards and guidelines, including minimum requirements for federal information systems, but such standards and guidelines shall not apply to national security systems without the express approval of appropriate federal officials exercising policy authority over such systems. This guideline is consistent with the requirements of the Office of Management and Budget (OMB) Circular A-130, Section 8b(3), *Securing Agency Information Systems*, as analyzed in Circular A-130, Appendix IV: *Analysis of Key Sections*. Supplemental information is provided in Circular A-130, Appendix III, *Security of Federal Automated Information Resources*.

Nothing in this publication should be taken to contradict the standards and guidelines made mandatory and binding on federal agencies by the Secretary of Commerce under statutory authority. Nor should these guidelines be interpreted as altering or superseding the existing authorities of the Secretary of Commerce, Director of the OMB, or any other federal official. This publication may be used by nongovernmental organizations on a voluntary basis and is not subject to copyright in the United States. Attribution would, however, be appreciated by NIST.

National Institute of Standards and Technology Special Publication 800-53, Revision 4
462 pages (April 2013)
CODEN: NSPUE2

This publication is available free of charge from: http://dx.doi.org/10.6028/NIST.SP.800-53r4

Certain commercial entities, equipment, or materials may be identified in this document in order to describe an experimental procedure or concept adequately. Such identification is not intended to imply recommendation or endorsement by NIST, nor is it intended to imply that the entities, materials, or equipment are necessarily the best available for the purpose.

There may be references in this publication to other publications currently under development by NIST in accordance with its assigned statutory responsibilities. The information in this publication, including concepts and methodologies, may be used by Federal agencies even before the completion of such companion publications. Thus, until each publication is completed, current requirements, guidelines, and procedures, where they exist, remain operative. For planning and transition purposes, Federal agencies may wish to closely follow the development of these new publications by NIST.

Organizations are encouraged to review all draft publications during public comment periods and provide feedback to NIST. All NIST Computer Security Division publications, other than the ones noted above, are available at http://csrc.nist.gov/publications.

Comments on this publication may be submitted to:

National Institute of Standards and Technology
Attn: Computer Security Division, Information Technology Laboratory
100 Bureau Drive (Mail Stop 8930) Gaithersburg, MD 20899-8930
Electronic Mail: **sec-cert@nist.gov**

Reports on Computer Systems Technology

The Information Technology Laboratory (ITL) at the National Institute of Standards and Technology (NIST) promotes the U.S. economy and public welfare by providing technical leadership for the Nation's measurement and standards infrastructure. ITL develops tests, test methods, reference data, proof of concept implementations, and technical analyses to advance the development and productive use of information technology. ITL's responsibilities include the development of management, administrative, technical, and physical standards and guidelines for the cost-effective security and privacy of other than national security-related information in federal information systems. The Special Publication 800-series reports on ITL's research, guidelines, and outreach efforts in information system security, and its collaborative activities with industry, government, and academic organizations.

Abstract

This publication provides a catalog of security and privacy controls for federal information systems and organizations and a process for selecting controls to protect organizational operations (including mission, functions, image, and reputation), organizational assets, individuals, other organizations, and the Nation from a diverse set of threats including hostile cyber attacks, natural disasters, structural failures, and human errors. The controls are customizable and implemented as part of an organization-wide process that manages information security and privacy risk. The controls address a diverse set of security and privacy requirements across the federal government and critical infrastructure, derived from legislation, Executive Orders, policies, directives, regulations, standards, and/or mission/business needs. The publication also describes how to develop specialized sets of controls, or overlays, tailored for specific types of missions/business functions, technologies, or environments of operation. Finally, the catalog of security controls addresses security from both a functionality perspective (the strength of security functions and mechanisms provided) and an assurance perspective (the measures of confidence in the implemented security capability). Addressing both security functionality and security assurance ensures that information technology products and the information systems built from those products using sound systems and security engineering principles are sufficiently trustworthy.

Keywords

Assurance; computer security; FIPS Publication 199; FIPS Publication 200, FISMA; Privacy Act; Risk Management Framework; security controls; security requirements.

Acknowledgements

This publication was developed by the *Joint Task Force Transformation Initiative* Interagency Working Group with representatives from the Civil, Defense, and Intelligence Communities in an ongoing effort to produce a unified information security framework for the federal government. The National Institute of Standards and Technology wishes to acknowledge and thank the senior leaders from the Departments of Commerce and Defense, the Office of the Director of National Intelligence, the Committee on National Security Systems, and the members of the interagency technical working group whose dedicated efforts contributed significantly to the publication. The senior leaders, interagency working group members, and their organizational affiliations include:

Department of Defense

Teresa M. Takai
DoD Chief Information Officer

Robert J. Carey
Principal Deputy DoD Chief Information Officer

Richard Hale
Deputy Chief Information Officer for Cybersecurity

Dominic Cussatt
Deputy Director, Cybersecurity Policy

National Institute of Standards and Technology

Charles H. Romine
Director, Information Technology Laboratory

Donna Dodson
Cybersecurity Advisor, Information Technology Laboratory

Donna Dodson
Chief, Computer Security Division

Ron Ross
FISMA Implementation Project Leader

Office of the Director of National Intelligence

Adolpho Tarasiuk Jr.
Assistant DNI and Intelligence Community Chief Information Officer

Charlene Leubecker
Deputy Intelligence Community Chief Information Officer

Catherine A. Henson
Director, Data Management

Greg Hall
Chief, Risk Management and Information Security Programs Division

Committee on National Security Systems

Teresa M. Takai
Chair, CNSS

Richard Spires
Co-Chair, CNSS

Dominic Cussatt
CNSS Subcommittee Tri-Chair

Jeffrey Wilk
CNSS Subcommittee Tri-Chair

Richard Tannich
CNSS Subcommittee Tri-Chair

Joint Task Force Transformation Initiative Interagency Working Group

Ron Ross *NIST, JTF Leader*	Gary Stoneburner *Johns Hopkins APL*	Richard Graubart *The MITRE Corporation*	Kelley Dempsey *NIST*
Esten Porter *The MITRE Corporation*	Bennett Hodge *Booz Allen Hamilton*	Karen Quigg *The MITRE Corporation*	Christian Enloe *NIST*
Kevin Stine *NIST*	Jennifer Fabius *The MITRE Corporation*	Daniel Faigin *The Aerospace Corporation*	Arnold Johnson *NIST*
Lisa Kaiser *DHS*	Pam Miller *The MITRE Corporation*	Sandra Miravalle *The MITRE Corporation*	Victoria Pillitteri *NIST*

In addition to the above acknowledgments, a special note of thanks goes to Peggy Himes and Elizabeth Lennon of NIST for their superb technical editing and administrative support. The authors also wish to recognize Marshall Abrams, Nadya Bartol, Frank Belz, Deb Bodeau, Dawn Cappelli, Corinne Castanza, Matt Coose, George Dinolt, Kurt Eleam, Jennifer Guild, Cynthia Irvine, Cass Kelly, Steve LaFountain, Steve Lipner, Tom Macklin, Tim McChesney, Michael

McEvilley, John Mildner, Joji Montelibano, George Moore, LouAnna Notargiacomo, Dorian Pappas, Roger Schell, Carol Woody, and the research staff from the NIST Computer Security Division for their exceptional contributions in helping to improve the content of the publication. And finally, the authors also gratefully acknowledge and appreciate the significant contributions from individuals, working groups, and organizations in the public and private sectors, both nationally and internationally, whose thoughtful and constructive comments improved the overall quality, thoroughness, and usefulness of this publication.

> **FIPS 200 AND SP 800-53**
>
> IMPLEMENTING INFORMATION SECURITY STANDARDS AND GUIDELINES
>
> FIPS Publication 200, *Minimum Security Requirements for Federal Information and Information Systems*, is a mandatory federal standard developed by NIST in response to FISMA. To comply with the federal standard, organizations first determine the security category of their information system in accordance with FIPS Publication 199, *Standards for Security Categorization of Federal Information and Information Systems*, derive the information system impact level from the security category in accordance with FIPS 200, and then apply the appropriately tailored set of baseline security controls in NIST Special Publication 800-53, *Security and Privacy Controls for Federal Information Systems and Organizations*. Organizations have flexibility in applying the baseline security controls in accordance with the guidance provided in Special Publication 800-53. This allows organizations to tailor the relevant security control baseline so that it more closely aligns with their mission and business requirements and environments of operation.
>
> FIPS 200 and NIST Special Publication 800-53, in combination, ensure that appropriate security requirements and security controls are applied to all federal information and information systems. An organizational assessment of risk validates the initial security control selection and determines if additional controls are needed to protect organizational operations (including mission, functions, image, or reputation), organizational assets, individuals, other organizations, or the Nation. The resulting set of security controls establishes a level of security due diligence for the organization.

> **DEVELOPING COMMON INFORMATION SECURITY FOUNDATIONS**
>
> COLLABORATION AMONG PUBLIC AND PRIVATE SECTOR ENTITIES
>
> In developing standards and guidelines required by FISMA, NIST consults with other federal agencies and the private sector to improve information security, avoid unnecessary and costly duplication of effort, and ensure that its publications are complementary with the standards and guidelines employed for the protection of national security systems. In addition to a comprehensive public review and vetting process, NIST is collaborating with the Office of the Director of National Intelligence (ODNI), the Department of Defense (DoD), and the Committee on National Security Systems (CNSS) to establish a unified information security framework for the federal government. A common foundation for information security will provide the Civil, Defense, and Intelligence sectors of the federal government and their contractors, more cost-effective and consistent ways to manage information security-related risk to organizational operations and assets, individuals, other organizations, and the Nation. The unified framework will also provide a strong basis for reciprocal acceptance of authorization decisions and facilitate information sharing. NIST is also working with many public and private sector entities to establish mappings and relationships between the security standards and guidelines developed by NIST and the International Organization for Standardization and International Electrotechnical Commission (ISO/IEC).

> **SECURITY REQUIREMENTS**
>
> FROM THE PERSPECTIVE OF DIFFERENT COMMUNITIES OF INTEREST
>
> The term *security requirement* is used by different communities and groups in different ways and may require additional explanation to establish the particular context for the various use cases. Security requirements can be stated at a very high level of abstraction, for example, in legislation, Executive Orders, directives, policies, standards, and mission/business needs statements. FISMA and FIPS Publication 200 articulate security requirements at such a level.
>
> Acquisition personnel develop security requirements for contracting purposes that address the protections necessary to achieve mission/business needs. Systems/security engineers, system developers, and systems integrators develop the security design requirements for the information system, develop the system security architecture and the architecture-specific derived security requirements, and subsequently implement specific security functions at the hardware, software, and firmware component level.
>
> Security requirements are also reflected in various nontechnical security controls that address such matters as policy and procedures at the management and operational elements within organizations, again at differing levels of detail. It is important to define the context for each use of the term security requirement so the respective communities (including individuals responsible for policy, architecture, acquisition, engineering, and mission/business protection) can clearly communicate their intent.
>
> Organizations may define certain *security capabilities* needed to satisfy security requirements and provide appropriate mission and business protection. Security capabilities are typically defined by bringing together a specific set of safeguards/countermeasures (i.e., security controls) derived from the appropriately tailored baselines that together produce the needed capability.

TECHNOLOGY AND POLICY NEUTRALITY
CHARACTERISTICS OF SECURITY CONTROLS

The security controls in the catalog with few exceptions, have been designed to be policy- and technology-neutral. This means that security controls and control enhancements focus on the fundamental safeguards and countermeasures necessary to protect information during processing, while in storage, and during transmission. Therefore, it is beyond the scope of this publication to provide guidance on the application of security controls to specific technologies, environments of operation, communities of interest, or missions/business functions. Application-specific areas are addressed by the use of the tailoring process described in Chapter Three and the use of overlays described in Appendix I. It should also be noted that while the security controls are largely policy- and technology-neutral, that does not imply that the controls are policy- and technology-unaware. Understanding policy and technology is necessary so that the controls are meaningful and relevant when implemented.

In the few cases where specific technologies are called out in security controls (e.g., mobile, PKI, wireless, VOIP), organizations are cautioned that the need to provide adequate security goes well beyond the requirements in a single control associated with a particular technology. Many of the needed safeguards and countermeasures are obtained from the other security controls in the catalog allocated to the initial control baselines as starting points for the development of security plans and overlays using the tailoring process. There may also be some overlap in the protections articulated by the security controls within the different control families.

In addition to the customer-driven development of specialized security plans and overlays, NIST Special Publications and Interagency Reports may provide guidance on recommended security controls for specific technologies and sector-specific applications (e.g., Smart Grid, healthcare, Industrial Control Systems, and mobile).

Employing a technology- and policy-neutral security control catalog has the following benefits:

- It encourages organizations to focus on the *security capabilities* required for mission/business success and the protection of information, irrespective of the information technologies that are employed in organizational information systems.

- It encourages organizations to analyze each security control for its applicability to specific technologies, environments of operation, missions/business functions, and communities of interest.

- It encourages organizations to specify security policies as part of the tailoring process for security controls that have variable parameters.

The specialization of security plans using the tailoring guidance and overlays, together with a robust set of technology- and policy-neutral security controls, promotes cost-effective, risk-based information security for organizations—in any sector, for any technology, and in any operating environment.

INFORMATION SECURITY DUE DILIGENCE

MANAGING THE RISK TO ORGANIZATIONAL MISSIONS/BUSINESS FUNCTIONS

The security controls in NIST Special Publication 800-53 are designed to facilitate compliance with applicable federal laws, Executive Orders, directives, policies, regulations, standards, and guidance. Compliance is *not* about adhering to static checklists or generating unnecessary FISMA reporting paperwork. Rather, compliance necessitates organizations executing *due diligence* with regard to information security and risk management. Information security due diligence includes using all appropriate information as part of an organization-wide risk management program to effectively use the tailoring guidance and inherent flexibility in NIST publications so that the selected security controls documented in organizational security plans meet the mission and business requirements of organizations. Using the risk management tools and techniques that are available to organizations is essential in developing, implementing, and maintaining the safeguards and countermeasures with the necessary and sufficient strength of mechanism to address the current threats to organizational operations and assets, individuals, other organizations, and the Nation. Employing effective risk-based processes, procedures, and technologies will help ensure that all federal information systems and organizations have the necessary resilience to support ongoing federal responsibilities, critical infrastructure applications, and continuity of government.

> **PRIVACY CONTROLS**
>
> PROVIDING PRIVACY PROTECTION FOR FEDERAL INFORMATION
>
> Appendix J, *Privacy Control Catalog*, is a new addition to NIST Special Publication 800-53. It is intended to address the privacy needs of federal agencies. The Privacy Appendix:
>
> - Provides a structured set of privacy controls, based on best practices, that help organizations comply with applicable federal laws, Executive Orders, directives, instructions, regulations, policies, standards, guidance, and organization-specific issuances;
>
> - Establishes a linkage and relationship between privacy and security controls for purposes of enforcing respective privacy and security requirements which may overlap in concept and in implementation within federal information systems, programs, and organizations;
>
> - Demonstrates the applicability of the NIST Risk Management Framework in the selection, implementation, assessment, and ongoing monitoring of privacy controls deployed in federal information systems, programs, and organizations; and
>
> - Promotes closer cooperation between privacy and security officials within the federal government to help achieve the objectives of senior leaders/executives in enforcing the requirements in federal privacy legislation, policies, regulations, directives, standards, and guidance.
>
> There is a strong similarity in the structure of the privacy controls in Appendix J and the security controls in Appendices F and G. For example, the control AR-1 (Governance and Privacy Program) requires organizations to develop privacy plans that can be implemented at the organizational or program level. These plans can also be used in conjunction with security plans to provide an opportunity for organizations to select the appropriate set of security and privacy controls in accordance with organizational mission/business requirements and the environments in which the organizations operate. Incorporating the same concepts used in managing information security risk, helps organizations implement privacy controls in a more cost-effective, risked-based manner while simultaneously protecting individual privacy and meeting compliance requirements. Standardized privacy controls provide a more disciplined and structured approach for satisfying federal privacy requirements and demonstrating compliance to those requirements.

CAUTIONARY NOTE

IMPLEMENTING CHANGES BASED ON REVISIONS TO SPECIAL PUBLICATION 800-53

When NIST publishes revisions to Special Publication 800-53, there are four primary types of changes made to the document: (i) security controls or control enhancements are added to or withdrawn from Appendices F and G and/or to the low, moderate, and high baselines; (ii) supplemental guidance is modified; (iii) material in the main chapters or appendices is modified; and (iv) language is clarified and/or updated throughout the document.

When modifying existing tailored security control baselines at Tier 3 in the risk management hierarchy (as described in Special Publication 800-39) and updating security controls at any tier as a result of Special Publication 800-53 revisions, organizations should take a measured, risk-based approach in accordance with organizational risk tolerance and current risk assessments. Unless otherwise directed by OMB policy, the following activities are recommended to implement changes to Special Publication 800-53:

- First, organizations determine if any added security controls/control enhancements are applicable to organizational information systems or environments of operation following tailoring guidelines in this publication.

- Next, organizations review changes to the supplemental guidance, guidance in the main chapters and appendices, and updated/clarified language throughout the publication to determine if changes apply to any organizational information systems and if any immediate actions are required.

- Finally, once organizations have determined the entirety of changes necessitated by the revisions to the publication, the changes are integrated into the established continuous monitoring process to the greatest extent possible. The implementation of new or modified security controls to address specific, active threats is always the highest priority for sequencing and implementing changes. Modifications such as changes to templates or minor language changes in policy or procedures are generally the lowest priority and are made in conjunction with established review cycles.

Table of Contents

CHAPTER ONE INTRODUCTION 1
    1.1 PURPOSE AND APPLICABILITY 2
    1.2 TARGET AUDIENCE 3
    1.3 RELATIONSHIP TO OTHER SECURITY CONTROL PUBLICATIONS 3
    1.4 ORGANIZATIONAL RESPONSIBILITIES 4
    1.5 ORGANIZATION OF THIS SPECIAL PUBLICATION 6

CHAPTER TWO THE FUNDAMENTALS 7
    2.1 MULTITIERED RISK MANAGEMENT 7
    2.2 SECURITY CONTROL STRUCTURE 9
    2.3 SECURITY CONTROL BASELINES 12
    2.4 SECURITY CONTROL DESIGNATIONS 14
    2.5 EXTERNAL SERVICE PROVIDERS 17
    2.6 ASSURANCE AND TRUSTWORTHINESS 20
    2.7 REVISIONS AND EXTENSIONS 26

CHAPTER THREE THE PROCESS 28
    3.1 SELECTING SECURITY CONTROL BASELINES 28
    3.2 TAILORING BASELINE SECURITY CONTROLS 30
    3.3 CREATING OVERLAYS 40
    3.4 DOCUMENTING THE CONTROL SELECTION PROCESS 42
    3.5 NEW DEVELOPMENT AND LEGACY SYSTEMS 44

APPENDIX A REFERENCES A-1
APPENDIX B GLOSSARY B-1
APPENDIX C ACRONYMS C-1
APPENDIX D SECURITY CONTROL BASELINES – SUMMARY D-1
APPENDIX E ASSURANCE AND TRUSTWORTHINESS E-1
APPENDIX F SECURITY CONTROL CATALOG F-1
APPENDIX G INFORMATION SECURITY PROGRAMS G-1
APPENDIX H INTERNATIONAL INFORMATION SECURITY STANDARDS H-1
APPENDIX I OVERLAY TEMPLATE I-1
APPENDIX J PRIVACY CONTROL CATALOG J-1

Prologue

"...Through the process of risk management, leaders must consider risk to US interests from adversaries using cyberspace to their advantage and from our own efforts to employ the global nature of cyberspace to achieve objectives in military, intelligence, and business operations... "

"...For operational plans development, the combination of threats, vulnerabilities, and impacts must be evaluated in order to identify important trends and decide where effort should be applied to eliminate or reduce threat capabilities; eliminate or reduce vulnerabilities; and assess, coordinate, and deconflict all cyberspace operations..."

"...Leaders at all levels are accountable for ensuring readiness and security to the same degree as in any other domain..."

-- THE NATIONAL STRATEGY FOR CYBERSPACE OPERATIONS
   OFFICE OF THE CHAIRMAN, JOINT CHIEFS OF STAFF, U.S. DEPARTMENT OF DEFENSE

Foreword

NIST Special Publication 800-53, Revision 4, represents the most comprehensive update to the security controls catalog since its inception in 2005. The publication was developed by NIST, the Department of Defense, the Intelligence Community, and the Committee on National Security Systems as part of the Joint Task Force, an interagency partnership formed in 2009. This update was motivated principally by the expanding threat space—characterized by the increasing sophistication of cyber attacks and the operations tempo of adversaries (i.e., the frequency of such attacks, the professionalism of the attackers, and the persistence of targeting by attackers). State-of-the-practice security controls and control enhancements have been developed and integrated into the catalog addressing such areas as: mobile and cloud computing; applications security; trustworthiness, assurance, and resiliency of information systems; insider threat; supply chain security; and the advanced persistent threat. In addition, Special Publication 800-53 has been expanded to include eight new families of privacy controls based on the internationally accepted Fair Information Practice Principles.

Special Publication 800-53, Revision 4, provides a more *holistic* approach to information security and risk management by providing organizations with the breadth and depth of security controls necessary to fundamentally strengthen their information systems and the environments in which those systems operate—contributing to systems that are more resilient in the face of cyber attacks and other threats. This "Build It Right" strategy is coupled with a variety of security controls for "Continuous Monitoring" to give organizations near real-time information that is essential for senior leaders making ongoing *risk-based* decisions affecting their critical missions and business functions.

To take advantage of the expanded set of security and privacy controls, and to give organizations greater flexibility and agility in defending their information systems, the concept of *overlays* was introduced in this revision. Overlays provide a structured approach to help organizations tailor security control baselines and develop specialized security plans that can be applied to specific missions/business functions, environments of operation, and/or technologies. This specialization approach is important as the number of threat-driven controls and control enhancements in the catalog increases and organizations develop risk management strategies to address their specific protection needs within defined risk tolerances.

Finally, there have been several new features added to this revision to facilitate ease of use by organizations. These include:

- Assumptions relating to security control baseline development;
- Expanded, updated, and streamlined tailoring guidance;
- Additional assignment and selection statement options for security and privacy controls;
- Descriptive names for security and privacy control enhancements;
- Consolidated tables for security controls and control enhancements by family with baseline allocations;
- Tables for security controls that support development, evaluation, and operational assurance; and
- Mapping tables for international security standard ISO/IEC 15408 (Common Criteria).

The security and privacy controls in Special Publication 800-53, Revision 4, have been designed to be largely policy/technology-neutral to facilitate flexibility in implementation. The controls are well positioned to support the integration of information security and privacy into organizational processes including enterprise architecture, systems engineering, system development life cycle, and acquisition/procurement. Successful integration of security and privacy controls into ongoing organizational processes will demonstrate a greater maturity of security and privacy programs and provide a tighter coupling of security and privacy investments to core organizational missions and business functions.

The Joint Task Force

Errata

The following changes have been incorporated into Special Publication 800-53, Revision 4.

DATE	TYPE	CHANGE	PAGE
05-07-2013	Editorial	Changed CA-9 Priority Code from P1 to P2 in Table D-2.	D-3
05-07-2013	Editorial	Changed CM-10 Priority Code from P1 to P2 in Table D-2.	D-4
05-07-2013	Editorial	Changed MA-6 Priority Code from P1 to P2 in Table D-2.	D-5
05-07-2013	Editorial	Changed MP-3 Priority Code from P1 to P2 in Table D-2.	D-5
05-07-2013	Editorial	Changed PE-5 Priority Code from P1 to P2 in Table D-2.	D-5
05-07-2013	Editorial	Changed PE-16 Priority Code from P1 to P2 in Table D-2.	D-5
05-07-2013	Editorial	Changed PE-17 Priority Code from P1 to P2 in Table D-2.	D-5
05-07-2013	Editorial	Changed PE-18 Priority Code from P2 to P3 in Table D-2.	D-5
05-07-2013	Editorial	Changed PL-4 Priority Code from P1 to P2 in Table D-2.	D-6
05-07-2013	Editorial	Changed PS-4 Priority Code from P2 to P1 in Table D-2.	D-6
05-07-2013	Editorial	Changed SA-11 Priority Code from P2 to P1 in Table D-2.	D-6
05-07-2013	Editorial	Changed SC-18 Priority Code from P1 to P2 in Table D-2.	D-7
05-07-2013	Editorial	Changed SI-8 Priority Code from P1 to P2 in Table D-2.	D-8
05-07-2013	Editorial	Deleted reference to SA-5(6) in Table D-17.	D-32
05-07-2013	Editorial	Deleted CM-4(3) from Table E-2.	E-4
05-07-2013	Editorial	Deleted CM-4(3) from Table E-3.	E-5
05-07-2013	Editorial	Deleted reference to SA-5(6).	F-161
05-07-2013	Editorial	Changed SI-16 Priority Code from P0 to P1.	F-233
01-15-2014	Editorial	Deleted "(both intentional and unintentional)" in line 5 in Abstract.	iii
01-15-2014	Editorial	Deleted "security and privacy" in line 5 in Abstract.	iii
01-15-2014	Editorial	Changed "an initial set of baseline security controls" to "the applicable security control baseline" in Section 2.1, RMF Step 2.	9
01-15-2014	Editorial	Deleted the following paragraph: "The security control enhancements section provides…in Appendix F."	11
01-15-2014	Editorial	Changed "baseline security controls" to "the security control baselines" in Section 2.3, 2nd paragraph, line 6.	13
01-15-2014	Editorial	Changed "an initial set of security controls" to "the applicable security control baseline" in Section 3.1, paragraph 2, line 4.	28
01-15-2014	Editorial	Changed "security control baselines" to "baselines identified in Appendix D" in Section 3.1, paragraph 2, line 5.	28
01-15-2014	Editorial	Changed "an appropriate set of baseline controls" to "the appropriate security control baseline" in Section 3.1, paragraph 3, line 3.	29
01-15-2014	Editorial	Deleted "initial" before "security control baseline" and added "FIPS 200" before "impact level" in Section 3.1, paragraph 3, line 4.	29
01-15-2014	Editorial	Changed "sets of baseline security controls" to "security control baselines" in Section 3.1, paragraph 3, line 6.	29
01-15-2014	Editorial	Changed "initial set of baseline security controls" to "applicable security control baseline" in Section 3.2, paragraph 1, line 1.	30
01-15-2014	Editorial	Changed "initial set of baseline security controls" to "applicable security control baseline" in Section 3.2, paragraph 3, line 5.	31
01-15-2014	Editorial	Deleted "set of" before "security controls" in Section 3.2, Applying Scoping Considerations, Mobility paragraph, line 1.	33

DATE	TYPE	CHANGE	PAGE
01-15-2014	Editorial	Deleted "initial" before "set of" in Section 3.2, Applying Scoping Considerations, Mobility paragraph, line 2.	33
01-15-2014	Editorial	Changed "the baselines" to "each baseline" in Section 3.2, Applying Scoping Considerations, Mobility paragraph, line 3.	33
01-15-2014	Editorial	Changed "initial set of security controls" to "security control baseline" in Section 3.2, Applying Scoping Considerations, Mobility paragraph, line 5.	33
01-15-2014	Editorial	Added "specific" before "locations" in Section 3.2, Applying Scoping Considerations, Mobility paragraph, line 6.	33
01-15-2014	Editorial	Changed "initial" to "three" in Section 3.2, Applying Scoping Considerations, Mobility paragraph, line 8.	33
01-15-2014	Editorial	Changed "initial set of baseline security controls" to "applicable security control baseline" in Section 3.2, Selecting Compensating Security Controls, line 10.	36
01-15-2014	Editorial	Changed "a set of initial baseline security controls" to "security control baselines" in Section 3.3, line 1.	40
01-15-2014	Editorial	Added "." after "C.F.R" in #3, Policies, Directives, Instructions, Regulations, and Memoranda.	A-1
01-15-2014	Editorial	Added "Revision 1 (Draft)" to NIST Special Publication 800-52 in References.	A-7
01-15-2014	Editorial	Added "Configuration," to title of NIST Special Publication 800-52, Revision 1.	A-7
01-15-2014	Editorial	Changed date for NIST Special Publication 800-52, Revision 1 to September 2013.	A-7
01-15-2014	Editorial	Moved definition for Information Security Risk after Information Security Program Plan in Glossary.	B-11
01-15-2014	Editorial	Added AC-2(11) to high baseline in Table D-2.	D-2
01-15-2014	Editorial	Changed AC-10 Priority Code from P2 to P3 in Table D-2.	D-2
01-15-2014	Editorial	Changed AC-14 Priority Code from P1 to P3 in Table D-2.	D-2
01-15-2014	Editorial	Changed AC-22 Priority Code from P2 to P3 in Table D-2.	D-2
01-15-2014	Editorial	Changed AU-10 Priority Code from P1 to P2 in Table D-2.	D-3
01-15-2014	Editorial	Changed CA-6 Priority Code from P3 to P2 in Table D-2.	D-3
01-15-2014	Editorial	Changed CA-7 Priority Code from P3 to P2 in Table D-2.	D-3
01-15-2014	Editorial	Changed CA-8 Priority Code from P1 to P2 in Table D-2.	D-3
01-15-2014	Editorial	Changed IA-6 Priority Code from P1 to P2 in Table D-2.	D-4
01-15-2014	Editorial	Changed IR-7 Priority Code from P3 to P2 in Table D-2.	D-5
01-15-2014	Editorial	Changed MA-3 Priority Code from P2 to P3 in Table D-2.	D-5
01-15-2014	Editorial	Changed MA-4 Priority Code from P1 to P2 in Table D-2.	D-5
01-15-2014	Editorial	Changed MA-5 Priority Code from P1 to P2 in Table D-2.	D-5
01-15-2014	Editorial	Deleted Program Management Controls from Table D-2.	D-8/9
01-15-2014	Editorial	Deleted the following sentence at end of paragraph: "There is no summary table provided for the Program Management (PM) family since PM controls are not associated with any particular security control baseline."	D-9
01-15-2014	Editorial	Added AC-2(12) and AC-2(13) to high baseline in Table D-3.	D-10
01-15-2014	Editorial	Changed AC-17(5) incorporated into reference from AC-17 to SI-4 in Table D-3.	D-12
01-15-2014	Editorial	Changed AC-17(7) incorporated into reference from AC-3 to AC-3(10) in Table D-3.	D-12
01-15-2014	Editorial	Changed AC-6 to AC-6(9) in AU-2(4) withdrawal notice in Table D-5.	D-15
01-15-2014	Editorial	Changed "Training" to "Scanning" in SA-19(4) title in Table D-17.	D-34
01-15-2014	Editorial	Deleted SC-9(1), SC-9(2), SC-9(3), and SC-9(4) from Table D-18.	D-37
01-15-2014	Editorial	Added AC-2 and AC-5 to SC-14 and deleted SI-9 from SC-14 in Table D-18.	D-37

DATE	TYPE	CHANGE	PAGE
01-15-2014	Editorial	Deleted CA-3(5) from Table E-2.	E-4
01-15-2014	Editorial	Added CM-3(2) to Table E-2.	E-4
01-15-2014	Editorial	Added RA-5(2) and RA-5(5) to Table E-2.	E-4
01-15-2014	Editorial	Deleted CA-3(5) from Table E-3.	E-5
01-15-2014	Editorial	Added CM-3(2) to Table E-3.	E-5
01-15-2014	Editorial	Deleted bold text from RA-5(2) and RA-5(5) in Table E-3.	E-5
01-15-2014	Editorial	Added CM-8(9) to Table E-4.	E-7
01-15-2014	Editorial	Added CP-4(4) to Table E-4.	E-7
01-15-2014	Editorial	Added IR-3(1) to Table E-4.	E-7
01-15-2014	Editorial	Added RA-5(3) to Table E-4.	E-7
01-15-2014	Editorial	Deleted SA-4(4) from Table E-4.	E-7
01-15-2014	Editorial	Changed SA-21(1) from "enhancements" to "enhancement" in Table E-4.	E-7
01-15-2014	Editorial	Deleted SI-4(8) from Table E-4.	E-7
01-15-2014	Editorial	Changed "risk management process" to "RMF" in Using the Catalog, line 4.	F-6
01-15-2014	Editorial	Changed "an appropriate set of security controls" to "the appropriate security control baselines" in Using the Catalog, line 5.	F-6
01-15-2014	Editorial	Deleted extraneous "," from AC-2 g.	F-7
01-15-2014	Editorial	Added AC-2(11) to high baseline.	F-10
01-15-2014	Substantive	Added the following text to AC-3(2) Supplemental Guidance: "Dual authorization may also be known as two-person control."	F-11
01-15-2014	Editorial	Changed "ucdmo.gov" to "None" in AC-4 References.	F-18
01-15-2014	Editorial	Added "." after "C.F.R" in AT-2 References.	F-38
01-15-2014	Editorial	Changed AC-6 to AC-6(9) in AU-2(4) withdrawal notice.	F-42
01-15-2014	Editorial	Deleted "csrc.nist.gov/pcig/cig.html" and added "http://" to URL in AU-2 References.	F-42
01-15-2014	Editorial	Changed "identify" to "identity" in AU-6(6) Supplemental Guidance.	F-46
01-15-2014	Substantive	Added the following text to AU-9(5) Supplemental Guidance: "Dual authorization may also be known as two-person control."	F-49
01-15-2014	Editorial	Added "Control Enhancements: None." to AU-15.	F-53
01-15-2014	Editorial	Deleted extraneous "." from CM-2(7) Supplemental Guidance.	F-66
01-15-2014	Editorial	Added ")" after "board" in CM-3 g.	F-66
01-15-2014	Substantive	Added CA-7 to related controls list in CM-3.	F-66
01-15-2014	Substantive	Added the following text to CM-5(4) Supplemental Guidance: "Dual authorization may also be known as two-person control."	F-69
01-15-2014	Editorial	Added "http://" to URLs in CM-6 References.	F-71
01-15-2014	Editorial	Added "component" before "inventories" in CM-8(5).	F-74
01-15-2014	Editorial	Changed "tsp.ncs.gov" to "http://www.dhs.gov/telecommunications-service-priority-tsp" in CP-8 References.	F-86
01-15-2014	Substantive	Added the following text to CP-9(7) Supplemental Guidance: "Dual authorization may also be known as two-person control."	F-87
01-15-2014	Editorial	Changed "HSPD 12" to "HSPD-12" and added "http://" to URL in IA-2 References.	F-93
01-15-2014	Editorial	Changed "encrypted representations of" to "cryptographically-protected" in IA-5(1) (c).	F-96
01-15-2014	Editorial	Changed "Encrypted representations of" to "Cryptographically-protected" in IA-5(1) Supplemental Guidance.	F-97

DATE	TYPE	CHANGE	PAGE
01-15-2014	Substantive	Added the following text to IA-5(1) Supplemental Guidance: "To mitigate certain brute force attacks against passwords, organizations may also consider salting passwords."	F-97
01-15-2014	Editorial	Added "http://" to URL in IA-5 References.	F-99
01-15-2014	Editorial	Added "http://" to URL in IA-7 References.	F-99
01-15-2014	Editorial	Added "http://" to URL in IA-8 References.	F-101
01-15-2014	Editorial	Changed ":" to ";" after "800-61" and added "http://" to URL in IR-6 References.	F-108
01-15-2014	Substantive	Added the following text to MP-6(7) Supplemental Guidance: "Dual authorization may also be known as two-person control."	F-124
01-15-2014	Editorial	Added "http://" to URL in MP-6 References.	F-124
01-15-2014	Editorial	Changed "DoDI" to "DoD Instruction" and added "http://" to URLs in PE-3 References.	F-130
01-15-2014	Editorial	Deleted "and supplementation" after "tailoring" in PL-2 a. 8.	F-140
01-15-2014	Editorial	Added "Special" before "Publication" in PL-4 References.	F-141
01-15-2014	Editorial	Added "Control Enhancements: None." to PL-7.	F-142
01-15-2014	Editorial	Deleted AT-5, AC-19(6), AC-19(8), and AC-19(9) from PL-9 Supplemental Guidance.	F-144
01-15-2014	Editorial	Added "Control Enhancements: None." to PL-9.	F-144
01-15-2014	Editorial	Added "Special" before "Publication" in PL-9 References.	F-144
01-15-2014	Editorial	Changed "731.106(a)" to "731.106" in PS-2 References.	F-145
01-15-2014	Editorial	Changed "Publication" to "Publications" and added "http://" to URL in RA-3 References.	F-153
01-15-2014	Editorial	Added "http://" to URLs in RA-5 References.	F-155
01-15-2014	Editorial	Added "http://" to URLs in SA-4 References.	F-160
01-15-2014	Substantive	Added the following text to SA-11(8) Supplemental Guidance: "To understand the scope of dynamic code analysis and hence the assurance provided, organizations may also consider conducting code coverage analysis (checking the degree to which the code has been tested using metrics such as percent of subroutines tested or percent of program statements called during execution of the test suite) and/or concordance analysis (checking for words that are out of place in software code such as non-English language words or derogatory terms)."	F-169
01-15-2014	Editorial	Added "http://" to URLs in SA-11 References.	F-169
01-15-2014	Editorial	Added "Control Enhancements: None." to SA-16.	F-177
01-15-2014	Editorial	Changed "Training" to "Scanning" in SA-19(4) title.	F-181
01-15-2014	Editorial	Changed "physical" to "protected" in SC-8 Supplemental Guidance.	F-193
01-15-2014	Editorial	Changed "140-2" to "140" and added "http://" to URLs in SC-13 References.	F-196
01-15-2014	Editorial	Added "authentication" after "data origin" in SC-20, Part a.	F-199
01-15-2014	Editorial	Added "verification" after "integrity" in SC-20, Part a.	F-199
01-15-2014	Editorial	Added "Control Enhancements: None." to SC-35.	F-209
01-15-2014	Editorial	Deleted extraneous "References: None" from SI-7.	F-228

DATE	TYPE	CHANGE	PAGE
01-15-2014	Substantive	Added the following text as new third paragraph in Appendix G:: "Table G-1 provides a summary of the security controls in the program management family from Appendix G. Organizations can use the recommended *priority code* designation associated with each program management control to assist in making sequencing decisions for implementation (i.e., a Priority Code 1 [P1] control has a higher priority for implementation than a Priority Code 2 [P2] control; and a Priority Code 2 [P2] control has a higher priority for implementation than a Priority Code 3 [P3] control."	G-1/2
01-15-2014	Editorial	Added Table G-1 to Appendix G.	G-2
01-15-2014	Editorial	Added "http://" to URL in PM-5 References.	G-5
01-15-2014	Editorial	Deleted "Web: www.fsam.gov" from PM-7 References.	G-5
01-15-2014	Editorial	Added "http://" to URL in Footnote 124.	J-22
01-22-2015	Editorial	Changed security control enhancement naming convention (i.e., format) by deleting space between base security control and numbered enhancement designation.	Global
01-22-2015	Editorial	Changed "(iv) and" to "and (iv)" in Glossary definition for Developer.	B-6
01-22-2015	Editorial	Changed "an IR-2 (1) in the high baseline entry for the IR-2 security control" to "the IR-2 (1) (2) entry in the high baseline for IR-2" in Appendix D, paragraph 1, line 8.	D-1
01-22-2015	Editorial	Changed "enhancement (1)" to "enhancements (1) and (2)" in Appendix D, paragraph 1, line 10.	D-1
01-22-2015	Editorial	Deleted "in the security control catalog" in Appendix D, paragraph 1, line 10.	D-1
01-22-2015	Editorial	Changed "SHARED GROUPS / ACCOUNTS" to "SHARED / GROUP ACCOUNTS" in Table D-3, AC-2(9) title.	D-10
01-22-2015	Editorial	Added "ROLE-BASED" before "SECURITY TRAINING" in Table D-4, AT-3(1) title.	D-14
01-22-2015	Editorial	Added "ROLE-BASED" before "SECURITY TRAINING" in Table D-4, AT-3(2) title.	D-14
01-22-2015	Editorial	Added "ROLE-BASED" before "SECURITY TRAINING" in Table D-4, AT-3(3) title.	D-14
01-22-2015	Editorial	Added "ROLE-BASED" before "SECURITY TRAINING" in Table D-4, AT-3(4) title.	D-14
01-22-2015	Editorial	Added "-BASED" to "BIOMETRIC" in Table D-9, IA-5(12) title.	D-23
01-22-2015	Editorial	Deleted "/ ANALYSIS" after "PENETRATION TESTING" in Table D-17, SA-11(5) title.	D-33
01-22-2015	Editorial	Changed "(1)" from normal font to bold font in Table E-4, SI-4(1).	E-7
01-22-2015	Editorial	Changed "SHARED GROUPS / ACCOUNTS" to "SHARED / GROUP ACCOUNTS" in AC-2(9) title.	F-10
01-22-2015	Editorial	Changed "use" to "usage" in AC-2(12) part (a).	F-10
01-22-2015	Editorial	Changed "policies" to "policy" in AC-3(3).	F-11
01-22-2015	Editorial	Deleted "specifies that" in AC-3(3).	F-11
01-22-2015	Editorial	Changed "The policy is" to "Is" in AC-3(3) part (a).	F-11
01-22-2015	Editorial	Changed "A" to "Specifies that a" in AC-3(3) part (b).	F-11
01-22-2015	Editorial	Added "Specifies that" to AC-3(3) part (c).	F-11
01-22-2015	Editorial	Changed "Organized-defined" to "organization-defined" in AC-3(3) part (c).	F-11
01-22-2015	Editorial	Changed "policies" to "policy" in AC-3(4).	F-12
01-22-2015	Editorial	Added "information" before "flows" in AC-4(7).	F-15
01-22-2015	Editorial	Added "ROLE-BASED" before "SECURITY TRAINING" in AT-3(1) title.	F-39
01-22-2015	Editorial	Added "ROLE-BASED" before "SECURITY TRAINING" in AT-3(2) title.	F-39
01-22-2015	Editorial	Added "ROLE-BASED" before "SECURITY TRAINING" in AT-3(3) title.	F-39
01-22-2015	Editorial	Added "ROLE-BASED" before "SECURITY TRAINING" in AT-3(4) title.	F-39
01-22-2015	Editorial	Added "the" before "relationship" in AU-12(1).	F-52

DATE	TYPE	CHANGE	PAGE
01-22-2015	Editorial	Moved "." outside of closing bracket in Withdrawn section.	F-61
01-22-2015	Editorial	Changed "that" to "those" in CP-7 part c.	F-84
01-22-2015	Editorial	Deleted "list of" in IA-2(10).	F-92
01-22-2015	Editorial	Deleted "such as documentary evidence or a combination of documents and biometrics" in IA-4(3).	F-95
01-22-2015	Editorial	Added ", such as documentary evidence or a combination of documents and biometrics," in IA-4(3) Supplemental Guidance.	F-95
01-22-2015	Editorial	Added "-BASED" to "BIOMETRIC" in IA-5(12) title.	F-98
01-22-2015	Editorial	Changed "testing/exercises" to "testing" in IR-4 part c.	F-105
01-22-2015	Editorial	Deleted "and" before "prior" in MA-4(3) part (b).	F-115
01-22-2015	Editorial	Changed "Sanitation" to "Sanitization" in MP-7(2) Supplemental Guidance (two instances).	F-125
01-22-2015	Editorial	Changed "resign" to "re-sign" in PL-4 part d.	F-141
01-22-2015	Editorial	Deleted "security categorization decision is reviewed and approved by the" before "authorizing" (first instance) in RA-2 part c.	F-151
01-22-2015	Editorial	Added "reviews and approves the security categorization decision" after "representative" RA-2 part c.	F-151
01-22-2015	Editorial	Changed ";" to "," after IA-2 in SA-4(10) Supplemental Guidance.	F-160
01-22-2015	Editorial	Added "takes" before assignment statement in SA-5 part c.	F-161
01-22-2015	Editorial	Changed "either is" to "is either" in SA-11(3) part (b).	F-167
01-22-2015	Editorial	Deleted "has been" before "granted" in SA-11(3) part (b).	F-167
01-22-2015	Editorial	Deleted "/ ANALYSIS" after "PENETRATION TESTING" in SA-11(5) title.	F-168
01-22-2015	Editorial	Deleted "enhancement" after "control" in SA-12 Supplemental Guidance.	F-169
01-22-2015	Editorial	Deleted "Related control: PE-21." from SA-12(9) Supplemental Guidance.	F-171
01-22-2015	Editorial	Changed "reference to source" to "references to sources" in SC-5.	F-187
01-22-2015	Editorial	Added "to be" before "routed to" in SC-7(11).	F-190
01-22-2015	Editorial	Changed "i" to "1" and "ii" to "2" in SI-4 part c.	F-219
01-22-2015	Editorial	Changed "USER" to "USERS" in SI-4(20) title.	F-223
01-22-2015	Editorial	Deleted "for" in SI-6(2).	F-225
01-22-2015	Editorial	Changed "interfaces" to "interactions" in SI-10(4) Supplemental Guidance.	F-229
01-22-2015	Editorial	Changed "-" to "," after AU-7 in PM-12 Supplemental Guidance.	G-8
01-22-2015	Substantive	Updated the introduction to Appendix H and Tables H-1 and H-2 in accordance with the 2013 version of ISO/IEC 27001 and revised security control mapping methodology.	H-1 through H-12
01-22-2015	Editorial	Deleted UL-3 from related controls list in SE-1.	J-20

CHAPTER ONE

INTRODUCTION

THE NEED TO PROTECT INFORMATION AND INFORMATION SYSTEMS

The selection and implementation of *security controls* for information systems[1] and organizations are important tasks that can have major implications on the operations[2] and assets of organizations[3] as well as the welfare of individuals and the Nation. Security controls are the safeguards/countermeasures prescribed for information systems or organizations that are designed to: (i) protect the confidentiality, integrity, and availability of information that is processed, stored, and transmitted by those systems/organizations; and (ii) satisfy a set of defined security requirements.[4] There are several key questions that should be answered by organizations when addressing the information security considerations for information systems:

- What security controls are needed to satisfy the security requirements and to adequately mitigate risk incurred by using information and information systems in the execution of organizational missions and business functions?

- Have the security controls been implemented, or is there an implementation plan in place?

- What is the desired or required level of assurance that the selected security controls, as implemented, are effective in their application?[5]

The answers to these questions are not given in isolation but rather in the context of an effective *risk management process* for the organization that identifies, mitigates as deemed necessary, and monitors on an ongoing basis, risks[6] arising from its information and information systems. NIST Special Publication 800-39 provides guidance on managing information security risk at three distinct tiers—the organization level, mission/business process level, and information system level. The security controls defined in this publication and recommended for use by organizations to satisfy their information security requirements should be employed as part of a well-defined risk management process that supports organizational information security programs.[7]

---

[1] An information system is a discrete set of *information resources* organized expressly for the collection, processing, maintenance, use, sharing, dissemination, or disposition of information. Information systems also include specialized systems such as industrial/process controls systems, telephone switching/private branch exchange (PBX) systems, and environmental control systems.

[2] Organizational operations include mission, functions, image, and reputation.

[3] The term *organization* describes an entity of any size, complexity, or positioning within an organizational structure (e.g., a federal agency or, as appropriate, any of its operational elements).

[4] Security requirements are derived from mission/business needs, laws, Executive Orders, directives, regulations, policies, instructions, standards, guidance, and/or procedures to ensure the confidentiality, integrity, and availability of the information being processed, stored, or transmitted by organizational information systems.

[5] Security control *effectiveness* addresses the extent to which the controls are implemented correctly, operating as intended, and producing the desired outcome with respect to meeting the security requirements for the information system in its operational environment or enforcing/mediating established security policies.

[6] Information security-related risks are those risks that arise from the loss of confidentiality, integrity, or availability of information or information systems and consider the potential adverse impacts to organizational operations and assets, individuals, other organizations, and the Nation.

[7] The program management controls (Appendix G) complement the security controls for an information system (Appendix F) by focusing on the organization-wide information security requirements that are independent of any particular information system and are essential for managing information security programs.

It is of paramount importance that responsible officials understand the risks and other factors that could adversely affect organizational operations and assets, individuals, other organizations, and the Nation.[8] These officials must also understand the current status of their security programs and the security controls planned or in place to protect their information and information systems in order to make informed judgments and investments that mitigate risks to an acceptable level. The ultimate objective is to conduct the day-to-day operations of the organization and accomplish the organization's stated missions and business functions with what the OMB Circular A-130 defines as *adequate security*, or security commensurate with risk resulting from the unauthorized access, use, disclosure, disruption, modification, or destruction of information.

1.1 PURPOSE AND APPLICABILITY

The purpose of this publication is to provide guidelines for selecting and specifying security controls for organizations and information systems supporting the executive agencies of the federal government to meet the requirements of FIPS Publication 200, *Minimum Security Requirements for Federal Information and Information Systems*. The guidelines apply to all components[9] of an information system that process, store, or transmit federal information. The guidelines have been developed to achieve more secure information systems and effective risk management within the federal government by:

- Facilitating a more consistent, comparable, and repeatable approach for selecting and specifying security controls for information systems and organizations;

- Providing a stable, yet flexible catalog of security controls to meet current information protection needs and the demands of future protection needs based on changing threats, requirements, and technologies;

- Providing a recommendation for security controls for information systems categorized in accordance with FIPS Publication 199, *Standards for Security Categorization of Federal Information and Information Systems*;

- Creating a foundation for the development of assessment methods and procedures for determining security control effectiveness; and

- Improving communication among organizations by providing a common lexicon that supports discussion of risk management concepts.

In addition to the security controls described above, this publication: (i) provides a set of information security program management (PM) controls that are typically implemented at the organization level and not directed at individual organizational information systems; (ii) provides a set of privacy controls based on international standards and best practices that help organizations enforce privacy requirements derived from federal legislation, directives, policies, regulations, and standards; and (iii) establishes a linkage and relationship between privacy and security controls for purposes of enforcing respective privacy and security requirements which may overlap in concept and in implementation within federal information systems, programs, and organizations. Standardized privacy controls provide a more disciplined and structured approach for satisfying federal privacy requirements and demonstrating compliance to those

---

[8] This includes risk to critical infrastructure/key resources described in Homeland Security Presidential Directive 7.

[9] Information system components include, for example, mainframes, workstations, servers (e.g., database, electronic mail, authentication, web, proxy, file, domain name), input/output devices (e.g., scanners, copiers, printers), network components (e.g., firewalls, routers, gateways, voice and data switches, process controllers, wireless access points, network appliances, sensors), operating systems, virtual machines, middleware, and applications.

requirements. Incorporating the same concepts used in managing information security risk, helps organizations implement privacy controls in a more cost-effective, risked-based manner.

The guidelines in this special publication are applicable to all federal information systems[10] other than those systems designated as national security systems as defined in 44 U.S.C., Section 3542.[11] The guidelines have been broadly developed from a technical perspective to complement similar guidelines for national security systems and may be used for such systems with the approval of appropriate federal officials exercising policy authority over such systems.[12] State, local, and tribal governments, as well as private sector organizations are encouraged to consider using these guidelines, as appropriate.

1.2 TARGET AUDIENCE

This publication is intended to serve a diverse audience of information system and information security professionals including:

- Individuals with information system, security, and/or risk management and oversight responsibilities (e.g., authorizing officials, chief information officers, senior information security officers,[13] information system managers, information security managers);

- Individuals with information system development responsibilities (e.g., program managers, system designers and developers, information security engineers, systems integrators);

- Individuals with information security implementation and operational responsibilities (e.g., mission/business owners, information system owners, common control providers, information owners/stewards, system administrators, information system security officers);

- Individuals with information security assessment and monitoring responsibilities (e.g., auditors, Inspectors General, system evaluators, assessors, independent verifiers/validators, analysts, information system owners); and

- Commercial companies producing information technology products and systems, creating information security-related technologies, or providing information security services.

1.3 RELATIONSHIP TO OTHER SECURITY CONTROL PUBLICATIONS

To create a technically sound and broadly applicable set of security controls for information systems and organizations, a variety of sources were considered during the development of this special publication. The sources included security controls from the defense, audit, financial, healthcare, industrial/process control, and intelligence communities as well as controls defined by

---

[10] A *federal information system* is an information system used or operated by an executive agency, by a contractor of an executive agency, or by another organization on behalf of an executive agency.

[11] A *national security system* is any information system (including any telecommunications system) used or operated by an agency or by a contractor of an agency, or other organization on behalf of an agency: (i) the function, operation, or use of which involves intelligence activities; involves cryptologic activities related to national security; involves command and control of military forces; involves equipment that is an integral part of a weapon or weapons system; or is critical to the direct fulfillment of military or intelligence missions (excluding a system that is to be used for routine administrative and business applications, e.g., payroll, finance, logistics, and personnel management applications); or (ii) is protected at all times by procedures established for information that have been specifically authorized under criteria established by an Executive Order or an Act of Congress to be kept classified in the interest of national defense or foreign policy.

[12] CNSS Instruction 1253 provides implementing guidance for *national security systems*.

[13] At the *agency* level, this position is known as the Senior Agency Information Security Officer. Organizations may also refer to this position as the *Senior Information Security Officer* or the *Chief Information Security Officer*.

national and international standards organizations. The objective of NIST Special Publication 800-53 is to provide a set of security controls that can satisfy the breadth and depth of security requirements[14] levied on organizations, mission/business processes, and information systems and that is consistent with and complementary to other established information security standards.

The catalog of security controls in Special Publication 800-53 can be effectively used to protect information and information systems from traditional and advanced persistent threats in varied operational, environmental, and technical scenarios. The controls can also be used to demonstrate compliance with a variety of governmental, organizational, or institutional security requirements. Organizations have the responsibility to select the appropriate security controls, to implement the controls correctly, and to demonstrate the effectiveness of the controls in satisfying established security requirements.[15] The security controls facilitate the development of assessment methods and procedures that can be used to demonstrate control effectiveness in a consistent/repeatable manner—thus contributing to the organization's confidence that security requirements continue to be satisfied on an ongoing basis. In addition, security controls can be used in developing *overlays* for specialized information systems, information technologies, environments of operation, or communities of interest (see Appendix I).

1.4 ORGANIZATIONAL RESPONSIBILITIES

Organizations use FIPS Publication 199 to categorize their information and information systems. Security categorization is accomplished as an organization-wide activity[16] with the involvement of senior-level organizational personnel including, for example, authorizing officials, chief information officers, senior information security officers, information owners and/or stewards, information system owners, and risk executive (function).[17] Information is categorized at Tier 1 (organization level) and at Tier 2 (mission/business process level). In accordance with FIPS Publication 200, organizations use the security categorization results from Tiers 1 and 2 to designate organizational information systems at Tier 3 (information system level) as low-impact, moderate-impact, or high-impact systems. For each organizational information system at Tier 3, the recommendation for security controls from the *baseline* controls defined in Appendix D is the starting point for the security control *tailoring* process. While the security control selection process is generally focused on information systems at Tier 3, the process is generally applicable across all three tiers of risk management.

FIPS Publication 199 security categorization associates information and the operation and use of information systems with the potential worst-case adverse impact on organizational operations and assets, individuals, other organizations, and the Nation.[18] Organizational assessments of risk, including the use of specific and credible threat information, vulnerability information, and the likelihood of such threats exploiting vulnerabilities to cause adverse impacts, guide and inform

---

[14] Security requirements are those requirements levied on an information system that are derived from laws, Executive Orders, directives, policies, instructions, regulations, standards, guidelines, or organizational (mission) needs to ensure the confidentiality, integrity, and availability of the information being processed, stored, or transmitted.

[15] NIST Special Publication 800-53A provides guidance on assessing the effectiveness of security controls.

[16] See FIPS Publication 200, Footnote 7.

[17] Organizations typically exercise managerial, operational, and financial control over their information systems and the security provided to those systems, including the authority and capability to implement or require the security controls deemed necessary to protect organizational operations and assets, individuals, other organizations, and the Nation.

[18] Considerations for potential national-level impacts and impacts to other organizations in categorizing organizational information systems derive from the USA PATRIOT Act and Homeland Security Presidential Directives (HSPDs).

the tailoring process and the final selection of security controls.[19] The final, agreed-upon set of security controls addressing specific organizational mission/business needs and tolerance for risk is documented with appropriate rationale in the security plan for the information system.[20] The use of security controls from Special Publication 800-53 (including the baseline controls as a starting point in the control selection process), facilitates a more consistent level of security for federal information systems and organizations, while simultaneously preserving the flexibility and agility organizations need to address an increasingly sophisticated and hostile threat space, specific organizational missions/business functions, rapidly changing technologies, and in some cases, unique environments of operation.

Achieving adequate information security for organizations, mission/business processes, and information systems is a multifaceted undertaking that requires:

- Clearly articulated security requirements and security specifications;
- Well-designed and well-built information technology products based on state-of-the-practice hardware, firmware, and software development processes;
- Sound systems/security engineering principles and practices to effectively integrate information technology products into organizational information systems;
- Sound security practices that are well documented and seamlessly integrated into the training requirements and daily routines of organizational personnel with security responsibilities;
- Continuous monitoring of organizations and information systems to determine the ongoing effectiveness of deployed security controls, changes in information systems and environments of operation, and compliance with legislation, directives, policies, and standards;[21] and
- Information security planning and system development life cycle management.[22]

From an engineering viewpoint, information security is just one of many required operational capabilities for information systems that support organizational mission/business processes—capabilities that must be funded by organizations throughout the system development life cycle in order to achieve mission/business success. It is important that organizations *realistically* assess the risk to organizational operations and assets, individuals, other organizations, and the Nation arising from mission/business processes and by placing information systems into operation or continuing operations. Realistic assessment of risk requires an understanding of threats to and vulnerabilities within organizations and the likelihood and potential adverse impacts of successful exploitations of such vulnerabilities by those threats.[23] Finally, information security requirements must be satisfied with the full knowledge and consideration of the risk management strategy of

---

[19] Risk assessments can be accomplished in a variety of ways depending on the specific needs of organizations. NIST Special Publication 800-30 provides guidance on the assessment of risk as part of an overall risk management process.

[20] Authorizing officials or designated representatives, by accepting the completed security plans, agree to the set of security controls proposed to meet the security requirements for organizations (including mission/business processes) and/or designated information systems.

[21] NIST Special Publication 800-137 provides guidance on continuous monitoring of organizational information systems and environments of operation.

[22] NIST Special Publication 800-64 provides guidance on the information security considerations in the system development life cycle.

[23] NIST Special Publication 800-30 provides guidance on the risk assessment process.

the organization, in light of the potential cost, schedule, and performance issues associated with the acquisition, deployment, and operation of organizational information systems.[24]

1.5 ORGANIZATION OF THIS SPECIAL PUBLICATION

The remainder of this special publication is organized as follows:

- **Chapter Two** describes the fundamental concepts associated with security control selection and specification including: (i) multitiered risk management; (ii) the structure of security controls and how the controls are organized into families; (iii) security control baselines as starting points for the tailoring process; (iv) the use of common controls and inheritance of security capabilities; (v) external environments and service providers; (vi) assurance and trustworthiness; and (vii) revisions and extensions to security controls and control baselines.

- **Chapter Three** describes the process of selecting and specifying security controls for organizational information systems including: (i) selecting appropriate security control baselines; (ii) tailoring the baseline controls including developing specialized overlays; (iii) documenting the security control selection process; and (iv) applying the selection process to new and legacy systems.

- **Supporting appendices** provide essential security control selection and specification-related information including: (i) general references;[25] (ii) definitions and terms; (iii) acronyms; (iv) baseline security controls for low-impact, moderate-impact, and high-impact information systems; (v) guidance on assurance and trustworthiness in information systems; (vi) a catalog of security controls;[26] (vii) a catalog of information security program management controls; (viii) mappings to international information security standards; (ix) guidance for developing overlays by organizations or communities of interest; and (x) a catalog of privacy controls.

---

[24] In addition to information security requirements, organizations must also address privacy requirements that derive from federal legislation and policies. Organizations can employ the privacy controls in Appendix J in conjunction with the security controls in Appendix F to achieve comprehensive security and privacy protection.

[25] Unless otherwise stated, all references to NIST publications in this document (i.e., Federal Information Processing Standards and Special Publications) are to the most recent version of the publication.

[26] The security controls in Special Publication 800-53 are available online and can be downloaded in various formats from the NIST web site at: http://web.nvd.nist.gov/view/800-53/home.

CHAPTER TWO

THE FUNDAMENTALS
SECURITY CONTROL STRUCTURE, ORGANIZATION, BASELINES, AND ASSURANCE

This chapter presents the fundamental concepts associated with security control selection and specification including: (i) three-tiered risk management; (ii) the structure of security controls and the organization of the controls in the control catalog; (iii) security control baselines; (iv) the identification and use of common security controls; (v) security controls in external environments; (vi) security control assurance; and (vii) future revisions to the security controls, the control catalog, and baseline controls.

2.1 MULTITIERED RISK MANAGEMENT

The selection and specification of security controls for an information system is accomplished as part of an organization-wide information security program for the management of risk—that is, the risk to organizational operations and assets, individuals, other organizations, and the Nation associated with the operation of information systems. Risk-based approaches to security control selection and specification consider effectiveness, efficiency, and constraints due to applicable federal laws, Executive Orders, directives, policies, regulations, standards, and guidelines. To integrate the risk management process throughout the organization and more effectively address mission/business concerns, a three-tiered approach is employed that addresses risk at the: (i) *organization* level; (ii) *mission/business process* level; and (iii) *information system* level. The risk management process is carried out across the three tiers with the overall objective of continuous improvement in the organization's risk-related activities and effective inter-tier and intra-tier communication among all stakeholders having a shared interest in the mission/business success of the organization. Figure 1 illustrates the three-tiered approach to risk management.

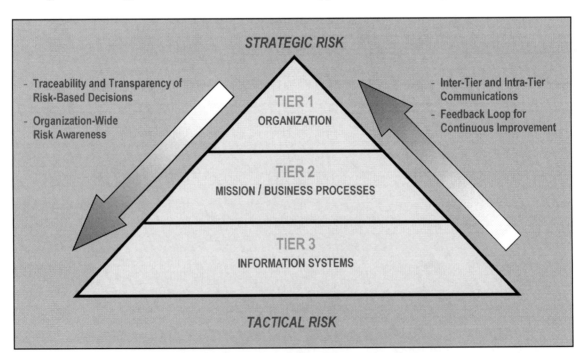

FIGURE 1: THREE-TIERED RISK MANAGEMENT APPROACH

Tier 1 provides a prioritization of organizational missions/business functions which in turn drives investment strategies and funding decisions—promoting cost-effective, efficient information technology solutions consistent with the strategic goals and objectives of the organization and measures of performance. Tier 2 includes: (i) defining the mission/business processes needed to support the organizational missions/business functions; (ii) determining the security categories of the information systems needed to execute the mission/business processes; (iii) incorporating information security requirements into the mission/business processes; and (iv) establishing an enterprise architecture (including an embedded information security architecture) to facilitate the allocation of security controls to organizational information systems and the environments in which those systems operate. The Risk Management Framework (RMF), depicted in Figure 2, is the primary means for addressing risk at Tier 3.[27] This publication focuses on Step 2 of the RMF, the security control selection process, in the context of the three tiers in the organizational risk management hierarchy.

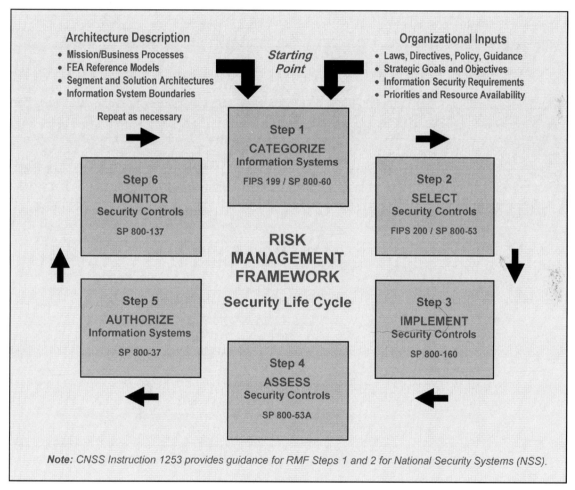

FIGURE 2: RISK MANAGEMENT FRAMEWORK

The RMF addresses the security concerns of organizations related to the design, development, implementation, operation, and disposal of information systems and the environments in which those systems operate. The RMF consists of the following six steps:

---

[27] NIST Special Publication 800-37 provides guidance on the implementation of the Risk Management Framework. A complete listing of all publications supporting the RMF and referenced in Figure 2 is provided in Appendix A.

Step 1: *Categorize* the information system based on a FIPS Publication 199 impact assessment;[28]

Step 2: *Select* the applicable security control baseline based on the results of the security categorization and apply tailoring guidance (including the potential use of overlays);

Step 3: *Implement* the security controls and document the design, development, and implementation details for the controls;

Step 4: *Assess* the security controls to determine the extent to which the controls are implemented correctly, operating as intended, and producing the desired outcome with respect to meeting the security requirements for the system;[29]

Step 5: *Authorize* information system operation based on a determination of risk to organizational operations and assets, individuals, other organizations, and the Nation resulting from the operation and use of the information system and the decision that this risk is acceptable; and

Step 6: *Monitor* the security controls in the information system and environment of operation on an ongoing basis to determine control effectiveness, changes to the system/environment, and compliance to legislation, Executive Orders, directives, policies, regulations, and standards.

2.2 SECURITY CONTROL STRUCTURE

Security controls described in this publication have a well-defined organization and structure. For ease of use in the security control selection and specification process, controls are organized into eighteen *families*.[30] Each family contains security controls related to the general security topic of the family. A two-character identifier uniquely identifies security control families, for example, PS (Personnel Security). Security controls may involve aspects of policy, oversight, supervision, manual processes, actions by individuals, or automated mechanisms implemented by information systems/devices. Table 1 lists the security control families and the associated family identifiers in the security control catalog.[31]

TABLE 1: SECURITY CONTROL IDENTIFIERS AND FAMILY NAMES

ID	FAMILY	ID	FAMILY
AC	Access Control	MP	Media Protection
AT	Awareness and Training	PE	Physical and Environmental Protection
AU	Audit and Accountability	PL	Planning
CA	Security Assessment and Authorization	PS	Personnel Security
CM	Configuration Management	RA	Risk Assessment
CP	Contingency Planning	SA	System and Services Acquisition
IA	Identification and Authentication	SC	System and Communications Protection
IR	Incident Response	SI	System and Information Integrity
MA	Maintenance	PM	Program Management

---

[28] CNSS Instruction 1253 provides security categorization guidance for national security systems.

[29] NIST Special Publication 800-53A provides guidance on assessing the effectiveness of security controls.

[30] Of the eighteen security control families in NIST Special Publication 800-53, seventeen families are described in the security control catalog in Appendix F, and are closely aligned with the seventeen minimum security requirements for federal information and information systems in FIPS Publication 200. One additional family (Program Management [PM] family) provides controls for information security programs required by FISMA. This family, while not specifically referenced in FIPS Publication 200, provides security controls at the organization level rather than the information system level. See Appendix G for a description of and implementation guidance for the PM controls.

[31] *Privacy controls* listed in Appendix J, have an organization and structure similar to security controls, including the use of two-character identifiers for the eight privacy families.

The security control structure consists of the following components: (i) a *control* section; (ii) a *supplemental guidance* section; (iii) a *control enhancements* section; (iv) a *references* section; and (v) a *priority* and *baseline allocation* section. The following example from the Auditing and Accountability family illustrates the structure of a typical security control.

AU-3 CONTENT OF AUDIT RECORDS

Control: The information system generates audit records containing information that establishes what type of event occurred, when the event occurred, where the event occurred, the source of the event, the outcome of the event, and the identity of any individuals or subjects associated with the event.

Supplemental Guidance: Audit record content that may be necessary to satisfy the requirement of this control includes, for example, time stamps, source and destination addresses, user/process identifiers, event descriptions, success/fail indications, filenames involved, and access control or flow control rules invoked. Event outcomes can include indicators of event success or failure and event-specific results (e.g., the security state of the information system after the event occurred). Related controls: AU-2, AU-8, AU-12, SI-11.

Control Enhancements:

(1) CONTENT OF AUDIT RECORDS | ADDITIONAL AUDIT INFORMATION

The information system generates audit records containing the following additional information: [*Assignment: organization-defined additional, more detailed information*].

Supplemental Guidance: Detailed information that organizations may consider in audit records includes, for example, full-text recording of privileged commands or the individual identities of group account users. Organizations consider limiting the additional audit information to only that information explicitly needed for specific audit requirements. This facilitates the use of audit trails and audit logs by not including information that could potentially be misleading or could make it more difficult to locate information of interest.

(2) CONTENT OF AUDIT RECORDS | CENTRALIZED MANAGEMENT OF PLANNED AUDIT RECORD CONTENT

The information system provides centralized management and configuration of the content to be captured in audit records generated by [*Assignment: organization-defined information system components*].

Supplemental Guidance: This control enhancement requires that the content to be captured in audit records be configured from a central location (necessitating automation). Organizations coordinate the selection of required audit content to support the centralized management and configuration capability provided by the information system. Related controls: AU-6, AU-7.

References: None.

Priority and Baseline Allocation:

P1	LOW AU-3	MOD AU-3 (1)	HIGH AU-3 (1) (2)

The control section prescribes specific security-related activities or actions to be carried out by organizations or by information systems. The term *information system* refers to those functions that generally involve the implementation of information technology (e.g., hardware, software, and firmware). Conversely, the term *organization* refers to activities that are generally process-driven or entity-driven—that is, the security control is generally implemented through human or procedural-based actions. Security controls that use the term organization may still require some degree of automation to be fulfilled. Similarly, security controls that use the term information system may have some elements that are process-driven or entity-driven. Using the terms organization and/or information system does not preclude the application of security controls at any of the tiers in the risk management hierarchy (i.e., organization level, mission/business process level, information system level), as appropriate.

For some security controls in the control catalog, a degree of flexibility is provided by allowing organizations to define values for certain parameters associated with the controls. This flexibility is achieved through the use of *assignment* and *selection* statements embedded within the security controls and control enhancements. Assignment and selection statements provide organizations with the capability to tailor security controls and control enhancements based on: (i) security requirements to support organizational missions/business functions and operational needs; (ii) risk assessments and organizational risk tolerance; and (iii) security requirements originating in federal laws, Executive Orders, directives, policies, regulations, standards, or guidelines.[32]

For example, organizations can specify additional information needed for audit records to support audit event processing. See the AU-3(1) example above (i.e., [*Assignment: organization-defined additional, more detailed information*]). These assignments may include particular actions to be taken by information systems in the event of audit failures, the frequency of conducting system backups, restrictions on password use, or the distribution list for organizational policies and procedures.[33] Once specified,[34] the organization-defined values for assignment and selection statements become part of the security control, and the control implementation is assessed against the completed control statement. Assignment statements offer a high degree of flexibility by allowing organizations to specify parameter values, without requiring those values to be one of two or more specific predefined choices. In contrast, selection statements narrow the potential input values by providing a specific list of items from which organizations must choose.[35]

The supplemental guidance section provides non-prescriptive, additional information for a specific security control. Organizations can apply the supplemental guidance as appropriate, when defining, developing, and/or implementing security controls. The supplemental guidance can provide important considerations for implementing security controls in the context of operational environments, mission/business requirements, or assessments of risk and can also explain the purpose or meaning of particular controls. Security control enhancements may also contain supplemental guidance when the guidance is not applicable to the entire control but instead focused on a particular control enhancement. The supplemental guidance sections for security controls and control enhancements may contain a list of *related controls*. Related controls: (i) directly impact or support the implementation of a particular security control or control enhancement; (ii) address a closely related *security capability*; or (iii) are referenced in the supplemental guidance. Security control enhancements are by definition related to the base control. Related controls that are listed in the supplemental guidance for the base controls are not repeated in the supplemental guidance for the control enhancements. However, there may be related controls identified for control enhancements that are not listed in the base control.

The security control enhancements section provides statements of security capability to: (i) add functionality/specificity to a control; and/or (ii) increase the strength of a control. In both cases, control enhancements are used in information systems and environments of operation requiring

---

[32] In general, organization-defined *parameters* used in assignment and selection statements in the basic security controls apply also to all control enhancements associated with those controls.

[33] Organizations determine whether specific assignment or selection statements are completed at Tier 1 (organization level), Tier 2 (mission/business process level), Tier 3 (information system level), or a combination thereof.

[34] Organizations may choose to define specific values for security control parameters in policies, procedures, or guidance (which may be applicable to more than one information system) referencing the source documents in the security plan in lieu of explicitly completing the assignment/selection statements within the control as part of the plan.

[35] Security controls are generally designed to be *technology*- and *implementation*-independent, and therefore do not contain specific requirements in these areas. Organizations provide such requirements as deemed necessary in the security plan for the information system.

greater protection than provided by the base control due to the potential adverse organizational impacts or when organizations seek additions to the base control functionality/specificity based on organizational assessments of risk. Security control enhancements are numbered sequentially within each control so that the enhancements can be easily identified when selected to supplement the base control. Each security control enhancement has a short subtitle to indicate the intended security capability provided by the control enhancement. In the AU-3 example, if the first control enhancement is selected, the control designation becomes AU-3(1). The numerical designation of a control enhancement is used only to identify the particular enhancement within the control. The designation is not indicative of either the strength of the control enhancement or any hierarchical relationship among the enhancements. Control enhancements are not intended to be selected independently (i.e., if a control enhancement is selected, then the corresponding base security control must also be selected). This intent is reflected in the baseline specifications in Appendix D and in the baseline allocation section under each control in Appendix F.

The references section includes a list of applicable federal laws, Executive Orders, directives, policies, regulations, standards, and guidelines (e.g., OMB Circulars/Memoranda, Homeland Security Presidential Directives, FIPS Publications, and NIST Special Publications) that are relevant to a particular security control.[36] The references provide federal legislative and policy mandates as well as supporting information for the implementation of security controls and control enhancements. The references section also contains pertinent websites for organizations to use in obtaining additional information for security control implementation and assessment.

The priority and security control baseline allocation section provides: (i) the recommended priority codes used for sequencing decisions during security control implementation; and (ii) the initial allocation of security controls and control enhancements to the baselines. Organizations can use the *priority code* designation associated with each security control to assist in making sequencing decisions for control implementation (i.e., a Priority Code 1 [P1] control has a higher priority for implementation than a Priority Code 2 [P2] control, a Priority Code 2 [P2] control has a higher priority for implementation than a Priority Code 3 [P3] control, and a Priority Code 0 [P0] indicates the security control is not selected in any baseline). This recommended sequencing prioritization helps to ensure that the foundational security controls upon which other controls depend are implemented first, thus enabling organizations to deploy controls in a more structured and timely manner in accordance with available resources. The implementation of security controls by sequence priority code does not imply the achievement of any defined level of risk mitigation until *all* of the security controls in the security plan have been implemented. The priority codes are intended only for implementation sequencing, not for making security control selection decisions.

2.3 SECURITY CONTROL BASELINES

Organizations are required to adequately mitigate the risk arising from use of information and information systems in the execution of missions and business functions. A significant challenge for organizations is to determine the most cost-effective, appropriate set of security controls, which if implemented and determined to be effective, would mitigate risk while complying with security requirements defined by applicable federal laws, Executive Orders, regulations, policies, directives, or standards (e.g., FISMA, OMB Circular A-130, HSPD-12, FIPS Publication 200). There is no one correct set of security controls that addresses all organizational security concerns in all situations. Selecting the most appropriate set of security controls for a specific situation or

---

[36] Publications listed in the *references section* refer to the most recent versions of the publications. References are provided to assist organizations in applying the security controls and are not intended to be inclusive or complete.

information system to adequately mitigate risk is an important task that requires a fundamental understanding of organizational mission/business priorities, the mission and business functions the information systems will support, and the environments of operation where the systems will reside. With that understanding, organizations can demonstrate how to most effectively assure the confidentiality, integrity, and availability of organizational information and information systems in a manner that supports mission/business needs while demonstrating due diligence. Selecting, implementing, and maintaining an appropriate set of security controls to adequately protect the information systems employed by organizations requires strong collaboration with system owners to understand ongoing changes to missions/business functions, environments of operation, and how the systems are used.

To assist organizations in making the appropriate selection of security controls for information systems, the concept of *baseline* controls is introduced. Baseline controls are the starting point for the security control selection process described in this document and are chosen based on the security category and associated impact level of information systems determined in accordance with FIPS Publication 199 and FIPS Publication 200, respectively.[37] Appendix D provides a listing of the security control baselines. Three security control baselines have been identified corresponding to the low-impact, moderate-impact, and high-impact information systems using the high water mark defined in FIPS Publication 200 and used in Section 3.1 of this document to provide an initial set of security controls for each impact level.[38]

Appendix F provides a comprehensive catalog of security controls for information systems and organizations, arranged by control families. Chapter Three provides additional information on how to use FIPS Publication 199 security categories and FIPS Publication 200 system impact levels in applying the tailoring guidance to the baseline security controls to achieve adequate risk mitigation. Tailoring guidance, described in Section 3.2, helps organizations to customize the security control baselines selected using the results from organizational assessments of risk. Baseline tailoring actions include: (i) identifying and designating common controls; (ii) applying scoping considerations; (iii) selecting compensating controls; (iv) assigning specific values to security control parameters; (v) supplementing initial baselines with additional security controls or control enhancements; and (vi) providing additional information for control implementation.

Implementation Tip

There are security controls and control enhancements that appear in the security control catalog (Appendix F) that are found in only higher-impact baselines or are not used in any of the baselines. These additional security controls and control enhancements for information systems are available to organizations and can be used in tailoring security control baselines to achieve the needed level of protection in accordance with organizational assessments of risk. The set of security controls in the security plan must be sufficient to adequately mitigate risks to organizational operations and assets, individuals, other organizations, and the Nation based on the organizational risk tolerance.

---

[37] CNSS Instruction 1253 provides guidance on security control baselines for national security systems.

[38] The baseline security controls contained in Appendix D are not necessarily absolutes in that the guidance described in Section 3.2 provides organizations with the ability to tailor controls in accordance with the terms and conditions established by their authorizing officials and documented in their respective security plans.

2.4 SECURITY CONTROL DESIGNATIONS

There are three distinct types of designations related to the security controls in Appendix F that define: (i) the scope of applicability for the control; (ii) the shared nature of the control; and (iii) the responsibility for control development, implementation, assessment, and authorization. These designations include *common* controls, *system-specific* controls, and *hybrid* controls.

Common controls are security controls whose implementation results in a security capability that is *inheritable* by one or more organizational information systems. Security controls are deemed inheritable by information systems or information system components when the systems or components receive protection from the implemented controls but the controls are developed, implemented, assessed, authorized, and monitored by entities other than those responsible for the systems or components—entities internal or external to the organizations where the systems or components reside. Security capabilities provided by common controls can be inherited from many sources including, for example, organizations, organizational mission/business lines, sites, enclaves, environments of operation, or other information systems. Many of the controls needed to protect organizational information systems (e.g., security awareness training, incident response plans, physical access to facilities, rules of behavior) are excellent candidates for common control status. In addition, there can also be a variety of technology-based common controls (e.g., Public Key Infrastructure [PKI], authorized secure standard configurations for clients/servers, access control systems, boundary protection, cross-domain solutions). By centrally managing and documenting the development, implementation, assessment, authorization, and monitoring of common controls, security costs can be amortized across multiple information systems.

The organization assigns responsibility for common controls to appropriate organizational officials (i.e., common control providers) and coordinates the development, implementation, assessment, authorization, and monitoring of the controls.[39] The identification of common controls is most effectively accomplished as an organization-wide exercise with the active involvement of chief information officers, senior information security officers, the risk executive (function), authorizing officials, information owners/stewards, information system owners, and information system security officers. The organization-wide exercise considers the security categories of the information systems within the organization and the security controls necessary to adequately mitigate the risks arising from the use of those systems (see *baseline* security controls in Section 2.3).[40] Common control identification for the controls that impact multiple information systems, but not all systems across the organization could benefit from taking a similar approach. Key stakeholders collaborate to identify opportunities to effectively employ common controls at the mission/business line, site, or enclave level.

When common controls protect multiple organizational information systems of differing impact levels, the controls are implemented with regard to the highest impact level among the systems. If the common controls are not implemented at the highest impact level of the information systems, system owners will need to factor this situation into their assessments of risk and take appropriate risk mitigation actions (e.g., adding security controls or control enhancements, changing assigned values of security control parameters, implementing compensating controls, or changing certain aspects of mission/business processes). Implementing common controls that are less than

---

[39] The Chief Information Officer, Senior Information Security Officer, or other designated organizational officials at the senior leadership level assign responsibility for the development, implementation, assessment, authorization, and monitoring of common controls to appropriate entities (either internal or external to the organization).

[40] Each common control identified by the organization is reviewed for applicability to each specific organizational information system, typically by information system owners and authorizing officials.

effective or that provide insufficient security capability for higher-impact information systems can have a significant adverse impact on organizational missions or business functions.

Common controls are generally documented in the organization-wide *information security program plan* unless implemented as part of a specific information system, in which case the controls are documented in the security plan for that system.[41] Organizations have the flexibility to describe common controls in a single document or in multiple documents with references or pointers, as appropriate. In the case of multiple documents, the documents describing common controls are included as attachments to the information security program plan. If the information security program plan contains multiple documents, organizations specify in each document the organizational officials responsible for development, implementation, assessment, authorization, and monitoring of the respective common controls. For example, the organization may require that the Facilities Management Office develop, implement, assess, authorize, and continuously monitor physical and environmental protection controls from the PE family when such controls are not associated with a particular information system but instead, support multiple systems. When common controls are included in a separate security plan for an information system (e.g., security controls employed as part of an intrusion detection system providing boundary protection inherited by one or more organizational information systems), the information security program plan indicates which separate security plan contains a description of the common controls.

> **Implementation Tip**
>
> The selection of common controls is most effectively accomplished on an organization-wide basis with the involvement of senior leadership (i.e., mission/business owners, authorizing officials, chief information officers, senior information security officers, information system owners, information owners/stewards, risk executives). These individuals have the collective knowledge to understand organizational priorities, the importance of organizational operations and assets, and the importance of the information systems that support those operations/assets. The senior leaders are also in the best position to select the common controls for each security control baseline and assign specific responsibilities for developing, implementing, assessing, authorizing, and monitoring those controls.

Common controls, whether employed in organizational information systems or environments of operation, are authorized by senior officials with at least the same level of authority/responsibility for managing risk as the authorization officials for information systems inheriting the controls. Authorization results for common controls are shared with the appropriate information system owners and authorizing officials. A plan of action and milestones is developed and maintained for common controls that have been determined through independent assessments, to be less than effective. Information system owners dependent on common controls that are less than effective consider whether they are willing to accept the associated risk or if additional tailoring is required to address the weaknesses or deficiencies in the controls. Such risk-based decisions are influenced by available resources, the trust models employed by the organization, and the risk tolerance of authorizing officials and the organization.[42]

---

[41] Information security program plans are described in Appendix G. Organizations ensure that any security capabilities provided by common controls (i.e., security capabilities inheritable by other organizational entities) are described in sufficient detail to facilitate adequate understanding of the control implementation by inheriting entities.

[42] NIST Special Publication 800-39 provides guidance on trust models, including validated, direct historical, mediated, and mandated trust models.

Common controls are subject to the same assessment and monitoring requirements as system-specific controls employed in individual organizational information systems. Because common controls impact more than one system, a higher degree of confidence regarding the effectiveness of those controls may be required.

Security controls not designated as common controls are considered *system-specific* or *hybrid* controls. System-specific controls are the primary responsibility of information system owners and their respective authorizing officials. Organizations assign a *hybrid* status to security controls when one part of the control is common and another part of the control is system-specific. For example, an organization may choose to implement the Incident Response Policy and Procedures security control (IR-1) as a hybrid control with the policy portion of the control designated as common and the procedures portion of the control designated as system-specific. Hybrid controls may also serve as predefined templates for further control refinement. Organizations may choose, for example, to implement the Contingency Planning security control (CP-2) as a predefined template for a generalized contingency plan for all organizational information systems with information system owners tailoring the plan, where appropriate, for system-specific uses.

Partitioning security controls into common, hybrid, and system-specific controls can result in significant savings to organizations in implementation and assessment costs as well as a more consistent application of security controls organization-wide. While security control partitioning into common, hybrid, and system-specific controls is straightforward and intuitive conceptually, the actual application takes a significant amount of planning and coordination. At the information system level, determination of common, hybrid, or system-specific security controls follows the development of a tailored baseline. It is necessary to first determine what security capability is needed before organizations assign responsibility for how security controls are implemented, operated, and maintained.

Security plans for individual information systems identify which security controls required for those systems have been designated by organizations as common controls and which controls have been designated as system-specific or hybrid controls. Information system owners are responsible for any system-specific implementation details associated with common controls. These implementation details are identified and described in the security plans for the individual information systems. Senior information security officers for organizations coordinate with *common control providers* (e.g., facility/site managers, human resources managers, intrusion detection system owners) to ensure that the required controls are developed, implemented, and assessed for effectiveness. Collectively, the security plans for individual information systems and the organization-wide information security program plans provide complete coverage for all security controls employed within organizations.

The determination as to whether a security control is a common, hybrid, or system-specific is context-based. Security controls cannot be determined to be common, hybrid, or system-specific simply based on reviewing the language of the control. For example, a control may be system-specific for a particular information system, but at the same time that control could be a common control for another system, which would inherit the control from the first system. One indicator of whether a system-specific control may also be a common control for other information systems is to consider who or what depends on the functionality of that particular control. If a certain part of an information system or solution external to the system boundary depends on the control, then that control may be a candidate for common control identification.

> ***Implementation Tip***
>
> - Organizations consider the *inherited risk* from the use of common controls. Security plans, security assessment reports, and plans of action and milestones for common controls (or a summary of such information) are made available to information system owners (for systems *inheriting* the controls) after the information is reviewed and approved by the senior official or executive responsible and accountable for the controls.
>
> - Organizations ensure that common control providers keep control status information current since the controls typically support multiple organizational information systems. Security plans, security assessment reports, and plans of action and milestones for common controls are used by authorizing officials to make risk-based decisions in the security authorization process for their information systems and therefore, inherited risk from common controls is a significant factor in such risk-based decisions.
>
> - Organizations ensure that common control providers have the capability to rapidly broadcast changes in the status of common controls that adversely affect the protections being provided by and expected of the common controls. Common control providers inform system owners when problems arise in the inherited common controls (e.g., when an assessment or reassessment of a common control indicates the control is flawed or deficient in some manner, or when a new threat or attack method arises that renders the common control less than effective in protecting against the new threat or attack method).
>
> - Organizations are encouraged to employ automated management systems to maintain records of the specific common controls employed in each organizational information system to enhance the ability of common control providers to rapidly communicate with system owners.
>
> - If common controls are provided to organizations by entities *external* to the organization (e.g., shared and/or external service providers), arrangements are made with the external/shared service providers by the organization to obtain information on the effectiveness of the deployed controls. Information obtained from external organizations regarding effectiveness of common controls is factored into authorization decisions.

2.5 EXTERNAL SERVICE PROVIDERS

Organizations are becoming increasingly reliant on information system services provided by external providers to conduct important missions and business functions. External information system services are computing and information technology services implemented outside of the traditional security authorization boundaries established by organizations for their information systems. Those traditional authorization boundaries linked to physical space and control of assets, are being extended (both physically and logically) with the growing use of external services. In this context, external services can be provided by: (i) entities within the organization but outside of the security authorization boundaries established for organizational information systems; (ii) entities outside of the organization either in the public sector (e.g., federal agencies) or private sector (e.g., commercial service providers); or (iii) some combination of the public and private sector options. External information system services include, for example, the use of service-oriented architectures (SOAs), cloud-based services (infrastructure, platform, software), or data center operations. External information system services may be used by, but are typically not part of, organizational information systems. In some situations, external information system services may completely replace or heavily augment the routine functionality of internal organizational information systems.

FISMA and OMB policies require that federal agencies using external service providers to process, store, or transmit federal information or operate information systems on behalf of the federal government, assure that such use meets the same security requirements that federal agencies are required to meet. Security requirements for external service providers including the security controls for external information systems are expressed in contracts or other formal agreements.[43] Organizations are responsible and accountable for the information security risk incurred by the use of information system services provided by external providers. Such risk is addressed by incorporating the Risk Management Framework (RMF) as part of the terms and conditions of the contracts with external providers. Organizations can require external providers to implement all steps in the RMF except the security authorization step, which remains an inherent federal responsibility directly linked to managing the information security risk related to the use of external information system services.[44] Organizations can also require external providers to provide appropriate evidence to demonstrate that they have complied with the RMF in protecting federal information. However, federal agencies take direct responsibility for the overall security of such services by authorizing the information systems providing the services.

Relationships with external service providers are established in a variety of ways, for example, through joint ventures, business partnerships, outsourcing arrangements (i.e., through contracts, interagency agreements, lines of business arrangements, service-level agreements), licensing agreements, and/or supply chain exchanges. The growing use of external service providers and new relationships being forged with those providers present new and difficult challenges for organizations, especially in the area of information system security. These challenges include:

- Defining the types of external information system services provided to organizations;
- Describing how those external services are protected in accordance with the information security requirements of organizations; and
- Obtaining the necessary assurances that the risk to organizational operations and assets, individuals, other organizations, and the Nation arising from the use of the external services is acceptable.

The degree of confidence that the risk from using external services is at an acceptable level depends on the trust that organizations place in external service providers. In some cases, the level of trust is based on the amount of direct control organizations are able to exert on external service providers with regard to employment of security controls necessary for the protection of the service/information and the evidence brought forth as to the effectiveness of those controls.[45] The level of control is usually established by the terms and conditions of the contracts or service-level agreements with the external service providers and can range from extensive control (e.g., negotiating contracts or agreements that specify detailed security requirements for the providers) to very limited control (e.g., using contracts or service-level agreements to obtain commodity

---

[43] Organizations consult the Federal Risk and Authorization Management Program (FedRAMP) when acquiring cloud services from external providers. FedRAMP addresses required security controls and independent assessments for a variety of cloud services. Additional information is available at http://www.fedramp.gov.

[44] To effectively manage information security risk, organizations *authorize* information systems of external providers that are part of the information technologies or services (e.g., infrastructure, platform, or software) provided to the federal government. Security authorization requirements are expressed in the terms and conditions of contracts with external providers of those information technologies and services.

[45] The level of trust that organizations place in external service providers can vary widely, ranging from those who are highly trusted (e.g., business partners in a joint venture that share a common business model and common goals) to those who are less trusted and represent greater sources of risk (e.g., business partners in one endeavor who are also competitors in another market sector). NIST Special Publication 800-39 describes different trust models that can be employed by organizations when establishing relationships with external service providers.

services such as commercial telecommunications services).[46] In other cases, levels of trust are based on factors that convince organizations that required security controls have been employed and that determinations of control effectiveness exist. For example, separately authorized external information system services provided to organizations through well-established lines of business relationships may provide degrees of trust in such services within the tolerable risk range of the authorizing officials and organizations using the services.

The provision of services by external providers may result in certain services without explicit agreements between organizations and the providers. Whenever explicit agreements are feasible and practical (e.g., through contracts, service-level agreements), organizations develop such agreements and require the use of the security controls in Appendix F of this publication. When organizations are not in a position to require explicit agreements with external service providers (e.g., services are imposed on organizations, services are commodity services), organizations establish and document explicit assumptions about service capabilities with regard to security. In situations where organizations are procuring information system services through centralized acquisition vehicles (e.g., governmentwide contracts by the General Services Administration or other preferred and/or mandatory acquisition organizations), it may be more efficient and cost-effective for contract originators to establish and maintain stated levels of trust with external service providers (including the definition of required security controls and level of assurance with regard to the provision of such controls). Organizations subsequently acquiring information system services from centralized contracts can take advantage of the negotiated levels of trust established by the procurement originators and thus avoid costly repetition of activities necessary to establish such trust.[47] Centralized acquisition vehicles (e.g., contracts) may also require the active participation of organizations. For example, organizations may be required by provisions in contracts or agreements to install public key encryption-enabled client software recommended by external service providers.

Ultimately, the responsibility for adequately mitigating unacceptable risks arising from the use of external information system services remains with authorizing officials. Organizations require that appropriate *chains of trust* be established with external service providers when dealing with the many issues associated with information system security. Organizations establish and retain a level of trust that participating service providers in the potentially complex consumer-provider relationship provide adequate protection for the services rendered to organizations. The chain of trust can be complicated due to the number of entities participating in the consumer-provider relationship and the types of relationships between the parties. External service providers may also outsource selected services to other external entities, making the chain of trust more difficult and complicated to manage. Depending on the nature of the services, organizations may find it impossible to place significant trust in external providers. This situation is due not to any inherent untrustworthiness on the part of providers, but to the intrinsic level of risk in the services.[48]

---

[46] Commercial providers of commodity-type services typically organize their business models and services around the concept of shared resources and devices for a broad and diverse customer base. Therefore, unless organizations obtain fully dedicated services from commercial service providers, there may be a need for greater reliance on compensating security controls to provide the necessary protections for the information system that relies on those external services. Organizational assessments of risk and risk mitigation activities reflect this situation.

[47] For example, procurement originators could authorize information systems providing external services to the federal government under the specific terms and conditions of the contracts. Federal agencies requesting such services under the terms of the contracts would not be required to reauthorize the information systems when acquiring such services (unless the request included services outside the scope of the original contracts).

[48] There may also be risk in disallowing certain functionality because of security concerns. Security is merely one of multiple considerations in an overall risk determination.

Where a sufficient level of trust cannot be established in the external services and/or providers, organizations can: (i) mitigate the risk by employing compensating controls; (ii) accept the risk within the level of organizational risk tolerance; (iii) transfer risk by obtaining insurance to cover potential losses; or (iv) avoid risk by choosing not to obtain the services from certain providers (resulting in performance of missions/business operations with reduced levels of functionality or possibly no functionality at all).[49] For example, in the case of cloud-based information systems and/or services, organizations might require as a compensating control, that all information stored in the cloud be encrypted for added security of the information. Alternatively, organizations may require encrypting some of the information stored in the cloud (depending on the criticality or sensitivity of such information)—accepting additional risk but limiting the risk of not storing all information in an unencrypted form.

2.6 ASSURANCE AND TRUSTWORTHINESS

Assurance and trustworthiness of information systems, system components, and information system services are becoming an increasingly important part of the risk management strategies developed by organizations. Whether information systems are deployed to support, for example, the operations of the national air traffic control system, a major financial institution, a nuclear power plant providing electricity for a large city, or the military services and warfighters, the systems must be reliable, trustworthy, and resilient in the face of increasingly sophisticated and pervasive threats. To understand how organizations achieve trustworthy systems and the role assurance plays in the trustworthiness factor, it is important to first define the term *trust*. Trust, in general, is the *belief* that an entity will behave in a predictable manner while performing specific functions, in specific environments, and under specified conditions or circumstances. The entity may be a person, process, information system, system component, system-of-systems, or any combination thereof.

From an information security perspective, trust is the belief that a security-relevant entity will behave in a predictable manner when satisfying a defined set of security requirements under specified conditions/circumstances and while subjected to disruptions, human errors, component faults and failures, and purposeful attacks that may occur in the environment of operation. Trust is usually determined relative to a specific *security capability*[50] and can be decided relative to an individual system component or the entire information system. However, trust at the information system level is not achieved as a result of composing a security capability from a set of trusted system components—rather, trust at the system level is an inherently subjective determination that is derived from the complex interactions among entities (i.e., technical components, physical components, and individuals), taking into account the life cycle activities that govern, develop, operate, and sustain the system. In essence, to have trust in a security capability requires that there is a sufficient basis for trust, or *trustworthiness,* in the set of security-relevant entities that are to be composed to provide such capability.

Trustworthiness with respect to information systems, expresses the degree to which the systems can be expected to preserve with some degree of confidence, the confidentiality, integrity, and availability of the information that is being processed, stored, or transmitted by the systems across a range of threats. Trustworthy information systems are systems that are believed to be capable of operating within a defined risk tolerance despite the environmental disruptions, human errors,

---

[49] Alternative providers offering a higher basis for trust, usually at a higher cost, may be available.

[50] A *security capability* is a combination of mutually reinforcing security controls (i.e., safeguards/countermeasures) implemented by technical means (i.e., functionality in hardware, software, and firmware), physical means (i.e., physical devices and protective measures), and/or procedural means (i.e., procedures performed by individuals).

structural failures, and purposeful attacks that are expected to occur in the environments in which the systems operate—systems that have the trustworthiness to successfully carry out assigned missions/business functions under conditions of stress and uncertainty.[51]

Security Capability

Organizations can consider defining a set of security capabilities as a precursor to the security control selection process. The concept of *security capability* is a construct that recognizes that the protection of information being processed, stored, or transmitted by information systems, seldom derives from a single safeguard or countermeasure (i.e., security control). In most cases, such protection results from the selection and implementation of a set of mutually reinforcing security controls. For example, organizations may wish to define a security capability for secure remote authentication. This capability can be achieved by the selection and implementation of a set of security controls from Appendix F (e.g., IA-2[1], IA-2[2], IA-2[8], IA-2[9], and SC-8[1]). Moreover, security capabilities can address a variety of areas that can include, for example, technical means, physical means, procedural means, or any combination thereof. Thus, in addition to the above functional capability for secure remote access, organizations may also need security capabilities that address physical means such as tamper detection on a cryptographic module or anomaly detection/analysis on an orbiting spacecraft.

As the number of security controls in Appendix F grows over time in response to an increasingly sophisticated threat space, it is important for organizations to have the ability to describe key security capabilities needed to protect core organizational missions/business functions, and to subsequently define a set of security controls that if properly designed, developed, and implemented, produce such capabilities. This simplifies how the protection problem is viewed conceptually. In essence, using the construct of security capability provides a shorthand method of grouping security controls that are employed for a common purpose or to achieve a common objective. This becomes an important consideration, for example, when assessing security controls for effectiveness.

Traditionally, assessments have been conducted on a control-by-control basis producing results that are characterized as pass (i.e., control satisfied) or fail (i.e., control not satisfied). However, the failure of a single control or in some cases, the failure of multiple controls, may not affect the overall security capability needed by an organization. Moreover, employing the broader construct of security capability allows an organization to assess the severity of vulnerabilities discovered in its information systems and determine if the failure of a particular security control (associated with a vulnerability) or the decision not to deploy a certain control, affects the overall capability needed for mission/business protection. It also facilitates conducting *root cause* analyses to determine if the failure of one security control can be traced to the failure of other controls based on the established relationships among controls. Ultimately, authorization decisions (i.e., risk acceptance decisions) are made based on the degree to which the desired security capabilities have been effectively achieved and are meeting the security requirements defined by an organization. These risk-based decisions are directly related to organizational risk tolerance that is defined as part of an organization's risk management strategy.

Two fundamental components affecting the trustworthiness of information systems are *security functionality* and *security assurance*. Security functionality is typically defined in terms of the security features, functions, mechanisms, services, procedures, and architectures implemented within organizational information systems or the environments in which those systems operate. Security assurance is the measure of confidence that the security functionality is implemented correctly, operating as intended, and producing the desired outcome with respect to meeting the security requirements for the system—thus possessing the capability to accurately mediate and enforce established security policies. Security controls address both security functionality and

---

[51] While information is the primary area of concern, trustworthiness applies to the protections for all *assets* deemed critical by organizations. Furthermore, protections are provided by technology (i.e., hardware, software, firmware), physical elements (i.e., doors, locks, surveillance), and human elements (i.e., people, processes, procedures).

security assurance. Some controls focus primarily on security functionality (e.g., PE-3, Physical Access Control; IA-2, Identification and Authentication; SC-13, Cryptographic Protection; AC-2, Account Management). Other controls focus primarily on security assurance (e.g., CA-2, Security Assessment; SA-17, Developer Security Architecture and Design; CM-3, Configuration Change Control). Finally, certain security controls can support security functionality and assurance (e.g., RA-5, Vulnerability Scanning; SC-3, Security Function Isolation; AC-25, Reference Monitor). Security controls related to functionality are combined to develop a security capability with the assurance-related controls implemented to provide a degree of confidence in the capability within the organizational risk tolerance.

Assurance Evidence—From Developmental and Operational Activities

Organizations obtain security assurance by the *actions* taken by information system developers, implementers, operators, maintainers, and assessors. Actions by individuals and/or groups during the development/operation of information systems produce *security evidence* that contributes to the assurance, or measures of confidence, in the security functionality needed to deliver the security capability. The depth and coverage of these actions (as described in Appendix E) also contribute to the efficacy of the evidence and measures of confidence. The evidence produced by developers, implementers, operators, assessors, and maintainers during the system development life cycle (e.g., design/development artifacts, assessment results, warranties, and certificates of evaluation/validation) contributes to the understanding of the security controls implemented by organizations.

The *strength* of security functionality[52] plays an important part in being able to achieve the needed security capability and subsequently satisfying the security requirements of organizations. Information system developers can increase the strength of security functionality by employing as part of the hardware/software/firmware development process: (i) well-defined security policies and policy models; (ii) structured/rigorous design and development techniques; and (iii) sound system/security engineering principles. The artifacts generated by these development activities (e.g., functional specifications, high-level/low-level designs, implementation representations [source code and hardware schematics], the results from static/dynamic testing and code analysis) can provide important evidence that the information systems (including the components that compose those systems) will be more reliable and trustworthy. Security evidence can also be generated from security testing conducted by independent, accredited, third-party assessment organizations (e.g., Common Criteria Testing Laboratories, Cryptographic/Security Testing Laboratories, and other assessment activities by government and private sector organizations).[53]

In addition to the evidence produced in the development environment, organizations can produce evidence from the operational environment that contributes to the assurance of functionality and ultimately, security capability. Operational evidence includes, for example, flaw reports, records of remediation actions, the results of security incident reporting, and the results of organizational continuous monitoring activities. Such evidence helps to determine the effectiveness of deployed security controls, changes to information systems and environments of operation, and compliance with federal legislation, policies, directives, regulations, and standards. Security evidence,

---

[52] The *security strength* of an information system component (i.e., hardware, software, or firmware) is determined by the degree to which the security functionality implemented within that component is correct, complete, resistant to direct attacks (strength of mechanism), and resistant to bypass or tampering.

[53] For example, third-party assessment organizations assess cloud services and service providers in support of the Federal Risk and Authorization Management Program (FedRAMP). Common Criteria Testing Laboratories test and evaluate information technology products using ISO/IEC standard 15408. Cryptographic/Security Testing Laboratories test cryptographic modules using the FIPS 140-2 standard.

whether obtained from development or operational activities, provides a better understanding of security controls implemented and used by organizations. Together, the actions taken during the system development life cycle by developers, implementers, operators, maintainers, and assessors and the evidence produced as part of those actions, help organizations to determine the extent to which the security functionality within their information systems is implemented correctly, operating as intended, and producing the desired outcome with respect to meeting stated security requirements and enforcing or mediating established security policies—thus providing greater confidence in the security capability.

The Compelling Argument for Assurance

Organizations specify assurance-related controls to define activities performed to generate relevant and credible evidence about the functionality and behavior of organizational information systems and to trace the evidence to the elements that provide such functionality/behavior. This evidence is used to obtain a degree of confidence that the systems satisfy stated security requirements—and do so while effectively supporting the organizational missions/business functions while being subjected to threats in the intended environments of operation.

With regard to the security evidence produced, the *depth* and *coverage* of such evidence can affect the level of assurance in the functionality implemented. Depth and coverage are attributes associated with assessment methods and the generation of security evidence. Assessment methods can be applied to developmental and operational assurance. For developmental assurance, depth is associated with the rigor, level of detail, and formality of the artifacts produced during the design and development of the hardware, software, and firmware components of information systems (e.g., functional specifications, high-level design, low-level design, source code). The level of detail available in development artifacts can affect the type of testing, evaluation, and analysis conducted during the system development life cycle (e.g., black-box testing, gray-box testing, white-box testing, static/dynamic analysis). For operational assurance, the depth attribute addresses the number and types of assurance-related security controls selected and implemented. In contrast, the coverage attribute is associated with the assessment methods employed during development and operations, addressing the scope and breadth of assessment objects included in the assessments (e.g., number/types of tests conducted on source code, number of software modules reviewed, number of network nodes/mobile devices scanned for vulnerabilities, number of individuals interviewed to check basic understanding of contingency responsibilities).[54]

Addressing assurance-related controls during acquisition and system development can help organizations to obtain sufficiently trustworthy information systems and components that are more reliable and less likely to fail. These controls include ensuring that developers employ sound systems security engineering principles and processes including, for example, providing a comprehensive security architecture, and enforcing strict configuration management and control of information system and software changes. Once information systems are deployed, assurance-related controls can help organizations to continue to have confidence in the trustworthiness of the systems. These controls include, for example, conducting integrity checks on software and firmware components, conducting penetration testing to find vulnerabilities in organizational

---

[54] NIST Special Publication 800-53A provides guidance on the generation of security evidence related to security assessments conducted during the system development life cycle.

information systems, monitoring established secure configuration settings, and developing policies/procedures that support the operation and use of the systems.

The concepts described above, including security requirements, security capability, security controls, security functionality, and security assurance, are brought together in a model for trustworthiness for information systems and system components. Figure 3 illustrates the key components in the model and the relationship among the components.

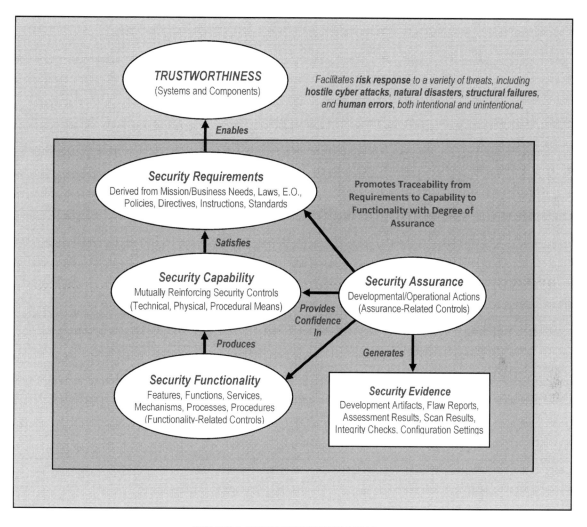

FIGURE 3: TRUSTWORTHINESS MODEL

Developmental and Operational Activities to Achieve High Assurance

Raising the bar on assurance can be difficult and costly for organizations—but sometimes essential for critical applications, missions, or business functions. Determining what parts of the organization's information technology infrastructure demand higher assurance of implemented security functionality is a Tier 1/Tier 2 risk management activity (see Figure 1 in Chapter Two). This type of activity occurs when organizations determine the *security requirements* necessary to protect organizational operations (i.e., mission, functions, image, and reputation), organizational assets, individuals, other organizations, and the Nation. Determining security requirements and the associated *security capabilities* needed to generate the appropriate protection is an integral part of the organizational risk management process described in NIST Special Publication 800-39—specifically, in the development of the *risk response strategy* following the risk framing and risk assessment steps (where organizations establish priorities, assumptions, constraints, risk tolerance and assess threats, vulnerabilities, mission/business impacts, and likelihood of threat occurrence). After the security requirements and security capabilities are determined at Tiers 1 and 2 (including the necessary assurance requirements to provide measures of confidence in the desired capabilities), those requirements/capabilities are reflected in the design of the enterprise architecture, the associated mission/business processes, and the organizational information systems that are needed to support those processes. Organizations can use the Risk Management Framework (RMF), described in NIST Special Publication 800-37, to ensure that the appropriate assurance levels are achieved for the information systems and system components deployed to carry out core missions and business functions. This is primarily a Tier 3 activity but can have some overlap with Tiers 1 and 2, for example, in the area of common control selection.

Trustworthy information systems are difficult to build from a software and systems development perspective. However, there are a number of design, architectural, and implementation principles that, if used, can result in more trustworthy systems. These core *security principles* include, for example, simplicity, modularity, layering, domain isolation, least privilege, least functionality, and resource isolation/encapsulation. Information technology products and systems exhibiting a higher degree of trustworthiness (i.e., products/systems having the requisite security functionality and security assurance) are expected to exhibit a lower rate of latent design/implementation flaws and a higher degree of penetration resistance against a range of threats including, for example, sophisticated cyber attacks, natural disasters, accidents, and intentional/unintentional errors.[55] The vulnerability and susceptibility of organizational missions/business functions and supporting information systems to known threats, the environments of operation where those systems are deployed, and the maximum acceptable level of information security risk, guide the degree of trustworthiness needed.

Appendix E describes the minimum assurance requirements for federal information systems and organizations and highlights the assurance-related controls in the security control baselines in Appendix D needed to ensure that the requirements are satisfied.[56]

---

[55] Organizations also rely to a great extent on security assurance from an operational perspective as illustrated by the assurance-related controls in Tables E-1 through E-3. Operational assurance is obtained by other than developmental actions including for example, defining and applying security configuration settings on information technology products, establishing policies and procedures, assessing security controls, and conducting a rigorous continuous monitoring program. In some situations, to achieve the necessary security capability with weak or deficient information technology, organizations compensate by increasing their operational assurance.

[56] CNSS Instruction 1253 designates security control baselines for national security systems. Therefore, the assurance-related controls in the baselines established for the national security community, if so designated, may differ from those controls designated for non-national security systems.

> **Why Assurance Matters**
>
> The importance of security assurance can be described by using the example of a light switch on a wall in the living room of your house. Individuals can observe that by simply turning the switch on and off, the switch appears to be performing according to its functional specification. This is analogous to conducting black-box testing of security functionality in an information system or system component. However, the more important questions might be—
>
> - Does the light switch do anything else besides what it is supposed to do?
> - What does the light switch look like from behind the wall?
> - What types of components were used to construct the light switch and how was the switch assembled?
> - Did the switch manufacturer follow industry best practices in the development process?
>
> This example is analogous to the many developmental activities that address the quality of the security functionality in an information system or system component including, for example, design principles, coding techniques, code analysis, testing, and evaluation.
>
> The security assurance requirements and associated assurance-related controls in Appendix E address the light switch problem from the *front of the wall perspective*, and potentially from the *behind the wall perspective*, depending on the measure of confidence needed about the component in question. For organizational missions/business functions that are less critical (i.e., low impact), lower levels of assurance might be appropriate. However, as missions/business functions become more important (i.e., moderate or high impact) and information systems and organizations become susceptible to advanced persistent threats by high-end adversaries, increased levels of assurance may be required. In addition, as organizations become more dependent on external information system services and providers, assurance becomes more important—providing greater insight and measures of confidence to organizations in understanding and verifying the security capability of external providers and the services provided to the federal government. Thus, when the potential impact to organizational operations and assets, individuals, other organizations, or the Nation is great, an increasing level of effort must be directed at what is happening behind the wall.

2.7 REVISIONS AND EXTENSIONS

The security controls listed in this publication represent the state-of-the-practice safeguards and countermeasures for federal information systems and organizations. The security controls[57] will be carefully reviewed and revised periodically to reflect:

- Experience gained from using the controls;
- New federal legislation, Executive Orders, directives, regulations, or policies;
- Changing security requirements;
- Emerging threats, vulnerabilities, and attack methods; and
- Availability of new technologies.

The security controls in the security control catalog are expected to change over time, as controls are withdrawn, revised, and added. The security controls defined in the low, moderate, and high baselines are also expected to change over time as the level of security and due diligence for mitigating risks within organizations changes. In addition to the need for change, the need for stability is addressed by requiring that proposed modifications to security controls go through a

---

[57] The privacy controls listed in Appendix J will also be updated on a regular basis using similar criteria.

rigorous public review process to obtain both public and private sector feedback and to build consensus for such change. This provides over time, a stable, flexible, and technically sound set of security controls for the federal government, contractors, and any other organizations using the security control catalog.

CHAPTER THREE

THE PROCESS

SELECTION AND SPECIFICATION OF SECURITY CONTROLS

This chapter describes the process of selecting and specifying security controls and control enhancements for organizational information systems to include: (i) selecting appropriate security control baselines; (ii) tailoring the baselines; (iii) documenting the security control selection process; and (iv) applying the control selection process to new development and legacy systems.

3.1 SELECTING SECURITY CONTROL BASELINES

In preparation for selecting and specifying the appropriate security controls for organizational information systems and their respective environments of operation, organizations first determine the criticality and sensitivity of the information to be processed, stored, or transmitted by those systems. This process, known as security categorization, is described in FIPS Publication 199.[58] The security categorization standard is based on a simple and well-established concept—that is, determining the potential adverse impact for organizational information systems. The results of security categorization help guide and inform the selection of appropriate security controls (i.e., safeguards and countermeasures) to adequately protect those information systems. The security controls selected for information systems are commensurate with the potential adverse impact on organizational operations and assets, individuals, other organizations, or the Nation if there is a loss of confidentiality, integrity, or availability. FIPS Publication 199 requires organizations to categorize information systems as low-impact, moderate-impact, or high-impact for the stated security objectives of confidentiality, integrity, and availability (**RMF Step 1**). The potential impact values assigned to the security objectives are the highest values (i.e., high water mark) from the security categories that have been determined for each type of information processed, stored, or transmitted by those information systems.[59] The generalized format for expressing the security category (SC) of an information system is:

$$SC_{\text{information system}} = \{(\textbf{confidentiality}, \textit{impact}), (\textbf{integrity}, \textit{impact}), (\textbf{availability}, \textit{impact})\},$$

where the acceptable values for potential impact are low, moderate, or high.

Since the potential impact values for confidentiality, integrity, and availability may not always be the same for a particular information system, the high water mark concept (introduced in FIPS Publication 199) is used in FIPS Publication 200 to determine the impact level of the information system for the express purpose of selecting the applicable security control baseline from one of the three baselines identified in Appendix D.[60] Thus, a *low-impact* system is defined as an information system in which all three of the security objectives are low. A *moderate-impact* system is an information system in which at least one of the security objectives is moderate and

---

[58] CNSS Instruction 1253 provides security categorization guidance for national security systems.

[59] NIST Special Publication 800-60, *Guide for Mapping Types of Information and Information Systems to Security Categories*, provides guidance on the assignment of security categories to information systems.

[60] The high water mark concept is employed because there are significant dependencies among the security objectives of confidentiality, integrity, and availability. In most cases, a compromise in one security objective ultimately affects the other security objectives as well. Accordingly, security controls are not categorized by security objective. Rather, the security controls are grouped into baselines to provide a general protection capability for classes of information systems based on impact level.

no security objective is greater than moderate. Finally, a *high-impact* system is an information system in which at least one security objective is high.

Implementation Tip

To determine the impact level of an information system:

- First, determine the different types of information that are processed, stored, or transmitted by the information system. NIST Special Publication 800-60 provides common information types.
- Second, using the impact values in FIPS Publication 199 and the recommendations of NIST Special Publication 800-60, categorize the confidentiality, integrity, and availability of each information type.
- Third, determine the information system security categorization, that is, the highest impact value for each security objective (confidentiality, integrity, availability) from among the categorizations for the information types associated with the information system.
- Fourth, determine the overall impact level of the information system from the highest impact value among the three security objectives in the system security categorization.

Note: *For national security systems, organizations use CNSSI 1253 for security categorization.*

Once the impact level of the information system is determined, organizations begin the security control selection process (**RMF Step 2**). The first step in selecting and specifying security controls for the information system is to choose the appropriate security control baseline.[61] The selection of the security control baseline is based on the FIPS 200 impact level of the information system as determined by the security categorization process described above. The organization selects one of three security control baselines from Appendix D corresponding to the low-impact, moderate-impact, or high-impact rating of the information system.[62] Note that not all security controls are assigned to baselines, as indicated in Table D-2 by the phrase *not selected*. Similarly, as illustrated in Tables D-3 through D-19, not all control enhancements are assigned to baselines. Those control enhancements that are assigned to baselines are so indicated by an "**x**" in the low, moderate, or high columns. The use of the term *baseline* is intentional. The security controls and control enhancements in the baselines are a starting point from which controls/enhancements may be removed, added, or specialized based on the tailoring guidance in Section 3.2.

The security control baselines in Appendix D address the security needs of a broad and diverse set of constituencies (including individual users and organizations). Some *assumptions* that generally underlie the baselines in Appendix D include, for example: (i) the environments in which organizational information systems operate; (ii) the nature of operations conducted by organizations; (iii) the functionality employed within information systems; (iv) the types of threats facing organizations, missions/business processes, and information systems; and (v) the type of information processed, stored, or transmitted by information systems. Articulating the underlying assumptions is a key element in the initial *risk framing* step of the risk management process described in NIST Special Publication 800-39. Some of the assumptions that underlie the baselines in Appendix D include:

---

[61] The general security control selection process may be augmented or further detailed by additional sector-specific guidance as described in Section 3.3, *Creating Overlays*, and Appendix I, *template* for developing overlays.

[62] CNSS Instruction 1253 provides security control baselines for national security systems.

- Information systems are located in physical facilities;
- User data/information in organizational information systems is relatively persistent;[63]
- Information systems are multi-user (either serially or concurrently) in operation;
- Some user data/information in organizational information systems is not shareable with other users who have authorized access to the same systems;
- Information systems exist in networked environments;
- Information systems are general purpose in nature; and
- Organizations have the necessary structure, resources, and infrastructure to implement the controls.[64]

If one or more of these assumptions is not valid, then some of the security controls assigned to the initial baselines in Appendix D may not be applicable—a situation that can be readily addressed by applying the tailoring guidance in Section 3.2 and the results of organizational assessments of risk. Conversely, there are also some possible situations that are specifically not addressed in the baselines. These include:

- Insider threats exist within organizations;
- Classified data/information is processed, stored, or transmitted by information systems;
- Advanced persistent threats (APTs) exist within organizations;
- Selected data/information requires specialized protection based on federal legislation, directives, regulations, or policies; and
- Information systems need to communicate with other systems across different security domains.

If any of the above assumptions apply, then additional security controls from Appendix F would likely be needed to ensure adequate protection—a situation that can also be effectively addressed by applying the tailoring guidance in Section 3.2 (specifically, security control supplementation) and the results of organizational assessments of risk.

3.2 TAILORING BASELINE SECURITY CONTROLS

After selecting the applicable security control baseline from Appendix D, organizations initiate the tailoring process to modify appropriately and align the controls more closely with the specific conditions within the organization (i.e., conditions related to organizational missions/business functions, information systems, or environments of operation). The tailoring process includes:

- Identifying and designating common controls in initial security control baselines;
- Applying scoping considerations to the remaining baseline security controls;
- Selecting compensating security controls, if needed;

---

[63] Persistent data/information refers to data/information with utility for a relatively long duration (e.g., days, weeks).

[64] In general, federal departments and agencies will satisfy this assumption. The assumption becomes more of an issue for nonfederal entities such as municipalities, first responders, and small (business) contractors. Such entities may not be large enough or sufficiently resourced to have elements dedicated to providing the range of security capabilities that are assumed by the baselines. Organizations consider such factors in their risk-based decisions.

- Assigning specific values to organization-defined security control parameters via explicit assignment and selection statements;
- Supplementing baselines with additional security controls and control enhancements, if needed; and
- Providing additional specification information for control implementation, if needed.

The tailoring process, as an integral part of security control selection and specification, is part of a comprehensive organizational risk management process—framing, assessing, responding to, and monitoring information security risk. Organizations use risk management guidance to facilitate risk-based decision making regarding the applicability of security controls in the security control baselines. Ultimately, organizations use the tailoring process to achieve cost-effective, risk-based security that supports organizational mission/business needs. Tailoring activities are approved by authorizing officials in coordination with selected organizational officials (e.g., risk executive [function], chief information officers, senior information security officers, information system owners, common control providers) prior to implementing the security controls. Organizations have the flexibility to perform the tailoring process at the organization level for all information systems (either as a required tailored baseline or as the starting point for system-specific tailoring activities), in support of a particular line of business or mission/business process, at the individual information system level, or by using a combination of the above.[65]

Conversely, organizations do not remove security controls for operational convenience. Tailoring decisions regarding security controls should be defensible based on mission/business needs and accompanied by explicit risk-based determinations.[66] Tailoring decisions, including the specific rationale for those decisions, are documented in the security plans for organizational information systems. Every security control from the applicable security control baseline is accounted for either by the organization (e.g., common control provider) or by the information system owner. If certain security controls are tailored out, then the associated rationale is recorded in security plans (or references/pointers to other relevant documentation are provided) for the information systems and approved by the responsible organizational officials as part of the security plan approval process.[67]

Documenting significant risk management decisions in the security control selection process is imperative in order for authorizing officials to have the necessary information to make credible, risk-based decisions with regard to the authorization of information systems. Since information systems, environments of operation, and personnel associated with the system development life cycle are subject to change, providing the assumptions, constraints, and rationale supporting those important risk decisions allows for a better understanding in the future of the security state of the information systems or environments of operation at the time the original risk decisions were made and facilitates identifying changes, when previous risk decisions are revisited.

---

[65] See also Section 3.3, *Creating Overlays*, and Appendix I, *template* for developing overlays.

[66] Tailoring decisions can also be based on timing and applicability of selected security controls under certain defined conditions. That is, security controls may not apply in every situation or the parameter values for assignment statements may change under certain circumstances. Overlays can define these special situations, conditions, or timing-related considerations.

[67] The level of detail required in documenting tailoring decisions in the security control selection process is at the discretion of organizations and reflects the impact levels of the respective information systems implementing or inheriting the controls.

Identifying and Designating Common Controls

Common controls are controls that may be inherited by one or more organizational information systems. If an information system inherits a common control, then that system does not need to explicitly implement that control—that is, the security capability is being provided by another entity. Therefore, when the security controls in Appendix F call for an information system to implement or perform a particular security function, it should not be interpreted to mean that all systems that are part of larger, more complex systems or all components of a particular system need to implement the control or function. Organizational decisions on which security controls are designated as common controls may greatly affect the responsibilities of individual system owners with regard to the implementation of controls in a particular baseline. Common control selection can also affect the overall resource expenditures by organizations (i.e., the greater the number of common controls implemented, the greater potential cost savings).

Applying Scoping Considerations

Scoping considerations, when applied in conjunction with risk management guidance, provide organizations with a more granular foundation with which to make risk-based decisions.[68] The application of scoping considerations can eliminate unnecessary security controls from the initial security control baselines and help to ensure that organizations select *only* those controls that are needed to provide the appropriate level of protection for organizational information systems— protection based on the missions and business functions being supported by those systems and the environments in which the systems operate. Organizations may apply the scoping considerations described below to assist with making risk-based decisions regarding security control selection and specification—decisions that can potentially affect how the baseline security controls are applied and implemented by organizations:

- CONTROL ALLOCATION AND PLACEMENT CONSIDERATIONS—

  The term *information system* can refer to systems at multiple levels of abstraction ranging from system-of-systems to individual single-user systems. The growing complexity of many information systems requires careful analysis in the allocation/placement of security controls within the three tiers in the risk management hierarchy (organization level, mission/business process level, and information system level) without imposing any specific architectural views or solutions.[69] Security controls in the initial baselines represent an information system-wide set of controls that may not be applicable to every component in the system. Security controls are applicable only to information system components that provide or support the information security capability addressed by the controls.[70] Organizations make explicit risk-based decisions about where to apply or allocate specific security controls in organizational information systems in order to achieve the needed security capability and to satisfy security requirements.[71] An example of this type of allocation is applying the

---

[68] The scoping considerations listed in this section are exemplary and *not* intended to limit organizations in rendering risk-based decisions based on other organization-defined considerations with appropriate rationale.

[69] This is especially true with the advent of service-oriented architectures where specific services are provided to implement a single function.

[70] For example, auditing controls are typically applied to components of an information system that provide auditing capability (e.g., servers, etc.) and are not necessarily applied to every user-level workstation within the organization. Organizations should carefully assess the inventory of components that compose their information systems to determine which security controls are applicable to the various components.

[71] As information technology advances, more powerful and diverse functionality can be found in smart phones, tablets, and other types of mobile devices. While tailor guidance may support not allocating a particular security control to a specific technology or device, any residual risk associated with the absence of that control must be addressed in risk assessments to adequately protect organizational operations and assets, individuals, other organizations, and the Nation.

requirement from AC-18(1) (i.e., protecting wireless access to information systems using authentication/encryption) to all wireless access except for wireless access to visitor subnetworks which are not connected to other system components.

- OPERATIONAL/ENVIRONMENTAL-RELATED CONSIDERATIONS—
  Several of the security controls in the baselines are based on the assumption of the existence of certain operational/environmental factors. Where these factors are absent or significantly diverge from the baseline assumptions, it is justifiable to tailor the baseline. Some of the more common operational/environmental factors include:

  - *Mobility*

    The mobility of physical hosting environments can impact the security controls selected for organizational information systems. As noted above, the set of security controls assigned to each baseline in Appendix D assumes the operation of information systems in fixed facilities and nonmobile locations. If those information systems operate primarily in mobile environments, the security control baseline should be tailored appropriately to account for the differences in mobility and accessibility of the specific locations where the systems reside. For example, many of the security controls in the Physical and Environmental Protection (PE) family that are selected in all three baselines reflect the assumption that the information systems reside in physical facilities/complexes that require appropriate physical protections. Such controls would likely not provide added value for mobile environments such as ships, aircraft, automobiles, vans, or space-based systems.[72]

  - *Single-User Systems and Operations*

    For information systems that are designed to operate as single-user systems (e.g., smart phones), several of the security controls that address sharing among users may not be needed. A single-user system or device refers to a system/device that is only intended to be used by a single individual over time (i.e., exclusive use). Systems or devices that are shared by multiple users over time are not considered single-user. Security controls such as AC-10, Concurrent Session Control, SC-4, Information in Shared Resources, and AC-3, Access Enforcement[73] may not be required in single-user systems/operations and could reasonably be tailored out of the baseline at the discretion of organizations.

  - *Data Connectivity and Bandwidth*

    While many information systems are interconnected, there are some systems which for security or operational reasons, lack networking capabilities—that is, the systems are *air gapped* from the network. For nonnetworked systems, security controls such as AC-17, Remote Access, SC-8, Transmission Confidentiality and Integrity, and SC-7, Boundary Protection, are not applicable and may be tailored out of the security control baselines at the discretion of organizations. In addition to nonnetworked information systems, there are systems that have very limited or sporadic bandwidth (e.g., tactical systems that support warfighter or law enforcement missions). For such systems, the application of security controls would need to be examined carefully as the limited and/or sporadic bandwidth could impact the practicality of implementing those controls and the viability of adversaries staging cyber attacks over the limited bandwidth.

---

[72] The mobile nature of devices means that it is possible that, for some period of time, the devices may reside in fixed facilities or complexes in fixed locations. During that time, the PE controls would likely apply.

[73] Organizations consider whether individual users have administrator privileges before removing AC-3 from security control baselines.

- *Limited Functionality Systems or System Components*

    What constitutes an information system under the E-Government Act of 2002 is quite broad. Fax machines, printers, scanners, pagers, smart phones, tablets, E-readers, and digital cameras can all be categorized as information systems (or system components). These types of systems and components may lack the general processing capabilities assumed in the security control baselines. The nature of these constraints may limit the types of threats that these systems face, and hence the appropriateness of some of the security controls. Thus, a control such as SI-3, Malicious Code Protection (required in all control baselines) may not be practical for information systems or components that are not capable of executing code (e.g., text-only pagers). However, because there is often no clear delineation between these types of information systems or components (e.g., smart phones combine the digital capabilities of telephones, cameras, and computers), it is important that the application of security controls to limited functionality systems or components be done judiciously and always take into account the intended use of the systems, system capabilities, and the risk of compromise.

- *Information and System Non-Persistence*

    There is often an assumption that user information within organizational information systems is persistent for a considerable period of time. However, for some applications and environments of operation (e.g., tactical systems, industrial control systems), the persistence of user information is often very limited in duration. For information systems processing, storing, or transmitting such non-persistent information, several security controls in the Contingency Planning (CP) family such as CP-6, Alternate Storage Site, CP-7, Alternate Processing Site, and CP-9, Information System Backup, may not be practical and can be tailored out at the discretion of organizations. For similar reasons, controls such as MP-6, Media Sanitization, and SC-28, Protection of Information at Rest, are good candidates for removal through tailoring.[74] In addition to the non-persistence of information, the information systems/services may be non-persistent as well. This can be achieved by the use of virtualization techniques to establish non-persistent instantiations of operating systems and applications. Depending on the duration of the instantiations, some baseline controls might not be applicable.

- *Public Access*

    When public access to organizational information systems is allowed, security controls should be applied with discretion since some security controls from the specified control baselines (e.g., identification and authentication, personnel security controls) may not be applicable for public access. Thus, in the case of the general public accessing federal government websites (e.g., to download publically accessible information such as forms, emergency preparedness information), security controls such as AC-7, Unsuccessful Logon Attempts, AC-17, Remote Access, IA-2, Identification and Authentication, IA-4, Identifier Management, and IA-5, Authenticator Management, typically would not be relevant for validating access authorizations or privileges. However, many of these controls would still be needed for identifying and authenticating organizational personnel that maintain and support information systems providing such public access websites and services. Similarly, many of the security controls may still be required for users accessing nonpublic information systems through such public interfaces, for example, to access or change personal information.

---

[74] Organizations balance information persistence with the sensitivity of the information. Non-persistent information may still require sanitization after deletion. In addition, organizations consider the duration of information sensitivity—some information may be persistent, but only be sensitive for a limited time.

- SECURITY OBJECTIVE-RELATED CONSIDERATIONS—

    Security controls that support only one or two of the confidentiality, integrity, or availability security objectives may be downgraded to the corresponding control in a lower baseline (or modified or eliminated if not defined in a lower baseline) only if the downgrading action: (i) reflects the FIPS Publication 199 security category for the supported security objective(s) before moving to the FIPS Publication 200 impact level (i.e., high water mark);[75] (ii) is supported by an organizational assessment of risk; and (iii) does not adversely affect the level of protection for the security-relevant information within the information system.[76] For example, if an information system is categorized as moderate impact using the high water mark concept because confidentiality and/or integrity are moderate but availability is low, there are several controls that only support the availability security objective and that potentially could be downgraded to low baseline requirements—that is, it may be appropriate *not* to implement CP-2(1) because the control enhancement supports only availability and is selected in the moderate baseline but not in the low baseline. The following security controls and control enhancements are potential candidates for downgrading:[77]

    - *Confidentiality:* AC-21, MA-3(3), MP-3, MP-4, MP-5, MP-5(4), MP-6(1), MP-6(2), PE-4, PE-5, SC-4, SC-8, SC-8(1);

    - *Integrity:* CM-5, CM-5(1), CM-5(3), SC-8, SC-8(1), SI-7, SI-7(1), SI-7(5), SI-10; and

    - *Availability:* CP-2(1), CP-2(2), CP-2(3), CP-2(4), CP-2(5), CP-2(8), CP-3(1), CP-4(1), CP-4(2), CP-6, CP-6(1), CP-6(2), CP-6(3), CP-7, CP-7(1), CP-7(2), CP-7(3), CP-7(4), CP-8, CP-8(1), CP-8(2), CP-8(3), CP-8(4), CP-9(1), CP-9(2), CP-9(3), CP-9(5), CP-10(2), CP-10(4), MA-6, PE-9, PE-10, PE-11, PE-11(1), PE-13(1), PE-13(2), PE-13(3), PE-15(1).

- TECHNOLOGY-RELATED CONSIDERATIONS—

    Security controls that refer to specific technologies (e.g., wireless, cryptography, public key infrastructure) are applicable only if those technologies are employed or are required to be employed within organizational information systems. Security controls that can be explicitly or implicitly supported by automated mechanisms do not require the development of such mechanisms if the mechanisms do not already exist or are not readily available in commercial or government off-the-shelf products. If automated mechanisms are not readily available,

---

[75] When applying the high water mark in Section 3.1, some of the original FIPS Publication 199 confidentiality, integrity, or availability security objectives may have been upgraded to a higher security control baseline. As part of this process, security controls that uniquely support the confidentiality, integrity, or availability security objectives may have been upgraded unnecessarily. Consequently, it is recommended that organizations consider appropriate and allowable downgrading actions to ensure cost-effective, risk-based application of security controls.

[76] Information that is security-relevant at the information system level (e.g., password files, network routing tables, cryptographic key management information) is distinguished from user-level information within the same system. Certain security controls are used to support the security objectives of confidentiality and integrity for both user-level and system-level information. Caution should be exercised in downgrading confidentiality or integrity-related security controls to ensure that downgrading actions do not result in insufficient protection for the security-relevant information within the information system. Security-relevant information must be protected at the high water mark in order to achieve a similar level of protection for any of the security objectives related to user-level information.

[77] Downgrading actions apply only to the moderate and high baselines. Security controls that are uniquely attributable to confidentiality, integrity, or availability that would ordinarily be considered as potential candidates for downgrading (e.g., AC-16, AU-10, IA-7, PE-12, PE-14, SC-5, SC-13, SC-16) are eliminated from consideration because the controls are either selected for use in all baselines and have no enhancements that could be downgraded, or the controls are optional and not selected for use in any baseline. Organizations should exercise caution when downgrading security controls that do not appear in the list in Section 3.2 to ensure that downgrading actions do not affect security objectives other than the objectives targeted for downgrading.

cost-effective, or technically feasible, compensating security controls, implemented through nonautomated mechanisms or procedures, are used to satisfy specified security controls or control enhancements (see terms and conditions for applying compensating controls below).

- MISSION REQUIREMENTS-RELATED CONSIDERATIONS—

  Some security controls may not be applicable (or appropriate) if implementing those controls has the potential to degrade, debilitate, or otherwise hamper critical organizational missions and/or business functions. For example, if the mission requires that an uninterrupted display of mission-critical information be available at an operator console (e.g., air traffic controller console), the implementation of AC-11, Session Lock, or SC-10, Network Disconnect, may not be appropriate.

Selecting Compensating Security Controls

Organizations may find it necessary on occasion to employ compensating security controls. Compensating controls are alternative security controls employed by organizations in lieu of specific controls in the low, moderate, or high baselines described in Appendix D—controls that provide equivalent or comparable protection for organizational information systems and the information processed, stored, or transmitted by those systems.[78] This may occur, for example, when organizations are unable to effectively implement specific security controls in the baselines or when, due to the specific nature of the information systems or environments of operation, the controls in the baselines are not a cost-effective means of obtaining the needed risk mitigation. Compensating controls are typically selected after applying the scoping considerations in the tailoring guidance to the applicable security control baseline. Compensating controls may be employed by organizations under the following conditions:

- Organizations select compensating controls from Appendix F; if appropriate compensating controls are not available, organizations adopt suitable compensating controls from other sources;[79]
- Organizations provide supporting rationale for how compensating controls provide equivalent security capabilities for organizational information systems and why the baseline security controls could not be employed; and
- Organizations assess and accept the risk associated with implementing compensating controls in organizational information systems.

Assigning Security Control Parameter Values

Security controls and control enhancements containing embedded parameters (i.e., assignment and selection statements) give organizations the flexibility to define certain portions of controls and enhancements to support specific organizational requirements. After the initial application of scoping considerations and the selection of compensating controls, organizations review the security controls and control enhancements for assignment/selection statements and determine appropriate organization-defined values for the identified parameters. Parameter values may be prescribed by applicable federal laws, Executive Orders, directives, regulations, policies, or standards. Once organizations define the parameter values for security controls and control

---

[78] More than one compensating control may be required to provide the equivalent protection for a particular security control in Appendix F. For example, organizations with significant staff limitations may compensate for the separation of duty security control by strengthening the audit, accountability, and personnel security controls.

[79] Organizations should make every attempt to select compensating controls from the security control catalog in Appendix F. Organization-defined compensating controls are employed *only* when organizations determine that the security control catalog does not contain suitable compensating controls.

enhancements, the assignments and selections become a part of the control and enhancement.[80] Organizations may choose to specify the values for security control parameters before selecting compensating controls since the specification of the parameters completes the control definitions and may affect compensating control requirements. There can also be significant benefits in collaborating on the development of parameter values. For organizations that work together on a frequent basis, it may be useful for those organizations to develop a mutually agreeable set of uniform values for security control parameters. Doing so may assist organizations in achieving a greater degree of reciprocity when depending upon the information systems and/or services offered by other organizations.

Supplementing Security Control Baselines

The final determination of the appropriate set of security controls necessary to provide adequate security for organizational information systems and the environments in which those systems operate is a function of the assessment of risk and what is required to sufficiently mitigate the risks to organizational operations and assets, individuals, other organizations, and the Nation.[81] In many cases, additional security controls or control enhancements (beyond those controls and enhancements contained in the baselines in Appendix D) will be required to address specific threats to and vulnerabilities in organizations, mission/business processes, and/or information systems and to satisfy the requirements of applicable federal laws, Executive Orders, directives, policies, standards, or regulations.[82] The risk assessment in the security control selection process provides essential information in determining the necessity and sufficiency of the security controls and control enhancements in the initial baselines. Organizations are encouraged to make maximum use of Appendix F to facilitate the process of supplementing the initial baselines with additional security controls and/or control enhancements.[83]

Situations Requiring Potential Baseline Supplementation

Organizations may be subject to conditions that, from an operational, environmental, or threat perspective, warrant the selection and implementation of additional (supplemental) controls to achieve adequate protection of organizational missions/business functions and the information systems supporting those missions/functions. Examples of conditions and additional controls that might be required are provided below.

- ADVANCED PERSISTENT THREAT

    Security control baselines do not assume that the current threat environment is one where adversaries have achieved a significant foothold and presence within organizations and organizational information systems—that is, organizations are dealing with an advanced persistent threat (APT). Adversaries continue to attack organizational information systems and the information technology infrastructure and are successful in some aspects of such attacks. To more fully address the advanced persistent threat, concepts such as insider threat

---

[80] CNSS Instruction 1253 provides assignment of minimum values for organization-defined variables applicable to national security systems. Parameter values can also be defined as part of overlays described in Section 3.4.

[81] Considerations for potential national-level impacts and impacts to other organizations in categorizing organizational information systems derive from the USA PATRIOT Act and Homeland Security Presidential Directives.

[82] In previous versions of Special Publication 800-53, tailoring referred only to the removal of security controls from baselines and supplementation referred only to the addition of controls to baselines. In this document, the term tailoring has been redefined to include both the addition of security controls to baselines (i.e., tailoring up) and the removal of controls from baselines (i.e., tailoring down).

[83] Security controls and control enhancements selected to supplement baselines are allocated to appropriate information system components in the same manner as the control allocations carried out by organizations in the initial baselines.

protection (CM-5(4)), heterogeneity (SC-29), deception (SC-26 and SC-30), non-persistence (SC-25 and SC-34), and segmentation (SC-7(13)) can be considered.

- CROSS-DOMAIN SERVICES

    Security control baselines do not assume that information systems have to operate across multiple security domains. The baselines assume a flat view of information flows (i.e., the same security policies in different domains when information moves across authorization boundaries). To address cross-domain services and transactions, some subset of the AC-4 security control enhancements can be considered to ensure adequate protection of information when transferred between information systems with different security policies.

- MOBILITY

    The use of mobile devices might result in the need for additional security controls and control enhancements not selected in the initial baselines. For example, AC-7(2), which requires the purging/wiping of information after an organization-defined number of unsuccessful logon attempts, or MP-6 (8), which requires the capability for remote purging/wiping, could be selected in order to address the threat of theft or loss of mobile devices.

- CLASSIFIED INFORMATION

    In some environments, classified and sensitive information[84] may be resident on national security systems without all users having the necessary authorizations to access all of the information. In those situations, additional security controls are required to ensure that information requiring strict separation is not accessed by unauthorized users. More stringent access controls include, for example, AC-3(3) and AC-16. When classified information is being processed, stored, or transmitted on information systems that are jointly owned by multiple entities (e.g., coalition partners in military alliances), more restrictive controls for maintenance personnel may be required including, for example, MA-5(4).

Processes for Identifying Additional Needed Security Controls

Organizations can employ a *requirements definition* approach or a *gap analysis* approach in selecting security controls and control enhancements to supplement initial baselines. In the requirements definition approach, organizations obtain specific and credible threat[85] information (or make reasonable assumptions) about the activities of adversaries with certain capabilities or attack potential (e.g., skill levels, expertise, available resources). To effectively withstand cyber attacks from adversaries with the stated capabilities or attack potential, organizations strive to achieve a certain level of defensive capability or cyber preparedness. Organizations can select additional security controls and control enhancements from Appendix F to obtain such defensive capability or level of preparedness. In contrast to the requirements definition approach, the gap analysis approach begins with an organizational assessment of its current defensive capability or level of cyber preparedness. From that initial capability assessment, organizations determine the types of threats they can reasonably expect to counter. If the current organizational defensive capabilities or levels of cyber preparedness are insufficient, the gap analysis determines the required capabilities and levels of preparedness. Organizations subsequently define the security controls and control enhancements from Appendix F needed to achieve the desired capabilities or cyber-preparedness levels. Both of the approaches described above require timely and accurate

---

[84] The example is illustrative only. CNSS Instruction 1253 provides specific guidance regarding security controls required for national security systems.

[85] While this example focuses on threats to information systems from purposeful attacks, the threat space of concern to organizations also includes environmental disruptions and human errors.

threat information. It is essential that organizations work with the appropriate threat identification component to obtain such information.

During the tailoring process, organizations consider reevaluating the priority codes from the security control baselines to determine if any changes to those priorities are appropriate. This is especially important when adding security controls that are not included in any of the baselines, because those controls have priority codes of P0. The reevaluation of priority codes can be based on organizational assessments of risk or design/developmental decisions related to the security architecture or the systems and security engineering process that may require certain sequencing in security control implementation.

Enhancing Information Security without Changing Control Selection

There may be situations in which organizations cannot apply sufficient security controls within their information systems to adequately reduce or mitigate risk (e.g., when using certain types of information technologies or employing certain computing paradigms). Therefore, alternative strategies are needed to prevent organizational missions/business functions from being adversely affected— strategies that consider the mission and business risks resulting from an aggressive use of information technology. Restrictions on the types of technologies used and how organizational information systems are employed provide an alternative method to reduce or mitigate risk that may be used in conjunction with, or instead of, supplemental security controls. Restrictions on the use of information systems and specific information technologies may be, in some situations, the only practical or reasonable actions organizations can take in order to have the capability to carry out assigned missions/business functions in the face of determined adversaries. Examples of use restrictions include:

- Limiting the information that information systems can process, store, or transmit or the manner in which organizational missions/business functions are automated;

- Prohibiting external access to organizational information by removing selected information system components from networks (i.e., air gapping); and

- Prohibiting moderate- or high-impact information on organizational information system components to which the public has access, unless an explicit risk determination is made authorizing such access.

Providing Additional Specification Information for Control Implementation

Since security controls are statements of security capability at higher levels of abstraction, the controls may lack sufficient information for successful implementation. Therefore, additional detail may be necessary to fully define the intent of a given security control for implementation purposes and to ensure that the security requirements related to that control are satisfied. For example, additional information may be provided as part of the process of moving from control to specification requirement, and may involve *refinement* of implementation details, *refinement* of scope, or *iteration* to apply the same control differently to different scopes. Organizations ensure that if existing security control information (e.g., selection and assignment statements) is not sufficient to fully define the intended application of the control, such information is provided. Organizations have the flexibility to determine whether additional detail is included as a part of the control statement, in supplemental guidance, or in a separate control addendum section. When providing additional detail, organizations are cautioned not to change the intent of the security control or modify the original language in the control. The additional implementation information can be documented either in security plans or systems and security engineering plans. The type of additional detail that might be necessary to fully specify a security control for implementation purposes is provided in the SI-7(6) example below:

SI-7   SOFTWARE, FIRMWARE, AND INFORMATION INTEGRITY

(6) *SOFTWARE, FIRMWARE, AND INFORMATION INTEGRITY | CRYPTOGRAPHIC PROTECTION*
   The information system implements cryptographic mechanisms to detect unauthorized changes to software, firmware, and information.

   Supplemental Guidance: Cryptographic mechanisms used for the protection of integrity include, for example, digital signatures and the computation and application of signed hashes using asymmetric cryptography, protecting the confidentiality of the key used to generate the hash, and using the public key to verify the hash information. Related control: SC-13.

   Additional implementation detail for SI-7(6):

   Digital signatures are applied to all traffic for which non-repudiation is required employing SHA-256 or another approved NIST algorithm demonstrably of at least the same strength of mechanism.

3.3 CREATING OVERLAYS

The previous sections described the process of tailoring security control baselines to achieve a more focused and relevant security capability for organizations. In certain situations, it may be beneficial for organizations to apply tailoring guidance to the baselines to develop a set of security controls for community-wide use or to address specialized requirements, technologies, or unique missions/environments of operation.[86] For example, the federal government may decide to establish a governmentwide set of security controls and implementation guidance for: (i) public key infrastructure (PKI) systems that could be uniformly applied to all PKI systems implemented within federal agencies; (ii) cloud-based information systems that are uniformly applied to all federal agencies procuring or implementing cloud services; or (iii) industrial control systems (ICSs) at federal facilities producing electric power or controlling environmental systems in federal facilities. Alternatively, to address particular communities of interest with specialized requirements, the Department of Defense, for example, may decide to establish a set of security controls and implementation guidance for its tactical operations and environments by applying the tailoring guidance to the standard security control baselines for national security systems to achieve more specialized solutions. In each of the above examples, tailored baselines can be developed for each information technology area or for the unique circumstances/environments and promulgated to large communities of interest—thus achieving standardized security capabilities, consistency of implementation, and cost-effective security solutions.

To address the need for developing community-wide and specialized sets of security controls for information systems and organizations, the concept of *overlay* is introduced. An overlay is a fully specified set of security controls, control enhancements, and supplemental guidance derived from the application of tailoring guidance in Section 3.2 to security control baselines in Appendix D.[87] Overlays complement the initial security control baselines by: (i) providing the opportunity to add or eliminate controls; (ii) providing security control applicability and interpretations for specific information technologies, computing paradigms, environments of operation, types of information systems, types of missions/operations, operating modes, industry sectors, and statutory/regulatory requirements; (iii) establishing community-wide parameter values for assignment and/or selection statements in security controls and control enhancements; and (iv) extending the supplemental guidance for security controls, where necessary. Organizations typically use the overlay concept

---

[86] This type of tailoring can be conducted at the federal level or by individual organizations.

[87] CNSS Instruction 1253 provides tailoring guidance and security control baselines for national security systems.

when there is divergence from the basic assumptions used to create the initial security control baselines (see Section 3.1). If organizations are not divergent from the basic assumptions for the initial baselines, there is likely no need to create an overlay. Alternatively, the baselines may be missing key assumptions which would justify creating an overlay with additional assumptions.

The full range of tailoring activities can be employed by organizations to provide a disciplined and structured approach for developing tailored baselines supporting the areas described above. Overlays provide an opportunity to build consensus across communities of interest and develop security plans for organizational information systems that have broad-based support for very specific circumstances, situations, and/or conditions. Categories of overlays that may be useful include, for example:

- Communities of interest, industry sectors, or coalitions/partnerships (e.g., healthcare, law enforcement, intelligence, financial, transportation, energy, allied collaboration/sharing);
- Information technologies/computing paradigms (e.g., cloud/mobile, PKI, Smart Grid, cross-domain solutions);
- Environments of operation (e.g., space, tactical);
- Types of information systems and operating modes (e.g., industrial/process control systems, weapons systems, single-user systems, standalone systems);
- Types of missions/operations (e.g., counterterrorism, first responders, research, development, test, and evaluation); and
- Statutory/regulatory requirements (e.g., Foreign Intelligence Surveillance Act, Health Insurance Portability and Accountability Act, Privacy Act).

Organizations can effectively use the risk management concepts defined in NIST Special Publication 800-39 when developing overlays. The successful development of overlays requires the involvement of: (i) information security professionals who understand the specific subject area that is the focus of the overlay development effort; and (ii) subject matter experts in the overlay area who understand the security controls in Appendix F and the initial baselines in Appendix D. The format and structure for developing overlays is provided in Appendix I.

Multiple overlays can be applied to a single security control baseline. The tailored baselines that result from the overlay development process may be more or less stringent than the original security control baselines. Risk assessments provide information necessary to determine if the risk from implementing the tailored baselines falls within the risk tolerance of the organizations or communities of interest developing the overlays. If multiple overlays are employed, it is possible that there could be a conflict between the overlays. If the use of multiple overlays results in conflicts between the application or removal of security controls, the authorizing official (or designee), in coordination with the mission/business owner and/or information owner/steward, can resolve the conflict. In general, overlays are intended to reduce the need for ad hoc tailoring of baselines by organizations through the selection of a set of controls and control enhancements that more closely correspond to common circumstances, situations, and/or conditions. However, the use of overlays does not preclude organizations from performing further tailoring to reflect organization-specific needs, assumptions, or constraints. Tailoring of overlays is accomplished within the constraints defined within the overlay and may require the concurrence/approval of the authorizing official or other organization-designated individuals. For example, an overlay created for an industrial control system (ICS) may require tailoring for applicability to a specific type of ICS and its environment of operation. But it is anticipated that the use of overlays would greatly reduce the number and extent of organization-specific ad hoc tailoring.

3.4 DOCUMENTING THE CONTROL SELECTION PROCESS

Organizations document the relevant decisions taken during the security control selection process, providing a sound rationale for those decisions. This documentation is essential when examining the security considerations for organizational information systems with respect to the potential mission/business impact. The resulting set of security controls and the supporting rationale for the selection decisions (including any information system use restrictions required by organizations) are documented in the security plans. Documenting significant risk management decisions in the security control selection process is imperative so that authorizing officials can have access to the necessary information to make informed authorization decisions for organizational information systems.[88] Without such information, the understanding, assumptions, constraints, and rationale supporting those risk management decisions will, in all likelihood, not be available when the state of the information systems or environments of operation change, and the original risk decisions are revisited. Figure 4 summarizes the security control selection process, including the selection of initial baselines and the tailoring of the baselines by applying the guidance in Section 3.2.

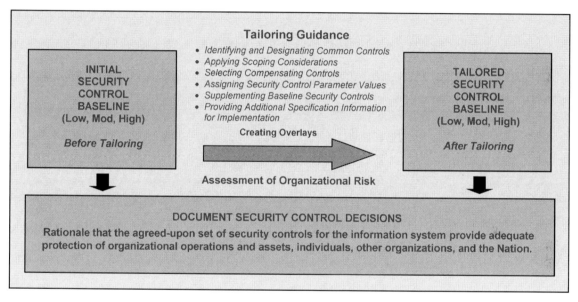

FIGURE 4: SECURITY CONTROL SELECTION PROCESS

Iterative and Dynamic Nature of Security Control Tailoring

The security control tailoring process described above, while appearing to be sequential in nature, can also have an iterative aspect. Organizations may choose to execute the tailoring steps in any order based on organizational needs and the information generated from risk assessments. For example, some organizations may establish the parameter values for security controls in the initial baselines prior to selecting compensating controls. Other organizations may delay completing assignment and selection statements in the controls until after the supplementation activities have been completed. Organizations may also discover that when fully specifying security controls for the intended environments of operation, there may be difficulties that arise which may trigger the need for additional (supplemental) controls. Finally, the security control tailoring process is not static—that is, organizations revisit the tailoring step as often as needed based on ongoing organizational assessments of risk.

---

[88] The security control selection process also applies to common control providers and the authorizing officials rendering authorization decisions for common controls deployed within organizations.

In addition to the iterative and dynamic nature of the security control tailoring process, there may also be side effects as controls are added and removed from the baselines. Security controls in Appendix F can have some degree of dependency and functional overlap with other controls. In many cases, security controls work together to achieve a security capability. Thus, removing a particular security control from a baseline during the tailoring process may have unintended side effects (and potentially adverse impacts) on the remaining controls. Alternatively, adding a new security control to a baseline during the tailoring process may eliminate or reduce the need for certain specific controls because the new control provides a better security capability than the capability provided by other controls. For example, if organizations implement SC-30(2) using virtualization techniques to randomly/frequently deploy diverse and changing operating systems and applications, this approach could potentially limit the requirement to update the security configurations in CM-2(2). Therefore, the addition or removal of security controls is viewed with regard to the totality of the information security needs of the organization and its information systems, and not simply with regard to the controls being added or removed.

> **Implementation Tip**
>
> In diverging from the security control baselines during the tailoring process, organizations consider some very important linkages between various controls and control enhancements. These linkages are captured in the selection of controls and enhancements in the baselines and are especially significant when developing overlays (described in Section 3.3 and Appendix I). In some instances, the linkages are such that it is not meaningful to include a security control or control enhancement without some other control or enhancement. The totality of the controls and enhancements provide a required *security capability*. Some linkages are obvious such as the linkage between Mandatory Access Control enhancement (AC-3(3)) and Security Attributes (AC-16). But other linkages may be more subtle. This is especially true in the case where the linkage is between security functionality-related controls and security assurance-related controls as described in Appendix E. For example, it is not particularly meaningful to implement AC-3(3) without also implementing a Reference Monitor (AC-25). Organizations are encouraged to pay careful attention to the *related controls* section of the *Supplemental Guidance* for the security controls to help in identifying such linkages.

Other Considerations

Organizational tailoring decisions are not carried out in a vacuum. While such decisions are rightly focused on information security considerations, it is important that the decisions be aligned with other risk factors that organizations address routinely. Risk factors such as cost, schedule, and performance are considered in the overall determination of which security controls to employ in organizational information systems and environments of operation. For example, in military command and control systems in which lives may be at stake, the adoption of security controls is balanced with operational necessity. With respect to the air traffic control system and consoles used by air traffic controllers, the need to access the consoles in real time to control the air space outweighs the security need for an AC-11, Session Lock. In short, the security control selection process (to include tailoring activities described in Section 3.2) should be integrated into the overall risk management process as described in NIST Special Publication 800-39.

Finally, organizations factor scalability into the security control selection process—that is, controls are scalable with regard to the extent/rigor of the implementation. Scalability is guided by the FIPS Publication 199 security categorizations and the associated FIPS Publication 200 impact levels of the information systems where the controls are to be applied. For example, contingency plans for high-impact information systems may contain significant amounts of implementation detail and be quite lengthy. In contrast, contingency plans for low-impact systems may contain considerably less detail and be quite succinct. Organizations use discretion in applying the security controls to organizational information systems, giving consideration to the scalability factors in particular operational environments. Scaling controls to the appropriate system impact level facilitates a more cost-effective, risk-based approach to security control implementation—expending only the level of resources necessary to achieve sufficient risk mitigation and adequate security.

> ***Implementation Tip***
>
> Maintaining a record of security control selection and control status can be addressed in one or multiple documents or security plans. If using multiple documents, consider providing references to the necessary information in the relevant documents rather than requiring duplication of information. Using references to relevant documentation reduces the amount of time and resources needed by organizations to generate such information. Other benefits include greater security awareness and understanding of the information system capabilities. Increased security awareness/understanding supports more effective integration of information security into organizational information systems.

3.5 NEW DEVELOPMENT AND LEGACY SYSTEMS

The security control selection process described in this section can be applied to organizational information systems from two different perspectives: (i) new development; and (ii) legacy. For new development systems, the security control selection process is applied from a *requirements definition* perspective since the systems do not yet exist and organizations are conducting initial security categorizations. The security controls included in the security plans for the information systems serve as a security specification and are expected to be incorporated into the systems during the development and implementation phases of the system development life cycle. In contrast, for legacy information systems, the security control selection process is applied from a *gap analysis* perspective when organizations are anticipating significant changes to the systems (e.g., during major upgrades, modifications, or outsourcing). Since the information systems already exist, organizations in all likelihood have completed the security categorization and security control selection processes resulting in the establishment of previously agreed-upon security controls in the respective security plans and the implementation of those controls within the information systems. Therefore, the gap analysis can be applied in the following manner:

- First, *reconfirm* or *update* as necessary, the security category and impact level for the information system based on the types of information that are *currently* being processed, stored, or transmitted by the system.

- Second, *review* the existing security plan that describes the security controls that are currently employed considering any updates to the security category and information system impact level as well as any changes to the organization, mission/business processes, the system, or the operational environment. Reassess the risk and revise the security plan as necessary, including documenting any additional security controls that *would* be needed by the system to ensure that the risk to organizational operations, organizational assets, individuals, other organizations, and the Nation, remains at an acceptable level.

- Third, *implement* the security controls described in the updated security plan, document in the plan of action and milestones any controls not implemented, and continue with the remaining steps in the Risk Management Framework in the same manner as a new development system.

Applying Gap Analyses to External Service Providers

The gap analysis perspective is also applied when interacting with external service providers. As described in Section 2.5, organizations are becoming increasingly reliant on external providers for information system services. Using the steps in the gap analysis described above, organizations can effectively use the acquisition process and appropriate contractual vehicles to require external providers to carry out the security categorization and security control selection steps in the RMF. The resulting information can help determine what security controls the external provider either has in place or intends to implement for the information system services that are to be provided. If a security control deficit exists, the responsibility for adequately mitigating unacceptable risks arising from the use of external information system services remains with authorizing officials. In such situations, organizations can reduce the organizational risk to an acceptable level by:

- Using the existing contractual vehicle to require the external provider to meet the additional security control requirements established by the organization;

- Negotiating with the provider for additional security controls if the existing contractual vehicle does not provide for such added requirements;

- Approving the use of compensating controls by the provider; or

- Employing alternative risk mitigation actions[89] within the organizational information system when a contract either does not exist or the contract does not provide the necessary leverage for organizations to obtain the needed security controls.

Implementation Tip

Many organizations operate and maintain complex information systems, often referred to as a system-of-systems. Enterprise architecture plays a key part in the security control selection process for these types of information systems. Organizations can address the complex system problem by dividing the system into two or more subsystems and applying the FIPS 199 security categorization and FIPS 200 impact level determination to each subsystem. Applying separate impact levels to each subsystem does not change the overall impact level of the information system; rather, it allows constituent subsystems to receive a separate allocation of security controls instead of deploying higher-impact controls across every subsystem. It is not valid to treat the subsystems as entirely independent entities, however, since the subsystems are interdependent and interconnected.

Organizations develop security architectures to allocate security controls among subsystems including monitoring and controlling communications at key internal boundaries within the system and provide system-wide controls that meet or exceed the highest information system impact level of the constituent subsystems inheriting security capabilities from those controls. Organizations also consider that replicated subsystems within complex systems may exhibit common vulnerabilities that can be exploited by common threat sources—thereby negating the redundancy that might be relied upon as a risk mitigation measure. The impact due to a security incident against one constituent subsystem might cascade and impact many subsystems at the same time.

---

[89] For example, local policies, procedures, and/or compensating controls could be established by organizations to serve as alternative mitigation actions for risks identified in a gap analysis.

APPENDIX A

REFERENCES

LAWS, POLICIES, DIRECTIVES, REGULATIONS, MEMORANDA, STANDARDS, AND GUIDELINES

LEGISLATION AND EXECUTIVE ORDERS

1. E-Government Act [includes FISMA] (P.L. 107-347), December 2002.
2. Federal Information Security Management Act (P.L. 107-347, Title III), December 2002.
3. Paperwork Reduction Act (P.L. 104-13), May 1995.
4. USA PATRIOT Act (P.L. 107-56), October 2001.
5. Privacy Act of 1974 (P.L. 93-579), December 1974.
6. Freedom of Information Act (FOIA), 5 U.S.C. § 552, As Amended By Public Law No. 104-231, 110 Stat. 3048, Electronic Freedom of Information Act Amendments of 1996.
7. Health Insurance Portability and Accountability Act (P.L. 104-191), August 1996.
8. The Atomic Energy Act of 1954 (P.L. 83-703), August 1954.
9. Executive Order 13556, Controlled Unclassified Information, November 2010.
10. Executive Order 13587, Structural Reforms to Improve the Security of Classified Networks and the Responsible Sharing and Safeguarding of Classified Information, October 2011.

POLICIES, DIRECTIVES, INSTRUCTIONS, REGULATIONS, AND MEMORANDA

1. Presidential Memorandum, National Insider Threat Policy and Minimum Standards for Executive Branch Insider Threat Programs, November 2012.
2. Code of Federal Regulations, Title 5, *Administrative Personnel*, Section 731.106, *Designation of Public Trust Positions and Investigative Requirements* (5 C.F.R. 731.106).
3. Code of Federal Regulations, Part 5 Administrative Personnel, Subpart C—Employees Responsible for the Management or Use of Federal Computer Systems, Section 930.301 through 930.305 (5 C.F.R. 930.301-305).
4. Committee on National Security Systems Policy (CNSSP) No. 11, *National Policy Governing the Acquisition of Information Assurance (IA) and IA-Enabled Information Technology (IT) Products*, July 2003.
5. Committee on National Security Systems Policy (CNSSP) No. 12, *National Information Assurance Policy for Space Systems Used to Support National Security Missions*, March 2007.
6. Committee on National Security Systems (CNSS) Instruction 4009, *National Information Assurance Glossary*, April 2010.
7. Committee on National Security Systems (CNSS) Instruction 1253, Version 2, *Security Categorization and Control Selection for National Security Systems*, March 2012.
8. Committee on National Security Systems Directive (CNSSD) No. 504, *Directive on Protecting National Security Systems from Insider Threat*, January 2012.
9. Department of Homeland Security, *National Infrastructure Protection Plan (NIPP)*, 2009.

10. Intelligence Community Directive (ICD) 705, *Sensitive Compartmented Information Facilities*, May 2010.

11. Federal Continuity Directive 1 (FCD 1), *Federal Executive Branch National Continuity Program and Requirements*, February 2008.

12. Executive Office of the President of the United States and Federal CIO Council, *Federal Identity, Credential, and Access Management (FICAM) Roadmap and Implementation Guidance*, December 2011.

13. Homeland Security Presidential Directive 7, *Critical Infrastructure Identification, Prioritization, and Protection*, December 2003.

14. Homeland Security Presidential Directive 12, *Policy for a Common Identification Standard for Federal Employees and Contractors*, August 2004.

15. Homeland Security Presidential Directive 20 (National Security Presidential Directive 51), *National Continuity Policy*, May 2007.

16. Intelligence Community Directive Number 704, *Personnel Security Standards and Procedures Governing Eligibility For Access To Sensitive Compartmented Information And Other Controlled Access Program Information*, October 2008.

17. National Communications System (NCS) Directive 3-10, *Minimum Requirements for Continuity Communications Capabilities*, July 2007.

18. National Security Telecommunications and Information Systems Security Instruction (NSTISSI) 7003, *Protective Distribution Systems (PDS)*, December 1996.

19. Office of Management and Budget Circular A-130, Appendix III, Transmittal Memorandum #4, *Management of Federal Information Resources*, November 2000.

20. Office of Management and Budget, Federal Enterprise Architecture Program Management Office, *FEA Consolidated Reference Model Document*, Version 2.3, October 2007.

21. Office of Management and Budget, *Federal Segment Architecture Methodology (FSAM)*, January 2009.

22. Office of Management and Budget Memorandum 01-05, *Guidance on Inter-Agency Sharing of Personal Data - Protecting Personal Privacy*, December 2000.

23. Office of Management and Budget Memorandum 02-01, *Guidance for Preparing and Submitting Security Plans of Action and Milestones*, October 2001.

24. Office of Management and Budget Memorandum 03-19, *Reporting Instructions for the Federal Information Security Management Act and Updated Guidance on Quarterly IT Security Reporting*, August 2003.

25. Office of Management and Budget Memorandum 03-22, *OMB Guidance for Implementing the Privacy Provisions of the E-Government Act of 2002*, September 2003.

26. Office of Management and Budget Memorandum 04-04, *E-Authentication Guidance for Federal Agencies*, December 2003.

27. Office of Management and Budget Memorandum 04-26, *Personal Use Policies and File Sharing Technology*, September 2004.

28. Office of Management and Budget Memorandum 05-08, *Designation of Senior Agency Officials for Privacy*, February 2005.

29. Office of Management and Budget Memorandum 05-24, *Implementation of Homeland Security Presidential Directive (HSPD) 12—Policy for a Common Identification Standard for Federal Employees and Contractors*, August 2005.

30. Office of Management and Budget Memorandum 06-15, *Safeguarding Personally Identifiable Information*, May 2006.

31. Office of Management and Budget Memorandum 06-16, *Protection of Sensitive Information*, June 2006.

32. Office of Management and Budget Memorandum 06-19, *Reporting Incidents Involving Personally Identifiable Information and Incorporating the Cost for Security in Agency Information Technology Investments*, July 2006.

33. Office of Management and Budget Memorandum, *Recommendations for Identity Theft Related Data Breach Notification Guidance*, September 2006.

34. Office of Management and Budget Memorandum 07-11, *Implementation of Commonly Accepted Security Configurations for Windows Operating Systems*, March 2007.

35. Office of Management and Budget Memorandum 07-16, *Safeguarding Against and Responding to the Breach of Personally Identifiable Information*, May 2007.

36. Office of Management and Budget Memorandum 07-18, *Ensuring New Acquisitions Include Common Security Configurations*, June 2007.

37. Office of Management and Budget Memorandum 08-22, *Guidance on the Federal Desktop Core Configuration (FDCC)*, August 2008.

38. Office of Management and Budget Memorandum 08-23, *Securing the Federal Government's Domain Name System Infrastructure*, August 2008.

39. The White House, Office of the Press Secretary, *Designation and Sharing of Controlled Unclassified Information (CUI)*, May 2008.

40. The White House, Office of the Press Secretary, *Classified Information and Controlled Unclassified Information*, May 2009.

41. Office of Management and Budget Memorandum 11-11, *Continued Implementation of Homeland Security Presidential Directive (HSPD) 12– Policy for a Common Identification Standard for Federal Employees and Contractors*, February 2011.

42. Office of Management and Budget Memorandum, *Requirements for Accepting Externally-Issued Identity Credentials*, October 2011.

43. Office of Management and Budget Memorandum 11-33, *FY 2011 Reporting Instructions for the Federal Information Security Management Act and Agency Privacy Management*, September 2011.

STANDARDS

1. International Organization for Standardization/International Electrotechnical Commission 27001:2005, *Security techniques -- Information security management systems -- Requirements*.

2. International Organization for Standardization/International Electrotechnical Commission 15408-1:2009, *Information technology -- Security techniques -- Evaluation criteria for IT security -- Part 1: Introduction and general model*.

3. International Organization for Standardization/International Electrotechnical Commission 15408-2:2008, *Information technology -- Security techniques -- Evaluation criteria for IT security -- Part 2: Security functional requirements*.

4. International Organization for Standardization/International Electrotechnical Commission 15408-3:2008, *Information technology -- Security techniques -- Evaluation criteria for IT security -- Part 3: Security assurance requirements*.

5. National Institute of Standards and Technology Federal Information Processing Standards Publication 140-2, *Security Requirements for Cryptographic Modules*, May 2001. National Institute of Standards and Technology Federal Information Processing Standards Publication 140-3 (Draft), *Security Requirements for Cryptographic Modules*, December 2009.

6. National Institute of Standards and Technology Federal Information Processing Standards Publication 180-4, *Secure Hash Standard (SHS)*, March 2012.

7. National Institute of Standards and Technology Federal Information Processing Standards Publication 186-3, *Digital Signature Standard (DSS)*, June 2009.

8. National Institute of Standards and Technology Federal Information Processing Standards Publication 188, *Standard Security Label for Information Transfer*, September 1994.

9. National Institute of Standards and Technology Federal Information Processing Standards Publication 190, *Guideline for the Use of Advanced Authentication Technology Alternatives*, September 1994.

10. National Institute of Standards and Technology Federal Information Processing Standards Publication 197, *Advanced Encryption Standard (AES)*, November 2001.

11. National Institute of Standards and Technology Federal Information Processing Standards Publication 198-1, *The Keyed-Hash Message Authentication Code (HMAC)*, July 2008.

12. National Institute of Standards and Technology Federal Information Processing Standards Publication 199, *Standards for Security Categorization of Federal Information and Information Systems*, February 2004.

13. National Institute of Standards and Technology Federal Information Processing Standards Publication 200, *Minimum Security Requirements for Federal Information and Information Systems*, March 2006.

14. National Institute of Standards and Technology Federal Information Processing Standards Publication 201-1, *Personal Identity Verification (PIV) of Federal Employees and Contractors*, March 2006.

GUIDELINES AND INTERAGENCY REPORTS

1. National Institute of Standards and Technology Special Publication 800-12, *An Introduction to Computer Security: The NIST Handbook*, October 1995.

2. National Institute of Standards and Technology Special Publication 800-13, *Telecommunications Security Guidelines for Telecommunications Management Network*, October 1995.

3. National Institute of Standards and Technology Special Publication 800-14, *Generally Accepted Principles and Practices for Securing Information Technology Systems*, September 1996.

4. National Institute of Standards and Technology Special Publication 800-15, *Minimum Interoperability Specification for PKI Components (MISPC)*, Version 1, January 1998.

5. National Institute of Standards and Technology Special Publication 800-16, *Information Security Training Requirements: A Role- and Performance-Based Model*, April 1998.

6. National Institute of Standards and Technology Special Publication 800-17, *Modes of Operation Validation System (MOVS): Requirements and Procedures*, February 1998.

7. National Institute of Standards and Technology Special Publication 800-18, Revision 1, *Guide for Developing Security Plans for Federal Information Systems*, February 2006.

8. National Institute of Standards and Technology Special Publication 800-19, *Mobile Agent Security*, October 1999.

9. National Institute of Standards and Technology Special Publication 800-20, *Modes of Operation Validation System for the Triple Data Encryption Algorithm (TMOVS): Requirements and Procedures*, October 1999.

10. National Institute of Standards and Technology Special Publication 800-21-1, *Second Edition, Guideline for Implementing Cryptography in the Federal Government*, December 2005.

11. National Institute of Standards and Technology Special Publication 800-22, Revision 1a, *A Statistical Test Suite for Random and Pseudorandom Number Generators for Cryptographic Applications*, April 2010.

12. National Institute of Standards and Technology Special Publication 800-23, *Guidelines to Federal Organizations on Security Assurance and Acquisition/Use of Tested/Evaluated Products*, August 2000.

13. National Institute of Standards and Technology Special Publication 800-24, *PBX Vulnerability Analysis: Finding Holes in Your PBX Before Someone Else Does*, August 2000.

14. National Institute of Standards and Technology Special Publication 800-25, *Federal Agency Use of Public Key Technology for Digital Signatures and Authentication*, October 2000.

15. National Institute of Standards and Technology Special Publication 800-27, Revision A, *Engineering Principles for Information Technology Security (A Baseline for Achieving Security)*, June 2004.

16. National Institute of Standards and Technology Special Publication 800-28, Version 2, *Guidelines on Active Content and Mobile Code*, March 2008.

17. National Institute of Standards and Technology Special Publication 800-29, *A Comparison of the Security Requirements for Cryptographic Modules in FIPS 140-1 and FIPS 140-2*, June 2001.

18. National Institute of Standards and Technology Special Publication 800-30, Revision 1, *Guide for Conducting Risk Assessments*, September 2012.

19. National Institute of Standards and Technology Special Publication 800-32, *Introduction to Public Key Technology and the Federal PKI Infrastructure*, February 2001.

20. National Institute of Standards and Technology Special Publication 800-33, *Underlying Technical Models for Information Technology Security*, December 2001.

21. National Institute of Standards and Technology Special Publication 800-34, Revision 1, *Contingency Planning Guide for Federal Information Systems*, May 2010.

22. National Institute of Standards and Technology Special Publication 800-35, *Guide to Information Technology Security Services*, October 2003.

23. National Institute of Standards and Technology Special Publication 800-36, *Guide to Selecting Information Security Products*, October 2003.

24. National Institute of Standards and Technology Special Publication 800-37, Revision 1, *Guide for Applying the Risk Management Framework to Federal Information Systems: A Security Life Cycle Approach*, February 2010.

25. National Institute of Standards and Technology Special Publication 800-38A—Addendum, *Recommendation for Block Cipher Modes of Operation: Three Variants of Ciphertext Stealing for CBC Mode*, October 2010.

26. National Institute of Standards and Technology Special Publication 800-38B, *Recommendation for Block Cipher Modes of Operation: The CMAC Mode for Authentication*, May 2005.

27. National Institute of Standards and Technology Special Publication 800-38C, *Recommendation for Block Cipher Modes of Operation: the CCM Mode for Authentication and Confidentiality*, May 2004.

28. National Institute of Standards and Technology Special Publication 800-38D, *Recommendation for Block Cipher Modes of Operation: Galois/Counter Mode (GCM) and GMAC*, November 2007.

29. National Institute of Standards and Technology Special Publication 800-38E, *Recommendation for Block Cipher Modes of Operation: The XTS-AES Mode for Confidentiality on Storage Devices*, January 2010.

30. National Institute of Standards and Technology Special Publication 800-38F, *Recommendation for Block Cipher Modes of Operation: Methods for Key Wrapping*, December 2012.

31. National Institute of Standards and Technology Special Publication 800-39, *Managing Information Security Risk: Organization, Mission, and Information System View*, March 2011.

32. National Institute of Standards and Technology Special Publication 800-40, Version 2, *Creating a Patch and Vulnerability Management Program*, November 2005.

33. National Institute of Standards and Technology Special Publication 800-41, Revision 1, *Guidelines on Firewalls and Firewall Policy*, September 2009.

34. National Institute of Standards and Technology Special Publication 800-43, *Systems Administration Guidance for Windows 2000 Professional System*, November 2002.

35. National Institute of Standards and Technology Special Publication 800-44, Version 2, *Guidelines on Securing Public Web Servers*, September 2007.

36. National Institute of Standards and Technology Special Publication 800-45, Version 2, *Guidelines on Electronic Mail Security*, February 2007.

37. National Institute of Standards and Technology Special Publication 800-46, Revision 1, *Guide to Enterprise Telework and Remote Access Security*, June 2009.

38. National Institute of Standards and Technology Special Publication 800-47, *Security Guide for Interconnecting Information Technology Systems*, August 2002.

39. National Institute of Standards and Technology Special Publication 800-48, Revision 1, *Guide to Securing Legacy IEEE 802.11 Wireless Networks*, July 2008.

40. National Institute of Standards and Technology Special Publication 800-49, *Federal S/MIME V3 Client Profile*, November 2002.

41. National Institute of Standards and Technology Special Publication 800-50, *Building an Information Technology Security Awareness and Training Program*, October 2003.

42. National Institute of Standards and Technology Special Publication 800-51, Revision 1, *Guide to Using Vulnerability Naming Schemes*, February 2011.

43. National Institute of Standards and Technology Special Publication 800-52, Revision 1 (Draft), *Guidelines for the Selection, Configuration, and Use of Transport Layer Security (TLS) Implementations*, September 2013.

44. National Institute of Standards and Technology Special Publication 800-53A, Revision 1, *Guide for Assessing the Security Controls in Federal Information Systems and Organizations: Building Effective Security Assessment Plans*, June 2010.

45. National Institute of Standards and Technology Special Publication 800-54, *Border Gateway Protocol Security*, July 2007.

46. National Institute of Standards and Technology Special Publication 800-55, Revision 1, *Performance Measurement Guide for Information Security*, July 2008.

47. National Institute of Standards and Technology Special Publication 800-56A (Revised), *Recommendation for Pair-Wise Key Establishment Schemes Using Discrete Logarithm Cryptography*, March 2007.

48. National Institute of Standards and Technology Special Publication 800-57 Revision 3, *Recommendation for Key Management*, July 2012.

49. National Institute of Standards and Technology Special Publication 800-58, *Security Considerations for Voice Over IP Systems*, January 2005.

50. National Institute of Standards and Technology Special Publication 800-59, *Guideline for Identifying an Information System as a National Security System*, August 2003.

51. National Institute of Standards and Technology Special Publication 800-60, Revision 1, *Guide for Mapping Types of Information and Information Systems to Security Categories*, August 2008.

52. National Institute of Standards and Technology Special Publication 800-61, Revision 2, *Computer Security Incident Handling Guide*, August 2012.

53. National Institute of Standards and Technology Special Publication 800-63-1, *Electronic Authentication Guideline*, December 2011.

54. National Institute of Standards and Technology Special Publication 800-64, Revision 2, *Security Considerations in the System Development Life Cycle*, October 2008.

55. National Institute of Standards and Technology Special Publication 800-65, *Integrating IT Security into the Capital Planning and Investment Control Process*, January 2005.

56. National Institute of Standards and Technology Special Publication 800-66, Revision 1, *An Introductory Resource Guide for Implementing the Health Insurance Portability and Accountability Act (HIPAA) Security Rule*, October 2008.

57. National Institute of Standards and Technology Special Publication 800-67, Revision 1, *Recommendation for the Triple Data Encryption Algorithm (TDEA) Block Cipher*, January 2012.

58. National Institute of Standards and Technology Special Publication 800-68, Revision 1, *Guide to Securing Microsoft Windows XP Systems for IT Professionals: A NIST Security Configuration Checklist*, October 2008.

59. National Institute of Standards and Technology Special Publication 800-69, *Guidance for Securing Microsoft Windows XP Home Edition: A NIST Security Configuration Checklist*, September 2006.

60. National Institute of Standards and Technology Special Publication 800-70, Revision 2, *National Checklist Program for IT Products--Guidelines for Checklist Users and Developers*, February 2011.

61. National Institute of Standards and Technology Special Publication 800-72, *Guidelines on PDA Forensics*, November 2004.

62. National Institute of Standards and Technology Special Publication 800-73-3, *Interfaces for Personal Identity Verification*, February 2010.

63. National Institute of Standards and Technology Special Publication 800-76-1, *Biometric Data Specification for Personal Identity Verification*, January 2007.

64. National Institute of Standards and Technology Special Publication 800-77, *Guide to IPsec VPNs*, December 2005.

65. National Institute of Standards and Technology Special Publication 800-78-3, *Cryptographic Algorithms and Key Sizes for Personal Identity Verification (PIV)*, December 2010.

66. National Institute of Standards and Technology Special Publication 800-79-1, *Guidelines for the Accreditation of Personal Identity Verification Card Issuers*, June 2008.

67. National Institute of Standards and Technology Special Publication 800-81, *Secure Domain Name System (DNS) Deployment Guide*, Revision 1, April 2010.

68. National Institute of Standards and Technology Special Publication 800-82, Revision 1, *Guide to Industrial Control Systems (ICS) Security*, April 2013.

69. National Institute of Standards and Technology Special Publication 800-83, *Guide to Malware Incident Prevention and Handling*, November 2005.

70. National Institute of Standards and Technology Special Publication 800-84, *Guide to Test, Training, and Exercise Programs for IT Plans and Capabilities*, September 2006.

71. National Institute of Standards and Technology Special Publication 800-85A-2, *PIV Card Application and Middleware Interface Test Guidelines (SP 800-73-3 Compliance)*, July 2010.

72. National Institute of Standards and Technology Special Publication 800-85B-1, (Draft) *PIV Data Model Test Guidelines*, September 2009.

73. National Institute of Standards and Technology Special Publication 800-86, *Guide to Integrating Forensic Techniques into Incident Response*, August 2006.
74. National Institute of Standards and Technology Special Publication 800-87, Revision 1, *Codes for the Identification of Federal and Federally-Assisted Organizations*, April 2008.
75. National Institute of Standards and Technology Special Publication 800-88, *Guidelines for Media Sanitization*, September 2006.
76. National Institute of Standards and Technology Special Publication 800-89, *Recommendation for Obtaining Assurances for Digital Signature Applications*, November 2006.
77. National Institute of Standards and Technology Special Publication 800-90A, *Recommendation for Random Number Generation Using Deterministic Random Bit Generators*, January 2012.
78. National Institute of Standards and Technology Special Publication 800-92, *Guide to Computer Security Log Management*, September 2006.
79. National Institute of Standards and Technology Special Publication 800-94, *Guide to Intrusion Detection and Prevention Systems (IDPS)*, February 2007.
80. National Institute of Standards and Technology Special Publication 800-95, *Guide to Secure Web Services*, August 2007.
81. National Institute of Standards and Technology Special Publication 800-96, *PIV Card / Reader Interoperability Guidelines*, September 2006.
82. National Institute of Standards and Technology Special Publication 800-97, *Establishing Robust Security Networks: A Guide to IEEE 802.11i*, February 2007.
83. National Institute of Standards and Technology Special Publication 800-98, *Guidelines for Securing Radio Frequency Identification (RFID) Systems*, April 2007.
84. National Institute of Standards and Technology Special Publication 800-100, *Information Security Handbook: A Guide for Managers*, October 2006.
85. National Institute of Standards and Technology Special Publication 800-101, *Guidelines on Cell Phone Forensics*, May 2007.
86. National Institute of Standards and Technology Special Publication 800-103 (Draft), *An Ontology of Identity Credentials, Part I: Background and Formulation*, October 2006.
87. National Institute of Standards and Technology Special Publication 800-104, *A Scheme for PIV Visual Card Topography*, June 2007.
88. National Institute of Standards and Technology Special Publication 800-106, *Randomized Hashing Digital Signatures*, February 2009.
89. National Institute of Standards and Technology Special Publication 800-107, *Recommendation for Applications Using Approved Hash Algorithms*, August 2012.
90. National Institute of Standards and Technology Special Publication 800-108, *Recommendation for Key Derivation Using Pseudorandom Functions*, October 2009.
91. National Institute of Standards and Technology Special Publication 800-111, *Guide to Storage Encryption Technologies for End User Devices*, November 2007.

92. National Institute of Standards and Technology Special Publication 800-113, *Guide to SSL VPNs*, July 2008.

93. National Institute of Standards and Technology Special Publication 800-114, *User's Guide to Securing External Devices for Telework and Remote Access*, November 2007.

94. National Institute of Standards and Technology Special Publication 800-115, *Technical Guide to Information Security Testing and Assessment*, September 2008.

95. National Institute of Standards and Technology Special Publication 800-116, *A Recommendation for the Use of PIV Credentials in Physical Access Control Systems (PACS)*, November 2008.

96. National Institute of Standards and Technology Special Publication 800-117, Version 1.0, *Guide to Adopting and Using the Security Content Automation Protocol (SCAP)*, July 2010.

97. National Institute of Standards and Technology Special Publication 800-118 (Draft), *Guide to Enterprise Password Management*, April 2009.

98. National Institute of Standards and Technology Special Publication 800-121, Revision 1, *Guide to Bluetooth Security*, June 2012.

99. National Institute of Standards and Technology Special Publication 800-122, *Guide to Protecting the Confidentiality of Personally Identifiable Information (PII)*, April 2010.

100. National Institute of Standards and Technology Special Publication 800-123, *Guide to General Server Security*, July 2008.

101. National Institute of Standards and Technology Special Publication 800-124, *Guidelines on Cell Phone and PDA Security*, October 2008.

102. National Institute of Standards and Technology Special Publication 800-125, *Guide to Security for Full Virtualization Technologies*, January 2011.

103. National Institute of Standards and Technology Special Publication 800-126, Revision 2, *The Technical Specification for the Security Content Automation Protocol (SCAP): SCAP Version 1.2*, September 2011.

104. National Institute of Standards and Technology Special Publication 800-127, *Guide to Securing WiMAX Wireless Communications*, September 2010.

105. National Institute of Standards and Technology Special Publication 800-128, *Guide for Security-Focused Configuration Management of Information Systems*, August 2011.

106. National Institute of Standards and Technology Special Publication 800-133, *Recommendation for Cryptographic Key Generation*, December 2012.

107. National Institute of Standards and Technology Special Publication 800-137, *Information Security Continuous Monitoring for Federal Information Systems and Organizations*, September 2011.

108. National Institute of Standards and Technology Special Publication 800-142, *Practical Combinatorial Testing*, October 2010.

109. National Institute of Standards and Technology Special Publication 800-144, *Guidelines for Security and Privacy in Public Cloud Computing*, December 2011.

110. National Institute of Standards and Technology Special Publication 800-145, *The NIST Definition of Cloud Computing*, September 2011.

111. National Institute of Standards and Technology Special Publication 800-146, *Cloud Computing Synopsis and Recommendations*, May 2012.

112. National Institute of Standards and Technology Special Publication 800-147, *Basic Input/Output System (BIOS) Protection Guidelines*, April 2011.

113. National Institute of Standards and Technology Special Publication 800-153, *Guidelines for Securing Wireless Local Area Networks (WLANs)*, September 2011.

114. National Institute of Standards and Technology Interagency Report 7622, *Notional Supply Chain Risk Management Practices for Federal Information Systems*, October 2012.

APPENDIX B

GLOSSARY

COMMON TERMS AND DEFINITIONS

Appendix B provides definitions for security terminology used within Special Publication 800-53. Unless specifically defined in this glossary, all terms used in this publication are consistent with the definitions contained in CNSS Instruction 4009, *National Information Assurance Glossary*.

Adequate Security [OMB Circular A-130, Appendix III, Adapted]	Security commensurate with the risk resulting from the loss, misuse, or unauthorized access to or modification of information.
Advanced Persistent Threat	An adversary that possesses sophisticated levels of expertise and significant resources which allow it to create opportunities to achieve its objectives by using multiple attack vectors (e.g., cyber, physical, and deception). These objectives typically include establishing and extending footholds within the information technology infrastructure of the targeted organizations for purposes of exfiltrating information, undermining or impeding critical aspects of a mission, program, or organization; or positioning itself to carry out these objectives in the future. The advanced persistent threat: (i) pursues its objectives repeatedly over an extended period of time; (ii) adapts to defenders' efforts to resist it; and (iii) is determined to maintain the level of interaction needed to execute its objectives.
Agency	See *Executive Agency*.
All Source Intelligence [Department of Defense, Joint Publication 1-02]	Intelligence products and/or organizations and activities that incorporate all sources of information, most frequently including human resources intelligence, imagery intelligence, measurement and signature intelligence, signals intelligence, and open source data in the production of finished intelligence.
Assessment	See *Security Control Assessment*.
Assessor	See *Security Control Assessor*.
Assurance [CNSSI 4009]	Measure of confidence that the security features, practices, procedures, and architecture of an information system accurately mediates and enforces the security policy.
Assurance Case [Software Engineering Institute, Carnegie Mellon University]	A structured set of arguments and a body of evidence showing that an information system satisfies specific claims with respect to a given quality attribute.
Audit Log [CNSSI 4009]	A chronological record of information system activities, including records of system accesses and operations performed in a given period.
Audit Record	An individual entry in an audit log related to an audited event.

Audit Reduction Tools [CNSSI 4009]	Preprocessors designed to reduce the volume of audit records to facilitate manual review. Before a security review, these tools can remove many audit records known to have little security significance. These tools generally remove records generated by specified classes of events, such as records generated by nightly backups.
Audit Trail [CNSSI 4009]	A chronological record that reconstructs and examines the sequence of activities surrounding or leading to a specific operation, procedure, or event in a security-relevant transaction from inception to final result.
Authentication [FIPS 200]	Verifying the identity of a user, process, or device, often as a prerequisite to allowing access to resources in an information system.
Authenticator	The means used to confirm the identity of a user, processor, or device (e.g., user password or token).
Authenticity	The property of being genuine and being able to be verified and trusted; confidence in the validity of a transmission, a message, or message originator. See *Authentication*.
Authorization (to operate)	The official management decision given by a senior organizational official to authorize operation of an information system and to explicitly accept the risk to organizational operations (including mission, functions, image, or reputation), organizational assets, individuals, other organizations, and the Nation based on the implementation of an agreed-upon set of security controls.
Authorization Boundary	All components of an information system to be authorized for operation by an authorizing official and excludes separately authorized systems, to which the information system is connected.
Authorize Processing	See *Authorization*.
Authorizing Official	A senior (federal) official or executive with the authority to formally assume responsibility for operating an information system at an acceptable level of risk to organizational operations (including mission, functions, image, or reputation), organizational assets, individuals, other organizations, and the Nation.
Availability [44 U.S.C., Sec. 3542]	Ensuring timely and reliable access to and use of information.
Baseline Configuration	A documented set of specifications for an information system, or a configuration item within a system, that has been formally reviewed and agreed on at a given point in time, and which can be changed only through change control procedures.

Blacklisting	The process used to identify: (i) software programs that are not authorized to execute on an information system; or (ii) prohibited Universal Resource Locators (URL)/websites.
Boundary Protection	Monitoring and control of communications at the external boundary of an information system to prevent and detect malicious and other unauthorized communications, through the use of boundary protection devices (e.g., gateways, routers, firewalls, guards, encrypted tunnels).
Boundary Protection Device	A device with appropriate mechanisms that: (i) facilitates the adjudication of different interconnected system security policies (e.g., controlling the flow of information into or out of an interconnected system); and/or (ii) provides information system boundary protection.
Central Management	The organization-wide management and implementation of selected security controls and related processes. Central management includes planning, implementing, assessing, authorizing, and monitoring the organization-defined, centrally managed security controls and processes.
Chief Information Officer [PL 104-106, Sec. 5125(b)]	Agency official responsible for: (i) Providing advice and other assistance to the head of the executive agency and other senior management personnel of the agency to ensure that information technology is acquired and information resources are managed in a manner that is consistent with laws, Executive Orders, directives, policies, regulations, and priorities established by the head of the agency; (ii) Developing, maintaining, and facilitating the implementation of a sound and integrated information technology architecture for the agency; and (iii) Promoting the effective and efficient design and operation of all major information resources management processes for the agency, including improvements to work processes of the agency. Note: Organizations subordinate to federal agencies may use the term *Chief Information Officer* to denote individuals filling positions with similar security responsibilities to agency-level Chief Information Officers.
Chief Information Security Officer	See *Senior Agency Information Security Officer*.
Chief Privacy Officer	See *Senior Agency Official for Privacy*.
Classified Information	Information that has been determined: (i) pursuant to Executive Order 12958 as amended by Executive Order 13526, or any predecessor Order, to be classified national security information; or (ii) pursuant to the Atomic Energy Act of 1954, as amended, to be Restricted Data (RD).

Commodity Service	An information system service (e.g., telecommunications service) provided by a commercial service provider typically to a large and diverse set of consumers. The organization acquiring and/or receiving the commodity service possesses limited visibility into the management structure and operations of the provider, and while the organization may be able to negotiate service-level agreements, the organization is typically not in a position to require that the provider implement specific security controls.
Common Carrier	In a telecommunications context, a telecommunications company that holds itself out to the public for hire to provide communications transmission services. Note: In the United States, such companies are usually subject to regulation by federal and state regulatory commissions.
Common Control [NIST SP 800-37; CNSSI 4009]	A security control that is inheritable by one or more organizational information systems. See *Security Control Inheritance*.
Common Control Provider [NIST SP 800-37]	An organizational official responsible for the development, implementation, assessment, and monitoring of common controls (i.e., security controls inheritable by information systems).
Common Criteria [CNSSI 4009]	Governing document that provides a comprehensive, rigorous method for specifying security function and assurance requirements for products and systems.
Common Secure Configuration	A recognized standardized and established benchmark that stipulates specific secure configuration settings for a given information technology platform.
Compensating Security Controls [CNSSI 4009, Adapted]	The security controls employed in lieu of the recommended controls in the security control baselines described in NIST Special Publication 800-53 and CNSS Instruction 1253 that provide equivalent or comparable protection for an information system or organization.
Computer Matching Agreement	An agreement entered into by an organization in connection with a computer matching program to which the organization is a party, as required by the Computer Matching and Privacy Protection Act of 1988. With certain exceptions, a computer matching program is any computerized comparison of two or more automated systems of records or a system of records with nonfederal records for the purpose of establishing or verifying the eligibility of, or continuing compliance with, statutory and regulatory requirements by, applicants for, recipients or beneficiaries of, participants in, or providers of services with respect to cash or in-kind assistance or payments under federal benefit programs or computerized comparisons of two or more automated federal personnel or payroll systems of records or a system of federal personnel or payroll records with non-federal records.

Confidentiality [44 U.S.C., Sec. 3542]	Preserving authorized restrictions on information access and disclosure, including means for protecting personal privacy and proprietary information.
Configuration Control [CNSSI 4009]	Process for controlling modifications to hardware, firmware, software, and documentation to protect the information system against improper modifications before, during, and after system implementation.
Configuration Item	An aggregation of information system components that is designated for configuration management and treated as a single entity in the configuration management process.
Configuration Management	A collection of activities focused on establishing and maintaining the integrity of information technology products and information systems, through control of processes for initializing, changing, and monitoring the configurations of those products and systems throughout the system development life cycle.
Configuration Settings	The set of parameters that can be changed in hardware, software, or firmware that affect the security posture and/or functionality of the information system.
Controlled Area	Any area or space for which an organization has confidence that the physical and procedural protections provided are sufficient to meet the requirements established for protecting the information and/or information system.
Controlled Interface [CNSSI 4009]	A boundary with a set of mechanisms that enforces the security policies and controls the flow of information between interconnected information systems.
Controlled Unclassified Information [E.O. 13556]	A categorical designation that refers to unclassified information that does not meet the standards for National Security Classification under Executive Order 12958, as amended, but is (i) pertinent to the national interests of the United States or to the important interests of entities outside the federal government, and (ii) under law or policy requires protection from unauthorized disclosure, special handling safeguards, or prescribed limits on exchange or dissemination.
Countermeasures [CNSSI 4009]	Actions, devices, procedures, techniques, or other measures that reduce the vulnerability of an information system. Synonymous with security controls and safeguards.
Covert Channel Analysis [CNSSI 4009]	Determination of the extent to which the security policy model and subsequent lower-level program descriptions may allow unauthorized access to information.
Covert Storage Channel [CNSSI 4009]	Covert channel involving the direct or indirect writing to a storage location by one process and the direct or indirect reading of the storage location by another process. Covert storage channels typically involve a finite resource (e.g., sectors on a disk) that is shared by two subjects at different security levels.

Covert Timing Channel [CNSSI 4009]	Covert channel in which one process signals information to another process by modulating its own use of system resources (e.g., central processing unit time) in such a way that this manipulation affects the real response time observed by the second process.
Cross Domain Solution [CNSSI 4009]	A form of controlled interface that provides the ability to manually and/or automatically access and/or transfer information between different security domains.
Cyber Attack [CNSSI 4009]	An attack, via cyberspace, targeting an enterprise's use of cyberspace for the purpose of disrupting, disabling, destroying, or maliciously controlling a computing environment/infrastructure; or destroying the integrity of the data or stealing controlled information.
Cyber Security [CNSSI 4009]	The ability to protect or defend the use of cyberspace from cyber attacks.
Cyberspace [CNSSI 4009]	A global domain within the information environment consisting of the interdependent network of information systems infrastructures including the Internet, telecommunications networks, computer systems, and embedded processors and controllers.
Data Mining/Harvesting	An analytical process that attempts to find correlations or patterns in large data sets for the purpose of data or knowledge discovery.
Defense-in-Breadth [CNSSI 4009]	A planned, systematic set of multidisciplinary activities that seek to identify, manage, and reduce risk of exploitable vulnerabilities at every stage of the system, network, or subcomponent life cycle (system, network, or product design and development; manufacturing; packaging; assembly; system integration; distribution; operations; maintenance; and retirement).
Defense-in-Depth	Information security strategy integrating people, technology, and operations capabilities to establish variable barriers across multiple layers and missions of the organization.
Developer	A general term that includes: (i) developers or manufacturers of information systems, system components, or information system services; (ii) systems integrators; (iii) vendors; and (iv) product resellers. Development of systems, components, or services can occur internally within organizations (i.e., in-house development) or through external entities.
Digital Media	A form of electronic media where data are stored in digital (as opposed to analog) form.

Discretionary Access Control	An access control policy that is enforced over all subjects and objects in an information system where the policy specifies that a subject that has been granted access to information can do one or more of the following: (i) pass the information to other subjects or objects; (ii) grant its privileges to other subjects; (iii) change security attributes on subjects, objects, information systems, or system components; (iv) choose the security attributes to be associated with newly-created or revised objects; or (v) change the rules governing access control. Mandatory access controls restrict this capability.
[CNSSI 4009]	A means of restricting access to objects (e.g., files, data entities) based on the identity and need-to-know of subjects (e.g., users, processes) and/or groups to which the object belongs. The controls are discretionary in the sense that a subject with a certain access permission is capable of passing that permission (perhaps indirectly) on to any other subject (unless restrained by mandatory access control).
Domain [CNSSI 4009]	An environment or context that includes a set of system resources and a set of system entities that have the right to access the resources as defined by a common security policy, security model, or security architecture. See *Security Domain*.
Enterprise [CNSSI 4009]	An organization with a defined mission/goal and a defined boundary, using information systems to execute that mission, and with responsibility for managing its own risks and performance. An enterprise may consist of all or some of the following business aspects: acquisition, program management, financial management (e.g., budgets), human resources, security, and information systems, information and mission management. See *Organization*.
Enterprise Architecture [44 U.S.C. Sec. 3601]	A strategic information asset base, which defines the mission; the information necessary to perform the mission; the technologies necessary to perform the mission; and the transitional processes for implementing new technologies in response to changing mission needs; and includes a baseline architecture; a target architecture; and a sequencing plan.
Environment of Operation [NIST SP 800-37]	The physical surroundings in which an information system processes, stores, and transmits information.
Event [CNSSI 4009, Adapted]	Any observable occurrence in an information system.
Executive Agency [41 U.S.C., Sec. 403]	An executive department specified in 5 U.S.C., Sec. 101; a military department specified in 5 U.S.C., Sec. 102; an independent establishment as defined in 5 U.S.C., Sec. 104(1); and a wholly owned Government corporation fully subject to the provisions of 31 U.S.C., Chapter 91.
Exfiltration	The unauthorized transfer of information from an information system.

External Information System (or Component)	An information system or component of an information system that is outside of the authorization boundary established by the organization and for which the organization typically has no direct control over the application of required security controls or the assessment of security control effectiveness.
External Information System Service	An information system service that is implemented outside of the authorization boundary of the organizational information system (i.e., a service that is used by, but not a part of, the organizational information system) and for which the organization typically has no direct control over the application of required security controls or the assessment of security control effectiveness.
External Information System Service Provider	A provider of external information system services to an organization through a variety of consumer-producer relationships including but not limited to: joint ventures; business partnerships; outsourcing arrangements (i.e., through contracts, interagency agreements, lines of business arrangements); licensing agreements; and/or supply chain exchanges.
External Network	A network not controlled by the organization.
Failover	The capability to switch over automatically (typically without human intervention or warning) to a redundant or standby information system upon the failure or abnormal termination of the previously active system.
Fair Information Practice Principles	Principles that are widely accepted in the United States and internationally as a general framework for privacy and that are reflected in various federal and international laws and policies. In a number of organizations, the principles serve as the basis for analyzing privacy risks and determining appropriate mitigation strategies.
Federal Agency	See *Executive Agency*.
Federal Enterprise Architecture [FEA Program Management Office]	A business-based framework for governmentwide improvement developed by the Office of Management and Budget that is intended to facilitate efforts to transform the federal government to one that is citizen-centered, results-oriented, and market-based.
Federal Information System [40 U.S.C., Sec. 11331]	An information system used or operated by an executive agency, by a contractor of an executive agency, or by another organization on behalf of an executive agency.
FIPS-Validated Cryptography	A cryptographic module validated by the Cryptographic Module Validation Program (CMVP) to meet requirements specified in FIPS Publication 140-2 (as amended). As a prerequisite to CMVP validation, the cryptographic module is required to employ a cryptographic algorithm implementation that has successfully passed validation testing by the Cryptographic Algorithm Validation Program (CAVP). See *NSA-Approved Cryptography*.

Firmware [CNSSI 4009]	Computer programs and data stored in hardware - typically in read-only memory (ROM) or programmable read-only memory (PROM) - such that the programs and data cannot be dynamically written or modified during execution of the programs.
Guard (System) [CNSSI 4009, Adapted]	A mechanism limiting the exchange of information between information systems or subsystems.
Hardware [CNSSI 4009]	The physical components of an information system. See *Software* and *Firmware*.
High-Impact System [FIPS 200]	An information system in which at least one security objective (i.e., confidentiality, integrity, or availability) is assigned a FIPS Publication 199 potential impact value of high.
Hybrid Security Control [CNSSI 4009]	A security control that is implemented in an information system in part as a common control and in part as a system-specific control. See *Common Control* and *System-Specific Security Control*.
Impact	The effect on organizational operations, organizational assets, individuals, other organizations, or the Nation (including the national security interests of the United States) of a loss of confidentiality, integrity, or availability of information or an information system.
Impact Value	The assessed potential impact resulting from a compromise of the confidentiality, integrity, or availability of information expressed as a value of low, moderate or high.
Incident [FIPS 200]	An occurrence that actually or potentially jeopardizes the confidentiality, integrity, or availability of an information system or the information the system processes, stores, or transmits or that constitutes a violation or imminent threat of violation of security policies, security procedures, or acceptable use policies.
Industrial Control System	An information system used to control industrial processes such as manufacturing, product handling, production, and distribution. Industrial control systems include supervisory control and data acquisition (SCADA) systems used to control geographically dispersed assets, as well as distributed control systems (DCSs) and smaller control systems using programmable logic controllers to control localized processes.
Information [CNSSI 4009]	Any communication or representation of knowledge such as facts, data, or opinions in any medium or form, including textual, numerical, graphic, cartographic, narrative, or audiovisual.
[FIPS 199]	An instance of an information type.
Information Leakage	The intentional or unintentional release of information to an untrusted environment.
Information Owner [CNSSI 4009]	Official with statutory or operational authority for specified information and responsibility for establishing the controls for its generation, collection, processing, dissemination, and disposal.

Information Resources [44 U.S.C., Sec. 3502]	Information and related resources, such as personnel, equipment, funds, and information technology.
Information Security [44 U.S.C., Sec. 3542]	The protection of information and information systems from unauthorized access, use, disclosure, disruption, modification, or destruction in order to provide confidentiality, integrity, and availability.
Information Security Architecture	An embedded, integral part of the enterprise architecture that describes the structure and behavior for an enterprise's security processes, information security systems, personnel and organizational subunits, showing their alignment with the enterprise's mission and strategic plans.
Information Security Policy [CNSSI 4009]	Aggregate of directives, regulations, rules, and practices that prescribes how an organization manages, protects, and distributes information.
Information Security Program Plan	Formal document that provides an overview of the security requirements for an organization-wide information security program and describes the program management controls and common controls in place or planned for meeting those requirements.
Information Security Risk	The risk to organizational operations (including mission, functions, image, reputation), organizational assets, individuals, other organizations, and the Nation due to the potential for unauthorized access, use, disclosure, disruption, modification, or destruction of information and/or information systems.
Information Steward [CNSSI 4009]	An agency official with statutory or operational authority for specified information and responsibility for establishing the controls for its generation, collection, processing, dissemination, and disposal.
Information System [44 U.S.C., Sec. 3502]	A discrete set of information resources organized for the collection, processing, maintenance, use, sharing, dissemination, or disposition of information. Note: Information systems also include specialized systems such as industrial/process controls systems, telephone switching and private branch exchange (PBX) systems, and environmental control systems.
Information System Boundary	See *Authorization Boundary*.
Information System Component [NIST SP 800-128, Adapted]	A discrete, identifiable information technology asset (e.g., hardware, software, firmware) that represents a building block of an information system. Information system components include commercial information technology products.
Information System Owner (or Program Manager)	Official responsible for the overall procurement, development, integration, modification, or operation and maintenance of an information system.

Information System Resilience	The ability of an information system to continue to: (i) operate under adverse conditions or stress, even if in a degraded or debilitated state, while maintaining essential operational capabilities; and (ii) recover to an effective operational posture in a time frame consistent with mission needs.
Information System Security Officer [CNSSI 4009]	Individual with assigned responsibility for maintaining the appropriate operational security posture for an information system or program.
Information System Service	A capability provided by an information system that facilitates information processing, storage, or transmission.
Information System-Related Security Risks	Risks that arise through the loss of confidentiality, integrity, or availability of information or information systems and that considers impacts to the organization (including assets, mission, functions, image, or reputation), individuals, other organizations, and the Nation. See *Risk*.
Information Technology [40 U.S.C., Sec. 1401]	Any equipment or interconnected system or subsystem of equipment that is used in the automatic acquisition, storage, manipulation, management, movement, control, display, switching, interchange, transmission, or reception of data or information by the executive agency. For purposes of the preceding sentence, equipment is used by an executive agency if the equipment is used by the executive agency directly or is used by a contractor under a contract with the executive agency which: (i) requires the use of such equipment; or (ii) requires the use, to a significant extent, of such equipment in the performance of a service or the furnishing of a product. The term *information technology* includes computers, ancillary equipment, software, firmware, and similar procedures, services (including support services), and related resources.
Information Technology Product	See *Information System Component*.
Information Type [FIPS 199]	A specific category of information (e.g., privacy, medical, proprietary, financial, investigative, contractor-sensitive, security management) defined by an organization or in some instances, by a specific law, Executive Order, directive, policy, or regulation.
Insider [Presidential Memorandum, National Insider Threat Policy and Minimum Standards for Executive Branch Insider Threat Programs]	Any person with authorized access to any U.S. Government resource, to include personnel, facilities, information, equipment, networks, or systems.

Insider Threat [Presidential Memorandum, National Insider Threat Policy and Minimum Standards for Executive Branch Insider Threat Programs]	The threat that an insider will use her/his authorized access, wittingly or unwittingly, to do harm to the security of United States. This threat can include damage to the United States through espionage, terrorism, unauthorized disclosure of national security information, or through the loss or degradation of departmental resources or capabilities.
[CNSSI 4009]	An entity with authorized access (i.e., within the security domain) that has the potential to harm an information system or enterprise through destruction, disclosure, modification of data, and/or denial of service.
Insider Threat Program [Presidential Memorandum, National Insider Threat Policy and Minimum Standards for Executive Branch Insider Threat Programs]	A coordinated group of capabilities under centralized management that is organized to detect and prevent the unauthorized disclosure of sensitive information. At a minimum, for departments and agencies that handle classified information, an insider threat program shall consist of capabilities that provide access to information; centralized information integration, analysis, and response; employee insider threat awareness training; and the monitoring of user activity on government computers. For department and agencies that do not handle classified information, these can be employed effectively for safeguarding information that is unclassified but sensitive.
Integrity [44 U.S.C., Sec. 3542]	Guarding against improper information modification or destruction, and includes ensuring information non-repudiation and authenticity.
Internal Network	A network where: (i) the establishment, maintenance, and provisioning of security controls are under the direct control of organizational employees or contractors; or (ii) cryptographic encapsulation or similar security technology implemented between organization-controlled endpoints, provides the same effect (at least with regard to confidentiality and integrity). An internal network is typically organization-owned, yet may be organization-controlled while not being organization-owned.
Label	See *Security Label*.
Line of Business	The following OMB-defined process areas common to virtually all federal agencies: Case Management, Financial Management, Grants Management, Human Resources Management, Federal Health Architecture, Information Systems Security, Budget Formulation and Execution, Geospatial, and IT Infrastructure.
Local Access	Access to an organizational information system by a user (or process acting on behalf of a user) communicating through a direct connection without the use of a network.

Logical Access Control System [FICAM Roadmap and Implementation Guidance]	An automated system that controls an individual's ability to access one or more computer system resources such as a workstation, network, application, or database. A logical access control system requires validation of an individual's identity through some mechanism such as a PIN, card, biometric, or other token. It has the capability to assign different access privileges to different persons depending on their roles and responsibilities in an organization.
Low-Impact System [FIPS 200]	An information system in which all three security objectives (i.e., confidentiality, integrity, and availability) are assigned a FIPS Publication 199 potential impact value of low.
Malicious Code	Software or firmware intended to perform an unauthorized process that will have adverse impact on the confidentiality, integrity, or availability of an information system. A virus, worm, Trojan horse, or other code-based entity that infects a host. Spyware and some forms of adware are also examples of malicious code.
Malware	See *Malicious Code*.
Managed Interface	An interface within an information system that provides boundary protection capability using automated mechanisms or devices.
Mandatory Access Control	An access control policy that is uniformly enforced across all subjects and objects within the boundary of an information system. A subject that has been granted access to information is constrained from doing any of the following: (i) passing the information to unauthorized subjects or objects; (ii) granting its privileges to other subjects; (iii) changing one or more security attributes on subjects, objects, the information system, or system components; (iv) choosing the security attributes to be associated with newly-created or modified objects; or (v) changing the rules governing access control. Organization-defined subjects may explicitly be granted organization-defined privileges (i.e., they are trusted subjects) such that they are not limited by some or all of the above constraints.
[CNSSI 4009]	A means of restricting access to objects based on the sensitivity (as represented by a security label) of the information contained in the objects and the formal authorization (i.e., clearance, formal access approvals, and need-to-know) of subjects to access information of such sensitivity. Mandatory Access Control is a type of nondiscretionary access control.
Marking	See *Security Marking*.
Media [FIPS 200]	Physical devices or writing surfaces including, but not limited to, magnetic tapes, optical disks, magnetic disks, Large-Scale Integration (LSI) memory chips, and printouts (but not including display media) onto which information is recorded, stored, or printed within an information system.

Metadata	Information describing the characteristics of data including, for example, structural metadata describing data structures (e.g., data format, syntax, and semantics) and descriptive metadata describing data contents (e.g., information security labels).
Mobile Code	Software programs or parts of programs obtained from remote information systems, transmitted across a network, and executed on a local information system without explicit installation or execution by the recipient.
Mobile Code Technologies	Software technologies that provide the mechanisms for the production and use of mobile code (e.g., Java, JavaScript, ActiveX, VBScript).
Mobile Device	A portable computing device that: (i) has a small form factor such that it can easily be carried by a single individual; (ii) is designed to operate without a physical connection (e.g., wirelessly transmit or receive information); (iii) possesses local, non-removable or removable data storage; and (iv) includes a self-contained power source. Mobile devices may also include voice communication capabilities, on-board sensors that allow the devices to capture information, and/or built-in features for synchronizing local data with remote locations. Examples include smart phones, tablets, and E-readers.
Moderate-Impact System [FIPS 200]	An information system in which at least one security objective (i.e., confidentiality, integrity, or availability) is assigned a FIPS Publication 199 potential impact value of moderate and no security objective is assigned a FIPS Publication 199 potential impact value of high.
Multifactor Authentication	Authentication using two or more different factors to achieve authentication. Factors include: (i) something you know (e.g., password/PIN); (ii) something you have (e.g., cryptographic identification device, token); or (iii) something you are (e.g., biometric). See *Authenticator*.
Multilevel Security [CNSSI 4009]	Concept of processing information with different classifications and categories that simultaneously permits access by users with different security clearances and denies access to users who lack authorization.
Multiple Security Levels [CNSSI 4009]	Capability of an information system that is trusted to contain, and maintain separation between, resources (particularly stored data) of different security domains.
National Security Emergency Preparedness Telecommunications Services [47 C.F.R., Part 64, App A]	Telecommunications services that are used to maintain a state of readiness or to respond to and manage any event or crisis (local, national, or international) that causes or could cause injury or harm to the population, damage to or loss of property, or degrade or threaten the national security or emergency preparedness posture of the United States.

National Security System [44 U.S.C., Sec. 3542]	Any information system (including any telecommunications system) used or operated by an agency or by a contractor of an agency, or other organization on behalf of an agency—(i) the function, operation, or use of which involves intelligence activities; involves cryptologic activities related to national security; involves command and control of military forces; involves equipment that is an integral part of a weapon or weapons system; or is critical to the direct fulfillment of military or intelligence missions (excluding a system that is to be used for routine administrative and business applications, for example, payroll, finance, logistics, and personnel management applications); or (ii) is protected at all times by procedures established for information that have been specifically authorized under criteria established by an Executive Order or an Act of Congress to be kept classified in the interest of national defense or foreign policy.
Network [CNSSI 4009]	Information system(s) implemented with a collection of interconnected components. Such components may include routers, hubs, cabling, telecommunications controllers, key distribution centers, and technical control devices.
Network Access	Access to an information system by a user (or a process acting on behalf of a user) communicating through a network (e.g., local area network, wide area network, Internet).
Nondiscretionary Access Control	See *Mandatory Access Control*.
Nonlocal Maintenance	Maintenance activities conducted by individuals communicating through a network, either an external network (e.g., the Internet) or an internal network.
Non-Organizational User	A user who is not an organizational user (including public users).
Non-repudiation	Protection against an individual falsely denying having performed a particular action. Provides the capability to determine whether a given individual took a particular action such as creating information, sending a message, approving information, and receiving a message.
NSA-Approved Cryptography	Cryptography that consists of: (i) an approved algorithm; (ii) an implementation that has been approved for the protection of classified information and/or controlled unclassified information in a particular environment; and (iii) a supporting key management infrastructure.
Object	Passive information system-related entity (e.g., devices, files, records, tables, processes, programs, domains) containing or receiving information. Access to an object (by a subject) implies access to the information it contains. See *Subject*.

Operations Security [CNSSI 4009]	Systematic and proven process by which potential adversaries can be denied information about capabilities and intentions by identifying, controlling, and protecting generally unclassified evidence of the planning and execution of sensitive activities. The process involves five steps: identification of critical information, analysis of threats, analysis of vulnerabilities, assessment of risks, and application of appropriate countermeasures.
Organization [FIPS 200, Adapted]	An entity of any size, complexity, or positioning within an organizational structure (e.g., a federal agency or, as appropriate, any of its operational elements).
Organizational User	An organizational employee or an individual the organization deems to have equivalent status of an employee including, for example, contractor, guest researcher, individual detailed from another organization. Policy and procedures for granting equivalent status of employees to individuals may include need-to-know, relationship to the organization, and citizenship.
Overlay	A specification of security controls, control enhancements, supplemental guidance, and other supporting information employed during the tailoring process, that is intended to complement (and further refine) security control baselines. The overlay specification may be more stringent or less stringent than the original security control baseline specification and can be applied to multiple information systems.
Penetration Testing	A test methodology in which assessors, typically working under specific constraints, attempt to circumvent or defeat the security features of an information system.
Personally Identifiable Information [OMB Memorandum 07-16]	Information which can be used to distinguish or trace the identity of an individual (e.g., name, social security number, biometric records, etc.) alone, or when combined with other personal or identifying information which is linked or linkable to a specific individual (e.g., date and place of birth, mother's maiden name, etc.).
Physical Access Control System [FICAM Roadmap and Implementation Guidance]	An automated system that manages the passage of people or assets through an opening(s) in a secure perimeter(s) based on a set of authorization rules.
Plan of Action and Milestones [OMB Memorandum 02-01]	A document that identifies tasks needing to be accomplished. It details resources required to accomplish the elements of the plan, any milestones in meeting the tasks, and scheduled completion dates for the milestones.
Portable Storage Device	An information system component that can be inserted into and removed from an information system, and that is used to store data or information (e.g., text, video, audio, and/or image data). Such components are typically implemented on magnetic, optical, or solid state devices (e.g., floppy disks, compact/digital video disks, flash/thumb drives, external hard disk drives, and flash memory cards/drives that contain non-volatile memory).

Potential Impact [FIPS 199]	The loss of confidentiality, integrity, or availability could be expected to have: (i) a *limited* adverse effect (FIPS Publication 199 low); (ii) a *serious* adverse effect (FIPS Publication 199 moderate); or (iii) a *severe or catastrophic* adverse effect (FIPS Publication 199 high) on organizational operations, organizational assets, or individuals.
Privacy Act Statement	A disclosure statement required by Section (e)(3) of the Privacy Act of 1974, as amended, to appear on documents used by organizations to collect personally identifiable information from individuals to be maintained in a Privacy Act System of Records (SORN).
Privacy Impact Assessment [OMB Memorandum 03-22]	An analysis of how information is handled: (i) to ensure handling conforms to applicable legal, regulatory, and policy requirements regarding privacy; (ii) to determine the risks and effects of collecting, maintaining, and disseminating information in identifiable form in an electronic information system; and (iii) to examine and evaluate protections and alternative processes for handling information to mitigate potential privacy risks.
Privileged Account	An information system account with authorizations of a privileged user.
Privileged Command	A human-initiated command executed on an information system involving the control, monitoring, or administration of the system including security functions and associated security-relevant information.
Privileged User [CNSSI 4009]	A user that is authorized (and therefore, trusted) to perform security-relevant functions that ordinary users are not authorized to perform.
Protective Distribution System	Wire line or fiber optic system that includes adequate safeguards and/or countermeasures (e.g., acoustic, electric, electromagnetic, and physical) to permit its use for the transmission of unencrypted information.
Provenance	The records describing the possession of, and changes to, components, component processes, information, systems, organization, and organizational processes. Provenance enables all changes to the baselines of components, component processes, information, systems, organizations, and organizational processes, to be reported to specific actors, functions, locales, or activities.
Public Key Infrastructure [CNSSI 4009]	The framework and services that provide for the generation, production, distribution, control, accounting, and destruction of public key certificates. Components include the personnel, policies, processes, server platforms, software, and workstations used for the purpose of administering certificates and public-private key pairs, including the ability to issue, maintain, recover, and revoke public key certificates.

Purge	Rendering sanitized data unrecoverable by laboratory attack methods.
Reciprocity [CNSSI 4009]	Mutual agreement among participating organizations to accept each other's security assessments in order to reuse information system resources and/or to accept each other's assessed security posture in order to share information.
Records	The recordings (automated and/or manual) of evidence of activities performed or results achieved (e.g., forms, reports, test results), which serve as a basis for verifying that the organization and the information system are performing as intended. Also used to refer to units of related data fields (i.e., groups of data fields that can be accessed by a program and that contain the complete set of information on particular items).
Red Team Exercise	An exercise, reflecting real-world conditions, that is conducted as a simulated adversarial attempt to compromise organizational missions and/or business processes to provide a comprehensive assessment of the security capability of the information system and organization.
Reference Monitor	A set of design requirements on a reference validation mechanism which as key component of an operating system, enforces an access control policy over all subjects and objects. A reference validation mechanism must be: (i) always invoked (i.e., complete mediation); (ii) tamperproof; and (iii) small enough to be subject to analysis and tests, the completeness of which can be assured (i.e., verifiable).
Remote Access	Access to an organizational information system by a user (or a process acting on behalf of a user) communicating through an external network (e.g., the Internet).
Remote Maintenance	Maintenance activities conducted by individuals communicating through an external network (e.g., the Internet).
Resilience	See *Information System Resilience*.
Restricted Data [Atomic Energy Act of 1954]	All data concerning (i) design, manufacture, or utilization of atomic weapons; (ii) the production of special nuclear material; or (iii) the use of special nuclear material in the production of energy, but shall not include data declassified or removed from the Restricted Data category pursuant to Section 142 [of the Atomic Energy Act of 1954].

Risk [FIPS 200, Adapted]	A measure of the extent to which an entity is threatened by a potential circumstance or event, and typically a function of: (i) the adverse impacts that would arise if the circumstance or event occurs; and (ii) the likelihood of occurrence. Information system-related security risks are those risks that arise from the loss of confidentiality, integrity, or availability of information or information systems and reflect the potential adverse impacts to organizational operations (including mission, functions, image, or reputation), organizational assets, individuals, other organizations, and the Nation.
Risk Assessment	The process of identifying risks to organizational operations (including mission, functions, image, reputation), organizational assets, individuals, other organizations, and the Nation, resulting from the operation of an information system. Part of risk management, incorporates threat and vulnerability analyses, and considers mitigations provided by security controls planned or in place. Synonymous with risk analysis.
Risk Executive (Function) [CNSSI 4009]	An individual or group within an organization that helps to ensure that: (i) security risk-related considerations for individual information systems, to include the authorization decisions for those systems, are viewed from an organization-wide perspective with regard to the overall strategic goals and objectives of the organization in carrying out its missions and business functions; and (ii) managing risk from individual information systems is consistent across the organization, reflects organizational risk tolerance, and is considered along with other organizational risks affecting mission/business success.
Risk Management [CNSSI 4009, adapted]	The program and supporting processes to manage information security risk to organizational operations (including mission, functions, image, reputation), organizational assets, individuals, other organizations, and the Nation, and includes: (i) establishing the context for risk-related activities; (ii) assessing risk; (iii) responding to risk once determined; and (iv) monitoring risk over time.
Risk Mitigation [CNSSI 4009]	Prioritizing, evaluating, and implementing the appropriate risk-reducing controls/countermeasures recommended from the risk management process.
Risk Monitoring	Maintaining ongoing awareness of an organization's risk environment, risk management program, and associated activities to support risk decisions.
Risk Response	Accepting, avoiding, mitigating, sharing, or transferring risk to organizational operations (i.e., mission, functions, image, or reputation), organizational assets, individuals, other organizations, or the Nation.

Role-Based Access Control	Access control based on user roles (i.e., a collection of access authorizations a user receives based on an explicit or implicit assumption of a given role). Role permissions may be inherited through a role hierarchy and typically reflect the permissions needed to perform defined functions within an organization. A given role may apply to a single individual or to several individuals.
Safeguards [CNSSI 4009]	Protective measures prescribed to meet the security requirements (i.e., confidentiality, integrity, and availability) specified for an information system. Safeguards may include security features, management constraints, personnel security, and security of physical structures, areas, and devices. Synonymous with security controls and countermeasures.
Sanitization	Actions taken to render data written on media unrecoverable by both ordinary and, for some forms of sanitization, extraordinary means. Process to remove information from media such that data recovery is not possible. It includes removing all classified labels, markings, and activity logs.
Scoping Considerations	A part of tailoring guidance providing organizations with specific considerations on the applicability and implementation of security controls in the security control baseline. Areas of consideration include policy/regulatory, technology, physical infrastructure, system component allocation, operational/environmental, public access, scalability, common control, and security objective.
Security [CNSSI 4009]	A condition that results from the establishment and maintenance of protective measures that enable an enterprise to perform its mission or critical functions despite risks posed by threats to its use of information systems. Protective measures may involve a combination of deterrence, avoidance, prevention, detection, recovery, and correction that should form part of the enterprise's risk management approach.
Security Assessment	See *Security Control Assessment*.
Security Assessment Plan	The objectives for the security control assessment and a detailed roadmap of how to conduct such an assessment.
Security Assurance	See *Assurance*.
Security Attribute	An abstraction representing the basic properties or characteristics of an entity with respect to safeguarding information; typically associated with internal data structures (e.g., records, buffers, files) within the information system and used to enable the implementation of access control and flow control policies, reflect special dissemination, handling or distribution instructions, or support other aspects of the information security policy.

Security Authorization	See *Authorization*.
Security Authorization Boundary	See *Authorization Boundary*.
Security Capability	A combination of mutually-reinforcing security controls (i.e., safeguards and countermeasures) implemented by technical means (i.e., functionality in hardware, software, and firmware), physical means (i.e., physical devices and protective measures), and procedural means (i.e., procedures performed by individuals).
Security Categorization	The process of determining the security category for information or an information system. Security categorization methodologies are described in CNSS Instruction 1253 for national security systems and in FIPS Publication 199 for other than national security systems. See *Security Category*.
Security Category [FIPS 199, Adapted; CNSSI 4009]	The characterization of information or an information system based on an assessment of the potential impact that a loss of confidentiality, integrity, or availability of such information or information system would have on organizational operations, organizational assets, individuals, other organizations, and the Nation.
Security Control [FIPS 199, Adapted]	A safeguard or countermeasure prescribed for an information system or an organization designed to protect the confidentiality, integrity, and availability of its information and to meet a set of defined security requirements.
Security Control Assessment [CNSSI 4009, Adapted]	The testing or evaluation of security controls to determine the extent to which the controls are implemented correctly, operating as intended, and producing the desired outcome with respect to meeting the security requirements for an information system or organization.
Security Control Assessor	The individual, group, or organization responsible for conducting a security control assessment.
Security Control Baseline [FIPS 200, Adapted]	The set of minimum security controls defined for a low-impact, moderate-impact, or high-impact information system that provides a starting point for the tailoring process.
Security Control Enhancement	Augmentation of a security control to: (i) build in additional, but related, functionality to the control; (ii) increase the strength of the control; or (iii) add assurance to the control.
Security Control Inheritance [CNSSI 4009]	A situation in which an information system or application receives protection from security controls (or portions of security controls) that are developed, implemented, assessed, authorized, and monitored by entities other than those responsible for the system or application; entities either internal or external to the organization where the system or application resides. See *Common Control*.
Security Control Overlay	See *Overlay*.

Security Domain [CNSSI 4009]	A domain that implements a security policy and is administered by a single authority.
Security Functionality	The security-related features, functions, mechanisms, services, procedures, and architectures implemented within organizational information systems or the environments in which those systems operate.
Security Functions	The hardware, software, and/or firmware of the information system responsible for enforcing the system security policy and supporting the isolation of code and data on which the protection is based.
Security Impact Analysis [CNSSI 4009]	The analysis conducted by an organizational official to determine the extent to which changes to the information system have affected the security state of the system.
Security Incident	See *Incident*.
Security Kernel [CNSSI 4009]	Hardware, firmware, and software elements of a trusted computing base implementing the reference monitor concept. Security kernel must mediate all accesses, be protected from modification, and be verifiable as correct.
Security Label	The means used to associate a set of security attributes with a specific information object as part of the data structure for that object.
Security Marking	The means used to associate a set of security attributes with objects in a human-readable form, to enable organizational process-based enforcement of information security policies.
Security Objective [FIPS 199]	Confidentiality, integrity, or availability.
Security Plan	Formal document that provides an overview of the security requirements for an information system or an information security program and describes the security controls in place or planned for meeting those requirements. See *System Security Plan* or *Information Security Program Plan*.
Security Policy [CNSSI 4009]	A set of criteria for the provision of security services.
Security Policy Filter	A hardware and/or software component that performs one or more of the following functions: (i) content verification to ensure the data type of the submitted content; (ii) content inspection, analyzing the submitted content to verify it complies with a defined policy (e.g., allowed vs. disallowed file constructs and content portions); (iii) malicious content checker that evaluates the content for malicious code; (iv) suspicious activity checker that evaluates or executes the content in a safe manner, such as in a sandbox/detonation chamber and monitors for suspicious activity; or (v) content sanitization, cleansing, and transformation, which modifies the submitted content to comply with a defined policy.

Security Requirement [FIPS 200, Adapted]	A requirement levied on an information system or an organization that is derived from applicable laws, Executive Orders, directives, policies, standards, instructions, regulations, procedures, and/or mission/business needs to ensure the confidentiality, integrity, and availability of information that is being processed, stored, or transmitted. Note: Security requirements can be used in a variety of contexts from high-level policy-related activities to low-level implementation-related activities in system development and engineering disciplines.
Security Service [CNSSI 4009]	A capability that supports one, or more, of the security requirements (Confidentiality, Integrity, Availability). Examples of security services are key management, access control, and authentication.
Security-Relevant Information	Any information within the information system that can potentially impact the operation of security functions or the provision of security services in a manner that could result in failure to enforce the system security policy or maintain isolation of code and data.
Senior Agency Information Security Officer [44 U.S.C., Sec. 3544]	Official responsible for carrying out the Chief Information Officer responsibilities under FISMA and serving as the Chief Information Officer's primary liaison to the agency's authorizing officials, information system owners, and information system security officers. Note: Organizations subordinate to federal agencies may use the term *Senior Information Security Officer* or *Chief Information Security Officer* to denote individuals filling positions with similar responsibilities to Senior Agency Information Security Officers.
Senior Agency Official for Privacy	The senior organizational official with overall organization-wide responsibility for information privacy issues.
Senior Information Security Officer	See *Senior Agency Information Security Officer*.
Sensitive Information [CNSSI 4009, Adapted]	Information where the loss, misuse, or unauthorized access or modification could adversely affect the national interest or the conduct of federal programs, or the privacy to which individuals are entitled under 5 U.S.C. Section 552a (the Privacy Act); that has not been specifically authorized under criteria established by an Executive Order or an Act of Congress to be kept classified in the interest of national defense or foreign policy.
Sensitive Compartmented Information [CNSSI 4009]	Classified information concerning or derived from intelligence sources, methods, or analytical processes, which is required to be handled within formal access control systems established by the Director of National Intelligence.
Service-Oriented Architecture	A set of principles and methodologies for designing and developing software in the form of interoperable services. These services are well-defined business functions that are built as software components (i.e., discrete pieces of code and/or data structures) that can be reused for different purposes.

Software [CNSSI 4009]	Computer programs and associated data that may be dynamically written or modified during execution.
Spam	The abuse of electronic messaging systems to indiscriminately send unsolicited bulk messages.
Special Access Program [CNSSI 4009]	A program established for a specific class of classified information that imposes safeguarding and access requirements that exceed those normally required for information at the same classification level.
Spyware	Software that is secretly or surreptitiously installed into an information system to gather information on individuals or organizations without their knowledge; a type of malicious code.
Subject	Generally an individual, process, or device causing information to flow among objects or change to the system state. See *Object*.
Subsystem	A major subdivision or component of an information system consisting of information, information technology, and personnel that performs one or more specific functions.
Supplemental Guidance	Statements used to provide additional explanatory information for security controls or security control enhancements.
Supplementation	The process of adding security controls or control enhancements to a security control baseline as part of the tailoring process (during security control selection) in order to adequately meet the organization's risk management needs.
Supply Chain [ISO 28001, Adapted]	Linked set of resources and processes between multiple tiers of developers that begins with the sourcing of products and services and extends through the design, development, manufacturing, processing, handling, and delivery of products and services to the acquirer.
Supply Chain Element	An information technology product or product component that contains programmable logic and that is critically important to the functioning of an information system.
System	See *Information System*.
System of Records Notice	An official public notice of an organization's system(s) of records, as required by the Privacy Act of 1974, that identifies: (i) the purpose for the system of records; (ii) the individuals covered by information in the system of records; (iii) the categories of records maintained about individuals; and (iv) the ways in which the information is shared.
System Security Plan [NIST SP 800-18]	Formal document that provides an overview of the security requirements for an information system and describes the security controls in place or planned for meeting those requirements.

System-Specific Security Control	A security control for an information system that has not been designated as a common security control or the portion of a hybrid control that is to be implemented within an information system.
Tailored Security Control Baseline	A set of security controls resulting from the application of tailoring guidance to a security control baseline. See *Tailoring*.
Tailoring	The process by which security control baselines are modified by: (i) identifying and designating common controls; (ii) applying scoping considerations on the applicability and implementation of baseline controls; (iii) selecting compensating security controls; (iv) assigning specific values to organization-defined security control parameters; (v) supplementing baselines with additional security controls or control enhancements; and (vi) providing additional specification information for control implementation.
Threat [CNSSI 4009, Adapted]	Any circumstance or event with the potential to adversely impact organizational operations (including mission, functions, image, or reputation), organizational assets, individuals, other organizations, or the Nation through an information system via unauthorized access, destruction, disclosure, modification of information, and/or denial of service.
Threat Assessment [CNSSI 4009]	Formal description and evaluation of threat to an information system.
Threat Source [FIPS 200]	The intent and method targeted at the intentional exploitation of a vulnerability or a situation and method that may accidentally trigger a vulnerability. Synonymous with threat agent.
Trusted Path	A mechanism by which a user (through an input device) can communicate directly with the security functions of the information system with the necessary confidence to support the system security policy. This mechanism can only be activated by the user or the security functions of the information system and cannot be imitated by untrusted software.
Trustworthiness [CNSSI 4009]	The attribute of a person or enterprise that provides confidence to others of the qualifications, capabilities, and reliability of that entity to perform specific tasks and fulfill assigned responsibilities.
Trustworthiness (Information System)	The degree to which an information system (including the information technology components that are used to build the system) can be expected to preserve the confidentiality, integrity, and availability of the information being processed, stored, or transmitted by the system across the full range of threats. A trustworthy information system is a system that is believed to be capable of operating within defined levels of risk despite the environmental disruptions, human errors, structural failures, and purposeful attacks that are expected to occur in its environment of operation.

User [CNSSI 4009, adapted]	Individual, or (system) process acting on behalf of an individual, authorized to access an information system. See *Organizational User* and *Non-Organizational User*.
Virtual Private Network [CNSSI 4009]	Protected information system link utilizing tunneling, security controls, and endpoint address translation giving the impression of a dedicated line.
Vulnerability [CNSSI 4009]	Weakness in an information system, system security procedures, internal controls, or implementation that could be exploited or triggered by a threat source.
Vulnerability Analysis	See *Vulnerability Assessment*.
Vulnerability Assessment [CNSSI 4009]	Systematic examination of an information system or product to determine the adequacy of security measures, identify security deficiencies, provide data from which to predict the effectiveness of proposed security measures, and confirm the adequacy of such measures after implementation.
Whitelisting	The process used to identify: (i) software programs that are authorized to execute on an information system; or (ii) authorized Universal Resource Locators (URL)/websites.

APPENDIX C

ACRONYMS

COMMON ABBREVIATIONS

APT	Advanced Persistent Threat
CFR	Code of Federal Regulations
CIO	Chief Information Officer
CISO	Chief Information Security Officer
CAVP	Cryptographic Algorithm Validation Program
CMVP	Cryptographic Module Validation Program
CNSS	Committee on National Security Systems
CPO	Chief Privacy Officer
CUI	Controlled Unclassified Information
DCS	Distributed Control System
DNS	Domain Name System
DoD	Department of Defense
FAR	Federal Acquisition Regulation
FEA	Federal Enterprise Architecture
FICAM	Federal Identity, Credential, and Access Management
FIPP	Fair Information Practice Principles
FIPS	Federal Information Processing Standards
FISMA	Federal Information Security Management Act
HSPD	Homeland Security Presidential Directive
ICS	Industrial Control System
IEEE	Institute of Electrical and Electronics Engineers
IPsec	Internet Protocol Security
ISO/IEC	International Organization for Standardization/International Electrotechnical Commission
ITL	Information Technology Laboratory
LACS	Logical Access Control System
LSI	Large-Scale Integration
NIST	National Institute of Standards and Technology
NISTIR	National Institute of Standards and Technology Interagency or Internal Report
NSA	National Security Agency

NSTISSI	National Security Telecommunications and Information System Security Instruction
ODNI	Office of the Director of National Intelligence
OMB	Office of Management and Budget
OPSEC	Operations Security
PBX	Private Branch Exchange
PACS	Physical Access Control System
PIA	Privacy Impact Assessment
PII	Personally Identifiable Information
PIV	Personal Identity Verification
PKI	Public Key Infrastructure
RBAC	Role-Based Access Control
RD	Restricted Data
RMF	Risk Management Framework
SAISO	Senior Agency Information Security Officer
SAMI	Sources And Methods Information
SAOP	Senior Agency Official for Privacy
SAP	Special Access Program
SC	Security Category
SCADA	Supervisory Control and Data Acquisition
SCI	Sensitive Compartmented Information
SOA	Service-Oriented Architecture
SORN	System of Records Notice
SP	Special Publication
TCP/IP	Transmission Control Protocol/Internet Protocol
USB	Universal Serial Bus
VoIP	Voice over Internet Protocol
VPN	Virtual Private Network

APPENDIX D

SECURITY CONTROL BASELINES – SUMMARY
LOW-IMPACT, MODERATE-IMPACT, AND HIGH-IMPACT INFORMATION SYSTEMS

This appendix contains the security control baselines that represent the *starting point* in determining the security controls for low-impact, moderate-impact, and high-impact information systems.[90] The three security control baselines are hierarchical in nature with regard to the security controls employed in those baselines.[91] If a security control is selected for one of the baselines, the family identifier and control number are listed in the appropriate column. If a security control is not used in a particular baseline, the entry is marked *not selected*. Security control enhancements, when used to supplement security controls, are indicated by the number of the enhancement. For example, the IR-2 (1) (2) entry in the high baseline for IR-2 indicates that the second control from the Incident Response family has been selected along with control enhancements (1) and (2). Some security controls and enhancements are not used in any of the baselines in this appendix but are available for use by organizations if needed. This situation occurs, for example, when the results of a risk assessment indicate the need for additional security controls or control enhancements in order to adequately mitigate risk to organizational operations and assets, individuals, other organizations, and the Nation.

Organizations can use the recommended *priority code* designation associated with each security control in the baselines to assist in making sequencing decisions for control implementation (i.e., a Priority Code 1 [P1] control has a higher priority for implementation than a Priority Code 2 [P2] control; a Priority Code 2 [P2] control has a higher priority for implementation than a Priority Code 3 [P3] control, and a Priority Code 0 [P0] indicates the security control is not selected in any baseline). This recommended sequencing prioritization helps ensure that security controls upon which other controls depend are implemented first, thus enabling organizations to deploy controls in a more structured and timely manner in accordance with available resources. The implementation of security controls by sequence priority code does not imply any defined level of risk mitigation until *all* controls in the security plan have been implemented. The priority codes are used only for implementation sequencing, not for making security control selection decisions. Table D-1 summarizes sequence priority codes for the baseline security controls in Table D-2.

TABLE D-1: SECURITY CONTROL PRIORITIZATION CODES

Priority Code	Sequencing	Action
Priority Code 1 **(P1)**	FIRST	Implement P1 security controls first.
Priority Code 2 **(P2)**	NEXT	Implement P2 security controls after implementation of P1 controls.
Priority Code 3 **(P3)**	LAST	Implement P3 security controls after implementation of P1 and P2 controls.
Unspecified Priority Code **(P0)**	NONE	Security control not selected in any baseline.

---

[90] A complete description of all security controls is provided in Appendices F and G. In addition, separate documents for individual security control baselines (listed as Annexes 1, 2, and 3) are available at http://csrc.nist.gov/publications. An online version of the catalog of security controls is also available at http://web.nvd.nist.gov/view/800-53/home.

[91] The hierarchical nature applies to the security requirements of each control (i.e., the base control plus all of its enhancements) at the low-impact, moderate-impact, and high-impact level in that the control requirements at a particular impact level (e.g., CP-4 *Contingency Plan Testing*—Moderate: CP-4(1)) meets a stronger set of security requirements for that control than the next lower impact level of the same control (e.g., CP-4 *Contingency Plan Testing*—Low: CP-4).

Table D-2 provides a summary of the security controls and control enhancements from Appendix F that have been allocated to the initial security control baselines (i.e., low, moderate, and high). The sequence priority codes for security control implementation and those security controls that have been withdrawn from Appendix F are also indicated in Table D-2. In addition to Table D-2, the sequence priority codes and security control baselines are annotated in a priority and baseline allocation summary section below each security control in Appendix F.

TABLE D-2: SECURITY CONTROL BASELINES[92]

CNTL NO.	CONTROL NAME	PRIORITY	INITIAL CONTROL BASELINES		
			LOW	MOD	HIGH
Access Control					
AC-1	Access Control Policy and Procedures	P1	AC-1	AC-1	AC-1
AC-2	Account Management	P1	AC-2	AC-2 (1) (2) (3) (4)	AC-2 (1) (2) (3) (4) (5) (11) (12) (13)
AC-3	Access Enforcement	P1	AC-3	AC-3	AC-3
AC-4	Information Flow Enforcement	P1	Not Selected	AC-4	AC-4
AC-5	Separation of Duties	P1	Not Selected	AC-5	AC-5
AC-6	Least Privilege	P1	Not Selected	AC-6 (1) (2) (5) (9) (10)	AC-6 (1) (2) (3) (5) (9) (10)
AC-7	Unsuccessful Logon Attempts	P2	AC-7	AC-7	AC-7
AC-8	System Use Notification	P1	AC-8	AC-8	AC-8
AC-9	Previous Logon (Access) Notification	P0	Not Selected	Not Selected	Not Selected
AC-10	Concurrent Session Control	P3	Not Selected	Not Selected	AC-10
AC-11	Session Lock	P3	Not Selected	AC-11 (1)	AC-11 (1)
AC-12	Session Termination	P2	Not Selected	AC-12	AC-12
AC-13	**Withdrawn**	---	---	---	---
AC-14	Permitted Actions without Identification or Authentication	P3	AC-14	AC-14	AC-14
AC-15	**Withdrawn**	---	---	---	---
AC-16	Security Attributes	P0	Not Selected	Not Selected	Not Selected
AC-17	Remote Access	P1	AC-17	AC-17 (1) (2) (3) (4)	AC-17 (1) (2) (3) (4)
AC-18	Wireless Access	P1	AC-18	AC-18 (1)	AC-18 (1) (4) (5)
AC-19	Access Control for Mobile Devices	P1	AC-19	AC-19 (5)	AC-19 (5)
AC-20	Use of External Information Systems	P1	AC-20	AC-20 (1) (2)	AC-20 (1) (2)
AC-21	Information Sharing	P2	Not Selected	AC-21	AC-21
AC-22	Publicly Accessible Content	P3	AC-22	AC-22	AC-22
AC-23	Data Mining Protection	P0	Not Selected	Not Selected	Not Selected
AC-24	Access Control Decisions	P0	Not Selected	Not Selected	Not Selected
AC-25	Reference Monitor	P0	Not Selected	Not Selected	Not Selected

---

[92] The security control baselines in Table D-2 are the initial baselines selected by organizations prior to conducting the tailoring activities described in Section 3.2. The control baselines and priority codes are only applicable to non-national security systems. Security control baselines for national security systems are included in CNSS Instruction 1253.

CNTL NO.	CONTROL NAME	PRIORITY	INITIAL CONTROL BASELINES		
			LOW	MOD	HIGH
Awareness and Training					
AT-1	Security Awareness and Training Policy and Procedures	P1	AT-1	AT-1	AT-1
AT-2	Security Awareness Training	P1	AT-2	AT-2 (2)	AT-2 (2)
AT-3	Role-Based Security Training	P1	AT-3	AT-3	AT-3
AT-4	Security Training Records	P3	AT-4	AT-4	AT-4
AT-5	**Withdrawn**	---	---	---	---
Audit and Accountability					
AU-1	Audit and Accountability Policy and Procedures	P1	AU-1	AU-1	AU-1
AU-2	Audit Events	P1	AU-2	AU-2 (3)	AU-2 (3)
AU-3	Content of Audit Records	P1	AU-3	AU-3 (1)	AU-3 (1) (2)
AU-4	Audit Storage Capacity	P1	AU-4	AU-4	AU-4
AU-5	Response to Audit Processing Failures	P1	AU-5	AU-5	AU-5 (1) (2)
AU-6	Audit Review, Analysis, and Reporting	P1	AU-6	AU-6 (1) (3)	AU-6 (1) (3) (5) (6)
AU-7	Audit Reduction and Report Generation	P2	Not Selected	AU-7 (1)	AU-7 (1)
AU-8	Time Stamps	P1	AU-8	AU-8 (1)	AU-8 (1)
AU-9	Protection of Audit Information	P1	AU-9	AU-9 (4)	AU-9 (2) (3) (4)
AU-10	Non-repudiation	P2	Not Selected	Not Selected	AU-10
AU-11	Audit Record Retention	P3	AU-11	AU-11	AU-11
AU-12	Audit Generation	P1	AU-12	AU-12	AU-12 (1) (3)
AU-13	Monitoring for Information Disclosure	P0	Not Selected	Not Selected	Not Selected
AU-14	Session Audit	P0	Not Selected	Not Selected	Not Selected
AU-15	Alternate Audit Capability	P0	Not Selected	Not Selected	Not Selected
AU-16	Cross-Organizational Auditing	P0	Not Selected	Not Selected	Not Selected
Security Assessment and Authorization					
CA-1	Security Assessment and Authorization Policies and Procedures	P1	CA-1	CA-1	CA-1
CA-2	Security Assessments	P2	CA-2	CA-2 (1)	CA-2 (1) (2)
CA-3	System Interconnections	P1	CA-3	CA-3 (5)	CA-3 (5)
CA-4	**Withdrawn**	---	---	---	---
CA-5	Plan of Action and Milestones	P3	CA-5	CA-5	CA-5
CA-6	Security Authorization	P2	CA-6	CA-6	CA-6
CA-7	Continuous Monitoring	P2	CA-7	CA-7 (1)	CA-7 (1)
CA-8	Penetration Testing	P2	Not Selected	Not Selected	CA-8
CA-9	Internal System Connections	P2	CA-9	CA-9	CA-9
Configuration Management					
CM-1	Configuration Management Policy and Procedures	P1	CM-1	CM-1	CM-1
CM-2	Baseline Configuration	P1	CM-2	CM-2 (1) (3) (7)	CM-2 (1) (2) (3) (7)
CM-3	Configuration Change Control	P1	Not Selected	CM-3 (2)	CM-3 (1) (2)
CM-4	Security Impact Analysis	P2	CM-4	CM-4	CM-4 (1)
CM-5	Access Restrictions for Change	P1	Not Selected	CM-5	CM-5 (1) (2) (3)

CNTL NO.	CONTROL NAME	PRIORITY	INITIAL CONTROL BASELINES		
			LOW	MOD	HIGH
CM-6	Configuration Settings	P1	CM-6	CM-6	CM-6 (1) (2)
CM-7	Least Functionality	P1	CM-7	CM-7 (1) (2) (4)	CM-7 (1) (2) (5)
CM-8	Information System Component Inventory	P1	CM-8	CM-8 (1) (3) (5)	CM-8 (1) (2) (3) (4) (5)
CM-9	Configuration Management Plan	P1	Not Selected	CM-9	CM-9
CM-10	Software Usage Restrictions	P2	CM-10	CM-10	CM-10
CM-11	User-Installed Software	P1	CM-11	CM-11	CM-11
Contingency Planning					
CP-1	Contingency Planning Policy and Procedures	P1	CP-1	CP-1	CP-1
CP-2	Contingency Plan	P1	CP-2	CP-2 (1) (3) (8)	CP-2 (1) (2) (3) (4) (5) (8)
CP-3	Contingency Training	P2	CP-3	CP-3	CP-3 (1)
CP-4	Contingency Plan Testing	P2	CP-4	CP-4 (1)	CP-4 (1) (2)
CP-5	Withdrawn	---	---	---	---
CP-6	Alternate Storage Site	P1	Not Selected	CP-6 (1) (3)	CP-6 (1) (2) (3)
CP-7	Alternate Processing Site	P1	Not Selected	CP-7 (1) (2) (3)	CP-7 (1) (2) (3) (4)
CP-8	Telecommunications Services	P1	Not Selected	CP-8 (1) (2)	CP-8 (1) (2) (3) (4)
CP-9	Information System Backup	P1	CP-9	CP-9 (1)	CP-9 (1) (2) (3) (5)
CP-10	Information System Recovery and Reconstitution	P1	CP-10	CP-10 (2)	CP-10 (2) (4)
CP-11	Alternate Communications Protocols	P0	Not Selected	Not Selected	Not Selected
CP-12	Safe Mode	P0	Not Selected	Not Selected	Not Selected
CP-13	Alternative Security Mechanisms	P0	Not Selected	Not Selected	Not Selected
Identification and Authentication					
IA-1	Identification and Authentication Policy and Procedures	P1	IA-1	IA-1	IA-1
IA-2	Identification and Authentication (Organizational Users)	P1	IA-2 (1) (12)	IA-2 (1) (2) (3) (8) (11) (12)	IA-2 (1) (2) (3) (4) (8) (9) (11) (12)
IA-3	Device Identification and Authentication	P1	Not Selected	IA-3	IA-3
IA-4	Identifier Management	P1	IA-4	IA-4	IA-4
IA-5	Authenticator Management	P1	IA-5 (1) (11)	IA-5 (1) (2) (3) (11)	IA-5 (1) (2) (3) (11)
IA-6	Authenticator Feedback	P2	IA-6	IA-6	IA-6
IA-7	Cryptographic Module Authentication	P1	IA-7	IA-7	IA-7
IA-8	Identification and Authentication (Non-Organizational Users)	P1	IA-8 (1) (2) (3) (4)	IA-8 (1) (2) (3) (4)	IA-8 (1) (2) (3) (4)
IA-9	Service Identification and Authentication	P0	Not Selected	Not Selected	Not Selected
IA-10	Adaptive Identification and Authentication	P0	Not Selected	Not Selected	Not Selected
IA-11	Re-authentication	P0	Not Selected	Not Selected	Not Selected
Incident Response					
IR-1	Incident Response Policy and Procedures	P1	IR-1	IR-1	IR-1
IR-2	Incident Response Training	P2	IR-2	IR-2	IR-2 (1) (2)

CNTL NO.	CONTROL NAME	PRIORITY	INITIAL CONTROL BASELINES		
			LOW	MOD	HIGH
IR-3	Incident Response Testing	P2	Not Selected	IR-3 (2)	IR-3 (2)
IR-4	Incident Handling	P1	IR-4	IR-4 (1)	IR-4 (1) (4)
IR-5	Incident Monitoring	P1	IR-5	IR-5	IR-5 (1)
IR-6	Incident Reporting	P1	IR-6	IR-6 (1)	IR-6 (1)
IR-7	Incident Response Assistance	P2	IR-7	IR-7 (1)	IR-7 (1)
IR-8	Incident Response Plan	P1	IR-8	IR-8	IR-8
IR-9	Information Spillage Response	P0	Not Selected	Not Selected	Not Selected
IR-10	Integrated Information Security Analysis Team	P0	Not Selected	Not Selected	Not Selected
Maintenance					
MA-1	System Maintenance Policy and Procedures	P1	MA-1	MA-1	MA-1
MA-2	Controlled Maintenance	P2	MA-2	MA-2	MA-2 (2)
MA-3	Maintenance Tools	P3	Not Selected	MA-3 (1) (2)	MA-3 (1) (2) (3)
MA-4	Nonlocal Maintenance	P2	MA-4	MA-4 (2)	MA-4 (2) (3)
MA-5	Maintenance Personnel	P2	MA-5	MA-5	MA-5 (1)
MA-6	Timely Maintenance	P2	Not Selected	MA-6	MA-6
Media Protection					
MP-1	Media Protection Policy and Procedures	P1	MP-1	MP-1	MP-1
MP-2	Media Access	P1	MP-2	MP-2	MP-2
MP-3	Media Marking	P2	Not Selected	MP-3	MP-3
MP-4	Media Storage	P1	Not Selected	MP-4	MP-4
MP-5	Media Transport	P1	Not Selected	MP-5 (4)	MP-5 (4)
MP-6	Media Sanitization	P1	MP-6	MP-6	MP-6 (1) (2) (3)
MP-7	Media Use	P1	MP-7	MP-7 (1)	MP-7 (1)
MP-8	Media Downgrading	P0	Not Selected	Not Selected	Not Selected
Physical and Environmental Protection					
PE-1	Physical and Environmental Protection Policy and Procedures	P1	PE-1	PE-1	PE-1
PE-2	Physical Access Authorizations	P1	PE-2	PE-2	PE-2
PE-3	Physical Access Control	P1	PE-3	PE-3	PE-3 (1)
PE-4	Access Control for Transmission Medium	P1	Not Selected	PE-4	PE-4
PE-5	Access Control for Output Devices	P2	Not Selected	PE-5	PE-5
PE-6	Monitoring Physical Access	P1	PE-6	PE-6 (1)	PE-6 (1) (4)
PE-7	**Withdrawn**	---	---	---	---
PE-8	Visitor Access Records	P3	PE-8	PE-8	PE-8 (1)
PE-9	Power Equipment and Cabling	P1	Not Selected	PE-9	PE-9
PE-10	Emergency Shutoff	P1	Not Selected	PE-10	PE-10
PE-11	Emergency Power	P1	Not Selected	PE-11	PE-11 (1)
PE-12	Emergency Lighting	P1	PE-12	PE-12	PE-12
PE-13	Fire Protection	P1	PE-13	PE-13 (3)	PE-13 (1) (2) (3)
PE-14	Temperature and Humidity Controls	P1	PE-14	PE-14	PE-14
PE-15	Water Damage Protection	P1	PE-15	PE-15	PE-15 (1)
PE-16	Delivery and Removal	P2	PE-16	PE-16	PE-16

CNTL NO.	CONTROL NAME	PRIORITY	INITIAL CONTROL BASELINES		
			LOW	MOD	HIGH
PE-17	Alternate Work Site	P2	Not Selected	PE-17	PE-17
PE-18	Location of Information System Components	P3	Not Selected	Not Selected	PE-18
PE-19	Information Leakage	P0	Not Selected	Not Selected	Not Selected
PE-20	Asset Monitoring and Tracking	P0	Not Selected	Not Selected	Not Selected
Planning					
PL-1	Security Planning Policy and Procedures	P1	PL-1	PL-1	PL-1
PL-2	System Security Plan	P1	PL-2	PL-2 (3)	PL-2 (3)
PL-3	Withdrawn	---	---	---	---
PL-4	Rules of Behavior	P2	PL-4	PL-4 (1)	PL-4 (1)
PL-5	Withdrawn	---	---	---	---
PL-6	Withdrawn	---	---	---	---
PL-7	Security Concept of Operations	P0	Not Selected	Not Selected	Not Selected
PL-8	Information Security Architecture	P1	Not Selected	PL-8	PL-8
PL-9	Central Management	P0	Not Selected	Not Selected	Not Selected
Personnel Security					
PS-1	Personnel Security Policy and Procedures	P1	PS-1	PS-1	PS-1
PS-2	Position Risk Designation	P1	PS-2	PS-2	PS-2
PS-3	Personnel Screening	P1	PS-3	PS-3	PS-3
PS-4	Personnel Termination	P1	PS-4	PS-4	PS-4 (2)
PS-5	Personnel Transfer	P2	PS-5	PS-5	PS-5
PS-6	Access Agreements	P3	PS-6	PS-6	PS-6
PS-7	Third-Party Personnel Security	P1	PS-7	PS-7	PS-7
PS-8	Personnel Sanctions	P3	PS-8	PS-8	PS-8
Risk Assessment					
RA-1	Risk Assessment Policy and Procedures	P1	RA-1	RA-1	RA-1
RA-2	Security Categorization	P1	RA-2	RA-2	RA-2
RA-3	Risk Assessment	P1	RA-3	RA-3	RA-3
RA-4	Withdrawn	---	---	---	---
RA-5	Vulnerability Scanning	P1	RA-5	RA-5 (1) (2) (5)	RA-5 (1) (2) (4) (5)
RA-6	Technical Surveillance Countermeasures Survey	P0	Not Selected	Not Selected	Not Selected
System and Services Acquisition					
SA-1	System and Services Acquisition Policy and Procedures	P1	SA-1	SA-1	SA-1
SA-2	Allocation of Resources	P1	SA-2	SA-2	SA-2
SA-3	System Development Life Cycle	P1	SA-3	SA-3	SA-3
SA-4	Acquisition Process	P1	SA-4 (10)	SA-4 (1) (2) (9) (10)	SA-4 (1) (2) (9) (10)
SA-5	Information System Documentation	P2	SA-5	SA-5	SA-5
SA-6	Withdrawn	---	---	---	---
SA-7	Withdrawn	---	---	---	---
SA-8	Security Engineering Principles	P1	Not Selected	SA-8	SA-8
SA-9	External Information System Services	P1	SA-9	SA-9 (2)	SA-9 (2)

CNTL NO.	CONTROL NAME	PRIORITY	INITIAL CONTROL BASELINES		
			LOW	MOD	HIGH
SA-10	Developer Configuration Management	P1	Not Selected	SA-10	SA-10
SA-11	Developer Security Testing and Evaluation	P1	Not Selected	SA-11	SA-11
SA-12	Supply Chain Protection	P1	Not Selected	Not Selected	SA-12
SA-13	Trustworthiness	P0	Not Selected	Not Selected	Not Selected
SA-14	Criticality Analysis	P0	Not Selected	Not Selected	Not Selected
SA-15	Development Process, Standards, and Tools	P2	Not Selected	Not Selected	SA-15
SA-16	Developer-Provided Training	P2	Not Selected	Not Selected	SA-16
SA-17	Developer Security Architecture and Design	P1	Not Selected	Not Selected	SA-17
SA-18	Tamper Resistance and Detection	P0	Not Selected	Not Selected	Not Selected
SA-19	Component Authenticity	P0	Not Selected	Not Selected	Not Selected
SA-20	Customized Development of Critical Components	P0	Not Selected	Not Selected	Not Selected
SA-21	Developer Screening	P0	Not Selected	Not Selected	Not Selected
SA-22	Unsupported System Components	P0	Not Selected	Not Selected	Not Selected
System and Communications Protection					
SC-1	System and Communications Protection Policy and Procedures	P1	SC-1	SC-1	SC-1
SC-2	Application Partitioning	P1	Not Selected	SC-2	SC-2
SC-3	Security Function Isolation	P1	Not Selected	Not Selected	SC-3
SC-4	Information in Shared Resources	P1	Not Selected	SC-4	SC-4
SC-5	Denial of Service Protection	P1	SC-5	SC-5	SC-5
SC-6	Resource Availability	P0	Not Selected	Not Selected	Not Selected
SC-7	Boundary Protection	P1	SC-7	SC-7 (3) (4) (5) (7)	SC-7 (3) (4) (5) (7) (8) (18) (21)
SC-8	Transmission Confidentiality and Integrity	P1	Not Selected	SC-8 (1)	SC-8 (1)
SC-9	Withdrawn	---	---	---	---
SC-10	Network Disconnect	P2	Not Selected	SC-10	SC-10
SC-11	Trusted Path	P0	Not Selected	Not Selected	Not Selected
SC-12	Cryptographic Key Establishment and Management	P1	SC-12	SC-12	SC-12 (1)
SC-13	Cryptographic Protection	P1	SC-13	SC-13	SC-13
SC-14	Withdrawn	---	---	---	---
SC-15	Collaborative Computing Devices	P1	SC-15	SC-15	SC-15
SC-16	Transmission of Security Attributes	P0	Not Selected	Not Selected	Not Selected
SC-17	Public Key Infrastructure Certificates	P1	Not Selected	SC-17	SC-17
SC-18	Mobile Code	P2	Not Selected	SC-18	SC-18
SC-19	Voice Over Internet Protocol	P1	Not Selected	SC-19	SC-19
SC-20	Secure Name /Address Resolution Service (Authoritative Source)	P1	SC-20	SC-20	SC-20
SC-21	Secure Name /Address Resolution Service (Recursive or Caching Resolver)	P1	SC-21	SC-21	SC-21
SC-22	Architecture and Provisioning for Name/Address Resolution Service	P1	SC-22	SC-22	SC-22
SC-23	Session Authenticity	P1	Not Selected	SC-23	SC-23
SC-24	Fail in Known State	P1	Not Selected	Not Selected	SC-24

CNTL NO.	CONTROL NAME	PRIORITY	INITIAL CONTROL BASELINES		
			LOW	MOD	HIGH
SC-25	Thin Nodes	P0	Not Selected	Not Selected	Not Selected
SC-26	Honeypots	P0	Not Selected	Not Selected	Not Selected
SC-27	Platform-Independent Applications	P0	Not Selected	Not Selected	Not Selected
SC-28	Protection of Information at Rest	P1	Not Selected	SC-28	SC-28
SC-29	Heterogeneity	P0	Not Selected	Not Selected	Not Selected
SC-30	Concealment and Misdirection	P0	Not Selected	Not Selected	Not Selected
SC-31	Covert Channel Analysis	P0	Not Selected	Not Selected	Not Selected
SC-32	Information System Partitioning	P0	Not Selected	Not Selected	Not Selected
SC-33	**Withdrawn**	---	---	---	---
SC-34	Non-Modifiable Executable Programs	P0	Not Selected	Not Selected	Not Selected
SC-35	Honeyclients	P0	Not Selected	Not Selected	Not Selected
SC-36	Distributed Processing and Storage	P0	Not Selected	Not Selected	Not Selected
SC-37	Out-of-Band Channels	P0	Not Selected	Not Selected	Not Selected
SC-38	Operations Security	P0	Not Selected	Not Selected	Not Selected
SC-39	Process Isolation	P1	SC-39	SC-39	SC-39
SC-40	Wireless Link Protection	P0	Not Selected	Not Selected	Not Selected
SC-41	Port and I/O Device Access	P0	Not Selected	Not Selected	Not Selected
SC-42	Sensor Capability and Data	P0	Not Selected	Not Selected	Not Selected
SC-43	Usage Restrictions	P0	Not Selected	Not Selected	Not Selected
SC-44	Detonation Chambers	P0	Not Selected	Not Selected	Not Selected
System and Information Integrity					
SI-1	System and Information Integrity Policy and Procedures	P1	SI-1	SI-1	SI-1
SI-2	Flaw Remediation	P1	SI-2	SI-2 (2)	SI-2 (1) (2)
SI-3	Malicious Code Protection	P1	SI-3	SI-3 (1) (2)	SI-3 (1) (2)
SI-4	Information System Monitoring	P1	SI-4	SI-4 (2) (4) (5)	SI-4 (2) (4) (5)
SI-5	Security Alerts, Advisories, and Directives	P1	SI-5	SI-5	SI-5 (1)
SI-6	Security Function Verification	P1	Not Selected	Not Selected	SI-6
SI-7	Software, Firmware, and Information Integrity	P1	Not Selected	SI-7 (1) (7)	SI-7 (1) (2) (5) (7) (14)
SI-8	Spam Protection	P2	Not Selected	SI-8 (1) (2)	SI-8 (1) (2)
SI-9	**Withdrawn**	---	---	---	---
SI-10	Information Input Validation	P1	Not Selected	SI-10	SI-10
SI-11	Error Handling	P2	Not Selected	SI-11	SI-11
SI-12	Information Handling and Retention	P2	SI-12	SI-12	SI-12
SI-13	Predictable Failure Prevention	P0	Not Selected	Not Selected	Not Selected
SI-14	Non-Persistence	P0	Not Selected	Not Selected	Not Selected
SI-15	Information Output Filtering	P0	Not Selected	Not Selected	Not Selected
SI-16	Memory Protection	P1	Not Selected	SI-16	SI-16
SI-17	Fail-Safe Procedures	P0	Not Selected	Not Selected	Not Selected

Tables D-3 through D-19 provide a more detailed summary of the security controls and control enhancements in Appendix F. Each table focuses on a different security control family. Whereas Table D-2 includes only those security controls and control enhancements allocated to the three security control baselines, Tables D-3 through D-19 include all controls and enhancements for the respective security control families. The tables include the following information: (i) the security controls and control enhancements that have been selected for the security control baselines as indicated by an "x" in the column for the selected baseline;[93] (ii) the security controls and control enhancements that have not been selected for any security control baseline (i.e., the controls and control enhancements available for selection to achieve greater protection) as indicated by blank cells in the baseline columns; (iii) the security controls and control enhancements that have been withdrawn from Appendix F as indicated by an "x" in the respective withdrawn column; and (iv) the security controls and control enhancements that have assurance-related characteristics or properties (i.e., assurance-related controls) as indicated by an "x" in the respective assurance column. Assurance-related controls are discussed in greater detail in Appendix E to include the allocation of such controls to security control baselines (see Tables E-1 through E-3).

---

[93] The security control baselines in Tables D-3 through D-19 are only applicable to non-national security systems. Security control baselines for national security systems are included in CNSS Instruction 1253.

TABLE D-3: SUMMARY — ACCESS CONTROLS

CNTL NO.	CONTROL NAME *Control Enhancement Name*	WITHDRAWN	ASSURANCE	CONTROL BASELINES		
				LOW	MOD	HIGH
AC-1	**Access Control Policy and Procedures**		x	x	x	x
AC-2	**Account Management**		x	x	x	x
AC-2(1)	ACCOUNT MANAGEMENT | AUTOMATED SYSTEM ACCOUNT MANAGEMENT				x	x
AC-2(2)	ACCOUNT MANAGEMENT | REMOVAL OF TEMPORARY / EMERGENCY ACCOUNTS				x	x
AC-2(3)	ACCOUNT MANAGEMENT | DISABLE INACTIVE ACCOUNTS				x	x
AC-2(4)	ACCOUNT MANAGEMENT | AUTOMATED AUDIT ACTIONS				x	x
AC-2(5)	ACCOUNT MANAGEMENT | INACTIVITY LOGOUT					x
AC-2(6)	ACCOUNT MANAGEMENT | DYNAMIC PRIVILEGE MANAGEMENT					
AC-2(7)	ACCOUNT MANAGEMENT | ROLE-BASED SCHEMES					
AC-2(8)	ACCOUNT MANAGEMENT | DYNAMIC ACCOUNT CREATION					
AC-2(9)	ACCOUNT MANAGEMENT | RESTRICTIONS ON USE OF SHARED / GROUP ACCOUNTS					
AC-2(10)	ACCOUNT MANAGEMENT | SHARED / GROUP ACCOUNT CREDENTIAL TERMINATION					
AC-2(11)	ACCOUNT MANAGEMENT | USAGE CONDITIONS					x
AC-2(12)	ACCOUNT MANAGEMENT | ACCOUNT MONITORING / ATYPICAL USAGE					x
AC-2(13)	ACCOUNT MANAGEMENT | DISABLE ACCOUNTS FOR HIGH-RISK INDIVIDUALS					x
AC-3	**Access Enforcement**			x	x	x
AC-3(1)	ACCESS ENFORCEMENT | RESTRICTED ACCESS TO PRIVILEGED FUNCTIONS	x	Incorporated into AC-6.			
AC-3(2)	ACCESS ENFORCEMENT | DUAL AUTHORIZATION					
AC-3(3)	ACCESS ENFORCEMENT | MANDATORY ACCESS CONTROL					
AC-3(4)	ACCESS ENFORCEMENT | DISCRETIONARY ACCESS CONTROL					
AC-3(5)	ACCESS ENFORCEMENT | SECURITY-RELEVANT INFORMATION					
AC-3(6)	ACCESS ENFORCEMENT | PROTECTION OF USER AND SYSTEM INFORMATION	x	Incorporated into MP-4 and SC-28.			
AC-3(7)	ACCESS ENFORCEMENT | ROLE-BASED ACCESS CONTROL					
AC-3(8)	ACCESS ENFORCEMENT | REVOCATION OF ACCESS AUTHORIZATIONS					
AC-3(9)	ACCESS ENFORCEMENT | CONTROLLED RELEASE					
AC-3(10)	ACCESS ENFORCEMENT | AUDITED OVERRIDE OF ACCESS CONTROL MECHANISMS					
AC-4	**Information Flow Enforcement**				x	x
AC-4(1)	INFORMATION FLOW ENFORCEMENT | OBJECT SECURITY ATTRIBUTES					
AC-4(2)	INFORMATION FLOW ENFORCEMENT | PROCESSING DOMAINS					
AC-4(3)	INFORMATION FLOW ENFORCEMENT | DYNAMIC INFORMATION FLOW CONTROL					
AC-4(4)	INFORMATION FLOW ENFORCEMENT | CONTENT CHECK ENCRYPTED INFORMATION					
AC-4(5)	INFORMATION FLOW ENFORCEMENT | EMBEDDED DATA TYPES					
AC-4(6)	INFORMATION FLOW ENFORCEMENT | METADATA					
AC-4(7)	INFORMATION FLOW ENFORCEMENT | ONE-WAY FLOW MECHANISMS					
AC-4(8)	INFORMATION FLOW ENFORCEMENT | SECURITY POLICY FILTERS					
AC-4(9)	INFORMATION FLOW ENFORCEMENT | HUMAN REVIEWS					
AC-4(10)	INFORMATION FLOW ENFORCEMENT | ENABLE / DISABLE SECURITY POLICY FILTERS					

CNTL NO.	CONTROL NAME *Control Enhancement Name*	WITHDRAWN	ASSURANCE	CONTROL BASELINES		
				LOW	MOD	HIGH
AC-4(11)	*INFORMATION FLOW ENFORCEMENT	CONFIGURATION OF SECURITY POLICY FILTERS*					
AC-4(12)	*INFORMATION FLOW ENFORCEMENT	DATA TYPE IDENTIFIERS*					
AC-4(13)	*INFORMATION FLOW ENFORCEMENT	DECOMPOSITION INTO POLICY-RELEVANT SUBCOMPONENTS*					
AC-4(14)	*INFORMATION FLOW ENFORCEMENT	SECURITY POLICY FILTER CONSTRAINTS*					
AC-4(15)	*INFORMATION FLOW ENFORCEMENT	DETECTION OF UNSANCTIONED INFORMATION*					
AC-4(16)	*INFORMATION FLOW ENFORCEMENT	INFORMATION TRANSFERS ON INTERCONNECTED SYSTEMS*	X	Incorporated into AC-4.			
AC-4(17)	*INFORMATION FLOW ENFORCEMENT	DOMAIN AUTHENTICATION*					
AC-4(18)	*INFORMATION FLOW ENFORCEMENT	SECURITY ATTRIBUTE BINDING*					
AC-4(19)	*INFORMATION FLOW ENFORCEMENT	VALIDATION OF METADATA*					
AC-4(20)	*INFORMATION FLOW ENFORCEMENT	APPROVED SOLUTIONS*					
AC-4(21)	*INFORMATION FLOW ENFORCEMENT	PHYSICAL / LOGICAL SEPARATION OF INFORMATION FLOWS*					
AC-4(22)	*INFORMATION FLOW ENFORCEMENT	ACCESS ONLY*					
AC-5	**Separation of Duties**				X	X
AC-6	**Least Privilege**				X	X
AC-6(1)	*LEAST PRIVILEGE	AUTHORIZE ACCESS TO SECURITY FUNCTIONS*				X	X
AC-6(2)	*LEAST PRIVILEGE	NON-PRIVILEGED ACCESS FOR NONSECURITY FUNCTIONS*				X	X
AC-6(3)	*LEAST PRIVILEGE	NETWORK ACCESS TO PRIVILEGED COMMANDS*					X
AC-6(4)	*LEAST PRIVILEGE	SEPARATE PROCESSING DOMAINS*					
AC-6(5)	*LEAST PRIVILEGE	PRIVILEGED ACCOUNTS*				X	X
AC-6(6)	*LEAST PRIVILEGE	PRIVILEGED ACCESS BY NON-ORGANIZATIONAL USERS*					
AC-6(7)	*LEAST PRIVILEGE	REVIEW OF USER PRIVILEGES*					
AC-6(8)	*LEAST PRIVILEGE	PRIVILEGE LEVELS FOR CODE EXECUTION*					
AC-6(9)	*LEAST PRIVILEGE	AUDITING USE OF PRIVILEGED FUNCTIONS*				X	X
AC-6(10)	*LEAST PRIVILEGE	PROHIBIT NON-PRIVILEGED USERS FROM EXECUTING PRIVILEGED FUNCTIONS*				X	X
AC-7	**Unsuccessful Logon Attempts**			X	X	X
AC-7(1)	*UNSUCCESSFUL LOGON ATTEMPTS	AUTOMATIC ACCOUNT LOCK*	X	Incorporated into AC-7.			
AC-7(2)	*UNSUCCESSFUL LOGON ATTEMPTS	PURGE / WIPE MOBILE DEVICE*					
AC-8	**System Use Notification**			X	X	X
AC-9	**Previous Logon (Access) Notification**					
AC-9(1)	*PREVIOUS LOGON NOTIFICATION	UNSUCCESSFUL LOGONS*					
AC-9(2)	*PREVIOUS LOGON NOTIFICATION	SUCCESSFUL / UNSUCCESSFUL LOGONS*					
AC-9(3)	*PREVIOUS LOGON NOTIFICATION	NOTIFICATION OF ACCOUNT CHANGES*					
AC-9(4)	*PREVIOUS LOGON NOTIFICATION	ADDITIONAL LOGON INFORMATION*					
AC-10	**Concurrent Session Control**					X
AC-11	**Session Lock**				X	X
AC-11(1)	*SESSION LOCK	PATTERN-HIDING DISPLAYS*				X	X
AC-12	**Session Termination**				X	X

CNTL NO.	CONTROL NAME *Control Enhancement Name*	WITHDRAWN	ASSURANCE	CONTROL BASELINES		
				LOW	MOD	HIGH
AC-12(1)	*SESSION TERMINATION	USER-INITIATED LOGOUTS / MESSAGE DISPLAYS*					
AC-13	**Supervision and Review — Access Control**	x	Incorporated into AC-2 and AU-6.			
AC-14	**Permitted Actions without Identification or Authentication**			x	x	x
AC-14(1)	*PERMITTED ACTIONS WITHOUT IDENTIFICATION OR AUTHENTICATION	NECESSARY USES*	x	Incorporated into AC-14.			
AC-15	**Automated Marking**	x	Incorporated into MP-3.			
AC-16	**Security Attributes**					
AC-16(1)	*SECURITY ATTRIBUTES	DYNAMIC ATTRIBUTE ASSOCIATION*					
AC-16(2)	*SECURITY ATTRIBUTES	ATTRIBUTE VALUE CHANGES BY AUTHORIZED INDIVIDUALS*					
AC-16(3)	*SECURITY ATTRIBUTES	MAINTENANCE OF ATTRIBUTE ASSOCIATIONS BY INFORMATION SYSTEM*					
AC-16(4)	*SECURITY ATTRIBUTES	ASSOCIATION OF ATTRIBUTES BY AUTHORIZED INDIVIDUALS*					
AC-16(5)	*SECURITY ATTRIBUTES	ATTRIBUTE DISPLAYS FOR OUTPUT DEVICES*					
AC-16(6)	*SECURITY ATTRIBUTES	MAINTENANCE OF ATTRIBUTE ASSOCIATION BY ORGANIZATION*					
AC-16(7)	*SECURITY ATTRIBUTES	CONSISTENT ATTRIBUTE INTERPRETATION*					
AC-16(8)	*SECURITY ATTRIBUTES	ASSOCIATION TECHNIQUES / TECHNOLOGIES*					
AC-16(9)	*SECURITY ATTRIBUTES	ATTRIBUTE REASSIGNMENT*					
AC-16(10)	*SECURITY ATTRIBUTES	ATTRIBUTE CONFIGURATION BY AUTHORIZED INDIVIDUALS*					
AC-17	**Remote Access**			x	x	x
AC-17(1)	*REMOTE ACCESS	AUTOMATED MONITORING / CONTROL*				x	x
AC-17(2)	*REMOTE ACCESS	PROTECTION OF CONFIDENTIALITY / INTEGRITY USING ENCRYPTION*				x	x
AC-17(3)	*REMOTE ACCESS	MANAGED ACCESS CONTROL POINTS*				x	x
AC-17(4)	*REMOTE ACCESS	PRIVILEGED COMMANDS / ACCESS*				x	x
AC-17(5)	*REMOTE ACCESS	MONITORING FOR UNAUTHORIZED CONNECTIONS*	x	Incorporated into SI-4.			
AC-17(6)	*REMOTE ACCESS	PROTECTION OF INFORMATION*					
AC-17(7)	*REMOTE ACCESS	ADDITIONAL PROTECTION FOR SECURITY FUNCTION ACCESS*	x	Incorporated into AC-3(10).			
AC-17(8)	*REMOTE ACCESS	DISABLE NONSECURE NETWORK PROTOCOLS*	x	Incorporated into CM-7.			
AC-17(9)	*REMOTE ACCESS	DISCONNECT / DISABLE ACCESS*					
AC-18	**Wireless Access**			x	x	x
AC-18(1)	*WIRELESS ACCESS	AUTHENTICATION AND ENCRYPTION*				x	x
AC-18(2)	*WIRELESS ACCESS	MONITORING UNAUTHORIZED CONNECTIONS*	x	Incorporated into SI-4.			
AC-18(3)	*WIRELESS ACCESS	DISABLE WIRELESS NETWORKING*					
AC-18(4)	*WIRELESS ACCESS	RESTRICT CONFIGURATIONS BY USERS*					x
AC-18(5)	*WIRELESS ACCESS	ANTENNAS / TRANSMISSION POWER LEVELS*					x
AC-19	**Access Control for Mobile Devices**			x	x	x
AC-19(1)	*ACCESS CONTROL FOR MOBILE DEVICES	USE OF WRITABLE / PORTABLE STORAGE DEVICES*	x	Incorporated into MP-7.			
AC-19(2)	*ACCESS CONTROL FOR MOBILE DEVICES	USE OF PERSONALLY OWNED PORTABLE STORAGE DEVICES*	x	Incorporated into MP-7.			
AC-19(3)	*ACCESS CONTROL FOR MOBILE DEVICES	USE OF PORTABLE STORAGE DEVICES WITH NO IDENTIFIABLE OWNER*	x	Incorporated into MP-7.			

CNTL NO.	CONTROL NAME *Control Enhancement Name*	WITHDRAWN	ASSURANCE	CONTROL BASELINES		
				LOW	MOD	HIGH
AC-19(4)	ACCESS CONTROL FOR MOBILE DEVICES | RESTRICTIONS FOR CLASSIFIED INFORMATION					
AC-19(5)	ACCESS CONTROL FOR MOBILE DEVICES | FULL DEVICE / CONTAINER-BASED ENCRYPTION				X	X
AC-20	**Use of External Information Systems**			X	X	X
AC-20(1)	USE OF EXTERNAL INFORMATION SYSTEMS | LIMITS ON AUTHORIZED USE				X	X
AC-20(2)	USE OF EXTERNAL INFORMATION SYSTEMS | PORTABLE STORAGE DEVICES				X	X
AC-20(3)	USE OF EXTERNAL INFORMATION SYSTEMS | NON-ORGANIZATIONALLY OWNED SYSTEMS / COMPONENTS / DEVICES					
AC-20(4)	USE OF EXTERNAL INFORMATION SYSTEMS | NETWORK ACCESSIBLE STORAGE DEVICES					
AC-21	**Information Sharing**				X	X
AC-21(1)	INFORMATION SHARING | AUTOMATED DECISION SUPPORT					
AC-21(2)	INFORMATION SHARING | INFORMATION SEARCH AND RETRIEVAL					
AC-22	**Publicly Accessible Content**			X	X	X
AC-23	**Data Mining Protection**					
AC-24	**Access Control Decisions**					
AC-24(1)	ACCESS CONTROL DECISIONS | TRANSMIT ACCESS AUTHORIZATION INFORMATION					
AC-24(2)	ACCESS CONTROL DECISIONS | NO USER OR PROCESS IDENTITY					
AC-25	**Reference Monitor**		X			

TABLE D-4: SUMMARY — AWARENESS AND TRAINING CONTROLS

CNTL NO.	CONTROL NAME *Control Enhancement Name*	WITHDRAWN	ASSURANCE	CONTROL BASELINES		
				LOW	MOD	HIGH
AT-1	Security Awareness and Training Policy and Procedures		x	x	x	x
AT-2	Security Awareness Training		x	x	x	x
AT-2(1)	*SECURITY AWARENESS	PRACTICAL EXERCISES*		x			
AT-2(2)	*SECURITY AWARENESS	INSIDER THREAT*		x		x	x
AT-3	Role-Based Security Training		x	x	x	x
AT-3(1)	*ROLE-BASED SECURITY TRAINING	ENVIRONMENTAL CONTROLS*		x			
AT-3(2)	*ROLE-BASED SECURITY TRAINING	PHYSICAL SECURITY CONTROLS*		x			
AT-3(3)	*ROLE-BASED SECURITY TRAINING	PRACTICAL EXERCISES*		x			
AT-3(4)	*ROLE-BASED SECURITY TRAINING	SUSPICIOUS COMMUNICATIONS AND ANOMALOUS SYSTEM BEHAVIOR*		x			
AT-4	Security Training Records		x	x	x	x
AT-5	Contacts with Security Groups and Associations	x	Incorporated into PM-15.			

TABLE D-5: SUMMARY — AUDIT AND ACCOUNTABILITY CONTROLS

CNTL NO.	CONTROL NAME *Control Enhancement Name*	WITHDRAWN	ASSURANCE	CONTROL BASELINES		
				LOW	MOD	HIGH
AU-1	**Audit and Accountability Policy and Procedures**		X	X	X	X
AU-2	**Audit Events**			X	X	X
AU-2(1)	*AUDIT EVENTS	COMPILATION OF AUDIT RECORDS FROM MULTIPLE SOURCES*	X	Incorporated into AU-12.			
AU-2(2)	*AUDIT EVENTS	SELECTION OF AUDIT EVENTS BY COMPONENT*	X	Incorporated into AU-12.			
AU-2(3)	*AUDIT EVENTS	REVIEWS AND UPDATES*				X	X
AU-2(4)	*AUDIT EVENTS	PRIVILEGED FUNCTIONS*	X	Incorporated into AC-6(9).			
AU-3	**Content of Audit Records**			X	X	X
AU-3(1)	*CONTENT OF AUDIT RECORDS	ADDITIONAL AUDIT INFORMATION*				X	X
AU-3(2)	*CONTENT OF AUDIT RECORDS	CENTRALIZED MANAGEMENT OF PLANNED AUDIT RECORD CONTENT*					X
AU-4	**Audit Storage Capacity**			X	X	X
AU-4(1)	*AUDIT STORAGE CAPACITY	TRANSFER TO ALTERNATE STORAGE*					
AU-5	**Response to Audit Processing Failures**			X	X	X
AU-5(1)	*RESPONSE TO AUDIT PROCESSING FAILURES	AUDIT STORAGE CAPACITY*					X
AU-5(2)	*RESPONSE TO AUDIT PROCESSING FAILURES	REAL-TIME ALERTS*					X
AU-5(3)	*RESPONSE TO AUDIT PROCESSING FAILURES	CONFIGURABLE TRAFFIC VOLUME THRESHOLDS*					
AU-5(4)	*RESPONSE TO AUDIT PROCESSING FAILURES	SHUTDOWN ON FAILURE*					
AU-6	**Audit Review, Analysis, and Reporting**		X	X	X	X
AU-6(1)	*AUDIT REVIEW, ANALYSIS, AND REPORTING	PROCESS INTEGRATION*		X		X	X
AU-6(2)	*AUDIT REVIEW, ANALYSIS, AND REPORTING	AUTOMATED SECURITY ALERTS*	X	Incorporated into SI-4.			
AU-6(3)	*AUDIT REVIEW, ANALYSIS, AND REPORTING	CORRELATE AUDIT REPOSITORIES*		X		X	X
AU-6(4)	*AUDIT REVIEW, ANALYSIS, AND REPORTING	CENTRAL REVIEW AND ANALYSIS*		X			
AU-6(5)	*AUDIT REVIEW, ANALYSIS, AND REPORTING	INTEGRATION / SCANNING AND MONITORING CAPABILITIES*		X			X
AU-6(6)	*AUDIT REVIEW, ANALYSIS, AND REPORTING	CORRELATION WITH PHYSICAL MONITORING*		X			X
AU-6(7)	*AUDIT REVIEW, ANALYSIS, AND REPORTING	PERMITTED ACTIONS*		X			
AU-6(8)	*AUDIT REVIEW, ANALYSIS, AND REPORTING	FULL TEXT ANALYSIS OF PRIVILEGED COMMANDS*		X			
AU-6(9)	*AUDIT REVIEW, ANALYSIS, AND REPORTING	CORRELATION WITH INFORMATION FROM NONTECHNICAL SOURCES*		X			
AU-6(10)	*AUDIT REVIEW, ANALYSIS, AND REPORTING	AUDIT LEVEL ADJUSTMENT*		X			
AU-7	**Audit Reduction and Report Generation**		X		X	X
AU-7(1)	*AUDIT REDUCTION AND REPORT GENERATION	AUTOMATIC PROCESSING*		X		X	X
AU-7(2)	*AUDIT REDUCTION AND REPORT GENERATION	AUTOMATIC SORT AND SEARCH*					
AU-8	**Time Stamps**			X	X	X
AU-8(1)	*TIME STAMPS	SYNCHRONIZATION WITH AUTHORITATIVE TIME SOURCE*				X	X
AU-8(2)	*TIME STAMPS	SECONDARY AUTHORITATIVE TIME SOURCE*					

CNTL NO.	CONTROL NAME *Control Enhancement Name*	WITHDRAWN	ASSURANCE	CONTROL BASELINES		
				LOW	MOD	HIGH
AU-9	Protection of Audit Information			x	x	x
AU-9(1)	PROTECTION OF AUDIT INFORMATION | HARDWARE WRITE-ONCE MEDIA					
AU-9(2)	PROTECTION OF AUDIT INFORMATION | AUDIT BACKUP ON SEPARATE PHYSICAL SYSTEMS / COMPONENTS					x
AU-9(3)	PROTECTION OF AUDIT INFORMATION | CRYPTOGRAPHIC PROTECTION					x
AU-9(4)	PROTECTION OF AUDIT INFORMATION | ACCESS BY SUBSET OF PRIVILEGED USERS				x	x
AU-9(5)	PROTECTION OF AUDIT INFORMATION | DUAL AUTHORIZATION					
AU-9(6)	PROTECTION OF AUDIT INFORMATION | READ-ONLY ACCESS					
AU-10	Non-repudiation		x			x
AU-10(1)	NON-REPUDIATION | ASSOCIATION OF IDENTITIES		x			
AU-10(2)	NON-REPUDIATION | VALIDATE BINDING OF INFORMATION PRODUCER IDENTITY		x			
AU-10(3)	NON-REPUDIATION | CHAIN OF CUSTODY		x			
AU-10(4)	NON-REPUDIATION | VALIDATE BINDING OF INFORMATION REVIEWER IDENTITY		x			
AU-10(5)	NON-REPUDIATION | DIGITAL SIGNATURES	x	Incorporated into SI-7.			
AU-11	Audit Record Retention			x	x	x
AU-11(1)	AUDIT RECORD RETENTION | LONG-TERM RETRIEVAL CAPABILITY		x			
AU-12	Audit Generation			x	x	x
AU-12(1)	AUDIT GENERATION | SYSTEM-WIDE / TIME-CORRELATED AUDIT TRAIL					x
AU-12(2)	AUDIT GENERATION | STANDARDIZED FORMATS					
AU-12(3)	AUDIT GENERATION | CHANGES BY AUTHORIZED INDIVIDUALS					x
AU-13	Monitoring for Information Disclosure		x			
AU-13(1)	MONITORING FOR INFORMATION DISCLOSURE | USE OF AUTOMATED TOOLS		x			
AU-13(2)	MONITORING FOR INFORMATION DISCLOSURE | REVIEW OF MONITORED SITES		x			
AU-14	Session Audit		x			
AU-14(1)	SESSION AUDIT | SYSTEM START-UP		x			
AU-14(2)	SESSION AUDIT | CAPTURE/RECORD AND LOG CONTENT		x			
AU-14(3)	SESSION AUDIT | REMOTE VIEWING / LISTENING		x			
AU-15	Alternate Audit Capability					
AU-16	Cross-Organizational Auditing					
AU-16(1)	CROSS-ORGANIZATIONAL AUDITING | IDENTITY PRESERVATION					
AU-16(2)	CROSS-ORGANIZATIONAL AUDITING | SHARING OF AUDIT INFORMATION					

TABLE D-6: SUMMARY — SECURITY ASSESSMENT AND AUTHORIZATION CONTROLS

CNTL NO.	CONTROL NAME *Control Enhancement Name*	WITHDRAWN	ASSURANCE	CONTROL BASELINES		
				LOW	MOD	HIGH
CA-1	Security Assessment and Authorization Policies and Procedures		X	X	X	X
CA-2	Security Assessments		X	X	X	X
CA-2(1)	*SECURITY ASSESSMENTS	INDEPENDENT ASSESSORS*		X		X	X
CA-2(2)	*SECURITY ASSESSMENTS	SPECIALIZED ASSESSMENTS*		X			X
CA-2(3)	*SECURITY ASSESSMENTS	EXTERNAL ORGANIZATIONS*		X			
CA-3	System Interconnections		X	X	X	X
CA-3(1)	*SYSTEM INTERCONNECTIONS	UNCLASSIFIED NATIONAL SECURITY SYSTEM CONNECTIONS*					
CA-3(2)	*SYSTEM INTERCONNECTIONS	CLASSIFIED NATIONAL SECURITY SYSTEM CONNECTIONS*					
CA-3(3)	*SYSTEM INTERCONNECTIONS	UNCLASSIFIED NON-NATIONAL SECURITY SYSTEM CONNECTIONS*					
CA-3(4)	*SYSTEM INTERCONNECTIONS	CONNECTIONS TO PUBLIC NETWORKS*					
CA-3(5)	*SYSTEM INTERCONNECTIONS	RESTRICTIONS ON EXTERNAL SYSTEM CONNECTIONS*				X	X
CA-4	Security Certification	X	Incorporated into CA-2.			
CA-5	Plan of Action and Milestones		X	X	X	X
CA-5(1)	*PLAN OF ACTION AND MILESTONES	AUTOMATION SUPPORT FOR ACCURACY / CURRENCY*		X			
CA-6	Security Authorization		X	X	X	X
CA-7	Continuous Monitoring		X	X	X	X
CA-7(1)	*CONTINUOUS MONITORING	INDEPENDENT ASSESSMENT*		X		X	X
CA-7(2)	*CONTINUOUS MONITORING	TYPES OF ASSESSMENTS*	X	Incorporated into CA-2.			
CA-7(3)	*CONTINUOUS MONITORING	TREND ANALYSES*		X			
CA-8	Penetration Testing		X			X
CA-8(1)	*PENETRATION TESTING	INDEPENDENT PENETRATION AGENT OR TEAM*		X			
CA-8(2)	*PENETRATION TESTING	RED TEAM EXERCISES*		X			
CA-9	Internal System Connections		X	X	X	X
CA-9(1)	*INTERNAL SYSTEM CONNECTIONS	SECURITY COMPLIANCE CHECKS*		X			

TABLE D-7: SUMMARY — CONFIGURATION MANAGEMENT CONTROLS

CNTL NO.	CONTROL NAME *Control Enhancement Name*	WITHDRAWN	ASSURANCE	CONTROL BASELINES		
				LOW	MOD	HIGH
CM-1	**Configuration Management Policy and Procedures**		X	X	X	X
CM-2	**Baseline Configuration**		X	X	X	X
CM-2(1)	*BASELINE CONFIGURATION	REVIEWS AND UPDATES*		X		X	X
CM-2(2)	*BASELINE CONFIGURATION	AUTOMATION SUPPORT FOR ACCURACY / CURRENCY*		X			X
CM-2(3)	*BASELINE CONFIGURATION	RETENTION OF PREVIOUS CONFIGURATIONS*		X		X	X
CM-2(4)	*BASELINE CONFIGURATION	UNAUTHORIZED SOFTWARE*	X	Incorporated into CM-7.			
CM-2(5)	*BASELINE CONFIGURATION	AUTHORIZED SOFTWARE*	X	Incorporated into CM-7.			
CM-2(6)	*BASELINE CONFIGURATION	DEVELOPMENT AND TEST ENVIRONMENTS*		X			
CM-2(7)	*BASELINE CONFIGURATION	CONFIGURE SYSTEMS, COMPONENTS, OR DEVICES FOR HIGH-RISK AREAS*		X		X	X
CM-3	**Configuration Change Control**		X		X	X
CM-3(1)	*CONFIGURATION CHANGE CONTROL	AUTOMATED DOCUMENT / NOTIFICATION / PROHIBITION OF CHANGES*		X			X
CM-3(2)	*CONFIGURATION CHANGE CONTROL	TEST / VALIDATE / DOCUMENT CHANGES*		X		X	X
CM-3(3)	*CONFIGURATION CHANGE CONTROL	AUTOMATED CHANGE IMPLEMENTATION*					
CM-3(4)	*CONFIGURATION CHANGE CONTROL	SECURITY REPRESENTATIVE*					
CM-3(5)	*CONFIGURATION CHANGE CONTROL	AUTOMATED SECURITY RESPONSE*					
CM-3(6)	*CONFIGURATION CHANGE CONTROL	CRYPTOGRAPHY MANAGEMENT*					
CM-4	**Security Impact Analysis**		X	X	X	X
CM-4(1)	*SECURITY IMPACT ANALYSIS	SEPARATE TEST ENVIRONMENTS*		X			X
CM-4(2)	*SECURITY IMPACT ANALYSIS	VERIFICATION OF SECURITY FUNCTIONS*		X			
CM-5	**Access Restrictions for Change**				X	X
CM-5(1)	*ACCESS RESTRICTIONS FOR CHANGE	AUTOMATED ACCESS ENFORCEMENT / AUDITING*					X
CM-5(2)	*ACCESS RESTRICTIONS FOR CHANGE	REVIEW SYSTEM CHANGES*					X
CM-5(3)	*ACCESS RESTRICTIONS FOR CHANGE	SIGNED COMPONENTS*					X
CM-5(4)	*ACCESS RESTRICTIONS FOR CHANGE	DUAL AUTHORIZATION*					
CM-5(5)	*ACCESS RESTRICTIONS FOR CHANGE	LIMIT PRODUCTION / OPERATIONAL PRIVILEGES*					
CM-5(6)	*ACCESS RESTRICTIONS FOR CHANGE	LIMIT LIBRARY PRIVILEGES*					
CM-5(7)	*ACCESS RESTRICTIONS FOR CHANGE	AUTOMATIC IMPLEMENTATION OF SECURITY SAFEGUARDS*	X	Incorporated into SI-7.			
CM-6	**Configuration Settings**				X	X	X
CM-6(1)	*CONFIGURATION SETTINGS	AUTOMATED CENTRAL MANAGEMENT / APPLICATION / VERIFICATION*					X
CM-6(2)	*CONFIGURATION SETTINGS	RESPOND TO UNAUTHORIZED CHANGES*					X
CM-6(3)	*CONFIGURATION SETTINGS	UNAUTHORIZED CHANGE DETECTION*	X	Incorporated into SI-7.			
CM-6(4)	*CONFIGURATION SETTINGS	CONFORMANCE DEMONSTRATION*	X	Incorporated into CM-4.			
CM-7	**Least Functionality**				X	X	X
CM-7(1)	*LEAST FUNCTIONALITY	PERIODIC REVIEW*				X	X
CM-7(2)	*LEAST FUNCTIONALITY	PREVENT PROGRAM EXECUTION*				X	X

CNTL NO.	CONTROL NAME *Control Enhancement Name*	WITHDRAWN	ASSURANCE	CONTROL BASELINES		
				LOW	MOD	HIGH
CM-7(3)	*LEAST FUNCTIONALITY	REGISTRATION COMPLIANCE*					
CM-7(4)	*LEAST FUNCTIONALITY	UNAUTHORIZED SOFTWARE / BLACKLISTING*				x	
CM-7(5)	*LEAST FUNCTIONALITY	AUTHORIZED SOFTWARE / WHITELISTING*					x
CM-8	**Information System Component Inventory**		x	x	x	x
CM-8(1)	*INFORMATION SYSTEM COMPONENT INVENTORY	UPDATES DURING INSTALLATIONS / REMOVALS*		x		x	x
CM-8(2)	*INFORMATION SYSTEM COMPONENT INVENTORY	AUTOMATED MAINTENANCE*		x			x
CM-8(3)	*INFORMATION SYSTEM COMPONENT INVENTORY	AUTOMATED UNAUTHORIZED COMPONENT DETECTION*		x		x	x
CM-8(4)	*INFORMATION SYSTEM COMPONENT INVENTORY	ACCOUNTABILITY INFORMATION*		x			x
CM-8(5)	*INFORMATION SYSTEM COMPONENT INVENTORY	NO DUPLICATE ACCOUNTING OF COMPONENTS*		x		x	x
CM-8(6)	*INFORMATION SYSTEM COMPONENT INVENTORY	ASSESSED CONFIGURATIONS / APPROVED DEVIATIONS*		x			
CM-8(7)	*INFORMATION SYSTEM COMPONENT INVENTORY	CENTRALIZED REPOSITORY*		x			
CM-8(8)	*INFORMATION SYSTEM COMPONENT INVENTORY	AUTOMATED LOCATION TRACKING*		x			
CM-8(9)	*INFORMATION SYSTEM COMPONENT INVENTORY	ASSIGNMENT OF COMPONENTS TO SYSTEMS*		x			
CM-9	**Configuration Management Plan**				x	x
CM-9(1)	*CONFIGURATION MANAGEMENT PLAN	ASSIGNMENT OF RESPONSIBILITY*					
CM-10	**Software Usage Restrictions**			x	x	x
CM-10(1)	*SOFTWARE USAGE RESTRICTIONS	OPEN SOURCE SOFTWARE*					
CM-11	**User-Installed Software**			x	x	x
CM-11(1)	*USER-INSTALLED SOFTWARE	ALERTS FOR UNAUTHORIZED INSTALLATIONS*					
CM-11(2)	*USER-INSTALLED SOFTWARE	PROHIBIT INSTALLATION WITHOUT PRIVILEGED STATUS*					

TABLE D-9: SUMMARY — IDENTIFICATION AND AUTHENTICATION CONTROLS

CNTL NO.	CONTROL NAME *Control Enhancement Name*	WITHDRAWN	ASSURANCE	CONTROL BASELINES		
				LOW	MOD	HIGH
IA-1	**Identification and Authentication Policy and Procedures**		x	x	x	x
IA-2	**Identification and Authentication (Organizational Users)**			x	x	x
IA-2(1)	*IDENTIFICATION AND AUTHENTICATION (ORGANIZATIONAL USERS)	NETWORK ACCESS TO PRIVILEGED ACCOUNTS*			x	x	x
IA-2(2)	*IDENTIFICATION AND AUTHENTICATION (ORGANIZATIONAL USERS)	NETWORK ACCESS TO NON-PRIVILEGED ACCOUNTS*				x	x
IA-2(3)	*IDENTIFICATION AND AUTHENTICATION (ORGANIZATIONAL USERS)	LOCAL ACCESS TO PRIVILEGED ACCOUNTS*				x	x
IA-2(4)	*IDENTIFICATION AND AUTHENTICATION (ORGANIZATIONAL USERS)	LOCAL ACCESS TO NON-PRIVILEGED ACCOUNTS*					x
IA-2(5)	*IDENTIFICATION AND AUTHENTICATION (ORGANIZATIONAL USERS)	GROUP AUTHENTICATION*					
IA-2(6)	*IDENTIFICATION AND AUTHENTICATION (ORGANIZATIONAL USERS)	NETWORK ACCESS TO PRIVILEGED ACCOUNTS - SEPARATE DEVICE*					
IA-2(7)	*IDENTIFICATION AND AUTHENTICATION (ORGANIZATIONAL USERS)	NETWORK ACCESS TO NON-PRIVILEGED ACCOUNTS - SEPARATE DEVICE*					
IA-2(8)	*IDENTIFICATION AND AUTHENTICATION (ORGANIZATIONAL USERS)	NETWORK ACCESS TO PRIVILEGED ACCOUNTS - REPLAY RESISTANT*				x	x
IA-2(9)	*IDENTIFICATION AND AUTHENTICATION (ORGANIZATIONAL USERS)	NETWORK ACCESS TO NON-PRIVILEGED ACCOUNTS - REPLAY RESISTANT*					x
IA-2(10)	*IDENTIFICATION AND AUTHENTICATION (ORGANIZATIONAL USERS)	SINGLE SIGN-ON*					
IA-2(11)	*IDENTIFICATION AND AUTHENTICATION (ORGANIZATIONAL USERS)	REMOTE ACCESS - SEPARATE DEVICE*				x	x
IA-2(12)	*IDENTIFICATION AND AUTHENTICATION (ORGANIZATIONAL USERS)	ACCEPTANCE OF PIV CREDENTIALS*			x	x	x
IA-2(13)	*IDENTIFICATION AND AUTHENTICATION	OUT-OF-BAND AUTHENTICATION*					
IA-3	**Device Identification and Authentication**				x	x
IA-3(1)	*DEVICE IDENTIFICATION AND AUTHENTICATION	CRYPTOGRAPHIC BIDIRECTIONAL AUTHENTICATION*					
IA-3(2)	*DEVICE IDENTIFICATION AND AUTHENTICATION	CRYPTOGRAPHIC BIDIRECTIONAL NETWORK AUTHENTICATION*	x	Incorporated into IA-3(1).			
IA-3(3)	*DEVICE IDENTIFICATION AND AUTHENTICATION	DYNAMIC ADDRESS ALLOCATION*					
IA-3(4)	*DEVICE IDENTIFICATION AND AUTHENTICATION	DEVICE ATTESTATION*					
IA-4	**Identifier Management**			x	x	x
IA-4(1)	*IDENTIFIER MANAGEMENT	PROHIBIT ACCOUNT IDENTIFIERS AS PUBLIC IDENTIFIERS*					
IA-4(2)	*IDENTIFIER MANAGEMENT	SUPERVISOR AUTHORIZATION*					
IA-4(3)	*IDENTIFIER MANAGEMENT	MULTIPLE FORMS OF CERTIFICATION*					
IA-4(4)	*IDENTIFIER MANAGEMENT	IDENTIFY USER STATUS*					
IA-4(5)	*IDENTIFIER MANAGEMENT	DYNAMIC MANAGEMENT*					
IA-4(6)	*IDENTIFIER MANAGEMENT	CROSS-ORGANIZATION MANAGEMENT*					
IA-4(7)	*IDENTIFIER MANAGEMENT	IN-PERSON REGISTRATION*					
IA-5	**Authenticator Management**			x	x	x

CNTL NO.	CONTROL NAME *Control Enhancement Name*	WITHDRAWN	ASSURANCE	CONTROL BASELINES		
				LOW	MOD	HIGH
IA-5(1)	AUTHENTICATOR MANAGEMENT | PASSWORD-BASED AUTHENTICATION			X	X	X
IA-5(2)	AUTHENTICATOR MANAGEMENT | PKI-BASED AUTHENTICATION				X	X
IA-5(3)	AUTHENTICATOR MANAGEMENT | IN-PERSON OR TRUSTED THIRD-PARTY REGISTRATION				X	X
IA-5(4)	AUTHENTICATOR MANAGEMENT | AUTOMATED SUPPORT FOR PASSWORD STRENGTH DETERMINATION					
IA-5(5)	AUTHENTICATOR MANAGEMENT | CHANGE AUTHENTICATORS PRIOR TO DELIVERY					
IA-5(6)	AUTHENTICATOR MANAGEMENT | PROTECTION OF AUTHENTICATORS					
IA-5(7)	AUTHENTICATOR MANAGEMENT | NO EMBEDDED UNENCRYPTED STATIC AUTHENTICATORS					
IA-5(8)	AUTHENTICATOR MANAGEMENT | MULTIPLE INFORMATION SYSTEM ACCOUNTS					
IA-5(9)	AUTHENTICATOR MANAGEMENT | CROSS-ORGANIZATION CREDENTIAL MANAGEMENT					
IA-5(10)	AUTHENTICATOR MANAGEMENT | DYNAMIC CREDENTIAL ASSOCIATION					
IA-5(11)	AUTHENTICATOR MANAGEMENT | HARDWARE TOKEN-BASED AUTHENTICATION			X	X	X
IA-5(12)	AUTHENTICATOR MANAGEMENT | BIOMETRIC-BASED AUTHENTICATION					
IA-5(13)	AUTHENTICATOR MANAGEMENT | EXPIRATION OF CACHED AUTHENTICATORS					
IA-5(14)	AUTHENTICATOR MANAGEMENT | MANAGING CONTENT OF PKI TRUST STORES					
IA-5(15)	AUTHENTICATOR MANAGEMENT | FICAM-APPROVED PRODUCTS AND SERVICES					
IA-6	**Authenticator Feedback**			X	X	X
IA-7	**Cryptographic Module Authentication**			X	X	X
IA-8	**Identification and Authentication (Non-Organizational Users)**			X	X	X
IA-8(1)	IDENTIFICATION AND AUTHENTICATION (NON-ORGANIZATIONAL USERS) | ACCEPTANCE OF PIV CREDENTIALS FROM OTHER AGENCIES			X	X	X
IA-8(2)	IDENTIFICATION AND AUTHENTICATION (NON-ORGANIZATIONAL USERS) | ACCEPTANCE OF THIRD-PARTY CREDENTIALS			X	X	X
IA-8(3)	IDENTIFICATION AND AUTHENTICATION (NON-ORGANIZATIONAL USERS) | USE OF FICAM-APPROVED PRODUCTS			X	X	X
IA-8(4)	IDENTIFICATION AND AUTHENTICATION (NON-ORGANIZATIONAL USERS) | USE OF FICAM-ISSUED PROFILES			X	X	X
IA-8(5)	IDENTIFICATION AND AUTHENTICATION (NON-ORGANIZATIONAL USERS) | ACCEPTANCE OF PIV-I CREDENTIALS					
IA-9	**Service Identification and Authentication**					
IA-9(1)	SERVICE IDENTIFICATION AND AUTHENTICATION | INFORMATION EXCHANGE					
IA-9(2)	SERVICE IDENTIFICATION AND AUTHENTICATION | TRANSMISSION OF DECISIONS					
IA-10	**Adaptive Identification and Authentication**					
IA-11	**Re-authentication**					

TABLE D-10: SUMMARY — INCIDENT RESPONSE CONTROLS

CNTL NO.	CONTROL NAME *Control Enhancement Name*	WITHDRAWN	ASSURANCE	CONTROL BASELINES		
				LOW	MOD	HIGH
IR-1	Incident Response Policy and Procedures		x	x	x	x
IR-2	Incident Response Training		x	x	x	x
IR-2(1)	INCIDENT RESPONSE TRAINING | SIMULATED EVENTS		x			x
IR-2(2)	INCIDENT RESPONSE TRAINING | AUTOMATED TRAINING ENVIRONMENTS		x			x
IR-3	Incident Response Testing		x		x	x
IR-3(1)	INCIDENT RESPONSE TESTING | AUTOMATED TESTING		x			
IR-3(2)	INCIDENT RESPONSE TESTING | COORDINATION WITH RELATED PLANS		x		x	x
IR-4	Incident Handling			x	x	x
IR-4(1)	INCIDENT HANDLING | AUTOMATED INCIDENT HANDLING PROCESSES				x	x
IR-4(2)	INCIDENT HANDLING | DYNAMIC RECONFIGURATION					
IR-4(3)	INCIDENT HANDLING | CONTINUITY OF OPERATIONS					
IR-4(4)	INCIDENT HANDLING | INFORMATION CORRELATION					x
IR-4(5)	INCIDENT HANDLING | AUTOMATIC DISABLING OF INFORMATION SYSTEM					
IR-4(6)	INCIDENT HANDLING | INSIDER THREATS - SPECIFIC CAPABILITIES					
IR-4(7)	INCIDENT HANDLING | INSIDER THREATS - INTRA-ORGANIZATION COORDINATION					
IR-4(8)	INCIDENT HANDLING | CORRELATION WITH EXTERNAL ORGANIZATIONS					
IR-4(9)	INCIDENT HANDLING | DYNAMIC RESPONSE CAPABILITY					
IR-4(10)	INCIDENT HANDLING | SUPPLY CHAIN COORDINATION					
IR-5	Incident Monitoring		x	x	x	x
IR-5(1)	INCIDENT MONITORING | AUTOMATED TRACKING / DATA COLLECTION / ANALYSIS		x			x
IR-6	Incident Reporting			x	x	x
IR-6(1)	INCIDENT REPORTING | AUTOMATED REPORTING				x	x
IR-6(2)	INCIDENT REPORTING | VULNERABILITIES RELATED TO INCIDENTS					
IR-6(3)	INCIDENT REPORTING | COORDINATION WITH SUPPLY CHAIN					
IR-7	Incident Response Assistance			x	x	x
IR-7(1)	INCIDENT RESPONSE ASSISTANCE | AUTOMATION SUPPORT FOR AVAILABILITY OF INFORMATION / SUPPORT				x	x
IR-7(2)	INCIDENT RESPONSE ASSISTANCE | COORDINATION WITH EXTERNAL PROVIDERS					
IR-8	Incident Response Plan			x	x	x
IR-9	Information Spillage Response					
IR-9(1)	INFORMATION SPILLAGE RESPONSE | RESPONSIBLE PERSONNEL					
IR-9(2)	INFORMATION SPILLAGE RESPONSE | TRAINING					
IR-9(3)	INFORMATION SPILLAGE RESPONSE | POST-SPILL OPERATIONS					
IR-9(4)	INFORMATION SPILLAGE RESPONSE | EXPOSURE TO UNAUTHORIZED PERSONNEL					
IR-10	Integrated Information Security Analysis Team					

TABLE D-11: SUMMARY — MAINTENANCE CONTROLS

CNTL NO.	CONTROL NAME *Control Enhancement Name*	WITHDRAWN	ASSURANCE	CONTROL BASELINES		
				LOW	MOD	HIGH
MA-1	**System Maintenance Policy and Procedures**		X	X	X	X
MA-2	**Controlled Maintenance**			X	X	X
MA-2(1)	*CONTROLLED MAINTENANCE	RECORD CONTENT*	X	Incorporated into MA-2.			
MA-2(2)	*CONTROLLED MAINTENANCE	AUTOMATED MAINTENANCE ACTIVITIES*					X
MA-3	**Maintenance Tools**				X	X
MA-3(1)	*MAINTENANCE TOOLS	INSPECT TOOLS*				X	X
MA-3(2)	*MAINTENANCE TOOLS	INSPECT MEDIA*				X	X
MA-3(3)	*MAINTENANCE TOOLS	PREVENT UNAUTHORIZED REMOVAL*					X
MA-3(4)	*MAINTENANCE TOOLS	RESTRICTED TOOL USE*					
MA-4	**Nonlocal Maintenance**			X	X	X
MA-4(1)	*NONLOCAL MAINTENANCE	AUDITING AND REVIEW*					
MA-4(2)	*NONLOCAL MAINTENANCE	DOCUMENT NONLOCAL MAINTENANCE*				X	X
MA-4(3)	*NONLOCAL MAINTENANCE	COMPARABLE SECURITY / SANITIZATION*					X
MA-4(4)	*NONLOCAL MAINTENANCE	AUTHENTICATION / SEPARATION OF MAINTENANCE SESSIONS*					
MA-4(5)	*NONLOCAL MAINTENANCE	APPROVALS AND NOTIFICATIONS*					
MA-4(6)	*NONLOCAL MAINTENANCE	CRYPTOGRAPHIC PROTECTION*					
MA-4(7)	*NONLOCAL MAINTENANCE	REMOTE DISCONNECT VERIFICATION*					
MA-5	**Maintenance Personnel**			X	X	X
MA-5(1)	*MAINTENANCE PERSONNEL	INDIVIDUALS WITHOUT APPROPRIATE ACCESS*					X
MA-5(2)	*MAINTENANCE PERSONNEL	SECURITY CLEARANCES FOR CLASSIFIED SYSTEMS*					
MA-5(3)	*MAINTENANCE PERSONNEL	CITIZENSHIP REQUIREMENTS FOR CLASSIFIED SYSTEMS*					
MA-5(4)	*MAINTENANCE PERSONNEL	FOREIGN NATIONALS*					
MA-5(5)	*MAINTENANCE PERSONNEL	NON-SYSTEM-RELATED MAINTENANCE*					
MA-6	**Timely Maintenance**				X	X
MA-6(1)	*TIMELY MAINTENANCE	PREVENTIVE MAINTENANCE*					
MA-6(2)	*TIMELY MAINTENANCE	PREDICTIVE MAINTENANCE*					
MA-6(3)	*TIMELY MAINTENANCE	AUTOMATED SUPPORT FOR PREDICTIVE MAINTENANCE*					

TABLE D-12: SUMMARY — MEDIA PROTECTION CONTROLS

CNTL NO.	CONTROL NAME *Control Enhancement Name*	WITHDRAWN	ASSURANCE	CONTROL BASELINES		
				LOW	MOD	HIGH
MP-1	**Media Protection Policy and Procedures**		x	x	x	x
MP-2	**Media Access**			x	x	x
MP-2(1)	*MEDIA ACCESS	AUTOMATED RESTRICTED ACCESS*	x	Incorporated into MP-4(2).			
MP-2(2)	*MEDIA ACCESS	CRYPTOGRAPHIC PROTECTION*	x	Incorporated into SC-28(1).			
MP-3	**Media Marking**				x	x
MP-4	**Media Storage**				x	x
MP-4(1)	*MEDIA STORAGE	CRYPTOGRAPHIC PROTECTION*	x	Incorporated into SC-28(1).			
MP-4(2)	*MEDIA STORAGE	AUTOMATED RESTRICTED ACCESS*					
MP-5	**Media Transport**				x	x
MP-5(1)	*MEDIA TRANSPORT	PROTECTION OUTSIDE OF CONTROLLED AREAS*	x	Incorporated into MP-5.			
MP-5(2)	*MEDIA TRANSPORT	DOCUMENTATION OF ACTIVITIES*	x	Incorporated into MP-5.			
MP-5(3)	*MEDIA TRANSPORT	CUSTODIANS*					
MP-5(4)	*MEDIA TRANSPORT	CRYPTOGRAPHIC PROTECTION*				x	x
MP-6	**Media Sanitization**			x	x	x
MP-6(1)	*MEDIA SANITIZATION	REVIEW / APPROVE / TRACK / DOCUMENT / VERIFY*					x
MP-6(2)	*MEDIA SANITIZATION	EQUIPMENT TESTING*					x
MP-6(3)	*MEDIA SANITIZATION	NONDESTRUCTIVE TECHNIQUES*					x
MP-6(4)	*MEDIA SANITIZATION	CONTROLLED UNCLASSIFIED INFORMATION*	x	Incorporated into MP-6.			
MP-6(5)	*MEDIA SANITIZATION	CLASSIFIED INFORMATION*	x	Incorporated into MP-6.			
MP-6(6)	*MEDIA SANITIZATION	MEDIA DESTRUCTION*	x	Incorporated into MP-6.			
MP-6(7)	*MEDIA SANITIZATION	DUAL AUTHORIZATION*					
MP-6(8)	*MEDIA SANITIZATION	REMOTE PURGING / WIPING OF INFORMATION*					
MP-7	**Media Use**			x	x	x
MP-7(1)	*MEDIA USE	PROHIBIT USE WITHOUT OWNER*				x	x
MP-7(2)	*MEDIA USE	PROHIBIT USE OF SANITIZATION-RESISTANT MEDIA*					
MP-8	**Media Downgrading**					
MP-8(1)	*MEDIA DOWNGRADING	DOCUMENTATION OF PROCESS*					
MP-8(2)	*MEDIA DOWNGRADING	EQUIPMENT TESTING*					
MP-8(3)	*MEDIA DOWNGRADING	CONTROLLED UNCLASSIFIED INFORMATION*					
MP-8(4)	*MEDIA DOWNGRADING	CLASSIFIED INFORMATION*					

TABLE D-13: SUMMARY — PHYSICAL AND ENVIRONMENTAL PROTECTION CONTROLS

CNTL NO.	CONTROL NAME *Control Enhancement Name*	WITHDRAWN	ASSURANCE	CONTROL BASELINES		
				LOW	MOD	HIGH
PE-1	Physical and Environmental Protection Policy and Procedures		X	X	X	X
PE-2	Physical Access Authorizations			X	X	X
PE-2(1)	*PHYSICAL ACCESS AUTHORIZATIONS	ACCESS BY POSITION / ROLE*					
PE-2(2)	*PHYSICAL ACCESS AUTHORIZATIONS	TWO FORMS OF IDENTIFICATION*					
PE-2(3)	*PHYSICAL ACCESS AUTHORIZATIONS	RESTRICT UNESCORTED ACCESS*					
PE-3	Physical Access Control			X	X	X
PE-3(1)	*PHYSICAL ACCESS CONTROL	INFORMATION SYSTEM ACCESS*					X
PE-3(2)	*PHYSICAL ACCESS CONTROL	FACILITY / INFORMATION SYSTEM BOUNDARIES*					
PE-3(3)	*PHYSICAL ACCESS CONTROL	CONTINUOUS GUARDS / ALARMS / MONITORING*					
PE-3(4)	*PHYSICAL ACCESS CONTROL	LOCKABLE CASINGS*					
PE-3(5)	*PHYSICAL ACCESS CONTROL	TAMPER PROTECTION*					
PE-3(6)	*PHYSICAL ACCESS CONTROL	FACILITY PENETRATION TESTING*					
PE-4	Access Control for Transmission Medium				X	X
PE-5	Access Control for Output Devices				X	X
PE-5(1)	*ACCESS CONTROL FOR OUTPUT DEVICES	ACCESS TO OUTPUT BY AUTHORIZED INDIVIDUALS*					
PE-5(2)	*ACCESS CONTROL FOR OUTPUT DEVICES	ACCESS TO OUTPUT BY INDIVIDUAL IDENTITY*					
PE-5(3)	*ACCESS CONTROL FOR OUTPUT DEVICES	MARKING OUTPUT DEVICES*					
PE-6	Monitoring Physical Access		X	X	X	X
PE-6(1)	*MONITORING PHYSICAL ACCESS	INTRUSION ALARMS / SURVEILLANCE EQUIPMENT*		X		X	X
PE-6(2)	*MONITORING PHYSICAL ACCESS	AUTOMATED INTRUSION RECOGNITION / RESPONSES*		X			
PE-6(3)	*MONITORING PHYSICAL ACCESS	VIDEO SURVEILLANCE*		X			
PE-6(4)	*MONITORING PHYSICAL ACCESS	MONITORING PHYSICAL ACCESS TO INFORMATION SYSTEMS*		X			X
PE-7	Visitor Control	X	Incorporated into PE-2 and PE-3.			
PE-8	Visitor Access Records			X	X	X	X
PE-8(1)	*VISITOR ACCESS RECORDS	AUTOMATED RECORDS MAINTENANCE / REVIEW*					X
PE-8(2)	*VISITOR ACCESS RECORDS	PHYSICAL ACCESS RECORDS*	X	Incorporated into PE-2.			
PE-9	Power Equipment and Cabling				X	X
PE-9(1)	*POWER EQUIPMENT AND CABLING	REDUNDANT CABLING*					
PE-9(2)	*POWER EQUIPMENT AND CABLING	AUTOMATIC VOLTAGE CONTROLS*					
PE-10	Emergency Shutoff				X	X
PE-10(1)	*EMERGENCY SHUTOFF	ACCIDENTAL / UNAUTHORIZED ACTIVATION*	X	Incorporated into PE-10.			
PE-11	Emergency Power				X	X
PE-11(1)	*EMERGENCY POWER	LONG-TERM ALTERNATE POWER SUPPLY - MINIMAL OPERATIONAL CAPABILITY*					X
PE-11(2)	*EMERGENCY POWER	LONG-TERM ALTERNATE POWER SUPPLY - SELF-CONTAINED*					

CNTL NO.	CONTROL NAME *Control Enhancement Name*	WITHDRAWN	ASSURANCE	CONTROL BASELINES		
				LOW	MOD	HIGH
PE-12	**Emergency Lighting**			x	x	x
PE-12(1)	*EMERGENCY LIGHTING	ESSENTIAL MISSIONS / BUSINESS FUNCTIONS*					
PE-13	**Fire Protection**			x	x	x
PE-13(1)	*FIRE PROTECTION	DETECTION DEVICES / SYSTEMS*					x
PE-13(2)	*FIRE PROTECTION	SUPPRESSION DEVICES / SYSTEMS*					x
PE-13(3)	*FIRE PROTECTION	AUTOMATIC FIRE SUPPRESSION*				x	x
PE-13(4)	*FIRE PROTECTION	INSPECTIONS*					
PE-14	**Temperature and Humidity Controls**			x	x	x
PE-14(1)	*TEMPERATURE AND HUMIDITY CONTROLS	AUTOMATIC CONTROLS*					
PE-14(2)	*TEMPERATURE AND HUMIDITY CONTROLS	MONITORING WITH ALARMS / NOTIFICATIONS*					
PE-15	**Water Damage Protection**			x	x	x
PE-15(1)	*WATER DAMAGE PROTECTION	AUTOMATION SUPPORT*					x
PE-16	**Delivery and Removal**			x	x	x
PE-17	**Alternate Work Site**				x	x
PE-18	**Location of Information System Components**					x
PE-18(1)	*LOCATION OF INFORMATION SYSTEM COMPONENTS	FACILITY SITE*					
PE-19	**Information Leakage**					
PE-19(1)	*INFORMATION LEAKAGE	NATIONAL EMISSIONS / TEMPEST POLICIES AND PROCEDURES*					
PE-20	**Asset Monitoring and Tracking**					

TABLE D-14: SUMMARY — PLANNING CONTROLS

CNTL NO.	CONTROL NAME *Control Enhancement Name*	WITHDRAWN	ASSURANCE	CONTROL BASELINES		
				LOW	MOD	HIGH
PL-1	Security Planning Policy and Procedures		x	x	x	x
PL-2	System Security Plan		x	x	x	x
PL-2(1)	*SYSTEM SECURITY PLAN	CONCEPT OF OPERATIONS*	x	Incorporated into PL-7.			
PL-2(2)	*SYSTEM SECURITY PLAN	FUNCTIONAL ARCHITECTURE*	x	Incorporated into PL-8.			
PL-2(3)	*SYSTEM SECURITY PLAN	PLAN / COORDINATE WITH OTHER ORGANIZATIONAL ENTITIES*		x		x	x
PL-3	System Security Plan Update	x	Incorporated into PL-2.			
PL-4	Rules of Behavior		x	x	x	x
PL-4(1)	*RULES OF BEHAVIOR	SOCIAL MEDIA AND NETWORKING RESTRICTIONS*		x		x	x
PL-5	Privacy Impact Assessment	x	Incorporated into Appendix J, AR-2.			
PL-6	Security-Related Activity Planning	x	Incorporated into PL-2.			
PL-7	Security Concept of Operations					
PL-8	Information Security Architecture		x		x	x
PL-8(1)	*INFORMATION SECURITY ARCHITECTURE	DEFENSE-IN-DEPTH*		x			
PL-8(2)	*INFORMATION SECURITY ARCHITECTURE	SUPPLIER DIVERSITY*		x			
PL-9	Central Management		x			

TABLE D-15: SUMMARY — PERSONNEL SECURITY CONTROLS

CNTL NO.	CONTROL NAME *Control Enhancement Name*	WITHDRAWN	ASSURANCE	CONTROL BASELINES		
				LOW	MOD	HIGH
PS-1	Personnel Security Policy and Procedures		x	x	x	x
PS-2	Position Risk Designation			x	x	x
PS-3	Personnel Screening			x	x	x
PS-3(1)	*PERSONNEL SCREENING	CLASSIFIED INFORMATION*					
PS-3(2)	*PERSONNEL SCREENING	FORMAL INDOCTRINATION*					
PS-3(3)	*PERSONNEL SCREENING	INFORMATION WITH SPECIAL PROTECTION MEASURES*					
PS-4	Personnel Termination			x	x	x
PS-4(1)	*PERSONNEL TERMINATION	POST-EMPLOYMENT REQUIREMENTS*					
PS-4(2)	*PERSONNEL TERMINATION	AUTOMATED NOTIFICATION*					x
PS-5	Personnel Transfer			x	x	x
PS-6	Access Agreements		x	x	x	x
PS-6(1)	*ACCESS AGREEMENTS	INFORMATION REQUIRING SPECIAL PROTECTION*	x	Incorporated into PS-3.			
PS-6(2)	*ACCESS AGREEMENTS	CLASSIFIED INFORMATION REQUIRING SPECIAL PROTECTION*		x			
PS-6(3)	*ACCESS AGREEMENTS	POST-EMPLOYMENT REQUIREMENTS*		x			
PS-7	Third-Party Personnel Security		x	x	x	x
PS-8	Personnel Sanctions			x	x	x

TABLE D-16: SUMMARY — RISK ASSESSMENT CONTROLS

CNTL NO.	CONTROL NAME *Control Enhancement Name*	WITHDRAWN	ASSURANCE	CONTROL BASELINES		
				LOW	MOD	HIGH
RA-1	**Risk Assessment Policy and Procedures**		X	X	X	X
RA-2	**Security Categorization**			X	X	X
RA-3	**Risk Assessment**		X	X	X	X
RA-4	**Risk Assessment Update**	X	Incorporated into RA-3.			
RA-5	**Vulnerability Scanning**		X	X	X	X
RA-5(1)	*VULNERABILITY SCANNING	UPDATE TOOL CAPABILITY*		X		X	X
RA-5(2)	*VULNERABILITY SCANNING	UPDATE BY FREQUENCY / PRIOR TO NEW SCAN / WHEN IDENTIFIED*		X		X	X
RA-5(3)	*VULNERABILITY SCANNING	BREADTH / DEPTH OF COVERAGE*		X			
RA-5(4)	*VULNERABILITY SCANNING	DISCOVERABLE INFORMATION*		X			X
RA-5(5)	*VULNERABILITY SCANNING	PRIVILEGED ACCESS*		X		X	X
RA-5(6)	*VULNERABILITY SCANNING	AUTOMATED TREND ANALYSES*		X			
RA-5(7)	*VULNERABILITY SCANNING	AUTOMATED DETECTION AND NOTIFICATION OF UNAUTHORIZED COMPONENTS*	X	Incorporated into CM-8.			
RA-5(8)	*VULNERABILITY SCANNING	REVIEW HISTORIC AUDIT LOGS*		X			
RA-5(9)	*VULNERABILITY SCANNING	PENETRATION TESTING AND ANALYSES*	X	Incorporated into CA-8.			
RA-5(10)	*VULNERABILITY SCANNING	CORRELATE SCANNING INFORMATION*		X			
RA-6	**Technical Surveillance Countermeasures Survey**		X			

TABLE D-17: SUMMARY — SYSTEM AND SERVICES ACQUISITION CONTROLS

CNTL NO.	CONTROL NAME *Control Enhancement Name*	WITHDRAWN	ASSURANCE	CONTROL BASELINES		
				LOW	MOD	HIGH
SA-1	System and Services Acquisition Policy and Procedures		x	x	x	x
SA-2	Allocation of Resources		x	x	x	x
SA-3	System Development Life Cycle		x	x	x	x
SA-4	Acquisition Process		x	x	x	x
SA-4(1)	ACQUISITION PROCESS	FUNCTIONAL PROPERTIES OF SECURITY CONTROLS		x		x	x
SA-4(2)	ACQUISITION PROCESS	DESIGN / IMPLEMENTATION INFORMATION FOR SECURITY CONTROLS		x		x	x
SA-4(3)	ACQUISITION PROCESS	DEVELOPMENT METHODS / TECHNIQUES / PRACTICES		x			
SA-4(4)	ACQUISITION PROCESS	ASSIGNMENT OF COMPONENTS TO SYSTEMS	x	Incorporated into CM-8(9).			
SA-4(5)	ACQUISITION PROCESS	SYSTEM / COMPONENT / SERVICE CONFIGURATIONS		x			
SA-4(6)	ACQUISITION PROCESS	USE OF INFORMATION ASSURANCE PRODUCTS		x			
SA-4(7)	ACQUISITION PROCESS	NIAP-APPROVED PROTECTION PROFILES		x			
SA-4(8)	ACQUISITION PROCESS	CONTINUOUS MONITORING PLAN		x			
SA-4(9)	ACQUISITION PROCESS	FUNCTIONS / PORTS / PROTOCOLS / SERVICES IN USE		x		x	x
SA-4(10)	ACQUISITION PROCESS	USE OF APPROVED PIV PRODUCTS		x	x	x	x
SA-5	Information System Documentation		x	x	x	x
SA-5(1)	INFORMATION SYSTEM DOCUMENTATION	FUNCTIONAL PROPERTIES OF SECURITY CONTROLS	x	Incorporated into SA-4(1).			
SA-5(2)	INFORMATION SYSTEM DOCUMENTATION	SECURITY-RELEVANT EXTERNAL SYSTEM INTERFACES	x	Incorporated into SA-4(2).			
SA-5(3)	INFORMATION SYSTEM DOCUMENTATION	HIGH-LEVEL DESIGN	x	Incorporated into SA-4(2).			
SA-5(4)	INFORMATION SYSTEM DOCUMENTATION	LOW-LEVEL DESIGN	x	Incorporated into SA-4(2).			
SA-5(5)	INFORMATION SYSTEM DOCUMENTATION	SOURCE CODE	x	Incorporated into SA-4(2).			
SA-6	Software Usage Restrictions	x	Incorporated into CM-10 and SI-7.			
SA-7	User-Installed Software	x	Incorporated into CM-11 and SI-7.			
SA-8	Security Engineering Principles		x		x	x
SA-9	External Information System Services		x	x	x	x
SA-9(1)	EXTERNAL INFORMATION SYSTEMS	RISK ASSESSMENTS / ORGANIZATIONAL APPROVALS		x			
SA-9(2)	EXTERNAL INFORMATION SYSTEMS	IDENTIFICATION OF FUNCTIONS / PORTS / PROTOCOLS / SERVICES		x		x	x
SA-9(3)	EXTERNAL INFORMATION SYSTEMS	ESTABLISH / MAINTAIN TRUST RELATIONSHIP WITH PROVIDERS		x			
SA-9(4)	EXTERNAL INFORMATION SYSTEMS	CONSISTENT INTERESTS OF CONSUMERS AND PROVIDERS		x			
SA-9(5)	EXTERNAL INFORMATION SYSTEMS	PROCESSING, STORAGE, AND SERVICE LOCATION		x			
SA-10	Developer Configuration Management		x		x	x
SA-10(1)	DEVELOPER CONFIGURATION MANAGEMENT	SOFTWARE / FIRMWARE INTEGRITY VERIFICATION		x			
SA-10(2)	DEVELOPER CONFIGURATION MANAGEMENT	ALTERNATIVE CONFIGURATION MANAGEMENT PROCESSES		x			

CNTL NO.	CONTROL NAME *Control Enhancement Name*	WITHDRAWN	ASSURANCE	CONTROL BASELINES		
				LOW	MOD	HIGH
SA-10(3)	DEVELOPER CONFIGURATION MANAGEMENT | HARDWARE INTEGRITY VERIFICATION		X			
SA-10(4)	DEVELOPER CONFIGURATION MANAGEMENT | TRUSTED GENERATION		X			
SA-10(5)	DEVELOPER CONFIGURATION MANAGEMENT | MAPPING INTEGRITY FOR VERSION CONTROL		X			
SA-10(6)	DEVELOPER CONFIGURATION MANAGEMENT | TRUSTED DISTRIBUTION		X			
SA-11	**Developer Security Testing and Evaluation**		X		X	X
SA-11(1)	DEVELOPER SECURITY TESTING AND EVALUATION | STATIC CODE ANALYSIS		X			
SA-11(2)	DEVELOPER SECURITY TESTING AND EVALUATION | THREAT AND VULNERABILITY ANALYSES		X			
SA-11(3)	DEVELOPER SECURITY TESTING AND EVALUATION | INDEPENDENT VERIFICATION OF ASSESSMENT PLANS / EVIDENCE		X			
SA-11(4)	DEVELOPER SECURITY TESTING AND EVALUATION | MANUAL CODE REVIEWS		X			
SA-11(5)	DEVELOPER SECURITY TESTING AND EVALUATION | PENETRATION TESTING		X			
SA-11(6)	DEVELOPER SECURITY TESTING AND EVALUATION | ATTACK SURFACE REVIEWS		X			
SA-11(7)	DEVELOPER SECURITY TESTING AND EVALUATION | VERIFY SCOPE OF TESTING / EVALUATION		X			
SA-11(8)	DEVELOPER SECURITY TESTING AND EVALUATION | DYNAMIC CODE ANALYSIS		X			
SA-12	**Supply Chain Protection**		X			X
SA-12(1)	SUPPLY CHAIN PROTECTION | ACQUISITION STRATEGIES / TOOLS / METHODS		X			
SA-12(2)	SUPPLY CHAIN PROTECTION | SUPPLIER REVIEWS		X			
SA-12(3)	SUPPLY CHAIN PROTECTION | TRUSTED SHIPPING AND WAREHOUSING	X	Incorporated into SA-12(1).			
SA-12(4)	SUPPLY CHAIN PROTECTION | DIVERSITY OF SUPPLIERS	X	Incorporated into SA-12(13).			
SA-12(5)	SUPPLY CHAIN PROTECTION | LIMITATION OF HARM		X			
SA-12(6)	SUPPLY CHAIN PROTECTION | MINIMIZING PROCUREMENT TIME	X	Incorporated into SA-12(1).			
SA-12(7)	SUPPLY CHAIN PROTECTION | ASSESSMENTS PRIOR TO SELECTION / ACCEPTANCE / UPDATE		X			
SA-12(8)	SUPPLY CHAIN PROTECTION | USE OF ALL-SOURCE INTELLIGENCE		X			
SA-12(9)	SUPPLY CHAIN PROTECTION | OPERATIONS SECURITY		X			
SA-12(10)	SUPPLY CHAIN PROTECTION | VALIDATE AS GENUINE AND NOT ALTERED		X			
SA-12(11)	SUPPLY CHAIN PROTECTION | PENETRATION TESTING / ANALYSIS OF ELEMENTS, PROCESSES, AND ACTORS		X			
SA-12(12)	SUPPLY CHAIN PROTECTION | INTER-ORGANIZATIONAL AGREEMENTS		X			
SA-12(13)	SUPPLY CHAIN PROTECTION | CRITICAL INFORMATION SYSTEM COMPONENTS		X			
SA-12(14)	SUPPLY CHAIN PROTECTION | IDENTITY AND TRACEABILITY		X			
SA-12(15)	SUPPLY CHAIN PROTECTION | PROCESSES TO ADDRESS WEAKNESSES OR DEFICIENCIES		X			
SA-13	**Trustworthiness**		X			
SA-14	**Criticality Analysis**		X			
SA-14(1)	CRITICALITY ANALYSIS | CRITICAL COMPONENTS WITH NO VIABLE ALTERNATIVE SOURCING	X	Incorporated into SA-20.			

CNTL NO.	CONTROL NAME *Control Enhancement Name*	WITHDRAWN	ASSURANCE	CONTROL BASELINES		
				LOW	MOD	HIGH
SA-15	Development Process, Standards, and Tools		x			x
SA-15(1)	*DEVELOPMENT PROCESS, STANDARDS, AND TOOLS	QUALITY METRICS*		x			
SA-15(2)	*DEVELOPMENT PROCESS, STANDARDS, AND TOOLS	SECURITY TRACKING TOOLS*		x			
SA-15(3)	*DEVELOPMENT PROCESS, STANDARDS, AND TOOLS	CRITICALITY ANALYSIS*		x			
SA-15(4)	*DEVELOPMENT PROCESS, STANDARDS, AND TOOLS	THREAT MODELING / VULNERABILITY ANALYSIS*		x			
SA-15(5)	*DEVELOPMENT PROCESS, STANDARDS, AND TOOLS	ATTACK SURFACE REDUCTION*		x			
SA-15(6)	*DEVELOPMENT PROCESS, STANDARDS, AND TOOLS	CONTINUOUS IMPROVEMENT*		x			
SA-15(7)	*DEVELOPMENT PROCESS, STANDARDS, AND TOOLS	AUTOMATED VULNERABILITY ANALYSIS*		x			
SA-15(8)	*DEVELOPMENT PROCESS, STANDARDS, AND TOOLS	REUSE OF THREAT / VULNERABILITY INFORMATION*		x			
SA-15(9)	*DEVELOPMENT PROCESS, STANDARDS, AND TOOLS	USE OF LIVE DATA*		x			
SA-15(10)	*DEVELOPMENT PROCESS, STANDARDS, AND TOOLS	INCIDENT RESPONSE PLAN*		x			
SA-15(11)	*DEVELOPMENT PROCESS, STANDARDS, AND TOOLS	ARCHIVE INFORMATION SYSTEM / COMPONENT*		x			
SA-16	Developer-Provided Training		x			x
SA-17	Developer Security Architecture and Design		x			x
SA-17(1)	*DEVELOPER SECURITY ARCHITECTURE AND DESIGN	FORMAL POLICY MODEL*		x			
SA-17(2)	*DEVELOPER SECURITY ARCHITECTURE AND DESIGN	SECURITY-RELEVANT COMPONENTS*		x			
SA-17(3)	*DEVELOPER SECURITY ARCHITECTURE AND DESIGN	FORMAL CORRESPONDENCE*		x			
SA-17(4)	*DEVELOPER SECURITY ARCHITECTURE AND DESIGN	INFORMAL CORRESPONDENCE*		x			
SA-17(5)	*DEVELOPER SECURITY ARCHITECTURE AND DESIGN	CONCEPTUALLY SIMPLE DESIGN*		x			
SA-17(6)	*DEVELOPER SECURITY ARCHITECTURE AND DESIGN	STRUCTURE FOR TESTING*		x			
SA-17(7)	*DEVELOPER SECURITY ARCHITECTURE AND DESIGN	STRUCTURE FOR LEAST PRIVILEGE*		x			
SA-18	Tamper Resistance and Detection		x			
SA-18(1)	*TAMPER RESISTANCE AND DETECTION	MULTIPLE PHASES OF SDLC*		x			
SA-18(2)	*TAMPER RESISTANCE AND DETECTION	INSPECTION OF INFORMATION SYSTEMS, COMPONENTS, OR DEVICES*		x			
SA-19	Component Authenticity		x			
SA-19(1)	*COMPONENT AUTHENTICITY	ANTI-COUNTERFEIT TRAINING*		x			
SA-19(2)	*COMPONENT AUTHENTICITY	CONFIGURATION CONTROL FOR COMPONENT SERVICE / REPAIR*		x			
SA-19(3)	*COMPONENT AUTHENTICITY	COMPONENT DISPOSAL*		x			
SA-19(4)	*COMPONENT AUTHENTICITY	ANTI-COUNTERFEIT SCANNING*		x			
SA-20	Customized Development of Critical Components		x			
SA-21	Developer Screening		x			

CNTL NO.	**CONTROL NAME** *Control Enhancement Name*	WITHDRAWN	ASSURANCE	CONTROL BASELINES		
				LOW	MOD	HIGH
SA-21(1)	*DEVELOPER SCREENING | VALIDATION OF SCREENING*		X			
SA-22	**Unsupported System Components**		X			
SA-22(1)	*UNSUPPORTED SYSTEM COMPONENTS | ALTERNATIVE SOURCES FOR CONTINUED SUPPORT*		X			

TABLE D-18: SUMMARY — SYSTEM AND COMMUNICATIONS PROTECTION CONTROLS

CNTL NO.	CONTROL NAME *Control Enhancement Name*	WITHDRAWN	ASSURANCE	CONTROL BASELINES		
				LOW	MOD	HIGH
SC-1	System and Communications Protection Policy and Procedures		x	x	x	x
SC-2	Application Partitioning		x		x	x
SC-2(1)	*APPLICATION PARTITIONING	INTERFACES FOR NON-PRIVILEGED USERS*		x			
SC-3	Security Function Isolation		x			x
SC-3(1)	*SECURITY FUNCTION ISOLATION	HARDWARE SEPARATION*		x			
SC-3(2)	*SECURITY FUNCTION ISOLATION	ACCESS / FLOW CONTROL FUNCTIONS*		x			
SC-3(3)	*SECURITY FUNCTION ISOLATION	MINIMIZE NONSECURITY FUNCTIONALITY*		x			
SC-3(4)	*SECURITY FUNCTION ISOLATION	MODULE COUPLING AND COHESIVENESS*		x			
SC-3(5)	*SECURITY FUNCTION ISOLATION	LAYERED STRUCTURES*		x			
SC-4	Information in Shared Resources				x	x
SC-4(1)	*INFORMATION IN SHARED RESOURCES	SECURITY LEVELS*	x	Incorporated into SC-4.			
SC-4(2)	*INFORMATION IN SHARED RESOURCES	PERIODS PROCESSING*					
SC-5	Denial of Service Protection			x	x	x
SC-5(1)	*DENIAL OF SERVICE PROTECTION	RESTRICT INTERNAL USERS*					
SC-5(2)	*DENIAL OF SERVICE PROTECTION	EXCESS CAPACITY / BANDWIDTH / REDUNDANCY*					
SC-5(3)	*DENIAL OF SERVICE PROTECTION	DETECTION / MONITORING*					
SC-6	Resource Availability		x			
SC-7	Boundary Protection			x	x	x
SC-7(1)	*BOUNDARY PROTECTION	PHYSICALLY SEPARATED SUBNETWORKS*	x	Incorporated into SC-7.			
SC-7(2)	*BOUNDARY PROTECTION	PUBLIC ACCESS*	x	Incorporated into SC-7.			
SC-7(3)	*BOUNDARY PROTECTION	ACCESS POINTS*				x	x
SC-7(4)	*BOUNDARY PROTECTION	EXTERNAL TELECOMMUNICATIONS SERVICES*				x	x
SC-7(5)	*BOUNDARY PROTECTION	DENY BY DEFAULT / ALLOW BY EXCEPTION*				x	x
SC-7(6)	*BOUNDARY PROTECTION	RESPONSE TO RECOGNIZED FAILURES*	x	Incorporated into SC-7(18).			
SC-7(7)	*BOUNDARY PROTECTION	PREVENT SPLIT TUNNELING FOR REMOTE DEVICES*				x	x
SC-7(8)	*BOUNDARY PROTECTION	ROUTE TRAFFIC TO AUTHENTICATED PROXY SERVERS*					x
SC-7(9)	*BOUNDARY PROTECTION	RESTRICT THREATENING OUTGOING COMMUNICATIONS TRAFFIC*					
SC-7(10)	*BOUNDARY PROTECTION	PREVENT UNAUTHORIZED EXFILTRATION*					
SC-7(11)	*BOUNDARY PROTECTION	RESTRICT INCOMING COMMUNICATIONS TRAFFIC*					
SC-7(12)	*BOUNDARY PROTECTION	HOST-BASED PROTECTION*					
SC-7(13)	*BOUNDARY PROTECTION	ISOLATION OF SECURITY TOOLS / MECHANISMS / SUPPORT COMPONENTS*					
SC-7(14)	*BOUNDARY PROTECTION	PROTECTS AGAINST UNAUTHORIZED PHYSICAL CONNECTIONS*					
SC-7(15)	*BOUNDARY PROTECTION	ROUTE PRIVILEGED NETWORK ACCESSES*					
SC-7(16)	*BOUNDARY PROTECTION	PREVENT DISCOVERY OF COMPONENTS / DEVICES*					

CNTL NO.	CONTROL NAME *Control Enhancement Name*	WITHDRAWN	ASSURANCE	CONTROL BASELINES		
				LOW	MOD	HIGH
SC-7(17)	BOUNDARY PROTECTION | AUTOMATED ENFORCEMENT OF PROTOCOL FORMATS					
SC-7(18)	BOUNDARY PROTECTION | FAIL SECURE		x			x
SC-7(19)	BOUNDARY PROTECTION | BLOCKS COMMUNICATION FROM NON-ORGANIZATIONALLY CONFIGURED HOSTS					
SC-7(20)	BOUNDARY PROTECTION | DYNAMIC ISOLATION / SEGREGATION					
SC-7(21)	BOUNDARY PROTECTION | ISOLATION OF INFORMATION SYSTEM COMPONENTS		x			x
SC-7(22)	BOUNDARY PROTECTION | SEPARATE SUBNETS FOR CONNECTING TO DIFFERENT SECURITY DOMAINS		x			
SC-7(23)	BOUNDARY PROTECTION | DISABLE SENDER FEEDBACK ON PROTOCOL VALIDATION FAILURE					
SC-8	**Transmission Confidentiality and Integrity**				x	x
SC-8(1)	TRANSMISSION CONFIDENTIALITY AND INTEGRITY | CRYPTOGRAPHIC OR ALTERNATE PHYSICAL PROTECTION				x	x
SC-8(2)	TRANSMISSION CONFIDENTIALITY AND INTEGRITY | PRE / POST TRANSMISSION HANDLING					
SC-8(3)	TRANSMISSION CONFIDENTIALITY AND INTEGRITY | CRYPTOGRAPHIC PROTECTION FOR MESSAGE EXTERNALS					
SC-8(4)	TRANSMISSION CONFIDENTIALITY AND INTEGRITY | CONCEAL / RANDOMIZE COMMUNICATIONS					
SC-9	**Transmission Confidentiality**	x	Incorporated into SC-8.			
SC-10	**Network Disconnect**				x	x
SC-11	**Trusted Path**		x			
SC-11(1)	TRUSTED PATH | LOGICAL ISOLATION		x			
SC-12	**Cryptographic Key Establishment and Management**			x	x	x
SC-12(1)	CRYPTOGRAPHIC KEY ESTABLISHMENT AND MANAGEMENT | AVAILABILITY					x
SC-12(2)	CRYPTOGRAPHIC KEY ESTABLISHMENT AND MANAGEMENT | SYMMETRIC KEYS					
SC-12(3)	CRYPTOGRAPHIC KEY ESTABLISHMENT AND MANAGEMENT | ASYMMETRIC KEYS					
SC-12(4)	CRYPTOGRAPHIC KEY ESTABLISHMENT AND MANAGEMENT | PKI CERTIFICATES	x	Incorporated into SC-12.			
SC-12(5)	CRYPTOGRAPHIC KEY ESTABLISHMENT AND MANAGEMENT | PKI CERTIFICATES / HARDWARE TOKENS	x	Incorporated into SC-12.			
SC-13	**Cryptographic Protection**			x	x	x
SC-13(1)	CRYPTOGRAPHIC PROTECTION | FIPS-VALIDATED CRYPTOGRAPHY	x	Incorporated into SC-13.			
SC-13(2)	CRYPTOGRAPHIC PROTECTION | NSA-APPROVED CRYPTOGRAPHY	x	Incorporated into SC-13.			
SC-13(3)	CRYPTOGRAPHIC PROTECTION | INDIVIDUALS WITHOUT FORMAL ACCESS APPROVALS	x	Incorporated into SC-13.			
SC-13(4)	CRYPTOGRAPHIC PROTECTION | DIGITAL SIGNATURES	x	Incorporated into SC-13.			
SC-14	**Public Access Protections**	x	Capability provided by AC-2, AC-3, AC-5, SI-3, SI-4, SI-5, SI-7, SI-10.			
SC-15	**Collaborative Computing Devices**			x	x	x
SC-15(1)	COLLABORATIVE COMPUTING DEVICES | PHYSICAL DISCONNECT					
SC-15(2)	COLLABORATIVE COMPUTING DEVICES | BLOCKING INBOUND / OUTBOUND COMMUNICATIONS TRAFFIC	x	Incorporated into SC-7.			
SC-15(3)	COLLABORATIVE COMPUTING DEVICES | DISABLING / REMOVAL IN SECURE WORK AREAS					

CNTL NO.	CONTROL NAME *Control Enhancement Name*	WITHDRAWN	ASSURANCE	CONTROL BASELINES		
				LOW	MOD	HIGH
SC-15(4)	*COLLABORATIVE COMPUTING DEVICES	EXPLICITLY INDICATE CURRENT PARTICIPANTS*					
SC-16	**Transmission of Security Attributes**					
SC-16(1)	*TRANSMISSION OF SECURITY ATTRIBUTES	INTEGRITY VALIDATION*					
SC-17	**Public Key Infrastructure Certificates**				x	x
SC-18	**Mobile Code**				x	x
SC-18(1)	*MOBILE CODE	IDENTIFY UNACCEPTABLE CODE / TAKE CORRECTIVE ACTIONS*					
SC-18(2)	*MOBILE CODE	ACQUISITION / DEVELOPMENT / USE*					
SC-18(3)	*MOBILE CODE	PREVENT DOWNLOADING / EXECUTION*					
SC-18(4)	*MOBILE CODE	PREVENT AUTOMATIC EXECUTION*					
SC-18(5)	*MOBILE CODE	ALLOW EXECUTION ONLY IN CONFINED ENVIRONMENTS*					
SC-19	**Voice Over Internet Protocol**				x	x
SC-20	**Secure Name /Address Resolution Service (Authoritative Source)**			x	x	x
SC-20(1)	*SECURE NAME / ADDRESS RESOLUTION SERVICE (AUTHORITATIVE SOURCE)	CHILD SUBSPACES*	x	Incorporated into SC-20.			
SC-20(2)	*SECURE NAME / ADDRESS RESOLUTION SERVICE (AUTHORITATIVE SOURCE)	DATA ORIGIN / INTEGRITY*					
SC-21	**Secure Name /Address Resolution Service (Recursive or Caching Resolver)**			x	x	x
SC-21(1)	*SECURE NAME / ADDRESS RESOLUTION SERVICE (RECURSIVE OR CACHING RESOLVER)	DATA ORIGIN / INTEGRITY*	x	Incorporated into SC-21.			
SC-22	**Architecture and Provisioning for Name/Address Resolution Service**			x	x	x
SC-23	**Session Authenticity**				x	x
SC-23(1)	*SESSION AUTHENTICITY	INVALIDATE SESSION IDENTIFIERS AT LOGOUT*					
SC-23(2)	*SESSION AUTHENTICITY	USER-INITIATED LOGOUTS / MESSAGE DISPLAYS*	x	Incorporated into AC-12(1).			
SC-23(3)	*SESSION AUTHENTICITY	UNIQUE SESSION IDENTIFIERS WITH RANDOMIZATION*					
SC-23(4)	*SESSION AUTHENTICITY	UNIQUE SESSION IDENTIFIERS WITH RANDOMIZATION*	x	Incorporated into SC-23(3).			
SC-23(5)	*SESSION AUTHENTICITY	ALLOWED CERTIFICATE AUTHORITIES*					
SC-24	**Fail in Known State**		x			x
SC-25	**Thin Nodes**					
SC-26	**Honeypots**					
SC-26(1)	*HONEYPOTS	DETECTION OF MALICIOUS CODE*	x	Incorporated into SC-35.			
SC-27	**Platform-Independent Applications**					
SC-28	**Protection of Information at Rest**				x	x
SC-28(1)	*PROTECTION OF INFORMATION AT REST	CRYPTOGRAPHIC PROTECTION*					
SC-28(2)	*PROTECTION OF INFORMATION AT REST	OFF-LINE STORAGE*					
SC-29	**Heterogeneity**		x			
SC-29(1)	*HETEROGENEITY	VIRTUALIZATION TECHNIQUES*		x			
SC-30	**Concealment and Misdirection**		x			
SC-30(1)	*CONCEALMENT AND MISDIRECTION	VIRTUALIZATION TECHNIQUES*	x	Incorporated into SC-29(1).			

CNTL NO.	CONTROL NAME *Control Enhancement Name*	WITHDRAWN	ASSURANCE	CONTROL BASELINES		
				LOW	MOD	HIGH
SC-30(2)	CONCEALMENT AND MISDIRECTION | RANDOMNESS		X			
SC-30(3)	CONCEALMENT AND MISDIRECTION | CHANGE PROCESSING / STORAGE LOCATIONS		X			
SC-30(4)	CONCEALMENT AND MISDIRECTION | MISLEADING INFORMATION		X			
SC-30(5)	CONCEALMENT AND MISDIRECTION | CONCEALMENT OF SYSTEM COMPONENTS		X			
SC-31	Covert Channel Analysis		X			
SC-31(1)	COVERT CHANNEL ANALYSIS | TEST COVERT CHANNELS FOR EXPLOITABILITY		X			
SC-31(2)	COVERT CHANNEL ANALYSIS | MAXIMUM BANDWIDTH		X			
SC-31(3)	COVERT CHANNEL ANALYSIS | MEASURE BANDWIDTH IN OPERATIONAL ENVIRONMENTS		X			
SC-32	Information System Partitioning		X			
SC-33	Transmission Preparation Integrity	X	Incorporated into SC-8.			
SC-34	Non-Modifiable Executable Programs		X			
SC-34(1)	NON-MODIFIABLE EXECUTABLE PROGRAMS | NO WRITABLE STORAGE		X			
SC-34(2)	NON-MODIFIABLE EXECUTABLE PROGRAMS | INTEGRITY PROTECTION / READ-ONLY MEDIA		X			
SC-34(3)	NON-MODIFIABLE EXECUTABLE PROGRAMS | HARDWARE-BASED PROTECTION		X			
SC-35	Honeyclients					
SC-36	Distributed Processing and Storage		X			
SC-36(1)	DISTRIBUTED PROCESSING AND STORAGE | POLLING TECHNIQUES		X			
SC-37	Out-of-Band Channels		X			
SC-37(1)	OUT-OF-BAND CHANNELS | ENSURE DELIVERY / TRANSMISSION		X			
SC-38	Operations Security		X			
SC-39	Process Isolation		X	X	X	X
SC-39(1)	PROCESS ISOLATION | HARDWARE SEPARATION		X			
SC-39(2)	PROCESS ISOLATION | THREAD ISOLATION		X			
SC-40	Wireless Link Protection					
SC-40(1)	WIRELESS LINK PROTECTION | ELECTROMAGNETIC INTERFERENCE					
SC-40(2)	WIRELESS LINK PROTECTION | REDUCE DETECTION POTENTIAL					
SC-40(3)	WIRELESS LINK PROTECTION | IMITATIVE OR MANIPULATIVE COMMUNICATIONS DECEPTION					
SC-40(4)	WIRELESS LINK PROTECTION | SIGNAL PARAMETER IDENTIFICATION					
SC-41	Port and I/O Device Access					
SC-42	Sensor Capability and Data					
SC-42(1)	SENSOR CAPABILITY AND DATA | REPORTING TO AUTHORIZED INDIVIDUALS OR ROLES					
SC-42(2)	SENSOR CAPABILITY AND DATA | AUTHORIZED USE					
SC-42(3)	SENSOR CAPABILITY AND DATA | PROHIBIT USE OF DEVICES					
SC-43	Usage Restrictions					
SC-44	Detonation Chambers					

TABLE D-19: SUMMARY — SYSTEM AND INFORMATION INTEGRITY CONTROLS

CNTL NO.	CONTROL NAME *Control Enhancement Name*	WITHDRAWN	ASSURANCE	CONTROL BASELINES		
				LOW	MOD	HIGH
SI-1	**System and Information Integrity Policy and Procedures**		x	x	x	x
SI-2	**Flaw Remediation**			x	x	x
SI-2(1)	*FLAW REMEDIATION	CENTRAL MANAGEMENT*					x
SI-2(2)	*FLAW REMEDIATION	AUTOMATED FLAW REMEDIATION STATUS*				x	x
SI-2(3)	*FLAW REMEDIATION	TIME TO REMEDIATE FLAWS / BENCHMARKS FOR CORRECTIVE ACTIONS*					
SI-2(4)	*FLAW REMEDIATION	AUTOMATED PATCH MANAGEMENT TOOLS*	x	Incorporated into SI-2.			
SI-2(5)	*FLAW REMEDIATION	AUTOMATIC SOFTWARE / FIRMWARE UPDATES*					
SI-2(6)	*FLAW REMEDIATION	REMOVAL OF PREVIOUS VERSIONS OF SOFTWARE / FIRMWARE*					
SI-3	**Malicious Code Protection**			x	x	x
SI-3(1)	*MALICIOUS CODE PROTECTION	CENTRAL MANAGEMENT*				x	x
SI-3(2)	*MALICIOUS CODE PROTECTION	AUTOMATIC UPDATES*				x	x
SI-3(3)	*MALICIOUS CODE PROTECTION	NON-PRIVILEGED USERS*	x	Incorporated into AC-6(10).			
SI-3(4)	*MALICIOUS CODE PROTECTION	UPDATES ONLY BY PRIVILEGED USERS*					
SI-3(5)	*MALICIOUS CODE PROTECTION	PORTABLE STORAGE DEVICES*	x	Incorporated into MP-7.			
SI-3(6)	*MALICIOUS CODE PROTECTION	TESTING / VERIFICATION*					
SI-3(7)	*MALICIOUS CODE PROTECTION	NONSIGNATURE-BASED DETECTION*					
SI-3(8)	*MALICIOUS CODE PROTECTION	DETECT UNAUTHORIZED COMMANDS*					
SI-3(9)	*MALICIOUS CODE PROTECTION	AUTHENTICATE REMOTE COMMANDS*					
SI-3(10)	*MALICIOUS CODE PROTECTION	MALICIOUS CODE ANALYSIS*					
SI-4	**Information System Monitoring**		x	x	x	x
SI-4(1)	*INFORMATION SYSTEM MONITORING	SYSTEM-WIDE INTRUSION DETECTION SYSTEM*		x			
SI-4(2)	*INFORMATION SYSTEM MONITORING	AUTOMATED TOOLS FOR REAL-TIME ANALYSIS*		x		x	x
SI-4(3)	*INFORMATION SYSTEM MONITORING	AUTOMATED TOOL INTEGRATION*		x			
SI-4(4)	*INFORMATION SYSTEM MONITORING	INBOUND AND OUTBOUND COMMUNICATIONS TRAFFIC*		x		x	x
SI-4(5)	*INFORMATION SYSTEM MONITORING	SYSTEM-GENERATED ALERTS*		x		x	x
SI-4(6)	*INFORMATION SYSTEM MONITORING	RESTRICT NON-PRIVILEGED USERS*	x	Incorporated into AC-6(10).			
SI-4(7)	*INFORMATION SYSTEM MONITORING	AUTOMATED RESPONSE TO SUSPICIOUS EVENTS*		x			
SI-4(8)	*INFORMATION SYSTEM MONITORING	PROTECTION OF MONITORING INFORMATION*	x	Incorporated into SI-4.			
SI-4(9)	*INFORMATION SYSTEM MONITORING	TESTING OF MONITORING TOOLS*		x			
SI-4(10)	*INFORMATION SYSTEM MONITORING	VISIBILITY OF ENCRYPTED COMMUNICATIONS*		x			
SI-4(11)	*INFORMATION SYSTEM MONITORING	ANALYZE COMMUNICATIONS TRAFFIC ANOMALIES*		x			
SI-4(12)	*INFORMATION SYSTEM MONITORING	AUTOMATED ALERTS*		x			
SI-4(13)	*INFORMATION SYSTEM MONITORING	ANALYZE TRAFFIC / EVENT PATTERNS*		x			
SI-4(14)	*INFORMATION SYSTEM MONITORING	WIRELESS INTRUSION DETECTION*		x			

CNTL NO.	CONTROL NAME *Control Enhancement Name*	WITHDRAWN	ASSURANCE	CONTROL BASELINES		
				LOW	MOD	HIGH
SI-4(15)	INFORMATION SYSTEM MONITORING | WIRELESS TO WIRELINE COMMUNICATIONS		X			
SI-4(16)	INFORMATION SYSTEM MONITORING | CORRELATE MONITORING INFORMATION		X			
SI-4(17)	INFORMATION SYSTEM MONITORING | INTEGRATED SITUATIONAL AWARENESS		X			
SI-4(18)	INFORMATION SYSTEM MONITORING | ANALYZE TRAFFIC / COVERT EXFILTRATION		X			
SI-4(19)	INFORMATION SYSTEM MONITORING | INDIVIDUALS POSING GREATER RISK		X			
SI-4(20)	INFORMATION SYSTEM MONITORING | PRIVILEGED USER		X			
SI-4(21)	INFORMATION SYSTEM MONITORING | PROBATIONARY PERIODS		X			
SI-4(22)	INFORMATION SYSTEM MONITORING | UNAUTHORIZED NETWORK SERVICES		X			
SI-4(23)	INFORMATION SYSTEM MONITORING | HOST-BASED DEVICES		X			
SI-4(24)	INFORMATION SYSTEM MONITORING | INDICATORS OF COMPROMISE		X			
SI-5	**Security Alerts, Advisories, and Directives**		X	X	X	X
SI-5(1)	SECURITY ALERTS, ADVISORIES, AND DIRECTIVES | AUTOMATED ALERTS AND ADVISORIES		X			X
SI-6	**Security Function Verification**		X			X
SI-6(1)	SECURITY FUNCTION VERIFICATION | NOTIFICATION OF FAILED SECURITY TESTS	X	Incorporated into SI-6.			
SI-6(2)	SECURITY FUNCTION VERIFICATION | AUTOMATION SUPPORT FOR DISTRIBUTED TESTING					
SI-6(3)	SECURITY FUNCTION VERIFICATION | REPORT VERIFICATION RESULTS					
SI-7	**Software, Firmware, and Information Integrity**		X		X	X
SI-7(1)	SOFTWARE, FIRMWARE, AND INFORMATION INTEGRITY | INTEGRITY CHECKS		X		X	X
SI-7(2)	SOFTWARE, FIRMWARE, AND INFORMATION INTEGRITY | AUTOMATED NOTIFICATIONS OF INTEGRITY VIOLATIONS		X			X
SI-7(3)	SOFTWARE, FIRMWARE, AND INFORMATION INTEGRITY | CENTRALLY MANAGED INTEGRITY TOOLS		X			
SI-7(4)	SOFTWARE, FIRMWARE, AND INFORMATION INTEGRITY | TAMPER-EVIDENT PACKAGING	X	Incorporated into SA-12.			
SI-7(5)	SOFTWARE, FIRMWARE, AND INFORMATION INTEGRITY | AUTOMATED RESPONSE TO INTEGRITY VIOLATIONS		X			X
SI-7(6)	SOFTWARE, FIRMWARE, AND INFORMATION INTEGRITY | CRYPTOGRAPHIC PROTECTION		X			
SI-7(7)	SOFTWARE, FIRMWARE, AND INFORMATION INTEGRITY | INTEGRATION OF DETECTION AND RESPONSE		X		X	X
SI-7(8)	SOFTWARE, FIRMWARE, AND INFORMATION INTEGRITY | AUDITING CAPABILITY FOR SIGNIFICANT EVENTS		X			
SI-7(9)	SOFTWARE, FIRMWARE, AND INFORMATION INTEGRITY | VERIFY BOOT PROCESS		X			
SI-7(10)	SOFTWARE, FIRMWARE, AND INFORMATION INTEGRITY | PROTECTION OF BOOT FIRMWARE		X			
SI-7(11)	SOFTWARE, FIRMWARE, AND INFORMATION INTEGRITY | CONFINED ENVIRONMENTS WITH LIMITED PRIVILEGES		X			
SI-7(12)	SOFTWARE, FIRMWARE, AND INFORMATION INTEGRITY | INTEGRITY VERIFICATION		X			

CNTL NO.	CONTROL NAME *Control Enhancement Name*	WITHDRAWN	ASSURANCE	CONTROL BASELINES		
				LOW	MOD	HIGH
SI-7(13)	*SOFTWARE, FIRMWARE, AND INFORMATION INTEGRITY	CODE EXECUTION IN PROTECTED ENVIRONMENTS*		X			
SI-7(14)	*SOFTWARE, FIRMWARE, AND INFORMATION INTEGRITY	BINARY OR MACHINE EXECUTABLE CODE*		X			X
SI-7(15)	*SOFTWARE, FIRMWARE, AND INFORMATION INTEGRITY	CODE AUTHENTICATION*		X			
SI-7(16)	*SOFTWARE, FIRMWARE, AND INFORMATION INTEGRITY	TIME LIMIT ON PROCESS EXECUTION WITHOUT SUPERVISION*		X			
SI-8	**Spam Protection**				X	X
SI-8(1)	*SPAM PROTECTION	CENTRAL MANAGEMENT*				X	X
SI-8(2)	*SPAM PROTECTION	AUTOMATIC UPDATES*				X	X
SI-8(3)	*SPAM PROTECTION	CONTINUOUS LEARNING CAPABILITY*					
SI-9	**Information Input Restrictions**	X	Incorporated into AC-2, AC-3, AC-5, AC-6.			
SI-10	**Information Input Validation**		X		X	X
SI-10(1)	*INFORMATION INPUT VALIDATION	MANUAL OVERRIDE CAPABILITY*		X			
SI-10(2)	*INFORMATION INPUT VALIDATION	REVIEW / RESOLUTION OF ERRORS*		X			
SI-10(3)	*INFORMATION INPUT VALIDATION	PREDICTABLE BEHAVIOR*		X			
SI-10(4)	*INFORMATION INPUT VALIDATION	REVIEW / TIMING INTERACTIONS*		X			
SI-10(5)	*INFORMATION INPUT VALIDATION	REVIEW / RESTRICT INPUTS TO TRUSTED SOURCES AND APPROVED FORMATS*		X			
SI-11	**Error Handling**				X	X
SI-12	**Information Handling and Retention**			X	X	X
SI-13	**Predictable Failure Prevention**		X			
SI-13(1)	*PREDICTABLE FAILURE PREVENTION	TRANSFERRING COMPONENT RESPONSIBILITIES*		X			
SI-13(2)	*PREDICTABLE FAILURE PREVENTION	TIME LIMIT ON PROCESS EXECUTION WITHOUT SUPERVISION*	X	Incorporated into SI-7(16).			
SI-13(3)	*PREDICTABLE FAILURE PREVENTION	MANUAL TRANSFER BETWEEN COMPONENTS*		X			
SI-13(4)	*PREDICTABLE FAILURE PREVENTION	STANDBY COMPONENT INSTALLATION / NOTIFICATION*		X			
SI-13(5)	*PREDICTABLE FAILURE PREVENTION	FAILOVER CAPABILITY*		X			
SI-14	**Non-Persistence**		X			
SI-14(1)	*NON-PERSISTENCE	REFRESH FROM TRUSTED SOURCES*		X			
SI-15	**Information Output Filtering**		X			
SI-16	**Memory Protection**		X		X	X
SI-17	**Fail-Safe Procedures**		X			

> **ADJUSTMENTS TO SECURITY CONTROL BASELINES**
>
> ALLOCATION OF SECURITY CONTROLS AND ASSIGNMENT OF PRIORITY SEQUENCING CODES
>
> With each revision to SP 800-53, minor adjustments may occur with the security control baselines including, for example, allocating additional controls and/or control enhancements, eliminating selected controls/enhancements, and changing sequencing priority codes (P-codes). These changes reflect: (i) the ongoing receipt and analysis of threat information; (ii) the periodic reexamination of the initial assumptions that generated the security control baselines; (iii) the desire for common security control baseline starting points for national security and non-national security systems to achieve community-wide convergence (relying subsequently on specific overlays to describe any adjustments from the common starting points); and (iv) the periodic reassessment of priority codes to appropriately balance the workload of security control implementation. Over time, as the security control catalog expands to address the continuing challenges from a dynamic and growing threat space that is increasingly sophisticated, organizations will come to rely to a much greater degree on overlays to provide the needed specialization for their security plans.

APPENDIX E

ASSURANCE AND TRUSTWORTHINESS
MEASURES OF CONFIDENCE FOR INFORMATION SYSTEMS

Security assurance is a critical aspect in determining the trustworthiness of information systems. Assurance is the measure of confidence that the security functions, features, practices, policies, procedures, mechanisms, and architecture of organizational information systems accurately mediate and enforce established security policies.[94] The objective of this appendix is:

- To encourage organizations to include assurance requirements in procurements of information systems, system components, and services;

- To encourage hardware, software, and firmware developers to employ development practices that result in more trustworthy information technology products and systems;

- To encourage organizations to identify, select, and use information technology products that have been built with appropriate levels of assurance and to employ sound systems and security engineering techniques and methods during the system development life cycle process;

- To reduce information security risk by deploying more trustworthy information technology products within critical information systems or system components; and

- To encourage developers and organizations to obtain on an ongoing basis, assurance evidence for maintaining trustworthiness of information systems.

Minimum security requirements for federal information and information systems are defined in FIPS Publication 200. These requirements can be satisfied by selecting, tailoring, implementing, and obtaining assurance evidence for the security controls in the low, moderate, or high baselines in Appendix D.[95] The baselines also include the assurance-related controls for the minimum assurance requirements that are generally applicable to federal information and information systems.[96] However, considering the current threat space and the increasing risk to organizational operations and assets, individuals, other organizations, and the Nation, posed by the advanced persistent threat (APT), organizations may choose to implement additional assurance-related controls from Appendix F. These additional controls can be selected based on the tailoring guidance provided in Section 3.2. Organizations can also consider developing high-assurance overlays for critical missions/business functions, specialized environments of operation, and/or information technologies (see Section 3.3 and Appendix I). When assurance-related controls cannot be satisfied, organizations can propose compensating controls (e.g., procedural/operational

---

[94] Section 2.6 provides an introduction to the concepts of assurance and trustworthiness and how the two concepts are related. A trustworthiness model is illustrated in Figure 3.

[95] CNSS Instruction 1253 provides security control baselines for national security systems. Therefore, the assurance-related controls in the baselines established for the national security community, if so designated, may differ from those controls designated in Tables E-1 through E-3.

[96] It is difficult to determine if a given security control baseline from Appendix D provides the assurance needed across all information technologies, users, platforms, and organizations. For example, while the use of formal methods might be appropriate in a cross-domain product, different assurance techniques might be appropriate for a complex air traffic control system or for a web server providing emergency preparedness information from the Department of Homeland Security. Still, the existing baselines do have assurance aspects that reflect the minimum assurance that is anticipated to be common across all technologies, users, platforms, and organizations.

solutions to compensate for insufficient technology-based solutions) or assume a greater degree of risk with regard to the actual security capability achieved.

The New Look for Assurance

While previous versions of Special Publication 800-53 addressed minimum assurance requirements, the focus was on higher-level, more abstract requirements applied to the low, moderate, and high baselines. This revision takes a fundamentally different approach to assurance by defining specific assurance-related security controls in Appendix F that can be implemented by organizations based on the security categorizations of their information systems—making the assurance requirements more *actionable* and providing opportunities for increasing the levels of assurance based on mission and business needs, current/projected threats, unique operating environments, or the use of new technologies. The identification of specific assurance-related controls in the low, moderate, and high baselines in easy-to-read tables (Tables E-1, E-2, E-3) helps organizations to quickly define controls necessary to satisfy minimum assurance requirements. The optional assurance-related controls in Table E-4 provide organizations with specification language to use in acquisitions targeted at the developers of information systems, system components, and information system services. The controls address specific methodologies, techniques, design, and architectural considerations as well as sound system and security engineering principles to fundamentally improve the quality of hardware, software, and firmware components that will be integrated into organizational information systems or the critical infrastructure. The designation of assurance-related controls is not intended to imply a greater level of importance for such controls. Achieving adequate security for organizational information systems requires the correct combination of both functionality- and assurance-related security controls. Only by understanding the importance of the concept of assurance and recognizing which security controls are more assurance-oriented versus functionality-oriented can organizations select the most appropriate combination of controls to protect their organizational operations and assets, individuals, other organizations, and the Nation.

The following sections provide a description of the assurance-related controls that are included in each of the security control baselines in Appendix D. The criteria for whether a security control is assurance-related or functionality-related is based on the overall characteristics of the control. In general, assurance-related controls are controls that: (i) define processes, procedures, techniques, or methodologies for designing and developing information systems and system components (i.e., hardware, software, firmware); (ii) provide supporting operational processes including improving the quality of systems/components/processes; (iii) produce security evidence from developmental or operational activities; (iv) determine security control effectiveness or risk (e.g., audit, testing, evaluation, analysis, assessment, verification, validation, monitoring); or (v) improve personnel skills, expertise, and understanding (e.g., security awareness/training, incident response training, contingency training).

Security controls may be designated as assurance-related controls even when the controls exhibit some functional characteristics or properties (e.g., SI-4, Information System Monitoring). The distinction between functionality and assurance is less important when describing the assurance-related controls in the baselines—primarily because the security controls in the three baselines after the tailoring process is applied, become part of the security plans for information systems and for organizations.[97] However, the distinction becomes more important when organizations exercise the option of selecting additional security controls to increase the level of assurance (or the degree of confidence) in the security functionality and security capability.

---

[97] Organizations are cautioned to carefully examine the assurance-related controls in the baselines during the tailoring process, including the development of overlays, to help ensure that controls are not being inadvertently eliminated that provide the measures of confidence in the security functionality needed for mission/business protection.

Minimum Assurance Requirements – Low-Impact Systems

Assurance Requirement: The organization, based on its security requirements, security policies, and needed security capabilities, has an expectation of: (i) a **limited** strength of security functionality; and (ii) a **limited** degree of confidence supported by the depth and coverage of associated security evidence, that the security functionality is complete, consistent, and correct.

Supplemental Guidance: Security functionality and assurance for low-impact systems are achieved by the implementation of security controls from the tailored low baseline in Appendix D. Assurance requirements for low-impact systems (including the information technology components that are part of those systems), align with that which is readily achievable with unmodified, commercial off-the-shelf (COTS) products and services. Due to the limited strength of functionality expected for low-impact systems, the depth/coverage of security evidence[98] produced is minimal and is not expected to be more than what is routinely provided by COTS manufacturers, vendors, and resellers. The depth/coverage evidence is further supplemented by the results of security control assessments and the ongoing monitoring of organizational information systems and environments in which the systems operate. For other than technology-based functionality, the emphasis is on a limited degree of confidence in the completeness, correctness, and consistency of procedural and/or operational security functionality (e.g., policies, procedures, physical security, and personnel security). Assurance requirements specified in the form of developmental and operational assurance controls for low-impact systems are listed in Table E-1. Organizations, through the tailoring process (including an organizational assessment of risk), may choose to add other assurance-related controls and/or control enhancements to the set included in Table E-1.

TABLE E-1: ASSURANCE-RELATED CONTROLS FOR LOW-IMPACT SYSTEMS[99]

ID	CONTROLS	ID	CONTROLS
AC	AC-1	MP	MP-1
AT	AT-1, AT-2, AT-3, AT-4	PE	PE-1, PE-6, PE-8
AU	AU-1, AU-6	PL	PL-1, PL-2, PL-4
CA	CA-1, CA-2, CA-3, CA-5, CA-6, CA-7, CA-9	PS	PS-1, PS-6, PS-7
CM	CM-1, CM-2, CM-4, CM-8	RA	RA-1, RA-3, RA-5
CP	CP-1, CP-3, CP-4	SA	SA-1, SA-2, SA-3, SA-4, SA-4(10), SA-5, SA-9
IA	IA-1	SC	SC-1, SC-39
IR	IR-1, IR-2, IR-5	SI	SI-1, SI-4, SI-5
MA	MA-1		

---

[98] NIST Special Publication 800-53A provides additional information on depth and coverage in security control assessments.

[99] The assurance-related controls in Table E-1 are a *subset* of the security controls contained in the security control baseline for low-impact systems in Appendix D. Implementing the assurance-related controls in Table E-1 (including depth/coverage security evidence from NIST Special Publication 800-53A) will satisfy the minimum assurance requirements for low-impact systems mandated by FIPS Publication 200.

Minimum Assurance Requirements – Moderate-Impact Systems

Assurance Requirement: The organization, based on its security requirements, security policies, and needed security capabilities, has an expectation of: (i) a **moderate** strength of security functionality; and (ii) a **moderate** degree of confidence supported by the depth and coverage of associated security evidence, that the security functionality is complete, consistent, and correct.

Supplemental Guidance: Security functionality and assurance for moderate-impact systems are achieved by the implementation of security controls from the tailored moderate baseline in Appendix D. Assurance requirements for moderate-impact systems (including the information technology components that are part of those systems) add to the expectations at the low-assurance level by: (i) incorporating COTS security functionality with greater strength of mechanism and capability than the strength of mechanism and capability achieved in low-impact systems; (ii) requiring perhaps, some special development; (iii) establishing more secure configuration settings; and (iv) requiring some additional assessment of the implemented capability. Due to the moderate strength of functionality expected for moderate-impact systems, the depth/coverage of security evidence[100] produced is more substantial than the minimal evidence produced for low-impact systems but still in the range of what can be provided by COTS manufacturers, vendors, and resellers. The depth/coverage evidence is further supplemented by the results of additional security control assessments and the ongoing monitoring of organizational information systems and environments of operation. For other than technology-based functionality, the emphasis is on a moderate degree of confidence in the completeness, correctness, and consistency of procedural and/or operational security functionality (e.g., policies, procedures, physical security, and personnel security). Assurance requirements in the form of developmental and operational assurance controls for moderate-impact systems are listed in Table E-2. Organizations, through the tailoring process (including an organizational assessment of risk), may choose to add other assurance-related controls and/or control enhancements to the set included in Table E-2.

TABLE E-2: ASSURANCE-RELATED CONTROLS FOR MODERATE-IMPACT SYSTEMS[101]

ID	CONTROLS	ID	CONTROLS
AC	AC-1	MP	MP-1
AT	AT-1, AT-2, **AT-2(2)**, AT-3, AT-4	PE	PE-1, PE-6, **PE-6(1)**, PE-8
AU	AU-1, AU-6, **AU-6(1)**, **AU-6(3)**, AU-7, **AU-7(1)**	PL	PL-1, PL-2, **PL-2(3)**, PL-4, **PL-4(1)**, PL-8
CA	CA-1, CA-2, **CA-2(1)**, CA-3, CA-5, CA-6, CA-7, **CA-7(1)**, CA-9	PS	PS-1, PS-6, PS-7
CM	CM-1, CM-2, **CM-2(1)**, **CM-2(3)**, **CM-2(7)**, CM-3, **CM-3(2)**, CM-4, CM-8, **CM-8(1)**, **CM-8(3)**, **CM-8(5)**	RA	RA-1, RA-3, RA-5, **RA-5(1)**, **RA-5(2)**, **RA-5(5)**
CP	CP-1, CP-3, CP-4, **CP-4(1)**	SA	SA-1, SA-2, SA-3, SA-4, **SA-4(1)**, **SA-4(2)**, **SA-4(9)**, SA-4(10), SA-5, **SA-8**, SA-9, **SA-9(2)**, SA-10, SA-11
IA	IA-1	SC	SC-1, **SC-2**, SC-39
IR	IR-1, IR-2, **IR-3**, **IR-3(2)**, IR-5	SI	SI-1, SI-4, **SI-4(2)**, **SI-4(4)**, **SI-4(5)**, SI-5, **SI-7**, **SI-7(1)**, **SI-7(7)**, SI-10, SI-16
MA	MA-1		

---

[100] NIST Special Publication 800-53A provides additional information on depth and coverage in security control assessments.

[101] The assurance-related controls in Table E-2 are a *subset* of the security controls contained in the security control baseline for moderate-impact systems in Appendix D. Implementing the assurance-related controls in Table E-2 (including depth/coverage security evidence from NIST Special Publication 800-53A) will satisfy the minimum assurance requirements for moderate-impact systems mandated by FIPS Publication 200. The **bold** text indicates the *delta* from the low baseline (i.e., the assurance-related controls added to the low baseline to produce the increased level of assurance in the moderate baseline).

Minimum Assurance Requirements – High-Impact Systems

Assurance Requirement: The organization, based on its security requirements, security policies, and needed security capabilities, has an expectation of: (i) a **high** strength of security functionality; and (ii) a **high** degree of confidence supported by the depth and coverage of associated security evidence, that the security functionality is complete, consistent, and correct.

Supplemental Guidance: Security functionality and assurance for high-impact systems are achieved by the implementation of security controls from the tailored high baseline in Appendix D. Assurance requirements for high-impact systems (including the information technology components that are part of those systems), add to the expectations at the moderate assurance level by: (i) incorporating higher-end COTS security capabilities that result from the application of commonly accepted best commercial development practices for reducing latent flaw rates, some special development, and additional assessment of the implemented capability. Due to the high strength of functionality expected for high-impact systems, the depth/coverage of security evidence[102] produced is more comprehensive than the evidence produced for moderate-impact systems. Although the evidence may still be in the range of what can be provided by COTS manufacturers, vendors, and resellers, greater assurance from independent assessment providers may be required. The depth/coverage evidence is supplemented by the results of additional security control assessments and the ongoing monitoring of organizational information systems/environments of operation. For other than technology-based functionality, there is a high degree of confidence in the completeness, correctness, and consistency of procedural and/or operational security functionality (e.g., policies, procedures, physical security, and personnel security). Assurance requirements in the form of developmental and operational assurance controls for high-impact information systems are listed in Table E-3. Organizations, through the tailoring process (including an organizational assessment of risk), may choose to add other assurance-related controls and/or control enhancements to the set included in Table E-3.

TABLE E-3: ASSURANCE-RELATED CONTROLS FOR HIGH-IMPACT SYSTEMS[103]

ID	CONTROLS	ID	CONTROLS
AC	AC-1	MP	MP-1
AT	AT-1, AT-2, AT-2(2), AT-3, AT-4	PE	PE-1, PE-6, PE-6(1), **PE-6(4)**, PE-8
AU	AU-1, AU-6, AU-6(1), AU-6(3), **AU-6(5)**, **AU-6(6)**, AU-7, AU-7(1), **AU-10**	PL	PL-1, PL-2, PL-2(3), PL-4, PL-4(1), PL-8
CA	CA-1, CA-2, CA-2(1), **CA-2(2)**, CA-3, CA-5, CA-6, CA-7, CA-7(1), **CA-8**, CA-9	PS	PS-1, PS-6, PS-7
CM	CM-1, CM-2, CM-2(1), **CM-2(2)**, CM-2(3), CM-2(7), CM-3, **CM-3(1)**, CM-3(2), CM-4, **CM-4(1)**, CM-8, CM-8(1), **CM-8(2)**, CM-8(3), **CM-8(4)**, CM-8(5)	RA	RA-1, RA-3, RA-5, RA-5(1), RA-5(2), **RA-5(4)**, RA-5(5)
CP	CP-1, CP-3, **CP-3(1)**, CP-4, CP-4(1), **CP-4(2)**	SA	SA-1, SA-2, SA-3, SA-4, SA-4(1), SA-4(2), SA-4(9), SA-4(10), SA-5, SA-8, SA-9, SA-9(2), SA-10, SA-11, **SA-12**, **SA-15**, **SA-16**, **SA-17**
IA	IA-1	SC	SC-1, SC-2, **SC-3**, **SC-7(18)**, **SC-7(21)**, **SC-24**, SC-39
IR	IR-1, IR-2, **IR-2(1)**, **IR-2(2)**, IR-3, IR-3(2), IR-5, **IR-5(1)**	SI	SI-1, SI-4, SI-4(2), SI-4(4), SI-4(5), SI-5, **SI-5(1)**, **SI-6**, SI-7, SI-7(1), **SI-7(2)**, **SI-7(5)**, SI-7(7), **SI-7(14)**, SI-10, SI-16
MA	MA-1		

---

[102] NIST Special Publication 800-53A provides additional information on depth and coverage in security control assessments.

[103] The assurance-related controls in Table E-3 are a *subset* of the security controls contained in the security control baseline for high-impact systems in Appendix D. Implementing the assurance-related controls in Table E-3 (including depth/coverage security evidence from NIST Special Publication 800-53A) will satisfy the minimum assurance requirements for high-impact systems mandated by FIPS Publication 200. The **bold** text indicates the *delta* from the moderate baseline (i.e., the assurance-related controls added to the moderate baseline to produce the increased level of assurance in the high baseline).

Security Controls to Achieve Enhanced Assurance

While the assurance-related controls allocated to the low, moderate, and high baselines in the previous sections, represent minimum assurance requirements, organizations can, over time, choose to raise the level of assurance in their information systems—increasing the level of trustworthiness accordingly. This is accomplished by adding assurance-related controls to the controls in the baselines to increase both the strength of security functionality and degree of confidence that the functionality is correct, complete, and consistent—making the functionality highly resistant to penetration, tamper, or bypass. Security functionality that is highly resistant to penetration, tamper, and bypass requires a significant work factor on the part of adversaries to compromise the confidentiality, integrity, or availability of the information system or system components where that functionality is employed.

Since high-assurance information technology products may be more costly and difficult to obtain, organizations may choose to partition their information systems into distinct subsystems to isolate the critical components and focus the high-assurance efforts on a more narrowly defined subset of information resources. Organizations that find it difficult to achieve high-assurance information technology solutions may have to rely to a greater extent on procedural or operational protections to ensure mission and business success. This includes, for example, reengineering critical mission and business processes to be less susceptible to high-end threats. Table E-4 provides additional developmental and operational activities (e.g., in the SA, SI, and CM security control families), that organizations can select to achieve an enhanced level of assurance (up to and including high assurance). The list of assurance-related controls is not intended to be exhaustive. Organizations, during the tailoring process, may choose to designate other security controls as assurance-related and add to the exemplar set in Table E-4.

TABLE E-4: SECURITY CONTROLS FOR ENHANCED ASSURANCE[104]

ID	CONTROLS	ID	CONTROLS
AC	AC-25	MP	No additional controls.
AT	AT-2(1), AT-3 (all enhancements)	PE	PE-6(2), PE-6(3)
AU	AU-6(4), AU-6(7), AU-6(8), AU-6(9), AU-6(10), AU-10 (all enhancements), AU-11(1), AU-13 (plus enhancements), AU-14 (plus enhancements)	PL	PL-8 (all enhancements), PL-9
CA	CA-2(3), CA-5(1), CA-7(3), CA-8 (all enhancements), CA-9(1)	PS	PS-6(2), PS-6(3)
CM	CM-2(6), CM-4(2), CM-8(6), CM-8(7), CM-8(8), CM-8(9)	RA	RA-5(3), RA-5(6), RA-5(8), RA-5(10), RA-6
CP	CP-3(2), CP-4(3), CP-4(4), CP-12	SA	SA-4(3), SA-4(5), SA-4(6), SA-4(7), SA-4(8), SA-9(1), SA-9(3), SA-9(4), SA-9(5), SA-10 (all enhancements), SA-11 (all enhancements), SA-12 (all enhancements), SA-13, SA-14, SA-15 (all enhancements), SA-17 (all enhancements), SA-18 (plus enhancements), SA-19 (plus enhancements), SA-20, SA-21 (plus enhancement), SA-22 (plus enhancement)
IA	No additional controls.	SC	SC-2(1), SC-3 (all enhancements), SC-6, SC-7(22), SC-11 (plus enhancement), SC-29 (plus enhancement), SC-30 (plus enhancements), SC-31 (plus enhancements), SC-32, SC-34 (plus enhancements), SC-36 (plus enhancement), SC-37 (plus enhancement), SC-38, SC-39 (all enhancements)
IR	IR-3(1)	SI	SI-4(1), SI-4(3), SI-4(7), SI-4(9), SI-4(10), SI-4(11), SI-4(12), SI-4(13), SI-4(14), SI-4(15), SI-4(16), SI-4(17), SI-4(18), SI-4(19), SI-4(20), SI-4(21), SI-4(22), SI-4(23), SI-4(24), SI-7(3), SI-7(6), SI-7(8), SI-7(9), SI-7(10), SI-7(11), SI-7(12), SI-7(13), SI-7(15), SI-7(16), SI-10 (all enhancements), SI-13 (plus enhancements), SI-14 (plus enhancement), SI-15, SI-17
MA	No additional controls.		

---

[104] The assurance-related controls in Table E-4 represent the additional security controls needed to achieve enhanced levels of assurance (i.e., the controls needed to go beyond the minimum assurance levels that are represented by the assurance-related controls in Tables E-1, E-2, and E-3). When an assurance-related control is allocated to a baseline (i.e., listed in Tables E-1, E-2, or E-3), but all of its control enhancements are in Table E-4, it is designated in the table as **Control** (*all enhancements*). When an assurance-related control and all of its control enhancements are not allocated to baselines, it is designated in the table as **Control** (*plus enhancements*). When assurance-related control enhancements from a particular control are allocated to one of the baselines, the remaining unselected control enhancements are listed individually in Table E-4.

APPENDIX F

SECURITY CONTROL CATALOG

SECURITY CONTROLS, ENHANCEMENTS, AND SUPPLEMENTAL GUIDANCE

The catalog of security controls in this appendix provides a range of safeguards and countermeasures for organizations and information systems.[105] The security controls have been designed to facilitate compliance with applicable federal laws, Executive Orders, directives, policies, regulations, standards, and guidelines.[106] The organization of the security control catalog, the structure of the security controls, and the concept of allocating security controls and control enhancements to the initial baselines in Appendix D are described in Chapter Two. The security controls in the catalog with few exceptions, have been designed to be policy- and technology-neutral. This means that security controls and control enhancements focus on the fundamental safeguards and countermeasures necessary to protect information during processing, while in storage, and during transmission. Therefore, it is beyond the scope of this publication to provide guidance on the application of security controls to specific technologies, communities of interest, environments of operation, or missions/business functions. These areas are addressed by the use of the tailoring process described in Chapter Three and the development of overlays described in Appendix I.

In the few cases where specific technologies are called out in security controls (e.g., mobile, PKI, wireless, VOIP), organizations are cautioned that the need to provide adequate security goes well beyond the requirements in a single control associated with a particular technology. Many of the needed safeguards/countermeasures are obtained from the other security controls in the catalog allocated to the initial control baselines as the starting point for the development of security plans and overlays using the tailoring process. In addition to the organization-driven development of specialized security plans and overlays, NIST Special Publications and Interagency Reports may provide guidance on recommended security controls for specific technologies and sector-specific applications (e.g., Smart Grid, healthcare, Industrial Control Systems, and mobile).

Employing a policy- and technology-neutral security control catalog has the following benefits:

- It encourages organizations to focus on the *security capabilities* required for mission/business success and the protection of information, irrespective of the information technologies that are employed in organizational information systems;

- It encourages organizations to analyze each security control for its applicability to specific technologies, environments of operation, missions/business functions, and communities of interest; and

---

[105] An online version of the catalog of security controls is also available at http://web.nvd.nist.gov/view/800-53/home.

[106] Compliance necessitates organizations executing *due diligence* with regard to information security and risk management. Information security due diligence includes using all appropriate information as part of an organization-wide risk management program to effectively use the tailoring guidance and inherent flexibility in NIST publications so that the selected security controls documented in organizational security plans meet the specific mission and business requirements of organizations. Using the risk management tools and techniques that are available to organizations is essential in developing, implementing, and maintaining the safeguards and countermeasures with the necessary and sufficient strength of mechanism to address the current threats to organizational operations and assets, individuals, other organizations, and the Nation. Employing effective risk-based processes, procedures, and technologies will help ensure that all federal information systems and organizations have the necessary resilience to support ongoing federal responsibilities, critical infrastructure applications, and continuity of government.

- It encourages organizations to specify security policies as part of the tailoring process for security controls that have variable parameters.

For example, organizations using smart phones, tablets, or other types of mobile devices would start the tailoring process by assuming that *all* security controls and control enhancements in the appropriate baseline (low, moderate, or high) are needed. The tailoring process may result in certain security controls being eliminated for a variety of reasons, including, for example, the inability of the technology to support the implementation of the control. However, the elimination of such controls without understanding the potential adverse impacts to organizational missions and business functions can significantly increase information security risk and should be carefully analyzed. This type of analysis is essential in order for organizations to make effective risk-based decisions including the selection of appropriate compensating security controls, when considering the use of these emerging mobile devices and technologies. The specialization of security plans using the tailoring guidance and overlays, together with a comprehensive set of technology- and policy-neutral security controls, promotes cost-effective, risk-based information security for organizations—in any sector, for any technology, and in any operating environment.

The security controls in the catalog are expected to change over time, as controls are withdrawn, revised, and added. In order to maintain stability in security plans and automated tools supporting the implementation of Special Publication 800-53, security controls will not be renumbered each time a control is withdrawn. Rather, notations of security controls that have been withdrawn are maintained in the catalog for historical purposes. Security controls are withdrawn for a variety of reasons including, for example: the security capability provided by the withdrawn control has been incorporated into another control; the security capability provided by the withdrawn control is redundant to an existing control; or the security control is deemed to be no longer necessary.

There may, on occasion, be repetition in requirements that appear in the security controls and control enhancements that are part of the security control catalog. This repetition in requirements is intended to reinforce the security requirements from the perspective of multiple controls and/or enhancements. For example, the requirement for strong identification and authentication when conducting remote maintenance activities appears in the MA family in the specific context of systems maintenance activities conducted by organizations. The identification and authentication requirement also appears in a more general context in the IA family. While these requirements appear to be redundant (i.e., overlapping), they are, in fact, mutually reinforcing and not intended to require additional effort on the part of organizations in the development and implementation of security programs.

Implementation Tip

New security controls and control enhancements will be developed on a regular basis using state-of-the-practice information from national-level threat and vulnerability databases as well as information on the tactics, techniques, and procedures employed by adversaries in launching cyber attacks. The proposed modifications to security controls and security control baselines will be carefully weighed during each revision cycle, considering the desire for stability of the security control catalog and the need to respond to changing threats, vulnerabilities, attack methods, and information technologies. The overall objective is to raise the basic level of information security over time. Organizations may choose to develop new security controls when there is a specific security capability required and the appropriate controls are not available in Appendices F or G.

> **SECURITY CONTROL CLASS DESIGNATIONS**
>
> MANAGEMENT, OPERATIONAL, AND TECHNICAL REFERENCES
>
> Because many security controls within the security control families in Appendix F have various combinations of *management*, *operational*, and *technical* properties, the specific class designations have been removed from the security control families. Organizations may still find it useful to apply such designations to individual security controls and control enhancements or to individual sections within a particular control/enhancement. Organizations may find it beneficial to employ class designations as a way to group or refer to security controls. The class designations may also help organizations with the process of allocating security controls and control enhancements to: (i) responsible parties or information systems (e.g., as common or hybrid controls); (ii) specific roles; and/or (iii) specific components of a system. For example, organizations may determine that the responsibility for system-specific controls they have placed in the management class belong to the information system owner, controls placed in the operational class belong to the Information System Security Officer (ISSO), and controls placed in the technical class belong to one or more system administrators. This example is provided to illustrate the potential usefulness of designating classes for controls and/or control enhancements; it is not meant to suggest or require additional tasks for organizations.

> **CAUTIONARY NOTE**
>
> *DEVELOPMENT OF SYSTEMS, COMPONENTS, AND SERVICES*
>
> With the renewed emphasis on trustworthy information systems and supply chain security, it is essential that organizations have the capability to express their information security requirements with clarity and specificity in order to engage the information technology industry and obtain the systems, components, and services necessary for mission and business success. To ensure that organizations have such capability, Special Publication 800-53 provides a set of security controls in the System and Services Acquisition family (i.e., SA family) addressing requirements for the development of information systems, information technology products, and information system services. Therefore, many of the controls in the SA family are directed at developers of those systems, components, and services. It is important for organizations to recognize that the scope of the security controls in the SA family includes all system/component/service development and the developers associated with such development whether the development is conducted by internal organizational personnel or by external developers through the contracting/acquisition process. Affected controls include SA-8, SA-10, SA-11, SA-15, SA-16, SA-17, SA-20, and SA-21.

Fundamentals of the Catalog

Security controls and control enhancements in Appendices F and G are generally designed to be policy-neutral and technology/implementation-independent. Organizations provide information about security controls and control enhancements in two ways:

- By specifying security control implementation details (e.g., platform dependencies) in the associated security plan for the information system or security program plan for the organization; and
- By establishing specific values in the variable sections of selected security controls through the use of *assignment* and *selection* statements.

Assignment and selection statements provide organizations with the capability to specialize security controls and control enhancements based on organizational security requirements or requirements originating in federal laws, Executive Orders, directives, policies, regulations, standards, or guidelines. Organization-defined parameters used in assignment and selection statements in the basic security controls apply also to all control enhancements associated with those controls. Control enhancements strengthen the fundamental security capability in the base control but are not a substitute for using assignment or selection statements to provide greater specificity to the control. Assignment statements for security controls and control enhancements do not contain minimum or maximum values (e.g., testing contingency plans *at least annually*). Organizations should consult specific federal laws, Executive Orders, directives, regulations, policies, standards, or guidelines as the definitive sources for such information. The absence of minimum and maximum values from the security controls and control enhancements does not obviate the need for organizations to comply with requirements in the controlling source publications.

The first security control in each family (i.e., the dash-1 control) generates requirements for specific policies and procedures that are needed for the effective implementation of the other security controls in the family. Therefore, individual controls and control enhancements in a particular family do not call for the development of such policies and procedures. Supplemental guidance sections of security controls and control enhancements do not contain any requirements or references to FIPS or NIST Special Publications. NIST publications are, however, included in a *references* section for each security control.

In support of the Joint Task Force initiative to develop a unified information security framework for the federal government, security controls and control enhancements for national security systems are included in this appendix. The inclusion of such controls and enhancements is not intended to impose security requirements on organizations that operate national security systems. Rather, organizations can use the security controls and control enhancements on a voluntary basis with the approval of federal officials exercising policy authority over national security systems. In addition, the security control priorities and security control baselines listed in Appendix D and in the priority and baseline allocation summary boxes below each security control in Appendix F, apply to non-national security systems *only* unless otherwise directed by the federal officials with national security policy authority.

Using the Catalog

Organizations employ security controls[107] in federal information systems and the environments in which those systems operate in accordance with FIPS Publication 199, FIPS Publication 200, and NIST Special Publications 800-37 and 800-39. Security categorization of federal information and information systems, as required by FIPS Publication 199, is the first step in the RMF.[108] Next, organizations select the appropriate security control baselines for their information systems by satisfying the minimum security requirements set forth in FIPS Publication 200. Appendix D includes three security control baselines that are associated with the designated impact levels of information systems as determined during the security categorization process.[109] After baseline selection, organizations tailor the baselines by: (i) identifying/designating common controls; (ii) applying scoping considerations; (iii) selecting compensating controls, if needed; (iv) assigning control parameter values in selection and assignment statements; (v) supplementing the baseline controls with additional controls and control enhancements from the security control catalog; and (vi) providing additional information for control implementation. Organizations can also use the baseline tailoring process with the overlay concept that is described in Section 3.2 and Appendix I. Risk assessments, as described in NIST Special Publication 800-30, guide and inform the security control selection process.[110]

CAUTIONARY NOTE

USE OF CRYPTOGRAPHY

If cryptography is required for the protection of information based on the selection of security controls in Appendix F and subsequently implemented by organizational information systems, the cryptographic mechanisms comply with applicable federal laws, Executive Orders, directives, policies, regulations, standards, and guidance. This includes, for NSA-approved cryptography to protect classified information, FIPS-validated cryptography to protect unclassified information, and NSA-approved and FIPS-compliant key management technologies and processes. Security controls SC-12 and SC-13 provide specific information on the selection of appropriate cryptographic mechanisms, including the strength of such mechanisms.

---

[107] The security controls in Special Publication 800-53 are available online and can be downloaded in various formats from the NIST web site at: http://web.nvd.nist.gov/view/800-53/home.

[108] CNSS Instruction 1253 provides guidance for *security categorization* of national security systems.

[109] CNSS Instruction 1253 provides guidance on *security control baselines* for national security systems and specific tailoring requirements associated with such systems.

[110] There are additional security controls and control enhancements that appear in the catalog that are not used in any of the initial baselines. These additional controls and control enhancements are available to organizations and can be used in the tailoring process to achieve the needed level of protection in accordance with organizational risk assessments.

FAMILY: ACCESS CONTROL

AC-1   ACCESS CONTROL POLICY AND PROCEDURES

Control: The organization:

a. Develops, documents, and disseminates to [*Assignment: organization-defined personnel or roles*]:

1. An access control policy that addresses purpose, scope, roles, responsibilities, management commitment, coordination among organizational entities, and compliance; and

2. Procedures to facilitate the implementation of the access control policy and associated access controls; and

b. Reviews and updates the current:

1. Access control policy [*Assignment: organization-defined frequency*]; and

2. Access control procedures [*Assignment: organization-defined frequency*].

Supplemental Guidance: This control addresses the establishment of policy and procedures for the effective implementation of selected security controls and control enhancements in the AC family. Policy and procedures reflect applicable federal laws, Executive Orders, directives, regulations, policies, standards, and guidance. Security program policies and procedures at the organization level may make the need for system-specific policies and procedures unnecessary. The policy can be included as part of the general information security policy for organizations or conversely, can be represented by multiple policies reflecting the complex nature of certain organizations. The procedures can be established for the security program in general and for particular information systems, if needed. The organizational risk management strategy is a key factor in establishing policy and procedures. Related control: PM-9.

Control Enhancements: None.

References: NIST Special Publications 800-12, 800-100.

Priority and Baseline Allocation:

| P1 | LOW AC-1 | MOD AC-1 | HIGH AC-1 |

AC-2   ACCOUNT MANAGEMENT

Control: The organization:

a. Identifies and selects the following types of information system accounts to support organizational missions/business functions: [*Assignment: organization-defined information system account types*];

b. Assigns account managers for information system accounts;

c. Establishes conditions for group and role membership;

d. Specifies authorized users of the information system, group and role membership, and access authorizations (i.e., privileges) and other attributes (as required) for each account;

e. Requires approvals by [*Assignment: organization-defined personnel or roles*] for requests to create information system accounts;

f. Creates, enables, modifies, disables, and removes information system accounts in accordance with [*Assignment: organization-defined procedures or conditions*];

g. Monitors the use of information system accounts;

h. Notifies account managers:

   1. When accounts are no longer required;
   2. When users are terminated or transferred; and
   3. When individual information system usage or need-to-know changes;

i. Authorizes access to the information system based on:

   1. A valid access authorization;
   2. Intended system usage; and
   3. Other attributes as required by the organization or associated missions/business functions;

j. Reviews accounts for compliance with account management requirements [*Assignment: organization-defined frequency*]; and

k. Establishes a process for reissuing shared/group account credentials (if deployed) when individuals are removed from the group.

Supplemental Guidance: Information system account types include, for example, individual, shared, group, system, guest/anonymous, emergency, developer/manufacturer/vendor, temporary, and service. Some of the account management requirements listed above can be implemented by organizational information systems. The identification of authorized users of the information system and the specification of access privileges reflects the requirements in other security controls in the security plan. Users requiring administrative privileges on information system accounts receive additional scrutiny by appropriate organizational personnel (e.g., system owner, mission/business owner, or chief information security officer) responsible for approving such accounts and privileged access. Organizations may choose to define access privileges or other attributes by account, by type of account, or a combination of both. Other attributes required for authorizing access include, for example, restrictions on time-of-day, day-of-week, and point-of-origin. In defining other account attributes, organizations consider system-related requirements (e.g., scheduled maintenance, system upgrades) and mission/business requirements, (e.g., time zone differences, customer requirements, remote access to support travel requirements). Failure to consider these factors could affect information system availability. Temporary and emergency accounts are accounts intended for short-term use. Organizations establish temporary accounts as a part of normal account activation procedures when there is a need for short-term accounts without the demand for immediacy in account activation. Organizations establish emergency accounts in response to crisis situations and with the need for rapid account activation. Therefore, emergency account activation may bypass normal account authorization processes. Emergency and temporary accounts are not to be confused with infrequently used accounts (e.g., local logon accounts used for special tasks defined by organizations or when network resources are unavailable). Such accounts remain available and are not subject to automatic disabling or removal dates. Conditions for disabling or deactivating accounts include, for example: (i) when shared/group, emergency, or temporary accounts are no longer required; or (ii) when individuals are transferred or terminated. Some types of information system accounts may require specialized training. Related controls: AC-3, AC-4, AC-5, AC-6, AC-10, AC-17, AC-19, AC-20, AU-9, IA-2, IA-4, IA-5, IA-8, CM-5, CM-6, CM-11, MA-3, MA-4, MA-5, PL-4, SC-13.

Control Enhancements:

(1) ACCOUNT MANAGEMENT | AUTOMATED SYSTEM ACCOUNT MANAGEMENT

   The organization employs automated mechanisms to support the management of information system accounts.

   Supplemental Guidance: The use of automated mechanisms can include, for example: using email or text messaging to automatically notify account managers when users are terminated or transferred; using the information system to monitor account usage; and using telephonic notification to report atypical system account usage.

(2) ACCOUNT MANAGEMENT | REMOVAL OF TEMPORARY / EMERGENCY ACCOUNTS

The information system automatically [Selection: removes; disables] temporary and emergency accounts after [Assignment: organization-defined time period for each type of account].

Supplemental Guidance: This control enhancement requires the removal of both temporary and emergency accounts automatically after a predefined period of time has elapsed, rather than at the convenience of the systems administrator.

(3) ACCOUNT MANAGEMENT | DISABLE INACTIVE ACCOUNTS

The information system automatically disables inactive accounts after [Assignment: organization-defined time period].

(4) ACCOUNT MANAGEMENT | AUTOMATED AUDIT ACTIONS

The information system automatically audits account creation, modification, enabling, disabling, and removal actions, and notifies [Assignment: organization-defined personnel or roles].

Supplemental Guidance: Related controls: AU-2, AU-12.

(5) ACCOUNT MANAGEMENT | INACTIVITY LOGOUT

The organization requires that users log out when [Assignment: organization-defined time-period of expected inactivity or description of when to log out].

Supplemental Guidance: Related control: SC-23.

(6) ACCOUNT MANAGEMENT | DYNAMIC PRIVILEGE MANAGEMENT

The information system implements the following dynamic privilege management capabilities: [Assignment: organization-defined list of dynamic privilege management capabilities].

Supplemental Guidance: In contrast to conventional access control approaches which employ static information system accounts and predefined sets of user privileges, dynamic access control approaches (e.g., service-oriented architectures) rely on run time access control decisions facilitated by dynamic privilege management. While user identities may remain relatively constant over time, user privileges may change more frequently based on ongoing mission/business requirements and operational needs of organizations. Dynamic privilege management can include, for example, the immediate revocation of privileges from users, as opposed to requiring that users terminate and restart their sessions to reflect any changes in privileges. Dynamic privilege management can also refer to mechanisms that change the privileges of users based on dynamic rules as opposed to editing specific user profiles. This type of privilege management includes, for example, automatic adjustments of privileges if users are operating out of their normal work times, or if information systems are under duress or in emergency maintenance situations. This control enhancement also includes the ancillary effects of privilege changes, for example, the potential changes to encryption keys used for communications. Dynamic privilege management can support requirements for information system resiliency. Related control: AC-16.

(7) ACCOUNT MANAGEMENT | ROLE-BASED SCHEMES

The organization:

(a) Establishes and administers privileged user accounts in accordance with a role-based access scheme that organizes allowed information system access and privileges into roles;

(b) Monitors privileged role assignments; and

(c) Takes [Assignment: organization-defined actions] when privileged role assignments are no longer appropriate.

Supplemental Guidance: Privileged roles are organization-defined roles assigned to individuals that allow those individuals to perform certain security-relevant functions that ordinary users are not authorized to perform. These privileged roles include, for example, key management, account management, network and system administration, database administration, and web administration.

(8) ACCOUNT MANAGEMENT | DYNAMIC ACCOUNT CREATION

The information system creates [Assignment: organization-defined information system accounts] dynamically.

Supplemental Guidance: Dynamic approaches for creating information system accounts (e.g., as implemented within service-oriented architectures) rely on establishing accounts (identities) at run time for entities that were previously unknown. Organizations plan for dynamic creation of information system accounts by establishing trust relationships and mechanisms with the appropriate authorities to validate related authorizations and privileges. Related control: AC-16.

(9) ACCOUNT MANAGEMENT | RESTRICTIONS ON USE OF SHARED / GROUP ACCOUNTS

The organization only permits the use of shared/group accounts that meet [*Assignment: organization-defined conditions for establishing shared/group accounts*].

(10) ACCOUNT MANAGEMENT | SHARED / GROUP ACCOUNT CREDENTIAL TERMINATION

The information system terminates shared/group account credentials when members leave the group.

(11) ACCOUNT MANAGEMENT | USAGE CONDITIONS

The information system enforces [*Assignment: organization-defined circumstances and/or usage conditions*] for [*Assignment: organization-defined information system accounts*].

Supplemental Guidance: Organizations can describe the specific conditions or circumstances under which information system accounts can be used, for example, by restricting usage to certain days of the week, time of day, or specific durations of time.

(12) ACCOUNT MANAGEMENT | ACCOUNT MONITORING / ATYPICAL USAGE

The organization:

(a) Monitors information system accounts for [*Assignment: organization-defined atypical usage*]; and

(b) Reports atypical usage of information system accounts to [*Assignment: organization-defined personnel or roles*].

Supplemental Guidance: Atypical usage includes, for example, accessing information systems at certain times of the day and from locations that are not consistent with the normal usage patterns of individuals working in organizations. Related control: CA-7.

(13) ACCOUNT MANAGEMENT | DISABLE ACCOUNTS FOR HIGH-RISK INDIVIDUALS

The organization disables accounts of users posing a significant risk within [*Assignment: organization-defined time period*] of discovery of the risk.

Supplemental Guidance: Users posing a significant risk to organizations include individuals for whom reliable evidence or intelligence indicates either the intention to use authorized access to information systems to cause harm or through whom adversaries will cause harm. Harm includes potential adverse impacts to organizational operations and assets, individuals, other organizations, or the Nation. Close coordination between authorizing officials, information system administrators, and human resource managers is essential in order for timely execution of this control enhancement. Related control: PS-4.

References: None.

Priority and Baseline Allocation:

P1	LOW AC-2	MOD AC-2 (1) (2) (3) (4)	HIGH AC-2 (1) (2) (3) (4) (5) (11) (12) (13)

AC-3 ACCESS ENFORCEMENT

Control: The information system enforces approved authorizations for logical access to information and system resources in accordance with applicable access control policies.

Supplemental Guidance: Access control policies (e.g., identity-based policies, role-based policies, control matrices, cryptography) control access between active entities or subjects (i.e., users or processes acting on behalf of users) and passive entities or objects (e.g., devices, files, records, domains) in information systems. In addition to enforcing authorized access at the information system level and recognizing that information systems can host many applications and services in support of organizational missions and business operations, access enforcement mechanisms can also be employed at the application and service level to provide increased information security.

Related controls: AC-2, AC-4, AC-5, AC-6, AC-16, AC-17, AC-18, AC-19, AC-20, AC-21, AC-22, AU-9, CM-5, CM-6, CM-11, MA-3, MA-4, MA-5, PE-3.

Control Enhancements:

(1) ACCESS ENFORCEMENT | RESTRICTED ACCESS TO PRIVILEGED FUNCTIONS

[Withdrawn: Incorporated into AC-6].

(2) ACCESS ENFORCEMENT | DUAL AUTHORIZATION

The information system enforces dual authorization for [*Assignment: organization-defined privileged commands and/or other organization-defined actions*].

Supplemental Guidance: Dual authorization mechanisms require the approval of two authorized individuals in order to execute. Organizations do not require dual authorization mechanisms when immediate responses are necessary to ensure public and environmental safety. Dual authorization may also be known as two-person control. Related controls: CP-9, MP-6.

(3) ACCESS ENFORCEMENT | MANDATORY ACCESS CONTROL

The information system enforces [*Assignment: organization-defined mandatory access control policy*] over all subjects and objects where the policy:

(a) Is uniformly enforced across all subjects and objects within the boundary of the information system;

(b) Specifies that a subject that has been granted access to information is constrained from doing any of the following;

   (1) Passing the information to unauthorized subjects or objects;

   (2) Granting its privileges to other subjects;

   (3) Changing one or more security attributes on subjects, objects, the information system, or information system components;

   (4) Choosing the security attributes and attribute values to be associated with newly created or modified objects; or

   (5) Changing the rules governing access control; and

(c) Specifies that [*Assignment: organization-defined subjects*] may explicitly be granted [*Assignment: organization-defined privileges (i.e., they are trusted subjects)*] such that they are not limited by some or all of the above constraints.

Supplemental Guidance: Mandatory access control as defined in this control enhancement is synonymous with nondiscretionary access control, and is not constrained only to certain historical uses (e.g., implementations using the Bell-LaPadula Model). The above class of mandatory access control policies constrains what actions subjects can take with information obtained from data objects for which they have already been granted access, thus preventing the subjects from passing the information to unauthorized subjects and objects. This class of mandatory access control policies also constrains what actions subjects can take with respect to the propagation of access control privileges; that is, a subject with a privilege cannot pass that privilege to other subjects. The policy is uniformly enforced over all subjects and objects to which the information system has control. Otherwise, the access control policy can be circumvented. This enforcement typically is provided via an implementation that meets the reference monitor concept (see AC-25). The policy is bounded by the information system boundary (i.e., once the information is passed outside of the control of the system, additional means may be required to ensure that the constraints on the information remain in effect). The trusted subjects described above are granted privileges consistent with the concept of least privilege (see AC-6). Trusted subjects are only given the minimum privileges relative to the above policy necessary for satisfying organizational mission/business needs. The control is most applicable when there is some policy mandate (e.g., law, Executive Order, directive, or regulation) that establishes a policy regarding access to sensitive/classified information and some users of the information system are not authorized access to all sensitive/classified information resident in the information system. This control can operate in conjunction with AC-3 (4). A subject that is constrained in its operation by policies governed by this control is still able to operate under the less rigorous constraints of AC-3 (4), but policies governed by this control take precedence over the less rigorous constraints of AC-3 (4). For example, while a mandatory access control policy imposes a constraint preventing a subject from passing information to another subject operating at a different sensitivity label, AC-3 (4) permits the subject to pass the information to any subject with the same sensitivity label as the subject. Related controls: AC-25, SC-11.

(4) ACCESS ENFORCEMENT | DISCRETIONARY ACCESS CONTROL

The information system enforces [*Assignment: organization-defined discretionary access control policy*] over defined subjects and objects where the policy specifies that a subject that has been granted access to information can do one or more of the following:

(a) Pass the information to any other subjects or objects;

(b) Grant its privileges to other subjects;

(c) Change security attributes on subjects, objects, the information system, or the information system's components;

(d) Choose the security attributes to be associated with newly created or revised objects; or

(e) Change the rules governing access control.

Supplemental Guidance: When discretionary access control policies are implemented, subjects are not constrained with regard to what actions they can take with information for which they have already been granted access. Thus, subjects that have been granted access to information are not prevented from passing (i.e., the subjects have the discretion to pass) the information to other subjects or objects. This control enhancement can operate in conjunction with AC-3 (3). A subject that is constrained in its operation by policies governed by AC-3 (3) is still able to operate under the less rigorous constraints of this control enhancement. Thus, while AC-3 (3) imposes constraints preventing a subject from passing information to another subject operating at a different sensitivity level, AC-3 (4) permits the subject to pass the information to any subject at the same sensitivity level. The policy is bounded by the information system boundary. Once the information is passed outside of the control of the information system, additional means may be required to ensure that the constraints remain in effect. While the older, more traditional definitions of discretionary access control require identity-based access control, that limitation is not required for this use of discretionary access control.

(5) ACCESS ENFORCEMENT | SECURITY-RELEVANT INFORMATION

The information system prevents access to [*Assignment: organization-defined security-relevant information*] except during secure, non-operable system states.

Supplemental Guidance: Security-relevant information is any information within information systems that can potentially impact the operation of security functions or the provision of security services in a manner that could result in failure to enforce system security policies or maintain the isolation of code and data. Security-relevant information includes, for example, filtering rules for routers/firewalls, cryptographic key management information, configuration parameters for security services, and access control lists. Secure, non-operable system states include the times in which information systems are not performing mission/business-related processing (e.g., the system is off-line for maintenance, troubleshooting, boot-up, shut down). Related control: CM-3.

(6) ACCESS ENFORCEMENT | PROTECTION OF USER AND SYSTEM INFORMATION

[Withdrawn: Incorporated into MP-4 and SC-28].

(7) ACCESS ENFORCEMENT | ROLE-BASED ACCESS CONTROL

The information system enforces a role-based access control policy over defined subjects and objects and controls access based upon [*Assignment: organization-defined roles and users authorized to assume such roles*].

Supplemental Guidance: Role-based access control (RBAC) is an access control policy that restricts information system access to authorized users. Organizations can create specific roles based on job functions and the authorizations (i.e., privileges) to perform needed operations on organizational information systems associated with the organization-defined roles. When users are assigned to the organizational roles, they inherit the authorizations or privileges defined for those roles. RBAC simplifies privilege administration for organizations because privileges are not assigned directly to every user (which can be a significant number of individuals for mid- to large-size organizations) but are instead acquired through role assignments. RBAC can be implemented either as a mandatory or discretionary form of access control. For organizations implementing RBAC with mandatory access controls, the requirements in AC-3 (3) define the scope of the subjects and objects covered by the policy.

(8) ACCESS ENFORCEMENT | REVOCATION OF ACCESS AUTHORIZATIONS

The information system enforces the revocation of access authorizations resulting from changes to the security attributes of subjects and objects based on [*Assignment: organization-defined rules governing the timing of revocations of access authorizations*].

Supplemental Guidance: Revocation of access rules may differ based on the types of access revoked. For example, if a subject (i.e., user or process) is removed from a group, access may not be revoked until the next time the object (e.g., file) is opened or until the next time the subject attempts a new access to the object. Revocation based on changes to security labels may take effect immediately. Organizations can provide alternative approaches on how to make revocations immediate if information systems cannot provide such capability and immediate revocation is necessary.

(9) ACCESS ENFORCEMENT | CONTROLLED RELEASE

The information system does not release information outside of the established system boundary unless:

(a) **The receiving [*Assignment: organization-defined information system or system component*] provides [*Assignment: organization-defined security safeguards*]; and**

(b) **[*Assignment: organization-defined security safeguards*] are used to validate the appropriateness of the information designated for release.**

Supplemental Guidance: Information systems can only protect organizational information within the confines of established system boundaries. Additional security safeguards may be needed to ensure that such information is adequately protected once it is passed beyond the established information system boundaries. Examples of information leaving the system boundary include transmitting information to an external information system or printing the information on one of its printers. In cases where the information system is unable to make a determination of the adequacy of the protections provided by entities outside its boundary, as a mitigating control, organizations determine procedurally whether the external information systems are providing adequate security. The means used to determine the adequacy of the security provided by external information systems include, for example, conducting inspections or periodic testing, establishing agreements between the organization and its counterpart organizations, or some other process. The means used by external entities to protect the information received need not be the same as those used by the organization, but the means employed are sufficient to provide consistent adjudication of the security policy to protect the information. This control enhancement requires information systems to employ technical or procedural means to validate the information prior to releasing it to external systems. For example, if the information system passes information to another system controlled by another organization, technical means are employed to validate that the security attributes associated with the exported information are appropriate for the receiving system. Alternatively, if the information system passes information to a printer in organization-controlled space, procedural means can be employed to ensure that only appropriately authorized individuals gain access to the printer. This control enhancement is most applicable when there is some policy mandate (e.g., law, Executive Order, directive, or regulation) that establishes policy regarding access to the information, and that policy applies beyond the realm of a particular information system or organization.

(10) ACCESS ENFORCEMENT | AUDITED OVERRIDE OF ACCESS CONTROL MECHANISMS

The organization employs an audited override of automated access control mechanisms under [*Assignment: organization-defined conditions*].

Supplemental Guidance: Related controls: AU-2, AU-6.

References: None.

Priority and Baseline Allocation:

| P1 | LOW AC-3 | MOD AC-3 | HIGH AC-3 |

AC-4 **INFORMATION FLOW ENFORCEMENT**

Control: The information system enforces approved authorizations for controlling the flow of information within the system and between interconnected systems based on [*Assignment: organization-defined information flow control policies*].

Supplemental Guidance: Information flow control regulates where information is allowed to travel within an information system and between information systems (as opposed to who is allowed to access the information) and without explicit regard to subsequent accesses to that information. Flow control restrictions include, for example, keeping export-controlled information from being transmitted in the clear to the Internet, blocking outside traffic that claims to be from within the organization, restricting web requests to the Internet that are not from the internal web proxy server, and limiting information transfers between organizations based on data structures and content. Transferring information between information systems representing different security domains with different security policies introduces risk that such transfers violate one or more domain security policies. In such situations, information owners/stewards provide guidance at designated policy enforcement points between interconnected systems. Organizations consider mandating specific architectural solutions when required to enforce specific security policies. Enforcement includes, for example: (i) prohibiting information transfers between interconnected systems (i.e., allowing access only); (ii) employing hardware mechanisms to enforce one-way information flows; and (iii) implementing trustworthy regrading mechanisms to reassign security attributes and security labels.

Organizations commonly employ information flow control policies and enforcement mechanisms to control the flow of information between designated sources and destinations (e.g., networks, individuals, and devices) within information systems and between interconnected systems. Flow control is based on the characteristics of the information and/or the information path. Enforcement occurs, for example, in boundary protection devices (e.g., gateways, routers, guards, encrypted tunnels, firewalls) that employ rule sets or establish configuration settings that restrict information system services, provide a packet-filtering capability based on header information, or message-filtering capability based on message content (e.g., implementing key word searches or using document characteristics). Organizations also consider the trustworthiness of filtering/inspection mechanisms (i.e., hardware, firmware, and software components) that are critical to information flow enforcement. Control enhancements 3 through 22 primarily address cross-domain solution needs which focus on more advanced filtering techniques, in-depth analysis, and stronger flow enforcement mechanisms implemented in cross-domain products, for example, high-assurance guards. Such capabilities are generally not available in commercial off-the-shelf information technology products. Related controls: AC-3, AC-17, AC-19, AC-21, CM-6, CM-7, SA-8, SC-2, SC-5, SC-7, SC-18.

Control Enhancements:

(1) *INFORMATION FLOW ENFORCEMENT | OBJECT SECURITY ATTRIBUTES*

   The information system uses [*Assignment: organization-defined security attributes*] associated with [*Assignment: organization-defined information, source, and destination objects*] to enforce [*Assignment: organization-defined information flow control policies*] as a basis for flow control decisions.

   Supplemental Guidance: Information flow enforcement mechanisms compare security attributes associated with information (data content and data structure) and source/destination objects, and respond appropriately (e.g., block, quarantine, alert administrator) when the mechanisms encounter information flows not explicitly allowed by information flow policies. For example, an information object labeled *Secret* would be allowed to flow to a destination object labeled *Secret*, but an information object labeled *Top Secret* would not be allowed to flow to a destination object labeled *Secret*. Security attributes can also include, for example, source and destination addresses employed in traffic filter firewalls. Flow enforcement using explicit security attributes can be used, for example, to control the release of certain types of information. Related control: AC-16.

(2) INFORMATION FLOW ENFORCEMENT | PROCESSING DOMAINS

The information system uses protected processing domains to enforce [*Assignment: organization-defined information flow control policies*] as a basis for flow control decisions.

Supplemental Guidance: Within information systems, protected processing domains are processing spaces that have controlled interactions with other processing spaces, thus enabling control of information flows between these spaces and to/from data/information objects. A protected processing domain can be provided, for example, by implementing domain and type enforcement. In domain and type enforcement, information system processes are assigned to domains; information is identified by types; and information flows are controlled based on allowed information accesses (determined by domain and type), allowed signaling among domains, and allowed process transitions to other domains.

(3) INFORMATION FLOW ENFORCEMENT | DYNAMIC INFORMATION FLOW CONTROL

The information system enforces dynamic information flow control based on [*Assignment: organization-defined policies*].

Supplemental Guidance: Organizational policies regarding dynamic information flow control include, for example, allowing or disallowing information flows based on changing conditions or mission/operational considerations. Changing conditions include, for example, changes in organizational risk tolerance due to changes in the immediacy of mission/business needs, changes in the threat environment, and detection of potentially harmful or adverse events. Related control: SI-4.

(4) INFORMATION FLOW ENFORCEMENT | CONTENT CHECK ENCRYPTED INFORMATION

The information system prevents encrypted information from bypassing content-checking mechanisms by [*Selection (one or more): decrypting the information; blocking the flow of the encrypted information; terminating communications sessions attempting to pass encrypted information; [Assignment: organization-defined procedure or method*]].

Supplemental Guidance: Related control: SI-4.

(5) INFORMATION FLOW ENFORCEMENT | EMBEDDED DATA TYPES

The information system enforces [*Assignment: organization-defined limitations*] on embedding data types within other data types.

Supplemental Guidance: Embedding data types within other data types may result in reduced flow control effectiveness. Data type embedding includes, for example, inserting executable files as objects within word processing files, inserting references or descriptive information into a media file, and compressed or archived data types that may include multiple embedded data types. Limitations on data type embedding consider the levels of embedding and prohibit levels of data type embedding that are beyond the capability of the inspection tools.

(6) INFORMATION FLOW ENFORCEMENT | METADATA

The information system enforces information flow control based on [*Assignment: organization-defined metadata*].

Supplemental Guidance: Metadata is information used to describe the characteristics of data. Metadata can include structural metadata describing data structures (e.g., data format, syntax, and semantics) or descriptive metadata describing data contents (e.g., age, location, telephone number). Enforcing allowed information flows based on metadata enables simpler and more effective flow control. Organizations consider the trustworthiness of metadata with regard to data accuracy (i.e., knowledge that the metadata values are correct with respect to the data), data integrity (i.e., protecting against unauthorized changes to metadata tags), and the binding of metadata to the data payload (i.e., ensuring sufficiently strong binding techniques with appropriate levels of assurance). Related controls: AC-16, SI-7.

(7) INFORMATION FLOW ENFORCEMENT | ONE-WAY FLOW MECHANISMS

The information system enforces [*Assignment: organization-defined one-way information flows*] using hardware mechanisms.

(8) *INFORMATION FLOW ENFORCEMENT | SECURITY POLICY FILTERS*

The information system enforces information flow control using [*Assignment: organization-defined security policy filters*] as a basis for flow control decisions for [*Assignment: organization-defined information flows*].

Supplemental Guidance: Organization-defined security policy filters can address data structures and content. For example, security policy filters for data structures can check for maximum file lengths, maximum field sizes, and data/file types (for structured and unstructured data). Security policy filters for data content can check for specific words (e.g., dirty/clean word filters), enumerated values or data value ranges, and hidden content. Structured data permits the interpretation of data content by applications. Unstructured data typically refers to digital information without a particular data structure or with a data structure that does not facilitate the development of rule sets to address the particular sensitivity of the information conveyed by the data or the associated flow enforcement decisions. Unstructured data consists of: (i) bitmap objects that are inherently non language-based (i.e., image, video, or audio files); and (ii) textual objects that are based on written or printed languages (e.g., commercial off-the-shelf word processing documents, spreadsheets, or emails). Organizations can implement more than one security policy filter to meet information flow control objectives (e.g., employing clean word lists in conjunction with dirty word lists may help to reduce false positives).

(9) *INFORMATION FLOW ENFORCEMENT | HUMAN REVIEWS*

The information system enforces the use of human reviews for [*Assignment: organization-defined information flows*] under the following conditions: [*Assignment: organization-defined conditions*].

Supplemental Guidance: Organizations define security policy filters for all situations where automated flow control decisions are possible. When a fully automated flow control decision is not possible, then a human review may be employed in lieu of, or as a complement to, automated security policy filtering. Human reviews may also be employed as deemed necessary by organizations.

(10) *INFORMATION FLOW ENFORCEMENT | ENABLE / DISABLE SECURITY POLICY FILTERS*

The information system provides the capability for privileged administrators to enable/disable [*Assignment: organization-defined security policy filters*] under the following conditions: [*Assignment: organization-defined conditions*].

Supplemental Guidance: For example, as allowed by the information system authorization, administrators can enable security policy filters to accommodate approved data types.

(11) *INFORMATION FLOW ENFORCEMENT | CONFIGURATION OF SECURITY POLICY FILTERS*

The information system provides the capability for privileged administrators to configure [*Assignment: organization-defined security policy filters*] to support different security policies.

Supplemental Guidance: For example, to reflect changes in security policies, administrators can change the list of "dirty words" that security policy mechanisms check in accordance with the definitions provided by organizations.

(12) *INFORMATION FLOW ENFORCEMENT | DATA TYPE IDENTIFIERS*

The information system, when transferring information between different security domains, uses [*Assignment: organization-defined data type identifiers*] to validate data essential for information flow decisions.

Supplemental Guidance: Data type identifiers include, for example, filenames, file types, file signatures/tokens, and multiple internal file signatures/tokens. Information systems may allow transfer of data only if compliant with data type format specifications.

(13) *INFORMATION FLOW ENFORCEMENT | DECOMPOSITION INTO POLICY-RELEVANT SUBCOMPONENTS*

The information system, when transferring information between different security domains, decomposes information into [*Assignment: organization-defined policy-relevant subcomponents*] for submission to policy enforcement mechanisms.

Supplemental Guidance: Policy enforcement mechanisms apply filtering, inspection, and/or sanitization rules to the policy-relevant subcomponents of information to facilitate flow enforcement prior to transferring such information to different security domains. Parsing transfer files facilitates policy decisions on source, destination, certificates, classification, attachments, and other security-related component differentiators.

(14) *INFORMATION FLOW ENFORCEMENT | SECURITY POLICY FILTER CONSTRAINTS*

The information system, when transferring information between different security domains, implements [*Assignment: organization-defined security policy filters*] requiring fully enumerated formats that restrict data structure and content.

Supplemental Guidance: Data structure and content restrictions reduce the range of potential malicious and/or unsanctioned content in cross-domain transactions. Security policy filters that restrict data structures include, for example, restricting file sizes and field lengths. Data content policy filters include, for example: (i) encoding formats for character sets (e.g., Universal Character Set Transformation Formats, American Standard Code for Information Interchange); (ii) restricting character data fields to only contain alpha-numeric characters; (iii) prohibiting special characters; and (iv) validating schema structures.

(15) *INFORMATION FLOW ENFORCEMENT | DETECTION OF UNSANCTIONED INFORMATION*

The information system, when transferring information between different security domains, examines the information for the presence of [*Assignment: organized-defined unsanctioned information*] and prohibits the transfer of such information in accordance with the [*Assignment: organization-defined security policy*].

Supplemental Guidance: Detection of unsanctioned information includes, for example, checking all information to be transferred for malicious code and dirty words. Related control: SI-3.

(16) *INFORMATION FLOW ENFORCEMENT | INFORMATION TRANSFERS ON INTERCONNECTED SYSTEMS*

[Withdrawn: Incorporated into AC-4].

(17) *INFORMATION FLOW ENFORCEMENT | DOMAIN AUTHENTICATION*

The information system uniquely identifies and authenticates source and destination points by [*Selection (one or more): organization, system, application, individual*] for information transfer.

Supplemental Guidance: Attribution is a critical component of a security concept of operations. The ability to identify source and destination points for information flowing in information systems, allows the forensic reconstruction of events when required, and encourages policy compliance by attributing policy violations to specific organizations/individuals. Successful domain authentication requires that information system labels distinguish among systems, organizations, and individuals involved in preparing, sending, receiving, or disseminating information. Related controls: IA-2, IA-3, IA-4, IA-5.

(18) *INFORMATION FLOW ENFORCEMENT | SECURITY ATTRIBUTE BINDING*

The information system binds security attributes to information using [*Assignment: organization-defined binding techniques*] to facilitate information flow policy enforcement.

Supplemental Guidance: Binding techniques implemented by information systems affect the strength of security attribute binding to information. Binding strength and the assurance associated with binding techniques play an important part in the trust organizations have in the information flow enforcement process. The binding techniques affect the number and degree of additional reviews required by organizations. Related controls: AC-16, SC-16.

(19) *INFORMATION FLOW ENFORCEMENT | VALIDATION OF METADATA*

The information system, when transferring information between different security domains, applies the same security policy filtering to metadata as it applies to data payloads.

Supplemental Guidance: This control enhancement requires the validation of metadata and the data to which the metadata applies. Some organizations distinguish between metadata and data payloads (i.e., only the data to which the metadata is bound). Other organizations do not make such distinctions, considering metadata and the data to which the metadata applies as part of the payload. All information (including metadata and the data to which the metadata applies) is subject to filtering and inspection.

(20) *INFORMATION FLOW ENFORCEMENT | APPROVED SOLUTIONS*

The organization employs [*Assignment: organization-defined solutions in approved configurations*] to control the flow of [*Assignment: organization-defined information*] across security domains.

Supplemental Guidance: Organizations define approved solutions and configurations in cross-domain policies and guidance in accordance with the types of information flows across classification boundaries. The Unified Cross Domain Management Office (UCDMO) provides a baseline listing of approved cross-domain solutions.

(21) INFORMATION FLOW ENFORCEMENT | PHYSICAL / LOGICAL SEPARATION OF INFORMATION FLOWS

The information system separates information flows logically or physically using [*Assignment: organization-defined mechanisms and/or techniques*] to accomplish [*Assignment: organization-defined required separations by types of information*].

Supplemental Guidance: Enforcing the separation of information flows by type can enhance protection by ensuring that information is not commingled while in transit and by enabling flow control by transmission paths perhaps not otherwise achievable. Types of separable information include, for example, inbound and outbound communications traffic, service requests and responses, and information of differing security categories.

(22) INFORMATION FLOW ENFORCEMENT | ACCESS ONLY

The information system provides access from a single device to computing platforms, applications, or data residing on multiple different security domains, while preventing any information flow between the different security domains.

Supplemental Guidance: The information system, for example, provides a desktop for users to access each connected security domain without providing any mechanisms to allow transfer of information between the different security domains.

References: None.

Priority and Baseline Allocation:

| P1 | LOW Not Selected | MOD AC-4 | HIGH AC-4 |

AC-5 SEPARATION OF DUTIES

Control: The organization:

a. Separates [*Assignment: organization-defined duties of individuals*];

b. Documents separation of duties of individuals; and

c. Defines information system access authorizations to support separation of duties.

Supplemental Guidance: Separation of duties addresses the potential for abuse of authorized privileges and helps to reduce the risk of malevolent activity without collusion. Separation of duties includes, for example: (i) dividing mission functions and information system support functions among different individuals and/or roles; (ii) conducting information system support functions with different individuals (e.g., system management, programming, configuration management, quality assurance and testing, and network security); and (iii) ensuring security personnel administering access control functions do not also administer audit functions. Related controls: AC-3, AC-6, PE-3, PE-4, PS-2.

Control Enhancements: None.

References: None.

Priority and Baseline Allocation:

| P1 | LOW Not Selected | MOD AC-5 | HIGH AC-5 |

AC-6 LEAST PRIVILEGE

Control: The organization employs the principle of least privilege, allowing only authorized accesses for users (or processes acting on behalf of users) which are necessary to accomplish assigned tasks in accordance with organizational missions and business functions.

Supplemental Guidance: Organizations employ least privilege for specific duties and information systems. The principle of least privilege is also applied to information system processes, ensuring that the processes operate at privilege levels no higher than necessary to accomplish required organizational missions/business functions. Organizations consider the creation of additional processes, roles, and information system accounts as necessary, to achieve least privilege. Organizations also apply least privilege to the development, implementation, and operation of organizational information systems. Related controls: AC-2, AC-3, AC-5, CM-6, CM-7, PL-2.

Control Enhancements:

(1) LEAST PRIVILEGE | AUTHORIZE ACCESS TO SECURITY FUNCTIONS

The organization explicitly authorizes access to [Assignment: organization-defined security functions (deployed in hardware, software, and firmware) and security-relevant information].

Supplemental Guidance: Security functions include, for example, establishing system accounts, configuring access authorizations (i.e., permissions, privileges), setting events to be audited, and setting intrusion detection parameters. Security-relevant information includes, for example, filtering rules for routers/firewalls, cryptographic key management information, configuration parameters for security services, and access control lists. Explicitly authorized personnel include, for example, security administrators, system and network administrators, system security officers, system maintenance personnel, system programmers, and other privileged users. Related controls: AC-17, AC-18, AC-19.

(2) LEAST PRIVILEGE | NON-PRIVILEGED ACCESS FOR NONSECURITY FUNCTIONS

The organization requires that users of information system accounts, or roles, with access to [Assignment: organization-defined security functions or security-relevant information], use non-privileged accounts or roles, when accessing nonsecurity functions.

Supplemental Guidance: This control enhancement limits exposure when operating from within privileged accounts or roles. The inclusion of roles addresses situations where organizations implement access control policies such as role-based access control and where a change of role provides the same degree of assurance in the change of access authorizations for both the user and all processes acting on behalf of the user as would be provided by a change between a privileged and non-privileged account. Related control: PL-4.

(3) LEAST PRIVILEGE | NETWORK ACCESS TO PRIVILEGED COMMANDS

The organization authorizes network access to [Assignment: organization-defined privileged commands] only for [Assignment: organization-defined compelling operational needs] and documents the rationale for such access in the security plan for the information system.

Supplemental Guidance: Network access is any access across a network connection in lieu of local access (i.e., user being physically present at the device). Related control: AC-17.

(4) LEAST PRIVILEGE | SEPARATE PROCESSING DOMAINS

The information system provides separate processing domains to enable finer-grained allocation of user privileges.

Supplemental Guidance: Providing separate processing domains for finer-grained allocation of user privileges includes, for example: (i) using virtualization techniques to allow additional privileges within a virtual machine while restricting privileges to other virtual machines or to the underlying actual machine; (ii) employing hardware and/or software domain separation mechanisms; and (iii) implementing separate physical domains. Related controls: AC-4, SC-3, SC-30, SC-32.

(5) LEAST PRIVILEGE | PRIVILEGED ACCOUNTS

The organization restricts privileged accounts on the information system to [Assignment: organization-defined personnel or roles].

Supplemental Guidance: Privileged accounts, including super user accounts, are typically described as system administrator for various types of commercial off-the-shelf operating systems. Restricting privileged accounts to specific personnel or roles prevents day-to-day users from having access to privileged information/functions. Organizations may differentiate in the application of this control enhancement between allowed privileges for local accounts and for domain accounts provided organizations retain the ability to control information system configurations for key security parameters and as otherwise necessary to sufficiently mitigate risk. Related control: CM-6.

(6) LEAST PRIVILEGE | PRIVILEGED ACCESS BY NON-ORGANIZATIONAL USERS

The organization prohibits privileged access to the information system by non-organizational users.

Supplemental Guidance: Related control: IA-8.

(7) LEAST PRIVILEGE | REVIEW OF USER PRIVILEGES

The organization:

(a) Reviews [*Assignment: organization-defined frequency*] the privileges assigned to [*Assignment: organization-defined roles or classes of users*] to validate the need for such privileges; and

(b) Reassigns or removes privileges, if necessary, to correctly reflect organizational mission/business needs.

Supplemental Guidance: The need for certain assigned user privileges may change over time reflecting changes in organizational missions/business function, environments of operation, technologies, or threat. Periodic review of assigned user privileges is necessary to determine if the rationale for assigning such privileges remains valid. If the need cannot be revalidated, organizations take appropriate corrective actions. Related control: CA-7.

(8) LEAST PRIVILEGE | PRIVILEGE LEVELS FOR CODE EXECUTION

The information system prevents [*Assignment: organization-defined software*] from executing at higher privilege levels than users executing the software.

Supplemental Guidance: In certain situations, software applications/programs need to execute with elevated privileges to perform required functions. However, if the privileges required for execution are at a higher level than the privileges assigned to organizational users invoking such applications/programs, those users are indirectly provided with greater privileges than assigned by organizations.

(9) LEAST PRIVILEGE | AUDITING USE OF PRIVILEGED FUNCTIONS

The information system audits the execution of privileged functions.

Supplemental Guidance: Misuse of privileged functions, either intentionally or unintentionally by authorized users, or by unauthorized external entities that have compromised information system accounts, is a serious and ongoing concern and can have significant adverse impacts on organizations. Auditing the use of privileged functions is one way to detect such misuse, and in doing so, help mitigate the risk from insider threats and the advanced persistent threat (APT). Related control: AU-2.

(10) LEAST PRIVILEGE | PROHIBIT NON-PRIVILEGED USERS FROM EXECUTING PRIVILEGED FUNCTIONS

The information system prevents non-privileged users from executing privileged functions to include disabling, circumventing, or altering implemented security safeguards/countermeasures.

Supplemental Guidance: Privileged functions include, for example, establishing information system accounts, performing system integrity checks, or administering cryptographic key management activities. Non-privileged users are individuals that do not possess appropriate authorizations. Circumventing intrusion detection and prevention mechanisms or malicious code protection mechanisms are examples of privileged functions that require protection from non-privileged users.

References: None.

Priority and Baseline Allocation:

| P1 | LOW Not Selected | MOD AC-6 (1) (2) (5) (9) (10) | HIGH AC-6 (1) (2) (3) (5) (9) (10) |

AC-7 UNSUCCESSFUL LOGON ATTEMPTS

Control: The information system:

a. Enforces a limit of [*Assignment: organization-defined number*] consecutive invalid logon attempts by a user during a [*Assignment: organization-defined time period*]; and

b. Automatically [*Selection: locks the account/node for an [Assignment: organization-defined time period]; locks the account/node until released by an administrator; delays next logon prompt according to [Assignment: organization-defined delay algorithm]*] when the maximum number of unsuccessful attempts is exceeded.

Supplemental Guidance: This control applies regardless of whether the logon occurs via a local or network connection. Due to the potential for denial of service, automatic lockouts initiated by information systems are usually temporary and automatically release after a predetermined time period established by organizations. If a delay algorithm is selected, organizations may choose to employ different algorithms for different information system components based on the capabilities of those components. Responses to unsuccessful logon attempts may be implemented at both the operating system and the application levels. Related controls: AC-2, AC-9, AC-14, IA-5.

Control Enhancements:

(1) UNSUCCESSFUL LOGON ATTEMPTS | AUTOMATIC ACCOUNT LOCK

[Withdrawn: Incorporated into AC-7].

(2) UNSUCCESSFUL LOGON ATTEMPTS | PURGE / WIPE MOBILE DEVICE

The information system purges/wipes information from [*Assignment: organization-defined mobile devices*] based on [*Assignment: organization-defined purging/wiping requirements/techniques*] after [*Assignment: organization-defined number*] consecutive, unsuccessful device logon attempts.

Supplemental Guidance: This control enhancement applies only to mobile devices for which a logon occurs (e.g., personal digital assistants, smart phones, tablets). The logon is to the mobile device, not to any one account on the device. Therefore, successful logons to any accounts on mobile devices reset the unsuccessful logon count to zero. Organizations define information to be purged/wiped carefully in order to avoid over purging/wiping which may result in devices becoming unusable. Purging/wiping may be unnecessary if the information on the device is protected with sufficiently strong encryption mechanisms. Related controls: AC-19, MP-5, MP-6, SC-13.

References: None.

Priority and Baseline Allocation:

| P2 | LOW AC-7 | MOD AC-7 | HIGH AC-7 |

AC-8 SYSTEM USE NOTIFICATION

Control: The information system:

a. Displays to users [*Assignment: organization-defined system use notification message or banner*] before granting access to the system that provides privacy and security notices consistent with applicable federal laws, Executive Orders, directives, policies, regulations, standards, and guidance and states that:

1. Users are accessing a U.S. Government information system;

2. Information system usage may be monitored, recorded, and subject to audit;

3. Unauthorized use of the information system is prohibited and subject to criminal and civil penalties; and

4. Use of the information system indicates consent to monitoring and recording;

b. Retains the notification message or banner on the screen until users acknowledge the usage conditions and take explicit actions to log on to or further access the information system; and

c. For publicly accessible systems:

1. Displays system use information [*Assignment: organization-defined conditions*], before granting further access;

2. Displays references, if any, to monitoring, recording, or auditing that are consistent with privacy accommodations for such systems that generally prohibit those activities; and

3. Includes a description of the authorized uses of the system.

Supplemental Guidance: System use notifications can be implemented using messages or warning banners displayed before individuals log in to information systems. System use notifications are used only for access via logon interfaces with human users and are not required when such human interfaces do not exist. Organizations consider system use notification messages/banners displayed in multiple languages based on specific organizational needs and the demographics of information system users. Organizations also consult with the Office of the General Counsel for legal review and approval of warning banner content.

Control Enhancements: None.

References: None.

Priority and Baseline Allocation:

P1	LOW AC-8	MOD AC-8	HIGH AC-8

AC-9 PREVIOUS LOGON (ACCESS) NOTIFICATION

Control: The information system notifies the user, upon successful logon (access) to the system, of the date and time of the last logon (access).

Supplemental Guidance: This control is applicable to logons to information systems via human user interfaces and logons to systems that occur in other types of architectures (e.g., service-oriented architectures). Related controls: AC-7, PL-4.

Control Enhancements:

(1) PREVIOUS LOGON NOTIFICATION | UNSUCCESSFUL LOGONS

The information system notifies the user, upon successful logon/access, of the number of unsuccessful logon/access attempts since the last successful logon/access.

(2) PREVIOUS LOGON NOTIFICATION | SUCCESSFUL / UNSUCCESSFUL LOGONS

The information system notifies the user of the number of [*Selection: successful logons/accesses; unsuccessful logon/access attempts; both*] during [*Assignment: organization-defined time period*].

(3) PREVIOUS LOGON NOTIFICATION | NOTIFICATION OF ACCOUNT CHANGES

The information system notifies the user of changes to [*Assignment: organization-defined security-related characteristics/parameters of the user's account*] during [*Assignment: organization-defined time period*].

(4) PREVIOUS LOGON NOTIFICATION | ADDITIONAL LOGON INFORMATION

The information system notifies the user, upon successful logon (access), of the following additional information: [*Assignment: organization-defined information to be included in addition to the date and time of the last logon (access)*].

Supplemental Guidance: This control enhancement permits organizations to specify additional information to be provided to users upon logon including, for example, the location of last logon. User location is defined as that information which can be determined by information systems, for example, IP addresses from which network logons occurred, device identifiers, or notifications of local logons.

References: None.

Priority and Baseline Allocation:

| P0 | LOW Not Selected | MOD Not Selected | HIGH Not Selected |

AC-10 CONCURRENT SESSION CONTROL

Control: The information system limits the number of concurrent sessions for each [*Assignment: organization-defined account and/or account type*] to [*Assignment: organization-defined number*].

Supplemental Guidance: Organizations may define the maximum number of concurrent sessions for information system accounts globally, by account type (e.g., privileged user, non-privileged user, domain, specific application), by account, or a combination. For example, organizations may limit the number of concurrent sessions for system administrators or individuals working in particularly sensitive domains or mission-critical applications. This control addresses concurrent sessions for information system accounts and does not address concurrent sessions by single users via multiple system accounts.

Control Enhancements: None.

References: None.

Priority and Baseline Allocation:

| P3 | LOW Not Selected | MOD Not Selected | HIGH AC-10 |

AC-11 SESSION LOCK

Control: The information system:

a. Prevents further access to the system by initiating a session lock after [*Assignment: organization-defined time period*] of inactivity or upon receiving a request from a user; and

b. Retains the session lock until the user reestablishes access using established identification and authentication procedures.

Supplemental Guidance: Session locks are temporary actions taken when users stop work and move away from the immediate vicinity of information systems but do not want to log out because of the temporary nature of their absences. Session locks are implemented where session activities can be determined. This is typically at the operating system level, but can also be at the application level. Session locks are not an acceptable substitute for logging out of information systems, for example, if organizations require users to log out at the end of workdays. Related control: AC-7.

Control Enhancements:

(1) SESSION LOCK | PATTERN-HIDING DISPLAYS

The information system conceals, via the session lock, information previously visible on the display with a publicly viewable image.

Supplemental Guidance: Publicly viewable images can include static or dynamic images, for example, patterns used with screen savers, photographic images, solid colors, clock, battery life indicator, or a blank screen, with the additional caveat that none of the images convey sensitive information.

References: OMB Memorandum 06-16.

Priority and Baseline Allocation:

P3	LOW Not Selected	MOD AC-11 (1)	HIGH AC-11 (1)

AC-12 SESSION TERMINATION

Control: The information system automatically terminates a user session after [*Assignment: organization-defined conditions or trigger events requiring session disconnect*].

Supplemental Guidance: This control addresses the termination of user-initiated logical sessions in contrast to SC-10 which addresses the termination of network connections that are associated with communications sessions (i.e., network disconnect). A logical session (for local, network, and remote access) is initiated whenever a user (or process acting on behalf of a user) accesses an organizational information system. Such user sessions can be terminated (and thus terminate user access) without terminating network sessions. Session termination terminates all processes associated with a user's logical session except those processes that are specifically created by the user (i.e., session owner) to continue after the session is terminated. Conditions or trigger events requiring automatic session termination can include, for example, organization-defined periods of user inactivity, targeted responses to certain types of incidents, time-of-day restrictions on information system use. Related controls: SC-10, SC-23.

Control Enhancements:

(1) SESSION TERMINATION | USER-INITIATED LOGOUTS / MESSAGE DISPLAYS

The information system:

(a) Provides a logout capability for user-initiated communications sessions whenever authentication is used to gain access to [*Assignment: organization-defined information resources*]; and

(b) Displays an explicit logout message to users indicating the reliable termination of authenticated communications sessions.

Supplemental Guidance: Information resources to which users gain access via authentication include, for example, local workstations, databases, and password-protected websites/web-based services. Logout messages for web page access, for example, can be displayed after authenticated sessions have been terminated. However, for some types of interactive sessions including, for example, file transfer protocol (FTP) sessions, information systems typically send logout messages as final messages prior to terminating sessions.

References: None.

Priority and Baseline Allocation:

P2	LOW Not Selected	MOD AC-12	HIGH AC-12

AC-13 SUPERVISION AND REVIEW — ACCESS CONTROL

[Withdrawn: Incorporated into AC-2 and AU-6].

AC-14 PERMITTED ACTIONS WITHOUT IDENTIFICATION OR AUTHENTICATION

Control: The organization:

a. Identifies [*Assignment: organization-defined user actions*] that can be performed on the information system without identification or authentication consistent with organizational missions/business functions; and

b. Documents and provides supporting rationale in the security plan for the information system, user actions not requiring identification or authentication.

Supplemental Guidance: This control addresses situations in which organizations determine that no identification or authentication is required in organizational information systems. Organizations may allow a limited number of user actions without identification or authentication including, for example, when individuals access public websites or other publicly accessible federal information systems, when individuals use mobile phones to receive calls, or when facsimiles are received. Organizations also identify actions that normally require identification or authentication but may under certain circumstances (e.g., emergencies), allow identification or authentication mechanisms to be bypassed. Such bypasses may occur, for example, via a software-readable physical switch that commands bypass of the logon functionality and is protected from accidental or unmonitored use. This control does not apply to situations where identification and authentication have already occurred and are not repeated, but rather to situations where identification and authentication have not yet occurred. Organizations may decide that there are no user actions that can be performed on organizational information systems without identification and authentication and thus, the values for assignment statements can be *none*. Related controls: CP-2, IA-2.

Control Enhancements: None.

(1) PERMITTED ACTIONS WITHOUT IDENTIFICATION OR AUTHENTICATION | NECESSARY USES
[Withdrawn: Incorporated into AC-14].

References: None.

Priority and Baseline Allocation:

| P3 | LOW AC-14 | MOD AC-14 | HIGH AC-14 |

AC-15 AUTOMATED MARKING

[Withdrawn: Incorporated into MP-3].

AC-16 SECURITY ATTRIBUTES

Control: The organization:

a. Provides the means to associate [*Assignment: organization-defined types of security attributes*] having [*Assignment: organization-defined security attribute values*] with information in storage, in process, and/or in transmission;

b. Ensures that the security attribute associations are made and retained with the information;

c. Establishes the permitted [*Assignment: organization-defined security attributes*] for [*Assignment: organization-defined information systems*]; and

d. Determines the permitted [*Assignment: organization-defined values or ranges*] for each of the established security attributes.

Supplemental Guidance: Information is represented internally within information systems using abstractions known as data structures. Internal data structures can represent different types of entities, both active and passive. Active entities, also known as *subjects*, are typically associated with individuals, devices, or processes acting on behalf of individuals. Passive entities, also known as *objects*, are typically associated with data structures such as records, buffers, tables, files, inter-process pipes, and communications ports. Security attributes, a form of metadata, are abstractions representing the basic properties or characteristics of active and passive entities with respect to safeguarding information. These attributes may be associated with active entities (i.e., subjects) that have the potential to send or receive information, to cause information to flow among objects, or to change the information system state. These attributes may also be associated with passive entities (i.e., objects) that contain or receive information. The association of security attributes to subjects and objects is referred to as *binding* and is typically inclusive of setting the attribute value and the attribute type. Security attributes when bound to data/information, enables the enforcement of information security policies for access control and information flow control, either through organizational processes or information system functions or mechanisms. The content or assigned values of security attributes can directly affect the ability of individuals to access organizational information.

Organizations can define the types of attributes needed for selected information systems to support missions/business functions. There is potentially a wide range of values that can be assigned to any given security attribute. Release markings could include, for example, US only, NATO, or NOFORN (not releasable to foreign nationals). By specifying permitted attribute ranges and values, organizations can ensure that the security attribute values are meaningful and relevant. The term *security labeling* refers to the association of security attributes with subjects and objects represented by internal data structures within organizational information systems, to enable information system-based enforcement of information security policies. Security labels include, for example, access authorizations, data life cycle protection (i.e., encryption and data expiration), nationality, affiliation as contractor, and classification of information in accordance with legal and compliance requirements. The term security marking refers to the association of security attributes with objects in a human-readable form, to enable organizational process-based enforcement of information security policies. The AC-16 base control represents the requirement for user-based attribute association (marking). The enhancements to AC-16 represent additional requirements including information system-based attribute association (labeling). Types of attributes include, for example, classification level for objects and clearance (access authorization) level for subjects. An example of a value for both of these attribute types is *Top Secret*. Related controls: AC-3, AC-4, AC-6, AC-21, AU-2, AU-10, SC-16, MP-3.

Control Enhancements:

(1) SECURITY ATTRIBUTES | DYNAMIC ATTRIBUTE ASSOCIATION

The information system dynamically associates security attributes with [*Assignment: organization-defined subjects and objects*] in accordance with [*Assignment: organization-defined security policies*] as information is created and combined.

Supplemental Guidance: Dynamic association of security attributes is appropriate whenever the security characteristics of information changes over time. Security attributes may change, for example, due to information aggregation issues (i.e., the security characteristics of individual information elements are different from the combined elements), changes in individual access authorizations (i.e., privileges), and changes in the security category of information. Related control: AC-4.

(2) SECURITY ATTRIBUTES | ATTRIBUTE VALUE CHANGES BY AUTHORIZED INDIVIDUALS

The information system provides authorized individuals (or processes acting on behalf of individuals) the capability to define or change the value of associated security attributes.

Supplemental Guidance: The content or assigned values of security attributes can directly affect the ability of individuals to access organizational information. Therefore, it is important for information systems to be able to limit the ability to create or modify security attributes to authorized individuals. Related controls: AC-6, AU-2.

(3) SECURITY ATTRIBUTES | MAINTENANCE OF ATTRIBUTE ASSOCIATIONS BY INFORMATION SYSTEM

The information system maintains the association and integrity of [*Assignment: organization-defined security attributes*] to [*Assignment: organization-defined subjects and objects*].

Supplemental Guidance: Maintaining the association and integrity of security attributes to subjects and objects with sufficient assurance helps to ensure that the attribute associations can be used as the basis of automated policy actions. Automated policy actions include, for example, access control decisions or information flow control decisions.

(4) SECURITY ATTRIBUTES | ASSOCIATION OF ATTRIBUTES BY AUTHORIZED INDIVIDUALS

The information system supports the association of [*Assignment: organization-defined security attributes*] with [*Assignment: organization-defined subjects and objects*] by authorized individuals (or processes acting on behalf of individuals).

Supplemental Guidance: The support provided by information systems can vary to include: (i) prompting users to select specific security attributes to be associated with specific information objects; (ii) employing automated mechanisms for categorizing information with appropriate attributes based on defined policies; or (iii) ensuring that the combination of selected security attributes selected is valid. Organizations consider the creation, deletion, or modification of security attributes when defining auditable events.

(5) SECURITY ATTRIBUTES | ATTRIBUTE DISPLAYS FOR OUTPUT DEVICES

The information system displays security attributes in human-readable form on each object that the system transmits to output devices to identify [*Assignment: organization-identified special dissemination, handling, or distribution instructions*] using [*Assignment: organization-identified human-readable, standard naming conventions*].

Supplemental Guidance: Information system outputs include, for example, pages, screens, or equivalent. Information system output devices include, for example, printers and video displays on computer workstations, notebook computers, and personal digital assistants.

(6) SECURITY ATTRIBUTES | MAINTENANCE OF ATTRIBUTE ASSOCIATION BY ORGANIZATION

The organization allows personnel to associate, and maintain the association of [*Assignment: organization-defined security attributes*] with [*Assignment: organization-defined subjects and objects*] in accordance with [*Assignment: organization-defined security policies*].

Supplemental Guidance: This control enhancement requires individual users (as opposed to the information system) to maintain associations of security attributes with subjects and objects.

(7) SECURITY ATTRIBUTES | CONSISTENT ATTRIBUTE INTERPRETATION

The organization provides a consistent interpretation of security attributes transmitted between distributed information system components.

Supplemental Guidance: In order to enforce security policies across multiple components in distributed information systems (e.g., distributed database management systems, cloud-based systems, and service-oriented architectures), organizations provide a consistent interpretation of security attributes that are used in access enforcement and flow enforcement decisions. Organizations establish agreements and processes to ensure that all distributed information system components implement security attributes with consistent interpretations in automated access/flow enforcement actions.

(8) SECURITY ATTRIBUTES | ASSOCIATION TECHNIQUES / TECHNOLOGIES

The information system implements [*Assignment: organization-defined techniques or technologies*] with [*Assignment: organization-defined level of assurance*] in associating security attributes to information.

Supplemental Guidance: The association (i.e., binding) of security attributes to information within information systems is of significant importance with regard to conducting automated access enforcement and flow enforcement actions. The association of such security attributes can be accomplished with technologies/techniques providing different levels of assurance. For example, information systems can cryptographically bind security attributes to information using digital signatures with the supporting cryptographic keys protected by hardware devices (sometimes known as hardware roots of trust).

(9) SECURITY ATTRIBUTES | ATTRIBUTE REASSIGNMENT

The organization ensures that security attributes associated with information are reassigned only via re-grading mechanisms validated using [*Assignment: organization-defined techniques or procedures*].

Supplemental Guidance: Validated re-grading mechanisms are employed by organizations to provide the requisite levels of assurance for security attribute reassignment activities. The validation is facilitated by ensuring that re-grading mechanisms are single purpose and of limited function. Since security attribute reassignments can affect security policy enforcement actions (e.g., access/flow enforcement decisions), using trustworthy re-grading mechanisms is necessary to ensure that such mechanisms perform in a consistent/correct mode of operation.

(10) SECURITY ATTRIBUTES | ATTRIBUTE CONFIGURATION BY AUTHORIZED INDIVIDUALS

The information system provides authorized individuals the capability to define or change the type and value of security attributes available for association with subjects and objects.

Supplemental Guidance: The content or assigned values of security attributes can directly affect the ability of individuals to access organizational information. Therefore, it is important for information systems to be able to limit the ability to create or modify security attributes to authorized individuals only.

References: None.

Priority and Baseline Allocation:

P0	LOW Not Selected	MOD Not Selected	HIGH Not Selected

AC-17 REMOTE ACCESS

Control: The organization:

a. Establishes and documents usage restrictions, configuration/connection requirements, and implementation guidance for each type of remote access allowed; and

b. Authorizes remote access to the information system prior to allowing such connections.

Supplemental Guidance: Remote access is access to organizational information systems by users (or processes acting on behalf of users) communicating through external networks (e.g., the Internet). Remote access methods include, for example, dial-up, broadband, and wireless. Organizations often employ encrypted virtual private networks (VPNs) to enhance confidentiality and integrity over remote connections. The use of encrypted VPNs does not make the access non-remote; however, the use of VPNs, when adequately provisioned with appropriate security controls (e.g., employing appropriate encryption techniques for confidentiality and integrity protection) may provide sufficient assurance to the organization that it can effectively treat such connections as internal networks. Still, VPN connections traverse external networks, and the encrypted VPN does not enhance the availability of remote connections. Also, VPNs with encrypted tunnels can affect the organizational capability to adequately monitor network communications traffic for malicious code. Remote access controls apply to information systems other than public web servers or systems designed for public access. This control addresses authorization prior to allowing remote access without specifying the formats for such authorization. While organizations may use interconnection security agreements to authorize remote access connections, such agreements are not required by this control. Enforcing access restrictions for remote connections is addressed in AC-3. Related controls: AC-2, AC-3, AC-18, AC-19, AC-20, CA-3, CA-7, CM-8, IA-2, IA-3, IA-8, MA-4, PE-17, PL-4, SC-10, SI-4.

Control Enhancements:

(1) REMOTE ACCESS | AUTOMATED MONITORING / CONTROL

The information system monitors and controls remote access methods.

Supplemental Guidance: Automated monitoring and control of remote access sessions allows organizations to detect cyber attacks and also ensure ongoing compliance with remote access policies by auditing connection activities of remote users on a variety of information system components (e.g., servers, workstations, notebook computers, smart phones, and tablets). Related controls: AU-2, AU-12.

(2) REMOTE ACCESS | PROTECTION OF CONFIDENTIALITY / INTEGRITY USING ENCRYPTION

The information system implements cryptographic mechanisms to protect the confidentiality and integrity of remote access sessions.

Supplemental Guidance: The encryption strength of mechanism is selected based on the security categorization of the information. Related controls: SC-8, SC-12, SC-13.

(3) REMOTE ACCESS | MANAGED ACCESS CONTROL POINTS

The information system routes all remote accesses through [*Assignment: organization-defined number*] managed network access control points.

Supplemental Guidance: Limiting the number of access control points for remote accesses reduces the attack surface for organizations. Organizations consider the Trusted Internet Connections (TIC) initiative requirements for external network connections. Related control: SC-7.

(4) REMOTE ACCESS | PRIVILEGED COMMANDS / ACCESS

The organization:

(a) Authorizes the execution of privileged commands and access to security-relevant information via remote access only for [*Assignment: organization-defined needs*]; and

(b) Documents the rationale for such access in the security plan for the information system.

Supplemental Guidance: Related control: AC-6.

(5) REMOTE ACCESS | MONITORING FOR UNAUTHORIZED CONNECTIONS

[Withdrawn: Incorporated into SI-4].

(6) REMOTE ACCESS | PROTECTION OF INFORMATION

The organization ensures that users protect information about remote access mechanisms from unauthorized use and disclosure.

Supplemental Guidance: Related controls: AT-2, AT-3, PS-6.

(7) REMOTE ACCESS | ADDITIONAL PROTECTION FOR SECURITY FUNCTION ACCESS

[Withdrawn: Incorporated into AC-3 (10)].

(8) REMOTE ACCESS | DISABLE NONSECURE NETWORK PROTOCOLS

[Withdrawn: Incorporated into CM-7].

(9) REMOTE ACCESS | DISCONNECT / DISABLE ACCESS

The organization provides the capability to expeditiously disconnect or disable remote access to the information system within [*Assignment: organization-defined time period*].

Supplemental Guidance: This control enhancement requires organizations to have the capability to rapidly disconnect current users remotely accessing the information system and/or disable further remote access. The speed of disconnect or disablement varies based on the criticality of missions/business functions and the need to eliminate immediate or future remote access to organizational information systems.

References: NIST Special Publications 800-46, 800-77, 800-113, 800-114, 800-121.

Priority and Baseline Allocation:

P1	LOW AC-17	MOD AC-17 (1) (2) (3) (4)	HIGH AC-17 (1) (2) (3) (4)

AC-18 **WIRELESS ACCESS**

Control: The organization:

a. Establishes usage restrictions, configuration/connection requirements, and implementation guidance for wireless access; and

b. Authorizes wireless access to the information system prior to allowing such connections.

Supplemental Guidance: Wireless technologies include, for example, microwave, packet radio (UHF/VHF), 802.11x, and Bluetooth. Wireless networks use authentication protocols (e.g., EAP/TLS, PEAP), which provide credential protection and mutual authentication. Related controls: AC-2, AC-3, AC-17, AC-19, CA-3, CA-7, CM-8, IA-2, IA-3, IA-8, PL-4, SI-4.

Control Enhancements:

(1) WIRELESS ACCESS | AUTHENTICATION AND ENCRYPTION

The information system protects wireless access to the system using authentication of [*Selection (one or more): users; devices*] and encryption.

Supplemental Guidance: Related controls: SC-8, SC-13.

(2) WIRELESS ACCESS | MONITORING UNAUTHORIZED CONNECTIONS

[Withdrawn: Incorporated into SI-4].

(3) WIRELESS ACCESS | DISABLE WIRELESS NETWORKING

The organization disables, when not intended for use, wireless networking capabilities internally embedded within information system components prior to issuance and deployment.

Supplemental Guidance: Related control: AC-19.

(4) WIRELESS ACCESS | RESTRICT CONFIGURATIONS BY USERS

The organization identifies and explicitly authorizes users allowed to independently configure wireless networking capabilities.

Supplemental Guidance: Organizational authorizations to allow selected users to configure wireless networking capability are enforced in part, by the access enforcement mechanisms employed within organizational information systems. Related controls: AC-3, SC-15.

(5) WIRELESS ACCESS | ANTENNAS / TRANSMISSION POWER LEVELS

The organization selects radio antennas and calibrates transmission power levels to reduce the probability that usable signals can be received outside of organization-controlled boundaries.

Supplemental Guidance: Actions that may be taken by organizations to limit unauthorized use of wireless communications outside of organization-controlled boundaries include, for example: (i) reducing the power of wireless transmissions so that the transmissions are less likely to emit a signal that can be used by adversaries outside of the physical perimeters of organizations; (ii) employing measures such as TEMPEST to control wireless emanations; and (iii) using directional/beam forming antennas that reduce the likelihood that unintended receivers will be able to intercept signals. Prior to taking such actions, organizations can conduct periodic wireless surveys to understand the radio frequency profile of organizational information systems as well as other systems that may be operating in the area. Related control: PE-19.

References: NIST Special Publications 800-48, 800-94, 800-97.

Priority and Baseline Allocation:

P1	LOW AC-18	MOD AC-18 (1)	HIGH AC-18 (1) (4) (5)

AC-19 ACCESS CONTROL FOR MOBILE DEVICES

Control: The organization:

a. Establishes usage restrictions, configuration requirements, connection requirements, and implementation guidance for organization-controlled mobile devices; and

b. Authorizes the connection of mobile devices to organizational information systems.

Supplemental Guidance: A mobile device is a computing device that: (i) has a small form factor such that it can easily be carried by a single individual; (ii) is designed to operate without a physical connection (e.g., wirelessly transmit or receive information); (iii) possesses local, non-removable or removable data storage; and (iv) includes a self-contained power source. Mobile devices may also include voice communication capabilities, on-board sensors that allow the device to capture information, and/or built-in features for synchronizing local data with remote locations. Examples include smart phones, E-readers, and tablets. Mobile devices are typically associated with a single individual and the device is usually in close proximity to the individual; however, the degree of proximity can vary depending upon on the form factor and size of the device. The processing, storage, and transmission capability of the mobile device may be comparable to or merely a subset of desktop systems, depending upon the nature and intended purpose of the device. Due to the large variety of mobile devices with different technical characteristics and capabilities, organizational restrictions may vary for the different classes/types of such devices. Usage restrictions and specific implementation guidance for mobile devices include, for example, configuration management, device identification and authentication, implementation of mandatory protective software (e.g., malicious code detection, firewall), scanning devices for malicious code, updating virus protection software, scanning for critical software updates and patches, conducting primary operating system (and possibly other resident software) integrity checks, and disabling unnecessary hardware (e.g., wireless, infrared). Organizations are cautioned that the need to provide adequate security for mobile devices goes beyond the requirements in this control. Many safeguards and countermeasures for mobile devices are reflected in other security controls in the catalog allocated in the initial control baselines as starting points for the development of security plans and overlays using the tailoring process. There may also be some degree of overlap in the requirements articulated by the security controls within the different families of controls. AC-20 addresses mobile devices that are not organization-controlled. Related controls: AC-3, AC-7, AC-18, AC-20, CA-9, CM-2, IA-2, IA-3, MP-2, MP-4, MP-5, PL-4, SC-7, SC-43, SI-3, SI-4.

Control Enhancements:

(1) ACCESS CONTROL FOR MOBILE DEVICES | USE OF WRITABLE / PORTABLE STORAGE DEVICES
[Withdrawn: Incorporated into MP-7].

(2) ACCESS CONTROL FOR MOBILE DEVICES | USE OF PERSONALLY OWNED PORTABLE STORAGE DEVICES
[Withdrawn: Incorporated into MP-7].

(3) ACCESS CONTROL FOR MOBILE DEVICES | USE OF PORTABLE STORAGE DEVICES WITH NO IDENTIFIABLE OWNER
[Withdrawn: Incorporated into MP-7].

(4) ACCESS CONTROL FOR MOBILE DEVICES | RESTRICTIONS FOR CLASSIFIED INFORMATION

The organization:

(a) Prohibits the use of unclassified mobile devices in facilities containing information systems processing, storing, or transmitting classified information unless specifically permitted by the authorizing official; and

(b) Enforces the following restrictions on individuals permitted by the authorizing official to use unclassified mobile devices in facilities containing information systems processing, storing, or transmitting classified information:

(1) Connection of unclassified mobile devices to classified information systems is prohibited;

(2) Connection of unclassified mobile devices to unclassified information systems requires approval from the authorizing official;

(3) Use of internal or external modems or wireless interfaces within the unclassified mobile devices is prohibited; and

(4) Unclassified mobile devices and the information stored on those devices are subject to random reviews and inspections by [Assignment: organization-defined security officials], and if classified information is found, the incident handling policy is followed.

(c) Restricts the connection of classified mobile devices to classified information systems in accordance with [Assignment: organization-defined security policies].

Supplemental Guidance: Related controls: CA-6, IR-4.

(5) ACCESS CONTROL FOR MOBILE DEVICES | FULL DEVICE / CONTAINER-BASED ENCRYPTION

The organization employs [Selection: full-device encryption; container encryption] to protect the confidentiality and integrity of information on [Assignment: organization-defined mobile devices].

Supplemental Guidance: Container-based encryption provides a more fine-grained approach to the encryption of data/information on mobile devices, including for example, encrypting selected data structures such as files, records, or fields. Related controls: MP-5, SC-13, SC-28.

References: OMB Memorandum 06-16; NIST Special Publications 800-114, 800-124, 800-164.

Priority and Baseline Allocation:

| P1 | LOW AC-19 | MOD AC-19 (5) | HIGH AC-19 (5) |

AC-20 USE OF EXTERNAL INFORMATION SYSTEMS

Control: The organization establishes terms and conditions, consistent with any trust relationships established with other organizations owning, operating, and/or maintaining external information systems, allowing authorized individuals to:

a. Access the information system from external information systems; and

b. Process, store, or transmit organization-controlled information using external information systems.

Supplemental Guidance: External information systems are information systems or components of information systems that are outside of the authorization boundary established by organizations and for which organizations typically have no direct supervision and authority over the application of required security controls or the assessment of control effectiveness. External information systems include, for example: (i) personally owned information systems/devices (e.g., notebook computers, smart phones, tablets, personal digital assistants); (ii) privately owned computing and communications devices resident in commercial or public facilities (e.g., hotels, train stations, convention centers, shopping malls, or airports); (iii) information systems owned or controlled by nonfederal governmental organizations; and (iv) federal information systems that are not owned by, operated by, or under the direct supervision and authority of organizations. This control also addresses the use of external information systems for the processing, storage, or transmission of organizational information, including, for example, accessing cloud services (e.g., infrastructure as a service, platform as a service, or software as a service) from organizational information systems.

For some external information systems (i.e., information systems operated by other federal agencies, including organizations subordinate to those agencies), the trust relationships that have been established between those organizations and the originating organization may be such, that no explicit terms and conditions are required. Information systems within these organizations would not be considered external. These situations occur when, for example, there are pre-existing sharing/trust agreements (either implicit or explicit) established between federal agencies or organizations subordinate to those agencies, or when such trust agreements are specified by applicable laws, Executive Orders, directives, or policies. Authorized individuals include, for example, organizational personnel, contractors, or other individuals with authorized access to organizational information systems and over which organizations have the authority to impose rules of behavior with regard to system access. Restrictions that organizations impose on authorized individuals need not be uniform, as those restrictions may vary depending upon the trust relationships between organizations. Therefore, organizations may choose to impose different security restrictions on contractors than on state, local, or tribal governments.

This control does not apply to the use of external information systems to access public interfaces to organizational information systems (e.g., individuals accessing federal information through www.usa.gov). Organizations establish terms and conditions for the use of external information systems in accordance with organizational security policies and procedures. Terms and conditions address as a minimum: types of applications that can be accessed on organizational information systems from external information systems; and the highest security category of information that can be processed, stored, or transmitted on external information systems. If terms and conditions with the owners of external information systems cannot be established, organizations may impose restrictions on organizational personnel using those external systems. Related controls: AC-3, AC-17, AC-19, CA-3, PL-4, SA-9.

Control Enhancements:

(1) USE OF EXTERNAL INFORMATION SYSTEMS | LIMITS ON AUTHORIZED USE

The organization permits authorized individuals to use an external information system to access the information system or to process, store, or transmit organization-controlled information only when the organization:

(a) Verifies the implementation of required security controls on the external system as specified in the organization's information security policy and security plan; or

(b) Retains approved information system connection or processing agreements with the organizational entity hosting the external information system.

Supplemental Guidance: This control enhancement recognizes that there are circumstances where individuals using external information systems (e.g., contractors, coalition partners) need to access organizational information systems. In those situations, organizations need confidence that the external information systems contain the necessary security safeguards (i.e., security controls), so as not to compromise, damage, or otherwise harm organizational information systems. Verification that the required security controls have been implemented can be achieved, for example, by third-party, independent assessments, attestations, or other means, depending on the confidence level required by organizations. Related control: CA-2.

(2) USE OF EXTERNAL INFORMATION SYSTEMS | PORTABLE STORAGE DEVICES

The organization [Selection: restricts; prohibits] the use of organization-controlled portable storage devices by authorized individuals on external information systems.

Supplemental Guidance: Limits on the use of organization-controlled portable storage devices in external information systems include, for example, complete prohibition of the use of such devices or restrictions on how the devices may be used and under what conditions the devices may be used.

(3) USE OF EXTERNAL INFORMATION SYSTEMS | NON-ORGANIZATIONALLY OWNED SYSTEMS / COMPONENTS / DEVICES

The organization [Selection: restricts; prohibits] the use of non-organizationally owned information systems, system components, or devices to process, store, or transmit organizational information.

Supplemental Guidance: Non-organizationally owned devices include devices owned by other organizations (e.g., federal/state agencies, contractors) and personally owned devices. There are risks to using non-organizationally owned devices. In some cases, the risk is sufficiently high as to prohibit such use. In other cases, it may be such that the use of non-organizationally owned devices is allowed but restricted in some way. Restrictions include, for example: (i) requiring the implementation of organization-approved security controls prior to authorizing such connections; (ii) limiting access to certain types of information, services, or applications; (iii) using virtualization techniques to limit processing and storage activities to servers or other system components provisioned by the organization; and (iv) agreeing to terms and conditions for usage. For personally owned devices, organizations consult with the Office of the General Counsel regarding legal issues associated with using such devices in operational environments, including, for example, requirements for conducting forensic analyses during investigations after an incident.

(4) USE OF EXTERNAL INFORMATION SYSTEMS | NETWORK ACCESSIBLE STORAGE DEVICES

The organization prohibits the use of [Assignment: organization-defined network accessible storage devices] in external information systems.

Supplemental Guidance: Network accessible storage devices in external information systems include, for example, online storage devices in public, hybrid, or community cloud-based systems.

References: FIPS Publication 199.

Priority and Baseline Allocation:

| P1 | LOW AC-20 | MOD AC-20 (1) (2) | HIGH AC-20 (1) (2) |

AC-21 INFORMATION SHARING

Control: The organization:

a. Facilitates information sharing by enabling authorized users to determine whether access authorizations assigned to the sharing partner match the access restrictions on the information for [*Assignment: organization-defined information sharing circumstances where user discretion is required*]; and

b. Employs [*Assignment: organization-defined automated mechanisms or manual processes*] to assist users in making information sharing/collaboration decisions.

Supplemental Guidance: This control applies to information that may be restricted in some manner (e.g., privileged medical information, contract-sensitive information, proprietary information, personally identifiable information, classified information related to special access programs or compartments) based on some formal or administrative determination. Depending on the particular information-sharing circumstances, sharing partners may be defined at the individual, group, or organizational level. Information may be defined by content, type, security category, or special access program/compartment. Related control: AC-3.

Control Enhancements:

(1) INFORMATION SHARING | AUTOMATED DECISION SUPPORT

The information system enforces information-sharing decisions by authorized users based on access authorizations of sharing partners and access restrictions on information to be shared.

(2) INFORMATION SHARING | INFORMATION SEARCH AND RETRIEVAL

The information system implements information search and retrieval services that enforce [*Assignment: organization-defined information sharing restrictions*].

References: None.

Priority and Baseline Allocation:

P2	LOW Not Selected	MOD AC-21	HIGH AC-21

AC-22 PUBLICLY ACCESSIBLE CONTENT

Control: The organization:

a. Designates individuals authorized to post information onto a publicly accessible information system;

b. Trains authorized individuals to ensure that publicly accessible information does not contain nonpublic information;

c. Reviews the proposed content of information prior to posting onto the publicly accessible information system to ensure that nonpublic information is not included; and

d. Reviews the content on the publicly accessible information system for nonpublic information [*Assignment: organization-defined frequency*] and removes such information, if discovered.

Supplemental Guidance: In accordance with federal laws, Executive Orders, directives, policies, regulations, standards, and/or guidance, the general public is not authorized access to nonpublic information (e.g., information protected under the Privacy Act and proprietary information). This control addresses information systems that are controlled by the organization and accessible to the general public, typically without identification or authentication. The posting of information on non-organization information systems is covered by organizational policy. Related controls: AC-3, AC-4, AT-2, AT-3, AU-13.

Control Enhancements: None.

References: None.

Priority and Baseline Allocation:

| P3 | LOW AC-22 | MOD AC-22 | HIGH AC-22 |

AC-23 DATA MINING PROTECTION

Control: The organization employs [*Assignment: organization-defined data mining prevention and detection techniques*] for [*Assignment: organization-defined data storage objects*] to adequately detect and protect against data mining.

Supplemental Guidance: Data storage objects include, for example, databases, database records, and database fields. Data mining prevention and detection techniques include, for example: (i) limiting the types of responses provided to database queries; (ii) limiting the number/frequency of database queries to increase the work factor needed to determine the contents of such databases; and (iii) notifying organizational personnel when atypical database queries or accesses occur. This control focuses on the protection of organizational information from data mining while such information resides in organizational data stores. In contrast, AU-13 focuses on monitoring for organizational information that may have been mined or otherwise obtained from data stores and is now available as open source information residing on external sites, for example, through social networking or social media websites.

Control Enhancements: None.

References: None.

Priority and Baseline Allocation:

| P0 | LOW Not Selected | MOD Not Selected | HIGH Not Selected |

AC-24 ACCESS CONTROL DECISIONS

Control: The organization establishes procedures to ensure [*Assignment: organization-defined access control decisions*] are applied to each access request prior to access enforcement.

Supplemental Guidance: Access control decisions (also known as authorization decisions) occur when authorization information is applied to specific accesses. In contrast, access enforcement occurs when information systems enforce access control decisions. While it is very common to have access control decisions and access enforcement implemented by the same entity, it is not required and it is not always an optimal implementation choice. For some architectures and distributed information systems, different entities may perform access control decisions and access enforcement.

Control Enhancements:

(1) ACCESS CONTROL DECISIONS | TRANSMIT ACCESS AUTHORIZATION INFORMATION

The information system transmits [*Assignment: organization-defined access authorization information*] using [*Assignment: organization-defined security safeguards*] to [*Assignment: organization-defined information systems*] that enforce access control decisions.

Supplemental Guidance: In distributed information systems, authorization processes and access control decisions may occur in separate parts of the systems. In such instances, authorization information is transmitted securely so timely access control decisions can be enforced at the appropriate locations. To support the access control decisions, it may be necessary to transmit as part of the access authorization information, supporting security attributes. This is due to the fact that in distributed information systems, there are various access control decisions that need to be made and different entities (e.g., services) make these decisions in a serial fashion, each requiring some security attributes to make the decisions. Protecting access authorization information (i.e., access control decisions) ensures that such information cannot be altered, spoofed, or otherwise compromised during transmission.

(2) ACCESS CONTROL DECISIONS | NO USER OR PROCESS IDENTITY

The information system enforces access control decisions based on [*Assignment: organization-defined security attributes*] that do not include the identity of the user or process acting on behalf of the user.

Supplemental Guidance: In certain situations, it is important that access control decisions can be made without information regarding the identity of the users issuing the requests. These are generally instances where preserving individual privacy is of paramount importance. In other situations, user identification information is simply not needed for access control decisions and, especially in the case of distributed information systems, transmitting such information with the needed degree of assurance may be very expensive or difficult to accomplish.

References: None.

Priority and Baseline Allocation:

| P0 | LOW Not Selected | MOD Not Selected | HIGH Not Selected |

AC-25 REFERENCE MONITOR

Control: The information system implements a reference monitor for [*Assignment: organization-defined access control policies*] that is tamperproof, always invoked, and small enough to be subject to analysis and testing, the completeness of which can be assured.

Supplemental Guidance: Information is represented internally within information systems using abstractions known as data structures. Internal data structures can represent different types of entities, both active and passive. Active entities, also known as *subjects*, are typically associated with individuals, devices, or processes acting on behalf of individuals. Passive entities, also known as *objects*, are typically associated with data structures such as records, buffers, tables, files, inter-process pipes, and communications ports. Reference monitors typically enforce mandatory access control policies—a type of access control that restricts access to objects based on the identity of subjects or groups to which the subjects belong. The access controls are mandatory because subjects with certain privileges (i.e., access permissions) are restricted from passing those privileges on to any other subjects, either directly or indirectly—that is, the information system strictly enforces the access control policy based on the rule set established by the policy. The *tamperproof* property of the reference monitor prevents adversaries from compromising the functioning of the mechanism. The *always invoked* property prevents adversaries from bypassing the mechanism and hence violating the security policy. The *smallness* property helps to ensure the completeness in the analysis and testing of the mechanism to detect weaknesses or deficiencies (i.e., latent flaws) that would prevent the enforcement of the security policy. Related controls: AC-3, AC-16, SC-3, SC-39.

Control Enhancements: None.

References: None.

Priority and Baseline Allocation:

| P0 | LOW Not Selected | MOD Not Selected | HIGH Not Selected |

FAMILY: AWARENESS AND TRAINING

AT-1   SECURITY AWARENESS AND TRAINING POLICY AND PROCEDURES

Control: The organization:

a. Develops, documents, and disseminates to [*Assignment: organization-defined personnel or roles*]:

 1. A security awareness and training policy that addresses purpose, scope, roles, responsibilities, management commitment, coordination among organizational entities, and compliance; and

 2. Procedures to facilitate the implementation of the security awareness and training policy and associated security awareness and training controls; and

b. Reviews and updates the current:

 1. Security awareness and training policy [*Assignment: organization-defined frequency*]; and

 2. Security awareness and training procedures [*Assignment: organization-defined frequency*].

Supplemental Guidance: This control addresses the establishment of policy and procedures for the effective implementation of selected security controls and control enhancements in the AT family. Policy and procedures reflect applicable federal laws, Executive Orders, directives, regulations, policies, standards, and guidance. Security program policies and procedures at the organization level may make the need for system-specific policies and procedures unnecessary. The policy can be included as part of the general information security policy for organizations or conversely, can be represented by multiple policies reflecting the complex nature of certain organizations. The procedures can be established for the security program in general and for particular information systems, if needed. The organizational risk management strategy is a key factor in establishing policy and procedures. Related control: PM-9.

Control Enhancements: None.

References: NIST Special Publications 800-12, 800-16, 800-50, 800-100.

Priority and Baseline Allocation:

| P1 | LOW AT-1 | MOD AT-1 | HIGH AT-1 |

AT-2   SECURITY AWARENESS TRAINING

Control: The organization provides basic security awareness training to information system users (including managers, senior executives, and contractors):

a. As part of initial training for new users;

b. When required by information system changes; and

c. [*Assignment: organization-defined frequency*] thereafter.

Supplemental Guidance: Organizations determine the appropriate content of security awareness training and security awareness techniques based on the specific organizational requirements and the information systems to which personnel have authorized access. The content includes a basic understanding of the need for information security and user actions to maintain security and to respond to suspected security incidents. The content also addresses awareness of the need for operations security. Security awareness techniques can include, for example, displaying posters, offering supplies inscribed with security reminders, generating email advisories/notices from senior organizational officials, displaying logon screen messages, and conducting information security awareness events. Related controls: AT-3, AT-4, PL-4.

Control Enhancements:

(1) SECURITY AWARENESS | PRACTICAL EXERCISES

The organization includes practical exercises in security awareness training that simulate actual cyber attacks.

Supplemental Guidance: Practical exercises may include, for example, no-notice social engineering attempts to collect information, gain unauthorized access, or simulate the adverse impact of opening malicious email attachments or invoking, via spear phishing attacks, malicious web links. Related controls: CA-2, CA-7, CP-4, IR-3.

(2) SECURITY AWARENESS | INSIDER THREAT

The organization includes security awareness training on recognizing and reporting potential indicators of insider threat.

Supplemental Guidance: Potential indicators and possible precursors of insider threat can include behaviors such as inordinate, long-term job dissatisfaction, attempts to gain access to information not required for job performance, unexplained access to financial resources, bullying or sexual harassment of fellow employees, workplace violence, and other serious violations of organizational policies, procedures, directives, rules, or practices. Security awareness training includes how to communicate employee and management concerns regarding potential indicators of insider threat through appropriate organizational channels in accordance with established organizational policies and procedures. Related controls: PL-4, PM-12, PS-3, PS-6.

References: C.F.R. Part 5 Subpart C (5 C.F.R. 930.301); Executive Order 13587; NIST Special Publication 800-50.

Priority and Baseline Allocation:

P1	LOW AT-2	MOD AT-2 (2)	HIGH AT-2 (2)

AT-3 ROLE-BASED SECURITY TRAINING

Control: The organization provides role-based security training to personnel with assigned security roles and responsibilities:

a. Before authorizing access to the information system or performing assigned duties;

b. When required by information system changes; and

c. [*Assignment: organization-defined frequency*] thereafter.

Supplemental Guidance: Organizations determine the appropriate content of security training based on the assigned roles and responsibilities of individuals and the specific security requirements of organizations and the information systems to which personnel have authorized access. In addition, organizations provide enterprise architects, information system developers, software developers, acquisition/procurement officials, information system managers, system/network administrators, personnel conducting configuration management and auditing activities, personnel performing independent verification and validation activities, security control assessors, and other personnel having access to system-level software, adequate security-related technical training specifically tailored for their assigned duties. Comprehensive role-based training addresses management, operational, and technical roles and responsibilities covering physical, personnel, and technical safeguards and countermeasures. Such training can include for example, policies, procedures, tools, and artifacts for the organizational security roles defined. Organizations also provide the training necessary for individuals to carry out their responsibilities related to operations and supply chain security within the context of organizational information security programs. Role-based security training also applies to contractors providing services to federal agencies. Related controls: AT-2, AT-4, PL-4, PS-7, SA-3, SA-12, SA-16.

Control Enhancements:

(1) ROLE-BASED SECURITY TRAINING | ENVIRONMENTAL CONTROLS

The organization provides [*Assignment: organization-defined personnel or roles*] with initial and [*Assignment: organization-defined frequency*] training in the employment and operation of environmental controls.

Supplemental Guidance: Environmental controls include, for example, fire suppression and detection devices/systems, sprinkler systems, handheld fire extinguishers, fixed fire hoses, smoke detectors, temperature/humidity, HVAC, and power within the facility. Organizations identify personnel with specific roles and responsibilities associated with environmental controls requiring specialized training. Related controls: PE-1, PE-13, PE-14, PE-15.

(2) ROLE-BASED SECURITY TRAINING | PHYSICAL SECURITY CONTROLS

The organization provides [*Assignment: organization-defined personnel or roles*] with initial and [*Assignment: organization-defined frequency*] training in the employment and operation of physical security controls.

Supplemental Guidance: Physical security controls include, for example, physical access control devices, physical intrusion alarms, monitoring/surveillance equipment, and security guards (deployment and operating procedures). Organizations identify personnel with specific roles and responsibilities associated with physical security controls requiring specialized training. Related controls: PE-2, PE-3, PE-4, PE-5.

(3) ROLE-BASED SECURITY TRAINING | PRACTICAL EXERCISES

The organization includes practical exercises in security training that reinforce training objectives.

Supplemental Guidance: Practical exercises may include, for example, security training for software developers that includes simulated cyber attacks exploiting common software vulnerabilities (e.g., buffer overflows), or spear/whale phishing attacks targeted at senior leaders/executives. These types of practical exercises help developers better understand the effects of such vulnerabilities and appreciate the need for security coding standards and processes.

(4) ROLE-BASED SECURITY TRAINING | SUSPICIOUS COMMUNICATIONS AND ANOMALOUS SYSTEM BEHAVIOR

The organization provides training to its personnel on [*Assignment: organization-defined indicators of malicious code*] to recognize suspicious communications and anomalous behavior in organizational information systems.

Supplemental Guidance: A well-trained workforce provides another organizational safeguard that can be employed as part of a defense-in-depth strategy to protect organizations against malicious code coming in to organizations via email or the web applications. Personnel are trained to look for indications of potentially suspicious email (e.g., receiving an unexpected email, receiving an email containing strange or poor grammar, or receiving an email from an unfamiliar sender but who appears to be from a known sponsor or contractor). Personnel are also trained on how to respond to such suspicious email or web communications (e.g., not opening attachments, not clicking on embedded web links, and checking the source of email addresses). For this process to work effectively, all organizational personnel are trained and made aware of what constitutes suspicious communications. Training personnel on how to recognize anomalous behaviors in organizational information systems can potentially provide early warning for the presence of malicious code. Recognition of such anomalous behavior by organizational personnel can supplement automated malicious code detection and protection tools and systems employed by organizations.

References: C.F.R. Part 5 Subpart C (5 C.F.R. 930.301); NIST Special Publications 800-16, 800-50.

Priority and Baseline Allocation:

| P1 | LOW AT-3 | MOD AT-3 | HIGH AT-3 |

AT-4 **SECURITY TRAINING RECORDS**

Control: The organization:

a. Documents and monitors individual information system security training activities including basic security awareness training and specific information system security training; and

b. Retains individual training records for [*Assignment: organization-defined time period*].

Supplemental Guidance: Documentation for specialized training may be maintained by individual supervisors at the option of the organization. Related controls: AT-2, AT-3, PM-14.

Control Enhancements: None.

References: None.

Priority and Baseline Allocation:

| P3 | LOW AT-4 | MOD AT-4 | HIGH AT-4 |

AT-5 **CONTACTS WITH SECURITY GROUPS AND ASSOCIATIONS**

[Withdrawn: Incorporated into PM-15].

FAMILY: AUDIT AND ACCOUNTABILITY

AU-1   AUDIT AND ACCOUNTABILITY POLICY AND PROCEDURES

Control: The organization:

a.   Develops, documents, and disseminates to [*Assignment: organization-defined personnel or roles*]:

1.   An audit and accountability policy that addresses purpose, scope, roles, responsibilities, management commitment, coordination among organizational entities, and compliance; and

2.   Procedures to facilitate the implementation of the audit and accountability policy and associated audit and accountability controls; and

b.   Reviews and updates the current:

1.   Audit and accountability policy [*Assignment: organization-defined frequency*]; and

2.   Audit and accountability procedures [*Assignment: organization-defined frequency*].

Supplemental Guidance: This control addresses the establishment of policy and procedures for the effective implementation of selected security controls and control enhancements in the AU family. Policy and procedures reflect applicable federal laws, Executive Orders, directives, regulations, policies, standards, and guidance. Security program policies and procedures at the organization level may make the need for system-specific policies and procedures unnecessary. The policy can be included as part of the general information security policy for organizations or conversely, can be represented by multiple policies reflecting the complex nature of certain organizations. The procedures can be established for the security program in general and for particular information systems, if needed. The organizational risk management strategy is a key factor in establishing policy and procedures. Related control: PM-9.

Control Enhancements: None.

References: NIST Special Publications 800-12, 800-100.

Priority and Baseline Allocation:

| P1 | LOW AU-1 | MOD AU-1 | HIGH AU-1 |

AU-2   AUDIT EVENTS

Control: The organization:

a.   Determines that the information system is capable of auditing the following events: [*Assignment: organization-defined auditable events*];

b.   Coordinates the security audit function with other organizational entities requiring audit-related information to enhance mutual support and to help guide the selection of auditable events;

c.   Provides a rationale for why the auditable events are deemed to be adequate to support after-the-fact investigations of security incidents; and

d.   Determines that the following events are to be audited within the information system: [*Assignment: organization-defined audited events (the subset of the auditable events defined in AU-2 a.) along with the frequency of (or situation requiring) auditing for each identified event*].

Supplemental Guidance: An event is any observable occurrence in an organizational information system. Organizations identify audit events as those events which are significant and relevant to the security of information systems and the environments in which those systems operate in order to meet specific and ongoing audit needs. Audit events can include, for example, password changes, failed logons, or failed accesses related to information systems, administrative privilege usage, PIV credential usage, or third-party credential usage. In determining the set of auditable events, organizations consider the auditing appropriate for each of the security controls to be implemented. To balance auditing requirements with other information system needs, this control also requires identifying that subset of *auditable* events that are *audited* at a given point in time. For example, organizations may determine that information systems must have the capability to log every file access both successful and unsuccessful, but not activate that capability except for specific circumstances due to the potential burden on system performance. Auditing requirements, including the need for auditable events, may be referenced in other security controls and control enhancements. Organizations also include auditable events that are required by applicable federal laws, Executive Orders, directives, policies, regulations, and standards. Audit records can be generated at various levels of abstraction, including at the packet level as information traverses the network. Selecting the appropriate level of abstraction is a critical aspect of an audit capability and can facilitate the identification of root causes to problems. Organizations consider in the definition of auditable events, the auditing necessary to cover related events such as the steps in distributed, transaction-based processes (e.g., processes that are distributed across multiple organizations) and actions that occur in service-oriented architectures. Related controls: AC-6, AC-17, AU-3, AU-12, MA-4, MP-2, MP-4, SI-4.

Control Enhancements:

(1) *AUDIT EVENTS | COMPILATION OF AUDIT RECORDS FROM MULTIPLE SOURCES*
[Withdrawn: Incorporated into AU-12].

(2) *AUDIT EVENTS | SELECTION OF AUDIT EVENTS BY COMPONENT*
[Withdrawn: Incorporated into AU-12].

(3) *AUDIT EVENTS | REVIEWS AND UPDATES*

The organization reviews and updates the audited events [*Assignment: organization-defined frequency*].

Supplemental Guidance: Over time, the events that organizations believe should be audited may change. Reviewing and updating the set of audited events periodically is necessary to ensure that the current set is still necessary and sufficient.

(4) *AUDIT EVENTS | PRIVILEGED FUNCTIONS*
[Withdrawn: Incorporated into AC-6 (9)].

References: NIST Special Publication 800-92; Web: http://idmanagement.gov.

Priority and Baseline Allocation:

P1	LOW AU-2	MOD AU-2 (3)	HIGH AU-2 (3)

AU-3 CONTENT OF AUDIT RECORDS

Control: The information system generates audit records containing information that establishes what type of event occurred, when the event occurred, where the event occurred, the source of the event, the outcome of the event, and the identity of any individuals or subjects associated with the event.

Supplemental Guidance: Audit record content that may be necessary to satisfy the requirement of this control, includes, for example, time stamps, source and destination addresses, user/process identifiers, event descriptions, success/fail indications, filenames involved, and access control or flow control rules invoked. Event outcomes can include indicators of event success or failure and event-specific results (e.g., the security state of the information system after the event occurred). Related controls: AU-2, AU-8, AU-12, SI-11.

Control Enhancements:

(1) CONTENT OF AUDIT RECORDS | ADDITIONAL AUDIT INFORMATION

The information system generates audit records containing the following additional information: [*Assignment: organization-defined additional, more detailed information*].

Supplemental Guidance: Detailed information that organizations may consider in audit records includes, for example, full text recording of privileged commands or the individual identities of group account users. Organizations consider limiting the additional audit information to only that information explicitly needed for specific audit requirements. This facilitates the use of audit trails and audit logs by not including information that could potentially be misleading or could make it more difficult to locate information of interest.

(2) CONTENT OF AUDIT RECORDS | CENTRALIZED MANAGEMENT OF PLANNED AUDIT RECORD CONTENT

The information system provides centralized management and configuration of the content to be captured in audit records generated by [*Assignment: organization-defined information system components*].

Supplemental Guidance: This control enhancement requires that the content to be captured in audit records be configured from a central location (necessitating automation). Organizations coordinate the selection of required audit content to support the centralized management and configuration capability provided by the information system. Related controls: AU-6, AU-7.

References: None.

Priority and Baseline Allocation:

P1	LOW AU-3	MOD AU-3 (1)	HIGH AU-3 (1) (2)

AU-4 AUDIT STORAGE CAPACITY

Control: The organization allocates audit record storage capacity in accordance with [*Assignment: organization-defined audit record storage requirements*].

Supplemental Guidance: Organizations consider the types of auditing to be performed and the audit processing requirements when allocating audit storage capacity. Allocating sufficient audit storage capacity reduces the likelihood of such capacity being exceeded and resulting in the potential loss or reduction of auditing capability. Related controls: AU-2, AU-5, AU-6, AU-7, AU-11, SI-4.

Control Enhancements:

(1) AUDIT STORAGE CAPACITY | TRANSFER TO ALTERNATE STORAGE

The information system off-loads audit records [*Assignment: organization-defined frequency*] onto a different system or media than the system being audited.

Supplemental Guidance: Off-loading is a process designed to preserve the confidentiality and integrity of audit records by moving the records from the primary information system to a secondary or alternate system. It is a common process in information systems with limited audit storage capacity; the audit storage is used only in a transitory fashion until the system can communicate with the secondary or alternate system designated for storing the audit records, at which point the information is transferred.

References: None.

Priority and Baseline Allocation:

P1	LOW AU-4	MOD AU-4	HIGH AU-4

AU-5 RESPONSE TO AUDIT PROCESSING FAILURES

Control: The information system:

a. Alerts [*Assignment: organization-defined personnel or roles*] in the event of an audit processing failure; and

b. Takes the following additional actions: [*Assignment: organization-defined actions to be taken (e.g., shut down information system, overwrite oldest audit records, stop generating audit records)*].

Supplemental Guidance: Audit processing failures include, for example, software/hardware errors, failures in the audit capturing mechanisms, and audit storage capacity being reached or exceeded. Organizations may choose to define additional actions for different audit processing failures (e.g., by type, by location, by severity, or a combination of such factors). This control applies to each audit data storage repository (i.e., distinct information system component where audit records are stored), the total audit storage capacity of organizations (i.e., all audit data storage repositories combined), or both. Related controls: AU-4, SI-12.

Control Enhancements:

(1) *RESPONSE TO AUDIT PROCESSING FAILURES | AUDIT STORAGE CAPACITY*

The information system provides a warning to [*Assignment: organization-defined personnel, roles, and/or locations*] within [*Assignment: organization-defined time period*] when allocated audit record storage volume reaches [*Assignment: organization-defined percentage*] of repository maximum audit record storage capacity.

Supplemental Guidance: Organizations may have multiple audit data storage repositories distributed across multiple information system components, with each repository having different storage volume capacities.

(2) *RESPONSE TO AUDIT PROCESSING FAILURES | REAL-TIME ALERTS*

The information system provides an alert in [*Assignment: organization-defined real-time period*] to [*Assignment: organization-defined personnel, roles, and/or locations*] when the following audit failure events occur: [*Assignment: organization-defined audit failure events requiring real-time alerts*].

Supplemental Guidance: Alerts provide organizations with urgent messages. Real-time alerts provide these messages at information technology speed (i.e., the time from event detection to alert occurs in seconds or less).

(3) *RESPONSE TO AUDIT PROCESSING FAILURES | CONFIGURABLE TRAFFIC VOLUME THRESHOLDS*

The information system enforces configurable network communications traffic volume thresholds reflecting limits on auditing capacity and [*Selection: rejects; delays*] network traffic above those thresholds.

Supplemental Guidance: Organizations have the capability to reject or delay the processing of network communications traffic if auditing such traffic is determined to exceed the storage capacity of the information system audit function. The rejection or delay response is triggered by the established organizational traffic volume thresholds which can be adjusted based on changes to audit storage capacity.

(4) *RESPONSE TO AUDIT PROCESSING FAILURES | SHUTDOWN ON FAILURE*

The information system invokes a [*Selection: full system shutdown; partial system shutdown; degraded operational mode with limited mission/business functionality available*] in the event of [*Assignment: organization-defined audit failures*], unless an alternate audit capability exists.

Supplemental Guidance: Organizations determine the types of audit failures that can trigger automatic information system shutdowns or degraded operations. Because of the importance of ensuring mission/business continuity, organizations may determine that the nature of the audit failure is not so severe that it warrants a complete shutdown of the information system supporting the core organizational missions/business operations. In those instances, partial information system shutdowns or operating in a degraded mode with reduced capability may be viable alternatives. Related control: AU-15.

References: None.

Priority and Baseline Allocation:

| P1 | LOW AU-5 | MOD AU-5 | HIGH AU-5 (1) (2) |

AU-6 AUDIT REVIEW, ANALYSIS, AND REPORTING

Control: The organization:

a. Reviews and analyzes information system audit records [*Assignment: organization-defined frequency*] for indications of [*Assignment: organization-defined inappropriate or unusual activity*]; and

b. Reports findings to [*Assignment: organization-defined personnel or roles*].

Supplemental Guidance: Audit review, analysis, and reporting covers information security-related auditing performed by organizations including, for example, auditing that results from monitoring of account usage, remote access, wireless connectivity, mobile device connection, configuration settings, system component inventory, use of maintenance tools and nonlocal maintenance, physical access, temperature and humidity, equipment delivery and removal, communications at the information system boundaries, use of mobile code, and use of VoIP. Findings can be reported to organizational entities that include, for example, incident response team, help desk, information security group/department. If organizations are prohibited from reviewing and analyzing audit information or unable to conduct such activities (e.g., in certain national security applications or systems), the review/analysis may be carried out by other organizations granted such authority. Related controls: AC-2, AC-3, AC-6, AC-17, AT-3, AU-7, AU-16, CA-7, CM-5, CM-10, CM-11, IA-3, IA-5, IR-5, IR-6, MA-4, MP-4, PE-3, PE-6, PE-14, PE-16, RA-5, SC-7, SC-18, SC-19, SI-3, SI-4, SI-7.

Control Enhancements:

(1) AUDIT REVIEW, ANALYSIS, AND REPORTING | PROCESS INTEGRATION

The organization employs automated mechanisms to integrate audit review, analysis, and reporting processes to support organizational processes for investigation and response to suspicious activities.

Supplemental Guidance: Organizational processes benefiting from integrated audit review, analysis, and reporting include, for example, incident response, continuous monitoring, contingency planning, and Inspector General audits. Related controls: AU-12, PM-7.

(2) AUDIT REVIEW, ANALYSIS, AND REPORTING | AUTOMATED SECURITY ALERTS

[Withdrawn: Incorporated into SI-4].

(3) AUDIT REVIEW, ANALYSIS, AND REPORTING | CORRELATE AUDIT REPOSITORIES

The organization analyzes and correlates audit records across different repositories to gain organization-wide situational awareness.

Supplemental Guidance: Organization-wide situational awareness includes awareness across all three tiers of risk management (i.e., organizational, mission/business process, and information system) and supports cross-organization awareness. Related controls: AU-12, IR-4.

(4) AUDIT REVIEW, ANALYSIS, AND REPORTING | CENTRAL REVIEW AND ANALYSIS

The information system provides the capability to centrally review and analyze audit records from multiple components within the system.

Supplemental Guidance: Automated mechanisms for centralized reviews and analyses include, for example, Security Information Management products. Related controls: AU-2, AU-12.

(5) AUDIT REVIEW, ANALYSIS, AND REPORTING | INTEGRATION / SCANNING AND MONITORING CAPABILITIES

The organization integrates analysis of audit records with analysis of [*Selection (one or more): vulnerability scanning information; performance data; information system monitoring information; [Assignment: organization-defined data/information collected from other sources]*] to further enhance the ability to identify inappropriate or unusual activity.

Supplemental Guidance: This control enhancement does not require vulnerability scanning, the generation of performance data, or information system monitoring. Rather, the enhancement requires that the analysis of information being otherwise produced in these areas is integrated with the analysis of audit information. Security Event and Information Management System tools can facilitate audit record aggregation/consolidation from multiple information system components as well as audit record correlation and analysis. The use of standardized audit record analysis scripts developed by organizations (with localized script adjustments, as necessary) provides more cost-effective approaches for analyzing audit record information collected. The correlation of audit record information with vulnerability scanning information is important in determining the veracity of vulnerability scans and correlating attack detection events with scanning results. Correlation with performance data can help uncover denial of service attacks or cyber attacks resulting in unauthorized use of resources. Correlation with system monitoring information can assist in uncovering attacks and in better relating audit information to operational situations. Related controls: AU-12, IR-4, RA-5.

(6) AUDIT REVIEW, ANALYSIS, AND REPORTING | CORRELATION WITH PHYSICAL MONITORING

The organization correlates information from audit records with information obtained from monitoring physical access to further enhance the ability to identify suspicious, inappropriate, unusual, or malevolent activity.

Supplemental Guidance: The correlation of physical audit information and audit logs from information systems may assist organizations in identifying examples of suspicious behavior or supporting evidence of such behavior. For example, the correlation of an individual's identity for logical access to certain information systems with the additional physical security information that the individual was actually present at the facility when the logical access occurred, may prove to be useful in investigations.

(7) AUDIT REVIEW, ANALYSIS, AND REPORTING | PERMITTED ACTIONS

The organization specifies the permitted actions for each [Selection (one or more): information system process; role; user] associated with the review, analysis, and reporting of audit information.

Supplemental Guidance: Organizations specify permitted actions for information system processes, roles, and/or users associated with the review, analysis, and reporting of audit records through account management techniques. Specifying permitted actions on audit information is a way to enforce the principle of least privilege. Permitted actions are enforced by the information system and include, for example, read, write, execute, append, and delete.

(8) AUDIT REVIEW, ANALYSIS, AND REPORTING | FULL TEXT ANALYSIS OF PRIVILEGED COMMANDS

The organization performs a full text analysis of audited privileged commands in a physically distinct component or subsystem of the information system, or other information system that is dedicated to that analysis.

Supplemental Guidance: This control enhancement requires a distinct environment for the dedicated analysis of audit information related to privileged users without compromising such information on the information system where the users have elevated privileges including the capability to execute privileged commands. Full text analysis refers to analysis that considers the full text of privileged commands (i.e., commands and all parameters) as opposed to analysis that considers only the name of the command. Full text analysis includes, for example, the use of pattern matching and heuristics. Related controls: AU-3, AU-9, AU-11, AU-12.

(9) AUDIT REVIEW, ANALYSIS, AND REPORTING | CORRELATION WITH INFORMATION FROM NONTECHNICAL SOURCES

The organization correlates information from nontechnical sources with audit information to enhance organization-wide situational awareness.

Supplemental Guidance: Nontechnical sources include, for example, human resources records documenting organizational policy violations (e.g., sexual harassment incidents, improper use of organizational information assets). Such information can lead organizations to a more directed analytical effort to detect potential malicious insider activity. Due to the sensitive nature of the information available from nontechnical sources, organizations limit access to such information to minimize the potential for the inadvertent release of privacy-related information to individuals that do not have a need to know. Thus, correlation of information from nontechnical sources with audit information generally occurs only when individuals are suspected of being involved in a security incident. Organizations obtain legal advice prior to initiating such actions. Related control: AT-2.

(10) AUDIT REVIEW, ANALYSIS, AND REPORTING | AUDIT LEVEL ADJUSTMENT

The organization adjusts the level of audit review, analysis, and reporting within the information system when there is a change in risk based on law enforcement information, intelligence information, or other credible sources of information.

Supplemental Guidance: The frequency, scope, and/or depth of the audit review, analysis, and reporting may be adjusted to meet organizational needs based on new information received.

References: None.

Priority and Baseline Allocation:

P1	LOW AU-6	MOD AU-6 (1) (3)	HIGH AU-6 (1) (3) (5) (6)

AU-7 AUDIT REDUCTION AND REPORT GENERATION

Control: The information system provides an audit reduction and report generation capability that:

a. Supports on-demand audit review, analysis, and reporting requirements and after-the-fact investigations of security incidents; and

b. Does not alter the original content or time ordering of audit records.

Supplemental Guidance: Audit reduction is a process that manipulates collected audit information and organizes such information in a summary format that is more meaningful to analysts. Audit reduction and report generation capabilities do not always emanate from the same information system or from the same organizational entities conducting auditing activities. Audit reduction capability can include, for example, modern data mining techniques with advanced data filters to identify anomalous behavior in audit records. The report generation capability provided by the information system can generate customizable reports. Time ordering of audit records can be a significant issue if the granularity of the timestamp in the record is insufficient. Related control: AU-6.

Control Enhancements:

(1) AUDIT REDUCTION AND REPORT GENERATION | AUTOMATIC PROCESSING

The information system provides the capability to process audit records for events of interest based on [Assignment: organization-defined audit fields within audit records].

Supplemental Guidance: Events of interest can be identified by the content of specific audit record fields including, for example, identities of individuals, event types, event locations, event times, event dates, system resources involved, IP addresses involved, or information objects accessed. Organizations may define audit event criteria to any degree of granularity required, for example, locations selectable by general networking location (e.g., by network or subnetwork) or selectable by specific information system component. Related controls: AU-2, AU-12.

(2) AUDIT REDUCTION AND REPORT GENERATION | AUTOMATIC SORT AND SEARCH

The information system provides the capability to sort and search audit records for events of interest based on the content of [Assignment: organization-defined audit fields within audit records].

Supplemental Guidance: Sorting and searching of audit records may be based upon the contents of audit record fields, for example: (i) date/time of events; (ii) user identifiers; (iii) Internet Protocol (IP) addresses involved in the event; (iv) type of event; or (v) event success/failure.

References: None.

Priority and Baseline Allocation:

| P2 | LOW Not Selected | MOD AU-7 (1) | HIGH AU-7 (1) |

AU-8 TIME STAMPS

Control: The information system:

a. Uses internal system clocks to generate time stamps for audit records; and

b. Records time stamps for audit records that can be mapped to Coordinated Universal Time (UTC) or Greenwich Mean Time (GMT) and meets [Assignment: organization-defined granularity of time measurement].

Supplemental Guidance: Time stamps generated by the information system include date and time. Time is commonly expressed in Coordinated Universal Time (UTC), a modern continuation of Greenwich Mean Time (GMT), or local time with an offset from UTC. Granularity of time measurements refers to the degree of synchronization between information system clocks and reference clocks, for example, clocks synchronizing within hundreds of milliseconds or within tens of milliseconds. Organizations may define different time granularities for different system components. Time service can also be critical to other security capabilities such as access control and identification and authentication, depending on the nature of the mechanisms used to support those capabilities. Related controls: AU-3, AU-12.

Control Enhancements:

(1) TIME STAMPS | SYNCHRONIZATION WITH AUTHORITATIVE TIME SOURCE

   The information system:

   (a) Compares the internal information system clocks [Assignment: organization-defined frequency] with [Assignment: organization-defined authoritative time source]; and

   (b) Synchronizes the internal system clocks to the authoritative time source when the time difference is greater than [Assignment: organization-defined time period].

   Supplemental Guidance: This control enhancement provides uniformity of time stamps for information systems with multiple system clocks and systems connected over a network.

(2) TIME STAMPS | SECONDARY AUTHORITATIVE TIME SOURCE

   The information system identifies a secondary authoritative time source that is located in a different geographic region than the primary authoritative time source.

References: None.

Priority and Baseline Allocation:

| P1 | LOW AU-8 | MOD AU-8 (1) | HIGH AU-8 (1) |

AU-9 PROTECTION OF AUDIT INFORMATION

Control: The information system protects audit information and audit tools from unauthorized access, modification, and deletion.

Supplemental Guidance: Audit information includes all information (e.g., audit records, audit settings, and audit reports) needed to successfully audit information system activity. This control focuses on technical protection of audit information. Physical protection of audit information is addressed by media protection controls and physical and environmental protection controls. Related controls: AC-3, AC-6, MP-2, MP-4, PE-2, PE-3, PE-6.

Control Enhancements:

(1) *PROTECTION OF AUDIT INFORMATION | HARDWARE WRITE-ONCE MEDIA*
The information system writes audit trails to hardware-enforced, write-once media.

Supplemental Guidance: This control enhancement applies to the initial generation of audit trails (i.e., the collection of audit records that represents the audit information to be used for detection, analysis, and reporting purposes) and to the backup of those audit trails. The enhancement does not apply to the initial generation of audit records prior to being written to an audit trail. Write-once, read-many (WORM) media includes, for example, Compact Disk-Recordable (CD-R) and Digital Video Disk-Recordable (DVD-R). In contrast, the use of switchable write-protection media such as on tape cartridges or Universal Serial Bus (USB) drives results in write-protected, but not write-once, media. Related controls: AU-4, AU-5.

(2) *PROTECTION OF AUDIT INFORMATION | AUDIT BACKUP ON SEPARATE PHYSICAL SYSTEMS / COMPONENTS*
The information system backs up audit records [*Assignment: organization-defined frequency*] onto a physically different system or system component than the system or component being audited.

Supplemental Guidance: This control enhancement helps to ensure that a compromise of the information system being audited does not also result in a compromise of the audit records. Related controls: AU-4, AU-5, AU-11.

(3) *PROTECTION OF AUDIT INFORMATION | CRYPTOGRAPHIC PROTECTION*
The information system implements cryptographic mechanisms to protect the integrity of audit information and audit tools.

Supplemental Guidance: Cryptographic mechanisms used for protecting the integrity of audit information include, for example, signed hash functions using asymmetric cryptography enabling distribution of the public key to verify the hash information while maintaining the confidentiality of the secret key used to generate the hash. Related controls: AU-10, SC-12, SC-13.

(4) *PROTECTION OF AUDIT INFORMATION | ACCESS BY SUBSET OF PRIVILEGED USERS*
The organization authorizes access to management of audit functionality to only [*Assignment: organization-defined subset of privileged users*].

Supplemental Guidance: Individuals with privileged access to an information system and who are also the subject of an audit by that system, may affect the reliability of audit information by inhibiting audit activities or modifying audit records. This control enhancement requires that privileged access be further defined between audit-related privileges and other privileges, thus limiting the users with audit-related privileges. Related control: AC-5.

(5) *PROTECTION OF AUDIT INFORMATION | DUAL AUTHORIZATION*
The organization enforces dual authorization for [*Selection (one or more): movement; deletion*] of [*Assignment: organization-defined audit information*].

Supplemental Guidance: Organizations may choose different selection options for different types of audit information. Dual authorization mechanisms require the approval of two authorized individuals in order to execute. Dual authorization may also be known as two-person control. Related controls: AC-3, MP-2.

(6) *PROTECTION OF AUDIT INFORMATION | READ ONLY ACCESS*
The organization authorizes read-only access to audit information to [*Assignment: organization-defined subset of privileged users*].

Supplemental Guidance: Restricting privileged user authorizations to read-only helps to limit the potential damage to organizations that could be initiated by such users (e.g., deleting audit records to cover up malicious activity).

References: None.

Priority and Baseline Allocation:

P1	**LOW** AU-9	**MOD** AU-9 (4)	**HIGH** AU-9 (2) (3) (4)

AU-10 NON-REPUDIATION

Control: The information system protects against an individual (or process acting on behalf of an individual) falsely denying having performed [*Assignment: organization-defined actions to be covered by non-repudiation*].

Supplemental Guidance: Types of individual actions covered by non-repudiation include, for example, creating information, sending and receiving messages, approving information (e.g., indicating concurrence or signing a contract). Non-repudiation protects individuals against later claims by: (i) authors of not having authored particular documents; (ii) senders of not having transmitted messages; (iii) receivers of not having received messages; or (iv) signatories of not having signed documents. Non-repudiation services can be used to determine if information originated from a particular individual, or if an individual took specific actions (e.g., sending an email, signing a contract, approving a procurement request) or received specific information. Organizations obtain non-repudiation services by employing various techniques or mechanisms (e.g., digital signatures, digital message receipts). Related controls: SC-12, SC-8, SC-13, SC-16, SC-17, SC-23.

Control Enhancements:

(1) NON-REPUDIATION | ASSOCIATION OF IDENTITIES

The information system:

(a) Binds the identity of the information producer with the information to [*Assignment: organization-defined strength of binding*]; and

(b) Provides the means for authorized individuals to determine the identity of the producer of the information.

Supplemental Guidance: This control enhancement supports audit requirements that provide organizational personnel with the means to identify who produced specific information in the event of an information transfer. Organizations determine and approve the strength of the binding between the information producer and the information based on the security category of the information and relevant risk factors. Related controls: AC-4, AC-16.

(2) NON-REPUDIATION | VALIDATE BINDING OF INFORMATION PRODUCER IDENTITY

The information system:

(a) Validates the binding of the information producer identity to the information at [*Assignment: organization-defined frequency*]; and

(b) Performs [*Assignment: organization-defined actions*] in the event of a validation error.

Supplemental Guidance: This control enhancement prevents the modification of information between production and review. The validation of bindings can be achieved, for example, by the use of cryptographic checksums. Organizations determine if validations are in response to user requests or generated automatically. Related controls: AC-3, AC-4, AC-16.

(3) NON-REPUDIATION | CHAIN OF CUSTODY

The information system maintains reviewer/releaser identity and credentials within the established chain of custody for all information reviewed or released.

Supplemental Guidance: Chain of custody is a process that tracks the movement of evidence through its collection, safeguarding, and analysis life cycle by documenting each person who handled the evidence, the date and time it was collected or transferred, and the purpose for the transfer. If the reviewer is a human or if the review function is automated but separate from the release/transfer function, the information system associates the identity of the reviewer of the information to be released with the information and the information label. In the case of human reviews, this control enhancement provides organizational officials the means to identify who reviewed and released the information. In the case of automated reviews, this control enhancement ensures that only approved review functions are employed. Related controls: AC-4, AC-16.

(4) *NON-REPUDIATION | VALIDATE BINDING OF INFORMATION REVIEWER IDENTITY*

The information system:

(a) Validates the binding of the information reviewer identity to the information at the transfer or release points prior to release/transfer between [*Assignment: organization-defined security domains*]; and

(b) Performs [*Assignment: organization-defined actions*] in the event of a validation error.

Supplemental Guidance: This control enhancement prevents the modification of information between review and transfer/release. The validation of bindings can be achieved, for example, by the use of cryptographic checksums. Organizations determine validations are in response to user requests or generated automatically. Related controls: AC-4, AC-16.

(5) *NON-REPUDIATION | DIGITAL SIGNATURES*
[Withdrawn: Incorporated into SI-7].

References: None.

Priority and Baseline Allocation:

P2	LOW Not Selected	MOD Not Selected	HIGH AU-10

AU-11 AUDIT RECORD RETENTION

Control: The organization retains audit records for [*Assignment: organization-defined time period consistent with records retention policy*] to provide support for after-the-fact investigations of security incidents and to meet regulatory and organizational information retention requirements.

Supplemental Guidance: Organizations retain audit records until it is determined that they are no longer needed for administrative, legal, audit, or other operational purposes. This includes, for example, retention and availability of audit records relative to Freedom of Information Act (FOIA) requests, subpoenas, and law enforcement actions. Organizations develop standard categories of audit records relative to such types of actions and standard response processes for each type of action. The National Archives and Records Administration (NARA) General Records Schedules provide federal policy on record retention. Related controls: AU-4, AU-5, AU-9, MP-6.

Control Enhancements:

(1) *AUDIT RECORD RETENTION | LONG-TERM RETRIEVAL CAPABILITY*
The organization employs [*Assignment: organization-defined measures*] to ensure that long-term audit records generated by the information system can be retrieved.

Supplemental Guidance: Measures employed by organizations to help facilitate the retrieval of audit records include, for example, converting records to newer formats, retaining equipment capable of reading the records, and retaining necessary documentation to help organizational personnel understand how to interpret the records.

References: None.

Priority and Baseline Allocation:

P3	LOW AU-11	MOD AU-11	HIGH AU-11

AU-12 AUDIT GENERATION

Control: The information system:

a. Provides audit record generation capability for the auditable events defined in AU-2 a. at [*Assignment: organization-defined information system components*];

b. Allows [*Assignment: organization-defined personnel or roles*] to select which auditable events are to be audited by specific components of the information system; and

c. Generates audit records for the events defined in AU-2 d. with the content defined in AU-3.

Supplemental Guidance: Audit records can be generated from many different information system components. The list of audited events is the set of events for which audits are to be generated. These events are typically a subset of all events for which the information system is capable of generating audit records. Related controls: AC-3, AU-2, AU-3, AU-6, AU-7.

Control Enhancements:

(1) AUDIT GENERATION | SYSTEM-WIDE / TIME-CORRELATED AUDIT TRAIL

The information system compiles audit records from [*Assignment: organization-defined information system components*] into a system-wide (logical or physical) audit trail that is time-correlated to within [*Assignment: organization-defined level of tolerance for the relationship between time stamps of individual records in the audit trail*].

Supplemental Guidance: Audit trails are time-correlated if the time stamps in the individual audit records can be reliably related to the time stamps in other audit records to achieve a time ordering of the records within organizational tolerances. Related controls: AU-8, AU-12.

(2) AUDIT GENERATION | STANDARDIZED FORMATS

The information system produces a system-wide (logical or physical) audit trail composed of audit records in a standardized format.

Supplemental Guidance: Audit information that is normalized to common standards promotes interoperability and exchange of such information between dissimilar devices and information systems. This facilitates production of event information that can be more readily analyzed and correlated. Standard formats for audit records include, for example, system log records and audit records compliant with Common Event Expressions (CEE). If logging mechanisms within information systems do not conform to standardized formats, systems may convert individual audit records into standardized formats when compiling system-wide audit trails.

(3) AUDIT GENERATION | CHANGES BY AUTHORIZED INDIVIDUALS

The information system provides the capability for [*Assignment: organization-defined individuals or roles*] to change the auditing to be performed on [*Assignment: organization-defined information system components*] based on [*Assignment: organization-defined selectable event criteria*] within [*Assignment: organization-defined time thresholds*].

Supplemental Guidance: This control enhancement enables organizations to extend or limit auditing as necessary to meet organizational requirements. Auditing that is limited to conserve information system resources may be extended to address certain threat situations. In addition, auditing may be limited to a specific set of events to facilitate audit reduction, analysis, and reporting. Organizations can establish time thresholds in which audit actions are changed, for example, near real-time, within minutes, or within hours. Related control: AU-7.

References: None.

Priority and Baseline Allocation:

P1	LOW AU-12	MOD AU-12	HIGH AU-12 (1) (3)

AU-13 MONITORING FOR INFORMATION DISCLOSURE

Control: The organization monitors [*Assignment: organization-defined open source information and/or information sites*] [*Assignment: organization-defined frequency*] for evidence of unauthorized disclosure of organizational information.

Supplemental Guidance: Open source information includes, for example, social networking sites. Related controls: PE-3, SC-7.

Control Enhancements:

(1) MONITORING FOR INFORMATION DISCLOSURE | USE OF AUTOMATED TOOLS

The organization employs automated mechanisms to determine if organizational information has been disclosed in an unauthorized manner.

Supplemental Guidance: Automated mechanisms can include, for example, automated scripts to monitor new posts on selected websites, and commercial services providing notifications and alerts to organizations.

(2) MONITORING FOR INFORMATION DISCLOSURE | REVIEW OF MONITORED SITES

The organization reviews the open source information sites being monitored [*Assignment: organization-defined frequency*].

References: None.

Priority and Baseline Allocation:

| P0 | LOW Not Selected | MOD Not Selected | HIGH Not Selected |

AU-14 SESSION AUDIT

Control: The information system provides the capability for authorized users to select a user session to capture/record or view/hear.

Supplemental Guidance: Session audits include, for example, monitoring keystrokes, tracking websites visited, and recording information and/or file transfers. Session auditing activities are developed, integrated, and used in consultation with legal counsel in accordance with applicable federal laws, Executive Orders, directives, policies, regulations, or standards. Related controls: AC-3, AU-4, AU-5, AU-9, AU-11.

Control Enhancements:

(1) SESSION AUDIT | SYSTEM START-UP

The information system initiates session audits at system start-up.

(2) SESSION AUDIT | CAPTURE/RECORD AND LOG CONTENT

The information system provides the capability for authorized users to capture/record and log content related to a user session.

(3) SESSION AUDIT | REMOTE VIEWING / LISTENING

The information system provides the capability for authorized users to remotely view/hear all content related to an established user session in real time.

References: None.

Priority and Baseline Allocation:

| P0 | LOW Not Selected | MOD Not Selected | HIGH Not Selected |

AU-15 ALTERNATE AUDIT CAPABILITY

Control: The organization provides an alternate audit capability in the event of a failure in primary audit capability that provides [*Assignment: organization-defined alternate audit functionality*].

Supplemental Guidance: Since an alternate audit capability may be a short-term protection employed until the failure in the primary auditing capability is corrected, organizations may determine that the alternate audit capability need only provide a subset of the primary audit functionality that is impacted by the failure. Related control: AU-5.

Control Enhancements: None.

References: None.

Priority and Baseline Allocation:

| P0 | LOW Not Selected | MOD Not Selected | HIGH Not Selected |

AU-16 CROSS-ORGANIZATIONAL AUDITING

Control: The organization employs [*Assignment: organization-defined methods*] for coordinating [*Assignment: organization-defined audit information*] among external organizations when audit information is transmitted across organizational boundaries.

Supplemental Guidance: When organizations use information systems and/or services of external organizations, the auditing capability necessitates a coordinated approach across organizations. For example, maintaining the identity of individuals that requested particular services across organizational boundaries may often be very difficult, and doing so may prove to have significant performance ramifications. Therefore, it is often the case that cross-organizational auditing (e.g., the type of auditing capability provided by service-oriented architectures) simply captures the identity of individuals issuing requests at the initial information system, and subsequent systems record that the requests emanated from authorized individuals. Related control: AU-6.

Control Enhancements:

(1) CROSS-ORGANIZATIONAL AUDITING | IDENTITY PRESERVATION

The organization requires that the identity of individuals be preserved in cross-organizational audit trails.

Supplemental Guidance: This control enhancement applies when there is a need to be able to trace actions that are performed across organizational boundaries to a specific individual.

(2) CROSS-ORGANIZATIONAL AUDITING | SHARING OF AUDIT INFORMATION

The organization provides cross-organizational audit information to [*Assignment: organization-defined organizations*] based on [*Assignment: organization-defined cross-organizational sharing agreements*].

Supplemental Guidance: Because of the distributed nature of the audit information, cross-organization sharing of audit information may be essential for effective analysis of the auditing being performed. For example, the audit records of one organization may not provide sufficient information to determine the appropriate or inappropriate use of organizational information resources by individuals in other organizations. In some instances, only the home organizations of individuals have the appropriate knowledge to make such determinations, thus requiring the sharing of audit information among organizations.

References: None.

Priority and Baseline Allocation:

| P0 | LOW Not Selected | MOD Not Selected | HIGH Not Selected |

FAMILY: SECURITY ASSESSMENT AND AUTHORIZATION

CA-1 SECURITY ASSESSMENT AND AUTHORIZATION POLICY AND PROCEDURES

Control: The organization:

a. Develops, documents, and disseminates to [*Assignment: organization-defined personnel or roles*]:

1. A security assessment and authorization policy that addresses purpose, scope, roles, responsibilities, management commitment, coordination among organizational entities, and compliance; and

2. Procedures to facilitate the implementation of the security assessment and authorization policy and associated security assessment and authorization controls; and

b. Reviews and updates the current:

1. Security assessment and authorization policy [*Assignment: organization-defined frequency*]; and

2. Security assessment and authorization procedures [*Assignment: organization-defined frequency*].

Supplemental Guidance: This control addresses the establishment of policy and procedures for the effective implementation of selected security controls and control enhancements in the CA family. Policy and procedures reflect applicable federal laws, Executive Orders, directives, regulations, policies, standards, and guidance. Security program policies and procedures at the organization level may make the need for system-specific policies and procedures unnecessary. The policy can be included as part of the general information security policy for organizations or conversely, can be represented by multiple policies reflecting the complex nature of certain organizations. The procedures can be established for the security program in general and for particular information systems, if needed. The organizational risk management strategy is a key factor in establishing policy and procedures. Related control: PM-9.

Control Enhancements: None.

References: NIST Special Publications 800-12, 800-37, 800-53A, 800-100.

Priority and Baseline Allocation:

| P1 | LOW CA-1 | MOD CA-1 | HIGH CA-1 |

CA-2 SECURITY ASSESSMENTS

Control: The organization:

a. Develops a security assessment plan that describes the scope of the assessment including:

1. Security controls and control enhancements under assessment;

2. Assessment procedures to be used to determine security control effectiveness; and

3. Assessment environment, assessment team, and assessment roles and responsibilities;

b. Assesses the security controls in the information system and its environment of operation [*Assignment: organization-defined frequency*] to determine the extent to which the controls are implemented correctly, operating as intended, and producing the desired outcome with respect to meeting established security requirements;

c. Produces a security assessment report that documents the results of the assessment; and

d. Provides the results of the security control assessment to [*Assignment: organization-defined individuals or roles*].

Supplemental Guidance: Organizations assess security controls in organizational information systems and the environments in which those systems operate as part of: (i) initial and ongoing security authorizations; (ii) FISMA annual assessments; (iii) continuous monitoring; and (iv) system development life cycle activities. Security assessments: (i) ensure that information security is built into organizational information systems; (ii) identify weaknesses and deficiencies early in the development process; (iii) provide essential information needed to make risk-based decisions as part of security authorization processes; and (iv) ensure compliance to vulnerability mitigation procedures. Assessments are conducted on the implemented security controls from Appendix F (main catalog) and Appendix G (Program Management controls) as documented in System Security Plans and Information Security Program Plans. Organizations can use other types of assessment activities such as vulnerability scanning and system monitoring to maintain the security posture of information systems during the entire life cycle. Security assessment reports document assessment results in sufficient detail as deemed necessary by organizations, to determine the accuracy and completeness of the reports and whether the security controls are implemented correctly, operating as intended, and producing the desired outcome with respect to meeting security requirements. The FISMA requirement for assessing security controls at least annually does not require additional assessment activities to those activities already in place in organizational security authorization processes. Security assessment results are provided to the individuals or roles appropriate for the types of assessments being conducted. For example, assessments conducted in support of security authorization decisions are provided to authorizing officials or authorizing official designated representatives.

To satisfy annual assessment requirements, organizations can use assessment results from the following sources: (i) initial or ongoing information system authorizations; (ii) continuous monitoring; or (iii) system development life cycle activities. Organizations ensure that security assessment results are current, relevant to the determination of security control effectiveness, and obtained with the appropriate level of assessor independence. Existing security control assessment results can be reused to the extent that the results are still valid and can also be supplemented with additional assessments as needed. Subsequent to initial authorizations and in accordance with OMB policy, organizations assess security controls during continuous monitoring. Organizations establish the frequency for ongoing security control assessments in accordance with organizational continuous monitoring strategies. Information Assurance Vulnerability Alerts provide useful examples of vulnerability mitigation procedures. External audits (e.g., audits by external entities such as regulatory agencies) are outside the scope of this control. Related controls: CA-5, CA-6, CA-7, PM-9, RA-5, SA-11, SA-12, SI-4.

Control Enhancements:

(1) SECURITY ASSESSMENTS | INDEPENDENT ASSESSORS

The organization employs assessors or assessment teams with [*Assignment: organization-defined level of independence*] to conduct security control assessments.

Supplemental Guidance: Independent assessors or assessment teams are individuals or groups who conduct impartial assessments of organizational information systems. Impartiality implies that assessors are free from any perceived or actual conflicts of interest with regard to the development, operation, or management of the organizational information systems under assessment or to the determination of security control effectiveness. To achieve impartiality, assessors should not: (i) create a mutual or conflicting interest with the organizations where the assessments are being conducted; (ii) assess their own work; (iii) act as management or employees of the organizations they are serving; or (iv) place themselves in positions of advocacy for the organizations acquiring their services. Independent assessments can be obtained from elements within organizations or can be contracted to public or private sector entities outside of organizations. Authorizing officials determine the required level of independence based on the security categories of information systems and/or the ultimate risk to organizational operations, organizational assets, or individuals. Authorizing officials also determine if the level of assessor independence provides sufficient assurance that the results are sound and can be used to make credible, risk-based decisions. This includes determining whether contracted security assessment services have sufficient independence, for example, when information system owners are not directly involved in contracting processes or cannot unduly influence the impartiality of assessors conducting assessments. In special situations, for example, when organizations that own the information systems are small or organizational structures require that assessments are conducted by individuals that are in the developmental, operational, or management chain of system owners, independence in assessment processes can be achieved by ensuring that assessment results are carefully reviewed and analyzed by independent teams of experts to validate the completeness, accuracy, integrity, and reliability of the results. Organizations recognize that assessments performed for purposes other than direct support to authorization decisions are, when performed by assessors with sufficient independence, more likely to be useable for such decisions, thereby reducing the need to repeat assessments.

(2) SECURITY ASSESSMENTS | SPECIALIZED ASSESSMENTS

The organization includes as part of security control assessments, [Assignment: organization-defined frequency], [Selection: announced; unannounced], [Selection (one or more): in-depth monitoring; vulnerability scanning; malicious user testing; insider threat assessment; performance/load testing; [Assignment: organization-defined other forms of security assessment]].

Supplemental Guidance: Organizations can employ information system monitoring, insider threat assessments, malicious user testing, and other forms of testing (e.g., verification and validation) to improve readiness by exercising organizational capabilities and indicating current performance levels as a means of focusing actions to improve security. Organizations conduct assessment activities in accordance with applicable federal laws, Executive Orders, directives, policies, regulations, and standards. Authorizing officials approve the assessment methods in coordination with the organizational risk executive function. Organizations can incorporate vulnerabilities uncovered during assessments into vulnerability remediation processes. Related controls: PE-3, SI-2.

(3) SECURITY ASSESSMENTS | EXTERNAL ORGANIZATIONS

The organization accepts the results of an assessment of [Assignment: organization-defined information system] performed by [Assignment: organization-defined external organization] when the assessment meets [Assignment: organization-defined requirements].

Supplemental Guidance: Organizations may often rely on assessments of specific information systems by other (external) organizations. Utilizing such existing assessments (i.e., reusing existing assessment evidence) can significantly decrease the time and resources required for organizational assessments by limiting the amount of independent assessment activities that organizations need to perform. The factors that organizations may consider in determining whether to accept assessment results from external organizations can vary. Determinations for accepting assessment results can be based on, for example, past assessment experiences one organization has had with another organization, the reputation that organizations have with regard to assessments, the level of detail of supporting assessment documentation provided, or mandates imposed upon organizations by federal legislation, policies, or directives.

References: Executive Order 13587; FIPS Publication 199; NIST Special Publications 800-37, 800-39, 800-53A, 800-115, 800-137.

Priority and Baseline Allocation:

| P2 | LOW CA-2 | MOD CA-2 (1) | HIGH CA-2 (1) (2) |

CA-3 SYSTEM INTERCONNECTIONS

Control: The organization:

a. Authorizes connections from the information system to other information systems through the use of Interconnection Security Agreements;

b. Documents, for each interconnection, the interface characteristics, security requirements, and the nature of the information communicated; and

c. Reviews and updates Interconnection Security Agreements [*Assignment: organization-defined frequency*].

Supplemental Guidance: This control applies to dedicated connections between information systems (i.e., system interconnections) and does not apply to transitory, user-controlled connections such as email and website browsing. Organizations carefully consider the risks that may be introduced when information systems are connected to other systems with different security requirements and security controls, both within organizations and external to organizations. Authorizing officials determine the risk associated with information system connections and the appropriate controls employed. If interconnecting systems have the same authorizing official, organizations do not need to develop Interconnection Security Agreements. Instead, organizations can describe the interface characteristics between those interconnecting systems in their respective security plans. If interconnecting systems have different authorizing officials within the same organization, organizations can either develop Interconnection Security Agreements or describe the interface characteristics between systems in the security plans for the respective systems. Organizations may also incorporate Interconnection Security Agreement information into formal contracts, especially for interconnections established between federal agencies and nonfederal (i.e., private sector) organizations. Risk considerations also include information systems sharing the same networks. For certain technologies (e.g., space, unmanned aerial vehicles, and medical devices), there may be specialized connections in place during preoperational testing. Such connections may require Interconnection Security Agreements and be subject to additional security controls. Related controls: AC-3, AC-4, AC-20, AU-2, AU-12, AU-16, CA-7, IA-3, SA-9, SC-7, SI-4.

Control Enhancements:

(1) SYSTEM INTERCONNECTIONS | UNCLASSIFIED NATIONAL SECURITY SYSTEM CONNECTIONS

The organization prohibits the direct connection of an [*Assignment: organization-defined unclassified, national security system*] to an external network without the use of [*Assignment: organization-defined boundary protection device*].

Supplemental Guidance: Organizations typically do not have control over external networks (e.g., the Internet). Approved boundary protection devices (e.g., routers, firewalls) mediate communications (i.e., information flows) between unclassified national security systems and external networks. This control enhancement is required for organizations processing, storing, or transmitting Controlled Unclassified Information (CUI).

(2) SYSTEM INTERCONNECTIONS | CLASSIFIED NATIONAL SECURITY SYSTEM CONNECTIONS

The organization prohibits the direct connection of a classified, national security system to an external network without the use of [*Assignment: organization-defined boundary protection device*].

Supplemental Guidance: Organizations typically do not have control over external networks (e.g., the Internet). Approved boundary protection devices (e.g., routers, firewalls) mediate communications (i.e., information flows) between classified national security systems and external networks. In addition, approved boundary protection devices (typically managed interface/cross-domain systems) provide information flow enforcement from information systems to external networks.

(3) SYSTEM INTERCONNECTIONS | UNCLASSIFIED NON-NATIONAL SECURITY SYSTEM CONNECTIONS

The organization prohibits the direct connection of an [*Assignment: organization-defined unclassified, non-national security system*] to an external network without the use of [*Assignment; organization-defined boundary protection device*].

Supplemental Guidance: Organizations typically do not have control over external networks (e.g., the Internet). Approved boundary protection devices (e.g., routers, firewalls) mediate communications (i.e., information flows) between unclassified non-national security systems and external networks. This control enhancement is required for organizations processing, storing, or transmitting Controlled Unclassified Information (CUI).

(4) *SYSTEM INTERCONNECTIONS | CONNECTIONS TO PUBLIC NETWORKS*

The organization prohibits the direct connection of an [*Assignment: organization-defined information system*] to a public network.

Supplemental Guidance: A public network is any network accessible to the general public including, for example, the Internet and organizational extranets with public access.

(5) *SYSTEM INTERCONNECTIONS | RESTRICTIONS ON EXTERNAL SYSTEM CONNECTIONS*

The organization employs [*Selection: allow-all, deny-by-exception; deny-all, permit-by-exception*] policy for allowing [*Assignment: organization-defined information systems*] to connect to external information systems.

Supplemental Guidance: Organizations can constrain information system connectivity to external domains (e.g., websites) by employing one of two policies with regard to such connectivity: (i) allow-all, deny by exception, also known as *blacklisting* (the weaker of the two policies); or (ii) deny-all, allow by exception, also known as *whitelisting* (the stronger of the two policies). For either policy, organizations determine what exceptions, if any, are acceptable. Related control: CM-7.

References: FIPS Publication 199; NIST Special Publication 800-47.

Priority and Baseline Allocation:

P1	LOW CA-3	MOD CA-3 (5)	HIGH CA-3 (5)

CA-4 SECURITY CERTIFICATION

[Withdrawn: Incorporated into CA-2].

CA-5 PLAN OF ACTION AND MILESTONES

Control: The organization:

a. Develops a plan of action and milestones for the information system to document the organization's planned remedial actions to correct weaknesses or deficiencies noted during the assessment of the security controls and to reduce or eliminate known vulnerabilities in the system; and

b. Updates existing plan of action and milestones [*Assignment: organization-defined frequency*] based on the findings from security controls assessments, security impact analyses, and continuous monitoring activities.

Supplemental Guidance: Plans of action and milestones are key documents in security authorization packages and are subject to federal reporting requirements established by OMB. Related controls: CA-2, CA-7, CM-4, PM-4.

Control Enhancements:

(1) *PLAN OF ACTION AND MILESTONES | AUTOMATION SUPPORT FOR ACCURACY / CURRENCY*

The organization employs automated mechanisms to help ensure that the plan of action and milestones for the information system is accurate, up to date, and readily available.

References: OMB Memorandum 02-01; NIST Special Publication 800-37.

Priority and Baseline Allocation:

P3	LOW CA-5	MOD CA-5	HIGH CA-5

CA-6 **SECURITY AUTHORIZATION**

Control: The organization:

a. Assigns a senior-level executive or manager as the authorizing official for the information system;

b. Ensures that the authorizing official authorizes the information system for processing before commencing operations; and

c. Updates the security authorization [*Assignment: organization-defined frequency*].

Supplemental Guidance: Security authorizations are official management decisions, conveyed through authorization decision documents, by senior organizational officials or executives (i.e., authorizing officials) to authorize operation of information systems and to explicitly accept the risk to organizational operations and assets, individuals, other organizations, and the Nation based on the implementation of agreed-upon security controls. Authorizing officials provide budgetary oversight for organizational information systems or assume responsibility for the mission/business operations supported by those systems. The security authorization process is an inherently federal responsibility and therefore, authorizing officials must be federal employees. Through the security authorization process, authorizing officials assume responsibility and are accountable for security risks associated with the operation and use of organizational information systems. Accordingly, authorizing officials are in positions with levels of authority commensurate with understanding and accepting such information security-related risks. OMB policy requires that organizations conduct ongoing authorizations of information systems by implementing continuous monitoring programs. Continuous monitoring programs can satisfy three-year reauthorization requirements, so separate reauthorization processes are not necessary. Through the employment of comprehensive continuous monitoring processes, critical information contained in authorization packages (i.e., security plans, security assessment reports, and plans of action and milestones) is updated on an ongoing basis, providing authorizing officials and information system owners with an up-to-date status of the security state of organizational information systems and environments of operation. To reduce the administrative cost of security reauthorization, authorizing officials use the results of continuous monitoring processes to the maximum extent possible as the basis for rendering reauthorization decisions. Related controls: CA-2, CA-7, PM-9, PM-10.

Control Enhancements: None.

References: OMB Circular A-130; OMB Memorandum 11-33; NIST Special Publications 800-37, 800-137.

Priority and Baseline Allocation:

| P2 | LOW CA-6 | MOD CA-6 | HIGH CA-6 |

CA-7 **CONTINUOUS MONITORING**

Control: The organization develops a continuous monitoring strategy and implements a continuous monitoring program that includes:

a. Establishment of [*Assignment: organization-defined metrics*] to be monitored;

b. Establishment of [*Assignment: organization-defined frequencies*] for monitoring and [*Assignment: organization-defined frequencies*] for assessments supporting such monitoring;

c. Ongoing security control assessments in accordance with the organizational continuous monitoring strategy;

d. Ongoing security status monitoring of organization-defined metrics in accordance with the organizational continuous monitoring strategy;

e. Correlation and analysis of security-related information generated by assessments and monitoring;

f. Response actions to address results of the analysis of security-related information; and

g. Reporting the security status of organization and the information system to [*Assignment: organization-defined personnel or roles*] [*Assignment: organization-defined frequency*].

Supplemental Guidance: Continuous monitoring programs facilitate ongoing awareness of threats, vulnerabilities, and information security to support organizational risk management decisions. The terms *continuous* and *ongoing* imply that organizations assess/analyze security controls and information security-related risks at a frequency sufficient to support organizational risk-based decisions. The results of continuous monitoring programs generate appropriate risk response actions by organizations. Continuous monitoring programs also allow organizations to maintain the security authorizations of information systems and common controls over time in highly dynamic environments of operation with changing mission/business needs, threats, vulnerabilities, and technologies. Having access to security-related information on a continuing basis through reports/dashboards gives organizational officials the capability to make more effective and timely risk management decisions, including ongoing security authorization decisions. Automation supports more frequent updates to security authorization packages, hardware/software/firmware inventories, and other system information. Effectiveness is further enhanced when continuous monitoring outputs are formatted to provide information that is specific, measurable, actionable, relevant, and timely. Continuous monitoring activities are scaled in accordance with the security categories of information systems. Related controls: CA-2, CA-5, CA-6, CM-3, CM-4, PM-6, PM-9, RA-5, SA-11, SA-12, SI-2, SI-4.

Control Enhancements:

(1) CONTINUOUS MONITORING | INDEPENDENT ASSESSMENT

The organization employs assessors or assessment teams with [*Assignment: organization-defined level of independence*] to monitor the security controls in the information system on an ongoing basis.

Supplemental Guidance: Organizations can maximize the value of assessments of security controls during the continuous monitoring process by requiring that such assessments be conducted by assessors or assessment teams with appropriate levels of independence based on continuous monitoring strategies. Assessor independence provides a degree of impartiality to the monitoring process. To achieve such impartiality, assessors should not: (i) create a mutual or conflicting interest with the organizations where the assessments are being conducted; (ii) assess their own work; (iii) act as management or employees of the organizations they are serving; or (iv) place themselves in advocacy positions for the organizations acquiring their services.

(2) CONTINUOUS MONITORING | TYPES OF ASSESSMENTS

[Withdrawn: Incorporated into CA-2].

(3) CONTINUOUS MONITORING | TREND ANALYSES

The organization employs trend analyses to determine if security control implementations, the frequency of continuous monitoring activities, and/or the types of activities used in the continuous monitoring process need to be modified based on empirical data.

Supplemental Guidance: Trend analyses can include, for example, examining recent threat information regarding the types of threat events that have occurred within the organization or across the federal government, success rates of certain types of cyber attacks, emerging vulnerabilities in information technologies, evolving social engineering techniques, results from multiple security control assessments, the effectiveness of configuration settings, and findings from Inspectors General or auditors.

References: OMB Memorandum 11-33; NIST Special Publications 800-37, 800-39, 800-53A, 800-115, 800-137; US-CERT Technical Cyber Security Alerts; DoD Information Assurance Vulnerability Alerts.

Priority and Baseline Allocation:

| P2 | LOW CA-7 | MOD CA-7 (1) | HIGH CA-7 (1) |

CA-8 PENETRATION TESTING

Control: The organization conducts penetration testing [*Assignment: organization-defined frequency*] on [*Assignment: organization-defined information systems or system components*].

Supplemental Guidance: Penetration testing is a specialized type of assessment conducted on information systems or individual system components to identify vulnerabilities that could be exploited by adversaries. Such testing can be used to either validate vulnerabilities or determine the degree of resistance organizational information systems have to adversaries within a set of specified constraints (e.g., time, resources, and/or skills). Penetration testing attempts to duplicate the actions of adversaries in carrying out hostile cyber attacks against organizations and provides a more in-depth analysis of security-related weaknesses/deficiencies. Organizations can also use the results of vulnerability analyses to support penetration testing activities. Penetration testing can be conducted on the hardware, software, or firmware components of an information system and can exercise both physical and technical security controls. A standard method for penetration testing includes, for example: (i) pretest analysis based on full knowledge of the target system; (ii) pretest identification of potential vulnerabilities based on pretest analysis; and (iii) testing designed to determine exploitability of identified vulnerabilities. All parties agree to the rules of engagement before the commencement of penetration testing scenarios. Organizations correlate the penetration testing rules of engagement with the tools, techniques, and procedures that are anticipated to be employed by adversaries carrying out attacks. Organizational risk assessments guide decisions on the level of independence required for personnel conducting penetration testing. Related control: SA-12.

Control Enhancements:

(1) PENETRATION TESTING | INDEPENDENT PENETRATION AGENT OR TEAM

The organization employs an independent penetration agent or penetration team to perform penetration testing on the information system or system components.

Supplemental Guidance: Independent penetration agents or teams are individuals or groups who conduct impartial penetration testing of organizational information systems. Impartiality implies that penetration agents or teams are free from any perceived or actual conflicts of interest with regard to the development, operation, or management of the information systems that are the targets of the penetration testing. Supplemental guidance for CA-2 (1) provides additional information regarding independent assessments that can be applied to penetration testing. Related control: CA-2.

(2) PENETRATION TESTING | RED TEAM EXERCISES

The organization employs [*Assignment: organization-defined red team exercises*] to simulate attempts by adversaries to compromise organizational information systems in accordance with [*Assignment: organization-defined rules of engagement*].

Supplemental Guidance: Red team exercises extend the objectives of penetration testing by examining the security posture of organizations and their ability to implement effective cyber defenses. As such, red team exercises reflect simulated adversarial attempts to compromise organizational mission/business functions and provide a comprehensive assessment of the security state of information systems and organizations. Simulated adversarial attempts to compromise organizational missions/business functions and the information systems that support those missions/functions may include technology-focused attacks (e.g., interactions with hardware, software, or firmware components and/or mission/business processes) and social engineering-based attacks (e.g., interactions via email, telephone, shoulder surfing, or personal conversations). While penetration testing may be largely laboratory-based testing, organizations use red team exercises to provide more comprehensive assessments that reflect real-world conditions. Red team exercises can be used to improve security awareness and training and to assess levels of security control effectiveness.

References: None.

Priority and Baseline Allocation:

| P2 | LOW Not Selected | MOD Not Selected | HIGH CA-8 |

CA-9 INTERNAL SYSTEM CONNECTIONS

Control: The organization:

a. Authorizes internal connections of [*Assignment: organization-defined information system components or classes of components*] to the information system; and

b. Documents, for each internal connection, the interface characteristics, security requirements, and the nature of the information communicated.

Supplemental Guidance: This control applies to connections between organizational information systems and (separate) constituent system components (i.e., intra-system connections) including, for example, system connections with mobile devices, notebook/desktop computers, printers, copiers, facsimile machines, scanners, sensors, and servers. Instead of authorizing each individual internal connection, organizations can authorize internal connections for a class of components with common characteristics and/or configurations, for example, all digital printers, scanners, and copiers with a specified processing, storage, and transmission capability or all smart phones with a specific baseline configuration. Related controls: AC-3, AC-4, AC-18, AC-19, AU-2, AU-12, CA-7, CM-2, IA-3, SC-7, SI-4.

Control Enhancements:

(1) INTERNAL SYSTEM CONNECTIONS | SECURITY COMPLIANCE CHECKS

The information system performs security compliance checks on constituent system components prior to the establishment of the internal connection.

Supplemental Guidance: Security compliance checks may include, for example, verification of the relevant baseline configuration. Related controls: CM-6.

References: None.

Priority and Baseline Allocation:

| P2 | LOW CA-9 | MOD CA-9 | HIGH CA-9 |

FAMILY: CONFIGURATION MANAGEMENT

CM-1 CONFIGURATION MANAGEMENT POLICY AND PROCEDURES

Control: The organization:

a. Develops, documents, and disseminates to [*Assignment: organization-defined personnel or roles*]:

1. A configuration management policy that addresses purpose, scope, roles, responsibilities, management commitment, coordination among organizational entities, and compliance; and

2. Procedures to facilitate the implementation of the configuration management policy and associated configuration management controls; and

b. Reviews and updates the current:

1. Configuration management policy [*Assignment: organization-defined frequency*]; and

2. Configuration management procedures [*Assignment: organization-defined frequency*].

Supplemental Guidance: This control addresses the establishment of policy and procedures for the effective implementation of selected security controls and control enhancements in the CM family. Policy and procedures reflect applicable federal laws, Executive Orders, directives, regulations, policies, standards, and guidance. Security program policies and procedures at the organization level may make the need for system-specific policies and procedures unnecessary. The policy can be included as part of the general information security policy for organizations or conversely, can be represented by multiple policies reflecting the complex nature of certain organizations. The procedures can be established for the security program in general and for particular information systems, if needed. The organizational risk management strategy is a key factor in establishing policy and procedures. Related control: PM-9.

Control Enhancements: None.

References: NIST Special Publications 800-12, 800-100.

Priority and Baseline Allocation:

P1	LOW CM-1	MOD CM-1	HIGH CM-1

CM-2 BASELINE CONFIGURATION

Control: The organization develops, documents, and maintains under configuration control, a current baseline configuration of the information system.

Supplemental Guidance: This control establishes baseline configurations for information systems and system components including communications and connectivity-related aspects of systems. Baseline configurations are documented, formally reviewed and agreed-upon sets of specifications for information systems or configuration items within those systems. Baseline configurations serve as a basis for future builds, releases, and/or changes to information systems. Baseline configurations include information about information system components (e.g., standard software packages installed on workstations, notebook computers, servers, network components, or mobile devices; current version numbers and patch information on operating systems and applications; and configuration settings/parameters), network topology, and the logical placement of those components within the system architecture. Maintaining baseline configurations requires creating new baselines as organizational information systems change over time. Baseline configurations of information systems reflect the current enterprise architecture. Related controls: CM-3, CM-6, CM-8, CM-9, SA-10, PM-5, PM-7.

Control Enhancements:

(1) BASELINE CONFIGURATION | REVIEWS AND UPDATES

The organization reviews and updates the baseline configuration of the information system:

(a) [Assignment: organization-defined frequency];

(b) When required due to [Assignment organization-defined circumstances]; and

(c) As an integral part of information system component installations and upgrades.

Supplemental Guidance: Related control: CM-5.

(2) BASELINE CONFIGURATION | AUTOMATION SUPPORT FOR ACCURACY / CURRENCY

The organization employs automated mechanisms to maintain an up-to-date, complete, accurate, and readily available baseline configuration of the information system.

Supplemental Guidance: Automated mechanisms that help organizations maintain consistent baseline configurations for information systems include, for example, hardware and software inventory tools, configuration management tools, and network management tools. Such tools can be deployed and/or allocated as common controls, at the information system level, or at the operating system or component level (e.g., on workstations, servers, notebook computers, network components, or mobile devices). Tools can be used, for example, to track version numbers on operating system applications, types of software installed, and current patch levels. This control enhancement can be satisfied by the implementation of CM-8 (2) for organizations that choose to combine information system component inventory and baseline configuration activities. Related controls: CM-7, RA-5.

(3) BASELINE CONFIGURATION | RETENTION OF PREVIOUS CONFIGURATIONS

The organization retains [Assignment: organization-defined previous versions of baseline configurations of the information system] to support rollback.

Supplemental Guidance: Retaining previous versions of baseline configurations to support rollback may include, for example, hardware, software, firmware, configuration files, and configuration records.

(4) BASELINE CONFIGURATION | UNAUTHORIZED SOFTWARE

[Withdrawn: Incorporated into CM-7].

(5) BASELINE CONFIGURATION | AUTHORIZED SOFTWARE

[Withdrawn: Incorporated into CM-7].

(6) BASELINE CONFIGURATION | DEVELOPMENT AND TEST ENVIRONMENTS

The organization maintains a baseline configuration for information system development and test environments that is managed separately from the operational baseline configuration.

Supplemental Guidance: Establishing separate baseline configurations for development, testing, and operational environments helps protect information systems from unplanned/unexpected events related to development and testing activities. Separate baseline configurations allow organizations to apply the configuration management that is most appropriate for each type of configuration. For example, management of operational configurations typically emphasizes the need for stability, while management of development/test configurations requires greater flexibility. Configurations in the test environment mirror the configurations in the operational environment to the extent practicable so that the results of the testing are representative of the proposed changes to the operational systems. This control enhancement requires separate configurations but not necessarily separate physical environments. Related controls: CM-4, SC-3, SC-7.

(7) BASELINE CONFIGURATION | CONFIGURE SYSTEMS, COMPONENTS, OR DEVICES FOR HIGH-RISK AREAS

The organization:

(a) Issues [Assignment: organization-defined information systems, system components, or devices] with [Assignment: organization-defined configurations] to individuals traveling to locations that the organization deems to be of significant risk; and

(b) Applies [Assignment: organization-defined security safeguards] to the devices when the individuals return.

Supplemental Guidance: When it is known that information systems, system components, or devices (e.g., notebook computers, mobile devices) will be located in high-risk areas, additional security controls may be implemented to counter the greater threat in such areas coupled with the lack of physical security relative to organizational-controlled areas. For example, organizational policies and procedures for notebook computers used by individuals departing on and returning from travel include, for example, determining which locations are of concern, defining required configurations for the devices, ensuring that the devices are configured as intended before travel is initiated, and applying specific safeguards to the device after travel is completed. Specially configured notebook computers include, for example, computers with sanitized hard drives, limited applications, and additional hardening (e.g., more stringent configuration settings). Specified safeguards applied to mobile devices upon return from travel include, for example, examining the device for signs of physical tampering and purging/reimaging the hard disk drive. Protecting information residing on mobile devices is covered in the media protection family.

References: NIST Special Publication 800-128.

Priority and Baseline Allocation:

P1	LOW CM-2	MOD CM-2 (1) (3) (7)	HIGH CM-2 (1) (2) (3) (7)

CM-3 CONFIGURATION CHANGE CONTROL

Control: The organization:

a. Determines the types of changes to the information system that are configuration-controlled;

b. Reviews proposed configuration-controlled changes to the information system and approves or disapproves such changes with explicit consideration for security impact analyses;

c. Documents configuration change decisions associated with the information system;

d. Implements approved configuration-controlled changes to the information system;

e. Retains records of configuration-controlled changes to the information system for [*Assignment: organization-defined time period*];

f. Audits and reviews activities associated with configuration-controlled changes to the information system; and

g. Coordinates and provides oversight for configuration change control activities through [*Assignment: organization-defined configuration change control element (e.g., committee, board)*] that convenes [*Selection (one or more): [Assignment: organization-defined frequency]*]; [*Assignment: organization-defined configuration change conditions*]].

Supplemental Guidance: Configuration change controls for organizational information systems involve the systematic proposal, justification, implementation, testing, review, and disposition of changes to the systems, including system upgrades and modifications. Configuration change control includes changes to baseline configurations for components and configuration items of information systems, changes to configuration settings for information technology products (e.g., operating systems, applications, firewalls, routers, and mobile devices), unscheduled/unauthorized changes, and changes to remediate vulnerabilities. Typical processes for managing configuration changes to information systems include, for example, Configuration Control Boards that approve proposed changes to systems. For new development information systems or systems undergoing major upgrades, organizations consider including representatives from development organizations on the Configuration Control Boards. Auditing of changes includes activities before and after changes are made to organizational information systems and the auditing activities required to implement such changes. Related controls: CA-7, CM-2, CM-4, CM-5, CM-6, CM-9, SA-10, SI-2, SI-12.

Control Enhancements:

(1) CONFIGURATION CHANGE CONTROL | AUTOMATED DOCUMENT / NOTIFICATION / PROHIBITION OF CHANGES

The organization employs automated mechanisms to:

(a) Document proposed changes to the information system;

(b) Notify [Assignment: organized-defined approval authorities] of proposed changes to the information system and request change approval;

(c) Highlight proposed changes to the information system that have not been approved or disapproved by [Assignment: organization-defined time period];

(d) Prohibit changes to the information system until designated approvals are received;

(e) Document all changes to the information system; and

(f) Notify [Assignment: organization-defined personnel] when approved changes to the information system are completed.

(2) CONFIGURATION CHANGE CONTROL | TEST / VALIDATE / DOCUMENT CHANGES

The organization tests, validates, and documents changes to the information system before implementing the changes on the operational system.

Supplemental Guidance: Changes to information systems include modifications to hardware, software, or firmware components and configuration settings defined in CM-6. Organizations ensure that testing does not interfere with information system operations. Individuals/groups conducting tests understand organizational security policies and procedures, information system security policies and procedures, and the specific health, safety, and environmental risks associated with particular facilities/processes. Operational systems may need to be taken off-line, or replicated to the extent feasible, before testing can be conducted. If information systems must be taken off-line for testing, the tests are scheduled to occur during planned system outages whenever possible. If testing cannot be conducted on operational systems, organizations employ compensating controls (e.g., testing on replicated systems).

(3) CONFIGURATION CHANGE CONTROL | AUTOMATED CHANGE IMPLEMENTATION

The organization employs automated mechanisms to implement changes to the current information system baseline and deploys the updated baseline across the installed base.

(4) CONFIGURATION CHANGE CONTROL | SECURITY REPRESENTATIVE

The organization requires an information security representative to be a member of the [Assignment: organization-defined configuration change control element].

Supplemental Guidance: Information security representatives can include, for example, senior agency information security officers, information system security officers, or information system security managers. Representation by personnel with information security expertise is important because changes to information system configurations can have unintended side effects, some of which may be security-relevant. Detecting such changes early in the process can help avoid unintended, negative consequences that could ultimately affect the security state of organizational information systems. The configuration change control element in this control enhancement reflects the change control elements defined by organizations in CM-3.

(5) CONFIGURATION CHANGE CONTROL | AUTOMATED SECURITY RESPONSE

The information system implements [Assignment: organization-defined security responses] automatically if baseline configurations are changed in an unauthorized manner.

Supplemental Guidance: Security responses include, for example, halting information system processing, halting selected system functions, or issuing alerts/notifications to organizational personnel when there is an unauthorized modification of a configuration item.

(6) CONFIGURATION CHANGE CONTROL | CRYPTOGRAPHY MANAGEMENT

The organization ensures that cryptographic mechanisms used to provide [Assignment: organization-defined security safeguards] are under configuration management.

Supplemental Guidance: Regardless of the cryptographic means employed (e.g., public key, private key, shared secrets), organizations ensure that there are processes and procedures in place to effectively manage those means. For example, if devices use certificates as a basis for identification and authentication, there needs to be a process in place to address the expiration of those certificates. Related control: SC-13.

References: NIST Special Publication 800-128.

Priority and Baseline Allocation:

| P1 | LOW Not Selected | MOD CM-3 (2) | HIGH CM-3 (1) (2) |

CM-4 **SECURITY IMPACT ANALYSIS**

Control: The organization analyzes changes to the information system to determine potential security impacts prior to change implementation.

Supplemental Guidance: Organizational personnel with information security responsibilities (e.g., Information System Administrators, Information System Security Officers, Information System Security Managers, and Information System Security Engineers) conduct security impact analyses. Individuals conducting security impact analyses possess the necessary skills/technical expertise to analyze the changes to information systems and the associated security ramifications. Security impact analysis may include, for example, reviewing security plans to understand security control requirements and reviewing system design documentation to understand control implementation and how specific changes might affect the controls. Security impact analyses may also include assessments of risk to better understand the impact of the changes and to determine if additional security controls are required. Security impact analyses are scaled in accordance with the security categories of the information systems. Related controls: CA-2, CA-7, CM-3, CM-9, SA-4, SA-5, SA-10, SI-2.

Control Enhancements:

(1) *SECURITY IMPACT ANALYSIS | SEPARATE TEST ENVIRONMENTS*

The organization analyzes changes to the information system in a separate test environment before implementation in an operational environment, looking for security impacts due to flaws, weaknesses, incompatibility, or intentional malice.

Supplemental Guidance: Separate test environment in this context means an environment that is physically or logically isolated and distinct from the operational environment. The separation is sufficient to ensure that activities in the test environment do not impact activities in the operational environment, and information in the operational environment is not inadvertently transmitted to the test environment. Separate environments can be achieved by physical or logical means. If physically separate test environments are not used, organizations determine the strength of mechanism required when implementing logical separation (e.g., separation achieved through virtual machines). Related controls: SA-11, SC-3, SC-7.

(2) *SECURITY IMPACT ANALYSIS | VERIFICATION OF SECURITY FUNCTIONS*

The organization, after the information system is changed, checks the security functions to verify that the functions are implemented correctly, operating as intended, and producing the desired outcome with regard to meeting the security requirements for the system.

Supplemental Guidance: Implementation is this context refers to installing changed code in the operational information system. Related control: SA-11.

References: NIST Special Publication 800-128.

Priority and Baseline Allocation:

| P2 | LOW CM-4 | MOD CM-4 | HIGH CM-4 (1) |

CM-5 ACCESS RESTRICTIONS FOR CHANGE

Control: The organization defines, documents, approves, and enforces physical and logical access restrictions associated with changes to the information system.

Supplemental Guidance: Any changes to the hardware, software, and/or firmware components of information systems can potentially have significant effects on the overall security of the systems. Therefore, organizations permit only qualified and authorized individuals to access information systems for purposes of initiating changes, including upgrades and modifications. Organizations maintain records of access to ensure that configuration change control is implemented and to support after-the-fact actions should organizations discover any unauthorized changes. Access restrictions for change also include software libraries. Access restrictions include, for example, physical and logical access controls (see AC-3 and PE-3), workflow automation, media libraries, abstract layers (e.g., changes implemented into third-party interfaces rather than directly into information systems), and change windows (e.g., changes occur only during specified times, making unauthorized changes easy to discover). Related controls: AC-3, AC-6, PE-3.

Control Enhancements:

(1) ACCESS RESTRICTIONS FOR CHANGE | AUTOMATED ACCESS ENFORCEMENT / AUDITING

The information system enforces access restrictions and supports auditing of the enforcement actions.

Supplemental Guidance: Related controls: AU-2, AU-12, AU-6, CM-3, CM-6.

(2) ACCESS RESTRICTIONS FOR CHANGE | REVIEW SYSTEM CHANGES

The organization reviews information system changes [Assignment: organization-defined frequency] and [Assignment: organization-defined circumstances] to determine whether unauthorized changes have occurred.

Supplemental Guidance: Indications that warrant review of information system changes and the specific circumstances justifying such reviews may be obtained from activities carried out by organizations during the configuration change process. Related controls: AU-6, AU-7, CM-3, CM-5, PE-6, PE-8.

(3) ACCESS RESTRICTIONS FOR CHANGE | SIGNED COMPONENTS

The information system prevents the installation of [Assignment: organization-defined software and firmware components] without verification that the component has been digitally signed using a certificate that is recognized and approved by the organization.

Supplemental Guidance: Software and firmware components prevented from installation unless signed with recognized and approved certificates include, for example, software and firmware version updates, patches, service packs, device drivers, and basic input output system (BIOS) updates. Organizations can identify applicable software and firmware components by type, by specific items, or a combination of both. Digital signatures and organizational verification of such signatures, is a method of code authentication. Related controls: CM-7, SC-13, SI-7.

(4) ACCESS RESTRICTIONS FOR CHANGE | DUAL AUTHORIZATION

The organization enforces dual authorization for implementing changes to [Assignment: organization-defined information system components and system-level information].

Supplemental Guidance: Organizations employ dual authorization to ensure that any changes to selected information system components and information cannot occur unless two qualified individuals implement such changes. The two individuals possess sufficient skills/expertise to determine if the proposed changes are correct implementations of approved changes. Dual authorization may also be known as two-person control. Related controls: AC-5, CM-3.

(5) ACCESS RESTRICTIONS FOR CHANGE | LIMIT PRODUCTION / OPERATIONAL PRIVILEGES

The organization:

(a) Limits privileges to change information system components and system-related information within a production or operational environment; and

(b) Reviews and reevaluates privileges [Assignment: organization-defined frequency].

Supplemental Guidance: In many organizations, information systems support multiple core missions/business functions. Limiting privileges to change information system components with respect to operational systems is necessary because changes to a particular information system component may have far-reaching effects on mission/business processes supported by the system where the component resides. The complex, many-to-many relationships between systems and mission/business processes are in some cases, unknown to developers. Related control: AC-2.

(6) ACCESS RESTRICTIONS FOR CHANGE | LIMIT LIBRARY PRIVILEGES

The organization limits privileges to change software resident within software libraries.

Supplemental Guidance: Software libraries include privileged programs. Related control: AC-2.

(7) ACCESS RESTRICTIONS FOR CHANGE | AUTOMATIC IMPLEMENTATION OF SECURITY SAFEGUARDS

[Withdrawn: Incorporated into SI-7].

References: None.

Priority and Baseline Allocation:

| P1 | LOW Not Selected | MOD CM-5 | HIGH CM-5 (1) (2) (3) |

CM-6 **CONFIGURATION SETTINGS**

Control: The organization:

a. Establishes and documents configuration settings for information technology products employed within the information system using [*Assignment: organization-defined security configuration checklists*] that reflect the most restrictive mode consistent with operational requirements;

b. Implements the configuration settings;

c. Identifies, documents, and approves any deviations from established configuration settings for [*Assignment: organization-defined information system components*] based on [*Assignment: organization-defined operational requirements*]; and

d. Monitors and controls changes to the configuration settings in accordance with organizational policies and procedures.

Supplemental Guidance: Configuration settings are the set of parameters that can be changed in hardware, software, or firmware components of the information system that affect the security posture and/or functionality of the system. Information technology products for which security-related configuration settings can be defined include, for example, mainframe computers, servers (e.g., database, electronic mail, authentication, web, proxy, file, domain name), workstations, input/output devices (e.g., scanners, copiers, and printers), network components (e.g., firewalls, routers, gateways, voice and data switches, wireless access points, network appliances, sensors), operating systems, middleware, and applications. Security-related parameters are those parameters impacting the security state of information systems including the parameters required to satisfy other security control requirements. Security-related parameters include, for example: (i) registry settings; (ii) account, file, directory permission settings; and (iii) settings for functions, ports, protocols, services, and remote connections. Organizations establish organization-wide configuration settings and subsequently derive specific settings for information systems. The established settings become part of the systems configuration baseline.

Common secure configurations (also referred to as security configuration checklists, lockdown and hardening guides, security reference guides, security technical implementation guides) provide recognized, standardized, and established benchmarks that stipulate secure configuration settings for specific information technology platforms/products and instructions for configuring those information system components to meet operational requirements. Common secure configurations can be developed by a variety of organizations including, for example, information technology product developers, manufacturers, vendors, consortia, academia, industry, federal agencies, and other organizations in the public and private sectors. Common secure configurations include the

United States Government Configuration Baseline (USGCB) which affects the implementation of CM-6 and other controls such as AC-19 and CM-7. The Security Content Automation Protocol (SCAP) and the defined standards within the protocol (e.g., Common Configuration Enumeration) provide an effective method to uniquely identify, track, and control configuration settings. OMB establishes federal policy on configuration requirements for federal information systems. Related controls: AC-19, CM-2, CM-3, CM-7, SI-4.

Control Enhancements:

(1) CONFIGURATION SETTINGS | AUTOMATED CENTRAL MANAGEMENT / APPLICATION / VERIFICATION

The organization employs automated mechanisms to centrally manage, apply, and verify configuration settings for [*Assignment: organization-defined information system components*].

Supplemental Guidance: Related controls: CA-7, CM-4.

(2) CONFIGURATION SETTINGS | RESPOND TO UNAUTHORIZED CHANGES

The organization employs [*Assignment: organization-defined security safeguards*] to respond to unauthorized changes to [*Assignment: organization-defined configuration settings*].

Supplemental Guidance: Responses to unauthorized changes to configuration settings can include, for example, alerting designated organizational personnel, restoring established configuration settings, or in extreme cases, halting affected information system processing. Related controls: IR-4, SI-7.

(3) CONFIGURATION SETTINGS | UNAUTHORIZED CHANGE DETECTION

[Withdrawn: Incorporated into SI-7].

(4) CONFIGURATION SETTINGS | CONFORMANCE DEMONSTRATION

[Withdrawn: Incorporated into CM-4].

References: OMB Memoranda 07-11, 07-18, 08-22; NIST Special Publications 800-70, 800-128; Web: http://nvd.nist.gov, http://checklists.nist.gov, http://www.nsa.gov.

Priority and Baseline Allocation:

P1	LOW CM-6	MOD CM-6	HIGH CM-6 (1) (2)

CM-7 LEAST FUNCTIONALITY

Control: The organization:

a. Configures the information system to provide only essential capabilities; and

b. Prohibits or restricts the use of the following functions, ports, protocols, and/or services: [*Assignment: organization-defined prohibited or restricted functions, ports, protocols, and/or services*].

Supplemental Guidance: Information systems can provide a wide variety of functions and services. Some of the functions and services, provided by default, may not be necessary to support essential organizational operations (e.g., key missions, functions). Additionally, it is sometimes convenient to provide multiple services from single information system components, but doing so increases risk over limiting the services provided by any one component. Where feasible, organizations limit component functionality to a single function per device (e.g., email servers or web servers, but not both). Organizations review functions and services provided by information systems or individual components of information systems, to determine which functions and services are candidates for elimination (e.g., Voice Over Internet Protocol, Instant Messaging, auto-execute, and file sharing). Organizations consider disabling unused or unnecessary physical and logical ports/protocols (e.g., Universal Serial Bus, File Transfer Protocol, and Hyper Text Transfer Protocol) on information systems to prevent unauthorized connection of devices, unauthorized transfer of information, or unauthorized tunneling. Organizations can utilize network scanning tools, intrusion detection and prevention systems, and end-point protections such as firewalls and host-based intrusion detection systems to identify and prevent the use of prohibited functions, ports, protocols, and services. Related controls: AC-6, CM-2, RA-5, SA-5, SC-7.

Control Enhancements:

(1) LEAST FUNCTIONALITY | PERIODIC REVIEW

The organization:

(a) Reviews the information system [*Assignment: organization-defined frequency*] to identify unnecessary and/or nonsecure functions, ports, protocols, and services; and

(b) Disables [*Assignment: organization-defined functions, ports, protocols, and services within the information system deemed to be unnecessary and/or nonsecure*].

Supplemental Guidance: The organization can either make a determination of the relative security of the function, port, protocol, and/or service or base the security decision on the assessment of other entities. Bluetooth, FTP, and peer-to-peer networking are examples of less than secure protocols. Related controls: AC-18, CM-7, IA-2.

(2) LEAST FUNCTIONALITY | PREVENT PROGRAM EXECUTION

The information system prevents program execution in accordance with [*Selection (one or more): [Assignment: organization-defined policies regarding software program usage and restrictions]; rules authorizing the terms and conditions of software program usage*].

Supplemental Guidance: Related controls: CM-8, PM-5.

(3) LEAST FUNCTIONALITY | REGISTRATION COMPLIANCE

The organization ensures compliance with [*Assignment: organization-defined registration requirements for functions, ports, protocols, and services*].

Supplemental Guidance: Organizations use the registration process to manage, track, and provide oversight for information systems and implemented functions, ports, protocols, and services.

(4) LEAST FUNCTIONALITY | UNAUTHORIZED SOFTWARE / BLACKLISTING

The organization:

(a) Identifies [*Assignment: organization-defined software programs not authorized to execute on the information system*];

(b) Employs an allow-all, deny-by-exception policy to prohibit the execution of unauthorized software programs on the information system; and

(c) Reviews and updates the list of unauthorized software programs [*Assignment: organization-defined frequency*].

Supplemental Guidance: The process used to identify software programs that are not authorized to execute on organizational information systems is commonly referred to as *blacklisting*. Organizations can implement CM-7 (5) instead of this control enhancement if whitelisting (the stronger of the two policies) is the preferred approach for restricting software program execution. Related controls: CM-6, CM-8, PM-5.

(5) LEAST FUNCTIONALITY | AUTHORIZED SOFTWARE / WHITELISTING

The organization:

(a) Identifies [*Assignment: organization-defined software programs authorized to execute on the information system*];

(b) Employs a deny-all, permit-by-exception policy to allow the execution of authorized software programs on the information system; and

(c) Reviews and updates the list of authorized software programs [*Assignment: organization-defined frequency*].

Supplemental Guidance: The process used to identify software programs that are authorized to execute on organizational information systems is commonly referred to as *whitelisting*. In addition to whitelisting, organizations consider verifying the integrity of white-listed software programs using, for example, cryptographic checksums, digital signatures, or hash functions. Verification of white-listed software can occur either prior to execution or at system startup. Related controls: CM-2, CM-6, CM-8, PM-5, SA-10, SC-34, SI-7.

References: DoD Instruction 8551.01.

Priority and Baseline Allocation:

| P1 | LOW CM-7 | MOD CM-7 (1) (2) (4) | HIGH CM-7 (1) (2) (5) |

CM-8   INFORMATION SYSTEM COMPONENT INVENTORY

Control: The organization:

a. Develops and documents an inventory of information system components that:

   1. Accurately reflects the current information system;

   2. Includes all components within the authorization boundary of the information system;

   3. Is at the level of granularity deemed necessary for tracking and reporting; and

   4. Includes [*Assignment: organization-defined information deemed necessary to achieve effective information system component accountability*]; and

b. Reviews and updates the information system component inventory [*Assignment: organization-defined frequency*].

Supplemental Guidance: Organizations may choose to implement centralized information system component inventories that include components from all organizational information systems. In such situations, organizations ensure that the resulting inventories include system-specific information required for proper component accountability (e.g., information system association, information system owner). Information deemed necessary for effective accountability of information system components includes, for example, hardware inventory specifications, software license information, software version numbers, component owners, and for networked components or devices, machine names and network addresses. Inventory specifications include, for example, manufacturer, device type, model, serial number, and physical location. Related controls: CM-2, CM-6, PM-5.

Control Enhancements:

(1) INFORMATION SYSTEM COMPONENT INVENTORY | UPDATES DURING INSTALLATIONS / REMOVALS

   The organization updates the inventory of information system components as an integral part of component installations, removals, and information system updates.

(2) INFORMATION SYSTEM COMPONENT INVENTORY | AUTOMATED MAINTENANCE

   The organization employs automated mechanisms to help maintain an up-to-date, complete, accurate, and readily available inventory of information system components.

   Supplemental Guidance: Organizations maintain information system inventories to the extent feasible. Virtual machines, for example, can be difficult to monitor because such machines are not visible to the network when not in use. In such cases, organizations maintain as up-to-date, complete, and accurate an inventory as is deemed reasonable. This control enhancement can be satisfied by the implementation of CM-2 (2) for organizations that choose to combine information system component inventory and baseline configuration activities. Related control: SI-7.

(3) INFORMATION SYSTEM COMPONENT INVENTORY | AUTOMATED UNAUTHORIZED COMPONENT DETECTION

   The organization:

   (a) **Employs automated mechanisms [*Assignment: organization-defined frequency*] to detect the presence of unauthorized hardware, software, and firmware components within the information system; and**

   (b) **Takes the following actions when unauthorized components are detected: [*Selection (one or more): disables network access by such components; isolates the components; notifies [Assignment: organization-defined personnel or roles]*].**

Supplemental Guidance: This control enhancement is applied in addition to the monitoring for unauthorized remote connections and mobile devices. Monitoring for unauthorized system components may be accomplished on an ongoing basis or by the periodic scanning of systems for that purpose. Automated mechanisms can be implemented within information systems or in other separate devices. Isolation can be achieved, for example, by placing unauthorized information system components in separate domains or subnets or otherwise quarantining such components. This type of component isolation is commonly referred to as sandboxing. Related controls: AC-17, AC-18, AC-19, CA-7, SI-3, SI-4, SI-7, RA-5.

(4) INFORMATION SYSTEM COMPONENT INVENTORY | ACCOUNTABILITY INFORMATION

The organization includes in the information system component inventory information, a means for identifying by [*Selection (one or more): name; position; role*], individuals responsible/accountable for administering those components.

Supplemental Guidance: Identifying individuals who are both responsible and accountable for administering information system components helps to ensure that the assigned components are properly administered and organizations can contact those individuals if some action is required (e.g., component is determined to be the source of a breach/compromise, component needs to be recalled/replaced, or component needs to be relocated).

(5) INFORMATION SYSTEM COMPONENT INVENTORY | NO DUPLICATE ACCOUNTING OF COMPONENTS

The organization verifies that all components within the authorization boundary of the information system are not duplicated in other information system component inventories.

Supplemental Guidance: This control enhancement addresses the potential problem of duplicate accounting of information system components in large or complex interconnected systems.

(6) INFORMATION SYSTEM COMPONENT INVENTORY | ASSESSED CONFIGURATIONS / APPROVED DEVIATIONS

The organization includes assessed component configurations and any approved deviations to current deployed configurations in the information system component inventory.

Supplemental Guidance: This control enhancement focuses on configuration settings established by organizations for information system components, the specific components that have been assessed to determine compliance with the required configuration settings, and any approved deviations from established configuration settings. Related controls: CM-2, CM-6.

(7) INFORMATION SYSTEM COMPONENT INVENTORY | CENTRALIZED REPOSITORY

The organization provides a centralized repository for the inventory of information system components.

Supplemental Guidance: Organizations may choose to implement centralized information system component inventories that include components from all organizational information systems. Centralized repositories of information system component inventories provide opportunities for efficiencies in accounting for organizational hardware, software, and firmware assets. Such repositories may also help organizations rapidly identify the location and responsible individuals of system components that have been compromised, breached, or are otherwise in need of mitigation actions. Organizations ensure that the resulting centralized inventories include system-specific information required for proper component accountability (e.g., information system association, information system owner).

(8) INFORMATION SYSTEM COMPONENT INVENTORY | AUTOMATED LOCATION TRACKING

The organization employs automated mechanisms to support tracking of information system components by geographic location.

Supplemental Guidance: The use of automated mechanisms to track the location of information system components can increase the accuracy of component inventories. Such capability may also help organizations rapidly identify the location and responsible individuals of system components that have been compromised, breached, or are otherwise in need of mitigation actions.

(9) INFORMATION SYSTEM COMPONENT INVENTORY | ASSIGNMENT OF COMPONENTS TO SYSTEMS

The organization:

(a) Assigns [*Assignment: organization-defined acquired information system components*] to an information system; and

(b) Receives an acknowledgement from the information system owner of this assignment.

Supplemental Guidance: Organizations determine the criteria for or types of information system components (e.g., microprocessors, motherboards, software, programmable logic controllers, and network devices) that are subject to this control enhancement. Related control: SA-4.

References: NIST Special Publication 800-128.

Priority and Baseline Allocation:

P1	LOW CM-8	MOD CM-8 (1) (3) (5)	HIGH CM-8 (1) (2) (3) (4) (5)

CM-9 CONFIGURATION MANAGEMENT PLAN

Control: The organization develops, documents, and implements a configuration management plan for the information system that:

a. Addresses roles, responsibilities, and configuration management processes and procedures;

b. Establishes a process for identifying configuration items throughout the system development life cycle and for managing the configuration of the configuration items;

c. Defines the configuration items for the information system and places the configuration items under configuration management; and

d. Protects the configuration management plan from unauthorized disclosure and modification.

Supplemental Guidance: Configuration management plans satisfy the requirements in configuration management policies while being tailored to individual information systems. Such plans define detailed processes and procedures for how configuration management is used to support system development life cycle activities at the information system level. Configuration management plans are typically developed during the development/acquisition phase of the system development life cycle. The plans describe how to move changes through change management processes, how to update configuration settings and baselines, how to maintain information system component inventories, how to control development, test, and operational environments, and how to develop, release, and update key documents. Organizations can employ templates to help ensure consistent and timely development and implementation of configuration management plans. Such templates can represent a master configuration management plan for the organization at large with subsets of the plan implemented on a system by system basis. Configuration management approval processes include designation of key management stakeholders responsible for reviewing and approving proposed changes to information systems, and personnel that conduct security impact analyses prior to the implementation of changes to the systems. Configuration items are the information system items (hardware, software, firmware, and documentation) to be configuration-managed. As information systems continue through the system development life cycle, new configuration items may be identified and some existing configuration items may no longer need to be under configuration control. Related controls: CM-2, CM-3, CM-4, CM-5, CM-8, SA-10.

Control Enhancements:

(1) CONFIGURATION MANAGEMENT PLAN | ASSIGNMENT OF RESPONSIBILITY

The organization assigns responsibility for developing the configuration management process to organizational personnel that are not directly involved in information system development.

Supplemental Guidance: In the absence of dedicated configuration management teams assigned within organizations, system developers may be tasked to develop configuration management processes using personnel who are not directly involved in system development or integration. This separation of duties ensures that organizations establish and maintain a sufficient degree of independence between the information system development and integration processes and configuration management processes to facilitate quality control and more effective oversight.

References: NIST Special Publication 800-128.

Priority and Baseline Allocation:

| P1 | LOW Not Selected | MOD CM-9 | HIGH CM-9 |

CM-10 SOFTWARE USAGE RESTRICTIONS

Control: The organization:

a. Uses software and associated documentation in accordance with contract agreements and copyright laws;

b. Tracks the use of software and associated documentation protected by quantity licenses to control copying and distribution; and

c. Controls and documents the use of peer-to-peer file sharing technology to ensure that this capability is not used for the unauthorized distribution, display, performance, or reproduction of copyrighted work.

Supplemental Guidance: Software license tracking can be accomplished by manual methods (e.g., simple spreadsheets) or automated methods (e.g., specialized tracking applications) depending on organizational needs. Related controls: AC-17, CM-8, SC-7.

Control Enhancements:

(1) SOFTWARE USAGE RESTRICTIONS | OPEN SOURCE SOFTWARE

The organization establishes the following restrictions on the use of open source software: [Assignment: organization-defined restrictions].

Supplemental Guidance: Open source software refers to software that is available in source code form. Certain software rights normally reserved for copyright holders are routinely provided under software license agreements that permit individuals to study, change, and improve the software. From a security perspective, the major advantage of open source software is that it provides organizations with the ability to examine the source code. However, there are also various licensing issues associated with open source software including, for example, the constraints on derivative use of such software.

References: None.

Priority and Baseline Allocation:

| P2 | LOW CM-10 | MOD CM-10 | HIGH CM-10 |

CM-11 USER-INSTALLED SOFTWARE

Control: The organization:

a. Establishes [Assignment: organization-defined policies] governing the installation of software by users;

b. Enforces software installation policies through [Assignment: organization-defined methods]; and

c. Monitors policy compliance at [Assignment: organization-defined frequency].

Supplemental Guidance: If provided the necessary privileges, users have the ability to install software in organizational information systems. To maintain control over the types of software installed, organizations identify permitted and prohibited actions regarding software installation. Permitted software installations may include, for example, updates and security patches to existing software and downloading applications from organization-approved "app stores." Prohibited software installations may include, for example, software with unknown or suspect pedigrees or software that organizations consider potentially malicious. The policies organizations select governing user-installed software may be organization-developed or provided by some external entity. Policy enforcement methods include procedural methods (e.g., periodic examination of user accounts), automated methods (e.g., configuration settings implemented on organizational information systems), or both. Related controls: AC-3, CM-2, CM-3, CM-5, CM-6, CM-7, PL-4.

Control Enhancements:

(1) USER-INSTALLED SOFTWARE | ALERTS FOR UNAUTHORIZED INSTALLATIONS

The information system alerts [*Assignment: organization-defined personnel or roles*] when the unauthorized installation of software is detected.

Supplemental Guidance: Related controls: CA-7, SI-4.

(2) USER-INSTALLED SOFTWARE | PROHIBIT INSTALLATION WITHOUT PRIVILEGED STATUS

The information system prohibits user installation of software without explicit privileged status.

Supplemental Guidance: Privileged status can be obtained, for example, by serving in the role of system administrator. Related control: AC-6.

References: None.

Priority and Baseline Allocation:

| P1 | LOW CM-11 | MOD CM-11 | HIGH CM-11 |

FAMILY: CONTINGENCY PLANNING

CP-1 CONTINGENCY PLANNING POLICY AND PROCEDURES

Control: The organization:

a. Develops, documents, and disseminates to [*Assignment: organization-defined personnel or roles*]:

1. A contingency planning policy that addresses purpose, scope, roles, responsibilities, management commitment, coordination among organizational entities, and compliance; and

2. Procedures to facilitate the implementation of the contingency planning policy and associated contingency planning controls; and

b. Reviews and updates the current:

1. Contingency planning policy [*Assignment: organization-defined frequency*]; and

2. Contingency planning procedures [*Assignment: organization-defined frequency*].

Supplemental Guidance: This control addresses the establishment of policy and procedures for the effective implementation of selected security controls and control enhancements in the CP family. Policy and procedures reflect applicable federal laws, Executive Orders, directives, regulations, policies, standards, and guidance. Security program policies and procedures at the organization level may make the need for system-specific policies and procedures unnecessary. The policy can be included as part of the general information security policy for organizations or conversely, can be represented by multiple policies reflecting the complex nature of certain organizations. The procedures can be established for the security program in general and for particular information systems, if needed. The organizational risk management strategy is a key factor in establishing policy and procedures. Related control: PM-9.

Control Enhancements: None.

References: Federal Continuity Directive 1; NIST Special Publications 800-12, 800-34, 800-100.

Priority and Baseline Allocation:

| P1 | LOW CP-1 | MOD CP-1 | HIGH CP-1 |

CP-2 CONTINGENCY PLAN

Control: The organization:

a. Develops a contingency plan for the information system that:

1. Identifies essential missions and business functions and associated contingency requirements;

2. Provides recovery objectives, restoration priorities, and metrics;

3. Addresses contingency roles, responsibilities, assigned individuals with contact information;

4. Addresses maintaining essential missions and business functions despite an information system disruption, compromise, or failure;

5. Addresses eventual, full information system restoration without deterioration of the security safeguards originally planned and implemented; and

6. Is reviewed and approved by [*Assignment: organization-defined personnel or roles*];

b. Distributes copies of the contingency plan to [*Assignment: organization-defined key contingency personnel (identified by name and/or by role) and organizational elements*];

c. Coordinates contingency planning activities with incident handling activities;

d. Reviews the contingency plan for the information system [*Assignment: organization-defined frequency*];

e. Updates the contingency plan to address changes to the organization, information system, or environment of operation and problems encountered during contingency plan implementation, execution, or testing;

f. Communicates contingency plan changes to [*Assignment: organization-defined key contingency personnel (identified by name and/or by role) and organizational elements*]; and

g. Protects the contingency plan from unauthorized disclosure and modification.

Supplemental Guidance: Contingency planning for information systems is part of an overall organizational program for achieving continuity of operations for mission/business functions. Contingency planning addresses both information system restoration and implementation of alternative mission/business processes when systems are compromised. The effectiveness of contingency planning is maximized by considering such planning throughout the phases of the system development life cycle. Performing contingency planning on hardware, software, and firmware development can be an effective means of achieving information system resiliency. Contingency plans reflect the degree of restoration required for organizational information systems since not all systems may need to fully recover to achieve the level of continuity of operations desired. Information system recovery objectives reflect applicable laws, Executive Orders, directives, policies, standards, regulations, and guidelines. In addition to information system availability, contingency plans also address other security-related events resulting in a reduction in mission and/or business effectiveness, such as malicious attacks compromising the confidentiality or integrity of information systems. Actions addressed in contingency plans include, for example, orderly/graceful degradation, information system shutdown, fallback to a manual mode, alternate information flows, and operating in modes reserved for when systems are under attack. By closely coordinating contingency planning with incident handling activities, organizations can ensure that the necessary contingency planning activities are in place and activated in the event of a security incident. Related controls: AC-14, CP-6, CP-7, CP-8, CP-9, CP-10, IR-4, IR-8, MP-2, MP-4, MP-5, PM-8, PM-11.

Control Enhancements:

(1) CONTINGENCY PLAN | COORDINATE WITH RELATED PLANS

The organization coordinates contingency plan development with organizational elements responsible for related plans.

Supplemental Guidance: Plans related to contingency plans for organizational information systems include, for example, Business Continuity Plans, Disaster Recovery Plans, Continuity of Operations Plans, Crisis Communications Plans, Critical Infrastructure Plans, Cyber Incident Response Plans, Insider Threat Implementation Plan, and Occupant Emergency Plans.

(2) CONTINGENCY PLAN | CAPACITY PLANNING

The organization conducts capacity planning so that necessary capacity for information processing, telecommunications, and environmental support exists during contingency operations.

Supplemental Guidance: Capacity planning is needed because different types of threats (e.g., natural disasters, targeted cyber attacks) can result in a reduction of the available processing, telecommunications, and support services originally intended to support the organizational missions/business functions. Organizations may need to anticipate degraded operations during contingency operations and factor such degradation into capacity planning.

(3) CONTINGENCY PLAN | RESUME ESSENTIAL MISSIONS / BUSINESS FUNCTIONS

The organization plans for the resumption of essential missions and business functions within [*Assignment: organization-defined time period*] of contingency plan activation.

Supplemental Guidance: Organizations may choose to carry out the contingency planning activities in this control enhancement as part of organizational business continuity planning including, for example, as part of business impact analyses. The time period for resumption of essential missions/business functions may be dependent on the severity/extent of disruptions to the information system and its supporting infrastructure. Related control: PE-12.

(4) CONTINGENCY PLAN | RESUME ALL MISSIONS / BUSINESS FUNCTIONS

The organization plans for the resumption of all missions and business functions within [*Assignment: organization-defined time period*] of contingency plan activation.

Supplemental Guidance: Organizations may choose to carry out the contingency planning activities in this control enhancement as part of organizational business continuity planning including, for example, as part of business impact analyses. The time period for resumption of all missions/business functions may be dependent on the severity/extent of disruptions to the information system and its supporting infrastructure. Related control: PE-12.

(5) CONTINGENCY PLAN | CONTINUE ESSENTIAL MISSIONS / BUSINESS FUNCTIONS

The organization plans for the continuance of essential missions and business functions with little or no loss of operational continuity and sustains that continuity until full information system restoration at primary processing and/or storage sites.

Supplemental Guidance: Organizations may choose to carry out the contingency planning activities in this control enhancement as part of organizational business continuity planning including, for example, as part of business impact analyses. Primary processing and/or storage sites defined by organizations as part of contingency planning may change depending on the circumstances associated with the contingency (e.g., backup sites may become primary sites). Related control: PE-12.

(6) CONTINGENCY PLAN | ALTERNATE PROCESSING / STORAGE SITE

The organization plans for the transfer of essential missions and business functions to alternate processing and/or storage sites with little or no loss of operational continuity and sustains that continuity through information system restoration to primary processing and/or storage sites.

Supplemental Guidance: Organizations may choose to carry out the contingency planning activities in this control enhancement as part of organizational business continuity planning including, for example, as part of business impact analyses. Primary processing and/or storage sites defined by organizations as part of contingency planning may change depending on the circumstances associated with the contingency (e.g., backup sites may become primary sites). Related control: PE-12.

(7) CONTINGENCY PLAN | COORDINATE WITH EXTERNAL SERVICE PROVIDERS

The organization coordinates its contingency plan with the contingency plans of external service providers to ensure that contingency requirements can be satisfied.

Supplemental Guidance: When the capability of an organization to successfully carry out its core missions/business functions is dependent on external service providers, developing a timely and comprehensive contingency plan may become more challenging. In this situation, organizations coordinate contingency planning activities with the external entities to ensure that the individual plans reflect the overall contingency needs of the organization. Related control: SA-9.

(8) CONTINGENCY PLAN | IDENTIFY CRITICAL ASSETS

The organization identifies critical information system assets supporting essential missions and business functions.

Supplemental Guidance: Organizations may choose to carry out the contingency planning activities in this control enhancement as part of organizational business continuity planning including, for example, as part of business impact analyses. Organizations identify critical information system assets so that additional safeguards and countermeasures can be employed (above and beyond those safeguards and countermeasures routinely implemented) to help ensure that organizational missions/business functions can continue to be conducted during contingency operations. In addition, the identification of critical information assets facilitates the prioritization of organizational resources. Critical information system assets include technical and operational aspects. Technical aspects include, for example, information technology services, information system components, information technology products, and mechanisms. Operational aspects include, for example, procedures (manually executed operations) and personnel (individuals operating technical safeguards and/or executing manual procedures). Organizational program protection plans can provide assistance in identifying critical assets. Related controls: SA-14, SA-15.

References: Federal Continuity Directive 1; NIST Special Publication 800-34.

Priority and Baseline Allocation:

P1	LOW CP-2	MOD CP-2 (1) (3) (8)	HIGH CP-2 (1) (2) (3) (4) (5) (8)

CP-3 **CONTINGENCY TRAINING**

Control: The organization provides contingency training to information system users consistent with assigned roles and responsibilities:

a. Within [*Assignment: organization-defined time period*] of assuming a contingency role or responsibility;

b. When required by information system changes; and

c. [*Assignment: organization-defined frequency*] thereafter.

Supplemental Guidance: Contingency training provided by organizations is linked to the assigned roles and responsibilities of organizational personnel to ensure that the appropriate content and level of detail is included in such training. For example, regular users may only need to know when and where to report for duty during contingency operations and if normal duties are affected; system administrators may require additional training on how to set up information systems at alternate processing and storage sites; and managers/senior leaders may receive more specific training on how to conduct mission-essential functions in designated off-site locations and how to establish communications with other governmental entities for purposes of coordination on contingency-related activities. Training for contingency roles/responsibilities reflects the specific continuity requirements in the contingency plan. Related controls: AT-2, AT-3, CP-2, IR-2.

Control Enhancements:

(1) CONTINGENCY TRAINING | SIMULATED EVENTS

The organization incorporates simulated events into contingency training to facilitate effective response by personnel in crisis situations.

(2) CONTINGENCY TRAINING | AUTOMATED TRAINING ENVIRONMENTS

The organization employs automated mechanisms to provide a more thorough and realistic contingency training environment.

References: Federal Continuity Directive 1; NIST Special Publications 800-16, 800-50.

Priority and Baseline Allocation:

P2	LOW CP-3	MOD CP-3	HIGH CP-3 (1)

CP-4 **CONTINGENCY PLAN TESTING**

Control: The organization:

a. Tests the contingency plan for the information system [*Assignment: organization-defined frequency*] using [*Assignment: organization-defined tests*] to determine the effectiveness of the plan and the organizational readiness to execute the plan;

b. Reviews the contingency plan test results; and

c. Initiates corrective actions, if needed.

Supplemental Guidance: Methods for testing contingency plans to determine the effectiveness of the plans and to identify potential weaknesses in the plans include, for example, walk-through and tabletop exercises, checklists, simulations (parallel, full interrupt), and comprehensive exercises. Organizations conduct testing based on the continuity requirements in contingency plans and include a determination of the effects on organizational operations, assets, and individuals arising due to contingency operations. Organizations have flexibility and discretion in the breadth, depth, and timelines of corrective actions. Related controls: CP-2, CP-3, IR-3.

Control Enhancements:

(1) CONTINGENCY PLAN TESTING | COORDINATE WITH RELATED PLANS

The organization coordinates contingency plan testing with organizational elements responsible for related plans.

Supplemental Guidance: Plans related to contingency plans for organizational information systems include, for example, Business Continuity Plans, Disaster Recovery Plans, Continuity of Operations Plans, Crisis Communications Plans, Critical Infrastructure Plans, Cyber Incident Response Plans, and Occupant Emergency Plans. This control enhancement does not require organizations to create organizational elements to handle related plans or to align such elements with specific plans. It does require, however, that if such organizational elements are responsible for related plans, organizations should coordinate with those elements. Related controls: IR-8, PM-8.

(2) CONTINGENCY PLAN TESTING | ALTERNATE PROCESSING SITE

The organization tests the contingency plan at the alternate processing site:

(a) To familiarize contingency personnel with the facility and available resources; and

(b) To evaluate the capabilities of the alternate processing site to support contingency operations.

Supplemental Guidance: Related control: CP-7.

(3) CONTINGENCY PLAN TESTING | AUTOMATED TESTING

The organization employs automated mechanisms to more thoroughly and effectively test the contingency plan.

Supplemental Guidance: Automated mechanisms provide more thorough and effective testing of contingency plans, for example: (i) by providing more complete coverage of contingency issues; (ii) by selecting more realistic test scenarios and environments; and (iii) by effectively stressing the information system and supported missions.

(4) CONTINGENCY PLAN TESTING | FULL RECOVERY / RECONSTITUTION

The organization includes a full recovery and reconstitution of the information system to a known state as part of contingency plan testing.

Supplemental Guidance: Related controls: CP-10, SC-24.

References: Federal Continuity Directive 1; FIPS Publication 199; NIST Special Publications 800-34, 800-84.

Priority and Baseline Allocation:

| P2 | LOW CP-4 | MOD CP-4 (1) | HIGH CP-4 (1) (2) |

CP-5 CONTINGENCY PLAN UPDATE

[Withdrawn: Incorporated into CP-2].

CP-6 ALTERNATE STORAGE SITE

Control: The organization:

a. Establishes an alternate storage site including necessary agreements to permit the storage and retrieval of information system backup information; and

b. Ensures that the alternate storage site provides information security safeguards equivalent to that of the primary site.

Supplemental Guidance: Alternate storage sites are sites that are geographically distinct from primary storage sites. An alternate storage site maintains duplicate copies of information and data in the event that the primary storage site is not available. Items covered by alternate storage site agreements include, for example, environmental conditions at alternate sites, access rules, physical and environmental protection requirements, and coordination of delivery/retrieval of backup media. Alternate storage sites reflect the requirements in contingency plans so that organizations can maintain essential missions/business functions despite disruption, compromise, or failure in organizational information systems. Related controls: CP-2, CP-7, CP-9, CP-10, MP-4.

Control Enhancements:

(1) ALTERNATE STORAGE SITE | SEPARATION FROM PRIMARY SITE

The organization identifies an alternate storage site that is separated from the primary storage site to reduce susceptibility to the same threats.

Supplemental Guidance: Threats that affect alternate storage sites are typically defined in organizational assessments of risk and include, for example, natural disasters, structural failures, hostile cyber attacks, and errors of omission/commission. Organizations determine what is considered a sufficient degree of separation between primary and alternate storage sites based on the types of threats that are of concern. For one particular type of threat (i.e., hostile cyber attack), the degree of separation between sites is less relevant. Related control: RA-3.

(2) ALTERNATE STORAGE SITE | RECOVERY TIME / POINT OBJECTIVES

The organization configures the alternate storage site to facilitate recovery operations in accordance with recovery time and recovery point objectives.

(3) ALTERNATE STORAGE SITE | ACCESSIBILITY

The organization identifies potential accessibility problems to the alternate storage site in the event of an area-wide disruption or disaster and outlines explicit mitigation actions.

Supplemental Guidance: Area-wide disruptions refer to those types of disruptions that are broad in geographic scope (e.g., hurricane, regional power outage) with such determinations made by organizations based on organizational assessments of risk. Explicit mitigation actions include, for example: (i) duplicating backup information at other alternate storage sites if access problems occur at originally designated alternate sites; or (ii) planning for physical access to retrieve backup information if electronic accessibility to the alternate site is disrupted. Related control: RA-3.

References: NIST Special Publication 800-34.

Priority and Baseline Allocation:

P1	LOW Not Selected	MOD CP-6 (1) (3)	HIGH CP-6 (1) (2) (3)

CP-7 ALTERNATE PROCESSING SITE

Control: The organization:

a. Establishes an alternate processing site including necessary agreements to permit the transfer and resumption of [Assignment: organization-defined information system operations] for essential missions/business functions within [Assignment: organization-defined time period *consistent with recovery time and recovery point objectives*] when the primary processing capabilities are unavailable;

b. Ensures that equipment and supplies required to transfer and resume operations are available at the alternate processing site or contracts are in place to support delivery to the site within the organization-defined time period for transfer/resumption; and

c. Ensures that the alternate processing site provides information security safeguards equivalent to those of the primary site.

Supplemental Guidance: Alternate processing sites are sites that are geographically distinct from primary processing sites. An alternate processing site provides processing capability in the event that the primary processing site is not available. Items covered by alternate processing site agreements include, for example, environmental conditions at alternate sites, access rules, physical and environmental protection requirements, and coordination for the transfer/assignment of personnel. Requirements are specifically allocated to alternate processing sites that reflect the requirements in contingency plans to maintain essential missions/business functions despite disruption, compromise, or failure in organizational information systems. Related controls: CP-2, CP-6, CP-8, CP-9, CP-10, MA-6.

Control Enhancements:

(1) ALTERNATE PROCESSING SITE | SEPARATION FROM PRIMARY SITE

The organization identifies an alternate processing site that is separated from the primary processing site to reduce susceptibility to the same threats.

Supplemental Guidance: Threats that affect alternate processing sites are typically defined in organizational assessments of risk and include, for example, natural disasters, structural failures, hostile cyber attacks, and errors of omission/commission. Organizations determine what is considered a sufficient degree of separation between primary and alternate processing sites based on the types of threats that are of concern. For one particular type of threat (i.e., hostile cyber attack), the degree of separation between sites is less relevant. Related control: RA-3.

(2) ALTERNATE PROCESSING SITE | ACCESSIBILITY

The organization identifies potential accessibility problems to the alternate processing site in the event of an area-wide disruption or disaster and outlines explicit mitigation actions.

Supplemental Guidance: Area-wide disruptions refer to those types of disruptions that are broad in geographic scope (e.g., hurricane, regional power outage) with such determinations made by organizations based on organizational assessments of risk. Related control: RA-3.

(3) ALTERNATE PROCESSING SITE | PRIORITY OF SERVICE

The organization develops alternate processing site agreements that contain priority-of-service provisions in accordance with organizational availability requirements (including recovery time objectives).

Supplemental Guidance: Priority-of-service agreements refer to negotiated agreements with service providers that ensure that organizations receive priority treatment consistent with their availability requirements and the availability of information resources at the alternate processing site.

(4) ALTERNATE PROCESSING SITE | PREPARATION FOR USE

The organization prepares the alternate processing site so that the site is ready to be used as the operational site supporting essential missions and business functions.

Supplemental Guidance: Site preparation includes, for example, establishing configuration settings for information system components at the alternate processing site consistent with the requirements for such settings at the primary site and ensuring that essential supplies and other logistical considerations are in place. Related controls: CM-2, CM-6.

(5) ALTERNATE PROCESSING SITE | EQUIVALENT INFORMATION SECURITY SAFEGUARDS
[Withdrawn: Incorporated into CP-7].

(6) *ALTERNATE PROCESSING SITE | INABILITY TO RETURN TO PRIMARY SITE*

The organization plans and prepares for circumstances that preclude returning to the primary processing site.

References: NIST Special Publication 800-34.

Priority and Baseline Allocation:

P1	LOW Not Selected	MOD CP-7 (1) (2) (3)	HIGH CP-7 (1) (2) (3) (4)

CP-8 TELECOMMUNICATIONS SERVICES

Control: The organization establishes alternate telecommunications services including necessary agreements to permit the resumption of [*Assignment: organization-defined information system operations*] for essential missions and business functions within [*Assignment: organization-defined time period*] when the primary telecommunications capabilities are unavailable at either the primary or alternate processing or storage sites.

Supplemental Guidance: This control applies to telecommunications services (data and voice) for primary and alternate processing and storage sites. Alternate telecommunications services reflect the continuity requirements in contingency plans to maintain essential missions/business functions despite the loss of primary telecommunications services. Organizations may specify different time periods for primary/alternate sites. Alternate telecommunications services include, for example, additional organizational or commercial ground-based circuits/lines or satellites in lieu of ground-based communications. Organizations consider factors such as availability, quality of service, and access when entering into alternate telecommunications agreements. Related controls: CP-2, CP-6, CP-7.

Control Enhancements:

(1) *TELECOMMUNICATIONS SERVICES | PRIORITY OF SERVICE PROVISIONS*

The organization:

(a) Develops primary and alternate telecommunications service agreements that contain priority-of-service provisions in accordance with organizational availability requirements (including recovery time objectives); and

(b) Requests Telecommunications Service Priority for all telecommunications services used for national security emergency preparedness in the event that the primary and/or alternate telecommunications services are provided by a common carrier.

Supplemental Guidance: Organizations consider the potential mission/business impact in situations where telecommunications service providers are servicing other organizations with similar priority-of-service provisions.

(2) *TELECOMMUNICATIONS SERVICES | SINGLE POINTS OF FAILURE*

The organization obtains alternate telecommunications services to reduce the likelihood of sharing a single point of failure with primary telecommunications services.

(3) *TELECOMMUNICATIONS SERVICES | SEPARATION OF PRIMARY / ALTERNATE PROVIDERS*

The organization obtains alternate telecommunications services from providers that are separated from primary service providers to reduce susceptibility to the same threats.

Supplemental Guidance: Threats that affect telecommunications services are typically defined in organizational assessments of risk and include, for example, natural disasters, structural failures, hostile cyber/physical attacks, and errors of omission/commission. Organizations seek to reduce common susceptibilities by, for example, minimizing shared infrastructure among telecommunications service providers and achieving sufficient geographic separation between services. Organizations may consider using a single service provider in situations where the service provider can provide alternate telecommunications services meeting the separation needs addressed in the risk assessment.

(4) *TELECOMMUNICATIONS SERVICES | PROVIDER CONTINGENCY PLAN*

The organization:

(a) Requires primary and alternate telecommunications service providers to have contingency plans;

(b) Reviews provider contingency plans to ensure that the plans meet organizational contingency requirements; and

(c) Obtains evidence of contingency testing/training by providers [*Assignment: organization-defined frequency*].

Supplemental Guidance: Reviews of provider contingency plans consider the proprietary nature of such plans. In some situations, a summary of provider contingency plans may be sufficient evidence for organizations to satisfy the review requirement. Telecommunications service providers may also participate in ongoing disaster recovery exercises in coordination with the Department of Homeland Security, state, and local governments. Organizations may use these types of activities to satisfy evidentiary requirements related to service provider contingency plan reviews, testing, and training.

(5) *TELECOMMUNICATIONS SERVICES | ALTERNATE TELECOMMUNICATION SERVICE TESTING*

The organization tests alternate telecommunication services [*Assignment: organization-defined frequency*].

References: NIST Special Publication 800-34; National Communications Systems Directive 3-10; Web: http://www.dhs.gov/telecommunications-service-priority-tsp.

Priority and Baseline Allocation:

P1	LOW Not Selected	MOD CP-8 (1) (2)	HIGH CP-8 (1) (2) (3) (4)

CP-9 INFORMATION SYSTEM BACKUP

Control: The organization:

a. Conducts backups of user-level information contained in the information system [*Assignment: organization-defined frequency consistent with recovery time and recovery point objectives*];

b. Conducts backups of system-level information contained in the information system [*Assignment: organization-defined frequency consistent with recovery time and recovery point objectives*];

c. Conducts backups of information system documentation including security-related documentation [*Assignment: organization-defined frequency consistent with recovery time and recovery point objectives*]; and

d. Protects the confidentiality, integrity, and availability of backup information at storage locations.

Supplemental Guidance: System-level information includes, for example, system-state information, operating system and application software, and licenses. User-level information includes any information other than system-level information. Mechanisms employed by organizations to protect the integrity of information system backups include, for example, digital signatures and cryptographic hashes. Protection of system backup information while in transit is beyond the scope of this control. Information system backups reflect the requirements in contingency plans as well as other organizational requirements for backing up information. Related controls: CP-2, CP-6, MP-4, MP-5, SC-13.

Control Enhancements:

(1) *INFORMATION SYSTEM BACKUP | TESTING FOR RELIABILITY / INTEGRITY*

The organization tests backup information [*Assignment: organization-defined frequency*] to verify media reliability and information integrity.

Supplemental Guidance: Related control: CP-4.

(2) INFORMATION SYSTEM BACKUP | TEST RESTORATION USING SAMPLING

The organization uses a sample of backup information in the restoration of selected information system functions as part of contingency plan testing.

Supplemental Guidance: Related control: CP-4.

(3) INFORMATION SYSTEM BACKUP | SEPARATE STORAGE FOR CRITICAL INFORMATION

The organization stores backup copies of [Assignment: organization-defined critical information system software and other security-related information] in a separate facility or in a fire-rated container that is not collocated with the operational system.

Supplemental Guidance: Critical information system software includes, for example, operating systems, cryptographic key management systems, and intrusion detection/prevention systems. Security-related information includes, for example, organizational inventories of hardware, software, and firmware components. Alternate storage sites typically serve as separate storage facilities for organizations. Related controls: CM-2, CM-8.

(4) INFORMATION SYSTEM BACKUP | PROTECTION FROM UNAUTHORIZED MODIFICATION

[Withdrawn: Incorporated into CP-9].

(5) INFORMATION SYSTEM BACKUP | TRANSFER TO ALTERNATE STORAGE SITE

The organization transfers information system backup information to the alternate storage site [Assignment: organization-defined time period and transfer rate consistent with the recovery time and recovery point objectives].

Supplemental Guidance: Information system backup information can be transferred to alternate storage sites either electronically or by physical shipment of storage media.

(6) INFORMATION SYSTEM BACKUP | REDUNDANT SECONDARY SYSTEM

The organization accomplishes information system backup by maintaining a redundant secondary system that is not collocated with the primary system and that can be activated without loss of information or disruption to operations.

Supplemental Guidance: Related controls: CP-7, CP-10.

(7) INFORMATION SYSTEM BACKUP | DUAL AUTHORIZATION

The organization enforces dual authorization for the deletion or destruction of [Assignment: organization-defined backup information].

Supplemental Guidance: Dual authorization ensures that the deletion or destruction of backup information cannot occur unless two qualified individuals carry out the task. Individuals deleting/destroying backup information possess sufficient skills/expertise to determine if the proposed deletion/destruction of backup information reflects organizational policies and procedures. Dual authorization may also be known as two-person control. Related controls: AC-3, MP-2.

References: NIST Special Publication 800-34.

Priority and Baseline Allocation:

P1	LOW CP-9	MOD CP-9 (1)	HIGH CP-9 (1) (2) (3) (5)

CP-10 INFORMATION SYSTEM RECOVERY AND RECONSTITUTION

Control: The organization provides for the recovery and reconstitution of the information system to a known state after a disruption, compromise, or failure.

Supplemental Guidance: Recovery is executing information system contingency plan activities to restore organizational missions/business functions. Reconstitution takes place following recovery and includes activities for returning organizational information systems to fully operational states. Recovery and reconstitution operations reflect mission and business priorities, recovery point/time and reconstitution objectives, and established organizational metrics consistent with contingency plan requirements. Reconstitution includes the deactivation of any interim information system capabilities that may have been needed during recovery operations. Reconstitution also includes assessments of fully restored information system capabilities, reestablishment of continuous monitoring activities, potential information system reauthorizations, and activities to prepare the systems against future disruptions, compromises, or failures. Recovery/reconstitution capabilities employed by organizations can include both automated mechanisms and manual procedures. Related controls: CA-2, CA-6, CA-7, CP-2, CP-6, CP-7, CP-9, SC-24.

Control Enhancements:

(1) INFORMATION SYSTEM RECOVERY AND RECONSTITUTION | CONTINGENCY PLAN TESTING
[Withdrawn: Incorporated into CP-4].

(2) INFORMATION SYSTEM RECOVERY AND RECONSTITUTION | TRANSACTION RECOVERY
The information system implements transaction recovery for systems that are transaction-based.

Supplemental Guidance: Transaction-based information systems include, for example, database management systems and transaction processing systems. Mechanisms supporting transaction recovery include, for example, transaction rollback and transaction journaling.

(3) INFORMATION SYSTEM RECOVERY AND RECONSTITUTION | COMPENSATING SECURITY CONTROLS
[Withdrawn: Addressed through tailoring procedures].

(4) INFORMATION SYSTEM RECOVERY AND RECONSTITUTION | RESTORE WITHIN TIME PERIOD
The organization provides the capability to restore information system components within [Assignment: organization-defined restoration time-periods] from configuration-controlled and integrity-protected information representing a known, operational state for the components.

Supplemental Guidance: Restoration of information system components includes, for example, reimaging which restores components to known, operational states. Related control: CM-2.

(5) INFORMATION SYSTEM RECOVERY AND RECONSTITUTION | FAILOVER CAPABILITY
[Withdrawn: Incorporated into SI-13].

(6) INFORMATION SYSTEM RECOVERY AND RECONSTITUTION | COMPONENT PROTECTION
The organization protects backup and restoration hardware, firmware, and software.

Supplemental Guidance: Protection of backup and restoration hardware, firmware, and software components includes both physical and technical safeguards. Backup and restoration software includes, for example, router tables, compilers, and other security-relevant system software. Related controls: AC-3, AC-6, PE-3.

References: Federal Continuity Directive 1; NIST Special Publication 800-34.

Priority and Baseline Allocation:

P1	LOW CP-10	MOD CP-10 (2)	HIGH CP-10 (2) (4)

CP-11 ALTERNATE COMMUNICATIONS PROTOCOLS

Control: The information system provides the capability to employ [Assignment: organization-defined alternative communications protocols] in support of maintaining continuity of operations.

Supplemental Guidance: Contingency plans and the associated training and testing for those plans, incorporate an alternate communications protocol capability as part of increasing the resilience of organizational information systems. Alternate communications protocols include, for example, switching from Transmission Control Protocol/Internet Protocol (TCP/IP) Version 4 to TCP/IP Version 6. Switching communications protocols may affect software applications and therefore, the potential side effects of introducing alternate communications protocols are analyzed prior to implementation.

Control Enhancements: None.

References: None.

Priority and Baseline Allocation:

| P0 | LOW Not Selected | MOD Not Selected | HIGH Not Selected |

CP-12 **SAFE MODE**

Control: The information system, when [*Assignment: organization-defined conditions*] are detected, enters a safe mode of operation with [*Assignment: organization-defined restrictions of safe mode of operation*].

Supplemental Guidance: For information systems supporting critical missions/business functions including, for example, military operations and weapons systems, civilian space operations, nuclear power plant operations, and air traffic control operations (especially real-time operational environments), organizations may choose to identify certain conditions under which those systems revert to a predefined safe mode of operation. The safe mode of operation, which can be activated automatically or manually, restricts the types of activities or operations information systems could execute when those conditions are encountered. Restriction includes, for example, allowing only certain functions that could be carried out under limited power or with reduced communications bandwidth.

Control Enhancements: None.

References: None.

Priority and Baseline Allocation:

| P0 | LOW Not Selected | MOD Not Selected | HIGH Not Selected |

CP-13 **ALTERNATIVE SECURITY MECHANISMS**

Control: The organization employs [*Assignment: organization-defined alternative or supplemental security mechanisms*] for satisfying [*Assignment: organization-defined security functions*] when the primary means of implementing the security function is unavailable or compromised.

Supplemental Guidance: This control supports information system resiliency and contingency planning/continuity of operations. To ensure mission/business continuity, organizations can implement alternative or supplemental security mechanisms. These mechanisms may be less effective than the primary mechanisms (e.g., not as easy to use, not as scalable, or not as secure). However, having the capability to readily employ these alternative/supplemental mechanisms enhances overall mission/business continuity that might otherwise be adversely impacted if organizational operations had to be curtailed until the primary means of implementing the functions was restored. Given the cost and level of effort required to provide such alternative capabilities, this control would typically be applied only to critical security capabilities provided by information systems, system components, or information system services. For example, an organization may issue to senior executives and system administrators one-time pads in case multifactor tokens, the organization's standard means for secure remote authentication, is compromised. Related control: CP-2.

Control Enhancements: None.

References: None.

Priority and Baseline Allocation:

| P0 | LOW Not Selected | MOD Not Selected | HIGH Not Selected |

FAMILY: IDENTIFICATION AND AUTHENTICATION

IA-1 IDENTIFICATION AND AUTHENTICATION POLICY AND PROCEDURES

Control: The organization:

a. Develops, documents, and disseminates to [*Assignment: organization-defined personnel or roles*]:

   1. An identification and authentication policy that addresses purpose, scope, roles, responsibilities, management commitment, coordination among organizational entities, and compliance; and

   2. Procedures to facilitate the implementation of the identification and authentication policy and associated identification and authentication controls; and

b. Reviews and updates the current:

   1. Identification and authentication policy [*Assignment: organization-defined frequency*]; and

   2. Identification and authentication procedures [*Assignment: organization-defined frequency*].

Supplemental Guidance: This control addresses the establishment of policy and procedures for the effective implementation of selected security controls and control enhancements in the IA family. Policy and procedures reflect applicable federal laws, Executive Orders, directives, regulations, policies, standards, and guidance. Security program policies and procedures at the organization level may make the need for system-specific policies and procedures unnecessary. The policy can be included as part of the general information security policy for organizations or conversely, can be represented by multiple policies reflecting the complex nature of certain organizations. The procedures can be established for the security program in general and for particular information systems, if needed. The organizational risk management strategy is a key factor in establishing policy and procedures. Related control: PM-9.

Control Enhancements: None.

References: FIPS Publication 201; NIST Special Publications 800-12, 800-63, 800-73, 800-76, 800-78, 800-100.

Priority and Baseline Allocation:

| P1 | LOW IA-1 | MOD IA-1 | HIGH IA-1 |

IA-2 IDENTIFICATION AND AUTHENTICATION (ORGANIZATIONAL USERS)

Control: The information system uniquely identifies and authenticates organizational users (or processes acting on behalf of organizational users).

Supplemental Guidance: Organizational users include employees or individuals that organizations deem to have equivalent status of employees (e.g., contractors, guest researchers). This control applies to all accesses other than: (i) accesses that are explicitly identified and documented in AC-14; and (ii) accesses that occur through authorized use of group authenticators without individual authentication. Organizations may require unique identification of individuals in group accounts (e.g., shared privilege accounts) or for detailed accountability of individual activity. Organizations employ passwords, tokens, or biometrics to authenticate user identities, or in the case multifactor authentication, or some combination thereof. Access to organizational information systems is defined as either local access or network access. Local access is any access to organizational information systems by users (or processes acting on behalf of users) where such access is obtained by direct connections without the use of networks. Network access is access to organizational information systems by users (or processes acting on behalf of users) where such access is obtained through network connections (i.e., nonlocal accesses). Remote access is a type of network access that involves communication through external networks (e.g., the Internet). Internal networks include local area networks and wide area networks. In addition, the use of encrypted virtual private networks (VPNs) for network connections between organization-controlled endpoints and non-organization controlled endpoints may be treated as internal networks from the perspective of protecting the confidentiality and integrity of information traversing the network.

Organizations can satisfy the identification and authentication requirements in this control by complying with the requirements in Homeland Security Presidential Directive 12 consistent with the specific organizational implementation plans. Multifactor authentication requires the use of two or more different factors to achieve authentication. The factors are defined as: (i) something you know (e.g., password, personal identification number [PIN]); (ii) something you have (e.g., cryptographic identification device, token); or (iii) something you are (e.g., biometric). Multifactor solutions that require devices separate from information systems gaining access include, for example, hardware tokens providing time-based or challenge-response authenticators and smart cards such as the U.S. Government Personal Identity Verification card and the DoD common access card. In addition to identifying and authenticating users at the information system level (i.e., at logon), organizations also employ identification and authentication mechanisms at the application level, when necessary, to provide increased information security. Identification and authentication requirements for other than organizational users are described in IA-8. Related controls: AC-2, AC-3, AC-14, AC-17, AC-18, IA-4, IA-5, IA-8.

Control Enhancements:

(1) IDENTIFICATION AND AUTHENTICATION | NETWORK ACCESS TO PRIVILEGED ACCOUNTS

The information system implements multifactor authentication for network access to privileged accounts.

Supplemental Guidance: Related control: AC-6.

(2) IDENTIFICATION AND AUTHENTICATION | NETWORK ACCESS TO NON-PRIVILEGED ACCOUNTS

The information system implements multifactor authentication for network access to non-privileged accounts.

(3) IDENTIFICATION AND AUTHENTICATION | LOCAL ACCESS TO PRIVILEGED ACCOUNTS

The information system implements multifactor authentication for local access to privileged accounts.

Supplemental Guidance: Related control: AC-6.

(4) IDENTIFICATION AND AUTHENTICATION | LOCAL ACCESS TO NON-PRIVILEGED ACCOUNTS

The information system implements multifactor authentication for local access to non-privileged accounts.

(5) IDENTIFICATION AND AUTHENTICATION | GROUP AUTHENTICATION

The organization requires individuals to be authenticated with an individual authenticator when a group authenticator is employed.

Supplemental Guidance: Requiring individuals to use individual authenticators as a second level of authentication helps organizations to mitigate the risk of using group authenticators.

(6) IDENTIFICATION AND AUTHENTICATION | NETWORK ACCESS TO PRIVILEGED ACCOUNTS - SEPARATE DEVICE

The information system implements multifactor authentication for network access to privileged accounts such that one of the factors is provided by a device separate from the system gaining access and the device meets [*Assignment: organization-defined strength of mechanism requirements*].

Supplemental Guidance: Related control: AC-6.

(7) IDENTIFICATION AND AUTHENTICATION | NETWORK ACCESS TO NON-PRIVILEGED ACCOUNTS - SEPARATE DEVICE

The information system implements multifactor authentication for network access to non-privileged accounts such that one of the factors is provided by a device separate from the system gaining access and the device meets [*Assignment: organization-defined strength of mechanism requirements*].

(8) *IDENTIFICATION AND AUTHENTICATION | NETWORK ACCESS TO PRIVILEGED ACCOUNTS - REPLAY RESISTANT*

The information system implements replay-resistant authentication mechanisms for network access to privileged accounts.

Supplemental Guidance: Authentication processes resist replay attacks if it is impractical to achieve successful authentications by replaying previous authentication messages. Replay-resistant techniques include, for example, protocols that use nonces or challenges such as Transport Layer Security (TLS) and time synchronous or challenge-response one-time authenticators.

(9) *IDENTIFICATION AND AUTHENTICATION | NETWORK ACCESS TO NON-PRIVILEGED ACCOUNTS - REPLAY RESISTANT*

The information system implements replay-resistant authentication mechanisms for network access to non-privileged accounts.

Supplemental Guidance: Authentication processes resist replay attacks if it is impractical to achieve successful authentications by recording/replaying previous authentication messages. Replay-resistant techniques include, for example, protocols that use nonces or challenges such as Transport Layer Security (TLS) and time synchronous or challenge-response one-time authenticators.

(10) *IDENTIFICATION AND AUTHENTICATION | SINGLE SIGN-ON*

The information system provides a single sign-on capability for [*Assignment: organization-defined information system accounts and services*].

Supplemental Guidance: Single sign-on enables users to log in once and gain access to multiple information system resources. Organizations consider the operational efficiencies provided by single sign-on capabilities with the increased risk from disclosures of single authenticators providing access to multiple system resources.

(11) *IDENTIFICATION AND AUTHENTICATION | REMOTE ACCESS - SEPARATE DEVICE*

The information system implements multifactor authentication for remote access to privileged and non-privileged accounts such that one of the factors is provided by a device separate from the system gaining access and the device meets [*Assignment: organization-defined strength of mechanism requirements*].

Supplemental Guidance: For remote access to privileged/non-privileged accounts, the purpose of requiring a device that is separate from the information system gaining access for one of the factors during multifactor authentication is to reduce the likelihood of compromising authentication credentials stored on the system. For example, adversaries deploying malicious code on organizational information systems can potentially compromise such credentials resident on the system and subsequently impersonate authorized users. Related control: AC-6.

(12) *IDENTIFICATION AND AUTHENTICATION | ACCEPTANCE OF PIV CREDENTIALS*

The information system accepts and electronically verifies Personal Identity Verification (PIV) credentials.

Supplemental Guidance: This control enhancement applies to organizations implementing logical access control systems (LACS) and physical access control systems (PACS). Personal Identity Verification (PIV) credentials are those credentials issued by federal agencies that conform to FIPS Publication 201 and supporting guidance documents. OMB Memorandum 11-11 requires federal agencies to continue implementing the requirements specified in HSPD-12 to enable agency-wide use of PIV credentials. Related controls: AU-2, PE-3, SA-4.

(13) *IDENTIFICATION AND AUTHENTICATION | OUT-OF-BAND AUTHENTICATION*

The information system implements [*Assignment: organization-defined out-of-band authentication*] under [*Assignment: organization-defined conditions*].

Supplemental Guidance: Out-of-band authentication (OOBA) refers to the use of two separate communication paths to identify and authenticate users or devices to an information system. The first path (i.e., the in-band path), is used to identify and authenticate users or devices, and generally is the path through which information flows. The second path (i.e., the out-of-band path) is used to independently verify the authentication and/or requested action. For example, a user authenticates via a notebook computer to a remote server to which the user desires access, and requests some action of the server via that communication path. Subsequently, the server contacts the user via the user's cell phone to verify that the requested action originated from the user. The user may either confirm the intended action to an individual on the telephone or provide an authentication code via the telephone. This type of authentication can be employed by organizations to mitigate actual or suspected man-in the-middle attacks. The conditions for activation can include, for example, suspicious activities, new threat indicators or elevated threat levels, or the impact level or classification level of information in requested transactions. Related controls: IA-10, IA-11, SC-37.

References: HSPD-12; OMB Memoranda 04-04, 06-16, 11-11; FIPS Publication 201; NIST Special Publications 800-63, 800-73, 800-76, 800-78; FICAM Roadmap and Implementation Guidance; Web: http://idmanagement.gov.

Priority and Baseline Allocation:

P1	LOW IA-2 (1) (12)	MOD IA-2 (1) (2) (3) (8) (11) (12)	HIGH IA-2 (1) (2) (3) (4) (8) (9) (11) (12)

IA-3 DEVICE IDENTIFICATION AND AUTHENTICATION

Control: The information system uniquely identifies and authenticates [*Assignment: organization-defined specific and/or types of devices*] before establishing a [*Selection (one or more): local; remote; network*] connection.

Supplemental Guidance: Organizational devices requiring unique device-to-device identification and authentication may be defined by type, by device, or by a combination of type/device. Information systems typically use either shared known information (e.g., Media Access Control [MAC] or Transmission Control Protocol/Internet Protocol [TCP/IP] addresses) for device identification or organizational authentication solutions (e.g., IEEE 802.1x and Extensible Authentication Protocol [EAP], Radius server with EAP-Transport Layer Security [TLS] authentication, Kerberos) to identify/authenticate devices on local and/or wide area networks. Organizations determine the required strength of authentication mechanisms by the security categories of information systems. Because of the challenges of applying this control on large scale, organizations are encouraged to only apply the control to those limited number (and type) of devices that truly need to support this capability. Related controls: AC-17, AC-18, AC-19, CA-3, IA-4, IA-5.

Control Enhancements:

(1) DEVICE IDENTIFICATION AND AUTHENTICATION | CRYPTOGRAPHIC BIDIRECTIONAL AUTHENTICATION

The information system authenticates [*Assignment: organization-defined specific devices and/or types of devices*] before establishing [*Selection (one or more): local; remote; network*] connection using bidirectional authentication that is cryptographically based.

Supplemental Guidance: A local connection is any connection with a device communicating without the use of a network. A network connection is any connection with a device that communicates through a network (e.g., local area or wide area network, Internet). A remote connection is any connection with a device communicating through an external network (e.g., the Internet). Bidirectional authentication provides stronger safeguards to validate the identity of other devices for connections that are of greater risk (e.g., remote connections). Related controls: SC-8, SC-12, SC-13.

(2) DEVICE IDENTIFICATION AND AUTHENTICATION | CRYPTOGRAPHIC BIDIRECTIONAL NETWORK AUTHENTICATION

[Withdrawn: Incorporated into IA-3 (1)].

(3) DEVICE IDENTIFICATION AND AUTHENTICATION | DYNAMIC ADDRESS ALLOCATION

The organization:

(a) **Standardizes dynamic address allocation lease information and the lease duration assigned to devices in accordance with [*Assignment: organization-defined lease information and lease duration*]; and**

(b) **Audits lease information when assigned to a device.**

Supplemental Guidance: DHCP-enabled clients obtaining *leases* for IP addresses from DHCP servers, is a typical example of dynamic address allocation for devices. Related controls: AU-2, AU-3, AU-6, AU-12.

(4) DEVICE IDENTIFICATION AND AUTHENTICATION | DEVICE ATTESTATION

The organization ensures that device identification and authentication based on attestation is handled by [*Assignment: organization-defined configuration management process*].

Supplemental Guidance: Device attestation refers to the identification and authentication of a device based on its configuration and known operating state. This might be determined via some cryptographic hash of the device. If device attestation is the means of identification and authentication, then it is important that patches and updates to the device are handled via a configuration management process such that the those patches/updates are done securely and at the same time do not disrupt the identification and authentication to other devices.

References: None.

Priority and Baseline Allocation:

P1	**LOW** Not Selected	**MOD** IA-3	**HIGH** IA-3

IA-4 IDENTIFIER MANAGEMENT

Control: The organization manages information system identifiers by:

a. Receiving authorization from [*Assignment: organization-defined personnel or roles*] to assign an individual, group, role, or device identifier;

b. Selecting an identifier that identifies an individual, group, role, or device;

c. Assigning the identifier to the intended individual, group, role, or device;

d. Preventing reuse of identifiers for [*Assignment: organization-defined time period*]; and

e. Disabling the identifier after [*Assignment: organization-defined time period of inactivity*].

Supplemental Guidance: Common device identifiers include, for example, media access control (MAC), Internet protocol (IP) addresses, or device-unique token identifiers. Management of individual identifiers is not applicable to shared information system accounts (e.g., guest and anonymous accounts). Typically, individual identifiers are the user names of the information system accounts assigned to those individuals. In such instances, the account management activities of AC-2 use account names provided by IA-4. This control also addresses individual identifiers not necessarily associated with information system accounts (e.g., identifiers used in physical security control databases accessed by badge reader systems for access to information systems). Preventing reuse of identifiers implies preventing the assignment of previously used individual, group, role, or device identifiers to different individuals, groups, roles, or devices. Related controls: AC-2, IA-2, IA-3, IA-5, IA-8, SC-37.

Control Enhancements:

(1) IDENTIFIER MANAGEMENT | PROHIBIT ACCOUNT IDENTIFIERS AS PUBLIC IDENTIFIERS

The organization prohibits the use of information system account identifiers that are the same as public identifiers for individual electronic mail accounts.

Supplemental Guidance: Prohibiting the use of information systems account identifiers that are the same as some public identifier such as the individual identifier section of an electronic mail address, makes it more difficult for adversaries to guess user identifiers on organizational information systems. Related control: AT-2.

(2) IDENTIFIER MANAGEMENT | SUPERVISOR AUTHORIZATION

The organization requires that the registration process to receive an individual identifier includes supervisor authorization.

(3) IDENTIFIER MANAGEMENT | MULTIPLE FORMS OF CERTIFICATION

The organization requires multiple forms of certification of individual identification be presented to the registration authority.

Supplemental Guidance: Requiring multiple forms of identification, such as documentary evidence or a combination of documents and biometrics, reduces the likelihood of individuals using fraudulent identification to establish an identity, or at least increases the work factor of potential adversaries.

(4) IDENTIFIER MANAGEMENT | IDENTIFY USER STATUS

The organization manages individual identifiers by uniquely identifying each individual as [*Assignment: organization-defined characteristic identifying individual status*].

Supplemental Guidance: Characteristics identifying the status of individuals include, for example, contractors and foreign nationals. Identifying the status of individuals by specific characteristics provides additional information about the people with whom organizational personnel are communicating. For example, it might be useful for a government employee to know that one of the individuals on an email message is a contractor. Related control: AT-2.

(5) IDENTIFIER MANAGEMENT | DYNAMIC MANAGEMENT

The information system dynamically manages identifiers.

Supplemental Guidance: In contrast to conventional approaches to identification which presume static accounts for preregistered users, many distributed information systems including, for example, service-oriented architectures, rely on establishing identifiers at run time for entities that were previously unknown. In these situations, organizations anticipate and provision for the dynamic establishment of identifiers. Preestablished trust relationships and mechanisms with appropriate authorities to validate identities and related credentials are essential. Related control: AC-16.

(6) IDENTIFIER MANAGEMENT | CROSS-ORGANIZATION MANAGEMENT

The organization coordinates with [*Assignment: organization-defined external organizations*] for cross-organization management of identifiers.

Supplemental Guidance: Cross-organization identifier management provides the capability for organizations to appropriately identify individuals, groups, roles, or devices when conducting cross-organization activities involving the processing, storage, or transmission of information.

(7) IDENTIFIER MANAGEMENT | IN-PERSON REGISTRATION

The organization requires that the registration process to receive an individual identifier be conducted in person before a designated registration authority.

Supplemental Guidance: In-person registration reduces the likelihood of fraudulent identifiers being issued because it requires the physical presence of individuals and actual face-to-face interactions with designated registration authorities.

References: FIPS Publication 201; NIST Special Publications 800-73, 800-76, 800-78.

Priority and Baseline Allocation:

| P1 | LOW IA-4 | MOD IA-4 | HIGH IA-4 |

IA-5 AUTHENTICATOR MANAGEMENT

Control: The organization manages information system authenticators by:

a. Verifying, as part of the initial authenticator distribution, the identity of the individual, group, role, or device receiving the authenticator;

b. Establishing initial authenticator content for authenticators defined by the organization;

c. Ensuring that authenticators have sufficient strength of mechanism for their intended use;

d. Establishing and implementing administrative procedures for initial authenticator distribution, for lost/compromised or damaged authenticators, and for revoking authenticators;

e. Changing default content of authenticators prior to information system installation;

f. Establishing minimum and maximum lifetime restrictions and reuse conditions for authenticators;

g. Changing/refreshing authenticators [*Assignment: organization-defined time period by authenticator type*];

h. Protecting authenticator content from unauthorized disclosure and modification;

i. Requiring individuals to take, and having devices implement, specific security safeguards to protect authenticators; and

j. Changing authenticators for group/role accounts when membership to those accounts changes.

Supplemental Guidance: Individual authenticators include, for example, passwords, tokens, biometrics, PKI certificates, and key cards. Initial authenticator content is the actual content (e.g., the initial password) as opposed to requirements about authenticator content (e.g., minimum password length). In many cases, developers ship information system components with factory default authentication credentials to allow for initial installation and configuration. Default authentication credentials are often well known, easily discoverable, and present a significant security risk. The requirement to protect individual authenticators may be implemented via control PL-4 or PS-6 for authenticators in the possession of individuals and by controls AC-3, AC-6, and SC-28 for authenticators stored within organizational information systems (e.g., passwords stored in hashed or encrypted formats, files containing encrypted or hashed passwords accessible with administrator privileges). Information systems support individual authenticator management by organization-defined settings and restrictions for various authenticator characteristics including, for example, minimum password length, password composition, validation time window for time synchronous one-time tokens, and number of allowed rejections during the verification stage of biometric authentication. Specific actions that can be taken to safeguard authenticators include, for example, maintaining possession of individual authenticators, not loaning or sharing individual authenticators with others, and reporting lost, stolen, or compromised authenticators immediately. Authenticator management includes issuing and revoking, when no longer needed, authenticators for temporary access such as that required for remote maintenance. Device authenticators include, for example, certificates and passwords. Related controls: AC-2, AC-3, AC-6, CM-6, IA-2, IA-4, IA-8, PL-4, PS-5, PS-6, SC-12, SC-13, SC-17, SC-28.

Control Enhancements:

(1) AUTHENTICATOR MANAGEMENT | PASSWORD-BASED AUTHENTICATION

The information system, for password-based authentication:

(a) Enforces minimum password complexity of [*Assignment: organization-defined requirements for case sensitivity, number of characters, mix of upper-case letters, lower-case letters, numbers, and special characters, including minimum requirements for each type*];

(b) Enforces at least the following number of changed characters when new passwords are created: [*Assignment: organization-defined number*];

(c) Stores and transmits only cryptographically-protected passwords;

(d) Enforces password minimum and maximum lifetime restrictions of [*Assignment: organization-defined numbers for lifetime minimum, lifetime maximum*];

(e) Prohibits password reuse for [*Assignment: organization-defined number*] generations; and

(f) Allows the use of a temporary password for system logons with an immediate change to a permanent password.

Supplemental Guidance: This control enhancement applies to single-factor authentication of individuals using passwords as individual or group authenticators, and in a similar manner, when passwords are part of multifactor authenticators. This control enhancement does *not* apply when passwords are used to unlock hardware authenticators (e.g., Personal Identity

Verification cards). The implementation of such password mechanisms may not meet all of the requirements in the enhancement. Cryptographically-protected passwords include, for example, encrypted versions of passwords and one-way cryptographic hashes of passwords. The number of changed characters refers to the number of changes required with respect to the total number of positions in the current password. Password lifetime restrictions do not apply to temporary passwords. To mitigate certain brute force attacks against passwords, organizations may also consider salting passwords. Related control: IA-6.

(2) AUTHENTICATOR MANAGEMENT | PKI-BASED AUTHENTICATION

The information system, for PKI-based authentication:

(a) Validates certifications by constructing and verifying a certification path to an accepted trust anchor including checking certificate status information;

(b) Enforces authorized access to the corresponding private key;

(c) Maps the authenticated identity to the account of the individual or group; and

(d) Implements a local cache of revocation data to support path discovery and validation in case of inability to access revocation information via the network.

Supplemental Guidance: Status information for certification paths includes, for example, certificate revocation lists or certificate status protocol responses. For PIV cards, validation of certifications involves the construction and verification of a certification path to the Common Policy Root trust anchor including certificate policy processing. Related control: IA-6.

(3) AUTHENTICATOR MANAGEMENT | IN-PERSON OR TRUSTED THIRD-PARTY REGISTRATION

The organization requires that the registration process to receive [Assignment: organization-defined types of and/or specific authenticators] be conducted [Selection: in person; by a trusted third party] before [Assignment: organization-defined registration authority] with authorization by [Assignment: organization-defined personnel or roles].

(4) AUTHENTICATOR MANAGEMENT | AUTOMATED SUPPORT FOR PASSWORD STRENGTH DETERMINATION

The organization employs automated tools to determine if password authenticators are sufficiently strong to satisfy [Assignment: organization-defined requirements].

Supplemental Guidance: This control enhancement focuses on the creation of strong passwords and the characteristics of such passwords (e.g., complexity) prior to use, the enforcement of which is carried out by organizational information systems in IA-5 (1). Related controls: CA-2, CA-7, RA-5.

(5) AUTHENTICATOR MANAGEMENT | CHANGE AUTHENTICATORS PRIOR TO DELIVERY

The organization requires developers/installers of information system components to provide unique authenticators or change default authenticators prior to delivery/installation.

Supplemental Guidance: This control enhancement extends the requirement for organizations to change default authenticators upon information system installation, by requiring developers and/or installers to provide unique authenticators or change default authenticators for system components prior to delivery and/or installation. However, it typically does not apply to the developers of commercial off-the-shelve information technology products. Requirements for unique authenticators can be included in acquisition documents prepared by organizations when procuring information systems or system components.

(6) AUTHENTICATOR MANAGEMENT | PROTECTION OF AUTHENTICATORS

The organization protects authenticators commensurate with the security category of the information to which use of the authenticator permits access.

Supplemental Guidance: For information systems containing multiple security categories of information without reliable physical or logical separation between categories, authenticators used to grant access to the systems are protected commensurate with the highest security category of information on the systems.

(7) AUTHENTICATOR MANAGEMENT | NO EMBEDDED UNENCRYPTED STATIC AUTHENTICATORS

The organization ensures that unencrypted static authenticators are not embedded in applications or access scripts or stored on function keys.

Supplemental Guidance: Organizations exercise caution in determining whether embedded or stored authenticators are in encrypted or unencrypted form. If authenticators are used in the manner stored, then those representations are considered unencrypted authenticators. This is irrespective of whether that representation is perhaps an encrypted version of something else (e.g., a password).

(8) AUTHENTICATOR MANAGEMENT | MULTIPLE INFORMATION SYSTEM ACCOUNTS

The organization implements [*Assignment: organization-defined security safeguards*] to manage the risk of compromise due to individuals having accounts on multiple information systems.

Supplemental Guidance: When individuals have accounts on multiple information systems, there is the risk that the compromise of one account may lead to the compromise of other accounts if individuals use the same authenticators. Possible alternatives include, for example: (i) having different authenticators on all systems; (ii) employing some form of single sign-on mechanism; or (iii) including some form of one-time passwords on all systems.

(9) AUTHENTICATOR MANAGEMENT | CROSS-ORGANIZATION CREDENTIAL MANAGEMENT

The organization coordinates with [*Assignment: organization-defined external organizations*] for cross-organization management of credentials.

Supplemental Guidance: Cross-organization management of credentials provides the capability for organizations to appropriately authenticate individuals, groups, roles, or devices when conducting cross-organization activities involving the processing, storage, or transmission of information.

(10) AUTHENTICATOR MANAGEMENT | DYNAMIC CREDENTIAL ASSOCIATION

The information system dynamically provisions identities.

Supplemental Guidance: Authentication requires some form of binding between an identity and the authenticator used to confirm the identity. In conventional approaches, this binding is established by pre-provisioning both the identity and the authenticator to the information system. For example, the binding between a username (i.e., identity) and a password (i.e., authenticator) is accomplished by provisioning the identity and authenticator as a pair in the information system. New authentication techniques allow the binding between the identity and the authenticator to be implemented outside an information system. For example, with smartcard credentials, the identity and the authenticator are bound together on the card. Using these credentials, information systems can authenticate identities that have not been pre-provisioned, dynamically provisioning the identity after authentication. In these situations, organizations can anticipate the dynamic provisioning of identities. Preestablished trust relationships and mechanisms with appropriate authorities to validate identities and related credentials are essential.

(11) AUTHENTICATOR MANAGEMENT | HARDWARE TOKEN-BASED AUTHENTICATION

The information system, for hardware token-based authentication, employs mechanisms that satisfy [*Assignment: organization-defined token quality requirements*].

Supplemental Guidance: Hardware token-based authentication typically refers to the use of PKI-based tokens, such as the U.S. Government Personal Identity Verification (PIV) card. Organizations define specific requirements for tokens, such as working with a particular PKI.

(12) AUTHENTICATOR MANAGEMENT | BIOMETRIC-BASED AUTHENTICATION

The information system, for biometric-based authentication, employs mechanisms that satisfy [*Assignment: organization-defined biometric quality requirements*].

Supplemental Guidance: Unlike password-based authentication which provides exact matches of user-input passwords to stored passwords, biometric authentication does not provide such exact matches. Depending upon the type of biometric and the type of collection mechanism, there is likely to be some divergence from the presented biometric and stored biometric which serves as the basis of comparison. There will likely be both false positives and false negatives when making such comparisons. The rate at which the false accept and false reject rates are equal is known as the crossover rate. Biometric quality requirements include, for example, acceptable crossover rates, as that essentially reflects the accuracy of the biometric.

(13) AUTHENTICATOR MANAGEMENT | EXPIRATION OF CACHED AUTHENTICATORS

The information system prohibits the use of cached authenticators after [*Assignment: organization-defined time period*].

(14) *AUTHENTICATOR MANAGEMENT | MANAGING CONTENT OF PKI TRUST STORES*

The organization, for PKI-based authentication, employs a deliberate organization-wide methodology for managing the content of PKI trust stores installed across all platforms including networks, operating systems, browsers, and applications.

(15) *AUTHENTICATOR MANAGEMENT | FICAM-APPROVED PRODUCTS AND SERVICES*

The organization uses only FICAM-approved path discovery and validation products and services.

Supplemental Guidance: Federal Identity, Credential, and Access Management (FICAM)-approved path discovery and validation products and services are those products and services that have been approved through the FICAM conformance program, where applicable.

References: OMB Memoranda 04-04, 11-11; FIPS Publication 201; NIST Special Publications 800-73, 800-63, 800-76, 800-78; FICAM Roadmap and Implementation Guidance; Web: http://idmanagement.gov.

Priority and Baseline Allocation:

P1	LOW IA-5 (1) (11)	MOD IA-5 (1) (2) (3) (11)	HIGH IA-5 (1) (2) (3) (11)

IA-6 AUTHENTICATOR FEEDBACK

Control: The information system obscures feedback of authentication information during the authentication process to protect the information from possible exploitation/use by unauthorized individuals.

Supplemental Guidance: The feedback from information systems does not provide information that would allow unauthorized individuals to compromise authentication mechanisms. For some types of information systems or system components, for example, desktops/notebooks with relatively large monitors, the threat (often referred to as shoulder surfing) may be significant. For other types of systems or components, for example, mobile devices with 2-4 inch screens, this threat may be less significant, and may need to be balanced against the increased likelihood of typographic input errors due to the small keyboards. Therefore, the means for obscuring the authenticator feedback is selected accordingly. Obscuring the feedback of authentication information includes, for example, displaying asterisks when users type passwords into input devices, or displaying feedback for a very limited time before fully obscuring it. Related control: PE-18.

Control Enhancements: None.

References: None.

Priority and Baseline Allocation:

P2	LOW IA-6	MOD IA-6	HIGH IA-6

IA-7 CRYPTOGRAPHIC MODULE AUTHENTICATION

Control: The information system implements mechanisms for authentication to a cryptographic module that meet the requirements of applicable federal laws, Executive Orders, directives, policies, regulations, standards, and guidance for such authentication.

Supplemental Guidance: Authentication mechanisms may be required within a cryptographic module to authenticate an operator accessing the module and to verify that the operator is authorized to assume the requested role and perform services within that role. Related controls: SC-12, SC-13.

Control Enhancements: None.

References: FIPS Publication 140; Web: http://csrc.nist.gov/groups/STM/cmvp/index.html.

Priority and Baseline Allocation:

| P1 | LOW IA-7 | MOD IA-7 | HIGH IA-7 |

IA-8 IDENTIFICATION AND AUTHENTICATION (NON-ORGANIZATIONAL USERS)

Control: The information system uniquely identifies and authenticates non-organizational users (or processes acting on behalf of non-organizational users).

Supplemental Guidance: Non-organizational users include information system users other than organizational users explicitly covered by IA-2. These individuals are uniquely identified and authenticated for accesses other than those accesses explicitly identified and documented in AC-14. In accordance with the E-Authentication E-Government initiative, authentication of non-organizational users accessing federal information systems may be required to protect federal, proprietary, or privacy-related information (with exceptions noted for national security systems). Organizations use risk assessments to determine authentication needs and consider scalability, practicality, and security in balancing the need to ensure ease of use for access to federal information and information systems with the need to protect and adequately mitigate risk. IA-2 addresses identification and authentication requirements for access to information systems by organizational users. Related controls: AC-2, AC-14, AC-17, AC-18, IA-2, IA-4, IA-5, MA-4, RA-3, SA-12, SC-8.

Control Enhancements:

(1) IDENTIFICATION AND AUTHENTICATION | ACCEPTANCE OF PIV CREDENTIALS FROM OTHER AGENCIES

The information system accepts and electronically verifies Personal Identity Verification (PIV) credentials from other federal agencies.

Supplemental Guidance: This control enhancement applies to logical access control systems (LACS) and physical access control systems (PACS). Personal Identity Verification (PIV) credentials are those credentials issued by federal agencies that conform to FIPS Publication 201 and supporting guidance documents. OMB Memorandum 11-11 requires federal agencies to continue implementing the requirements specified in HSPD-12 to enable agency-wide use of PIV credentials. Related controls: AU-2, PE-3, SA-4.

(2) IDENTIFICATION AND AUTHENTICATION | ACCEPTANCE OF THIRD-PARTY CREDENTIALS

The information system accepts only FICAM-approved third-party credentials.

Supplemental Guidance: This control enhancement typically applies to organizational information systems that are accessible to the general public, for example, public-facing websites. Third-party credentials are those credentials issued by nonfederal government entities approved by the Federal Identity, Credential, and Access Management (FICAM) Trust Framework Solutions initiative. Approved third-party credentials meet or exceed the set of minimum federal government-wide technical, security, privacy, and organizational maturity requirements. This allows federal government relying parties to trust such credentials at their approved assurance levels. Related control: AU-2.

(3) IDENTIFICATION AND AUTHENTICATION | USE OF FICAM-APPROVED PRODUCTS

The organization employs only FICAM-approved information system components in [*Assignment: organization-defined information systems*] to accept third-party credentials.

Supplemental Guidance: This control enhancement typically applies to information systems that are accessible to the general public, for example, public-facing websites. FICAM-approved information system components include, for example, information technology products and software libraries that have been approved by the Federal Identity, Credential, and Access Management conformance program. Related control: SA-4.

(4) IDENTIFICATION AND AUTHENTICATION | USE OF FICAM-ISSUED PROFILES

The information system conforms to FICAM-issued profiles.

Supplemental Guidance: This control enhancement addresses open identity management standards. To ensure that these standards are viable, robust, reliable, sustainable (e.g., available in commercial information technology products), and interoperable as documented, the United States Government assesses and scopes identity management standards and technology implementations against applicable federal legislation, directives, policies, and requirements. The result is FICAM-issued implementation profiles of approved protocols (e.g., FICAM authentication protocols such as SAML 2.0 and OpenID 2.0, as well as other protocols such as the FICAM Backend Attribute Exchange). Related control: SA-4.

(5) *IDENTIFICATION AND AUTHENTICATION | ACCEPTANCE OF PIV-I CREDENTIALS*

The information system accepts and electronically verifies Personal Identity Verification-I (PIV-I) credentials.

Supplemental Guidance: This control enhancement: (i) applies to logical and physical access control systems; and (ii) addresses Non-Federal Issuers (NFIs) of identity cards that desire to interoperate with United States Government Personal Identity Verification (PIV) information systems and that can be trusted by federal government-relying parties. The X.509 certificate policy for the Federal Bridge Certification Authority (FBCA) addresses PIV-I requirements. The PIV-I card is suitable for Assurance Level 4 as defined in OMB Memorandum 04-04 and NIST Special Publication 800-63, and multifactor authentication as defined in NIST Special Publication 800-116. PIV-I credentials are those credentials issued by a PIV-I provider whose PIV-I certificate policy maps to the Federal Bridge PIV-I Certificate Policy. A PIV-I provider is cross-certified (directly or through another PKI bridge) with the FBCA with policies that have been mapped and approved as meeting the requirements of the PIV-I policies defined in the FBCA certificate policy. Related control: AU-2.

References: OMB Memoranda 04-04, 11-11, 10-06-2011; FICAM Roadmap and Implementation Guidance; FIPS Publication 201; NIST Special Publications 800-63, 800-116; National Strategy for Trusted Identities in Cyberspace; Web: http://idmanagement.gov.

Priority and Baseline Allocation:

P1	LOW IA-8 (1) (2) (3) (4)	MOD IA-8 (1) (2) (3) (4)	HIGH IA-8 (1) (2) (3) (4)

IA-9 SERVICE IDENTIFICATION AND AUTHENTICATION

Control: The organization identifies and authenticates [*Assignment: organization-defined information system services*] using [*Assignment: organization-defined security safeguards*].

Supplemental Guidance: This control supports service-oriented architectures and other distributed architectural approaches requiring the identification and authentication of information system services. In such architectures, external services often appear dynamically. Therefore, information systems should be able to determine in a dynamic manner, if external providers and associated services are authentic. Safeguards implemented by organizational information systems to validate provider and service authenticity include, for example, information or code signing, provenance graphs, and/or electronic signatures indicating or including the sources of services.

Control Enhancements:

(1) *SERVICE IDENTIFICATION AND AUTHENTICATION | INFORMATION EXCHANGE*

The organization ensures that service providers receive, validate, and transmit identification and authentication information.

(2) *SERVICE IDENTIFICATION AND AUTHENTICATION | TRANSMISSION OF DECISIONS*

The organization ensures that identification and authentication decisions are transmitted between [*Assignment: organization-defined services*] consistent with organizational policies.

Supplemental Guidance: For distributed architectures (e.g., service-oriented architectures), the decisions regarding the validation of identification and authentication claims may be made by services separate from the services acting on those decisions. In such situations, it is necessary to provide the identification and authentication decisions (as opposed to the actual identifiers and authenticators) to the services that need to act on those decisions. Related control: SC-8.

References: None.

Priority and Baseline Allocation:

| P0 | LOW Not Selected | MOD Not Selected | HIGH Not Selected |

IA-10 ADAPTIVE IDENTIFICATION AND AUTHENTICATION

Control: The organization requires that individuals accessing the information system employ [*Assignment: organization-defined supplemental authentication techniques or mechanisms*] under specific [*Assignment: organization-defined circumstances or situations*].

Supplemental Guidance: Adversaries may compromise individual authentication mechanisms and subsequently attempt to impersonate legitimate users. This situation can potentially occur with any authentication mechanisms employed by organizations. To address this threat, organizations may employ specific techniques/mechanisms and establish protocols to assess suspicious behavior (e.g., individuals accessing information that they do not typically access as part of their normal duties, roles, or responsibilities, accessing greater quantities of information than the individuals would routinely access, or attempting to access information from suspicious network addresses). In these situations when certain preestablished conditions or triggers occur, organizations can require selected individuals to provide additional authentication information. Another potential use for adaptive identification and authentication is to increase the strength of mechanism based on the number and/or types of records being accessed. Related controls: AU-6, SI-4.

Control Enhancements: None.

References: None.

Priority and Baseline Allocation:

| P0 | LOW Not Selected | MOD Not Selected | HIGH Not Selected |

IA-11 RE-AUTHENTICATION

Control: The organization requires users and devices to re-authenticate when [*Assignment: organization-defined circumstances or situations requiring re-authentication*].

Supplemental Guidance: In addition to the re-authentication requirements associated with session locks, organizations may require re-authentication of individuals and/or devices in other situations including, for example: (i) when authenticators change; (ii), when roles change; (iii) when security categories of information systems change; (iv), when the execution of privileged functions occurs; (v) after a fixed period of time; or (vi) periodically. Related control: AC-11.

Control Enhancements: None.

References: None.

Priority and Baseline Allocation:

| P0 | LOW Not Selected | MOD Not Selected | HIGH Not Selected |

FAMILY: INCIDENT RESPONSE

IR-1 INCIDENT RESPONSE POLICY AND PROCEDURES

Control: The organization:

a. Develops, documents, and disseminates to [*Assignment: organization-defined personnel or roles*]:

1. An incident response policy that addresses purpose, scope, roles, responsibilities, management commitment, coordination among organizational entities, and compliance; and

2. Procedures to facilitate the implementation of the incident response policy and associated incident response controls; and

b. Reviews and updates the current:

1. Incident response policy [*Assignment: organization-defined frequency*]; and

2. Incident response procedures [*Assignment: organization-defined frequency*].

Supplemental Guidance: This control addresses the establishment of policy and procedures for the effective implementation of selected security controls and control enhancements in the IR family. Policy and procedures reflect applicable federal laws, Executive Orders, directives, regulations, policies, standards, and guidance. Security program policies and procedures at the organization level may make the need for system-specific policies and procedures unnecessary. The policy can be included as part of the general information security policy for organizations or conversely, can be represented by multiple policies reflecting the complex nature of certain organizations. The procedures can be established for the security program in general and for particular information systems, if needed. The organizational risk management strategy is a key factor in establishing policy and procedures. Related control: PM-9.

Control Enhancements: None.

References: NIST Special Publications 800-12, 800-61, 800-83, 800-100.

Priority and Baseline Allocation:

| P1 | LOW IR-1 | MOD IR-1 | HIGH IR-1 |

IR-2 INCIDENT RESPONSE TRAINING

Control: The organization provides incident response training to information system users consistent with assigned roles and responsibilities:

a. Within [*Assignment: organization-defined time period*] of assuming an incident response role or responsibility;

b. When required by information system changes; and

c. [*Assignment: organization-defined frequency*] thereafter.

Supplemental Guidance: Incident response training provided by organizations is linked to the assigned roles and responsibilities of organizational personnel to ensure the appropriate content and level of detail is included in such training. For example, regular users may only need to know who to call or how to recognize an incident on the information system; system administrators may require additional training on how to handle/remediate incidents; and incident responders may receive more specific training on forensics, reporting, system recovery, and restoration. Incident response training includes user training in the identification and reporting of suspicious activities, both from external and internal sources. Related controls: AT-3, CP-3, IR-8.

Control Enhancements:

(1) INCIDENT RESPONSE TRAINING | SIMULATED EVENTS

The organization incorporates simulated events into incident response training to facilitate effective response by personnel in crisis situations.

(2) INCIDENT RESPONSE TRAINING | AUTOMATED TRAINING ENVIRONMENTS

The organization employs automated mechanisms to provide a more thorough and realistic incident response training environment.

References: NIST Special Publications 800-16, 800-50.

Priority and Baseline Allocation:

P2	LOW IR-2	MOD IR-2	HIGH IR-2 (1) (2)

IR-3 INCIDENT RESPONSE TESTING

Control: The organization tests the incident response capability for the information system [*Assignment: organization-defined frequency*] using [*Assignment: organization-defined tests*] to determine the incident response effectiveness and documents the results.

Supplemental Guidance: Organizations test incident response capabilities to determine the overall effectiveness of the capabilities and to identify potential weaknesses or deficiencies. Incident response testing includes, for example, the use of checklists, walk-through or tabletop exercises, simulations (parallel/full interrupt), and comprehensive exercises. Incident response testing can also include a determination of the effects on organizational operations (e.g., reduction in mission capabilities), organizational assets, and individuals due to incident response. Related controls: CP-4, IR-8.

Control Enhancements:

(1) INCIDENT RESPONSE TESTING | AUTOMATED TESTING

The organization employs automated mechanisms to more thoroughly and effectively test the incident response capability.

Supplemental Guidance: Organizations use automated mechanisms to more thoroughly and effectively test incident response capabilities, for example: (i) by providing more complete coverage of incident response issues; (ii) by selecting more realistic test scenarios and test environments; and (iii) by stressing the response capability. Related control: AT-2.

(2) INCIDENT RESPONSE TESTING | COORDINATION WITH RELATED PLANS

The organization coordinates incident response testing with organizational elements responsible for related plans.

Supplemental Guidance: Organizational plans related to incident response testing include, for example, Business Continuity Plans, Contingency Plans, Disaster Recovery Plans, Continuity of Operations Plans, Crisis Communications Plans, Critical Infrastructure Plans, and Occupant Emergency Plans.

References: NIST Special Publications 800-84, 800-115.

Priority and Baseline Allocation:

P2	LOW Not Selected	MOD IR-3 (2)	HIGH IR-3 (2)

IR-4 **INCIDENT HANDLING**

Control: The organization:

a. Implements an incident handling capability for security incidents that includes preparation, detection and analysis, containment, eradication, and recovery;

b. Coordinates incident handling activities with contingency planning activities; and

c. Incorporates lessons learned from ongoing incident handling activities into incident response procedures, training, and testing, and implements the resulting changes accordingly.

Supplemental Guidance: Organizations recognize that incident response capability is dependent on the capabilities of organizational information systems and the mission/business processes being supported by those systems. Therefore, organizations consider incident response as part of the definition, design, and development of mission/business processes and information systems. Incident-related information can be obtained from a variety of sources including, for example, audit monitoring, network monitoring, physical access monitoring, user/administrator reports, and reported supply chain events. Effective incident handling capability includes coordination among many organizational entities including, for example, mission/business owners, information system owners, authorizing officials, human resources offices, physical and personnel security offices, legal departments, operations personnel, procurement offices, and the risk executive (function). Related controls: AU-6, CM-6, CP-2, CP-4, IR-2, IR-3, IR-8, PE-6, SC-5, SC-7, SI-3, SI-4, SI-7.

Control Enhancements:

(1) *INCIDENT HANDLING | AUTOMATED INCIDENT HANDLING PROCESSES*

The organization employs automated mechanisms to support the incident handling process.

Supplemental Guidance: Automated mechanisms supporting incident handling processes include, for example, online incident management systems.

(2) *INCIDENT HANDLING | DYNAMIC RECONFIGURATION*

The organization includes dynamic reconfiguration of [*Assignment: organization-defined information system components*] as part of the incident response capability.

Supplemental Guidance: Dynamic reconfiguration includes, for example, changes to router rules, access control lists, intrusion detection/prevention system parameters, and filter rules for firewalls and gateways. Organizations perform dynamic reconfiguration of information systems, for example, to stop attacks, to misdirect attackers, and to isolate components of systems, thus limiting the extent of the damage from breaches or compromises. Organizations include time frames for achieving the reconfiguration of information systems in the definition of the reconfiguration capability, considering the potential need for rapid response in order to effectively address sophisticated cyber threats. Related controls: AC-2, AC-4, AC-16, CM-2, CM-3, CM-4.

(3) *INCIDENT HANDLING | CONTINUITY OF OPERATIONS*

The organization identifies [*Assignment: organization-defined classes of incidents*] and [*Assignment: organization-defined actions to take in response to classes of incidents*] to ensure continuation of organizational missions and business functions.

Supplemental Guidance: Classes of incidents include, for example, malfunctions due to design/implementation errors and omissions, targeted malicious attacks, and untargeted malicious attacks. Appropriate incident response actions include, for example, graceful degradation, information system shutdown, fall back to manual mode/alternative technology whereby the system operates differently, employing deceptive measures, alternate information flows, or operating in a mode that is reserved solely for when systems are under attack.

(4) *INCIDENT HANDLING | INFORMATION CORRELATION*

The organization correlates incident information and individual incident responses to achieve an organization-wide perspective on incident awareness and response.

Supplemental Guidance: Sometimes the nature of a threat event, for example, a hostile cyber attack, is such that it can only be observed by bringing together information from different sources including various reports and reporting procedures established by organizations.

(5) INCIDENT HANDLING | AUTOMATIC DISABLING OF INFORMATION SYSTEM

The organization implements a configurable capability to automatically disable the information system if [*Assignment: organization-defined security violations*] are detected.

(6) INCIDENT HANDLING | INSIDER THREATS - SPECIFIC CAPABILITIES

The organization implements incident handling capability for insider threats.

Supplemental Guidance: While many organizations address insider threat incidents as an inherent part of their organizational incident response capability, this control enhancement provides additional emphasis on this type of threat and the need for specific incident handling capabilities (as defined within organizations) to provide appropriate and timely responses.

(7) INCIDENT HANDLING | INSIDER THREATS - INTRA-ORGANIZATION COORDINATION

The organization coordinates incident handling capability for insider threats across [*Assignment: organization-defined components or elements of the organization*].

Supplemental Guidance: Incident handling for insider threat incidents (including preparation, detection and analysis, containment, eradication, and recovery) requires close coordination among a variety of organizational components or elements to be effective. These components or elements include, for example, mission/business owners, information system owners, human resources offices, procurement offices, personnel/physical security offices, operations personnel, and risk executive (function). In addition, organizations may require external support from federal, state, and local law enforcement agencies.

(8) INCIDENT HANDLING | CORRELATION WITH EXTERNAL ORGANIZATIONS

The organization coordinates with [*Assignment: organization-defined external organizations*] to correlate and share [*Assignment: organization-defined incident information*] to achieve a cross-organization perspective on incident awareness and more effective incident responses.

Supplemental Guidance: The coordination of incident information with external organizations including, for example, mission/business partners, military/coalition partners, customers, and multitiered developers, can provide significant benefits. Cross-organizational coordination with respect to incident handling can serve as an important risk management capability. This capability allows organizations to leverage critical information from a variety of sources to effectively respond to information security-related incidents potentially affecting the organization's operations, assets, and individuals.

(9) INCIDENT HANDLING | DYNAMIC RESPONSE CAPABILITY

The organization employs [*Assignment: organization-defined dynamic response capabilities*] to effectively respond to security incidents.

Supplemental Guidance: This control enhancement addresses the deployment of replacement or new capabilities in a timely manner in response to security incidents (e.g., adversary actions during hostile cyber attacks). This includes capabilities implemented at the mission/business process level (e.g., activating alternative mission/business processes) and at the information system level. Related control: CP-10.

(10) INCIDENT HANDLING | SUPPLY CHAIN COORDINATION

The organization coordinates incident handling activities involving supply chain events with other organizations involved in the supply chain.

Supplemental Guidance: Organizations involved in supply chain activities include, for example, system/product developers, integrators, manufacturers, packagers, assemblers, distributors, vendors, and resellers. Supply chain incidents include, for example, compromises/breaches involving information system components, information technology products, development processes or personnel, and distribution processes or warehousing facilities.

References: Executive Order 13587; NIST Special Publication 800-61.

Priority and Baseline Allocation:

| P1 | LOW IR-4 | MOD IR-4 (1) | HIGH IR-4 (1) (4) |

IR-5   INCIDENT MONITORING

Control: The organization tracks and documents information system security incidents.

Supplemental Guidance: Documenting information system security incidents includes, for example, maintaining records about each incident, the status of the incident, and other pertinent information necessary for forensics, evaluating incident details, trends, and handling. Incident information can be obtained from a variety of sources including, for example, incident reports, incident response teams, audit monitoring, network monitoring, physical access monitoring, and user/administrator reports. Related controls: AU-6, IR-8, PE-6, SC-5, SC-7, SI-3, SI-4, SI-7.

Control Enhancements:

(1) INCIDENT MONITORING | AUTOMATED TRACKING / DATA COLLECTION / ANALYSIS

   The organization employs automated mechanisms to assist in the tracking of security incidents and in the collection and analysis of incident information.

   Supplemental Guidance: Automated mechanisms for tracking security incidents and collecting/analyzing incident information include, for example, the Einstein network monitoring device and monitoring online Computer Incident Response Centers (CIRCs) or other electronic databases of incidents. Related controls: AU-7, IR-4.

References: NIST Special Publication 800-61.

Priority and Baseline Allocation:

P1	LOW IR-5	MOD IR-5	HIGH IR-5 (1)

IR-6   INCIDENT REPORTING

Control: The organization:

a. Requires personnel to report suspected security incidents to the organizational incident response capability within [Assignment: organization-defined time period]; and

b. Reports security incident information to [Assignment: organization-defined authorities].

Supplemental Guidance: The intent of this control is to address both specific incident reporting requirements within an organization and the formal incident reporting requirements for federal agencies and their subordinate organizations. Suspected security incidents include, for example, the receipt of suspicious email communications that can potentially contain malicious code. The types of security incidents reported, the content and timeliness of the reports, and the designated reporting authorities reflect applicable federal laws, Executive Orders, directives, regulations, policies, standards, and guidance. Current federal policy requires that all federal agencies (unless specifically exempted from such requirements) report security incidents to the United States Computer Emergency Readiness Team (US-CERT) within specified time frames designated in the US-CERT Concept of Operations for Federal Cyber Security Incident Handling. Related controls: IR-4, IR-5, IR-8.

Control Enhancements:

(1) INCIDENT REPORTING | AUTOMATED REPORTING

   The organization employs automated mechanisms to assist in the reporting of security incidents.

   Supplemental Guidance: Related control: IR-7.

(2) INCIDENT REPORTING | VULNERABILITIES RELATED TO INCIDENTS

   The organization reports information system vulnerabilities associated with reported security incidents to [Assignment: organization-defined personnel or roles].

(3) INCIDENT REPORTING | COORDINATION WITH SUPPLY CHAIN

   The organization provides security incident information to other organizations involved in the supply chain for information systems or information system components related to the incident.

Supplemental Guidance: Organizations involved in supply chain activities include, for example, system/product developers, integrators, manufacturers, packagers, assemblers, distributors, vendors, and resellers. Supply chain incidents include, for example, compromises/breaches involving information system components, information technology products, development processes or personnel, and distribution processes or warehousing facilities. Organizations determine the appropriate information to share considering the value gained from support by external organizations with the potential for harm due to sensitive information being released to outside organizations of perhaps questionable trustworthiness.

References: NIST Special Publication 800-61; Web: http://www.us-cert.gov.

Priority and Baseline Allocation:

| P1 | LOW IR-6 | MOD IR-6 (1) | HIGH IR-6 (1) |

IR-7 INCIDENT RESPONSE ASSISTANCE

Control: The organization provides an incident response support resource, integral to the organizational incident response capability that offers advice and assistance to users of the information system for the handling and reporting of security incidents.

Supplemental Guidance: Incident response support resources provided by organizations include, for example, help desks, assistance groups, and access to forensics services, when required. Related controls: AT-2, IR-4, IR-6, IR-8, SA-9.

Control Enhancements:

(1) INCIDENT RESPONSE ASSISTANCE | AUTOMATION SUPPORT FOR AVAILABILITY OF INFORMATION / SUPPORT

The organization employs automated mechanisms to increase the availability of incident response-related information and support.

Supplemental Guidance: Automated mechanisms can provide a push and/or pull capability for users to obtain incident response assistance. For example, individuals might have access to a website to query the assistance capability, or conversely, the assistance capability may have the ability to proactively send information to users (general distribution or targeted) as part of increasing understanding of current response capabilities and support.

(2) INCIDENT RESPONSE ASSISTANCE | COORDINATION WITH EXTERNAL PROVIDERS

The organization:

(a) **Establishes a direct, cooperative relationship between its incident response capability and external providers of information system protection capability; and**

(b) **Identifies organizational incident response team members to the external providers.**

Supplemental Guidance: External providers of information system protection capability include, for example, the Computer Network Defense program within the U.S. Department of Defense. External providers help to protect, monitor, analyze, detect, and respond to unauthorized activity within organizational information systems and networks.

References: None.

Priority and Baseline Allocation:

| P2 | LOW IR-7 | MOD IR-7 (1) | HIGH IR-7 (1) |

IR-8 INCIDENT RESPONSE PLAN

Control: The organization:

a. Develops an incident response plan that:

1. Provides the organization with a roadmap for implementing its incident response capability;
2. Describes the structure and organization of the incident response capability;
3. Provides a high-level approach for how the incident response capability fits into the overall organization;
4. Meets the unique requirements of the organization, which relate to mission, size, structure, and functions;
5. Defines reportable incidents;
6. Provides metrics for measuring the incident response capability within the organization;
7. Defines the resources and management support needed to effectively maintain and mature an incident response capability; and
8. Is reviewed and approved by [*Assignment: organization-defined personnel or roles*];

b. Distributes copies of the incident response plan to [*Assignment: organization-defined incident response personnel (identified by name and/or by role) and organizational elements*];

c. Reviews the incident response plan [*Assignment: organization-defined frequency*];

d. Updates the incident response plan to address system/organizational changes or problems encountered during plan implementation, execution, or testing;

e. Communicates incident response plan changes to [*Assignment: organization-defined incident response personnel (identified by name and/or by role) and organizational elements*]; and

f. Protects the incident response plan from unauthorized disclosure and modification.

Supplemental Guidance: It is important that organizations develop and implement a coordinated approach to incident response. Organizational missions, business functions, strategies, goals, and objectives for incident response help to determine the structure of incident response capabilities. As part of a comprehensive incident response capability, organizations consider the coordination and sharing of information with external organizations, including, for example, external service providers and organizations involved in the supply chain for organizational information systems. Related controls: MP-2, MP-4, MP-5.

Control Enhancements: None.

References: NIST Special Publication 800-61.

Priority and Baseline Allocation:

| P1 | LOW IR-8 | MOD IR-8 | HIGH IR-8 |

IR-9 **INFORMATION SPILLAGE RESPONSE**

Control: The organization responds to information spills by:

a. Identifying the specific information involved in the information system contamination;

b. Alerting [*Assignment: organization-defined personnel or roles*] of the information spill using a method of communication not associated with the spill;

c. Isolating the contaminated information system or system component;

d. Eradicating the information from the contaminated information system or component;

e. Identifying other information systems or system components that may have been subsequently contaminated; and

f. Performing other [*Assignment: organization-defined actions*].

Supplemental Guidance: Information spillage refers to instances where either classified or sensitive information is inadvertently placed on information systems that are not authorized to process such information. Such information spills often occur when information that is initially thought to be of lower sensitivity is transmitted to an information system and then is subsequently determined to be of higher sensitivity. At that point, corrective action is required. The nature of the organizational response is generally based upon the degree of sensitivity of the spilled information (e.g., security category or classification level), the security capabilities of the information system, the specific nature of contaminated storage media, and the access authorizations (e.g., security clearances) of individuals with authorized access to the contaminated system. The methods used to communicate information about the spill after the fact do not involve methods directly associated with the actual spill to minimize the risk of further spreading the contamination before such contamination is isolated and eradicated.

Control Enhancements:

(1) INFORMATION SPILLAGE RESPONSE | RESPONSIBLE PERSONNEL

The organization assigns [*Assignment: organization-defined personnel or roles*] with responsibility for responding to information spills.

(2) INFORMATION SPILLAGE RESPONSE | TRAINING

The organization provides information spillage response training [*Assignment: organization-defined frequency*].

(3) INFORMATION SPILLAGE RESPONSE | POST-SPILL OPERATIONS

The organization implements [*Assignment: organization-defined procedures*] to ensure that organizational personnel impacted by information spills can continue to carry out assigned tasks while contaminated systems are undergoing corrective actions.

Supplemental Guidance: Correction actions for information systems contaminated due to information spillages may be very time-consuming. During those periods, personnel may not have access to the contaminated systems, which may potentially affect their ability to conduct organizational business.

(4) INFORMATION SPILLAGE RESPONSE | EXPOSURE TO UNAUTHORIZED PERSONNEL

The organization employs [*Assignment: organization-defined security safeguards*] for personnel exposed to information not within assigned access authorizations.

Supplemental Guidance: Security safeguards include, for example, making personnel exposed to spilled information aware of the federal laws, directives, policies, and/or regulations regarding the information and the restrictions imposed based on exposure to such information.

References: None.

Priority and Baseline Allocation:

| P0 | LOW Not Selected | MOD Not Selected | HIGH Not Selected |

IR-10 INTEGRATED INFORMATION SECURITY ANALYSIS TEAM

Control: The organization establishes an integrated team of forensic/malicious code analysts, tool developers, and real-time operations personnel.

Supplemental Guidance: Having an integrated team for incident response facilitates information sharing. Such capability allows organizational personnel, including developers, implementers, and operators, to leverage the team knowledge of the threat in order to implement defensive measures that will enable organizations to deter intrusions more effectively. Moreover, it promotes the rapid detection of intrusions, development of appropriate mitigations, and the deployment of effective defensive measures. For example, when an intrusion is detected, the integrated security analysis team can rapidly develop an appropriate response for operators to implement, correlate the new incident with information on past intrusions, and augment ongoing intelligence development. This enables the team to identify adversary TTPs that are linked to the operations tempo or to specific missions/business functions, and to define responsive actions in a way that does not disrupt the mission/business operations. Ideally, information security analysis teams are distributed within organizations to make the capability more resilient.

Control Enhancements: None.

References: None.

Priority and Baseline Allocation:

| P0 | LOW Not Selected | MOD Not Selected | HIGH Not Selected |

FAMILY: MAINTENANCE

MA-1 SYSTEM MAINTENANCE POLICY AND PROCEDURES

Control: The organization:

a. Develops, documents, and disseminates to [*Assignment: organization-defined personnel or roles*]:

   1. A system maintenance policy that addresses purpose, scope, roles, responsibilities, management commitment, coordination among organizational entities, and compliance; and

   2. Procedures to facilitate the implementation of the system maintenance policy and associated system maintenance controls; and

b. Reviews and updates the current:

   1. System maintenance policy [*Assignment: organization-defined frequency*]; and

   2. System maintenance procedures [*Assignment: organization-defined frequency*].

Supplemental Guidance: This control addresses the establishment of policy and procedures for the effective implementation of selected security controls and control enhancements in the MA family. Policy and procedures reflect applicable federal laws, Executive Orders, directives, regulations, policies, standards, and guidance. Security program policies and procedures at the organization level may make the need for system-specific policies and procedures unnecessary. The policy can be included as part of the general information security policy for organizations or conversely, can be represented by multiple policies reflecting the complex nature of certain organizations. The procedures can be established for the security program in general and for particular information systems, if needed. The organizational risk management strategy is a key factor in establishing policy and procedures. Related control: PM-9.

Control Enhancements: None.

References: NIST Special Publications 800-12, 800-100.

Priority and Baseline Allocation:

P1	LOW MA-1	MOD MA-1	HIGH MA-1

MA-2 CONTROLLED MAINTENANCE

Control: The organization:

a. Schedules, performs, documents, and reviews records of maintenance and repairs on information system components in accordance with manufacturer or vendor specifications and/or organizational requirements;

b. Approves and monitors all maintenance activities, whether performed on site or remotely and whether the equipment is serviced on site or removed to another location;

c. Requires that [*Assignment: organization-defined personnel or roles*] explicitly approve the removal of the information system or system components from organizational facilities for off-site maintenance or repairs;

d. Sanitizes equipment to remove all information from associated media prior to removal from organizational facilities for off-site maintenance or repairs;

e. Checks all potentially impacted security controls to verify that the controls are still functioning properly following maintenance or repair actions; and

f. Includes [*Assignment: organization-defined maintenance-related information*] in organizational maintenance records.

Supplemental Guidance: This control addresses the information security aspects of the information system maintenance program and applies to all types of maintenance to any system component (including applications) conducted by any local or nonlocal entity (e.g., in-contract, warranty, in-house, software maintenance agreement). System maintenance also includes those components not directly associated with information processing and/or data/information retention such as scanners, copiers, and printers. Information necessary for creating effective maintenance records includes, for example: (i) date and time of maintenance; (ii) name of individuals or group performing the maintenance; (iii) name of escort, if necessary; (iv) a description of the maintenance performed; and (v) information system components/equipment removed or replaced (including identification numbers, if applicable). The level of detail included in maintenance records can be informed by the security categories of organizational information systems. Organizations consider supply chain issues associated with replacement components for information systems. Related controls: CM-3, CM-4, MA-4, MP-6, PE-16, SA-12, SI-2.

Control Enhancements:

(1) CONTROLLED MAINTENANCE | RECORD CONTENT
[Withdrawn: Incorporated into MA-2].

(2) CONTROLLED MAINTENANCE | AUTOMATED MAINTENANCE ACTIVITIES
The organization:

(a) Employs automated mechanisms to schedule, conduct, and document maintenance and repairs; and

(b) Produces up-to date, accurate, and complete records of all maintenance and repair actions requested, scheduled, in process, and completed.

Supplemental Guidance: Related controls: CA-7, MA-3.

References: None.

Priority and Baseline Allocation:

P2	LOW MA-2	MOD MA-2	HIGH MA-2 (2)

MA-3 MAINTENANCE TOOLS

Control: The organization approves, controls, and monitors information system maintenance tools.

Supplemental Guidance: This control addresses security-related issues associated with maintenance tools used specifically for diagnostic and repair actions on organizational information systems. Maintenance tools can include hardware, software, and firmware items. Maintenance tools are potential vehicles for transporting malicious code, either intentionally or unintentionally, into a facility and subsequently into organizational information systems. Maintenance tools can include, for example, hardware/software diagnostic test equipment and hardware/software packet sniffers. This control does not cover hardware/software components that may support information system maintenance, yet are a part of the system, for example, the software implementing "ping," "ls," "ipconfig," or the hardware and software implementing the monitoring port of an Ethernet switch. Related controls: MA-2, MA-5, MP-6.

Control Enhancements:

(1) MAINTENANCE TOOLS | INSPECT TOOLS
The organization inspects the maintenance tools carried into a facility by maintenance personnel for improper or unauthorized modifications.

Supplemental Guidance: If, upon inspection of maintenance tools, organizations determine that the tools have been modified in an improper/unauthorized manner or contain malicious code, the incident is handled consistent with organizational policies and procedures for incident handling. Related control: SI-7.

(2) MAINTENANCE TOOLS | INSPECT MEDIA

The organization checks media containing diagnostic and test programs for malicious code before the media are used in the information system.

Supplemental Guidance: If, upon inspection of media containing maintenance diagnostic and test programs, organizations determine that the media contain malicious code, the incident is handled consistent with organizational incident handling policies and procedures. Related control: SI-3.

(3) MAINTENANCE TOOLS | PREVENT UNAUTHORIZED REMOVAL

The organization prevents the unauthorized removal of maintenance equipment containing organizational information by:

(a) Verifying that there is no organizational information contained on the equipment;

(b) Sanitizing or destroying the equipment;

(c) Retaining the equipment within the facility; or

(d) Obtaining an exemption from [*Assignment: organization-defined personnel or roles*] explicitly authorizing removal of the equipment from the facility.

Supplemental Guidance: Organizational information includes all information specifically owned by organizations and information provided to organizations in which organizations serve as information stewards.

(4) MAINTENANCE TOOLS | RESTRICTED TOOL USE

The information system restricts the use of maintenance tools to authorized personnel only.

Supplemental Guidance: This control enhancement applies to information systems that are used to carry out maintenance functions. Related controls: AC-2, AC-3, AC-5, AC-6.

References: NIST Special Publication 800-88.

Priority and Baseline Allocation:

| P3 | LOW Not Selected | MOD MA-3 (1) (2) | HIGH MA-3 (1) (2) (3) |

MA-4 NONLOCAL MAINTENANCE

Control: The organization:

a. Approves and monitors nonlocal maintenance and diagnostic activities;

b. Allows the use of nonlocal maintenance and diagnostic tools only as consistent with organizational policy and documented in the security plan for the information system;

c. Employs strong authenticators in the establishment of nonlocal maintenance and diagnostic sessions;

d. Maintains records for nonlocal maintenance and diagnostic activities; and

e. Terminates session and network connections when nonlocal maintenance is completed.

Supplemental Guidance: Nonlocal maintenance and diagnostic activities are those activities conducted by individuals communicating through a network, either an external network (e.g., the Internet) or an internal network. Local maintenance and diagnostic activities are those activities carried out by individuals physically present at the information system or information system component and not communicating across a network connection. Authentication techniques used in the establishment of nonlocal maintenance and diagnostic sessions reflect the network access requirements in IA-2. Typically, strong authentication requires authenticators that are resistant to replay attacks and employ multifactor authentication. Strong authenticators include, for example, PKI where certificates are stored on a token protected by a password, passphrase, or biometric.

Enforcing requirements in MA-4 is accomplished in part by other controls. Related controls: AC-2, AC-3, AC-6, AC-17, AU-2, AU-3, IA-2, IA-4, IA-5, IA-8, MA-2, MA-5, MP-6, PL-2, SC-7, SC-10, SC-17.

Control Enhancements:

(1) NONLOCAL MAINTENANCE | AUDITING AND REVIEW

The organization:

(a) Audits nonlocal maintenance and diagnostic sessions [*Assignment: organization-defined audit events*]; and

(b) Reviews the records of the maintenance and diagnostic sessions.

Supplemental Guidance: Related controls: AU-2, AU-6, AU-12.

(2) NONLOCAL MAINTENANCE | DOCUMENT NONLOCAL MAINTENANCE

The organization documents in the security plan for the information system, the policies and procedures for the establishment and use of nonlocal maintenance and diagnostic connections.

(3) NONLOCAL MAINTENANCE | COMPARABLE SECURITY / SANITIZATION

The organization:

(a) Requires that nonlocal maintenance and diagnostic services be performed from an information system that implements a security capability comparable to the capability implemented on the system being serviced; or

(b) Removes the component to be serviced from the information system prior to nonlocal maintenance or diagnostic services, sanitizes the component (with regard to organizational information) before removal from organizational facilities, and after the service is performed, inspects and sanitizes the component (with regard to potentially malicious software) before reconnecting the component to the information system.

Supplemental Guidance: Comparable security capability on information systems, diagnostic tools, and equipment providing maintenance services implies that the implemented security controls on those systems, tools, and equipment are at least as comprehensive as the controls on the information system being serviced. Related controls: MA-3, SA-12, SI-3, SI-7.

(4) NONLOCAL MAINTENANCE | AUTHENTICATION / SEPARATION OF MAINTENANCE SESSIONS

The organization protects nonlocal maintenance sessions by:

(a) Employing [*Assignment: organization-defined authenticators that are replay resistant*]; and

(b) Separating the maintenance sessions from other network sessions with the information system by either:

(1) Physically separated communications paths; or

(2) Logically separated communications paths based upon encryption.

Supplemental Guidance: Related control: SC-13.

(5) NONLOCAL MAINTENANCE | APPROVALS AND NOTIFICATIONS

The organization:

(a) Requires the approval of each nonlocal maintenance session by [*Assignment: organization-defined personnel or roles*]; and

(b) Notifies [*Assignment: organization-defined personnel or roles*] of the date and time of planned nonlocal maintenance.

Supplemental Guidance: Notification may be performed by maintenance personnel. Approval of nonlocal maintenance sessions is accomplished by organizational personnel with sufficient information security and information system knowledge to determine the appropriateness of the proposed maintenance.

(6) NONLOCAL MAINTENANCE | CRYPTOGRAPHIC PROTECTION

The information system implements cryptographic mechanisms to protect the integrity and confidentiality of nonlocal maintenance and diagnostic communications.

Supplemental Guidance: Related controls: SC-8, SC-13.

(7) NONLOCAL MAINTENANCE | REMOTE DISCONNECT VERIFICATION

The information system implements remote disconnect verification at the termination of nonlocal maintenance and diagnostic sessions.

Supplemental Guidance: Remote disconnect verification ensures that remote connections from nonlocal maintenance sessions have been terminated and are no longer available for use. Related control: SC-13.

References: FIPS Publications 140-2, 197, 201; NIST Special Publications 800-63, 800-88; CNSS Policy 15.

Priority and Baseline Allocation:

P2	LOW MA-4	MOD MA-4 (2)	HIGH MA-4 (2) (3)

MA-5 MAINTENANCE PERSONNEL

Control: The organization:

a. Establishes a process for maintenance personnel authorization and maintains a list of authorized maintenance organizations or personnel;

b. Ensures that non-escorted personnel performing maintenance on the information system have required access authorizations; and

c. Designates organizational personnel with required access authorizations and technical competence to supervise the maintenance activities of personnel who do not possess the required access authorizations.

Supplemental Guidance: This control applies to individuals performing hardware or software maintenance on organizational information systems, while PE-2 addresses physical access for individuals whose maintenance duties place them within the physical protection perimeter of the systems (e.g., custodial staff, physical plant maintenance personnel). Technical competence of supervising individuals relates to the maintenance performed on the information systems while having required access authorizations refers to maintenance on and near the systems. Individuals not previously identified as authorized maintenance personnel, such as information technology manufacturers, vendors, systems integrators, and consultants, may require privileged access to organizational information systems, for example, when required to conduct maintenance activities with little or no notice. Based on organizational assessments of risk, organizations may issue temporary credentials to these individuals. Temporary credentials may be for one-time use or for very limited time periods. Related controls: AC-2, IA-8, MP-2, PE-2, PE-3, PE-4, RA-3.

Control Enhancements:

(1) MAINTENANCE PERSONNEL | INDIVIDUALS WITHOUT APPROPRIATE ACCESS

The organization:

(a) Implements procedures for the use of maintenance personnel that lack appropriate security clearances or are not U.S. citizens, that include the following requirements:

(1) Maintenance personnel who do not have needed access authorizations, clearances, or formal access approvals are escorted and supervised during the performance of maintenance and diagnostic activities on the information system by approved organizational personnel who are fully cleared, have appropriate access authorizations, and are technically qualified;

(2) Prior to initiating maintenance or diagnostic activities by personnel who do not have needed access authorizations, clearances or formal access approvals, all volatile information storage components within the information system are sanitized and all nonvolatile storage media are removed or physically disconnected from the system and secured; and

(b) Develops and implements alternate security safeguards in the event an information system component cannot be sanitized, removed, or disconnected from the system.

Supplemental Guidance: This control enhancement denies individuals who lack appropriate security clearances (i.e., individuals who do not possess security clearances or possess security clearances at a lower level than required) or who are not U.S. citizens, visual and electronic access to any classified information, Controlled Unclassified Information (CUI), or any other sensitive information contained on organizational information systems. Procedures for the use of maintenance personnel can be documented in security plans for the information systems. Related controls: MP-6, PL-2.

(2) MAINTENANCE PERSONNEL | SECURITY CLEARANCES FOR CLASSIFIED SYSTEMS

The organization ensures that personnel performing maintenance and diagnostic activities on an information system processing, storing, or transmitting classified information possess security clearances and formal access approvals for at least the highest classification level and for all compartments of information on the system.

Supplemental Guidance: Related control: PS-3.

(3) MAINTENANCE PERSONNEL | CITIZENSHIP REQUIREMENTS FOR CLASSIFIED SYSTEMS

The organization ensures that personnel performing maintenance and diagnostic activities on an information system processing, storing, or transmitting classified information are U.S. citizens.

Supplemental Guidance: Related control: PS-3.

(4) MAINTENANCE PERSONNEL | FOREIGN NATIONALS

The organization ensures that:

(a) Cleared foreign nationals (i.e., foreign nationals with appropriate security clearances), are used to conduct maintenance and diagnostic activities on classified information systems only when the systems are jointly owned and operated by the United States and foreign allied governments, or owned and operated solely by foreign allied governments; and

(b) Approvals, consents, and detailed operational conditions regarding the use of foreign nationals to conduct maintenance and diagnostic activities on classified information systems are fully documented within Memoranda of Agreements.

Supplemental Guidance: Related control: PS-3.

(5) MAINTENANCE PERSONNEL | NONSYSTEM-RELATED MAINTENANCE

The organization ensures that non-escorted personnel performing maintenance activities not directly associated with the information system but in the physical proximity of the system, have required access authorizations.

Supplemental Guidance: Personnel performing maintenance activities in other capacities not directly related to the information system include, for example, physical plant personnel and janitorial personnel.

References: None.

Priority and Baseline Allocation:

P2	LOW MA-5	MOD MA-5	HIGH MA-5 (1)

MA-6 TIMELY MAINTENANCE

Control: The organization obtains maintenance support and/or spare parts for [*Assignment: organization-defined information system components*] within [*Assignment: organization-defined time period*] of failure.

Supplemental Guidance: Organizations specify the information system components that result in increased risk to organizational operations and assets, individuals, other organizations, or the Nation when the functionality provided by those components is not operational. Organizational actions to obtain maintenance support typically include having appropriate contracts in place. Related controls: CM-8, CP-2, CP-7, SA-14, SA-15.

Control Enhancements:

(1) *TIMELY MAINTENANCE | PREVENTIVE MAINTENANCE*

The organization performs preventive maintenance on [*Assignment: organization-defined information system components*] at [*Assignment: organization-defined time intervals*].

Supplemental Guidance: Preventive maintenance includes proactive care and servicing of organizational information systems components for the purpose of maintaining equipment and facilities in satisfactory operating condition. Such maintenance provides for the systematic inspection, tests, measurements, adjustments, parts replacement, detection, and correction of incipient failures either before they occur or before they develop into major defects. The primary goal of preventive maintenance is to avoid/mitigate the consequences of equipment failures. Preventive maintenance is designed to preserve and restore equipment reliability by replacing worn components before they actually fail. Methods of determining what preventive (or other) failure management policies to apply include, for example, original equipment manufacturer (OEM) recommendations, statistical failure records, requirements of codes, legislation, or regulations within a jurisdiction, expert opinion, maintenance that has already been conducted on similar equipment, or measured values and performance indications.

(2) *TIMELY MAINTENANCE | PREDICTIVE MAINTENANCE*

The organization performs predictive maintenance on [*Assignment: organization-defined information system components*] at [*Assignment: organization-defined time intervals*].

Supplemental Guidance: Predictive maintenance, or condition-based maintenance, attempts to evaluate the condition of equipment by performing periodic or continuous (online) equipment condition monitoring. The goal of predictive maintenance is to perform maintenance at a scheduled point in time when the maintenance activity is most cost-effective and before the equipment loses performance within a threshold. The predictive component of predictive maintenance stems from the goal of predicting the future trend of the equipment's condition. This approach uses principles of statistical process control to determine at what point in the future maintenance activities will be appropriate. Most predictive maintenance inspections are performed while equipment is in service, thereby minimizing disruption of normal system operations. Predictive maintenance can result in substantial cost savings and higher system reliability. Predictive maintenance tends to include measurement of the item. To evaluate equipment condition, predictive maintenance utilizes nondestructive testing technologies such as infrared, acoustic (partial discharge and airborne ultrasonic), corona detection, vibration analysis, sound level measurements, oil analysis, and other specific online tests.

(3) *TIMELY MAINTENANCE | AUTOMATED SUPPORT FOR PREDICTIVE MAINTENANCE*

The organization employs automated mechanisms to transfer predictive maintenance data to a computerized maintenance management system.

Supplemental Guidance: A computerized maintenance management system maintains a computer database of information about the maintenance operations of organizations and automates processing equipment condition data in order to trigger maintenance planning, execution, and reporting.

References: None.

Priority and Baseline Allocation:

P2	**LOW** Not Selected	**MOD** MA-6	**HIGH** MA-6

FAMILY: MEDIA PROTECTION

MP-1 MEDIA PROTECTION POLICY AND PROCEDURES

Control: The organization:

a. Develops, documents, and disseminates to [*Assignment: organization-defined personnel or roles*]:

1. A media protection policy that addresses purpose, scope, roles, responsibilities, management commitment, coordination among organizational entities, and compliance; and

2. Procedures to facilitate the implementation of the media protection policy and associated media protection controls; and

b. Reviews and updates the current:

1. Media protection policy [*Assignment: organization-defined frequency*]; and

2. Media protection procedures [*Assignment: organization-defined frequency*].

Supplemental Guidance: This control addresses the establishment of policy and procedures for the effective implementation of selected security controls and control enhancements in the MP family. Policy and procedures reflect applicable federal laws, Executive Orders, directives, regulations, policies, standards, and guidance. Security program policies and procedures at the organization level may make the need for system-specific policies and procedures unnecessary. The policy can be included as part of the general information security policy for organizations or conversely, can be represented by multiple policies reflecting the complex nature of certain organizations. The procedures can be established for the security program in general and for particular information systems, if needed. The organizational risk management strategy is a key factor in establishing policy and procedures. Related control: PM-9.

Control Enhancements: None.

References: NIST Special Publications 800-12, 800-100.

Priority and Baseline Allocation:

| P1 | LOW MP-1 | MOD MP-1 | HIGH MP-1 |

MP-2 MEDIA ACCESS

Control: The organization restricts access to [*Assignment: organization-defined types of digital and/or non-digital media*] to [*Assignment: organization-defined personnel or roles*].

Supplemental Guidance: Information system media includes both digital and non-digital media. Digital media includes, for example, diskettes, magnetic tapes, external/removable hard disk drives, flash drives, compact disks, and digital video disks. Non-digital media includes, for example, paper and microfilm. Restricting non-digital media access includes, for example, denying access to patient medical records in a community hospital unless the individuals seeking access to such records are authorized healthcare providers. Restricting access to digital media includes, for example, limiting access to design specifications stored on compact disks in the media library to the project leader and the individuals on the development team. Related controls: AC-3, IA-2, MP-4, PE-2, PE-3, PL-2.

Control Enhancements:

(1) MEDIA ACCESS | AUTOMATED RESTRICTED ACCESS

[Withdrawn: Incorporated into MP-4 (2)].

(2) *MEDIA ACCESS | CRYPTOGRAPHIC PROTECTION*
[Withdrawn: Incorporated into SC-28 (1)].

References: FIPS Publication 199; NIST Special Publication 800-111.

Priority and Baseline Allocation:

P1	LOW MP-2	MOD MP-2	HIGH MP-2

MP-3 MEDIA MARKING

Control: The organization:

a. Marks information system media indicating the distribution limitations, handling caveats, and applicable security markings (if any) of the information; and

b. Exempts [*Assignment: organization-defined types of information system media*] from marking as long as the media remain within [*Assignment: organization-defined controlled areas*].

Supplemental Guidance: The term *security marking* refers to the application/use of human-readable security attributes. The term *security labeling* refers to the application/use of security attributes with regard to internal data structures within information systems (see AC-16). Information system media includes both digital and non-digital media. Digital media includes, for example, diskettes, magnetic tapes, external/removable hard disk drives, flash drives, compact disks, and digital video disks. Non-digital media includes, for example, paper and microfilm. Security marking is generally not required for media containing information determined by organizations to be in the public domain or to be publicly releasable. However, some organizations may require markings for public information indicating that the information is publicly releasable. Marking of information system media reflects applicable federal laws, Executive Orders, directives, policies, regulations, standards, and guidance. Related controls: AC-16, PL-2, RA-3.

Control Enhancements: None.

References: FIPS Publication 199.

Priority and Baseline Allocation:

P2	LOW Not Selected	MOD MP-3	HIGH MP-3

MP-4 MEDIA STORAGE

Control: The organization:

a. Physically controls and securely stores [*Assignment: organization-defined types of digital and/or non-digital media*] within [*Assignment: organization-defined controlled areas*]; and

b. Protects information system media until the media are destroyed or sanitized using approved equipment, techniques, and procedures.

Supplemental Guidance: Information system media includes both digital and non-digital media. Digital media includes, for example, diskettes, magnetic tapes, external/removable hard disk drives, flash drives, compact disks, and digital video disks. Non-digital media includes, for example, paper and microfilm. Physically controlling information system media includes, for example, conducting inventories, ensuring procedures are in place to allow individuals to check out and return media to the media library, and maintaining accountability for all stored media. Secure storage includes, for example, a locked drawer, desk, or cabinet, or a controlled media library. The type of media storage is commensurate with the security category and/or classification of the information residing on the media. Controlled areas are areas for which organizations provide sufficient physical and procedural safeguards to meet the requirements established for protecting information and/or information systems. For media containing information determined by organizations to be in the public domain, to be publicly releasable, or to have limited or no adverse impact on organizations or individuals if accessed by other than authorized personnel, fewer safeguards may be needed. In these situations, physical access controls provide adequate protection. Related controls: CP-6, CP-9, MP-2, MP-7, PE-3.

Control Enhancements:

(1) MEDIA STORAGE | CRYPTOGRAPHIC PROTECTION
[Withdrawn: Incorporated into SC-28 (1)].

(2) MEDIA STORAGE | AUTOMATED RESTRICTED ACCESS
The organization employs automated mechanisms to restrict access to media storage areas and to audit access attempts and access granted.

Supplemental Guidance: Automated mechanisms can include, for example, keypads on the external entries to media storage areas. Related controls: AU-2, AU-9, AU-6, AU-12.

References: FIPS Publication 199; NIST Special Publications 800-56, 800-57, 800-111.

Priority and Baseline Allocation:

| P1 | LOW Not Selected | MOD MP-4 | HIGH MP-4 |

MP-5 MEDIA TRANSPORT

Control: The organization:

a. Protects and controls [*Assignment: organization-defined types of information system media*] during transport outside of controlled areas using [*Assignment: organization-defined security safeguards*];

b. Maintains accountability for information system media during transport outside of controlled areas;

c. Documents activities associated with the transport of information system media; and

d. Restricts the activities associated with the transport of information system media to authorized personnel.

Supplemental Guidance: Information system media includes both digital and non-digital media. Digital media includes, for example, diskettes, magnetic tapes, external/removable hard disk drives, flash drives, compact disks, and digital video disks. Non-digital media includes, for example, paper and microfilm. This control also applies to mobile devices with information storage capability (e.g., smart phones, tablets, E-readers), that are transported outside of controlled areas. Controlled areas are areas or spaces for which organizations provide sufficient physical and/or procedural safeguards to meet the requirements established for protecting information and/or information systems.

Physical and technical safeguards for media are commensurate with the security category or classification of the information residing on the media. Safeguards to protect media during transport include, for example, locked containers and cryptography. Cryptographic mechanisms can provide confidentiality and integrity protections depending upon the mechanisms used. Activities associated with transport include the actual transport as well as those activities such as releasing media for transport and ensuring that media enters the appropriate transport processes. For the actual transport, authorized transport and courier personnel may include individuals from outside the organization (e.g., U.S. Postal Service or a commercial transport or delivery service). Maintaining accountability of media during transport includes, for example, restricting transport activities to authorized personnel, and tracking and/or obtaining explicit records of transport activities as the media moves through the transportation system to prevent and detect loss, destruction, or tampering. Organizations establish documentation requirements for activities associated with the transport of information system media in accordance with organizational assessments of risk to include the flexibility to define different record-keeping methods for the different types of media transport as part of an overall system of transport-related records. Related controls: AC-19, CP-9, MP-3, MP-4, RA-3, SC-8, SC-13, SC-28.

Control Enhancements:

(1) MEDIA TRANSPORT | PROTECTION OUTSIDE OF CONTROLLED AREAS
[Withdrawn: Incorporated into MP-5].

(2) MEDIA TRANSPORT | DOCUMENTATION OF ACTIVITIES
[Withdrawn: Incorporated into MP-5].

(3) MEDIA TRANSPORT | CUSTODIANS

The organization employs an identified custodian during transport of information system media outside of controlled areas.

Supplemental Guidance: Identified custodians provide organizations with specific points of contact during the media transport process and facilitate individual accountability. Custodial responsibilities can be transferred from one individual to another as long as an unambiguous custodian is identified at all times.

(4) MEDIA TRANSPORT | CRYPTOGRAPHIC PROTECTION

The information system implements cryptographic mechanisms to protect the confidentiality and integrity of information stored on digital media during transport outside of controlled areas.

Supplemental Guidance: This control enhancement applies to both portable storage devices (e.g., USB memory sticks, compact disks, digital video disks, external/removable hard disk drives) and mobile devices with storage capability (e.g., smart phones, tablets, E-readers). Related control: MP-2.

References: FIPS Publication 199; NIST Special Publication 800-60.

Priority and Baseline Allocation:

P1	LOW Not Selected	MOD MP-5 (4)	HIGH MP-5 (4)

MP-6 MEDIA SANITIZATION

Control: The organization:

a. Sanitizes [*Assignment: organization-defined information system media*] prior to disposal, release out of organizational control, or release for reuse using [*Assignment: organization-defined sanitization techniques and procedures*] in accordance with applicable federal and organizational standards and policies; and

b. Employs sanitization mechanisms with the strength and integrity commensurate with the security category or classification of the information.

Supplemental Guidance: This control applies to all information system media, both digital and non-digital, subject to disposal or reuse, whether or not the media is considered removable. Examples include media found in scanners, copiers, printers, notebook computers, workstations, network components, and mobile devices. The sanitization process removes information from the media such that the information cannot be retrieved or reconstructed. Sanitization techniques, including clearing, purging, cryptographic erase, and destruction, prevent the disclosure of information to unauthorized individuals when such media is reused or released for disposal. Organizations determine the appropriate sanitization methods recognizing that destruction is sometimes necessary when other methods cannot be applied to media requiring sanitization. Organizations use discretion on the employment of approved sanitization techniques and procedures for media containing information deemed to be in the public domain or publicly releasable, or deemed to have no adverse impact on organizations or individuals if released for reuse or disposal.

Sanitization of non-digital media includes, for example, removing a classified appendix from an otherwise unclassified document, or redacting selected sections or words from a document by obscuring the redacted sections/words in a manner equivalent in effectiveness to removing them from the document. NSA standards and policies control the sanitization process for media containing classified information. Related controls: MA-2, MA-4, RA-3, SC-4.

Control Enhancements:

(1) *MEDIA SANITIZATION | REVIEW / APPROVE / TRACK / DOCUMENT / VERIFY*

The organization reviews, approves, tracks, documents, and verifies media sanitization and disposal actions.

Supplemental Guidance: Organizations review and approve media to be sanitized to ensure compliance with records-retention policies. Tracking/documenting actions include, for example, listing personnel who reviewed and approved sanitization and disposal actions, types of media sanitized, specific files stored on the media, sanitization methods used, date and time of the sanitization actions, personnel who performed the sanitization, verification actions taken, personnel who performed the verification, and disposal action taken. Organizations verify that the sanitization of the media was effective prior to disposal. Related control: SI-12.

(2) *MEDIA SANITIZATION | EQUIPMENT TESTING*

The organization tests sanitization equipment and procedures [*Assignment: organization-defined frequency*] to verify that the intended sanitization is being achieved.

Supplemental Guidance: Testing of sanitization equipment and procedures may be conducted by qualified and authorized external entities (e.g., other federal agencies or external service providers).

(3) *MEDIA SANITIZATION | NONDESTRUCTIVE TECHNIQUES*

The organization applies nondestructive sanitization techniques to portable storage devices prior to connecting such devices to the information system under the following circumstances: [*Assignment: organization-defined circumstances requiring sanitization of portable storage devices*].

Supplemental Guidance: This control enhancement applies to digital media containing classified information and Controlled Unclassified Information (CUI). Portable storage devices can be the source of malicious code insertions into organizational information systems. Many of these devices are obtained from unknown and potentially untrustworthy sources and may contain malicious code that can be readily transferred to information systems through USB ports or other entry portals. While scanning such storage devices is always recommended, sanitization provides additional assurance that the devices are free of malicious code to include code capable of initiating zero-day attacks. Organizations consider nondestructive sanitization of portable storage devices when such devices are first purchased from the manufacturer or vendor prior to initial use or when organizations lose a positive chain of custody for the devices. Related control: SI-3.

(4) *MEDIA SANITIZATION | CONTROLLED UNCLASSIFIED INFORMATION*

[Withdrawn: Incorporated into MP-6].

(5) *MEDIA SANITIZATION | CLASSIFIED INFORMATION*

[Withdrawn: Incorporated into MP-6].

(6) *MEDIA SANITIZATION | MEDIA DESTRUCTION*

[Withdrawn: Incorporated into MP-6].

(7) *MEDIA SANITIZATION | DUAL AUTHORIZATION*

The organization enforces dual authorization for the sanitization of [*Assignment: organization-defined information system media*].

Supplemental Guidance: Organizations employ dual authorization to ensure that information system media sanitization cannot occur unless two technically qualified individuals conduct the task. Individuals sanitizing information system media possess sufficient skills/expertise to determine if the proposed sanitization reflects applicable federal/organizational standards, policies, and procedures. Dual authorization also helps to ensure that sanitization occurs as intended, both protecting against errors and false claims of having performed the sanitization actions. Dual authorization may also be known as two-person control. Related controls: AC-3, MP-2.

(8) MEDIA SANITIZATION | REMOTE PURGING / WIPING OF INFORMATION

The organization provides the capability to purge/wipe information from [*Assignment: organization-defined information systems, system components, or devices*] either remotely or under the following conditions: [*Assignment: organization-defined conditions*].

Supplemental Guidance: This control enhancement protects data/information on organizational information systems, system components, or devices (e.g., mobile devices) if such systems, components, or devices are obtained by unauthorized individuals. Remote purge/wipe commands require strong authentication to mitigate the risk of unauthorized individuals purging/wiping the system/component/device. The purge/wipe function can be implemented in a variety of ways including, for example, by overwriting data/information multiple times or by destroying the key necessary to decrypt encrypted data.

References: FIPS Publication 199; NIST Special Publications 800-60, 800-88;
Web: http://www.nsa.gov/ia/mitigation_guidance/media_destruction_guidance/index.shtml.

Priority and Baseline Allocation:

P1	LOW MP-6	MOD MP-6	HIGH MP-6 (1) (2) (3)

MP-7 **MEDIA USE**

Control: The organization [*Selection: restricts; prohibits*] the use of [*Assignment: organization-defined types of information system media*] on [*Assignment: organization-defined information systems or system components*] using [*Assignment: organization-defined security safeguards*].

Supplemental Guidance: Information system media includes both digital and non-digital media. Digital media includes, for example, diskettes, magnetic tapes, external/removable hard disk drives, flash drives, compact disks, and digital video disks. Non-digital media includes, for example, paper and microfilm. This control also applies to mobile devices with information storage capability (e.g., smart phones, tablets, E-readers). In contrast to MP-2, which restricts user access to media, this control restricts the use of certain types of media on information systems, for example, restricting/prohibiting the use of flash drives or external hard disk drives. Organizations can employ technical and nontechnical safeguards (e.g., policies, procedures, rules of behavior) to restrict the use of information system media. Organizations may restrict the use of portable storage devices, for example, by using physical cages on workstations to prohibit access to certain external ports, or disabling/removing the ability to insert, read or write to such devices. Organizations may also limit the use of portable storage devices to only approved devices including, for example, devices provided by the organization, devices provided by other approved organizations, and devices that are not personally owned. Finally, organizations may restrict the use of portable storage devices based on the type of device, for example, prohibiting the use of writeable, portable storage devices, and implementing this restriction by disabling or removing the capability to write to such devices. Related controls: AC-19, PL-4.

Control Enhancements:

(1) MEDIA USE | PROHIBIT USE WITHOUT OWNER

The organization prohibits the use of portable storage devices in organizational information systems when such devices have no identifiable owner.

Supplemental Guidance: Requiring identifiable owners (e.g., individuals, organizations, or projects) for portable storage devices reduces the risk of using such technologies by allowing organizations to assign responsibility and accountability for addressing known vulnerabilities in the devices (e.g., malicious code insertion). Related control: PL-4.

(2) *MEDIA USE | PROHIBIT USE OF SANITIZATION-RESISTANT MEDIA*

The organization prohibits the use of sanitization-resistant media in organizational information systems.

Supplemental Guidance: Sanitization-resistance applies to the capability to purge information from media. Certain types of media do not support sanitize commands, or if supported, the interfaces are not supported in a standardized way across these devices. Sanitization-resistant media include, for example, compact flash, embedded flash on boards and devices, solid state drives, and USB removable media. Related control: MP-6.

References: FIPS Publication 199; NIST Special Publication 800-111.

Priority and Baseline Allocation:

P1	LOW MP-7	MOD MP-7 (1)	HIGH MP-7 (1)

MP-8 MEDIA DOWNGRADING

Control: The organization:

a. Establishes [*Assignment: organization-defined information system media downgrading process*] that includes employing downgrading mechanisms with [*Assignment: organization-defined strength and integrity*];

b. Ensures that the information system media downgrading process is commensurate with the security category and/or classification level of the information to be removed and the access authorizations of the potential recipients of the downgraded information;

c. Identifies [*Assignment: organization-defined information system media requiring downgrading*]; and

d. Downgrades the identified information system media using the established process.

Supplemental Guidance: This control applies to all information system media, digital and non-digital, subject to release outside of the organization, whether or not the media is considered removable. The downgrading process, when applied to system media, removes information from the media, typically by security category or classification level, such that the information cannot be retrieved or reconstructed. Downgrading of media includes redacting information to enable wider release and distribution. Downgrading of media also ensures that empty space on the media (e.g., slack space within files) is devoid of information.

Control Enhancements:

(1) *MEDIA DOWNGRADING | DOCUMENTATION OF PROCESS*

The organization documents information system media downgrading actions.

Supplemental Guidance: Organizations can document the media downgrading process by providing information such as the downgrading technique employed, the identification number of the downgraded media, and the identity of the individual that authorized and/or performed the downgrading action.

(2) *MEDIA DOWNGRADING | EQUIPMENT TESTING*

The organization employs [*Assignment: organization-defined tests*] of downgrading equipment and procedures to verify correct performance [*Assignment: organization-defined frequency*].

(3) *MEDIA DOWNGRADING | CONTROLLED UNCLASSIFIED INFORMATION*

The organization downgrades information system media containing [*Assignment: organization-defined Controlled Unclassified Information (CUI)*] prior to public release in accordance with applicable federal and organizational standards and policies.

(4) *MEDIA DOWNGRADING | CLASSIFIED INFORMATION*

The organization downgrades information system media containing classified information prior to release to individuals without required access authorizations in accordance with NSA standards and policies.

Supplemental Guidance: Downgrading of classified information uses approved sanitization tools, techniques, and procedures to transfer information confirmed to be unclassified from classified information systems to unclassified media.

References: None.

Priority and Baseline Allocation:

P0	**LOW** Not Selected	**MOD** Not Selected	**HIGH** Not Selected

FAMILY: PHYSICAL AND ENVIRONMENTAL PROTECTION

PE-1 PHYSICAL AND ENVIRONMENTAL PROTECTION POLICY AND PROCEDURES

Control: The organization:

a. Develops, documents, and disseminates to [*Assignment: organization-defined personnel or roles*]:

   1. A physical and environmental protection policy that addresses purpose, scope, roles, responsibilities, management commitment, coordination among organizational entities, and compliance; and

   2. Procedures to facilitate the implementation of the physical and environmental protection policy and associated physical and environmental protection controls; and

b. Reviews and updates the current:

   1. Physical and environmental protection policy [*Assignment: organization-defined frequency*]; and

   2. Physical and environmental protection procedures [*Assignment: organization-defined frequency*].

Supplemental Guidance: This control addresses the establishment of policy and procedures for the effective implementation of selected security controls and control enhancements in the PE family. Policy and procedures reflect applicable federal laws, Executive Orders, directives, regulations, policies, standards, and guidance. Security program policies and procedures at the organization level may make the need for system-specific policies and procedures unnecessary. The policy can be included as part of the general information security policy for organizations or conversely, can be represented by multiple policies reflecting the complex nature of certain organizations. The procedures can be established for the security program in general and for particular information systems, if needed. The organizational risk management strategy is a key factor in establishing policy and procedures. Related control: PM-9.

Control Enhancements: None.

References: NIST Special Publications 800-12, 800-100.

Priority and Baseline Allocation:

| P1 | LOW PE-1 | MOD PE-1 | HIGH PE-1 |

PE-2 PHYSICAL ACCESS AUTHORIZATIONS

Control: The organization:

a. Develops, approves, and maintains a list of individuals with authorized access to the facility where the information system resides;

b. Issues authorization credentials for facility access;

c. Reviews the access list detailing authorized facility access by individuals [*Assignment: organization-defined frequency*]; and

d. Removes individuals from the facility access list when access is no longer required.

Supplemental Guidance: This control applies to organizational employees and visitors. Individuals (e.g., employees, contractors, and others) with permanent physical access authorization credentials are not considered visitors. Authorization credentials include, for example, badges, identification cards, and smart cards. Organizations determine the strength of authorization credentials needed (including level of forge-proof badges, smart cards, or identification cards) consistent with federal standards, policies, and procedures. This control only applies to areas within facilities that have not been designated as publicly accessible. Related controls: PE-3, PE-4, PS-3.

Control Enhancements:

(1) PHYSICAL ACCESS AUTHORIZATIONS | ACCESS BY POSITION / ROLE

The organization authorizes physical access to the facility where the information system resides based on position or role.

Supplemental Guidance: Related controls: AC-2, AC-3, AC-6.

(2) PHYSICAL ACCESS AUTHORIZATIONS | TWO FORMS OF IDENTIFICATION

The organization requires two forms of identification from [Assignment: organization-defined list of acceptable forms of identification] for visitor access to the facility where the information system resides.

Supplemental Guidance: Acceptable forms of government photo identification include, for example, passports, Personal Identity Verification (PIV) cards, and drivers' licenses. In the case of gaining access to facilities using automated mechanisms, organizations may use PIV cards, key cards, PINs, and biometrics. Related controls: IA-2, IA-4, IA-5.

(3) PHYSICAL ACCESS AUTHORIZATIONS | RESTRICT UNESCORTED ACCESS

The organization restricts unescorted access to the facility where the information system resides to personnel with [Selection (one or more): security clearances for all information contained within the system; formal access authorizations for all information contained within the system; need for access to all information contained within the system; [Assignment: organization-defined credentials]].

Supplemental Guidance: Due to the highly sensitive nature of classified information stored within certain facilities, it is important that individuals lacking sufficient security clearances, access approvals, or need to know, be escorted by individuals with appropriate credentials to ensure that such information is not exposed or otherwise compromised. Related controls: PS-2, PS-6.

References: None.

Priority and Baseline Allocation:

| P1 | LOW PE-2 | MOD PE-2 | HIGH PE-2 |

PE-3 PHYSICAL ACCESS CONTROL

Control: The organization:

a. Enforces physical access authorizations at [Assignment: organization-defined entry/exit points to the facility where the information system resides] by;

1. Verifying individual access authorizations before granting access to the facility; and

2. Controlling ingress/egress to the facility using [Selection (one or more): [Assignment: organization-defined physical access control systems/devices]; guards];

b. Maintains physical access audit logs for [Assignment: organization-defined entry/exit points];

c. Provides [Assignment: organization-defined security safeguards] to control access to areas within the facility officially designated as publicly accessible;

d. Escorts visitors and monitors visitor activity [Assignment: organization-defined circumstances requiring visitor escorts and monitoring];

e. Secures keys, combinations, and other physical access devices;

f. Inventories [Assignment: organization-defined physical access devices] every [Assignment: organization-defined frequency]; and

g. Changes combinations and keys [*Assignment: organization-defined frequency*] and/or when keys are lost, combinations are compromised, or individuals are transferred or terminated.

Supplemental Guidance: This control applies to organizational employees and visitors. Individuals (e.g., employees, contractors, and others) with permanent physical access authorization credentials are not considered visitors. Organizations determine the types of facility guards needed including, for example, professional physical security staff or other personnel such as administrative staff or information system users. Physical access devices include, for example, keys, locks, combinations, and card readers. Safeguards for publicly accessible areas within organizational facilities include, for example, cameras, monitoring by guards, and isolating selected information systems and/or system components in secured areas. Physical access control systems comply with applicable federal laws, Executive Orders, directives, policies, regulations, standards, and guidance. The Federal Identity, Credential, and Access Management Program provides implementation guidance for identity, credential, and access management capabilities for physical access control systems. Organizations have flexibility in the types of audit logs employed. Audit logs can be procedural (e.g., a written log of individuals accessing the facility and when such access occurred), automated (e.g., capturing ID provided by a PIV card), or some combination thereof. Physical access points can include facility access points, interior access points to information systems and/or components requiring supplemental access controls, or both. Components of organizational information systems (e.g., workstations, terminals) may be located in areas designated as publicly accessible with organizations safeguarding access to such devices. Related controls: AU-2, AU-6, MP-2, MP-4, PE-2, PE-4, PE-5, PS-3, RA-3.

Control Enhancements:

(1) PHYSICAL ACCESS CONTROL | INFORMATION SYSTEM ACCESS

The organization enforces physical access authorizations to the information system in addition to the physical access controls for the facility at [*Assignment: organization-defined physical spaces containing one or more components of the information system*].

Supplemental Guidance: This control enhancement provides additional physical security for those areas within facilities where there is a concentration of information system components (e.g., server rooms, media storage areas, data and communications centers). Related control: PS-2.

(2) PHYSICAL ACCESS CONTROL | FACILITY / INFORMATION SYSTEM BOUNDARIES

The organization performs security checks [*Assignment: organization-defined frequency*] at the physical boundary of the facility or information system for unauthorized exfiltration of information or removal of information system components.

Supplemental Guidance: Organizations determine the extent, frequency, and/or randomness of security checks to adequately mitigate risk associated with exfiltration. Related controls: AC-4, SC-7.

(3) PHYSICAL ACCESS CONTROL | CONTINUOUS GUARDS / ALARMS / MONITORING

The organization employs guards and/or alarms to monitor every physical access point to the facility where the information system resides 24 hours per day, 7 days per week.

Supplemental Guidance: Related controls: CP-6, CP-7.

(4) PHYSICAL ACCESS CONTROL | LOCKABLE CASINGS

The organization uses lockable physical casings to protect [*Assignment: organization-defined information system components*] from unauthorized physical access.

(5) PHYSICAL ACCESS CONTROL | TAMPER PROTECTION

The organization employs [*Assignment: organization-defined security safeguards*] to [*Selection (one or more): detect; prevent*] physical tampering or alteration of [*Assignment: organization-defined hardware components*] within the information system.

Supplemental Guidance: Organizations may implement tamper detection/prevention at selected hardware components or tamper detection at some components and tamper prevention at other components. Tamper detection/prevention activities can employ many types of anti-tamper technologies including, for example, tamper-detection seals and anti-tamper coatings. Anti-tamper programs help to detect hardware alterations through counterfeiting and other supply chain-related risks. Related control: SA-12.

(6) PHYSICAL ACCESS CONTROL | FACILITY PENETRATION TESTING

The organization employs a penetration testing process that includes [*Assignment: organization-defined frequency*], unannounced attempts to bypass or circumvent security controls associated with physical access points to the facility.

Supplemental Guidance: Related controls: CA-2, CA-7.

References: FIPS Publication 201; NIST Special Publications 800-73, 800-76, 800-78, 800-116; ICD 704, 705; DoD Instruction 5200.39; Personal Identity Verification (PIV) in Enterprise Physical Access Control System (E-PACS);
Web: http://idmanagement.gov, http://fips201ep.cio.gov.

Priority and Baseline Allocation:

P1	LOW PE-3	MOD PE-3	HIGH PE-3 (1)

PE-4 ACCESS CONTROL FOR TRANSMISSION MEDIUM

Control: The organization controls physical access to [*Assignment: organization-defined information system distribution and transmission lines*] within organizational facilities using [*Assignment: organization-defined security safeguards*].

Supplemental Guidance: Physical security safeguards applied to information system distribution and transmission lines help to prevent accidental damage, disruption, and physical tampering. In addition, physical safeguards may be necessary to help prevent eavesdropping or in transit modification of unencrypted transmissions. Security safeguards to control physical access to system distribution and transmission lines include, for example: (i) locked wiring closets; (ii) disconnected or locked spare jacks; and/or (iii) protection of cabling by conduit or cable trays. Related controls: MP-2, MP-4, PE-2, PE-3, PE-5, SC-7, SC-8.

Control Enhancements: None.

References: NSTISSI No. 7003.

Priority and Baseline Allocation:

P1	LOW Not Selected	MOD PE-4	HIGH PE-4

PE-5 ACCESS CONTROL FOR OUTPUT DEVICES

Control: The organization controls physical access to information system output devices to prevent unauthorized individuals from obtaining the output.

Supplemental Guidance: Controlling physical access to output devices includes, for example, placing output devices in locked rooms or other secured areas and allowing access to authorized individuals only, and placing output devices in locations that can be monitored by organizational personnel. Monitors, printers, copiers, scanners, facsimile machines, and audio devices are examples of information system output devices. Related controls: PE-2, PE-3, PE-4, PE-18.

Control Enhancements:

(1) ACCESS CONTROL FOR OUTPUT DEVICES | ACCESS TO OUTPUT BY AUTHORIZED INDIVIDUALS

The organization:

(a) Controls physical access to output from [*Assignment: organization-defined output devices*]; and

(b) Ensures that only authorized individuals receive output from the device.

Supplemental Guidance: Controlling physical access to selected output devices includes, for example, placing printers, copiers, and facsimile machines in controlled areas with keypad access controls or limiting access to individuals with certain types of badges.

(2) ACCESS CONTROL FOR OUTPUT DEVICES | ACCESS TO OUTPUT BY INDIVIDUAL IDENTITY

The information system:

(a) Controls physical access to output from [Assignment: organization-defined output devices]; and

(b) Links individual identity to receipt of the output from the device.

Supplemental Guidance: Controlling physical access to selected output devices includes, for example, installing security functionality on printers, copiers, and facsimile machines that allows organizations to implement authentication (e.g., using a PIN or hardware token) on output devices prior to the release of output to individuals.

(3) ACCESS CONTROL FOR OUTPUT DEVICES | MARKING OUTPUT DEVICES

The organization marks [Assignment: organization-defined information system output devices] indicating the appropriate security marking of the information permitted to be output from the device.

Supplemental Guidance: Outputs devices include, for example, printers, monitors, facsimile machines, scanners, copiers, and audio devices. This control enhancement is generally applicable to information system output devices other than mobiles devices.

References: None.

Priority and Baseline Allocation:

P2	LOW Not Selected	MOD PE-5	HIGH PE-5

PE-6 MONITORING PHYSICAL ACCESS

Control: The organization:

a. Monitors physical access to the facility where the information system resides to detect and respond to physical security incidents;

b. Reviews physical access logs [Assignment: organization-defined frequency] and upon occurrence of [Assignment: organization-defined events or potential indications of events]; and

c. Coordinates results of reviews and investigations with the organizational incident response capability.

Supplemental Guidance: Organizational incident response capabilities include investigations of and responses to detected physical security incidents. Security incidents include, for example, apparent security violations or suspicious physical access activities. Suspicious physical access activities include, for example: (i) accesses outside of normal work hours; (ii) repeated accesses to areas not normally accessed; (iii) accesses for unusual lengths of time; and (iv) out-of-sequence accesses. Related controls: CA-7, IR-4, IR-8.

Control Enhancements:

(1) MONITORING PHYSICAL ACCESS | INTRUSION ALARMS / SURVEILLANCE EQUIPMENT

The organization monitors physical intrusion alarms and surveillance equipment.

(2) MONITORING PHYSICAL ACCESS | AUTOMATED INTRUSION RECOGNITION / RESPONSES

The organization employs automated mechanisms to recognize [Assignment: organization-defined classes/types of intrusions] and initiate [Assignment: organization-defined response actions].

Supplemental Guidance: Related control: SI-4.

(3) *MONITORING PHYSICAL ACCESS | VIDEO SURVEILLANCE*

The organization employs video surveillance of [*Assignment: organization-defined operational areas*] and retains video recordings for [*Assignment: organization-defined time period*].

Supplemental Guidance: This control enhancement focuses on recording surveillance video for purposes of subsequent review, if circumstances so warrant (e.g., a break-in detected by other means). It does not require monitoring surveillance video although organizations may choose to do so. Note that there may be legal considerations when performing and retaining video surveillance, especially if such surveillance is in a public location.

(4) *MONITORING PHYSICAL ACCESS | MONITORING PHYSICAL ACCESS TO INFORMATION SYSTEMS*

The organization monitors physical access to the information system in addition to the physical access monitoring of the facility as [*Assignment: organization-defined physical spaces containing one or more components of the information system*].

Supplemental Guidance: This control enhancement provides additional monitoring for those areas within facilities where there is a concentration of information system components (e.g., server rooms, media storage areas, communications centers). Related controls: PS-2, PS-3.

References: None.

Priority and Baseline Allocation:

P1	LOW PE-6	MOD PE-6 (1)	HIGH PE-6 (1) (4)

PE-7 VISITOR CONTROL

[Withdrawn: Incorporated into PE-2 and PE-3].

PE-8 VISITOR ACCESS RECORDS

Control: The organization:

a. Maintains visitor access records to the facility where the information system resides for [*Assignment: organization-defined time period*]; and

b. Reviews visitor access records [*Assignment: organization-defined frequency*].

Supplemental Guidance: Visitor access records include, for example, names and organizations of persons visiting, visitor signatures, forms of identification, dates of access, entry and departure times, purposes of visits, and names and organizations of persons visited. Visitor access records are not required for publicly accessible areas.

Control Enhancements:

(1) *VISITOR ACCESS RECORDS | AUTOMATED RECORDS MAINTENANCE / REVIEW*

The organization employs automated mechanisms to facilitate the maintenance and review of visitor access records.

(2) *VISITOR ACCESS RECORDS | PHYSICAL ACCESS RECORDS*

[Withdrawn: Incorporated into PE-2].

References: None.

Priority and Baseline Allocation:

P3	LOW PE-8	MOD PE-8	HIGH PE-8 (1)

PE-9 POWER EQUIPMENT AND CABLING

Control: The organization protects power equipment and power cabling for the information system from damage and destruction.

Supplemental Guidance: Organizations determine the types of protection necessary for power equipment and cabling employed at different locations both internal and external to organizational facilities and environments of operation. This includes, for example, generators and power cabling outside of buildings, internal cabling and uninterruptable power sources within an office or data center, and power sources for self-contained entities such as vehicles and satellites. Related control: PE-4.

Control Enhancements:

(1) POWER EQUIPMENT AND CABLING | REDUNDANT CABLING
The organization employs redundant power cabling paths that are physically separated by [*Assignment: organization-defined distance*].

Supplemental Guidance: Physically separate, redundant power cables help to ensure that power continues to flow in the event one of the cables is cut or otherwise damaged.

(2) POWER EQUIPMENT AND CABLING | AUTOMATIC VOLTAGE CONTROLS
The organization employs automatic voltage controls for [*Assignment: organization-defined critical information system components*].

References: None.

Priority and Baseline Allocation:

| P1 | LOW Not Selected | MOD PE-9 | HIGH PE-9 |

PE-10 EMERGENCY SHUTOFF

Control: The organization:

a. Provides the capability of shutting off power to the information system or individual system components in emergency situations;

b. Places emergency shutoff switches or devices in [*Assignment: organization-defined location by information system or system component*] to facilitate safe and easy access for personnel; and

c. Protects emergency power shutoff capability from unauthorized activation.

Supplemental Guidance: This control applies primarily to facilities containing concentrations of information system resources including, for example, data centers, server rooms, and mainframe computer rooms. Related control: PE-15.

Control Enhancements:

(1) EMERGENCY SHUTOFF | ACCIDENTAL / UNAUTHORIZED ACTIVATION
[Withdrawn: Incorporated into PE-10].

References: None.

Priority and Baseline Allocation:

| P1 | LOW Not Selected | MOD PE-10 | HIGH PE-10 |

PE-11 EMERGENCY POWER

Control: The organization provides a short-term uninterruptible power supply to facilitate [*Selection (one or more): an orderly shutdown of the information system; transition of the information system to long-term alternate power*] in the event of a primary power source loss.

Supplemental Guidance: Related controls: AT-3, CP-2, CP-7.

Control Enhancements:

(1) EMERGENCY POWER | LONG-TERM ALTERNATE POWER SUPPLY - MINIMAL OPERATIONAL CAPABILITY

The organization provides a long-term alternate power supply for the information system that is capable of maintaining minimally required operational capability in the event of an extended loss of the primary power source.

Supplemental Guidance: This control enhancement can be satisfied, for example, by the use of a secondary commercial power supply or other external power supply. Long-term alternate power supplies for the information system can be either manually or automatically activated.

(2) EMERGENCY POWER | LONG-TERM ALTERNATE POWER SUPPLY - SELF-CONTAINED

The organization provides a long-term alternate power supply for the information system that is:

(a) Self-contained;

(b) Not reliant on external power generation; and

(c) Capable of maintaining [*Selection: minimally required operational capability; full operational capability*] in the event of an extended loss of the primary power source.

Supplemental Guidance: This control enhancement can be satisfied, for example, by the use of one or more generators with sufficient capacity to meet the needs of the organization. Long-term alternate power supplies for organizational information systems are either manually or automatically activated.

References: None.

Priority and Baseline Allocation:

P1	LOW Not Selected	MOD PE-11	HIGH PE-11 (1)

PE-12 EMERGENCY LIGHTING

Control: The organization employs and maintains automatic emergency lighting for the information system that activates in the event of a power outage or disruption and that covers emergency exits and evacuation routes within the facility.

Supplemental Guidance: This control applies primarily to facilities containing concentrations of information system resources including, for example, data centers, server rooms, and mainframe computer rooms. Related controls: CP-2, CP-7.

Control Enhancements:

(1) EMERGENCY LIGHTING | ESSENTIAL MISSIONS / BUSINESS FUNCTIONS

The organization provides emergency lighting for all areas within the facility supporting essential missions and business functions.

References: None.

Priority and Baseline Allocation:

P1	LOW PE-12	MOD PE-12	HIGH PE-12

PE-13 FIRE PROTECTION

Control: The organization employs and maintains fire suppression and detection devices/systems for the information system that are supported by an independent energy source.

Supplemental Guidance: This control applies primarily to facilities containing concentrations of information system resources including, for example, data centers, server rooms, and mainframe computer rooms. Fire suppression and detection devices/systems include, for example, sprinkler systems, handheld fire extinguishers, fixed fire hoses, and smoke detectors.

Control Enhancements:

(1) FIRE PROTECTION | DETECTION DEVICES / SYSTEMS

The organization employs fire detection devices/systems for the information system that activate automatically and notify [Assignment: organization-defined personnel or roles] and [Assignment: organization-defined emergency responders] in the event of a fire.

Supplemental Guidance: Organizations can identify specific personnel, roles, and emergency responders in the event that individuals on the notification list must have appropriate access authorizations and/or clearances, for example, to obtain access to facilities where classified operations are taking place or where there are information systems containing classified information.

(2) FIRE PROTECTION | SUPPRESSION DEVICES / SYSTEMS

The organization employs fire suppression devices/systems for the information system that provide automatic notification of any activation to Assignment: organization-defined personnel or roles] and [Assignment: organization-defined emergency responders].

Supplemental Guidance: Organizations can identify specific personnel, roles, and emergency responders in the event that individuals on the notification list must have appropriate access authorizations and/or clearances, for example, to obtain access to facilities where classified operations are taking place or where there are information systems containing classified information.

(3) FIRE PROTECTION | AUTOMATIC FIRE SUPPRESSION

The organization employs an automatic fire suppression capability for the information system when the facility is not staffed on a continuous basis.

(4) FIRE PROTECTION | INSPECTIONS

The organization ensures that the facility undergoes [Assignment: organization-defined frequency] inspections by authorized and qualified inspectors and resolves identified deficiencies within [Assignment: organization-defined time period].

References: None.

Priority and Baseline Allocation:

P1	LOW PE-13	MOD PE-13 (3)	HIGH PE-13 (1) (2) (3)

PE-14 TEMPERATURE AND HUMIDITY CONTROLS

Control: The organization:

a. Maintains temperature and humidity levels within the facility where the information system resides at [*Assignment: organization-defined acceptable levels*]; and

b. Monitors temperature and humidity levels [*Assignment: organization-defined frequency*].

Supplemental Guidance: This control applies primarily to facilities containing concentrations of information system resources, for example, data centers, server rooms, and mainframe computer rooms. Related control: AT-3.

Control Enhancements:

(1) *TEMPERATURE AND HUMIDITY CONTROLS | AUTOMATIC CONTROLS*

The organization employs automatic temperature and humidity controls in the facility to prevent fluctuations potentially harmful to the information system.

(2) *TEMPERATURE AND HUMIDITY CONTROLS | MONITORING WITH ALARMS / NOTIFICATIONS*

The organization employs temperature and humidity monitoring that provides an alarm or notification of changes potentially harmful to personnel or equipment.

References: None.

Priority and Baseline Allocation:

P1	LOW PE-14	MOD PE-14	HIGH PE-14

PE-15 WATER DAMAGE PROTECTION

Control: The organization protects the information system from damage resulting from water leakage by providing master shutoff or isolation valves that are accessible, working properly, and known to key personnel.

Supplemental Guidance: This control applies primarily to facilities containing concentrations of information system resources including, for example, data centers, server rooms, and mainframe computer rooms. Isolation valves can be employed in addition to or in lieu of master shutoff valves to shut off water supplies in specific areas of concern, without affecting entire organizations. Related control: AT-3.

Control Enhancements:

(1) *WATER DAMAGE PROTECTION | AUTOMATION SUPPORT*

The organization employs automated mechanisms to detect the presence of water in the vicinity of the information system and alerts [Assignment: organization-defined personnel or roles].

Supplemental Guidance: Automated mechanisms can include, for example, water detection sensors, alarms, and notification systems.

References: None.

Priority and Baseline Allocation:

P1	LOW PE-15	MOD PE-15	HIGH PE-15 (1)

PE-16 DELIVERY AND REMOVAL

Control: The organization authorizes, monitors, and controls [*Assignment: organization-defined types of information system components*] entering and exiting the facility and maintains records of those items.

Supplemental Guidance: Effectively enforcing authorizations for entry and exit of information system components may require restricting access to delivery areas and possibly isolating the areas from the information system and media libraries. Related controls: CM-3, MA-2, MA-3, MP-5, SA-12.

Control Enhancements: None.

References: None.

Priority and Baseline Allocation:

| P2 | LOW PE-16 | MOD PE-16 | HIGH PE-16 |

PE-17 ALTERNATE WORK SITE

Control: The organization:

a. Employs [*Assignment: organization-defined security controls*] at alternate work sites;

b. Assesses as feasible, the effectiveness of security controls at alternate work sites; and

c. Provides a means for employees to communicate with information security personnel in case of security incidents or problems.

Supplemental Guidance: Alternate work sites may include, for example, government facilities or private residences of employees. While commonly distinct from alternative processing sites, alternate work sites may provide readily available alternate locations as part of contingency operations. Organizations may define different sets of security controls for specific alternate work sites or types of sites depending on the work-related activities conducted at those sites. This control supports the contingency planning activities of organizations and the federal telework initiative. Related controls: AC-17, CP-7.

Control Enhancements: None.

References: NIST Special Publication 800-46.

Priority and Baseline Allocation:

| P2 | LOW Not Selected | MOD PE-17 | HIGH PE-17 |

PE-18 LOCATION OF INFORMATION SYSTEM COMPONENTS

Control: The organization positions information system components within the facility to minimize potential damage from [*Assignment: organization-defined physical and environmental hazards*] and to minimize the opportunity for unauthorized access.

Supplemental Guidance: Physical and environmental hazards include, for example, flooding, fire, tornados, earthquakes, hurricanes, acts of terrorism, vandalism, electromagnetic pulse, electrical interference, and other forms of incoming electromagnetic radiation. In addition, organizations consider the location of physical entry points where unauthorized individuals, while not being granted access, might nonetheless be in close proximity to information systems and therefore increase the potential for unauthorized access to organizational communications (e.g., through the use of wireless sniffers or microphones). Related controls: CP-2, PE-19, RA-3.

Control Enhancements:

(1) *LOCATION OF INFORMATION SYSTEM COMPONENTS | FACILITY SITE*

   The organization plans the location or site of the facility where the information system resides with regard to physical and environmental hazards and for existing facilities, considers the physical and environmental hazards in its risk mitigation strategy.

   Supplemental Guidance: Related control: PM-8.

References: None.

Priority and Baseline Allocation:

| P3 | LOW Not Selected | MOD Not Selected | HIGH PE-18 |

PE-19 INFORMATION LEAKAGE

Control: The organization protects the information system from information leakage due to electromagnetic signals emanations.

Supplemental Guidance: Information leakage is the intentional or unintentional release of information to an untrusted environment from electromagnetic signals emanations. Security categories or classifications of information systems (with respect to confidentiality) and organizational security policies guide the selection of security controls employed to protect systems against information leakage due to electromagnetic signals emanations.

Control Enhancements:

(1) INFORMATION LEAKAGE | NATIONAL EMISSIONS / TEMPEST POLICIES AND PROCEDURES

The organization ensures that information system components, associated data communications, and networks are protected in accordance with national emissions and TEMPEST policies and procedures based on the security category or classification of the information.

References: FIPS Publication 199.

Priority and Baseline Allocation:

| P0 | LOW Not Selected | MOD Not Selected | HIGH Not Selected |

PE-20 ASSET MONITORING AND TRACKING

Control: The organization:

a. Employs [*Assignment: organization-defined asset location technologies*] to track and monitor the location and movement of [*Assignment: organization-defined assets*] within [*Assignment: organization-defined controlled areas*]; and

b. Ensures that asset location technologies are employed in accordance with applicable federal laws, Executive Orders, directives, regulations, policies, standards, and guidance.

Supplemental Guidance: Asset location technologies can help organizations ensure that critical assets such as vehicles or essential information system components remain in authorized locations. Organizations consult with the Office of the General Counsel and the Senior Agency Official for Privacy (SAOP)/Chief Privacy Officer (CPO) regarding the deployment and use of asset location technologies to address potential privacy concerns. Related control: CM-8.

Control Enhancements: None.

References: None.

Priority and Baseline Allocation:

| P0 | LOW Not Selected | MOD Not Selected | HIGH Not Selected |

FAMILY: PLANNING

PL-1   SECURITY PLANNING POLICY AND PROCEDURES

Control: The organization:

a. Develops, documents, and disseminates to [*Assignment: organization-defined personnel or roles*]:

1. A security planning policy that addresses purpose, scope, roles, responsibilities, management commitment, coordination among organizational entities, and compliance; and

2. Procedures to facilitate the implementation of the security planning policy and associated security planning controls; and

b. Reviews and updates the current:

1. Security planning policy [*Assignment: organization-defined frequency*]; and

2. Security planning procedures [*Assignment: organization-defined frequency*].

Supplemental Guidance: This control addresses the establishment of policy and procedures for the effective implementation of selected security controls and control enhancements in the PL family. Policy and procedures reflect applicable federal laws, Executive Orders, directives, regulations, policies, standards, and guidance. Security program policies and procedures at the organization level may make the need for system-specific policies and procedures unnecessary. The policy can be included as part of the general information security policy for organizations or conversely, can be represented by multiple policies reflecting the complex nature of certain organizations. The procedures can be established for the security program in general and for particular information systems, if needed. The organizational risk management strategy is a key factor in establishing policy and procedures. Related control: PM-9.

Control Enhancements: None.

References: NIST Special Publications 800-12, 800-18, 800-100.

Priority and Baseline Allocation:

| P1 | LOW PL-1 | MOD PL-1 | HIGH PL-1 |

PL-2   SYSTEM SECURITY PLAN

Control: The organization:

a. Develops a security plan for the information system that:

1. Is consistent with the organization's enterprise architecture;

2. Explicitly defines the authorization boundary for the system;

3. Describes the operational context of the information system in terms of missions and business processes;

4. Provides the security categorization of the information system including supporting rationale;

5. Describes the operational environment for the information system and relationships with or connections to other information systems;

6. Provides an overview of the security requirements for the system;

7. Identifies any relevant overlays, if applicable;

8. Describes the security controls in place or planned for meeting those requirements including a rationale for the tailoring decisions; and

9. Is reviewed and approved by the authorizing official or designated representative prior to plan implementation;

b. Distributes copies of the security plan and communicates subsequent changes to the plan to [*Assignment: organization-defined personnel or roles*];

c. Reviews the security plan for the information system [*Assignment: organization-defined frequency*];

d. Updates the plan to address changes to the information system/environment of operation or problems identified during plan implementation or security control assessments; and

e. Protects the security plan from unauthorized disclosure and modification.

Supplemental Guidance: Security plans relate security requirements to a set of security controls and control enhancements. Security plans also describe, at a high level, how the security controls and control enhancements meet those security requirements, but do not provide detailed, technical descriptions of the specific design or implementation of the controls/enhancements. Security plans contain sufficient information (including the specification of parameter values for assignment and selection statements either explicitly or by reference) to enable a design and implementation that is unambiguously compliant with the intent of the plans and subsequent determinations of risk to organizational operations and assets, individuals, other organizations, and the Nation if the plan is implemented as intended. Organizations can also apply tailoring guidance to the security control baselines in Appendix D and CNSS Instruction 1253 to develop *overlays* for community-wide use or to address specialized requirements, technologies, or missions/environments of operation (e.g., DoD-tactical, Federal Public Key Infrastructure, or Federal Identity, Credential, and Access Management, space operations). Appendix I provides guidance on developing overlays.

Security plans need not be single documents; the plans can be a collection of various documents including documents that already exist. Effective security plans make extensive use of references to policies, procedures, and additional documents (e.g., design and implementation specifications) where more detailed information can be obtained. This reduces the documentation requirements associated with security programs and maintains security-related information in other established management/operational areas related to enterprise architecture, system development life cycle, systems engineering, and acquisition. For example, security plans do not contain detailed contingency plan or incident response plan information but instead provide explicitly or by reference, sufficient information to define what needs to be accomplished by those plans. Related controls: AC-2, AC-6, AC-14, AC-17, AC-20, CA-2, CA-3, CA-7, CM-9, CP-2, IR-8, MA-4, MA-5, MP-2, MP-4, MP-5, PL-7, PM-1, PM-7, PM-8, PM-9, PM-11, SA-5, SA-17.

Control Enhancements:

(1) SYSTEM SECURITY PLAN | CONCEPT OF OPERATIONS
[Withdrawn: Incorporated into PL-7].

(2) SYSTEM SECURITY PLAN | FUNCTIONAL ARCHITECTURE
[Withdrawn: Incorporated into PL-8].

(3) SYSTEM SECURITY PLAN | PLAN / COORDINATE WITH OTHER ORGANIZATIONAL ENTITIES
The organization plans and coordinates security-related activities affecting the information system with [*Assignment: organization-defined individuals or groups*] before conducting such activities in order to reduce the impact on other organizational entities.

Supplemental Guidance: Security-related activities include, for example, security assessments, audits, hardware and software maintenance, patch management, and contingency plan testing. Advance planning and coordination includes emergency and nonemergency (i.e., planned or nonurgent unplanned) situations. The process defined by organizations to plan and coordinate security-related activities can be included in security plans for information systems or other documents, as appropriate. Related controls: CP-4, IR-4.

References: NIST Special Publication 800-18.

Priority and Baseline Allocation:

| P1 | LOW PL-2 | MOD PL-2 (3) | HIGH PL-2 (3) |

PL-3 **SYSTEM SECURITY PLAN UPDATE**

[Withdrawn: Incorporated into PL-2].

PL-4 **RULES OF BEHAVIOR**

Control: The organization:

a. Establishes and makes readily available to individuals requiring access to the information system, the rules that describe their responsibilities and expected behavior with regard to information and information system usage;

b. Receives a signed acknowledgment from such individuals, indicating that they have read, understand, and agree to abide by the rules of behavior, before authorizing access to information and the information system;

c. Reviews and updates the rules of behavior [*Assignment: organization-defined frequency*]; and

d. Requires individuals who have signed a previous version of the rules of behavior to read and re-sign when the rules of behavior are revised/updated.

Supplemental Guidance: This control enhancement applies to organizational users. Organizations consider rules of behavior based on individual user roles and responsibilities, differentiating, for example, between rules that apply to privileged users and rules that apply to general users. Establishing rules of behavior for some types of non-organizational users including, for example, individuals who simply receive data/information from federal information systems, is often not feasible given the large number of such users and the limited nature of their interactions with the systems. Rules of behavior for both organizational and non-organizational users can also be established in AC-8, System Use Notification. PL-4 b. (the signed acknowledgment portion of this control) may be satisfied by the security awareness training and role-based security training programs conducted by organizations if such training includes rules of behavior. Organizations can use electronic signatures for acknowledging rules of behavior. Related controls: AC-2, AC-6, AC-8, AC-9, AC-17, AC-18, AC-19, AC-20, AT-2, AT-3, CM-11, IA-2, IA-4, IA-5, MP-7, PS-6, PS-8, SA-5.

Control Enhancements:

(1) *RULES OF BEHAVIOR | SOCIAL MEDIA AND NETWORKING RESTRICTIONS*

   The organization includes in the rules of behavior, explicit restrictions on the use of social media/networking sites and posting organizational information on public websites.

   Supplemental Guidance: This control enhancement addresses rules of behavior related to the use of social media/networking sites: (i) when organizational personnel are using such sites for official duties or in the conduct of official business; (ii) when organizational information is involved in social media/networking transactions; and (iii) when personnel are accessing social media/networking sites from organizational information systems. Organizations also address specific rules that prevent unauthorized entities from obtaining and/or inferring non-public organizational information (e.g., system account information, personally identifiable information) from social media/networking sites.

References: NIST Special Publication 800-18.

Priority and Baseline Allocation:

| P2 | LOW PL-4 | MOD PL-4 (1) | HIGH PL-4 (1) |

PL-5 PRIVACY IMPACT ASSESSMENT

[Withdrawn: Incorporated into Appendix J, AR-2].

PL-6 SECURITY-RELATED ACTIVITY PLANNING

[Withdrawn: Incorporated into PL-2].

PL-7 SECURITY CONCEPT OF OPERATIONS

Control: The organization:

a. Develops a security Concept of Operations (CONOPS) for the information system containing at a minimum, how the organization intends to operate the system from the perspective of information security; and

b. Reviews and updates the CONOPS [*Assignment: organization-defined frequency*].

Supplemental Guidance: The security CONOPS may be included in the security plan for the information system or in other system development life cycle-related documents, as appropriate. Changes to the CONOPS are reflected in ongoing updates to the security plan, the information security architecture, and other appropriate organizational documents (e.g., security specifications for procurements/acquisitions, system development life cycle documents, and systems/security engineering documents). Related control: PL-2.

Control Enhancements: None.

References: None.

Priority and Baseline Allocation:

| P0 | LOW Not Selected | MOD Not Selected | HIGH Not Selected |

PL-8 INFORMATION SECURITY ARCHITECTURE

Control: The organization:

a. Develops an information security architecture for the information system that:

  1. Describes the overall philosophy, requirements, and approach to be taken with regard to protecting the confidentiality, integrity, and availability of organizational information;

  2. Describes how the information security architecture is integrated into and supports the enterprise architecture; and

  3. Describes any information security assumptions about, and dependencies on, external services;

b. Reviews and updates the information security architecture [*Assignment: organization-defined frequency*] to reflect updates in the enterprise architecture; and

c. Ensures that planned information security architecture changes are reflected in the security plan, the security Concept of Operations (CONOPS), and organizational procurements/acquisitions.

Supplemental Guidance: This control addresses actions taken by organizations in the design and development of information systems. The information security architecture at the individual information system level is consistent with and complements the more global, organization-wide information security architecture described in PM-7 that is integral to and developed as part of the enterprise architecture. The information security architecture includes an architectural description, the placement/allocation of security functionality (including security controls), security-related information for external interfaces, information being exchanged across the interfaces, and the protection mechanisms associated with each interface. In addition, the security architecture can include other important security-related information, for example, user roles and access privileges assigned to each role, unique security requirements, the types of information processed, stored, and transmitted by the information system, restoration priorities of information and information system services, and any other specific protection needs.

In today's modern architecture, it is becoming less common for organizations to control all information resources. There are going to be key dependencies on external information services and service providers. Describing such dependencies in the information security architecture is important to developing a comprehensive mission/business protection strategy. Establishing, developing, documenting, and maintaining under configuration control, a baseline configuration for organizational information systems is critical to implementing and maintaining an effective information security architecture. The development of the information security architecture is coordinated with the Senior Agency Official for Privacy (SAOP)/Chief Privacy Officer (CPO) to ensure that security controls needed to support privacy requirements are identified and effectively implemented. PL-8 is primarily directed at organizations (i.e., internally focused) to help ensure that organizations develop an information security architecture for the information system, and that the security architecture is integrated with or tightly coupled to the enterprise architecture through the organization-wide information security architecture. In contrast, SA-17 is primarily directed at external information technology product/system developers and integrators (although SA-17 could be used internally within organizations for in-house system development). SA-17, which is complementary to PL-8, is selected when organizations outsource the development of information systems or information system components to external entities, and there is a need to demonstrate/show consistency with the organization's enterprise architecture and information security architecture. Related controls: CM-2, CM-6, PL-2, PM-7, SA-5, SA-17, Appendix J.

Control Enhancements:

(1) *INFORMATION SECURITY ARCHITECTURE | DEFENSE-IN-DEPTH*

　　The organization designs its security architecture using a defense-in-depth approach that:

　　(a) Allocates [*Assignment: organization-defined security safeguards*] to [*Assignment: organization-defined locations and architectural layers*]; and

　　(b) Ensures that the allocated security safeguards operate in a coordinated and mutually reinforcing manner.

Supplemental Guidance: Organizations strategically allocate security safeguards (procedural, technical, or both) in the security architecture so that adversaries have to overcome multiple safeguards to achieve their objective. Requiring adversaries to defeat multiple mechanisms makes it more difficult to successfully attack critical information resources (i.e., increases adversary work factor) and also increases the likelihood of detection. The coordination of allocated safeguards is essential to ensure that an attack that involves one safeguard does not create adverse unintended consequences (e.g., lockout, cascading alarms) by interfering with another safeguard. Placement of security safeguards is a key activity. Greater asset criticality or information value merits additional layering. Thus, an organization may choose to place anti-virus software at organizational boundary layers, email/web servers, notebook computers, and workstations to maximize the number of related safeguards adversaries must penetrate before compromising the information and information systems. Related controls: SC-29, SC-36.

(2) *INFORMATION SECURITY ARCHITECTURE | SUPPLIER DIVERSITY*

The organization requires that [*Assignment: organization-defined security safeguards*] allocated to [*Assignment: organization-defined locations and architectural layers*] are obtained from different suppliers.

Supplemental Guidance: Different information technology products have different strengths and weaknesses. Providing a broad spectrum of products complements the individual offerings. For example, vendors offering malicious code protection typically update their products at different times, often developing solutions for known viruses, Trojans, or worms according to their priorities and development schedules. By having different products at different locations (e.g., server, boundary, desktop) there is an increased likelihood that at least one will detect the malicious code. Related control: SA-12.

References: None.

Priority and Baseline Allocation:

| P1 | LOW Not Selected | MOD PL-8 | HIGH PL-8 |

PL-9 **CENTRAL MANAGEMENT**

Control: The organization centrally manages [*Assignment: organization-defined security controls and related processes*].

Supplemental Guidance: Central management refers to the organization-wide management and implementation of selected security controls and related processes. Central management includes planning, implementing, assessing, authorizing, and monitoring the organization-defined, centrally managed security controls and processes. As central management of security controls is generally associated with common controls, such management promotes and facilitates standardization of security control implementations and management and judicious use of organizational resources. Centrally-managed security controls and processes may also meet independence requirements for assessments in support of initial and ongoing authorizations to operate as part of organizational continuous monitoring. As part of the security control selection process, organizations determine which controls may be suitable for central management based on organizational resources and capabilities. Organizations consider that it may not always be possible to centrally manage every aspect of a security control. In such cases, the security control is treated as a hybrid control with the control managed and implemented either centrally or at the information system level. Controls and control enhancements that are candidates for full or partial central management include, but are not limited to: AC-2 (1) (2) (3) (4); AC-17 (1) (2) (3) (9); AC-18 (1) (3) (4) (5); AC-19 (4); AC-22; AC-23; AT-2 (1) (2); AT-3 (1) (2) (3); AT-4; AU-6 (1) (3) (5) (6) (9); AU-7 (1) (2); AU-11, AU-13, AU-16, CA-2 (1) (2) (3); CA-3 (1) (2) (3); CA-7 (1); CA-9; CM-2 (1) (2); CM-3 (1) (4); CM-4; CM-6 (1); CM-7 (4) (5); CM-8 (all); CM-9 (1); CM-10; CM-11; CP-7 (all); CP-8 (all); SC-43; SI-2; SI-3; SI-7; and SI-8.

Control Enhancements: None.

References: NIST Special Publication 800-37.

Priority and Baseline Allocation:

| P0 | LOW Not Selected | MOD Not Selected | HIGH Not Selected |

FAMILY: PERSONNEL SECURITY

PS-1 PERSONNEL SECURITY POLICY AND PROCEDURES

Control: The organization:

a. Develops, documents, and disseminates to [*Assignment: organization-defined personnel or roles*]:

   1. A personnel security policy that addresses purpose, scope, roles, responsibilities, management commitment, coordination among organizational entities, and compliance; and

   2. Procedures to facilitate the implementation of the personnel security policy and associated personnel security controls; and

b. Reviews and updates the current:

   1. Personnel security policy [*Assignment: organization-defined frequency*]; and

   2. Personnel security procedures [*Assignment: organization-defined frequency*].

Supplemental Guidance: This control addresses the establishment of policy and procedures for the effective implementation of selected security controls and control enhancements in the PS family. Policy and procedures reflect applicable federal laws, Executive Orders, directives, regulations, policies, standards, and guidance. Security program policies and procedures at the organization level may make the need for system-specific policies and procedures unnecessary. The policy can be included as part of the general information security policy for organizations or conversely, can be represented by multiple policies reflecting the complex nature of certain organizations. The procedures can be established for the security program in general and for particular information systems, if needed. The organizational risk management strategy is a key factor in establishing policy and procedures. Related control: PM-9.

Control Enhancements: None.

References: NIST Special Publications 800-12, 800-100.

Priority and Baseline Allocation:

| P1 | LOW PS-1 | MOD PS-1 | HIGH PS-1 |

PS-2 POSITION RISK DESIGNATION

Control: The organization:

a. Assigns a risk designation to all organizational positions;

b. Establishes screening criteria for individuals filling those positions; and

c. Reviews and updates position risk designations [*Assignment: organization-defined frequency*].

Supplemental Guidance: Position risk designations reflect Office of Personnel Management policy and guidance. Risk designations can guide and inform the types of authorizations individuals receive when accessing organizational information and information systems. Position screening criteria include explicit information security role appointment requirements (e.g., training, security clearances). Related controls: AT-3, PL-2, PS-3.

Control Enhancements: None.

References: 5 C.F.R. 731.106.

Priority and Baseline Allocation:

| P1 | LOW PS-2 | MOD PS-2 | HIGH PS-2 |

PS-3 PERSONNEL SCREENING

Control: The organization:

a. Screens individuals prior to authorizing access to the information system; and

b. Rescreens individuals according to [*Assignment: organization-defined conditions requiring rescreening and, where rescreening is so indicated, the frequency of such rescreening*].

Supplemental Guidance: Personnel screening and rescreening activities reflect applicable federal laws, Executive Orders, directives, regulations, policies, standards, guidance, and specific criteria established for the risk designations of assigned positions. Organizations may define different rescreening conditions and frequencies for personnel accessing information systems based on types of information processed, stored, or transmitted by the systems. Related controls: AC-2, IA-4, PE-2, PS-2.

Control Enhancements:

(1) PERSONNEL SCREENING | CLASSIFIED INFORMATION

The organization ensures that individuals accessing an information system processing, storing, or transmitting classified information are cleared and indoctrinated to the highest classification level of the information to which they have access on the system.

Supplemental Guidance: Related controls: AC-3, AC-4.

(2) PERSONNEL SCREENING | FORMAL INDOCTRINATION

The organization ensures that individuals accessing an information system processing, storing, or transmitting types of classified information which require formal indoctrination, are formally indoctrinated for all of the relevant types of information to which they have access on the system.

Supplemental Guidance: Types of classified information requiring formal indoctrination include, for example, Special Access Program (SAP), Restricted Data (RD), and Sensitive Compartment Information (SCI). Related controls: AC-3, AC-4.

(3) PERSONNEL SCREENING | INFORMATION WITH SPECIAL PROTECTION MEASURES

The organization ensures that individuals accessing an information system processing, storing, or transmitting information requiring special protection:

(a) Have valid access authorizations that are demonstrated by assigned official government duties; and

(b) Satisfy [*Assignment: organization-defined additional personnel screening criteria*].

Supplemental Guidance: Organizational information requiring special protection includes, for example, Controlled Unclassified Information (CUI) and Sources and Methods Information (SAMI). Personnel security criteria include, for example, position sensitivity background screening requirements.

References: 5 C.F.R. 731.106; FIPS Publications 199, 201; NIST Special Publications 800-60, 800-73, 800-76, 800-78; ICD 704.

Priority and Baseline Allocation:

| P1 | LOW PS-3 | MOD PS-3 | HIGH PS-3 |

PS-4 PERSONNEL TERMINATION

Control: The organization, upon termination of individual employment:

a. Disables information system access within [Assignment: organization-defined time period];

b. Terminates/revokes any authenticators/credentials associated with the individual;

c. Conducts exit interviews that include a discussion of [Assignment: organization-defined information security topics];

d. Retrieves all security-related organizational information system-related property;

e. Retains access to organizational information and information systems formerly controlled by terminated individual; and

f. Notifies [Assignment: organization-defined personnel or roles] within [Assignment: organization-defined time period].

Supplemental Guidance: Information system-related property includes, for example, hardware authentication tokens, system administration technical manuals, keys, identification cards, and building passes. Exit interviews ensure that terminated individuals understand the security constraints imposed by being former employees and that proper accountability is achieved for information system-related property. Security topics of interest at exit interviews can include, for example, reminding terminated individuals of nondisclosure agreements and potential limitations on future employment. Exit interviews may not be possible for some terminated individuals, for example, in cases related to job abandonment, illnesses, and nonavailability of supervisors. Exit interviews are important for individuals with security clearances. Timely execution of termination actions is essential for individuals terminated for cause. In certain situations, organizations consider disabling the information system accounts of individuals that are being terminated prior to the individuals being notified. Related controls: AC-2, IA-4, PE-2, PS-5, PS-6.

Control Enhancements:

(1) PERSONNEL TERMINATION | POST-EMPLOYMENT REQUIREMENTS

The organization:

(a) Notifies terminated individuals of applicable, legally binding post-employment requirements for the protection of organizational information; and

(b) Requires terminated individuals to sign an acknowledgment of post-employment requirements as part of the organizational termination process.

Supplemental Guidance: Organizations consult with the Office of the General Counsel regarding matters of post-employment requirements on terminated individuals.

(2) PERSONNEL TERMINATION | AUTOMATED NOTIFICATION

The organization employs automated mechanisms to notify [Assignment: organization-defined personnel or roles] upon termination of an individual.

Supplemental Guidance: In organizations with a large number of employees, not all personnel who need to know about termination actions receive the appropriate notifications—or, if such notifications are received, they may not occur in a timely manner. Automated mechanisms can be used to send automatic alerts or notifications to specific organizational personnel or roles (e.g., management personnel, supervisors, personnel security officers, information security officers, systems administrators, or information technology administrators) when individuals are terminated. Such automatic alerts or notifications can be conveyed in a variety of ways, including, for example, telephonically, via electronic mail, via text message, or via websites.

References: None.

Priority and Baseline Allocation:

| P1 | LOW PS-4 | MOD PS-4 | HIGH PS-4 (2) |

PS-5 **PERSONNEL TRANSFER**

Control: The organization:

a. Reviews and confirms ongoing operational need for current logical and physical access authorizations to information systems/facilities when individuals are reassigned or transferred to other positions within the organization;

b. Initiates [*Assignment: organization-defined transfer or reassignment actions*] within [*Assignment: organization-defined time period following the formal transfer action*];

c. Modifies access authorization as needed to correspond with any changes in operational need due to reassignment or transfer; and

d. Notifies [*Assignment: organization-defined personnel or roles*] within [*Assignment: organization-defined time period*].

Supplemental Guidance: This control applies when reassignments or transfers of individuals are permanent or of such extended durations as to make the actions warranted. Organizations define actions appropriate for the types of reassignments or transfers, whether permanent or extended. Actions that may be required for personnel transfers or reassignments to other positions within organizations include, for example: (i) returning old and issuing new keys, identification cards, and building passes; (ii) closing information system accounts and establishing new accounts; (iii) changing information system access authorizations (i.e., privileges); and (iv) providing for access to official records to which individuals had access at previous work locations and in previous information system accounts. Related controls: AC-2, IA-4, PE-2, PS-4.

Control Enhancements: None.

References: None.

Priority and Baseline Allocation:

| P2 | LOW PS-5 | MOD PS-5 | HIGH PS-5 |

PS-6 **ACCESS AGREEMENTS**

Control: The organization:

a. Develops and documents access agreements for organizational information systems;

b. Reviews and updates the access agreements [*Assignment: organization-defined frequency*]; and

c. Ensures that individuals requiring access to organizational information and information systems:

   1. Sign appropriate access agreements prior to being granted access; and

   2. Re-sign access agreements to maintain access to organizational information systems when access agreements have been updated or [*Assignment: organization-defined frequency*].

Supplemental Guidance: Access agreements include, for example, nondisclosure agreements, acceptable use agreements, rules of behavior, and conflict-of-interest agreements. Signed access agreements include an acknowledgement that individuals have read, understand, and agree to abide by the constraints associated with organizational information systems to which access is authorized. Organizations can use electronic signatures to acknowledge access agreements unless specifically prohibited by organizational policy. Related control: PL-4, PS-2, PS-3, PS-4, PS-8.

Control Enhancements:

(1) ACCESS AGREEMENTS | INFORMATION REQUIRING SPECIAL PROTECTION

[Withdrawn: Incorporated into PS-3].

(2) ACCESS AGREEMENTS | CLASSIFIED INFORMATION REQUIRING SPECIAL PROTECTION

The organization ensures that access to classified information requiring special protection is granted only to individuals who:

(a) Have a valid access authorization that is demonstrated by assigned official government duties;

(b) Satisfy associated personnel security criteria; and

(c) Have read, understood, and signed a nondisclosure agreement.

Supplemental Guidance: Classified information requiring special protection includes, for example, collateral information, Special Access Program (SAP) information, and Sensitive Compartmented Information (SCI). Personnel security criteria reflect applicable federal laws, Executive Orders, directives, regulations, policies, standards, and guidance.

(3) ACCESS AGREEMENTS | POST-EMPLOYMENT REQUIREMENTS

The organization:

(a) Notifies individuals of applicable, legally binding post-employment requirements for protection of organizational information; and

(b) Requires individuals to sign an acknowledgment of these requirements, if applicable, as part of granting initial access to covered information.

Supplemental Guidance: Organizations consult with the Office of the General Counsel regarding matters of post-employment requirements on terminated individuals.

References: None.

Priority and Baseline Allocation:

| P3 | LOW PS-6 | MOD PS-6 | HIGH PS-6 |

PS-7 THIRD-PARTY PERSONNEL SECURITY

Control: The organization:

a. Establishes personnel security requirements including security roles and responsibilities for third-party providers;

b. Requires third-party providers to comply with personnel security policies and procedures established by the organization;

c. Documents personnel security requirements;

d. Requires third-party providers to notify [Assignment: organization-defined personnel or roles] of any personnel transfers or terminations of third-party personnel who possess organizational credentials and/or badges, or who have information system privileges within [Assignment: organization-defined time period]; and

e. Monitors provider compliance.

Supplemental Guidance: Third-party providers include, for example, service bureaus, contractors, and other organizations providing information system development, information technology services, outsourced applications, and network and security management. Organizations explicitly include personnel security requirements in acquisition-related documents. Third-party providers may have personnel working at organizational facilities with credentials, badges, or information system privileges issued by organizations. Notifications of third-party personnel changes ensure appropriate termination of privileges and credentials. Organizations define the transfers and terminations deemed reportable by security-related characteristics that include, for example, functions, roles, and nature of credentials/privileges associated with individuals transferred or terminated. Related controls: PS-2, PS-3, PS-4, PS-5, PS-6, SA-9, SA-21.

Control Enhancements: None.

References: NIST Special Publication 800-35.

Priority and Baseline Allocation:

| P1 | LOW PS-7 | MOD PS-7 | HIGH PS-7 |

PS-8 **PERSONNEL SANCTIONS**

Control: The organization:

a. Employs a formal sanctions process for individuals failing to comply with established information security policies and procedures; and

b. Notifies [*Assignment: organization-defined personnel or roles*] within [*Assignment: organization-defined time period*] when a formal employee sanctions process is initiated, identifying the individual sanctioned and the reason for the sanction.

Supplemental Guidance: Organizational sanctions processes reflect applicable federal laws, Executive Orders, directives, regulations, policies, standards, and guidance. Sanctions processes are described in access agreements and can be included as part of general personnel policies and procedures for organizations. Organizations consult with the Office of the General Counsel regarding matters of employee sanctions. Related controls: PL-4, PS-6.

Control Enhancements: None.

References: None.

Priority and Baseline Allocation:

| P3 | LOW PS-8 | MOD PS-8 | HIGH PS-8 |

FAMILY: RISK ASSESSMENT

RA-1 RISK ASSESSMENT POLICY AND PROCEDURES

Control: The organization:

a. Develops, documents, and disseminates to [*Assignment: organization-defined personnel or roles*]:

1. A risk assessment policy that addresses purpose, scope, roles, responsibilities, management commitment, coordination among organizational entities, and compliance; and

2. Procedures to facilitate the implementation of the risk assessment policy and associated risk assessment controls; and

b. Reviews and updates the current:

1. Risk assessment policy [*Assignment: organization-defined frequency*]; and

2. Risk assessment procedures [*Assignment: organization-defined frequency*].

Supplemental Guidance: This control addresses the establishment of policy and procedures for the effective implementation of selected security controls and control enhancements in the RA family. Policy and procedures reflect applicable federal laws, Executive Orders, directives, regulations, policies, standards, and guidance. Security program policies and procedures at the organization level may make the need for system-specific policies and procedures unnecessary. The policy can be included as part of the general information security policy for organizations or conversely, can be represented by multiple policies reflecting the complex nature of certain organizations. The procedures can be established for the security program in general and for particular information systems, if needed. The organizational risk management strategy is a key factor in establishing policy and procedures. Related control: PM-9.

Control Enhancements: None.

References: NIST Special Publications 800-12, 800-30, 800-100.

Priority and Baseline Allocation:

P1	LOW RA-1	MOD RA-1	HIGH RA-1

RA-2 SECURITY CATEGORIZATION

Control: The organization:

a. Categorizes information and the information system in accordance with applicable federal laws, Executive Orders, directives, policies, regulations, standards, and guidance;

b. Documents the security categorization results (including supporting rationale) in the security plan for the information system; and

c. Ensures that the authorizing official or authorizing official designated representative reviews and approves the security categorization decision.

Supplemental Guidance: Clearly defined authorization boundaries are a prerequisite for effective security categorization decisions. Security categories describe the potential adverse impacts to organizational operations, organizational assets, and individuals if organizational information and information systems are comprised through a loss of confidentiality, integrity, or availability. Organizations conduct the security categorization process as an organization-wide activity with the involvement of chief information officers, senior information security officers, information system owners, mission/business owners, and information owners/stewards. Organizations also consider the potential adverse impacts to other organizations and, in accordance with the USA PATRIOT Act of 2001 and Homeland Security Presidential Directives, potential national-level adverse impacts. Security categorization processes carried out by organizations facilitate the development of inventories of information assets, and along with CM-8, mappings to specific information system components where information is processed, stored, or transmitted. Related controls: CM-8, MP-4, RA-3, SC-7.

Control Enhancements: None.

References: FIPS Publication 199; NIST Special Publications 800-30, 800-39, 800-60.

Priority and Baseline Allocation:

| P1 | LOW RA-2 | MOD RA-2 | HIGH RA-2 |

RA-3 **RISK ASSESSMENT**

Control: The organization:

a. Conducts an assessment of risk, including the likelihood and magnitude of harm, from the unauthorized access, use, disclosure, disruption, modification, or destruction of the information system and the information it processes, stores, or transmits;

b. Documents risk assessment results in [Selection: security plan; risk assessment report; [Assignment: organization-defined document]];

c. Reviews risk assessment results [Assignment: organization-defined frequency];

d. Disseminates risk assessment results to [Assignment: organization-defined personnel or roles]; and

e. Updates the risk assessment [Assignment: organization-defined frequency] or whenever there are significant changes to the information system or environment of operation (including the identification of new threats and vulnerabilities), or other conditions that may impact the security state of the system.

Supplemental Guidance: Clearly defined authorization boundaries are a prerequisite for effective risk assessments. Risk assessments take into account threats, vulnerabilities, likelihood, and impact to organizational operations and assets, individuals, other organizations, and the Nation based on the operation and use of information systems. Risk assessments also take into account risk from external parties (e.g., service providers, contractors operating information systems on behalf of the organization, individuals accessing organizational information systems, outsourcing entities). In accordance with OMB policy and related E-authentication initiatives, authentication of public users accessing federal information systems may also be required to protect nonpublic or privacy-related information. As such, organizational assessments of risk also address public access to federal information systems.

Risk assessments (either formal or informal) can be conducted at all three tiers in the risk management hierarchy (i.e., organization level, mission/business process level, or information system level) and at any phase in the system development life cycle. Risk assessments can also be conducted at various steps in the Risk Management Framework, including categorization, security control selection, security control implementation, security control assessment, information system authorization, and security control monitoring. RA-3 is noteworthy in that the control must be partially implemented prior to the implementation of other controls in order to complete the first two steps in the Risk Management Framework. Risk assessments can play an important role in security control selection processes, particularly during the application of tailoring guidance, which includes security control supplementation. Related controls: RA-2, PM-9.

Control Enhancements: None.

References: OMB Memorandum 04-04; NIST Special Publications 800-30, 800-39; Web: http://idmanagement.gov.

Priority and Baseline Allocation:

| P1 | LOW RA-3 | MOD RA-3 | HIGH RA-3 |

RA-4 RISK ASSESSMENT UPDATE

[Withdrawn: Incorporated into RA-3].

RA-5 VULNERABILITY SCANNING

Control: The organization:

a. Scans for vulnerabilities in the information system and hosted applications [*Assignment: organization-defined frequency and/or randomly in accordance with organization-defined process*] and when new vulnerabilities potentially affecting the system/applications are identified and reported;

b. Employs vulnerability scanning tools and techniques that facilitate interoperability among tools and automate parts of the vulnerability management process by using standards for:

   1. Enumerating platforms, software flaws, and improper configurations;

   2. Formatting checklists and test procedures; and

   3. Measuring vulnerability impact;

c. Analyzes vulnerability scan reports and results from security control assessments;

d. Remediates legitimate vulnerabilities [*Assignment: organization-defined response times*] in accordance with an organizational assessment of risk; and

e. Shares information obtained from the vulnerability scanning process and security control assessments with [*Assignment: organization-defined personnel or roles*] to help eliminate similar vulnerabilities in other information systems (i.e., systemic weaknesses or deficiencies).

Supplemental Guidance: Security categorization of information systems guides the frequency and comprehensiveness of vulnerability scans. Organizations determine the required vulnerability scanning for all information system components, ensuring that potential sources of vulnerabilities such as networked printers, scanners, and copiers are not overlooked. Vulnerability analyses for custom software applications may require additional approaches such as static analysis, dynamic analysis, binary analysis, or a hybrid of the three approaches. Organizations can employ these analysis approaches in a variety of tools (e.g., web-based application scanners, static analysis tools, binary analyzers) and in source code reviews. Vulnerability scanning includes, for example: (i) scanning for patch levels; (ii) scanning for functions, ports, protocols, and services that should not be accessible to users or devices; and (iii) scanning for improperly configured or incorrectly operating information flow control mechanisms. Organizations consider using tools that express vulnerabilities in the Common Vulnerabilities and Exposures (CVE) naming convention and that use the Open Vulnerability Assessment Language (OVAL) to determine/test for the presence of vulnerabilities. Suggested sources for vulnerability information include the Common Weakness Enumeration (CWE) listing and the National Vulnerability Database (NVD). In addition, security control assessments such as red team exercises provide other sources of potential vulnerabilities for which to scan. Organizations also consider using tools that express vulnerability impact by the Common Vulnerability Scoring System (CVSS). Related controls: CA-2, CA-7, CM-4, CM-6, RA-2, RA-3, SA-11, SI-2.

Control Enhancements:

(1) *VULNERABILITY SCANNING | UPDATE TOOL CAPABILITY*

The organization employs vulnerability scanning tools that include the capability to readily update the information system vulnerabilities to be scanned.

Supplemental Guidance: The vulnerabilities to be scanned need to be readily updated as new vulnerabilities are discovered, announced, and scanning methods developed. This updating process helps to ensure that potential vulnerabilities in the information system are identified and addressed as quickly as possible. Related controls: SI-3, SI-7.

(2) *VULNERABILITY SCANNING | UPDATE BY FREQUENCY / PRIOR TO NEW SCAN / WHEN IDENTIFIED*

The organization updates the information system vulnerabilities scanned [*Selection (one or more): [Assignment: organization-defined frequency]; prior to a new scan; when new vulnerabilities are identified and reported*].

Supplemental Guidance: Related controls: SI-3, SI-5.

(3) *VULNERABILITY SCANNING | BREADTH / DEPTH OF COVERAGE*

The organization employs vulnerability scanning procedures that can identify the breadth and depth of coverage (i.e., information system components scanned and vulnerabilities checked).

(4) *VULNERABILITY SCANNING | DISCOVERABLE INFORMATION*

The organization determines what information about the information system is discoverable by adversaries and subsequently takes [*Assignment: organization-defined corrective actions*].

Supplemental Guidance: Discoverable information includes information that adversaries could obtain without directly compromising or breaching the information system, for example, by collecting information the system is exposing or by conducting extensive searches of the web. Corrective actions can include, for example, notifying appropriate organizational personnel, removing designated information, or changing the information system to make designated information less relevant or attractive to adversaries. Related control: AU-13.

(5) *VULNERABILITY SCANNING | PRIVILEGED ACCESS*

The information system implements privileged access authorization to [*Assignment: organization-identified information system components*] for selected [*Assignment: organization-defined vulnerability scanning activities*].

Supplemental Guidance: In certain situations, the nature of the vulnerability scanning may be more intrusive or the information system component that is the subject of the scanning may contain highly sensitive information. Privileged access authorization to selected system components facilitates more thorough vulnerability scanning and also protects the sensitive nature of such scanning.

(6) *VULNERABILITY SCANNING | AUTOMATED TREND ANALYSES*

The organization employs automated mechanisms to compare the results of vulnerability scans over time to determine trends in information system vulnerabilities.

Supplemental Guidance: Related controls: IR-4, IR-5, SI-4.

(7) *VULNERABILITY SCANNING | AUTOMATED DETECTION AND NOTIFICATION OF UNAUTHORIZED COMPONENTS*

[Withdrawn: Incorporated into CM-8].

(8) *VULNERABILITY SCANNING | REVIEW HISTORIC AUDIT LOGS*

The organization reviews historic audit logs to determine if a vulnerability identified in the information system has been previously exploited.

Supplemental Guidance: Related control: AU-6.

(9) *VULNERABILITY SCANNING | PENETRATION TESTING AND ANALYSES*

[Withdrawn: Incorporated into CA-8].

(10) *VULNERABILITY SCANNING | CORRELATE SCANNING INFORMATION*

The organization correlates the output from vulnerability scanning tools to determine the presence of multi-vulnerability/multi-hop attack vectors.

References: NIST Special Publications 800-40, 800-70, 800-115; Web: http://cwe.mitre.org, http://nvd.nist.gov.

Priority and Baseline Allocation:

| P1 | LOW RA-5 | MOD RA-5 (1) (2) (5) | HIGH RA-5 (1) (2) (4) (5) |

RA-6 TECHNICAL SURVEILLANCE COUNTERMEASURES SURVEY

Control: The organization employs a technical surveillance countermeasures survey at [*Assignment: organization-defined locations*] [*Selection (one or more): [Assignment: organization-defined frequency]; [Assignment: organization-defined events or indicators occur]*].

Supplemental Guidance: Technical surveillance countermeasures surveys are performed by qualified personnel to detect the presence of technical surveillance devices/hazards and to identify technical security weaknesses that could aid in the conduct of technical penetrations of surveyed facilities. Such surveys provide evaluations of the technical security postures of organizations and facilities and typically include thorough visual, electronic, and physical examinations in and about surveyed facilities. The surveys also provide useful input into risk assessments and organizational exposure to potential adversaries.

Control Enhancements: None.

References: None.

Priority and Baseline Allocation:

| P0 | LOW Not Selected | MOD Not Selected | HIGH Not Selected |

FAMILY: SYSTEM AND SERVICES ACQUISITION

SA-1 SYSTEM AND SERVICES ACQUISITION POLICY AND PROCEDURES

Control: The organization:

a. Develops, documents, and disseminates to [*Assignment: organization-defined personnel or roles*]:

   1. A system and services acquisition policy that addresses purpose, scope, roles, responsibilities, management commitment, coordination among organizational entities, and compliance; and

   2. Procedures to facilitate the implementation of the system and services acquisition policy and associated system and services acquisition controls; and

b. Reviews and updates the current:

   1. System and services acquisition policy [*Assignment: organization-defined frequency*]; and

   2. System and services acquisition procedures [*Assignment: organization-defined frequency*].

Supplemental Guidance: This control addresses the establishment of policy and procedures for the effective implementation of selected security controls and control enhancements in the SA family. Policy and procedures reflect applicable federal laws, Executive Orders, directives, regulations, policies, standards, and guidance. Security program policies and procedures at the organization level may make the need for system-specific policies and procedures unnecessary. The policy can be included as part of the general information security policy for organizations or conversely, can be represented by multiple policies reflecting the complex nature of certain organizations. The procedures can be established for the security program in general and for particular information systems, if needed. The organizational risk management strategy is a key factor in establishing policy and procedures. Related control: PM-9.

Control Enhancements: None.

References: NIST Special Publications 800-12, 800-100.

Priority and Baseline Allocation:

| P1 | LOW SA-1 | MOD SA-1 | HIGH SA-1 |

SA-2 ALLOCATION OF RESOURCES

Control: The organization:

a. Determines information security requirements for the information system or information system service in mission/business process planning;

b. Determines, documents, and allocates the resources required to protect the information system or information system service as part of its capital planning and investment control process; and

c. Establishes a discrete line item for information security in organizational programming and budgeting documentation.

Supplemental Guidance: Resource allocation for information security includes funding for the initial information system or information system service acquisition and funding for the sustainment of the system/service. Related controls: PM-3, PM-11.

Control Enhancements: None.

References: NIST Special Publication 800-65.

Priority and Baseline Allocation:

| P1 | LOW SA-2 | MOD SA-2 | HIGH SA-2 |

SA-3 SYSTEM DEVELOPMENT LIFE CYCLE

Control: The organization:

a. Manages the information system using [*Assignment: organization-defined system development life cycle*] that incorporates information security considerations;

b. Defines and documents information security roles and responsibilities throughout the system development life cycle;

c. Identifies individuals having information security roles and responsibilities; and

d. Integrates the organizational information security risk management process into system development life cycle activities.

Supplemental Guidance: A well-defined system development life cycle provides the foundation for the successful development, implementation, and operation of organizational information systems. To apply the required security controls within the system development life cycle requires a basic understanding of information security, threats, vulnerabilities, adverse impacts, and risk to critical missions/business functions. The security engineering principles in SA-8 cannot be properly applied if individuals that design, code, and test information systems and system components (including information technology products) do not understand security. Therefore, organizations include qualified personnel, for example, chief information security officers, security architects, security engineers, and information system security officers in system development life cycle activities to ensure that security requirements are incorporated into organizational information systems. It is equally important that developers include individuals on the development team that possess the requisite security expertise and skills to ensure that needed security capabilities are effectively integrated into the information system. Security awareness and training programs can help ensure that individuals having key security roles and responsibilities have the appropriate experience, skills, and expertise to conduct assigned system development life cycle activities. The effective integration of security requirements into enterprise architecture also helps to ensure that important security considerations are addressed early in the system development life cycle and that those considerations are directly related to the organizational mission/business processes. This process also facilitates the integration of the information security architecture into the enterprise architecture, consistent with organizational risk management and information security strategies. Related controls: AT-3, PM-7, SA-8.

Control Enhancements: None.

References: NIST Special Publications 800-37, 800-64.

Priority and Baseline Allocation:

| P1 | LOW SA-3 | MOD SA-3 | HIGH SA-3 |

SA-4 ACQUISITION PROCESS

Control: The organization includes the following requirements, descriptions, and criteria, explicitly or by reference, in the acquisition contract for the information system, system component, or information system service in accordance with applicable federal laws, Executive Orders, directives, policies, regulations, standards, guidelines, and organizational mission/business needs:

a. Security functional requirements;

b. Security strength requirements;

c. Security assurance requirements;

d. Security-related documentation requirements;

e. Requirements for protecting security-related documentation;

f. Description of the information system development environment and environment in which the system is intended to operate; and

g. Acceptance criteria.

Supplemental Guidance: Information system components are discrete, identifiable information technology assets (e.g., hardware, software, or firmware) that represent the building blocks of an information system. Information system components include commercial information technology products. Security functional requirements include security capabilities, security functions, and security mechanisms. Security strength requirements associated with such capabilities, functions, and mechanisms include degree of correctness, completeness, resistance to direct attack, and resistance to tampering or bypass. Security assurance requirements include: (i) development processes, procedures, practices, and methodologies; and (ii) evidence from development and assessment activities providing grounds for confidence that the required security functionality has been implemented and the required security strength has been achieved. Security documentation requirements address all phases of the system development life cycle.

Security functionality, assurance, and documentation requirements are expressed in terms of security controls and control enhancements that have been selected through the tailoring process. The security control tailoring process includes, for example, the specification of parameter values through the use of assignment and selection statements and the specification of platform dependencies and implementation information. Security documentation provides user and administrator guidance regarding the implementation and operation of security controls. The level of detail required in security documentation is based on the security category or classification level of the information system and the degree to which organizations depend on the stated security capability, functions, or mechanisms to meet overall risk response expectations (as defined in the organizational risk management strategy). Security requirements can also include organizationally mandated configuration settings specifying allowed functions, ports, protocols, and services. Acceptance criteria for information systems, information system components, and information system services are defined in the same manner as such criteria for any organizational acquisition or procurement. The Federal Acquisition Regulation (FAR) Section 7.103 contains information security requirements from FISMA. Related controls: CM-6, PL-2, PS-7, SA-3, SA-5, SA-8, SA-11, SA-12.

Control Enhancements:

(1) ACQUISITION PROCESS | FUNCTIONAL PROPERTIES OF SECURITY CONTROLS

The organization requires the developer of the information system, system component, or information system service to provide a description of the functional properties of the security controls to be employed.

Supplemental Guidance: Functional properties of security controls describe the functionality (i.e., security capability, functions, or mechanisms) visible at the interfaces of the controls and specifically exclude functionality and data structures internal to the operation of the controls. Related control: SA-5.

(2) ACQUISITION PROCESS | DESIGN / IMPLEMENTATION INFORMATION FOR SECURITY CONTROLS

The organization requires the developer of the information system, system component, or information system service to provide design and implementation information for the security controls to be employed that includes: [Selection (one or more): security-relevant external system interfaces; high-level design; low-level design; source code or hardware schematics; [Assignment: organization-defined design/implementation information]] at [Assignment: organization-defined level of detail].

Supplemental Guidance: Organizations may require different levels of detail in design and implementation documentation for security controls employed in organizational information systems, system components, or information system services based on mission/business requirements, requirements for trustworthiness/resiliency, and requirements for analysis and testing. Information systems can be partitioned into multiple subsystems. Each subsystem within the system can contain one or more modules. The high-level design for the system is expressed in terms of multiple subsystems and the interfaces between subsystems providing security-relevant functionality. The low-level design for the system is expressed in terms of modules with particular emphasis on software and firmware (but not excluding hardware) and the interfaces between modules providing security-relevant functionality. Source code and hardware schematics are typically referred to as the implementation representation of the information system. Related control: SA-5.

(3) ACQUISITION PROCESS | DEVELOPMENT METHODS / TECHNIQUES / PRACTICES

The organization requires the developer of the information system, system component, or information system service to demonstrate the use of a system development life cycle that includes [*Assignment: organization-defined state-of-the-practice system/security engineering methods, software development methods, testing/evaluation/validation techniques, and quality control processes*].

Supplemental Guidance: Following a well-defined system development life cycle that includes state-of-the-practice software development methods, systems/security engineering methods, quality control processes, and testing, evaluation, and validation techniques helps to reduce the number and severity of latent errors within information systems, system components, and information system services. Reducing the number/severity of such errors reduces the number of vulnerabilities in those systems, components, and services. Related control: SA-12.

(4) ACQUISITION PROCESS | ASSIGNMENT OF COMPONENTS TO SYSTEMS

[Withdrawn: Incorporated into CM-8 (9)].

(5) ACQUISITION PROCESS | SYSTEM / COMPONENT / SERVICE CONFIGURATIONS

The organization requires the developer of the information system, system component, or information system service to:

(a) Deliver the system, component, or service with [*Assignment: organization-defined security configurations*] implemented; and

(b) Use the configurations as the default for any subsequent system, component, or service reinstallation or upgrade.

Supplemental Guidance: Security configurations include, for example, the U.S. Government Configuration Baseline (USGCB) and any limitations on functions, ports, protocols, and services. Security characteristics include, for example, requiring that all default passwords have been changed. Related control: CM-8.

(6) ACQUISITION PROCESS | USE OF INFORMATION ASSURANCE PRODUCTS

The organization:

(a) Employs only government off-the-shelf (GOTS) or commercial off-the-shelf (COTS) information assurance (IA) and IA-enabled information technology products that compose an NSA-approved solution to protect classified information when the networks used to transmit the information are at a lower classification level than the information being transmitted; and

(b) Ensures that these products have been evaluated and/or validated by NSA or in accordance with NSA-approved procedures.

Supplemental Guidance: COTS IA or IA-enabled information technology products used to protect classified information by cryptographic means may be required to use NSA-approved key management. Related controls: SC-8, SC-12, SC-13.

(7) ACQUISITION PROCESS | NIAP-APPROVED PROTECTION PROFILES

The organization:

(a) Limits the use of commercially provided information assurance (IA) and IA-enabled information technology products to those products that have been successfully evaluated against a National Information Assurance partnership (NIAP)-approved Protection Profile for a specific technology type, if such a profile exists; and

(b) Requires, if no NIAP-approved Protection Profile exists for a specific technology type but a commercially provided information technology product relies on cryptographic functionality to enforce its security policy, that the cryptographic module is FIPS-validated.

Supplemental Guidance: Related controls: SC-12, SC-13.

(8) ACQUISITION PROCESS | CONTINUOUS MONITORING PLAN

The organization requires the developer of the information system, system component, or information system service to produce a plan for the continuous monitoring of security control effectiveness that contains [*Assignment: organization-defined level of detail*].

Supplemental Guidance: The objective of continuous monitoring plans is to determine if the complete set of planned, required, and deployed security controls within the information system, system component, or information system service continue to be effective over time based on the inevitable changes that occur. Developer continuous monitoring plans include a sufficient level of detail such that the information can be incorporated into the continuous monitoring strategies and programs implemented by organizations. Related control: CA-7.

(9) ACQUISITION PROCESS | FUNCTIONS / PORTS / PROTOCOLS / SERVICES IN USE

The organization requires the developer of the information system, system component, or information system service to identify early in the system development life cycle, the functions, ports, protocols, and services intended for organizational use.

Supplemental Guidance: The identification of functions, ports, protocols, and services early in the system development life cycle (e.g., during the initial requirements definition and design phases) allows organizations to influence the design of the information system, information system component, or information system service. This early involvement in the life cycle helps organizations to avoid or minimize the use of functions, ports, protocols, or services that pose unnecessarily high risks and understand the trade-offs involved in blocking specific ports, protocols, or services (or when requiring information system service providers to do so). Early identification of functions, ports, protocols, and services avoids costly retrofitting of security controls after the information system, system component, or information system service has been implemented. SA-9 describes requirements for external information system services with organizations identifying which functions, ports, protocols, and services are provided from external sources. Related controls: CM-7, SA-9.

(10) ACQUISITION PROCESS | USE OF APPROVED PIV PRODUCTS

The organization employs only information technology products on the FIPS 201-approved products list for Personal Identity Verification (PIV) capability implemented within organizational information systems.

Supplemental Guidance: Related controls: IA-2, IA-8.

References: HSPD-12; ISO/IEC 15408; FIPS Publications 140-2, 201; NIST Special Publications 800-23, 800-35, 800-36, 800-37, 800-64, 800-70, 800-137; Federal Acquisition Regulation; Web: http://www.niap-ccevs.org, http://fips201ep.cio.gov, http://www.acquisition.gov/far.

Priority and Baseline Allocation:

P1	LOW SA-4 (10)	MOD SA-4 (1) (2) (9) (10)	HIGH SA-4 (1) (2) (9) (10)

SA-5 INFORMATION SYSTEM DOCUMENTATION

Control: The organization:

a. Obtains administrator documentation for the information system, system component, or information system service that describes:

1. Secure configuration, installation, and operation of the system, component, or service;

2. Effective use and maintenance of security functions/mechanisms; and

3. Known vulnerabilities regarding configuration and use of administrative (i.e., privileged) functions;

b. Obtains user documentation for the information system, system component, or information system service that describes:

   1. User-accessible security functions/mechanisms and how to effectively use those security functions/mechanisms;
   2. Methods for user interaction, which enables individuals to use the system, component, or service in a more secure manner; and
   3. User responsibilities in maintaining the security of the system, component, or service;

c. Documents attempts to obtain information system, system component, or information system service documentation when such documentation is either unavailable or nonexistent and takes [Assignment: organization-defined actions] in response;

d. Protects documentation as required, in accordance with the risk management strategy; and

e. Distributes documentation to [Assignment: organization-defined personnel or roles].

Supplemental Guidance: This control helps organizational personnel understand the implementation and operation of security controls associated with information systems, system components, and information system services. Organizations consider establishing specific measures to determine the quality/completeness of the content provided. The inability to obtain needed documentation may occur, for example, due to the age of the information system/component or lack of support from developers and contractors. In those situations, organizations may need to recreate selected documentation if such documentation is essential to the effective implementation or operation of security controls. The level of protection provided for selected information system, component, or service documentation is commensurate with the security category or classification of the system. For example, documentation associated with a key DoD weapons system or command and control system would typically require a higher level of protection than a routine administrative system. Documentation that addresses information system vulnerabilities may also require an increased level of protection. Secure operation of the information system, includes, for example, initially starting the system and resuming secure system operation after any lapse in system operation. Related controls: CM-6, CM-8, PL-2, PL-4, PS-2, SA-3, SA-4.

Control Enhancements:

(1) INFORMATION SYSTEM DOCUMENTATION | FUNCTIONAL PROPERTIES OF SECURITY CONTROLS
[Withdrawn: Incorporated into SA-4 (1)].

(2) INFORMATION SYSTEM DOCUMENTATION | SECURITY-RELEVANT EXTERNAL SYSTEM INTERFACES
[Withdrawn: Incorporated into SA-4 (2)].

(3) INFORMATION SYSTEM DOCUMENTATION | HIGH-LEVEL DESIGN
[Withdrawn: Incorporated into SA-4 (2)].

(4) INFORMATION SYSTEM DOCUMENTATION | LOW-LEVEL DESIGN
[Withdrawn: Incorporated into SA-4 (2)].

(5) INFORMATION SYSTEM DOCUMENTATION | SOURCE CODE
[Withdrawn: Incorporated into SA-4 (2)].

References: None.

Priority and Baseline Allocation:

| P2 | LOW SA-5 | MOD SA-5 | HIGH SA-5 |

SA-6 SOFTWARE USAGE RESTRICTIONS

[Withdrawn: Incorporated into CM-10 and SI-7].

SA-7   USER-INSTALLED SOFTWARE

[Withdrawn: Incorporated into CM-11 and SI-7].

SA-8   SECURITY ENGINEERING PRINCIPLES

Control: The organization applies information system security engineering principles in the specification, design, development, implementation, and modification of the information system.

Supplemental Guidance: Organizations apply security engineering principles primarily to new development information systems or systems undergoing major upgrades. For legacy systems, organizations apply security engineering principles to system upgrades and modifications to the extent feasible, given the current state of hardware, software, and firmware within those systems. Security engineering principles include, for example: (i) developing layered protections; (ii) establishing sound security policy, architecture, and controls as the foundation for design; (iii) incorporating security requirements into the system development life cycle; (iv) delineating physical and logical security boundaries; (v) ensuring that system developers are trained on how to build secure software; (vi) tailoring security controls to meet organizational and operational needs; (vii) performing threat modeling to identify use cases, threat agents, attack vectors, and attack patterns as well as compensating controls and design patterns needed to mitigate risk; and (viii) reducing risk to acceptable levels, thus enabling informed risk management decisions. Related controls: PM-7, SA-3, SA-4, SA-17, SC-2, SC-3.

Control Enhancements: None.

References: NIST Special Publication 800-27.

Priority and Baseline Allocation:

| P1 | LOW   Not Selected | MOD   SA-8 | HIGH   SA-8 |

SA-9   EXTERNAL INFORMATION SYSTEM SERVICES

Control: The organization:

a. Requires that providers of external information system services comply with organizational information security requirements and employ [*Assignment: organization-defined security controls*] in accordance with applicable federal laws, Executive Orders, directives, policies, regulations, standards, and guidance;

b. Defines and documents government oversight and user roles and responsibilities with regard to external information system services; and

c. Employs [*Assignment: organization-defined processes, methods, and techniques*] to monitor security control compliance by external service providers on an ongoing basis.

Supplemental Guidance: External information system services are services that are implemented outside of the authorization boundaries of organizational information systems. This includes services that are used by, but not a part of, organizational information systems. FISMA and OMB policy require that organizations using external service providers that are processing, storing, or transmitting federal information or operating information systems on behalf of the federal government ensure that such providers meet the same security requirements that federal agencies are required to meet. Organizations establish relationships with external service providers in a variety of ways including, for example, through joint ventures, business partnerships, contracts, interagency agreements, lines of business arrangements, licensing agreements, and supply chain exchanges. The responsibility for managing risks from the use of external information system services remains with authorizing officials. For services external to organizations, a chain of trust requires that organizations establish and retain a level of confidence that each participating provider in the potentially complex consumer-provider relationship provides adequate protection for the services rendered. The extent and nature of this chain of trust varies based on the relationships between organizations and the external providers. Organizations document the basis for trust relationships so the relationships can be monitored over time. External information system services documentation includes government, service providers, end user security roles and responsibilities, and service-level agreements. Service-level agreements define expectations of performance for security controls, describe measurable outcomes, and identify remedies and response requirements for identified instances of noncompliance. Related controls: CA-3, IR-7, PS-7.

Control Enhancements:

(1) EXTERNAL INFORMATION SYSTEMS | RISK ASSESSMENTS / ORGANIZATIONAL APPROVALS

   The organization:

   (a) Conducts an organizational assessment of risk prior to the acquisition or outsourcing of dedicated information security services; and

   (b) Ensures that the acquisition or outsourcing of dedicated information security services is approved by [Assignment: organization-defined personnel or roles].

   Supplemental Guidance: Dedicated information security services include, for example, incident monitoring, analysis and response, operation of information security-related devices such as firewalls, or key management services. Related controls: CA-6, RA-3.

(2) EXTERNAL INFORMATION SYSTEMS | IDENTIFICATION OF FUNCTIONS / PORTS / PROTOCOLS / SERVICES

   The organization requires providers of [Assignment: organization-defined external information system services] to identify the functions, ports, protocols, and other services required for the use of such services.

   Supplemental Guidance: Information from external service providers regarding the specific functions, ports, protocols, and services used in the provision of such services can be particularly useful when the need arises to understand the trade-offs involved in restricting certain functions/services or blocking certain ports/protocols. Related control: CM-7.

(3) EXTERNAL INFORMATION SYSTEMS | ESTABLISH / MAINTAIN TRUST RELATIONSHIP WITH PROVIDERS

   The organization establishes, documents, and maintains trust relationships with external service providers based on [Assignment: organization-defined security requirements, properties, factors, or conditions defining acceptable trust relationships].

   Supplemental Guidance: The degree of confidence that the risk from using external services is at an acceptable level depends on the trust that organizations place in the external providers, individually or in combination. Trust relationships can help organization to gain increased levels of confidence that participating service providers are providing adequate protection for the services rendered. Such relationships can be complicated due to the number of potential entities participating in the consumer-provider interactions, subordinate relationships and levels of trust, and the types of interactions between the parties. In some cases, the degree of trust is based on the amount of direct control organizations are able to exert on external service providers with regard to employment of security controls necessary for the protection of the service/information and the evidence brought forth as to the effectiveness of those controls. The level of control is typically established by the terms and conditions of the contracts or service-level agreements and can range from extensive control (e.g., negotiating contracts or agreements that specify security requirements for the providers) to very limited control (e.g., using contracts or service-level agreements to obtain commodity services such as commercial telecommunications services). In other cases, levels of trust are based on factors that convince organizations that required security controls have been employed and that determinations of control effectiveness exist. For example, separately authorized external information system services provided to organizations through well-established business relationships may provide degrees of trust in such services within the tolerable risk range of the organizations using the services. External service providers may also outsource selected services to other external entities, making the trust relationship more difficult and complicated to manage. Depending on the nature of the services, organizations may find it very difficult to place significant trust in external providers. This is not due to any inherent untrustworthiness on the part of providers, but to the intrinsic level of risk in the services.

(4) EXTERNAL INFORMATION SYSTEMS | CONSISTENT INTERESTS OF CONSUMERS AND PROVIDERS

The organization employs [*Assignment: organization-defined security safeguards*] to ensure that the interests of [*Assignment: organization-defined external service providers*] are consistent with and reflect organizational interests.

Supplemental Guidance: As organizations increasingly use external service providers, the possibility exists that the interests of the service providers may diverge from organizational interests. In such situations, simply having the correct technical, procedural, or operational safeguards in place may not be sufficient if the service providers that implement and control those safeguards are not operating in a manner consistent with the interests of the consuming organizations. Possible actions that organizations might take to address such concerns include, for example, requiring background checks for selected service provider personnel, examining ownership records, employing only trustworthy service providers (i.e., providers with which organizations have had positive experiences), and conducting periodic/unscheduled visits to service provider facilities.

(5) EXTERNAL INFORMATION SYSTEMS | PROCESSING, STORAGE, AND SERVICE LOCATION

The organization restricts the location of [*Selection (one or more): information processing; information/data; information system services*] to [*Assignment: organization-defined locations*] based on [*Assignment: organization-defined requirements or conditions*].

Supplemental Guidance: The location of information processing, information/data storage, or information system services that are critical to organizations can have a direct impact on the ability of those organizations to successfully execute their missions/business functions. This situation exists when external providers control the location of processing, storage or services. The criteria external providers use for the selection of processing, storage, or service locations may be different from organizational criteria. For example, organizations may want to ensure that data/information storage locations are restricted to certain locations to facilitate incident response activities (e.g., forensic analyses, after-the-fact investigations) in case of information security breaches/compromises. Such incident response activities may be adversely affected by the governing laws or protocols in the locations where processing and storage occur and/or the locations from which information system services emanate.

References: NIST Special Publication 800-35.

Priority and Baseline Allocation:

P1	LOW SA-9	MOD SA-9 (2)	HIGH SA-9 (2)

SA-10 DEVELOPER CONFIGURATION MANAGEMENT

Control: The organization requires the developer of the information system, system component, or information system service to:

a. Perform configuration management during system, component, or service [*Selection (one or more): design; development; implementation; operation*];

b. Document, manage, and control the integrity of changes to [*Assignment: organization-defined configuration items under configuration management*];

c. Implement only organization-approved changes to the system, component, or service;

d. Document approved changes to the system, component, or service and the potential security impacts of such changes; and

e. Track security flaws and flaw resolution within the system, component, or service and report findings to [*Assignment: organization-defined personnel*].

Supplemental Guidance: This control also applies to organizations conducting internal information systems development and integration. Organizations consider the quality and completeness of the configuration management activities conducted by developers as evidence of applying effective security safeguards. Safeguards include, for example, protecting from unauthorized modification or destruction, the master copies of all material used to generate security-relevant portions of the system hardware, software, and firmware. Maintaining the integrity of changes to the information system, information system component, or information system service requires configuration control throughout the system development life cycle to track authorized changes and prevent unauthorized changes. Configuration items that are placed under configuration management (if existence/use is required by other security controls) include: the formal model; the functional, high-level, and low-level design specifications; other design data; implementation documentation; source code and hardware schematics; the running version of the object code; tools for comparing new versions of security-relevant hardware descriptions and software/firmware source code with previous versions; and test fixtures and documentation. Depending on the mission/business needs of organizations and the nature of the contractual relationships in place, developers may provide configuration management support during the operations and maintenance phases of the life cycle. Related controls: CM-3, CM-4, CM-9, SA-12, SI-2.

Control Enhancements:

(1) *DEVELOPER CONFIGURATION MANAGEMENT | SOFTWARE / FIRMWARE INTEGRITY VERIFICATION*

The organization requires the developer of the information system, system component, or information system service to enable integrity verification of software and firmware components.

Supplemental Guidance: This control enhancement allows organizations to detect unauthorized changes to software and firmware components through the use of tools, techniques, and/or mechanisms provided by developers. Integrity checking mechanisms can also address counterfeiting of software and firmware components. Organizations verify the integrity of software and firmware components, for example, through secure one-way hashes provided by developers. Delivered software and firmware components also include any updates to such components. Related control: SI-7.

(2) *DEVELOPER CONFIGURATION MANAGEMENT | ALTERNATIVE CONFIGURATION MANAGEMENT PROCESSES*

The organization provides an alternate configuration management process using organizational personnel in the absence of a dedicated developer configuration management team.

Supplemental Guidance: Alternate configuration management processes may be required, for example, when organizations use commercial off-the-shelf (COTS) information technology products. Alternate configuration management processes include organizational personnel that: (i) are responsible for reviewing/approving proposed changes to information systems, system components, and information system services; and (ii) conduct security impact analyses prior to the implementation of any changes to systems, components, or services (e.g., a configuration control board that considers security impacts of changes during development and includes representatives of both the organization and the developer, when applicable).

(3) *DEVELOPER CONFIGURATION MANAGEMENT | HARDWARE INTEGRITY VERIFICATION*

The organization requires the developer of the information system, system component, or information system service to enable integrity verification of hardware components.

Supplemental Guidance: This control enhancement allows organizations to detect unauthorized changes to hardware components through the use of tools, techniques, and/or mechanisms provided by developers. Organizations verify the integrity of hardware components, for example, with hard-to-copy labels and verifiable serial numbers provided by developers, and by requiring the implementation of anti-tamper technologies. Delivered hardware components also include updates to such components. Related control: SI-7.

(4) *DEVELOPER CONFIGURATION MANAGEMENT | TRUSTED GENERATION*

The organization requires the developer of the information system, system component, or information system service to employ tools for comparing newly generated versions of security-relevant hardware descriptions and software/firmware source and object code with previous versions.

Supplemental Guidance: This control enhancement addresses changes to hardware, software, and firmware components between versions during development. In contrast, SA-10 (1) and SA-10 (3) allow organizations to detect unauthorized changes to hardware, software, and firmware components through the use of tools, techniques, and/or mechanisms provided by developers.

(5) DEVELOPER CONFIGURATION MANAGEMENT | MAPPING INTEGRITY FOR VERSION CONTROL

The organization requires the developer of the information system, system component, or information system service to maintain the integrity of the mapping between the master build data (hardware drawings and software/firmware code) describing the current version of security-relevant hardware, software, and firmware and the on-site master copy of the data for the current version.

Supplemental Guidance: This control enhancement addresses changes to hardware, software, and firmware components during initial development and during system life cycle updates. Maintaining the integrity between the master copies of security-relevant hardware, software, and firmware (including designs and source code) and the equivalent data in master copies on-site in operational environments is essential to ensure the availability of organizational information systems supporting critical missions and/or business functions.

(6) DEVELOPER CONFIGURATION MANAGEMENT | TRUSTED DISTRIBUTION

The organization requires the developer of the information system, system component, or information system service to execute procedures for ensuring that security-relevant hardware, software, and firmware updates distributed to the organization are exactly as specified by the master copies.

Supplemental Guidance: The trusted distribution of security-relevant hardware, software, and firmware updates helps to ensure that such updates are faithful representations of the master copies maintained by the developer and have not been tampered with during distribution.

References: NIST Special Publication 800-128.

Priority and Baseline Allocation:

P1	LOW Not Selected	MOD SA-10	HIGH SA-10

SA-11 DEVELOPER SECURITY TESTING AND EVALUATION

Control: The organization requires the developer of the information system, system component, or information system service to:

a. Create and implement a security assessment plan;

b. Perform [Selection (one or more): unit; integration; system; regression] testing/evaluation at [Assignment: organization-defined depth and coverage];

c. Produce evidence of the execution of the security assessment plan and the results of the security testing/evaluation;

d. Implement a verifiable flaw remediation process; and

e. Correct flaws identified during security testing/evaluation.

Supplemental Guidance: Developmental security testing/evaluation occurs at all post-design phases of the system development life cycle. Such testing/evaluation confirms that the required security controls are implemented correctly, operating as intended, enforcing the desired security policy, and meeting established security requirements. Security properties of information systems may be affected by the interconnection of system components or changes to those components. These interconnections or changes (e.g., upgrading or replacing applications and operating systems) may adversely affect previously implemented security controls. This control provides additional types of security testing/evaluation that developers can conduct to reduce or eliminate potential flaws. Testing custom software applications may require approaches such as static analysis, dynamic analysis, binary analysis, or a hybrid of the three approaches. Developers can employ these analysis approaches in a variety of tools (e.g., web-based application scanners, static analysis tools, binary analyzers) and in source code reviews. Security assessment plans provide the specific activities that developers plan to carry out including the types of analyses, testing, evaluation, and reviews of software and firmware components, the degree of rigor to be applied, and the types of artifacts produced during those processes. The *depth* of security testing/evaluation refers to the rigor and level of detail associated with the assessment process (e.g., black box, gray box, or white box testing). The *coverage* of security testing/evaluation refers to the scope (i.e., number and type) of the artifacts included in the assessment process. Contracts specify the acceptance criteria for security assessment plans, flaw remediation processes, and the evidence that the plans/processes have been diligently applied. Methods for reviewing and protecting assessment plans, evidence, and documentation are commensurate with the security category or classification level of the information system. Contracts may specify documentation protection requirements. Related controls: CA-2, CM-4, SA-3, SA-4, SA-5, SI-2.

Control Enhancements:

(1) DEVELOPER SECURITY TESTING AND EVALUATION | STATIC CODE ANALYSIS

The organization requires the developer of the information system, system component, or information system service to employ static code analysis tools to identify common flaws and document the results of the analysis.

Supplemental Guidance: Static code analysis provides a technology and methodology for security reviews. Such analysis can be used to identify security vulnerabilities and enforce security coding practices. Static code analysis is most effective when used early in the development process, when each code change can be automatically scanned for potential weaknesses. Static analysis can provide clear remediation guidance along with defects to enable developers to fix such defects. Evidence of correct implementation of static analysis can include, for example, aggregate defect density for critical defect types, evidence that defects were inspected by developers or security professionals, and evidence that defects were fixed. An excessively high density of ignored findings (commonly referred to as ignored or false positives) indicates a potential problem with the analysis process or tool. In such cases, organizations weigh the validity of the evidence against evidence from other sources.

(2) DEVELOPER SECURITY TESTING AND EVALUATION | THREAT AND VULNERABILITY ANALYSES

The organization requires the developer of the information system, system component, or information system service to perform threat and vulnerability analyses and subsequent testing/evaluation of the as-built system, component, or service.

Supplemental Guidance: Applications may deviate significantly from the functional and design specifications created during the requirements and design phases of the system development life cycle. Therefore, threat and vulnerability analyses of information systems, system components, and information system services prior to delivery are critical to the effective operation of those systems, components, and services. Threat and vulnerability analyses at this phase of the life cycle help to ensure that design or implementation changes have been accounted for, and that any new vulnerabilities created as a result of those changes have been reviewed and mitigated. Related controls: PM-15, RA-5.

(3) DEVELOPER SECURITY TESTING AND EVALUATION | INDEPENDENT VERIFICATION OF ASSESSMENT PLANS / EVIDENCE

The organization:

(a) **Requires an independent agent satisfying [*Assignment: organization-defined independence criteria*] to verify the correct implementation of the developer security assessment plan and the evidence produced during security testing/evaluation; and**

(b) **Ensures that the independent agent is either provided with sufficient information to complete the verification process or granted the authority to obtain such information.**

Supplemental Guidance: Independent agents have the necessary qualifications (i.e., expertise, skills, training, and experience) to verify the correct implementation of developer security assessment plans. Related controls: AT-3, CA-7, RA-5, SA-12.

(4) DEVELOPER SECURITY TESTING AND EVALUATION | MANUAL CODE REVIEWS

The organization requires the developer of the information system, system component, or information system service to perform a manual code review of [Assignment: *organization-defined specific code*] using [*Assignment: organization-defined processes, procedures, and/or techniques*].

Supplemental Guidance: Manual code reviews are usually reserved for the critical software and firmware components of information systems. Such code reviews are uniquely effective at identifying weaknesses that require knowledge of the application's requirements or context which are generally unavailable to more automated analytic tools and techniques such as static or dynamic analysis. Components benefiting from manual review include for example, verifying access control matrices against application controls and reviewing more detailed aspects of cryptographic implementations and controls.

(5) DEVELOPER SECURITY TESTING AND EVALUATION | PENETRATION TESTING

The organization requires the developer of the information system, system component, or information system service to perform penetration testing at [*Assignment: organization-defined breadth/depth*] and with [*Assignment: organization-defined constraints*].

Supplemental Guidance: Penetration testing is an assessment methodology in which assessors, using all available information technology product and/or information system documentation (e.g., product/system design specifications, source code, and administrator/operator manuals) and working under specific constraints, attempt to circumvent implemented security features of information technology products and information systems. Penetration testing can include, for example, white, gray, or black box testing with analyses performed by skilled security professionals simulating adversary actions. The objective of penetration testing is to uncover potential vulnerabilities in information technology products and information systems resulting from implementation errors, configuration faults, or other operational deployment weaknesses or deficiencies. Penetration tests can be performed in conjunction with automated and manual code reviews to provide greater levels of analysis than would ordinarily be possible.

(6) DEVELOPER SECURITY TESTING AND EVALUATION | ATTACK SURFACE REVIEWS

The organization requires the developer of the information system, system component, or information system service to perform attack surface reviews.

Supplemental Guidance: Attack surfaces of information systems are exposed areas that make those systems more vulnerable to cyber attacks. This includes any accessible areas where weaknesses or deficiencies in information systems (including the hardware, software, and firmware components) provide opportunities for adversaries to exploit vulnerabilities. Attack surface reviews ensure that developers: (i) analyze both design and implementation changes to information systems; and (ii) mitigate attack vectors generated as a result of the changes. Correction of identified flaws includes, for example, deprecation of unsafe functions.

(7) DEVELOPER SECURITY TESTING AND EVALUATION | VERIFY SCOPE OF TESTING / EVALUATION

The organization requires the developer of the information system, system component, or information system service to verify that the scope of security testing/evaluation provides complete coverage of required security controls at [*Assignment: organization-defined depth of testing/evaluation*].

Supplemental Guidance: Verifying that security testing/evaluation provides complete coverage of required security controls can be accomplished by a variety of analytic techniques ranging from informal to formal. Each of these techniques provides an increasing level of assurance corresponding to the degree of formality of the analysis. Rigorously demonstrating security control coverage at the highest levels of assurance can be provided by the use of formal modeling and analysis techniques including correlation between control implementation and corresponding test cases.

(8) DEVELOPER SECURITY TESTING AND EVALUATION | DYNAMIC CODE ANALYSIS

The organization requires the developer of the information system, system component, or information system service to employ dynamic code analysis tools to identify common flaws and document the results of the analysis.

Supplemental Guidance: Dynamic code analysis provides run-time verification of software programs, using tools capable of monitoring programs for memory corruption, user privilege issues, and other potential security problems. Dynamic code analysis employs run-time tools to help to ensure that security functionality performs in the manner in which it was designed. A specialized type of dynamic analysis, known as fuzz testing, induces program failures by deliberately introducing malformed or random data into software programs. Fuzz testing strategies derive from the intended use of applications and the functional and design specifications for the applications. To understand the scope of dynamic code analysis and hence the assurance provided, organizations may also consider conducting code coverage analysis (checking the degree to which the code has been tested using metrics such as percent of subroutines tested or percent of program statements called during execution of the test suite) and/or concordance analysis (checking for words that are out of place in software code such as non-English language words or derogatory terms).

References: ISO/IEC 15408; NIST Special Publication 800-53A;
Web: http://nvd.nist.gov, http://cwe.mitre.org, http://cve.mitre.org, http://capec.mitre.org.

Priority and Baseline Allocation:

P1	LOW Not Selected	MOD SA-11	HIGH SA-11

SA-12 SUPPLY CHAIN PROTECTION

Control: The organization protects against supply chain threats to the information system, system component, or information system service by employing [*Assignment: organization-defined security safeguards*] as part of a comprehensive, defense-in-breadth information security strategy.

Supplemental Guidance: Information systems (including system components that compose those systems) need to be protected throughout the system development life cycle (i.e., during design, development, manufacturing, packaging, assembly, distribution, system integration, operations, maintenance, and retirement). Protection of organizational information systems is accomplished through threat awareness, by the identification, management, and reduction of vulnerabilities at each phase of the life cycle and the use of complementary, mutually reinforcing strategies to respond to risk. Organizations consider implementing a standardized process to address supply chain risk with respect to information systems and system components, and to educate the acquisition workforce on threats, risk, and required security controls. Organizations use the acquisition/procurement processes to require supply chain entities to implement necessary security safeguards to: (i) reduce the likelihood of unauthorized modifications at each stage in the supply chain; and (ii) protect information systems and information system components, prior to taking delivery of such systems/components. This control also applies to information system services. Security safeguards include, for example: (i) security controls for development systems, development facilities, and external connections to development systems; (ii) vetting development personnel; and (iii) use of tamper-evident packaging during shipping/warehousing. Methods for reviewing and protecting development plans, evidence, and documentation are commensurate with the security category or classification level of the information system. Contracts may specify documentation protection requirements. Related controls: AT-3, CM-8, IR-4, PE-16, PL-8, SA-3, SA-4, SA-8, SA-10, SA-14, SA-15, SA-18, SA-19, SC-29, SC-30, SC-38, SI-7.

Control Enhancements:

(1) *SUPPLY CHAIN PROTECTION | ACQUISITION STRATEGIES / TOOLS / METHODS*

The organization employs [*Assignment: organization-defined tailored acquisition strategies, contract tools, and procurement methods*] for the purchase of the information system, system component, or information system service from suppliers.

Supplemental Guidance: The use of acquisition and procurement processes by organizations early in the system development life cycle provides an important vehicle to protect the supply chain. Organizations use available all-source intelligence analysis to inform the tailoring of acquisition strategies, tools, and methods. There are a number of different tools and techniques available (e.g., obscuring the end use of an information system or system component, using blind or filtered buys). Organizations also consider creating incentives for suppliers who: (i) implement required security safeguards; (ii) promote transparency into their organizational processes and security practices; (iii) provide additional vetting of the processes and security practices of subordinate suppliers, critical information system components, and services; (iv) restrict purchases from specific suppliers or countries; and (v) provide contract language regarding the prohibition of tainted or counterfeit components. In addition, organizations consider minimizing the time between purchase decisions and required delivery to limit opportunities for adversaries to corrupt information system components or products. Finally, organizations can use trusted/controlled distribution, delivery, and warehousing options to reduce supply chain risk (e.g., requiring tamper-evident packaging of information system components during shipping and warehousing). Related control: SA-19.

(2) SUPPLY CHAIN PROTECTION | SUPPLIER REVIEWS

The organization conducts a supplier review prior to entering into a contractual agreement to acquire the information system, system component, or information system service.

Supplemental Guidance: Supplier reviews include, for example: (i) analysis of supplier processes used to design, develop, test, implement, verify, deliver, and support information systems, system components, and information system services; and (ii) assessment of supplier training and experience in developing systems, components, or services with the required security capability. These reviews provide organizations with increased levels of visibility into supplier activities during the system development life cycle to promote more effective supply chain risk management. Supplier reviews can also help to determine whether primary suppliers have security safeguards in place and a practice for vetting subordinate suppliers, for example, second- and third-tier suppliers, and any subcontractors.

(3) SUPPLY CHAIN PROTECTION | TRUSTED SHIPPING AND WAREHOUSING

[Withdrawn: Incorporated into SA-12 (1)].

(4) SUPPLY CHAIN PROTECTION | DIVERSITY OF SUPPLIERS

[Withdrawn: Incorporated into SA-12 (13)].

(5) SUPPLY CHAIN PROTECTION | LIMITATION OF HARM

The organization employs [*Assignment: organization-defined security safeguards*] to limit harm from potential adversaries identifying and targeting the organizational supply chain.

Supplemental Guidance: Supply chain risk is part of the advanced persistent threat (APT). Security safeguards and countermeasures to reduce the probability of adversaries successfully identifying and targeting the supply chain include, for example: (i) avoiding the purchase of custom configurations to reduce the risk of acquiring information systems, components, or products that have been corrupted via supply chain actions targeted at specific organizations; (ii) employing a diverse set of suppliers to limit the potential harm from any given supplier in the supply chain; (iii) employing approved vendor lists with standing reputations in industry, and (iv) using procurement carve outs (i.e., exclusions to commitments or obligations).

(6) SUPPLY CHAIN PROTECTION | MINIMIZING PROCUREMENT TIME

[Withdrawn: Incorporated into SA-12 (1)].

(7) SUPPLY CHAIN PROTECTION | ASSESSMENTS PRIOR TO SELECTION / ACCEPTANCE / UPDATE

The organization conducts an assessment of the information system, system component, or information system service prior to selection, acceptance, or update.

Supplemental Guidance: Assessments include, for example, testing, evaluations, reviews, and analyses. Independent, third-party entities or organizational personnel conduct assessments of systems, components, products, tools, and services. Organizations conduct assessments to uncover unintentional vulnerabilities and intentional vulnerabilities including, for example, malicious code, malicious processes, defective software, and counterfeits. Assessments can include, for example, static analyses, dynamic analyses, simulations, white, gray, and black box testing, fuzz testing, penetration testing, and ensuring that components or services are genuine (e.g., using tags, cryptographic hash verifications, or digital signatures). Evidence generated during security assessments is documented for follow-on actions carried out by organizations. Related controls: CA-2, SA-11.

(8) SUPPLY CHAIN PROTECTION | USE OF ALL-SOURCE INTELLIGENCE

The organization uses all-source intelligence analysis of suppliers and potential suppliers of the information system, system component, or information system service.

Supplemental Guidance: All-source intelligence analysis is employed by organizations to inform engineering, acquisition, and risk management decisions. All-source intelligence consists of intelligence products and/or organizations and activities that incorporate all sources of information, most frequently including human intelligence, imagery intelligence, measurement and signature intelligence, signals intelligence, and open source data in the production of finished intelligence. Where available, such information is used to analyze the risk of both intentional and unintentional vulnerabilities from development, manufacturing, and delivery processes, people, and the environment. This review is performed on suppliers at multiple tiers in the supply chain sufficient to manage risks. Related control: SA-15.

(9) SUPPLY CHAIN PROTECTION | OPERATIONS SECURITY

The organization employs [*Assignment: organization-defined Operations Security (OPSEC) safeguards*] in accordance with classification guides to protect supply chain-related information for the information system, system component, or information system service.

Supplemental Guidance: Supply chain information includes, for example: user identities; uses for information systems, information system components, and information system services; supplier identities; supplier processes; security requirements; design specifications; testing and evaluation results; and system/component configurations. This control enhancement expands the scope of OPSEC to include suppliers and potential suppliers. OPSEC is a process of identifying critical information and subsequently analyzing friendly actions attendant to operations and other activities to: (i) identify those actions that can be observed by potential adversaries; (ii) determine indicators that adversaries might obtain that could be interpreted or pieced together to derive critical information in sufficient time to cause harm to organizations; (iii) implement safeguards or countermeasures to eliminate or reduce to an acceptable level, exploitable vulnerabilities; and (iv) consider how aggregated information may compromise the confidentiality of users or uses of the supply chain. OPSEC may require organizations to withhold critical mission/business information from suppliers and may include the use of intermediaries to hide the end use, or users, of information systems, system components, or information system services.

(10) SUPPLY CHAIN PROTECTION | VALIDATE AS GENUINE AND NOT ALTERED

The organization employs [*Assignment: organization-defined security safeguards*] to validate that the information system or system component received is genuine and has not been altered.

Supplemental Guidance: For some information system components, especially hardware, there are technical means to help determine if the components are genuine or have been altered. Security safeguards used to validate the authenticity of information systems and information system components include, for example, optical/nanotechnology tagging and side-channel analysis. For hardware, detailed bill of material information can highlight the elements with embedded logic complete with component and production location.

(11) SUPPLY CHAIN PROTECTION | PENETRATION TESTING / ANALYSIS OF ELEMENTS, PROCESSES, AND ACTORS

The organization employs [*Selection (one or more): organizational analysis, independent third-party analysis, organizational penetration testing, independent third-party penetration testing*] of [*Assignment: organization-defined supply chain elements, processes, and actors*] associated with the *information system, system component, or information system service*.

Supplemental Guidance: This control enhancement addresses analysis and/or testing of the supply chain, not just delivered items. Supply chain elements are information technology products or product components that contain programmable logic and that are critically important to information system functions. Supply chain processes include, for example: (i) hardware, software, and firmware development processes; (ii) shipping/handling procedures; (iii) personnel and physical security programs; (iv) configuration management tools/measures to maintain provenance; or (v) any other programs, processes, or procedures associated with the production/distribution of supply chain elements. Supply chain actors are individuals with specific roles and responsibilities in the supply chain. The evidence generated during analyses and testing of supply chain elements, processes, and actors is documented and used to inform organizational risk management activities and decisions. Related control: RA-5.

(12) SUPPLY CHAIN PROTECTION | INTER-ORGANIZATIONAL AGREEMENTS

The organization establishes inter-organizational agreements and procedures with entities involved in the supply chain for the information system, system component, or information system service.

Supplemental Guidance: The establishment of inter-organizational agreements and procedures provides for notification of supply chain compromises. Early notification of supply chain compromises that can potentially adversely affect or have adversely affected organizational information systems, including critical system components, is essential for organizations to provide appropriate responses to such incidents.

(13) SUPPLY CHAIN PROTECTION | CRITICAL INFORMATION SYSTEM COMPONENTS

The organization employs [Assignment: organization-defined security safeguards] to ensure an adequate supply of [Assignment: organization-defined critical information system components].

Supplemental Guidance: Adversaries can attempt to impede organizational operations by disrupting the supply of critical information system components or corrupting supplier operations. Safeguards to ensure adequate supplies of critical information system components include, for example: (i) the use of multiple suppliers throughout the supply chain for the identified critical components; and (ii) stockpiling of spare components to ensure operation during mission-critical times.

(14) SUPPLY CHAIN PROTECTION | IDENTITY AND TRACEABILITY

The organization establishes and retains unique identification of [Assignment: organization-defined supply chain elements, processes, and actors] for the information system, system component, or information system service.

Supplemental Guidance: Knowing who and what is in the supply chains of organizations is critical to gaining visibility into what is happening within such supply chains, as well as monitoring and identifying high-risk events and activities. Without reasonable visibility and traceability into supply chains (i.e., elements, processes, and actors), it is very difficult for organizations to understand and therefore manage risk, and to reduce the likelihood of adverse events. Uniquely identifying acquirer and integrator roles, organizations, personnel, mission and element processes, testing and evaluation procedures, delivery mechanisms, support mechanisms, communications/delivery paths, and disposal/final disposition activities as well as the components and tools used, establishes a foundational identity structure for assessment of supply chain activities. For example, labeling (using serial numbers) and tagging (using radio-frequency identification [RFID] tags) individual supply chain elements including software packages, modules, and hardware devices, and processes associated with those elements can be used for this purpose. Identification methods are sufficient to support the provenance in the event of a supply chain issue or adverse supply chain event.

(15) SUPPLY CHAIN PROTECTION | PROCESSES TO ADDRESS WEAKNESSES OR DEFICIENCIES

The organization establishes a process to address weaknesses or deficiencies in supply chain elements identified during independent or organizational assessments of such elements.

Supplemental Guidance: Evidence generated during independent or organizational assessments of supply chain elements (e.g., penetration testing, audits, verification/validation activities) is documented and used in follow-on processes implemented by organizations to respond to the risks related to the identified weaknesses and deficiencies. Supply chain elements include, for example, supplier development processes and supplier distribution systems.

References: NIST Special Publication 800-161; NIST Interagency Report 7622.

Priority and Baseline Allocation:

| P1 | LOW Not Selected | MOD Not Selected | HIGH SA-12 |

SA-13 TRUSTWORTHINESS

Control: The organization:

a. Describes the trustworthiness required in the [*Assignment: organization-defined information system, information system component, or information system service*] supporting its critical missions/business functions; and

b. Implements [*Assignment: organization-defined assurance overlay*] to achieve such trustworthiness.

Supplemental Guidance: This control helps organizations to make explicit trustworthiness decisions when designing, developing, and implementing information systems that are needed to conduct critical organizational missions/business functions. Trustworthiness is a characteristic/property of an information system that expresses the degree to which the system can be expected to preserve the confidentiality, integrity, and availability of the information it processes, stores, or transmits. Trustworthy information systems are systems that are capable of being trusted to operate within defined levels of *risk* despite the environmental disruptions, human errors, and purposeful attacks that are expected to occur in the specified environments of operation. Trustworthy systems are important to mission/business success. Two factors affecting the trustworthiness of information systems include: (i) security functionality (i.e., the security features, functions, and/or mechanisms employed within the system and its environment of operation); and (ii) security assurance (i.e., the grounds for confidence that the security functionality is effective in its application). Developers, implementers, operators, and maintainers of organizational information systems can increase the level of assurance (and trustworthiness), for example, by employing well-defined security policy models, structured and rigorous hardware, software, and firmware development techniques, sound system/security engineering principles, and secure configuration settings (defined by a set of assurance-related security controls in Appendix E).

Assurance is also based on the assessment of evidence produced during the system development life cycle. Critical missions/business functions are supported by high-impact systems and the associated assurance requirements for such systems. The additional assurance controls in Table E-4 in Appendix E (designated as optional) can be used to develop and implement high-assurance solutions for specific information systems and system components using the concept of overlays described in Appendix I. Organizations select assurance overlays that have been developed, validated, and approved for community adoption (e.g., cross-organization, governmentwide), limiting the development of such overlays on an organization-by-organization basis. Organizations can conduct criticality analyses as described in SA-14, to determine the information systems, system components, or information system services that require high-assurance solutions. Trustworthiness requirements and assurance overlays can be described in the security plans for organizational information systems. Related controls: RA-2, SA-4, SA-8, SA-14, SC-3.

Control Enhancements: None.

References: FIPS Publications 199, 200; NIST Special Publications 800-53, 800-53A, 800-60, 800-64.

Priority and Baseline Allocation:

P0	LOW Not Selected	MOD Not Selected	HIGH Not Selected

SA-14 CRITICALITY ANALYSIS

Control: The organization identifies critical information system components and functions by performing a criticality analysis for [*Assignment: organization-defined information systems, information system components, or information system services*] at [*Assignment: organization-defined decision points in the system development life cycle*].

Supplemental Guidance: Criticality analysis is a key tenet of supply chain risk management and informs the prioritization of supply chain protection activities such as attack surface reduction, use of all-source intelligence, and tailored acquisition strategies. Information system engineers can conduct an end-to-end functional decomposition of an information system to identify mission-critical functions and components. The functional decomposition includes the identification of core organizational missions supported by the system, decomposition into the specific functions to perform those missions, and traceability to the hardware, software, and firmware components that implement those functions, including when the functions are shared by many components within and beyond the information system boundary. Information system components that allow for unmediated access to critical components or functions are considered critical due to the inherent vulnerabilities such components create. Criticality is assessed in terms of the impact of the function or component failure on the ability of the component to complete the organizational missions supported by the information system. A criticality analysis is performed whenever an architecture or design is being developed or modified, including upgrades. Related controls: CP-2, PL-2, PL-8, PM-1, SA-8, SA-12, SA-13, SA-15, SA-20.

Control Enhancements: None.

(1) CRITICALITY ANALYSIS | CRITICAL COMPONENTS WITH NO VIABLE ALTERNATIVE SOURCING
    [Withdrawn: Incorporated into SA-20].

References: None.

Priority and Baseline Allocation:

P0	LOW Not Selected	MOD Not Selected	HIGH Not Selected

SA-15 DEVELOPMENT PROCESS, STANDARDS, AND TOOLS

Control: The organization:

a. Requires the developer of the information system, system component, or information system service to follow a documented development process that:

   1. Explicitly addresses security requirements;

   2. Identifies the standards and tools used in the development process;

   3. Documents the specific tool options and tool configurations used in the development process; and

   4. Documents, manages, and ensures the integrity of changes to the process and/or tools used in development; and

b. Reviews the development process, standards, tools, and tool options/configurations [Assignment: organization-defined frequency] to determine if the process, standards, tools, and tool options/configurations selected and employed can satisfy [Assignment: organization-defined security requirements].

Supplemental Guidance: Development tools include, for example, programming languages and computer-aided design (CAD) systems. Reviews of development processes can include, for example, the use of maturity models to determine the potential effectiveness of such processes. Maintaining the integrity of changes to tools and processes enables accurate supply chain risk assessment and mitigation, and requires robust configuration control throughout the life cycle (including design, development, transport, delivery, integration, and maintenance) to track authorized changes and prevent unauthorized changes. Related controls: SA-3, SA-8.

Control Enhancements:

(1) DEVELOPMENT PROCESS, STANDARDS, AND TOOLS | QUALITY METRICS

The organization requires the developer of the information system, system component, or information system service to:

(a) Define quality metrics at the beginning of the development process; and

(b) Provide evidence of meeting the quality metrics [*Selection (one or more):* [*Assignment: organization-defined frequency*]; [*Assignment: organization-defined program review milestones*]; *upon delivery*].

Supplemental Guidance: Organizations use quality metrics to establish minimum acceptable levels of information system quality. Metrics may include quality gates which are collections of completion criteria or sufficiency standards representing the satisfactory execution of particular phases of the system development project. A quality gate, for example, may require the elimination of all compiler warnings or an explicit determination that the warnings have no impact on the effectiveness of required security capabilities. During the execution phases of development projects, quality gates provide clear, unambiguous indications of progress. Other metrics apply to the entire development project. These metrics can include defining the severity thresholds of vulnerabilities, for example, requiring no known vulnerabilities in the delivered information system with a Common Vulnerability Scoring System (CVSS) severity of Medium or High.

(2) DEVELOPMENT PROCESS, STANDARDS, AND TOOLS | SECURITY TRACKING TOOLS

The organization requires the developer of the information system, system component, or information system service to select and employ a security tracking tool for use during the development process.

Supplemental Guidance: Information system development teams select and deploy security tracking tools, including, for example, vulnerability/work item tracking systems that facilitate assignment, sorting, filtering, and tracking of completed work items or tasks associated with system development processes.

(3) DEVELOPMENT PROCESS, STANDARDS, AND TOOLS | CRITICALITY ANALYSIS

The organization requires the developer of the information system, system component, or information system service to perform a criticality analysis at [*Assignment: organization-defined breadth/depth*] and at [*Assignment: organization-defined decision points in the system development life cycle*].

Supplemental Guidance: This control enhancement provides developer input to the criticality analysis performed by organizations in SA-14. Developer input is essential to such analysis because organizations may not have access to detailed design documentation for information system components that are developed as commercial off-the-shelf (COTS) information technology products (e.g., functional specifications, high-level designs, low-level designs, and source code/hardware schematics). Related controls: SA-4, SA-14.

(4) DEVELOPMENT PROCESS, STANDARDS, AND TOOLS | THREAT MODELING / VULNERABILITY ANALYSIS

The organization requires that developers perform threat modeling and a vulnerability analysis for the information system at [*Assignment: organization-defined breadth/depth*] that:

(a) Uses [*Assignment: organization-defined information concerning impact, environment of operations, known or assumed threats, and acceptable risk levels*];

(b) Employs [*Assignment: organization-defined tools and methods*]; and

(c) Produces evidence that meets [*Assignment: organization-defined acceptance criteria*].

Supplemental Guidance: Related control: SA-4.

(5) DEVELOPMENT PROCESS, STANDARDS, AND TOOLS | ATTACK SURFACE REDUCTION

The organization requires the developer of the information system, system component, or information system service to reduce attack surfaces to [*Assignment: organization-defined thresholds*].

Supplemental Guidance: Attack surface reduction is closely aligned with developer threat and vulnerability analyses and information system architecture and design. Attack surface reduction is a means of reducing risk to organizations by giving attackers less opportunity to exploit weaknesses or deficiencies (i.e., potential vulnerabilities) within information systems, information system components, and information system services. Attack surface reduction includes, for example, applying the principle of least privilege, employing layered defenses, applying the principle of least functionality (i.e., restricting ports, protocols, functions, and services), deprecating unsafe functions, and eliminating application programming interfaces (APIs) that are vulnerable to cyber attacks. Related control: CM-7.

(6) DEVELOPMENT PROCESS, STANDARDS, AND TOOLS | CONTINUOUS IMPROVEMENT

The organization requires the developer of the information system, system component, or information system service to implement an explicit process to continuously improve the development process.

Supplemental Guidance: Developers of information systems, information system components, and information system services consider the effectiveness/efficiency of current development processes for meeting quality objectives and addressing security capabilities in current threat environments.

(7) DEVELOPMENT PROCESS, STANDARDS, AND TOOLS | AUTOMATED VULNERABILITY ANALYSIS

The organization requires the developer of the information system, system component, or information system service to:

(a) **Perform an automated vulnerability analysis using [*Assignment: organization-defined tools*];**

(b) **Determine the exploitation potential for discovered vulnerabilities;**

(c) **Determine potential risk mitigations for delivered vulnerabilities; and**

(d) **Deliver the outputs of the tools and results of the analysis to [*Assignment: organization-defined personnel or roles*].**

Supplemental Guidance: Related control: RA-5.

(8) DEVELOPMENT PROCESS, STANDARDS, AND TOOLS | REUSE OF THREAT / VULNERABILITY INFORMATION

The organization requires the developer of the information system, system component, or information system service to use threat modeling and vulnerability analyses from similar systems, components, or services to inform the current development process.

Supplemental Guidance: Analysis of vulnerabilities found in similar software applications can inform potential design or implementation issues for information systems under development. Similar information systems or system components may exist within developer organizations. Authoritative vulnerability information is available from a variety of public and private sector sources including, for example, the National Vulnerability Database.

(9) DEVELOPMENT PROCESS, STANDARDS, AND TOOLS | USE OF LIVE DATA

The organization approves, documents, and controls the use of live data in development and test environments for the information system, system component, or information system service.

Supplemental Guidance: The use of live data in preproduction environments can result in significant risk to organizations. Organizations can minimize such risk by using test or dummy data during the development and testing of information systems, information system components, and information system services.

(10) DEVELOPMENT PROCESS, STANDARDS, AND TOOLS | INCIDENT RESPONSE PLAN

The organization requires the developer of the information system, system component, or information system service to provide an incident response plan.

Supplemental Guidance: The incident response plan for developers of information systems, system components, and information system services is incorporated into organizational incident response plans to provide the type of incident response information not readily available to organizations. Such information may be extremely helpful, for example, when organizations respond to vulnerabilities in commercial off-the-shelf (COTS) information technology products. Related control: IR-8.

(11) DEVELOPMENT PROCESS, STANDARDS, AND TOOLS | ARCHIVE INFORMATION SYSTEM / COMPONENT

The organization requires the developer of the information system or system component to archive the system or component to be released or delivered together with the corresponding evidence supporting the final security review.

Supplemental Guidance: Archiving relevant documentation from the development process can provide a readily available baseline of information that can be helpful during information system/component upgrades or modifications.

References: None.

Priority and Baseline Allocation:

| P2 | LOW Not Selected | MOD Not Selected | HIGH SA-15 |

SA-16 DEVELOPER-PROVIDED TRAINING

Control: The organization requires the developer of the information system, system component, or information system service to provide [*Assignment: organization-defined training*] on the correct use and operation of the implemented security functions, controls, and/or mechanisms.

Supplemental Guidance: This control applies to external and internal (in-house) developers. Training of personnel is an essential element to ensure the effectiveness of security controls implemented within organizational information systems. Training options include, for example, classroom-style training, web-based/computer-based training, and hands-on training. Organizations can also request sufficient training materials from developers to conduct in-house training or offer self-training to organizational personnel. Organizations determine the type of training necessary and may require different types of training for different security functions, controls, or mechanisms. Related controls: AT-2, AT-3, SA-5.

Control Enhancements: None.

References: None.

Priority and Baseline Allocation:

| P2 | LOW Not Selected | MOD Not Selected | HIGH SA-16 |

SA-17 DEVELOPER SECURITY ARCHITECTURE AND DESIGN

Control: The organization requires the developer of the information system, system component, or information system service to produce a design specification and security architecture that:

a. Is consistent with and supportive of the organization's security architecture which is established within and is an integrated part of the organization's enterprise architecture;

b. Accurately and completely describes the required security functionality, and the allocation of security controls among physical and logical components; and

c. Expresses how individual security functions, mechanisms, and services work together to provide required security capabilities and a unified approach to protection.

Supplemental Guidance: This control is primarily directed at external developers, although it could also be used for internal (in-house) development. In contrast, PL-8 is primarily directed at internal developers to help ensure that organizations develop an information security architecture and such security architecture is integrated or tightly coupled to the enterprise architecture. This distinction is important if/when organizations outsource the development of information systems, information system components, or information system services to external entities, and there is a requirement to demonstrate consistency with the organization's enterprise architecture and information security architecture. Related controls: PL-8, PM-7, SA-3, SA-8.

Control Enhancements:

(1) *DEVELOPER SECURITY ARCHITECTURE AND DESIGN | FORMAL POLICY MODEL*

The organization requires the developer of the information system, system component, or information system service to:

(a) Produce, as an integral part of the development process, a formal policy model describing the [*Assignment: organization-defined elements of organizational security policy*] to be enforced; and

(b) Prove that the formal policy model is internally consistent and sufficient to enforce the defined elements of the organizational security policy when implemented.

Supplemental Guidance: Formal models describe specific behaviors or security policies using formal languages, thus enabling the correctness of those behaviors/policies to be formally proven. Not all components of information systems can be modeled, and generally, formal specifications are scoped to specific behaviors or policies of interest (e.g., nondiscretionary access control policies). Organizations choose the particular formal modeling language and approach based on the nature of the behaviors/policies to be described and the available tools. Formal modeling tools include, for example, Gypsy and Zed.

(2) *DEVELOPER SECURITY ARCHITECTURE AND DESIGN | SECURITY-RELEVANT COMPONENTS*

The organization requires the developer of the information system, system component, or information system service to:

(a) Define security-relevant hardware, software, and firmware; and

(b) Provide a rationale that the definition for security-relevant hardware, software, and firmware is complete.

Supplemental Guidance: Security-relevant hardware, software, and firmware represent the portion of the information system, component, or service that must be trusted to perform correctly in order to maintain required security properties. Related control: SA-5.

(3) *DEVELOPER SECURITY ARCHITECTURE AND DESIGN | FORMAL CORRESPONDENCE*

The organization requires the developer of the information system, system component, or information system service to:

(a) Produce, as an integral part of the development process, a formal top-level specification that specifies the interfaces to security-relevant hardware, software, and firmware in terms of exceptions, error messages, and effects;

(b) Show via proof to the extent feasible with additional informal demonstration as necessary, that the formal top-level specification is consistent with the formal policy model;

(c) Show via informal demonstration, that the formal top-level specification completely covers the interfaces to security-relevant hardware, software, and firmware;

(d) Show that the formal top-level specification is an accurate description of the implemented security-relevant hardware, software, and firmware; and

(e) Describe the security-relevant hardware, software, and firmware mechanisms not addressed in the formal top-level specification but strictly internal to the security-relevant hardware, software, and firmware.

Supplemental Guidance: Correspondence is an important part of the assurance gained through modeling. It demonstrates that the implementation is an accurate transformation of the model, and that any additional code or implementation details present have no impact on the behaviors or policies being modeled. Formal methods can be used to show that the high-level security properties are satisfied by the formal information system description, and that the formal system description is correctly implemented by a description of some lower level, for example a hardware description. Consistency between the formal top-level specification and the formal policy models is generally not amenable to being fully proven. Therefore, a combination of formal/informal methods may be needed to show such consistency. Consistency between the formal top-level specification and the implementation may require the use of an informal demonstration due to limitations in the applicability of formal methods to prove that the specification accurately reflects the implementation. Hardware, software, and firmware mechanisms strictly internal to security-relevant hardware, software, and firmware include, for example, mapping registers and direct memory input/output. Related control: SA-5.

(4) DEVELOPER SECURITY ARCHITECTURE AND DESIGN | INFORMAL CORRESPONDENCE

The organization requires the developer of the information system, system component, or information system service to:

(a) Produce, as an integral part of the development process, an informal descriptive top-level specification that specifies the interfaces to security-relevant hardware, software, and firmware in terms of exceptions, error messages, and effects;

(b) Show via [Selection: informal demonstration, convincing argument with formal methods as feasible] that the descriptive top-level specification is consistent with the formal policy model;

(c) Show via informal demonstration, that the descriptive top-level specification completely covers the interfaces to security-relevant hardware, software, and firmware;

(d) Show that the descriptive top-level specification is an accurate description of the interfaces to security-relevant hardware, software, and firmware; and

(e) Describe the security-relevant hardware, software, and firmware mechanisms not addressed in the descriptive top-level specification but strictly internal to the security-relevant hardware, software, and firmware.

Supplemental Guidance: Correspondence is an important part of the assurance gained through modeling. It demonstrates that the implementation is an accurate transformation of the model, and that any additional code or implementation details present has no impact on the behaviors or policies being modeled. Consistency between the descriptive top-level specification (i.e., high-level/low-level design) and the formal policy model is generally not amenable to being fully proven. Therefore, a combination of formal/informal methods may be needed to show such consistency. Hardware, software, and firmware mechanisms strictly internal to security-relevant hardware, software, and firmware include, for example, mapping registers and direct memory input/output. Related control: SA-5.

(5) DEVELOPER SECURITY ARCHITECTURE AND DESIGN | CONCEPTUALLY SIMPLE DESIGN

The organization requires the developer of the information system, system component, or information system service to:

(a) Design and structure the security-relevant hardware, software, and firmware to use a complete, conceptually simple protection mechanism with precisely defined semantics; and

(b) Internally structure the security-relevant hardware, software, and firmware with specific regard for this mechanism.

Supplemental Guidance: Related control: SC-3.

(6) DEVELOPER SECURITY ARCHITECTURE AND DESIGN | STRUCTURE FOR TESTING

The organization requires the developer of the information system, system component, or information system service to structure security-relevant hardware, software, and firmware to facilitate testing.

Supplemental Guidance: Related control: SA-11.

(7) DEVELOPER SECURITY ARCHITECTURE AND DESIGN | STRUCTURE FOR LEAST PRIVILEGE

The organization requires the developer of the information system, system component, or information system service to structure security-relevant hardware, software, and firmware to facilitate controlling access with least privilege.

Supplemental Guidance: Related controls: AC-5, AC-6.

References: None.

Priority and Baseline Allocation:

| P1 | LOW Not Selected | MOD Not Selected | HIGH SA-17 |

SA-18 TAMPER RESISTANCE AND DETECTION

Control: The organization implements a tamper protection program for the information system, system component, or information system service.

Supplemental Guidance: Anti-tamper technologies and techniques provide a level of protection for critical information systems, system components, and information technology products against a number of related threats including modification, reverse engineering, and substitution. Strong identification combined with tamper resistance and/or tamper detection is essential to protecting information systems, components, and products during distribution and when in use. Related controls: PE-3, SA-12, SI-7.

Control Enhancements:

(1) TAMPER RESISTANCE AND DETECTION | MULTIPLE PHASES OF SDLC

The organization employs anti-tamper technologies and techniques during multiple phases in the system development life cycle including design, development, integration, operations, and maintenance.

Supplemental Guidance: Organizations use a combination of hardware and software techniques for tamper resistance and detection. Organizations employ obfuscation and self-checking, for example, to make reverse engineering and modifications more difficult, time-consuming, and expensive for adversaries. Customization of information systems and system components can make substitutions easier to detect and therefore limit damage. Related control: SA-3.

(2) TAMPER RESISTANCE AND DETECTION | INSPECTION OF INFORMATION SYSTEMS, COMPONENTS, OR DEVICES

The organization inspects [Assignment: organization-defined information systems, system components, or devices] [Selection (one or more): at random; at [Assignment: organization-defined frequency], upon [Assignment: organization-defined indications of need for inspection]] to detect tampering.

Supplemental Guidance: This control enhancement addresses both physical and logical tampering and is typically applied to mobile devices, notebook computers, or other system components taken out of organization-controlled areas. Indications of need for inspection include, for example, when individuals return from travel to high-risk locations. Related control: SI-4.

References: None.

Priority and Baseline Allocation:

P0	LOW Not Selected	MOD Not Selected	HIGH Not Selected

SA-19 COMPONENT AUTHENTICITY

Control: The organization:

a. Develops and implements anti-counterfeit policy and procedures that include the means to detect and prevent counterfeit components from entering the information system; and

b. Reports counterfeit information system components to [Selection (one or more): source of counterfeit component; [Assignment: organization-defined external reporting organizations]; [Assignment: organization-defined personnel or roles]].

Supplemental Guidance: Sources of counterfeit components include, for example, manufacturers, developers, vendors, and contractors. Anti-counterfeiting policy and procedures support tamper resistance and provide a level of protection against the introduction of malicious code. External reporting organizations include, for example, US-CERT. Related controls: PE-3, SA-12, SI-7.

Control Enhancements:

(1) COMPONENT AUTHENTICITY | ANTI-COUNTERFEIT TRAINING

The organization trains [Assignment: organization-defined personnel or roles] to detect counterfeit information system components (including hardware, software, and firmware).

(2) COMPONENT AUTHENTICITY | CONFIGURATION CONTROL FOR COMPONENT SERVICE / REPAIR

The organization maintains configuration control over [*Assignment: organization-defined information system components*] awaiting service/repair and serviced/repaired components awaiting return to service.

(3) COMPONENT AUTHENTICITY | COMPONENT DISPOSAL

The organization disposes of information system components using [*Assignment: organization-defined techniques and methods*].

Supplemental Guidance: Proper disposal of information system components helps to prevent such components from entering the gray market.

(4) COMPONENT AUTHENTICITY | ANTI-COUNTERFEIT SCANNING

The organization scans for counterfeit information system components [*Assignment: organization-defined frequency*].

References: None.

Priority and Baseline Allocation:

| P0 | LOW Not Selected | MOD Not Selected | HIGH Not Selected |

SA-20 CUSTOMIZED DEVELOPMENT OF CRITICAL COMPONENTS

Control: The organization re-implements or custom develops [*Assignment: organization-defined critical information system components*].

Supplemental Guidance: Organizations determine that certain information system components likely cannot be trusted due to specific threats to and vulnerabilities in those components, and for which there are no viable security controls to adequately mitigate the resulting risk. Re-implementation or custom development of such components helps to satisfy requirements for higher assurance. This is accomplished by initiating changes to system components (including hardware, software, and firmware) such that the standard attacks by adversaries are less likely to succeed. In situations where no alternative sourcing is available and organizations choose not to re-implement or custom develop critical information system components, additional safeguards can be employed (e.g., enhanced auditing, restrictions on source code and system utility access, and protection from deletion of system and application files. Related controls: CP-2, SA-8, SA-14.

Control Enhancements: None.

References: None.

Priority and Baseline Allocation:

| P0 | LOW Not Selected | MOD Not Selected | HIGH Not Selected |

SA-21 DEVELOPER SCREENING

Control: The organization requires that the developer of [*Assignment: organization-defined information system, system component, or information system service*]:

a. Have appropriate access authorizations as determined by assigned [*Assignment: organization-defined official government duties*]; and

b. Satisfy [*Assignment: organization-defined additional personnel screening criteria*].

Supplemental Guidance: Because the information system, system component, or information system service may be employed in critical activities essential to the national and/or economic security interests of the United States, organizations have a strong interest in ensuring that the developer is trustworthy. The degree of trust required of the developer may need to be consistent with that of the individuals accessing the information system/component/service once deployed. Examples of authorization and personnel screening criteria include clearance, satisfactory background checks, citizenship, and nationality. Trustworthiness of developers may also include a review and analysis of company ownership and any relationships the company has with entities potentially affecting the quality/reliability of the systems, components, or services being developed. Related controls: PS-3, PS-7.

Control Enhancements:

(1) DEVELOPER SCREENING | VALIDATION OF SCREENING

The organization requires the developer of the information system, system component, or information system service take [*Assignment: organization-defined actions*] to ensure that the required access authorizations and screening criteria are satisfied.

Supplemental Guidance: Satisfying required access authorizations and personnel screening criteria includes, for example, providing a listing of all the individuals authorized to perform development activities on the selected information system, system component, or information system service so that organizations can validate that the developer has satisfied the necessary authorization and screening requirements.

References: None.

Priority and Baseline Allocation:

| P0 | LOW Not Selected | MOD Not Selected | HIGH Not Selected |

SA-22 UNSUPPORTED SYSTEM COMPONENTS

Control: The organization:

a. Replaces information system components when support for the components is no longer available from the developer, vendor, or manufacturer; and

b. Provides justification and documents approval for the continued use of unsupported system components required to satisfy mission/business needs.

Supplemental Guidance: Support for information system components includes, for example, software patches, firmware updates, replacement parts, and maintenance contracts. Unsupported components (e.g., when vendors are no longer providing critical software patches), provide a substantial opportunity for adversaries to exploit new weaknesses discovered in the currently installed components. Exceptions to replacing unsupported system components may include, for example, systems that provide critical mission/business capability where newer technologies are not available or where the systems are so isolated that installing replacement components is not an option. Related controls: PL-2, SA-3.

Control Enhancements:

(1) UNSUPPORTED SYSTEM COMPONENTS | ALTERNATIVE SOURCES FOR CONTINUED SUPPORT

The organization provides [*Selection (one or more): in-house support;* [*Assignment: organization-defined support from external providers*]] for unsupported information system components.

Supplemental Guidance: This control enhancement addresses the need to provide continued support for selected information system components that are no longer supported by the original developers, vendors, or manufacturers when such components remain essential to mission/business operations. Organizations can establish in-house support, for example, by developing customized patches for critical software components or secure the services of external providers who through contractual relationships, provide ongoing support for the designated unsupported components. Such contractual relationships can include, for example, Open Source Software value-added vendors.

References: None.

Priority and Baseline Allocation:

P0	**LOW** Not Selected	**MOD** Not Selected	**HIGH** Not Selected

---

SYSTEM AND SERVICES ACQUISITION CONTROLS

DEVELOPMENT OF SYSTEMS, COMPONENTS, AND SERVICES

With the renewed emphasis on trustworthy information systems and supply chain security, it is essential that organizations have the capability to express their information security requirements with clarity and specificity in order to engage the information technology industry and obtain the systems, components, and services necessary for mission and business success. To ensure that organizations have such capability, this publication provides a set of security controls in the System and Services Acquisition family (i.e., SA family) addressing requirements for the development of information systems, information technology products, and information system services. Therefore, many of the controls in the SA family are directed at developers of those systems, components, and services. It is important for organizations to recognize that the scope of the security controls in the SA family includes all system/component/service development and the developers associated with such development whether the development is conducted by internal organizational personnel or by external developers through the contracting/acquisition process. Affected controls include SA-8, SA-10, SA-11, SA-15, SA-16, SA-17, SA-20, and SA-21.

FAMILY: SYSTEM AND COMMUNICATIONS PROTECTION

SC-1 SYSTEM AND COMMUNICATIONS PROTECTION POLICY AND PROCEDURES

Control: The organization:

a. Develops, documents, and disseminates to [*Assignment: organization-defined personnel or roles*]:

1. A system and communications protection policy that addresses purpose, scope, roles, responsibilities, management commitment, coordination among organizational entities, and compliance; and

2. Procedures to facilitate the implementation of the system and communications protection policy and associated system and communications protection controls; and

b. Reviews and updates the current:

1. System and communications protection policy [*Assignment: organization-defined frequency*]; and

2. System and communications protection procedures [*Assignment: organization-defined frequency*].

Supplemental Guidance: This control addresses the establishment of policy and procedures for the effective implementation of selected security controls and control enhancements in the SC family. Policy and procedures reflect applicable federal laws, Executive Orders, directives, regulations, policies, standards, and guidance. Security program policies and procedures at the organization level may make the need for system-specific policies and procedures unnecessary. The policy can be included as part of the general information security policy for organizations or conversely, can be represented by multiple policies reflecting the complex nature of certain organizations. The procedures can be established for the security program in general and for particular information systems, if needed. The organizational risk management strategy is a key factor in establishing policy and procedures. Related control: PM-9.

Control Enhancements: None.

References: NIST Special Publications 800-12, 800-100.

Priority and Baseline Allocation:

P1	LOW SC-1	MOD SC-1	HIGH SC-1

SC-2 APPLICATION PARTITIONING

Control: The information system separates user functionality (including user interface services) from information system management functionality.

Supplemental Guidance: Information system management functionality includes, for example, functions necessary to administer databases, network components, workstations, or servers, and typically requires privileged user access. The separation of user functionality from information system management functionality is either physical or logical. Organizations implement separation of system management-related functionality from user functionality by using different computers, different central processing units, different instances of operating systems, different network addresses, virtualization techniques, or combinations of these or other methods, as appropriate. This type of separation includes, for example, web administrative interfaces that use separate authentication methods for users of any other information system resources. Separation of system and user functionality may include isolating administrative interfaces on different domains and with additional access controls. Related controls: SA-4, SA-8, SC-3.

Control Enhancements:

(1) APPLICATION PARTITIONING | INTERFACES FOR NON-PRIVILEGED USERS

The information system prevents the presentation of information system management-related functionality at an interface for non-privileged users.

Supplemental Guidance: This control enhancement ensures that administration options (e.g., administrator privileges) are not available to general users (including prohibiting the use of the grey-out option commonly used to eliminate accessibility to such information). Such restrictions include, for example, not presenting administration options until users establish sessions with administrator privileges. Related control: AC-3.

References: None.

Priority and Baseline Allocation:

| P1 | LOW Not Selected | MOD SC-2 | HIGH SC-2 |

SC-3 SECURITY FUNCTION ISOLATION

Control: The information system isolates security functions from nonsecurity functions.

Supplemental Guidance: The information system isolates security functions from nonsecurity functions by means of an isolation boundary (implemented via partitions and domains). Such isolation controls access to and protects the integrity of the hardware, software, and firmware that perform those security functions. Information systems implement code separation (i.e., separation of security functions from nonsecurity functions) in a number of ways, including, for example, through the provision of security kernels via processor rings or processor modes. For non-kernel code, security function isolation is often achieved through file system protections that serve to protect the code on disk, and address space protections that protect executing code. Information systems restrict access to security functions through the use of access control mechanisms and by implementing least privilege capabilities. While the ideal is for all of the code within the security function isolation boundary to only contain security-relevant code, it is sometimes necessary to include nonsecurity functions within the isolation boundary as an exception. Related controls: AC-3, AC-6, SA-4, SA-5, SA-8, SA-13, SC-2, SC-7, SC-39.

Control Enhancements:

(1) SECURITY FUNCTION ISOLATION | HARDWARE SEPARATION

The information system utilizes underlying hardware separation mechanisms to implement security function isolation.

Supplemental Guidance: Underlying hardware separation mechanisms include, for example, hardware ring architectures, commonly implemented within microprocessors, and hardware-enforced address segmentation used to support logically distinct storage objects with separate attributes (i.e., readable, writeable).

(2) SECURITY FUNCTION ISOLATION | ACCESS / FLOW CONTROL FUNCTIONS

The information system isolates security functions enforcing access and information flow control from nonsecurity functions and from other security functions.

Supplemental Guidance: Security function isolation occurs as a result of implementation; the functions can still be scanned and monitored. Security functions that are potentially isolated from access and flow control enforcement functions include, for example, auditing, intrusion detection, and anti-virus functions.

(3) SECURITY FUNCTION ISOLATION | MINIMIZE NONSECURITY FUNCTIONALITY

The organization minimizes the number of nonsecurity functions included within the isolation boundary containing security functions.

Supplemental Guidance: In those instances where it is not feasible to achieve strict isolation of nonsecurity functions from security functions, it is necessary to take actions to minimize the nonsecurity-relevant functions within the security function boundary. Nonsecurity functions contained within the isolation boundary are considered security-relevant because errors or maliciousness in such software, by virtue of being within the boundary, can impact the security functions of organizational information systems. The design objective is that the specific portions of information systems providing information security are of minimal size/complexity. Minimizing the number of nonsecurity functions in the security-relevant components of information systems allows designers and implementers to focus only on those functions which are necessary to provide the desired security capability (typically access enforcement). By minimizing nonsecurity functions within the isolation boundaries, the amount of code that must be trusted to enforce security policies is reduced, thus contributing to understandability.

(4) SECURITY FUNCTION ISOLATION | MODULE COUPLING AND COHESIVENESS

The organization implements security functions as largely independent modules that maximize internal cohesiveness within modules and minimize coupling between modules.

Supplemental Guidance: The reduction in inter-module interactions helps to constrain security functions and to manage complexity. The concepts of coupling and cohesion are important with respect to modularity in software design. Coupling refers to the dependencies that one module has on other modules. Cohesion refers to the relationship between the different functions within a particular module. Good software engineering practices rely on modular decomposition, layering, and minimization to reduce and manage complexity, thus producing software modules that are highly cohesive and loosely coupled.

(5) SECURITY FUNCTION ISOLATION | LAYERED STRUCTURES

The organization implements security functions as a layered structure minimizing interactions between layers of the design and avoiding any dependence by lower layers on the functionality or correctness of higher layers.

Supplemental Guidance: The implementation of layered structures with minimized interactions among security functions and non-looping layers (i.e., lower-layer functions do not depend on higher-layer functions) further enables the isolation of security functions and management of complexity.

References: None.

Priority and Baseline Allocation:

| P1 | LOW Not Selected | MOD Not Selected | HIGH SC-3 |

SC-4   INFORMATION IN SHARED RESOURCES

Control: The information system prevents unauthorized and unintended information transfer via shared system resources.

Supplemental Guidance: This control prevents information, including encrypted representations of information, produced by the actions of prior users/roles (or the actions of processes acting on behalf of prior users/roles) from being available to any current users/roles (or current processes) that obtain access to shared system resources (e.g., registers, main memory, hard disks) after those resources have been released back to information systems. The control of information in shared resources is also commonly referred to as object reuse and residual information protection. This control does not address: (i) information remanence which refers to residual representation of data that has been nominally erased or removed; (ii) covert channels (including storage and/or timing channels) where shared resources are manipulated to violate information flow restrictions; or (iii) components within information systems for which there are only single users/roles. Related controls: AC-3, AC-4, MP-6.

Control Enhancements:

(1) INFORMATION IN SHARED RESOURCES | SECURITY LEVELS
    [Withdrawn: Incorporated into SC-4].

(2) *INFORMATION IN SHARED RESOURCES | PERIODS PROCESSING*

The information system prevents unauthorized information transfer via shared resources in accordance with [*Assignment: organization-defined procedures*] when system processing explicitly switches between different information classification levels or security categories.

Supplemental Guidance: This control enhancement applies when there are explicit changes in information processing levels during information system operations, for example, during multilevel processing and periods processing with information at different classification levels or security categories. Organization-defined procedures may include, for example, approved sanitization processes for electronically stored information.

References: None.

Priority and Baseline Allocation:

P1	LOW Not Selected	MOD SC-4	HIGH SC-4

SC-5   **DENIAL OF SERVICE PROTECTION**

Control: The information system protects against or limits the effects of the following types of denial of service attacks: [*Assignment: organization-defined types of denial of service attacks or references to sources for such information*] by employing [*Assignment: organization-defined security safeguards*].

Supplemental Guidance: A variety of technologies exist to limit, or in some cases, eliminate the effects of denial of service attacks. For example, boundary protection devices can filter certain types of packets to protect information system components on internal organizational networks from being directly affected by denial of service attacks. Employing increased capacity and bandwidth combined with service redundancy may also reduce the susceptibility to denial of service attacks. Related controls: SC-6, SC-7.

Control Enhancements:

(1) *DENIAL OF SERVICE PROTECTION | RESTRICT INTERNAL USERS*

The information system restricts the ability of individuals to launch [*Assignment: organization-defined denial of service attacks*] against other information systems.

Supplemental Guidance: Restricting the ability of individuals to launch denial of service attacks requires that the mechanisms used for such attacks are unavailable. Individuals of concern can include, for example, hostile insiders or external adversaries that have successfully breached the information system and are using the system as a platform to launch cyber attacks on third parties. Organizations can restrict the ability of individuals to connect and transmit arbitrary information on the transport medium (i.e., network, wireless spectrum). Organizations can also limit the ability of individuals to use excessive information system resources. Protection against individuals having the ability to launch denial of service attacks may be implemented on specific information systems or on boundary devices prohibiting egress to potential target systems.

(2) *DENIAL OF SERVICE PROTECTION | EXCESS CAPACITY / BANDWIDTH / REDUNDANCY*

The information system manages excess capacity, bandwidth, or other redundancy to limit the effects of information flooding denial of service attacks.

Supplemental Guidance: Managing excess capacity ensures that sufficient capacity is available to counter flooding attacks. Managing excess capacity may include, for example, establishing selected usage priorities, quotas, or partitioning.

(3) *DENIAL OF SERVICE PROTECTION | DETECTION / MONITORING*

The organization:

(a) **Employs [*Assignment: organization-defined monitoring tools*] to detect indicators of denial of service attacks against the information system; and**

(b) Monitors [*Assignment: organization-defined information system resources*] to determine if sufficient resources exist to prevent effective denial of service attacks.

Supplemental Guidance: Organizations consider utilization and capacity of information system resources when managing risk from denial of service due to malicious attacks. Denial of service attacks can originate from external or internal sources. Information system resources sensitive to denial of service include, for example, physical disk storage, memory, and CPU cycles. Common safeguards to prevent denial of service attacks related to storage utilization and capacity include, for example, instituting disk quotas, configuring information systems to automatically alert administrators when specific storage capacity thresholds are reached, using file compression technologies to maximize available storage space, and imposing separate partitions for system and user data. Related controls: CA-7, SI-4.

References: None.

Priority and Baseline Allocation:

P1	LOW SC-5	MOD SC-5	HIGH SC-5

SC-6 **RESOURCE AVAILABILITY**

Control: The information system protects the availability of resources by allocating [*Assignment: organization-defined resources*] by [*Selection (one or more); priority; quota; [Assignment: organization-defined security safeguards]*].

Supplemental Guidance: Priority protection helps prevent lower-priority processes from delaying or interfering with the information system servicing any higher-priority processes. Quotas prevent users or processes from obtaining more than predetermined amounts of resources. This control does not apply to information system components for which there are only single users/roles.

Control Enhancements: None.

References: None.

Priority and Baseline Allocation:

P0	LOW Not Selected	MOD Not Selected	HIGH Not Selected

SC-7 **BOUNDARY PROTECTION**

Control: The information system:

a. Monitors and controls communications at the external boundary of the system and at key internal boundaries within the system;

b. Implements subnetworks for publicly accessible system components that are [*Selection: physically; logically*] separated from internal organizational networks; and

c. Connects to external networks or information systems only through managed interfaces consisting of boundary protection devices arranged in accordance with an organizational security architecture.

Supplemental Guidance: Managed interfaces include, for example, gateways, routers, firewalls, guards, network-based malicious code analysis and virtualization systems, or encrypted tunnels implemented within a security architecture (e.g., routers protecting firewalls or application gateways residing on protected subnetworks). Subnetworks that are physically or logically separated from internal networks are referred to as demilitarized zones or DMZs. Restricting or prohibiting interfaces within organizational information systems includes, for example, restricting external web traffic to designated web servers within managed interfaces and prohibiting external traffic that appears to be spoofing internal addresses. Organizations consider the shared nature of commercial telecommunications services in the implementation of security controls associated with the use of such services. Commercial telecommunications services are commonly based on network components and consolidated management systems shared by all attached commercial customers, and may also include third party-provided access lines and other service elements. Such transmission services may represent sources of increased risk despite contract security provisions. Related controls: AC-4, AC-17, CA-3, CM-7, CP-8, IR-4, RA-3, SC-5, SC-13.

Control Enhancements:

(1) BOUNDARY PROTECTION | PHYSICALLY SEPARATED SUBNETWORKS
[Withdrawn: Incorporated into SC-7].

(2) BOUNDARY PROTECTION | PUBLIC ACCESS
[Withdrawn: Incorporated into SC-7].

(3) BOUNDARY PROTECTION | ACCESS POINTS
The organization limits the number of external network connections to the information system.

Supplemental Guidance: Limiting the number of external network connections facilitates more comprehensive monitoring of inbound and outbound communications traffic. The Trusted Internet Connection (TIC) initiative is an example of limiting the number of external network connections.

(4) BOUNDARY PROTECTION | EXTERNAL TELECOMMUNICATIONS SERVICES
The organization:

(a) Implements a managed interface for each external telecommunication service;

(b) Establishes a traffic flow policy for each managed interface;

(c) Protects the confidentiality and integrity of the information being transmitted across each interface;

(d) Documents each exception to the traffic flow policy with a supporting mission/business need and duration of that need; and

(e) Reviews exceptions to the traffic flow policy [Assignment: organization-defined frequency] and removes exceptions that are no longer supported by an explicit mission/business need.

Supplemental Guidance: Related control: SC-8.

(5) BOUNDARY PROTECTION | DENY BY DEFAULT / ALLOW BY EXCEPTION
The information system at managed interfaces denies network communications traffic by default and allows network communications traffic by exception (i.e., deny all, permit by exception).

Supplemental Guidance: This control enhancement applies to both inbound and outbound network communications traffic. A deny-all, permit-by-exception network communications traffic policy ensures that only those connections which are essential and approved are allowed.

(6) BOUNDARY PROTECTION | RESPONSE TO RECOGNIZED FAILURES
[Withdrawn: Incorporated into SC-7 (18)].

(7) BOUNDARY PROTECTION | PREVENT SPLIT TUNNELING FOR REMOTE DEVICES
The information system, in conjunction with a remote device, prevents the device from simultaneously establishing non-remote connections with the system and communicating via some other connection to resources in external networks.

Supplemental Guidance: This control enhancement is implemented within remote devices (e.g., notebook computers) through configuration settings to disable split tunneling in those devices, and by preventing those configuration settings from being readily configurable by users. This control enhancement is implemented within the information system by the detection of split tunneling (or of configuration settings that allow split tunneling) in the remote device, and by prohibiting the connection if the remote device is using split tunneling. Split tunneling might be desirable by remote users to communicate with local information system resources such as printers/file servers. However, split tunneling would in effect allow unauthorized external connections, making the system more vulnerable to attack and to exfiltration of organizational information. The use of VPNs for remote connections, when adequately provisioned with appropriate security controls, may provide the organization with sufficient assurance that it can effectively treat such connections as non-remote connections from the confidentiality and integrity perspective. VPNs thus provide a means for allowing non-remote communications paths from remote devices. The use of an adequately provisioned VPN does not eliminate the need for preventing split tunneling.

(8) BOUNDARY PROTECTION | ROUTE TRAFFIC TO AUTHENTICATED PROXY SERVERS

The information system routes [*Assignment: organization-defined internal communications traffic*] to [*Assignment: organization-defined external networks*] through authenticated proxy servers at managed interfaces.

Supplemental Guidance: External networks are networks outside of organizational control. A proxy server is a server (i.e., information system or application) that acts as an intermediary for clients requesting information system resources (e.g., files, connections, web pages, or services) from other organizational servers. Client requests established through an initial connection to the proxy server are evaluated to manage complexity and to provide additional protection by limiting direct connectivity. Web content filtering devices are one of the most common proxy servers providing access to the Internet. Proxy servers support logging individual Transmission Control Protocol (TCP) sessions and blocking specific Uniform Resource Locators (URLs), domain names, and Internet Protocol (IP) addresses. Web proxies can be configured with organization-defined lists of authorized and unauthorized websites. Related controls: AC-3, AU-2.

(9) BOUNDARY PROTECTION | RESTRICT THREATENING OUTGOING COMMUNICATIONS TRAFFIC

The information system:

(a) Detects and denies outgoing communications traffic posing a threat to external information systems; and

(b) Audits the identity of internal users associated with denied communications.

Supplemental Guidance: Detecting outgoing communications traffic from internal actions that may pose threats to external information systems is sometimes termed extrusion detection. Extrusion detection at information system boundaries as part of managed interfaces includes the analysis of incoming and outgoing communications traffic searching for indications of internal threats to the security of external systems. Such threats include, for example, traffic indicative of denial of service attacks and traffic containing malicious code. Related controls: AU-2, AU-6, SC-38, SC-44, SI-3, SI-4.

(10) BOUNDARY PROTECTION | PREVENT UNAUTHORIZED EXFILTRATION

The organization prevents the unauthorized exfiltration of information across managed interfaces.

Supplemental Guidance: Safeguards implemented by organizations to prevent unauthorized exfiltration of information from information systems include, for example: (i) strict adherence to protocol formats; (ii) monitoring for beaconing from information systems; (iii) monitoring for steganography; (iv) disconnecting external network interfaces except when explicitly needed; (v) disassembling and reassembling packet headers; and (vi) employing traffic profile analysis to detect deviations from the volume/types of traffic expected within organizations or call backs to command and control centers. Devices enforcing strict adherence to protocol formats include, for example, deep packet inspection firewalls and XML gateways. These devices verify adherence to protocol formats and specification at the application layer and serve to identify vulnerabilities that cannot be detected by devices operating at the network or transport layers. This control enhancement is closely associated with cross-domain solutions and system guards enforcing information flow requirements. Related control: SI-3.

(11) BOUNDARY PROTECTION | RESTRICT INCOMING COMMUNICATIONS TRAFFIC

The information system only allows incoming communications from [*Assignment: organization-defined authorized sources*] to be routed to [*Assignment: organization-defined authorized destinations*].

Supplemental Guidance: This control enhancement provides determinations that source and destination address pairs represent authorized/allowed communications. Such determinations can be based on several factors including, for example, the presence of source/destination address pairs in lists of authorized/allowed communications, the absence of address pairs in lists of unauthorized/disallowed pairs, or meeting more general rules for authorized/allowed source/destination pairs. Related control: AC-3.

(12) BOUNDARY PROTECTION | HOST-BASED PROTECTION

The organization implements [*Assignment: organization-defined host-based boundary protection mechanisms*] at [*Assignment: organization-defined information system components*].

Supplemental Guidance: Host-based boundary protection mechanisms include, for example, host-based firewalls. Information system components employing host-based boundary protection mechanisms include, for example, servers, workstations, and mobile devices.

(13) BOUNDARY PROTECTION | ISOLATION OF SECURITY TOOLS / MECHANISMS / SUPPORT COMPONENTS

The organization isolates [*Assignment: organization-defined information security tools, mechanisms, and support components*] from other internal information system components by implementing physically separate subnetworks with managed interfaces to other components of the system.

Supplemental Guidance: Physically separate subnetworks with managed interfaces are useful, for example, in isolating computer network defenses from critical operational processing networks to prevent adversaries from discovering the analysis and forensics techniques of organizations. Related controls: SA-8, SC-2, SC-3.

(14) BOUNDARY PROTECTION | PROTECTS AGAINST UNAUTHORIZED PHYSICAL CONNECTIONS

The organization protects against unauthorized physical connections at [*Assignment: organization-defined managed interfaces*].

Supplemental Guidance: Information systems operating at different security categories or classification levels may share common physical and environmental controls, since the systems may share space within organizational facilities. In practice, it is possible that these separate information systems may share common equipment rooms, wiring closets, and cable distribution paths. Protection against unauthorized physical connections can be achieved, for example, by employing clearly identified and physically separated cable trays, connection frames, and patch panels for each side of managed interfaces with physical access controls enforcing limited authorized access to these items. Related controls: PE-4, PE-19.

(15) BOUNDARY PROTECTION | ROUTE PRIVILEGED NETWORK ACCESSES

The information system routes all networked, privileged accesses through a dedicated, managed interface for purposes of access control and auditing.

Supplemental Guidance: Related controls: AC-2, AC-3, AU-2, SI-4.

(16) BOUNDARY PROTECTION | PREVENT DISCOVERY OF COMPONENTS / DEVICES

The information system prevents discovery of specific system components composing a managed interface.

Supplemental Guidance: This control enhancement protects network addresses of information system components that are part of managed interfaces from discovery through common tools and techniques used to identify devices on networks. Network addresses are not available for discovery (e.g., network address not published or entered in domain name systems), requiring prior knowledge for access. Another obfuscation technique is to periodically change network addresses.

(17) BOUNDARY PROTECTION | AUTOMATED ENFORCEMENT OF PROTOCOL FORMATS

The information system enforces adherence to protocol formats.

Supplemental Guidance: Information system components that enforce protocol formats include, for example, deep packet inspection firewalls and XML gateways. Such system components verify adherence to protocol formats/specifications (e.g., IEEE) at the application layer and identify significant vulnerabilities that cannot be detected by devices operating at the network or transport layers. Related control: SC-4.

(18) BOUNDARY PROTECTION | FAIL SECURE

The information system fails securely in the event of an operational failure of a boundary protection device.

Supplemental Guidance: Fail secure is a condition achieved by employing information system mechanisms to ensure that in the event of operational failures of boundary protection devices at managed interfaces (e.g., routers, firewalls, guards, and application gateways residing on protected subnetworks commonly referred to as demilitarized zones), information systems do not enter into unsecure states where intended security properties no longer hold. Failures of boundary protection devices cannot lead to, or cause information external to the devices to enter the devices, nor can failures permit unauthorized information releases. Related controls: CP-2, SC-24.

(19) BOUNDARY PROTECTION | BLOCKS COMMUNICATION FROM NON-ORGANIZATIONALLY CONFIGURED HOSTS

The information system blocks both inbound and outbound communications traffic between [*Assignment: organization-defined communication clients*] that are independently configured by end users and external service providers.

Supplemental Guidance: Communication clients independently configured by end users and external service providers include, for example, instant messaging clients. Traffic blocking does not apply to communication clients that are configured by organizations to perform authorized functions.

(20) BOUNDARY PROTECTION | DYNAMIC ISOLATION / SEGREGATION

The information system provides the capability to dynamically isolate/segregate [*Assignment: organization-defined information system components*] from other components of the system.

Supplemental Guidance: The capability to dynamically isolate or segregate certain internal components of organizational information systems is useful when it is necessary to partition or separate certain components of dubious origin from those components possessing greater trustworthiness. Component isolation reduces the attack surface of organizational information systems. Isolation of selected information system components is also a means of limiting the damage from successful cyber attacks when those attacks occur.

(21) BOUNDARY PROTECTION | ISOLATION OF INFORMATION SYSTEM COMPONENTS

The organization employs boundary protection mechanisms to separate [*Assignment: organization-defined information system components*] supporting [*Assignment: organization-defined missions and/or business functions*].

Supplemental Guidance: Organizations can isolate information system components performing different missions and/or business functions. Such isolation limits unauthorized information flows among system components and also provides the opportunity to deploy greater levels of protection for selected components. Separating system components with boundary protection mechanisms provides the capability for increased protection of individual components and to more effectively control information flows between those components. This type of enhanced protection limits the potential harm from cyber attacks and errors. The degree of separation provided varies depending upon the mechanisms chosen. Boundary protection mechanisms include, for example, routers, gateways, and firewalls separating system components into physically separate networks or subnetworks, cross-domain devices separating subnetworks, virtualization techniques, and encrypting information flows among system components using distinct encryption keys. Related controls: CA-9, SC-3.

(22) BOUNDARY PROTECTION | SEPARATE SUBNETS FOR CONNECTING TO DIFFERENT SECURITY DOMAINS

The information system implements separate network addresses (i.e., different subnets) to connect to systems in different security domains.

Supplemental Guidance: Decomposition of information systems into subnets helps to provide the appropriate level of protection for network connections to different security domains containing information with different security categories or classification levels.

(23) BOUNDARY PROTECTION | DISABLE SENDER FEEDBACK ON PROTOCOL VALIDATION FAILURE

The information system disables feedback to senders on protocol format validation failure.

Supplemental Guidance: Disabling feedback to senders when there is a failure in protocol validation format prevents adversaries from obtaining information which would otherwise be unavailable.

References: FIPS Publication 199; NIST Special Publications 800-41, 800-77.

Priority and Baseline Allocation:

| P1 | LOW SC-7 | MOD SC-7 (3) (4) (5) (7) | HIGH SC-7 (3) (4) (5) (7) (8) (18) (21) |

SC-8 TRANSMISSION CONFIDENTIALITY AND INTEGRITY

Control: The information system protects the [Selection (one or more): confidentiality; integrity] of transmitted information.

Supplemental Guidance: This control applies to both internal and external networks and all types of information system components from which information can be transmitted (e.g., servers, mobile devices, notebook computers, printers, copiers, scanners, facsimile machines). Communication paths outside the physical protection of a controlled boundary are exposed to the possibility of interception and modification. Protecting the confidentiality and/or integrity of organizational information can be accomplished by physical means (e.g., by employing protected distribution systems) or by logical means (e.g., employing encryption techniques). Organizations relying on commercial providers offering transmission services as commodity services rather than as fully dedicated services (i.e., services which can be highly specialized to individual customer needs), may find it difficult to obtain the necessary assurances regarding the implementation of needed security controls for transmission confidentiality/integrity. In such situations, organizations determine what types of confidentiality/integrity services are available in standard, commercial telecommunication service packages. If it is infeasible or impractical to obtain the necessary security controls and assurances of control effectiveness through appropriate contracting vehicles, organizations implement appropriate compensating security controls or explicitly accept the additional risk. Related controls: AC-17, PE-4.

Control Enhancements:

(1) TRANSMISSION CONFIDENTIALITY AND INTEGRITY | CRYPTOGRAPHIC OR ALTERNATE PHYSICAL PROTECTION

The information system implements cryptographic mechanisms to [Selection (one or more): prevent unauthorized disclosure of information; detect changes to information] during transmission unless otherwise protected by [Assignment: organization-defined alternative physical safeguards].

Supplemental Guidance: Encrypting information for transmission protects information from unauthorized disclosure and modification. Cryptographic mechanisms implemented to protect information integrity include, for example, cryptographic hash functions which have common application in digital signatures, checksums, and message authentication codes. Alternative physical security safeguards include, for example, protected distribution systems. Related control: SC-13.

(2) TRANSMISSION CONFIDENTIALITY AND INTEGRITY | PRE / POST TRANSMISSION HANDLING

The information system maintains the [Selection (one or more): confidentiality; integrity] of information during preparation for transmission and during reception.

Supplemental Guidance: Information can be either unintentionally or maliciously disclosed or modified during preparation for transmission or during reception including, for example, during aggregation, at protocol transformation points, and during packing/unpacking. These unauthorized disclosures or modifications compromise the confidentiality or integrity of the information. Related control: AU-10.

(3) TRANSMISSION CONFIDENTIALITY AND INTEGRITY | CRYPTOGRAPHIC PROTECTION FOR MESSAGE EXTERNALS

The information system implements cryptographic mechanisms to protect message externals unless otherwise protected by [Assignment: organization-defined alternative physical safeguards].

Supplemental Guidance: This control enhancement addresses protection against unauthorized disclosure of information. Message externals include, for example, message headers/routing information. This control enhancement prevents the exploitation of message externals and applies to both internal and external networks or links that may be visible to individuals who are not authorized users. Header/routing information is sometimes transmitted unencrypted because the information is not properly identified by organizations as having significant value or because encrypting the information can result in lower network performance and/or higher costs. Alternative physical safeguards include, for example, protected distribution systems. Related controls: SC-12, SC-13.

(4) *TRANSMISSION CONFIDENTIALITY AND INTEGRITY | CONCEAL / RANDOMIZE COMMUNICATIONS*

The information system implements cryptographic mechanisms to conceal or randomize communication patterns unless otherwise protected by [*Assignment: organization-defined alternative physical safeguards*].

Supplemental Guidance: This control enhancement addresses protection against unauthorized disclosure of information. Communication patterns include, for example, frequency, periods, amount, and predictability. Changes to communications patterns can reveal information having intelligence value especially when combined with other available information related to missions/business functions supported by organizational information systems. This control enhancement prevents the derivation of intelligence based on communications patterns and applies to both internal and external networks or links that may be visible to individuals who are not authorized users. Encrypting the links and transmitting in continuous, fixed/random patterns prevents the derivation of intelligence from the system communications patterns. Alternative physical safeguards include, for example, protected distribution systems. Related controls: SC-12, SC-13.

References: FIPS Publications 140-2, 197; NIST Special Publications 800-52, 800-77, 800-81, 800-113; CNSS Policy 15; NSTISSI No. 7003.

Priority and Baseline Allocation:

P1	LOW Not Selected	MOD SC-8 (1)	HIGH SC-8 (1)

SC-9 TRANSMISSION CONFIDENTIALITY

[Withdrawn: Incorporated into SC-8].

SC-10 NETWORK DISCONNECT

Control: The information system terminates the network connection associated with a communications session at the end of the session or after [*Assignment: organization-defined time period*] of inactivity.

Supplemental Guidance: This control applies to both internal and external networks. Terminating network connections associated with communications sessions include, for example, de-allocating associated TCP/IP address/port pairs at the operating system level, or de-allocating networking assignments at the application level if multiple application sessions are using a single, operating system-level network connection. Time periods of inactivity may be established by organizations and include, for example, time periods by type of network access or for specific network accesses.

Control Enhancements: None.

References: None.

Priority and Baseline Allocation:

P2	LOW Not Selected	MOD SC-10	HIGH SC-10

SC-11 TRUSTED PATH

Control: The information system establishes a trusted communications path between the user and the following security functions of the system: [*Assignment: organization-defined security functions to include at a minimum, information system authentication and re-authentication*].

Supplemental Guidance: Trusted paths are mechanisms by which users (through input devices) can communicate directly with security functions of information systems with the requisite assurance to support information security policies. The mechanisms can be activated only by users or the security functions of organizational information systems. User responses via trusted paths are protected from modifications by or disclosure to untrusted applications. Organizations employ trusted paths for high-assurance connections between security functions of information systems and users (e.g., during system logons). Enforcement of trusted communications paths is typically provided via an implementation that meets the reference monitor concept. Related controls: AC-16, AC-25.

Control Enhancements:

(1) TRUSTED PATH | LOGICAL ISOLATION

The information system provides a trusted communications path that is logically isolated and distinguishable from other paths.

References: None.

Priority and Baseline Allocation:

P0	LOW Not Selected	MOD Not Selected	HIGH Not Selected

SC-12 CRYPTOGRAPHIC KEY ESTABLISHMENT AND MANAGEMENT

Control: The organization establishes and manages cryptographic keys for required cryptography employed within the information system in accordance with [*Assignment: organization-defined requirements for key generation, distribution, storage, access, and destruction*].

Supplemental Guidance: Cryptographic key management and establishment can be performed using manual procedures or automated mechanisms with supporting manual procedures. Organizations define key management requirements in accordance with applicable federal laws, Executive Orders, directives, regulations, policies, standards, and guidance, specifying appropriate options, levels, and parameters. Organizations manage trust stores to ensure that only approved trust anchors are in such trust stores. This includes certificates with visibility external to organizational information systems and certificates related to the internal operations of systems. Related controls: SC-13, SC-17.

Control Enhancements:

(1) CRYPTOGRAPHIC KEY ESTABLISHMENT AND MANAGEMENT | AVAILABILITY

The organization maintains availability of information in the event of the loss of cryptographic keys by users.

Supplemental Guidance: Escrowing of encryption keys is a common practice for ensuring availability in the event of loss of keys (e.g., due to forgotten passphrase).

(2) CRYPTOGRAPHIC KEY ESTABLISHMENT AND MANAGEMENT | SYMMETRIC KEYS

The organization produces, controls, and distributes symmetric cryptographic keys using [*Selection: NIST FIPS-compliant; NSA-approved*] key management technology and processes.

(3) CRYPTOGRAPHIC KEY ESTABLISHMENT AND MANAGEMENT | ASYMMETRIC KEYS

The organization produces, controls, and distributes asymmetric cryptographic keys using [*Selection: NSA-approved key management technology and processes; approved PKI Class 3 certificates or prepositioned keying material; approved PKI Class 3 or Class 4 certificates and hardware security tokens that protect the user's private key*].

(4) *CRYPTOGRAPHIC KEY ESTABLISHMENT AND MANAGEMENT | PKI CERTIFICATES*
[Withdrawn: Incorporated into SC-12].

(5) *CRYPTOGRAPHIC KEY ESTABLISHMENT AND MANAGEMENT | PKI CERTIFICATES / HARDWARE TOKENS*
[Withdrawn: Incorporated into SC-12].

References: NIST Special Publications 800-56, 800-57.

Priority and Baseline Allocation:

P1	LOW SC-12	MOD SC-12	HIGH SC-12 (1)

SC-13 CRYPTOGRAPHIC PROTECTION

Control: The information system implements [*Assignment: organization-defined cryptographic uses and type of cryptography required for each use*] in accordance with applicable federal laws, Executive Orders, directives, policies, regulations, and standards.

Supplemental Guidance: Cryptography can be employed to support a variety of security solutions including, for example, the protection of classified and Controlled Unclassified Information, the provision of digital signatures, and the enforcement of information separation when authorized individuals have the necessary clearances for such information but lack the necessary formal access approvals. Cryptography can also be used to support random number generation and hash generation. Generally applicable cryptographic standards include FIPS-validated cryptography and NSA-approved cryptography. This control does not impose any requirements on organizations to use cryptography. However, if cryptography is required based on the selection of other security controls, organizations define each type of cryptographic use and the type of cryptography required (e.g., protection of classified information: NSA-approved cryptography; provision of digital signatures: FIPS-validated cryptography). Related controls: AC-2, AC-3, AC-7, AC-17, AC-18, AU-9, AU-10, CM-11, CP-9, IA-3, IA-7, MA-4, MP-2, MP-4, MP-5, SA-4, SC-8, SC-12, SC-28, SI-7.

Control Enhancements: None.

(1) *CRYPTOGRAPHIC PROTECTION | FIPS-VALIDATED CRYPTOGRAPHY*
[Withdrawn: Incorporated into SC-13].

(2) *CRYPTOGRAPHIC PROTECTION | NSA-APPROVED CRYPTOGRAPHY*
[Withdrawn: Incorporated into SC-13].

(3) *CRYPTOGRAPHIC PROTECTION | INDIVIDUALS WITHOUT FORMAL ACCESS APPROVALS*
[Withdrawn: Incorporated into SC-13].

(4) *CRYPTOGRAPHIC PROTECTION | DIGITAL SIGNATURES*
[Withdrawn: Incorporated into SC-13].

References: FIPS Publication 140; Web: http://csrc.nist.gov/cryptval, http://www.cnss.gov.

Priority and Baseline Allocation:

P1	LOW SC-13	MOD SC-13	HIGH SC-13

SC-14 PUBLIC ACCESS PROTECTIONS

[Withdrawn: Capability provided by AC-2, AC-3, AC-5, AC-6, SI-3, SI-4, SI-5, SI-7, SI-10].

SC-15 COLLABORATIVE COMPUTING DEVICES

Control: The information system:

a. Prohibits remote activation of collaborative computing devices with the following exceptions: [*Assignment: organization-defined exceptions where remote activation is to be allowed*]; and

b. Provides an explicit indication of use to users physically present at the devices.

Supplemental Guidance: Collaborative computing devices include, for example, networked white boards, cameras, and microphones. Explicit indication of use includes, for example, signals to users when collaborative computing devices are activated. Related control: AC-21.

Control Enhancements:

(1) COLLABORATIVE COMPUTING DEVICES | PHYSICAL DISCONNECT

The information system provides physical disconnect of collaborative computing devices in a manner that supports ease of use.

Supplemental Guidance: Failing to physically disconnect from collaborative computing devices can result in subsequent compromises of organizational information. Providing easy methods to physically disconnect from such devices after a collaborative computing session helps to ensure that participants actually carry out the disconnect activity without having to go through complex and tedious procedures.

(2) COLLABORATIVE COMPUTING DEVICES | BLOCKING INBOUND / OUTBOUND COMMUNICATIONS TRAFFIC

[Withdrawn: Incorporated into SC-7].

(3) COLLABORATIVE COMPUTING DEVICES | DISABLING / REMOVAL IN SECURE WORK AREAS

The organization disables or removes collaborative computing devices from [*Assignment: organization-defined information systems or information system components*] in [*Assignment: organization-defined secure work areas*].

Supplemental Guidance: Failing to disable or remove collaborative computing devices from information systems or information system components can result in subsequent compromises of organizational information including, for example, eavesdropping on conversations.

(4) COLLABORATIVE COMPUTING DEVICES | EXPLICITLY INDICATE CURRENT PARTICIPANTS

The information system provides an explicit indication of current participants in [*Assignment: organization-defined online meetings and teleconferences*].

Supplemental Guidance: This control enhancement helps to prevent unauthorized individuals from participating in collaborative computing sessions without the explicit knowledge of other participants.

References: None.

Priority and Baseline Allocation:

| P1 | LOW SC-15 | MOD SC-15 | HIGH SC-15 |

SC-16 TRANSMISSION OF SECURITY ATTRIBUTES

Control: The information system associates [*Assignment: organization-defined security attributes*] with information exchanged between information systems and between system components.

Supplemental Guidance: Security attributes can be explicitly or implicitly associated with the information contained in organizational information systems or system components. Related controls: AC-3, AC-4, AC-16.

Control Enhancements:

(1) TRANSMISSION OF SECURITY ATTRIBUTES | INTEGRITY VALIDATION

The information system validates the integrity of transmitted security attributes.

Supplemental Guidance: This control enhancement ensures that the verification of the integrity of transmitted information includes security attributes. Related controls: AU-10, SC-8.

References: None.

Priority and Baseline Allocation:

| P0 | LOW Not Selected | MOD Not Selected | HIGH Not Selected |

SC-17 **PUBLIC KEY INFRASTRUCTURE CERTIFICATES**

Control: The organization issues public key certificates under an [*Assignment: organization-defined certificate policy*] or obtains public key certificates from an approved service provider.

Supplemental Guidance: For all certificates, organizations manage information system trust stores to ensure only approved trust anchors are in the trust stores. This control addresses both certificates with visibility external to organizational information systems and certificates related to the internal operations of systems, for example, application-specific time services. Related control: SC-12.

Control Enhancements: None.

References: OMB Memorandum 05-24; NIST Special Publications 800-32, 800-63.

Priority and Baseline Allocation:

| P1 | LOW Not Selected | MOD SC-17 | HIGH SC-17 |

SC-18 **MOBILE CODE**

Control: The organization:

a. Defines acceptable and unacceptable mobile code and mobile code technologies;

b. Establishes usage restrictions and implementation guidance for acceptable mobile code and mobile code technologies; and

c. Authorizes, monitors, and controls the use of mobile code within the information system.

Supplemental Guidance: Decisions regarding the employment of mobile code within organizational information systems are based on the potential for the code to cause damage to the systems if used maliciously. Mobile code technologies include, for example, Java, JavaScript, ActiveX, Postscript, PDF, Shockwave movies, Flash animations, and VBScript. Usage restrictions and implementation guidance apply to both the selection and use of mobile code installed on servers and mobile code downloaded and executed on individual workstations and devices (e.g., smart phones). Mobile code policy and procedures address preventing the development, acquisition, or introduction of unacceptable mobile code within organizational information systems. Related controls: AU-2, AU-12, CM-2, CM-6, SI-3.

Control Enhancements:

(1) *MOBILE CODE | IDENTIFY UNACCEPTABLE CODE / TAKE CORRECTIVE ACTIONS*

The information system identifies [*Assignment: organization-defined unacceptable mobile code*] and takes [*Assignment: organization-defined corrective actions*].

Supplemental Guidance: Corrective actions when unacceptable mobile code is detected include, for example, blocking, quarantine, or alerting administrators. Blocking includes, for example, preventing transmission of word processing files with embedded macros when such macros have been defined to be unacceptable mobile code.

(2) MOBILE CODE | ACQUISITION / DEVELOPMENT / USE

The organization ensures that the acquisition, development, and use of mobile code to be deployed in the information system meets [*Assignment: organization-defined mobile code requirements*].

(3) MOBILE CODE | PREVENT DOWNLOADING / EXECUTION

The information system prevents the download and execution of [*Assignment: organization-defined unacceptable mobile code*].

(4) MOBILE CODE | PREVENT AUTOMATIC EXECUTION

The information system prevents the automatic execution of mobile code in [*Assignment: organization-defined software applications*] and enforces [*Assignment: organization-defined actions*] prior to executing the code.

Supplemental Guidance: Actions enforced before executing mobile code, include, for example, prompting users prior to opening electronic mail attachments. Preventing automatic execution of mobile code includes, for example, disabling auto execute features on information system components employing portable storage devices such as Compact Disks (CDs), Digital Video Disks (DVDs), and Universal Serial Bus (USB) devices.

(5) MOBILE CODE | ALLOW EXECUTION ONLY IN CONFINED ENVIRONMENTS

The organization allows execution of permitted mobile code only in confined virtual machine environments.

References: NIST Special Publication 800-28; DoD Instruction 8552.01.

Priority and Baseline Allocation:

| P2 | LOW Not Selected | MOD SC-18 | HIGH SC-18 |

SC-19 VOICE OVER INTERNET PROTOCOL

Control: The organization:

a. Establishes usage restrictions and implementation guidance for Voice over Internet Protocol (VoIP) technologies based on the potential to cause damage to the information system if used maliciously; and

b. Authorizes, monitors, and controls the use of VoIP within the information system.

Supplemental Guidance: Related controls: CM-6, SC-7, SC-15.

Control Enhancements: None.

References: NIST Special Publication 800-58.

Priority and Baseline Allocation:

| P1 | LOW Not Selected | MOD SC-19 | HIGH SC-19 |

SC-20 SECURE NAME / ADDRESS RESOLUTION SERVICE (AUTHORITATIVE SOURCE)

Control: The information system:

a. Provides additional data origin authentication and integrity verification artifacts along with the authoritative name resolution data the system returns in response to external name/address resolution queries; and

b. Provides the means to indicate the security status of child zones and (if the child supports secure resolution services) to enable verification of a chain of trust among parent and child domains, when operating as part of a distributed, hierarchical namespace.

Supplemental Guidance: This control enables external clients including, for example, remote Internet clients, to obtain origin authentication and integrity verification assurances for the host/service name to network address resolution information obtained through the service. Information systems that provide name and address resolution services include, for example, domain name system (DNS) servers. Additional artifacts include, for example, DNS Security (DNSSEC) digital signatures and cryptographic keys. DNS resource records are examples of authoritative data. The means to indicate the security status of child zones includes, for example, the use of delegation signer resource records in the DNS. The DNS security controls reflect (and are referenced from) OMB Memorandum 08-23. Information systems that use technologies other than the DNS to map between host/service names and network addresses provide other means to assure the authenticity and integrity of response data. Related controls: AU-10, SC-8, SC-12, SC-13, SC-21, SC-22.

Control Enhancements:

(1) SECURE NAME / ADDRESS RESOLUTION SERVICE (AUTHORITATIVE SOURCE) | CHILD SUBSPACES
[Withdrawn: Incorporated into SC-20].

(2) SECURE NAME / ADDRESS RESOLUTION SERVICE (AUTHORITATIVE SOURCE) | DATA ORIGIN / INTEGRITY
The information system provides data origin and integrity protection artifacts for internal name/address resolution queries.

References: OMB Memorandum 08-23; NIST Special Publication 800-81.

Priority and Baseline Allocation:

| P1 | LOW SC-20 | MOD SC-20 | HIGH SC-20 |

SC-21 **SECURE NAME / ADDRESS RESOLUTION SERVICE (RECURSIVE OR CACHING RESOLVER)**

Control: The information system requests and performs data origin authentication and data integrity verification on the name/address resolution responses the system receives from authoritative sources.

Supplemental Guidance: Each client of name resolution services either performs this validation on its own, or has authenticated channels to trusted validation providers. Information systems that provide name and address resolution services for local clients include, for example, recursive resolving or caching domain name system (DNS) servers. DNS client resolvers either perform validation of DNSSEC signatures, or clients use authenticated channels to recursive resolvers that perform such validations. Information systems that use technologies other than the DNS to map between host/service names and network addresses provide other means to enable clients to verify the authenticity and integrity of response data. Related controls: SC-20, SC-22.

Control Enhancements: None.

(1) SECURE NAME / ADDRESS RESOLUTION SERVICE (RECURSIVE OR CACHING RESOLVER) | DATA ORIGIN / INTEGRITY
[Withdrawn: Incorporated into SC-21].

References: NIST Special Publication 800-81.

Priority and Baseline Allocation:

| P1 | LOW SC-21 | MOD SC-21 | HIGH SC-21 |

SC-22 **ARCHITECTURE AND PROVISIONING FOR NAME / ADDRESS RESOLUTION SERVICE**

Control: The information systems that collectively provide name/address resolution service for an organization are fault-tolerant and implement internal/external role separation.

Supplemental Guidance: Information systems that provide name and address resolution services include, for example, domain name system (DNS) servers. To eliminate single points of failure and to enhance redundancy, organizations employ at least two authoritative domain name system servers, one configured as the primary server and the other configured as the secondary server. Additionally, organizations typically deploy the servers in two geographically separated network subnetworks (i.e., not located in the same physical facility). For role separation, DNS servers with internal roles only process name and address resolution requests from within organizations (i.e., from internal clients). DNS servers with external roles only process name and address resolution information requests from clients external to organizations (i.e., on external networks including the Internet). Organizations specify clients that can access authoritative DNS servers in particular roles (e.g., by address ranges, explicit lists). Related controls: SC-2, SC-20, SC-21, SC-24.

Control Enhancements: None.

References: NIST Special Publication 800-81.

Priority and Baseline Allocation:

P1	LOW SC-22	MOD SC-22	HIGH SC-22

SC-23 SESSION AUTHENTICITY

Control: The information system protects the authenticity of communications sessions.

Supplemental Guidance: This control addresses communications protection at the session, versus packet level (e.g., sessions in service-oriented architectures providing web-based services) and establishes grounds for confidence at both ends of communications sessions in ongoing identities of other parties and in the validity of information transmitted. Authenticity protection includes, for example, protecting against man-in-the-middle attacks/session hijacking and the insertion of false information into sessions. Related controls: SC-8, SC-10, SC-11.

Control Enhancements:

(1) SESSION AUTHENTICITY | INVALIDATE SESSION IDENTIFIERS AT LOGOUT

The information system invalidates session identifiers upon user logout or other session termination.

Supplemental Guidance: This control enhancement curtails the ability of adversaries from capturing and continuing to employ previously valid session IDs.

(2) SESSION AUTHENTICITY | USER-INITIATED LOGOUTS / MESSAGE DISPLAYS

[Withdrawn: Incorporated into AC-12 (1)].

(3) SESSION AUTHENTICITY | UNIQUE SESSION IDENTIFIERS WITH RANDOMIZATION

The information system generates a unique session identifier for each session with [*Assignment: organization-defined randomness requirements*] and recognizes only session identifiers that are system-generated.

Supplemental Guidance: This control enhancement curtails the ability of adversaries from reusing previously valid session IDs. Employing the concept of randomness in the generation of unique session identifiers helps to protect against brute-force attacks to determine future session identifiers. Related control: SC-13.

(4) SESSION AUTHENTICITY | UNIQUE SESSION IDENTIFIERS WITH RANDOMIZATION

[Withdrawn: Incorporated into SC-23 (3)].

(5) SESSION AUTHENTICITY | ALLOWED CERTIFICATE AUTHORITIES

The information system only allows the use of [*Assignment: organization-defined certificate authorities*] for verification of the establishment of protected sessions.

Supplemental Guidance: Reliance on certificate authorities (CAs) for the establishment of secure sessions includes, for example, the use of Secure Socket Layer (SSL) and/or Transport Layer Security (TLS) certificates. These certificates, after verification by the respective certificate authorities, facilitate the establishment of protected sessions between web clients and web servers. Related control: SC-13.

References: NIST Special Publications 800-52, 800-77, 800-95.

Priority and Baseline Allocation:

| P1 | LOW Not Selected | MOD SC-23 | HIGH SC-23 |

SC-24 **FAIL IN KNOWN STATE**

Control: The information system fails to a [*Assignment: organization-defined known-state*] for [*Assignment: organization-defined types of failures*] preserving [*Assignment: organization-defined system state information*] in failure.

Supplemental Guidance: Failure in a known state addresses security concerns in accordance with the mission/business needs of organizations. Failure in a known secure state helps to prevent the loss of confidentiality, integrity, or availability of information in the event of failures of organizational information systems or system components. Failure in a known safe state helps to prevent systems from failing to a state that may cause injury to individuals or destruction to property. Preserving information system state information facilitates system restart and return to the operational mode of organizations with less disruption of mission/business processes. Related controls: CP-2, CP-10, CP-12, SC-7, SC-22.

Control Enhancements: None.

References: None.

Priority and Baseline Allocation:

| P1 | LOW Not Selected | MOD Not Selected | HIGH SC-24 |

SC-25 **THIN NODES**

Control: The organization employs [*Assignment: organization-defined information system components*] with minimal functionality and information storage.

Supplemental Guidance: The deployment of information system components with reduced/minimal functionality (e.g., diskless nodes and thin client technologies) reduces the need to secure every user endpoint, and may reduce the exposure of information, information systems, and services to cyber attacks. Related control: SC-30.

Control Enhancements: None.

References: None.

Priority and Baseline Allocation:

| P0 | LOW Not Selected | MOD Not Selected | HIGH Not Selected |

SC-26 **HONEYPOTS**

Control: The information system includes components specifically designed to be the target of malicious attacks for the purpose of detecting, deflecting, and analyzing such attacks.

Supplemental Guidance: A honeypot is set up as a decoy to attract adversaries and to deflect their attacks away from the operational systems supporting organizational missions/business function.

Depending upon the specific usage of the honeypot, consultation with the Office of the General Counsel before deployment may be needed. Related controls: SC-30, SC-44, SI-3, SI-4.

Control Enhancements: None.

(1) HONEYPOTS | DETECTION OF MALICIOUS CODE
[Withdrawn: Incorporated into SC-35].

References: None.

Priority and Baseline Allocation:

| P0 | LOW Not Selected | MOD Not Selected | HIGH Not Selected |

SC-27 **PLATFORM-INDEPENDENT APPLICATIONS**

Control: The information system includes: [*Assignment: organization-defined platform-independent applications*].

Supplemental Guidance: Platforms are combinations of hardware and software used to run software applications. Platforms include: (i) operating systems; (ii) the underlying computer architectures, or (iii) both. Platform-independent applications are applications that run on multiple platforms. Such applications promote portability and reconstitution on different platforms, increasing the availability of critical functions within organizations while information systems with specific operating systems are under attack. Related control: SC-29.

Control Enhancements: None.

References: None.

Priority and Baseline Allocation:

| P0 | LOW Not Selected | MOD Not Selected | HIGH Not Selected |

SC-28 **PROTECTION OF INFORMATION AT REST**

Control: The information system protects the [*Selection (one or more): confidentiality; integrity*] of [*Assignment: organization-defined information at rest*].

Supplemental Guidance: This control addresses the confidentiality and integrity of information at rest and covers user information and system information. Information at rest refers to the state of information when it is located on storage devices as specific components of information systems. System-related information requiring protection includes, for example, configurations or rule sets for firewalls, gateways, intrusion detection/prevention systems, filtering routers, and authenticator content. Organizations may employ different mechanisms to achieve confidentiality and integrity protections, including the use of cryptographic mechanisms and file share scanning. Integrity protection can be achieved, for example, by implementing Write-Once-Read-Many (WORM) technologies. Organizations may also employ other security controls including, for example, secure off-line storage in lieu of online storage when adequate protection of information at rest cannot otherwise be achieved and/or continuous monitoring to identify malicious code at rest. Related controls: AC-3, AC-6, CA-7, CM-3, CM-5, CM-6, PE-3, SC-8, SC-13, SI-3, SI-7.

Control Enhancements:

(1) PROTECTION OF INFORMATION AT REST | CRYPTOGRAPHIC PROTECTION
 The information system implements cryptographic mechanisms to prevent unauthorized disclosure and modification of [*Assignment: organization-defined information*] on [*Assignment: organization-defined information system components*].

Supplemental Guidance: Selection of cryptographic mechanisms is based on the need to protect the confidentiality and integrity of organizational information. The strength of mechanism is commensurate with the security category and/or classification of the information. This control enhancement applies to significant concentrations of digital media in organizational areas designated for media storage and also to limited quantities of media generally associated with information system components in operational environments (e.g., portable storage devices, mobile devices). Organizations have the flexibility to either encrypt all information on storage devices (i.e., full disk encryption) or encrypt specific data structures (e.g., files, records, or fields). Organizations employing cryptographic mechanisms to protect information at rest also consider cryptographic key management solutions. Related controls: AC-19, SC-12.

(2) PROTECTION OF INFORMATION AT REST | OFF-LINE STORAGE

The organization removes from online storage and stores off-line in a secure location [*Assignment: organization-defined information*].

Supplemental Guidance: Removing organizational information from online information system storage to off-line storage eliminates the possibility of individuals gaining unauthorized access to the information through a network. Therefore, organizations may choose to move information to off-line storage in lieu of protecting such information in online storage.

References: NIST Special Publications 800-56, 800-57, 800-111.

Priority and Baseline Allocation:

| P1 | LOW Not Selected | MOD SC-28 | HIGH SC-28 |

SC-29 HETEROGENEITY

Control: The organization employs a diverse set of information technologies for [*Assignment: organization-defined information system components*] in the implementation of the information system.

Supplemental Guidance: Increasing the diversity of information technologies within organizational information systems reduces the impact of potential exploitations of specific technologies and also defends against common mode failures, including those failures induced by supply chain attacks. Diversity in information technologies also reduces the likelihood that the means adversaries use to compromise one information system component will be equally effective against other system components, thus further increasing the adversary work factor to successfully complete planned cyber attacks. An increase in diversity may add complexity and management overhead which could ultimately lead to mistakes and unauthorized configurations. Related controls: SA-12, SA-14, SC-27.

Control Enhancements:

(1) HETEROGENEITY | VIRTUALIZATION TECHNIQUES

The organization employs virtualization techniques to support the deployment of a diversity of operating systems and applications that are changed [*Assignment: organization-defined frequency*].

Supplemental Guidance: While frequent changes to operating systems and applications pose configuration management challenges, the changes can result in an increased work factor for adversaries in order to carry out successful cyber attacks. Changing virtual operating systems or applications, as opposed to changing actual operating systems/applications, provide virtual changes that impede attacker success while reducing configuration management efforts. In addition, virtualization techniques can assist organizations in isolating untrustworthy software and/or software of dubious provenance into confined execution environments.

References: None.

Priority and Baseline Allocation:

| P0 | **LOW** Not Selected | **MOD** Not Selected | **HIGH** Not Selected |

SC-30 CONCEALMENT AND MISDIRECTION

Control: The organization employs [*Assignment: organization-defined concealment and misdirection techniques*] for [*Assignment: organization-defined information systems*] at [*Assignment: organization-defined time periods*] to confuse and mislead adversaries.

Supplemental Guidance: Concealment and misdirection techniques can significantly reduce the targeting capability of adversaries (i.e., window of opportunity and available attack surface) to initiate and complete cyber attacks. For example, virtualization techniques provide organizations with the ability to disguise information systems, potentially reducing the likelihood of successful attacks without the cost of having multiple platforms. Increased use of concealment/misdirection techniques including, for example, randomness, uncertainty, and virtualization, may sufficiently confuse and mislead adversaries and subsequently increase the risk of discovery and/or exposing tradecraft. Concealment/misdirection techniques may also provide organizations additional time to successfully perform core missions and business functions. Because of the time and effort required to support concealment/misdirection techniques, it is anticipated that such techniques would be used by organizations on a very limited basis. Related controls: SC-26, SC-29, SI-14.

Control Enhancements:

(1) CONCEALMENT AND MISDIRECTION | VIRTUALIZATION TECHNIQUES

[Withdrawn: Incorporated into SC-29 (1)].

(2) CONCEALMENT AND MISDIRECTION | RANDOMNESS

The organization employs [*Assignment: organization-defined techniques*] to introduce randomness into organizational operations and assets.

Supplemental Guidance: Randomness introduces increased levels of uncertainty for adversaries regarding the actions organizations take in defending against cyber attacks. Such actions may impede the ability of adversaries to correctly target information resources of organizations supporting critical missions/business functions. Uncertainty may also cause adversaries to hesitate before initiating or continuing attacks. Misdirection techniques involving randomness include, for example, performing certain routine actions at different times of day, employing different information technologies (e.g., browsers, search engines), using different suppliers, and rotating roles and responsibilities of organizational personnel.

(3) CONCEALMENT AND MISDIRECTION | CHANGE PROCESSING / STORAGE LOCATIONS

The organization changes the location of [*Assignment: organization-defined processing and/or storage*] [*Selection: [Assignment: organization-defined time frequency]; at random time intervals*]].

Supplemental Guidance: Adversaries target critical organizational missions/business functions and the information resources supporting those missions and functions while at the same time, trying to minimize exposure of their existence and tradecraft. The static, homogeneous, and deterministic nature of organizational information systems targeted by adversaries, make such systems more susceptible to cyber attacks with less adversary cost and effort to be successful. Changing organizational processing and storage locations (sometimes referred to as moving target defense) addresses the advanced persistent threat (APT) using techniques such as virtualization, distributed processing, and replication. This enables organizations to relocate the information resources (i.e., processing and/or storage) supporting critical missions and business functions. Changing locations of processing activities and/or storage sites introduces uncertainty into the targeting activities by adversaries. This uncertainty increases the work factor of adversaries making compromises or breaches to organizational information systems much more difficult and time-consuming, and increases the chances that adversaries may inadvertently disclose aspects of tradecraft while attempting to locate critical organizational resources.

(4) CONCEALMENT AND MISDIRECTION | MISLEADING INFORMATION

The organization employs realistic, but misleading information in [*Assignment: organization-defined information system components*] with regard to its security state or posture.

Supplemental Guidance: This control enhancement misleads potential adversaries regarding the nature and extent of security safeguards deployed by organizations. As a result, adversaries may employ incorrect (and as a result ineffective) attack techniques. One way of misleading adversaries is for organizations to place misleading information regarding the specific security controls deployed in external information systems that are known to be accessed or targeted by adversaries. Another technique is the use of deception nets (e.g., honeynets, virtualized environments) that mimic actual aspects of organizational information systems but use, for example, out-of-date software configurations.

(5) CONCEALMENT AND MISDIRECTION | CONCEALMENT OF SYSTEM COMPONENTS

The organization employs [*Assignment: organization-defined techniques*] to hide or conceal [*Assignment: organization-defined information system components*].

Supplemental Guidance: By hiding, disguising, or otherwise concealing critical information system components, organizations may be able to decrease the probability that adversaries target and successfully compromise those assets. Potential means for organizations to hide and/or conceal information system components include, for example, configuration of routers or the use of honeynets or virtualization techniques.

References: None.

Priority and Baseline Allocation:

P0	LOW Not Selected	MOD Not Selected	HIGH Not Selected

SC-31 COVERT CHANNEL ANALYSIS

Control: The organization:

a. Performs a covert channel analysis to identify those aspects of communications within the information system that are potential avenues for covert [*Selection (one or more): storage; timing*] channels; and

b. Estimates the maximum bandwidth of those channels.

Supplemental Guidance: Developers are in the best position to identify potential areas within systems that might lead to covert channels. Covert channel analysis is a meaningful activity when there is the potential for unauthorized information flows across security domains, for example, in the case of information systems containing export-controlled information and having connections to external networks (i.e., networks not controlled by organizations). Covert channel analysis is also meaningful for multilevel secure (MLS) information systems, multiple security level (MSL) systems, and cross-domain systems. Related controls: AC-3, AC-4, PL-2.

Control Enhancements:

(1) COVERT CHANNEL ANALYSIS | TEST COVERT CHANNELS FOR EXPLOITABILITY

The organization tests a subset of the identified covert channels to determine which channels are exploitable.

(2) COVERT CHANNEL ANALYSIS | MAXIMUM BANDWIDTH

The organization reduces the maximum bandwidth for identified covert [*Selection (one or more); storage; timing*] channels to [*Assignment: organization-defined values*].

Supplemental Guidance: Information system developers are in the best position to reduce the maximum bandwidth for identified covert storage and timing channels.

(3) COVERT CHANNEL ANALYSIS | MEASURE BANDWIDTH IN OPERATIONAL ENVIRONMENTS

The organization measures the bandwidth of [*Assignment: organization-defined subset of identified covert channels*] in the operational environment of the information system.

Supplemental Guidance: This control enhancement addresses covert channel bandwidth in operational environments versus developmental environments. Measuring covert channel bandwidth in operational environments helps organizations to determine how much information can be covertly leaked before such leakage adversely affects organizational missions/business functions. Covert channel bandwidth may be significantly different when measured in those settings that are independent of the particular environments of operation (e.g., laboratories or development environments).

References: None.

Priority and Baseline Allocation:

| P0 | LOW Not Selected | MOD Not Selected | HIGH Not Selected |

SC-32 INFORMATION SYSTEM PARTITIONING

Control: The organization partitions the information system into [Assignment: organization-defined information system components] residing in separate physical domains or environments based on [Assignment: organization-defined circumstances for physical separation of components].

Supplemental Guidance: Information system partitioning is a part of a defense-in-depth protection strategy. Organizations determine the degree of physical separation of system components from physically distinct components in separate racks in the same room, to components in separate rooms for the more critical components, to more significant geographical separation of the most critical components. Security categorization can guide the selection of appropriate candidates for domain partitioning. Managed interfaces restrict or prohibit network access and information flow among partitioned information system components. Related controls: AC-4, SA-8, SC-2, SC-3, SC-7.

Control Enhancements: None.

References: FIPS Publication 199.

Priority and Baseline Allocation:

| P0 | LOW Not Selected | MOD Not Selected | HIGH Not Selected |

SC-33 TRANSMISSION PREPARATION INTEGRITY

[Withdrawn: Incorporated into SC-8].

SC-34 NON-MODIFIABLE EXECUTABLE PROGRAMS

Control: The information system at [Assignment: organization-defined information system components]:

a. Loads and executes the operating environment from hardware-enforced, read-only media; and

b. Loads and executes [Assignment: organization-defined applications] from hardware-enforced, read-only media.

Supplemental Guidance: The term *operating environment* is defined as the specific code that hosts applications, for example, operating systems, executives, or monitors including virtual machine monitors (i.e., hypervisors). It can also include certain applications running directly on hardware platforms. Hardware-enforced, read-only media include, for example, Compact Disk-Recordable

(CD-R)/Digital Video Disk-Recordable (DVD-R) disk drives and one-time programmable read-only memory. The use of non-modifiable storage ensures the integrity of software from the point of creation of the read-only image. The use of reprogrammable read-only memory can be accepted as read-only media provided: (i) integrity can be adequately protected from the point of initial writing to the insertion of the memory into the information system; and (ii) there are reliable hardware protections against reprogramming the memory while installed in organizational information systems. Related controls: AC-3, SI-7.

Control Enhancements:

(1) *NON-MODIFIABLE EXECUTABLE PROGRAMS | NO WRITABLE STORAGE*

   The organization employs [*Assignment: organization-defined information system components*] with no writeable storage that is persistent across component restart or power on/off.

   Supplemental Guidance: This control enhancement: (i) eliminates the possibility of malicious code insertion via persistent, writeable storage within the designated information system components; and (ii) applies to both fixed and removable storage, with the latter being addressed directly or as specific restrictions imposed through access controls for mobile devices. Related controls: AC-19, MP-7.

(2) *NON-MODIFIABLE EXECUTABLE PROGRAMS | INTEGRITY PROTECTION / READ-ONLY MEDIA*

   The organization protects the integrity of information prior to storage on read-only media and controls the media after such information has been recorded onto the media.

   Supplemental Guidance: Security safeguards prevent the substitution of media into information systems or the reprogramming of programmable read-only media prior to installation into the systems. Security safeguards include, for example, a combination of prevention, detection, and response. Related controls: AC-5, CM-3, CM-5, CM-9, MP-2, MP-4, MP-5, SA-12, SC-28, SI-3.

(3) *NON-MODIFIABLE EXECUTABLE PROGRAMS | HARDWARE-BASED PROTECTION*

   The organization:

   (a) **Employs hardware-based, write-protect for [*Assignment: organization-defined information system firmware components*]; and**

   (b) **Implements specific procedures for [*Assignment: organization-defined authorized individuals*] to manually disable hardware write-protect for firmware modifications and re-enable the write-protect prior to returning to operational mode.**

References: None.

Priority and Baseline Allocation:

| P0 | LOW Not Selected | MOD Not Selected | HIGH Not Selected |

SC-35 HONEYCLIENTS

Control: The information system includes components that proactively seek to identify malicious websites and/or web-based malicious code.

Supplemental Guidance: Honeyclients differ from honeypots in that the components actively probe the Internet in search of malicious code (e.g., worms) contained on external websites. As with honeypots, honeyclients require some supporting isolation measures (e.g., virtualization) to ensure that any malicious code discovered during the search and subsequently executed does not infect organizational information systems. Related controls: SC-26, SC-44, SI-3, SI-4.

Control Enhancements: None.

References: None.

Priority and Baseline Allocation:

| P0 | LOW Not Selected | MOD Not Selected | HIGH Not Selected |

SC-36 **DISTRIBUTED PROCESSING AND STORAGE**

Control: The organization distributes [*Assignment: organization-defined processing and storage*] across multiple physical locations.

Supplemental Guidance: Distributing processing and storage across multiple physical locations provides some degree of redundancy or overlap for organizations, and therefore increases the work factor of adversaries to adversely impact organizational operations, assets, and individuals. This control does not assume a single primary processing or storage location, and thus allows for parallel processing and storage. Related controls: CP-6, CP-7.

Control Enhancements:

(1) DISTRIBUTED PROCESSING AND STORAGE | POLLING TECHNIQUES

The organization employs polling techniques to identify potential faults, errors, or compromises to [*Assignment: organization-defined distributed processing and storage components*].

Supplemental Guidance: Distributed processing and/or storage may be employed to reduce opportunities for adversaries to successfully compromise the confidentiality, integrity, or availability of information and information systems. However, distribution of processing and/or storage components does not prevent adversaries from compromising one (or more) of the distributed components. Polling compares the processing results and/or storage content from the various distributed components and subsequently voting on the outcomes. Polling identifies potential faults, errors, or compromises in distributed processing and/or storage components. Related control: SI-4.

References: None.

Priority and Baseline Allocation:

| P0 | LOW Not Selected | MOD Not Selected | HIGH Not Selected |

SC-37 **OUT-OF-BAND CHANNELS**

Control: The organization employs [*Assignment: organization-defined out-of-band channels*] for the physical delivery or electronic transmission of [*Assignment: organization-defined information, information system components, or devices*] to [*Assignment: organization-defined individuals or information systems*].

Supplemental Guidance: Out-of-band channels include, for example, local (nonnetwork) accesses to information systems, network paths physically separate from network paths used for operational traffic, or nonelectronic paths such as the US Postal Service. This is in contrast with using the same channels (i.e., in-band channels) that carry routine operational traffic. Out-of-band channels do not have the same vulnerability/exposure as in-band channels, and hence the confidentiality, integrity, or availability compromises of in-band channels will not compromise the out-of-band channels. Organizations may employ out-of-band channels in the delivery or transmission of many organizational items including, for example, identifiers/authenticators, configuration management changes for hardware, firmware, or software, cryptographic key management information, security updates, system/data backups, maintenance information, and malicious code protection updates. Related controls: AC-2, CM-3, CM-5, CM-7, IA-4, IA-5, MA-4, SC-12, SI-3, SI-4, SI-7.

Control Enhancements:

(1) OUT-OF-BAND CHANNELS | ENSURE DELIVERY / TRANSMISSION

The organization employs [*Assignment: organization-defined security safeguards*] to ensure that only [*Assignment: organization-defined individuals or information systems*] receive the [*Assignment: organization-defined information, information system components, or devices*].

Supplemental Guidance: Techniques and/or methods employed by organizations to ensure that only designated information systems or individuals receive particular information, system components, or devices include, for example, sending authenticators via courier service but requiring recipients to show some form of government-issued photographic identification as a condition of receipt.

References: None.

Priority and Baseline Allocation:

P0	LOW Not Selected	MOD Not Selected	HIGH Not Selected

SC-38 OPERATIONS SECURITY

Control: The organization employs [*Assignment: organization-defined operations security safeguards*] to protect key organizational information throughout the system development life cycle.

Supplemental Guidance: Operations security (OPSEC) is a systematic process by which potential adversaries can be denied information about the capabilities and intentions of organizations by identifying, controlling, and protecting generally unclassified information that specifically relates to the planning and execution of sensitive organizational activities. The OPSEC process involves five steps: (i) identification of critical information (e.g., the security categorization process); (ii) analysis of threats; (iii) analysis of vulnerabilities; (iv) assessment of risks; and (v) the application of appropriate countermeasures. OPSEC safeguards are applied to both organizational information systems and the environments in which those systems operate. OPSEC safeguards help to protect the confidentiality of key information including, for example, limiting the sharing of information with suppliers and potential suppliers of information system components, information technology products and services, and with other non-organizational elements and individuals. Information critical to mission/business success includes, for example, user identities, element uses, suppliers, supply chain processes, functional and security requirements, system design specifications, testing protocols, and security control implementation details. Related controls: RA-2, RA-5, SA-12.

Control Enhancements: None.

References: None.

Priority and Baseline Allocation:

P0	LOW Not Selected	MOD Not Selected	HIGH Not Selected

SC-39 PROCESS ISOLATION

Control: The information system maintains a separate execution domain for each executing process.

Supplemental Guidance: Information systems can maintain separate execution domains for each executing process by assigning each process a separate address space. Each information system process has a distinct address space so that communication between processes is performed in a manner controlled through the security functions, and one process cannot modify the executing code of another process. Maintaining separate execution domains for executing processes can be achieved, for example, by implementing separate address spaces. This capability is available in most commercial operating systems that employ multi-state processor technologies. Related controls: AC-3, AC-4, AC-6, SA-4, SA-5, SA-8, SC-2, SC-3.

Control Enhancements:

(1) PROCESS ISOLATION | HARDWARE SEPARATION

The information system implements underlying hardware separation mechanisms to facilitate process separation.

Supplemental Guidance: Hardware-based separation of information system processes is generally less susceptible to compromise than software-based separation, thus providing greater assurance that the separation will be enforced. Underlying hardware separation mechanisms include, for example, hardware memory management.

(2) PROCESS ISOLATION | THREAD ISOLATION

The information system maintains a separate execution domain for each thread in [*Assignment: organization-defined multi-threaded processing*].

References: None.

Priority and Baseline Allocation:

| P1 | LOW SC-39 | MOD SC-39 | HIGH SC-39 |

SC-40 WIRELESS LINK PROTECTION

Control: The information system protects external and internal [*Assignment: organization-defined wireless links*] from [*Assignment: organization-defined types of signal parameter attacks or references to sources for such attacks*].

Supplemental Guidance: This control applies to internal and external wireless communication links that may be visible to individuals who are not authorized information system users. Adversaries can exploit the signal parameters of wireless links if such links are not adequately protected. There are many ways to exploit the signal parameters of wireless links to gain intelligence, deny service, or to spoof users of organizational information systems. This control reduces the impact of attacks that are unique to wireless systems. If organizations rely on commercial service providers for transmission services as commodity items rather than as fully dedicated services, it may not be possible to implement this control. Related controls: AC-18, SC-5.

Control Enhancements:

(1) WIRELESS LINK PROTECTION | ELECTROMAGNETIC INTERFERENCE

The information system implements cryptographic mechanisms that achieve [*Assignment: organization-defined level of protection*] against the effects of intentional electromagnetic interference.

Supplemental Guidance: This control enhancement protects against intentional jamming that might deny or impair communications by ensuring that wireless spread spectrum waveforms used to provide anti-jam protection are not predictable by unauthorized individuals. The control enhancement may also coincidentally help to mitigate the effects of unintentional jamming due to interference from legitimate transmitters sharing the same spectrum. Mission requirements, projected threats, concept of operations, and applicable legislation, directives, regulations, policies, standards, and guidelines determine levels of wireless link availability and performance/cryptography needed. Related controls: SC-12, SC-13.

(2) WIRELESS LINK PROTECTION | REDUCE DETECTION POTENTIAL

The information system implements cryptographic mechanisms to reduce the detection potential of wireless links to [*Assignment: organization-defined level of reduction*].

Supplemental Guidance: This control enhancement is needed for covert communications and protecting wireless transmitters from being geo-located by their transmissions. The control enhancement ensures that spread spectrum waveforms used to achieve low probability of detection are not predictable by unauthorized individuals. Mission requirements, projected threats, concept of operations, and applicable legislation, directives, regulations, policies, standards, and guidelines determine the levels to which wireless links should be undetectable. Related controls: SC-12, SC-13.

(3) WIRELESS LINK PROTECTION | IMITATIVE OR MANIPULATIVE COMMUNICATIONS DECEPTION

The information system implements cryptographic mechanisms to identify and reject wireless transmissions that are deliberate attempts to achieve imitative or manipulative communications deception based on signal parameters.

Supplemental Guidance: This control enhancement ensures that the signal parameters of wireless transmissions are not predictable by unauthorized individuals. Such unpredictability reduces the probability of imitative or manipulative communications deception based upon signal parameters alone. Related controls: SC-12, SC-13.

(4) WIRELESS LINK PROTECTION | SIGNAL PARAMETER IDENTIFICATION

The information system implements cryptographic mechanisms to prevent the identification of [Assignment: organization-defined wireless transmitters] by using the transmitter signal parameters.

Supplemental Guidance: Radio fingerprinting techniques identify the unique signal parameters of transmitters to fingerprint such transmitters for purposes of tracking and mission/user identification. This control enhancement protects against the unique identification of wireless transmitters for purposes of intelligence exploitation by ensuring that anti-fingerprinting alterations to signal parameters are not predictable by unauthorized individuals. This control enhancement helps assure mission success when anonymity is required. Related controls: SC-12, SC-13.

References: None.

Priority and Baseline Allocation:

P0	**LOW** Not Selected	**MOD** Not Selected	**HIGH** Not Selected

SC-41 **PORT AND I/O DEVICE ACCESS**

Control: The organization physically disables or removes [*Assignment: organization-defined connection ports or input/output devices*] on [*Assignment: organization-defined information systems or information system components*].

Supplemental Guidance: Connection ports include, for example, Universal Serial Bus (USB) and Firewire (IEEE 1394). Input/output (I/O) devices include, for example, Compact Disk (CD) and Digital Video Disk (DVD) drives. Physically disabling or removing such connection ports and I/O devices helps prevent exfiltration of information from information systems and the introduction of malicious code into systems from those ports/devices.

Control Enhancements: None.

References: None.

Priority and Baseline Allocation:

P0	**LOW** Not Selected	**MOD** Not Selected	**HIGH** Not Selected

SC-42 **SENSOR CAPABILITY AND DATA**

Control: The information system:

a. Prohibits the remote activation of environmental sensing capabilities with the following exceptions: [*Assignment: organization-defined exceptions where remote activation of sensors is allowed*]; and

b. Provides an explicit indication of sensor use to [*Assignment: organization-defined class of users*].

Supplemental Guidance: This control often applies to types of information systems or system components characterized as mobile devices, for example, smart phones, tablets, and E-readers. These systems often include sensors that can collect and record data regarding the environment where the system is in use. Sensors that are embedded within mobile devices include, for example, cameras, microphones, Global Positioning System (GPS) mechanisms, and accelerometers. While the sensors on mobiles devices provide an important function, if activated covertly, such devices can potentially provide a means for adversaries to learn valuable information about individuals and organizations. For example, remotely activating the GPS function on a mobile device could provide an adversary with the ability to track the specific movements of an individual.

Control Enhancements:

(1) SENSOR CAPABILITY AND DATA | REPORTING TO AUTHORIZED INDIVIDUALS OR ROLES

The organization ensures that the information system is configured so that data or information collected by the [*Assignment: organization-defined sensors*] is only reported to authorized individuals or roles.

Supplemental Guidance: In situations where sensors are activated by authorized individuals (e.g., end users), it is still possible that the data/information collected by the sensors will be sent to unauthorized entities.

(2) SENSOR CAPABILITY AND DATA | AUTHORIZED USE

The organization employs the following measures: [*Assignment: organization-defined measures*], so that data or information collected by [*Assignment: organization-defined sensors*] is only used for authorized purposes.

Supplemental Guidance: Information collected by sensors for a specific authorized purpose potentially could be misused for some unauthorized purpose. For example, GPS sensors that are used to support traffic navigation could be misused to track movements of individuals. Measures to mitigate such activities include, for example, additional training to ensure that authorized parties do not abuse their authority, or (in the case where sensor data/information is maintained by external parties) contractual restrictions on the use of the data/information.

(3) SENSOR CAPABILITY AND DATA | PROHIBIT USE OF DEVICES

The organization prohibits the use of devices possessing [*Assignment: organization-defined environmental sensing capabilities*] in [*Assignment: organization-defined facilities, areas, or systems*].

Supplemental Guidance: For example, organizations may prohibit individuals from bringing cell phones or digital cameras into certain facilities or specific controlled areas within facilities where classified information is stored or sensitive conversations are taking place.

References: None.

Priority and Baseline Allocation:

| P0 | **LOW** Not Selected | **MOD** Not Selected | **HIGH** Not Selected |

SC-43 **USAGE RESTRICTIONS**

Control: The organization:

a. Establishes usage restrictions and implementation guidance for [*Assignment: organization-defined information system components*] based on the potential to cause damage to the information system if used maliciously; and

b. Authorizes, monitors, and controls the use of such components within the information system.

Supplemental Guidance: Information system components include hardware, software, or firmware components (e.g., Voice Over Internet Protocol, mobile code, digital copiers, printers, scanners, optical devices, wireless technologies, mobile devices). Related controls: CM-6, SC-7.

Control Enhancements: None.

References: None.

Priority and Baseline Allocation:

| P0 | LOW Not Selected | MOD Not Selected | HIGH Not Selected |

SC-44 **DETONATION CHAMBERS**

Control: The organization employs a detonation chamber capability within [*Assignment: organization-defined information system, system component, or location*].

Supplemental Guidance: Detonation chambers, also known as dynamic execution environments, allow organizations to open email attachments, execute untrusted or suspicious applications, and execute Universal Resource Locator (URL) requests in the safety of an isolated environment or virtualized sandbox. These protected and isolated execution environments provide a means of determining whether the associated attachments/applications contain malicious code. While related to the concept of deception nets, the control is not intended to maintain a long-term environment in which adversaries can operate and their actions can be observed. Rather, it is intended to quickly identify malicious code and reduce the likelihood that the code is propagated to user environments of operation (or prevent such propagation completely). Related controls: SC-7, SC-25, SC-26, SC-30.

Control Enhancements: None.

References: None.

Priority and Baseline Allocation:

| P0 | LOW Not Selected | MOD Not Selected | HIGH Not Selected |

FAMILY: SYSTEM AND INFORMATION INTEGRITY

SI-1 **SYSTEM AND INFORMATION INTEGRITY POLICY AND PROCEDURES**

Control: The organization:

a. Develops, documents, and disseminates to [*Assignment: organization-defined personnel or roles*]:

1. A system and information integrity policy that addresses purpose, scope, roles, responsibilities, management commitment, coordination among organizational entities, and compliance; and

2. Procedures to facilitate the implementation of the system and information integrity policy and associated system and information integrity controls; and

b. Reviews and updates the current:

1. System and information integrity policy [*Assignment: organization-defined frequency*]; and

2. System and information integrity procedures [*Assignment: organization-defined frequency*].

Supplemental Guidance: This control addresses the establishment of policy and procedures for the effective implementation of selected security controls and control enhancements in the SI family. Policy and procedures reflect applicable federal laws, Executive Orders, directives, regulations, policies, standards, and guidance. Security program policies and procedures at the organization level may make the need for system-specific policies and procedures unnecessary. The policy can be included as part of the general information security policy for organizations or conversely, can be represented by multiple policies reflecting the complex nature of certain organizations. The procedures can be established for the security program in general and for particular information systems, if needed. The organizational risk management strategy is a key factor in establishing policy and procedures. Related control: PM-9.

Control Enhancements: None.

References: NIST Special Publications 800-12, 800-100.

Priority and Baseline Allocation:

| P1 | LOW SI-1 | MOD SI-1 | HIGH SI-1 |

SI-2 **FLAW REMEDIATION**

Control: The organization:

a. Identifies, reports, and corrects information system flaws;

b. Tests software and firmware updates related to flaw remediation for effectiveness and potential side effects before installation;

c. Installs security-relevant software and firmware updates within [*Assignment: organization-defined time period*] of the release of the updates; and

d. Incorporates flaw remediation into the organizational configuration management process.

Supplemental Guidance: Organizations identify information systems affected by announced software flaws including potential vulnerabilities resulting from those flaws, and report this information to designated organizational personnel with information security responsibilities. Security-relevant software updates include, for example, patches, service packs, hot fixes, and anti-virus signatures. Organizations also address flaws discovered during security assessments, continuous monitoring, incident response activities, and system error handling. Organizations take advantage of available resources such as the Common Weakness Enumeration (CWE) or Common Vulnerabilities and Exposures (CVE) databases in remediating flaws discovered in organizational information systems. By incorporating flaw remediation into ongoing configuration management processes, required/anticipated remediation actions can be tracked and verified. Flaw remediation actions that can be tracked and verified include, for example, determining whether organizations follow US-CERT guidance and Information Assurance Vulnerability Alerts. Organization-defined time periods for updating security-relevant software and firmware may vary based on a variety of factors including, for example, the security category of the information system or the criticality of the update (i.e., severity of the vulnerability related to the discovered flaw). Some types of flaw remediation may require more testing than other types. Organizations determine the degree and type of testing needed for the specific type of flaw remediation activity under consideration and also the types of changes that are to be configuration-managed. In some situations, organizations may determine that the testing of software and/or firmware updates is not necessary or practical, for example, when implementing simple anti-virus signature updates. Organizations may also consider in testing decisions, whether security-relevant software or firmware updates are obtained from authorized sources with appropriate digital signatures. Related controls: CA-2, CA-7, CM-3, CM-5, CM-8, MA-2, IR-4, RA-5, SA-10, SA-11, SI-11.

Control Enhancements:

(1) FLAW REMEDIATION | CENTRAL MANAGEMENT

   The organization centrally manages the flaw remediation process.

   Supplemental Guidance: Central management is the organization-wide management and implementation of flaw remediation processes. Central management includes planning, implementing, assessing, authorizing, and monitoring the organization-defined, centrally managed flaw remediation security controls.

(2) FLAW REMEDIATION | AUTOMATED FLAW REMEDIATION STATUS

   The organization employs automated mechanisms [Assignment: organization-defined frequency] to determine the state of information system components with regard to flaw remediation.

   Supplemental Guidance: Related controls: CM-6, SI-4.

(3) FLAW REMEDIATION | TIME TO REMEDIATE FLAWS / BENCHMARKS FOR CORRECTIVE ACTIONS

   The organization:

   (a) Measures the time between flaw identification and flaw remediation; and

   (b) Establishes [Assignment: organization-defined benchmarks] for taking corrective actions.

   Supplemental Guidance: This control enhancement requires organizations to determine the current time it takes on the average to correct information system flaws after such flaws have been identified, and subsequently establish organizational benchmarks (i.e., time frames) for taking corrective actions. Benchmarks can be established by type of flaw and/or severity of the potential vulnerability if the flaw can be exploited.

(4) FLAW REMEDIATION | AUTOMATED PATCH MANAGEMENT TOOLS

   [Withdrawn: Incorporated into SI-2].

(5) FLAW REMEDIATION | AUTOMATIC SOFTWARE / FIRMWARE UPDATES

   The organization installs [Assignment: organization-defined security-relevant software and firmware updates] automatically to [Assignment: organization-defined information system components].

   Supplemental Guidance: Due to information system integrity and availability concerns, organizations give careful consideration to the methodology used to carry out automatic updates. Organizations must balance the need to ensure that the updates are installed as soon as possible with the need to maintain configuration management and with any mission or operational impacts that automatic updates might impose.

(6) FLAW REMEDIATION | REMOVAL OF PREVIOUS VERSIONS OF SOFTWARE / FIRMWARE

   The organization removes [Assignment: organization-defined software and firmware components] after updated versions have been installed.

Supplemental Guidance: Previous versions of software and/or firmware components that are not removed from the information system after updates have been installed may be exploited by adversaries. Some information technology products may remove older versions of software and/or firmware automatically from the information system.

References: NIST Special Publications 800-40, 800-128.

Priority and Baseline Allocation:

P1	LOW SI-2	MOD SI-2 (2)	HIGH SI-2 (1) (2)

SI-3 **MALICIOUS CODE PROTECTION**

Control: The organization:

a. Employs malicious code protection mechanisms at information system entry and exit points to detect and eradicate malicious code;

b. Updates malicious code protection mechanisms whenever new releases are available in accordance with organizational configuration management policy and procedures;

c. Configures malicious code protection mechanisms to:

1. Perform periodic scans of the information system [*Assignment: organization-defined frequency*] and real-time scans of files from external sources at [*Selection (one or more); endpoint; network entry/exit points*] as the files are downloaded, opened, or executed in accordance with organizational security policy; and

2. [*Selection (one or more): block malicious code; quarantine malicious code; send alert to administrator; [Assignment: organization-defined action]*] in response to malicious code detection; and

d. Addresses the receipt of false positives during malicious code detection and eradication and the resulting potential impact on the availability of the information system.

Supplemental Guidance: Information system entry and exit points include, for example, firewalls, electronic mail servers, web servers, proxy servers, remote-access servers, workstations, notebook computers, and mobile devices. Malicious code includes, for example, viruses, worms, Trojan horses, and spyware. Malicious code can also be encoded in various formats (e.g., UUENCODE, Unicode), contained within compressed or hidden files, or hidden in files using steganography. Malicious code can be transported by different means including, for example, web accesses, electronic mail, electronic mail attachments, and portable storage devices. Malicious code insertions occur through the exploitation of information system vulnerabilities. Malicious code protection mechanisms include, for example, anti-virus signature definitions and reputation-based technologies. A variety of technologies and methods exist to limit or eliminate the effects of malicious code. Pervasive configuration management and comprehensive software integrity controls may be effective in preventing execution of unauthorized code. In addition to commercial off-the-shelf software, malicious code may also be present in custom-built software. This could include, for example, logic bombs, back doors, and other types of cyber attacks that could affect organizational missions/business functions. Traditional malicious code protection mechanisms cannot always detect such code. In these situations, organizations rely instead on other safeguards including, for example, secure coding practices, configuration management and control, trusted procurement processes, and monitoring practices to help ensure that software does not perform functions other than the functions intended. Organizations may determine that in response to the detection of malicious code, different actions may be warranted. For example, organizations can define actions in response to malicious code detection during periodic scans, actions in response to detection of malicious downloads, and/or actions in response to detection of maliciousness when attempting to open or execute files. Related controls: CM-3, MP-2, SA-4, SA-8, SA-12, SA-13, SC-7, SC-26, SC-44, SI-2, SI-4, SI-7.

Control Enhancements:

(1) *MALICIOUS CODE PROTECTION | CENTRAL MANAGEMENT*

The organization centrally manages malicious code protection mechanisms.

Supplemental Guidance: Central management is the organization-wide management and implementation of malicious code protection mechanisms. Central management includes planning, implementing, assessing, authorizing, and monitoring the organization-defined, centrally managed flaw malicious code protection security controls. Related controls: AU-2, SI-8.

(2) *MALICIOUS CODE PROTECTION | AUTOMATIC UPDATES*

The information system automatically updates malicious code protection mechanisms.

Supplemental Guidance: Malicious code protection mechanisms include, for example, signature definitions. Due to information system integrity and availability concerns, organizations give careful consideration to the methodology used to carry out automatic updates. Related control: SI-8.

(3) *MALICIOUS CODE PROTECTION | NON-PRIVILEGED USERS*

[Withdrawn: Incorporated into AC-6 (10)].

(4) *MALICIOUS CODE PROTECTION | UPDATES ONLY BY PRIVILEGED USERS*

The information system updates malicious code protection mechanisms only when directed by a privileged user.

Supplemental Guidance: This control enhancement may be appropriate for situations where for reasons of security or operational continuity, updates are only applied when selected/approved by designated organizational personnel. Related controls: AC-6, CM-5.

(5) *MALICIOUS CODE PROTECTION | PORTABLE STORAGE DEVICES*

[Withdrawn: Incorporated into MP-7].

(6) *MALICIOUS CODE PROTECTION | TESTING / VERIFICATION*

The organization:

(a) Tests malicious code protection mechanisms [*Assignment: organization-defined frequency*] by introducing a known benign, non-spreading test case into the information system; and

(b) Verifies that both detection of the test case and associated incident reporting occur.

Supplemental Guidance: Related controls: CA-2, CA-7, RA-5.

(7) *MALICIOUS CODE PROTECTION | NONSIGNATURE-BASED DETECTION*

The information system implements nonsignature-based malicious code detection mechanisms.

Supplemental Guidance: Nonsignature-based detection mechanisms include, for example, the use of heuristics to detect, analyze, and describe the characteristics or behavior of malicious code and to provide safeguards against malicious code for which signatures do not yet exist or for which existing signatures may not be effective. This includes polymorphic malicious code (i.e., code that changes signatures when it replicates). This control enhancement does not preclude the use of signature-based detection mechanisms.

(8) *MALICIOUS CODE PROTECTION | DETECT UNAUTHORIZED COMMANDS*

The information system detects [*Assignment: organization-defined unauthorized operating system commands*] through the kernel application programming interface at [*Assignment: organization-defined information system hardware components*] and [*Selection (one or more): issues a warning; audits the command execution; prevents the execution of the command*].

Supplemental Guidance: This control enhancement can also be applied to critical interfaces other than kernel-based interfaces, including for example, interfaces with virtual machines and privileged applications. Unauthorized operating system commands include, for example, commands for kernel functions from information system processes that are not trusted to initiate such commands, or commands for kernel functions that are suspicious even though commands of that type are reasonable for processes to initiate. Organizations can define the malicious commands to be detected by a combination of command types, command classes, or specific instances of commands. Organizations can define hardware components by specific component, component type, location in the network, or combination therein.

Organizations may select different actions for different types/classes/specific instances of potentially malicious commands. Related control: AU-6.

(9) MALICIOUS CODE PROTECTION | AUTHENTICATE REMOTE COMMANDS

The information system implements [*Assignment: organization-defined security safeguards*] to authenticate [*Assignment: organization-defined remote commands*].

Supplemental Guidance: This control enhancement protects against unauthorized commands and replay of authorized commands. This capability is important for those remote information systems whose loss, malfunction, misdirection, or exploitation would have immediate and/or serious consequences (e.g., injury or death, property damage, loss of high-valued assets or sensitive information, or failure of important missions/business functions). Authentication safeguards for remote commands help to ensure that information systems accept and execute in the order intended, only authorized commands, and that unauthorized commands are rejected. Cryptographic mechanisms can be employed, for example, to authenticate remote commands. Related controls: SC-12, SC-13, SC-23.

(10) MALICIOUS CODE PROTECTION | MALICIOUS CODE ANALYSIS

The organization:

(a) Employs [*Assignment: organization-defined tools and techniques*] to analyze the characteristics and behavior of malicious code; and

(b) Incorporates the results from malicious code analysis into organizational incident response and flaw remediation processes.

Supplemental Guidance: The application of selected malicious code analysis tools and techniques provides organizations with a more in-depth understanding of adversary tradecraft (i.e., tactics, techniques, and procedures) and the functionality and purpose of specific instances of malicious code. Understanding the characteristics of malicious code facilitates more effective organizational responses to current and future threats. Organizations can conduct malicious code analyses by using reverse engineering techniques or by monitoring the behavior of executing code.

References: NIST Special Publication 800-83.

Priority and Baseline Allocation:

P1	LOW SI-3	MOD SI-3 (1) (2)	HIGH SI-3 (1) (2)

SI-4 **INFORMATION SYSTEM MONITORING**

Control: The organization:

a. Monitors the information system to detect:

1. Attacks and indicators of potential attacks in accordance with [*Assignment: organization-defined monitoring objectives*]; and

2. Unauthorized local, network, and remote connections;

b. Identifies unauthorized use of the information system through [*Assignment: organization-defined techniques and methods*];

c. Deploys monitoring devices:

1. Strategically within the information system to collect organization-determined essential information; and

2. At ad hoc locations within the system to track specific types of transactions of interest to the organization;

d. Protects information obtained from intrusion-monitoring tools from unauthorized access, modification, and deletion;

e. Heightens the level of information system monitoring activity whenever there is an indication of increased risk to organizational operations and assets, individuals, other organizations, or the Nation based on law enforcement information, intelligence information, or other credible sources of information;

f. Obtains legal opinion with regard to information system monitoring activities in accordance with applicable federal laws, Executive Orders, directives, policies, or regulations; and

g. Provides [*Assignment: organization-defined information system monitoring information*] to [*Assignment: organization-defined personnel or roles*] [*Selection (one or more): as needed; [Assignment: organization-defined frequency*]].

Supplemental Guidance: Information system monitoring includes external and internal monitoring. External monitoring includes the observation of events occurring at the information system boundary (i.e., part of perimeter defense and boundary protection). Internal monitoring includes the observation of events occurring within the information system. Organizations can monitor information systems, for example, by observing audit activities in real time or by observing other system aspects such as access patterns, characteristics of access, and other actions. The monitoring objectives may guide determination of the events. Information system monitoring capability is achieved through a variety of tools and techniques (e.g., intrusion detection systems, intrusion prevention systems, malicious code protection software, scanning tools, audit record monitoring software, network monitoring software). Strategic locations for monitoring devices include, for example, selected perimeter locations and near server farms supporting critical applications, with such devices typically being employed at the managed interfaces associated with controls SC-7 and AC-17. Einstein network monitoring devices from the Department of Homeland Security can also be included as monitoring devices. The granularity of monitoring information collected is based on organizational monitoring objectives and the capability of information systems to support such objectives. Specific types of transactions of interest include, for example, Hyper Text Transfer Protocol (HTTP) traffic that bypasses HTTP proxies. Information system monitoring is an integral part of organizational continuous monitoring and incident response programs. Output from system monitoring serves as input to continuous monitoring and incident response programs. A network connection is any connection with a device that communicates through a network (e.g., local area network, Internet). A remote connection is any connection with a device communicating through an external network (e.g., the Internet). Local, network, and remote connections can be either wired or wireless. Related controls: AC-3, AC-4, AC-8, AC-17, AU-2, AU-6, AU-7, AU-9, AU-12, CA-7, IR-4, PE-3, RA-5, SC-7, SC-26, SC-35, SI-3, SI-7.

Control Enhancements:

(1) INFORMATION SYSTEM MONITORING | SYSTEM-WIDE INTRUSION DETECTION SYSTEM

The organization connects and configures individual intrusion detection tools into an information system-wide intrusion detection system.

(2) INFORMATION SYSTEM MONITORING | AUTOMATED TOOLS FOR REAL-TIME ANALYSIS

The organization employs automated tools to support near real-time analysis of events.

Supplemental Guidance: Automated tools include, for example, host-based, network-based, transport-based, or storage-based event monitoring tools or Security Information and Event Management (SIEM) technologies that provide real time analysis of alerts and/or notifications generated by organizational information systems.

(3) INFORMATION SYSTEM MONITORING | AUTOMATED TOOL INTEGRATION

The organization employs automated tools to integrate intrusion detection tools into access control and flow control mechanisms for rapid response to attacks by enabling reconfiguration of these mechanisms in support of attack isolation and elimination.

(4) INFORMATION SYSTEM MONITORING | INBOUND AND OUTBOUND COMMUNICATIONS TRAFFIC

The information system monitors inbound and outbound communications traffic [*Assignment: organization-defined frequency*] for unusual or unauthorized activities or conditions.

Supplemental Guidance: Unusual/unauthorized activities or conditions related to information system inbound and outbound communications traffic include, for example, internal traffic that indicates the presence of malicious code within organizational information systems or propagating among system components, the unauthorized exporting of information, or signaling to external information systems. Evidence of malicious code is used to identify potentially compromised information systems or information system components.

(5) INFORMATION SYSTEM MONITORING | SYSTEM-GENERATED ALERTS

The information system alerts [*Assignment: organization-defined personnel or roles*] when the following indications of compromise or potential compromise occur: [*Assignment: organization-defined compromise indicators*].

Supplemental Guidance: Alerts may be generated from a variety of sources, including, for example, audit records or inputs from malicious code protection mechanisms, intrusion detection or prevention mechanisms, or boundary protection devices such as firewalls, gateways, and routers. Alerts can be transmitted, for example, telephonically, by electronic mail messages, or by text messaging. Organizational personnel on the notification list can include, for example, system administrators, mission/business owners, system owners, or information system security officers. Related controls: AU-5, PE-6.

(6) INFORMATION SYSTEM MONITORING | RESTRICT NON-PRIVILEGED USERS

[Withdrawn: Incorporated into AC-6 (10)].

(7) INFORMATION SYSTEM MONITORING | AUTOMATED RESPONSE TO SUSPICIOUS EVENTS

The information system notifies [*Assignment: organization-defined incident response personnel (identified by name and/or by role)*] of detected suspicious events and takes [*Assignment: organization-defined least-disruptive actions to terminate suspicious events*].

Supplemental Guidance: Least-disruptive actions may include, for example, initiating requests for human responses.

(8) INFORMATION SYSTEM MONITORING | PROTECTION OF MONITORING INFORMATION

[Withdrawn: Incorporated into SI-4].

(9) INFORMATION SYSTEM MONITORING | TESTING OF MONITORING TOOLS

The organization tests intrusion-monitoring tools [*Assignment: organization-defined frequency*].

Supplemental Guidance: Testing intrusion-monitoring tools is necessary to ensure that the tools are operating correctly and continue to meet the monitoring objectives of organizations. The frequency of testing depends on the types of tools used by organizations and methods of deployment. Related control: CP-9.

(10) INFORMATION SYSTEM MONITORING | VISIBILITY OF ENCRYPTED COMMUNICATIONS

The organization makes provisions so that [*Assignment: organization-defined encrypted communications traffic*] is visible to [*Assignment: organization-defined information system monitoring tools*].

Supplemental Guidance: Organizations balance the potentially conflicting needs for encrypting communications traffic and for having insight into such traffic from a monitoring perspective. For some organizations, the need to ensure the confidentiality of communications traffic is paramount; for others, mission-assurance is of greater concern. Organizations determine whether the visibility requirement applies to internal encrypted traffic, encrypted traffic intended for external destinations, or a subset of the traffic types.

(11) INFORMATION SYSTEM MONITORING | ANALYZE COMMUNICATIONS TRAFFIC ANOMALIES

The organization analyzes outbound communications traffic at the external boundary of the information system and selected [*Assignment: organization-defined interior points within the system (e.g., subnetworks, subsystems)*] to discover anomalies.

Supplemental Guidance: Anomalies within organizational information systems include, for example, large file transfers, long-time persistent connections, unusual protocols and ports in use, and attempted communications with suspected malicious external addresses.

(12) INFORMATION SYSTEM MONITORING | AUTOMATED ALERTS

The organization employs automated mechanisms to alert security personnel of the following inappropriate or unusual activities with security implications: [*Assignment: organization-defined activities that trigger alerts*].

Supplemental Guidance: This control enhancement focuses on the security alerts generated by organizations and transmitted using automated means. In contrast to the alerts generated by information systems in SI-4 (5), which tend to focus on information sources internal to the systems (e.g., audit records), the sources of information for this enhancement can include other entities as well (e.g., suspicious activity reports, reports on potential insider threats). Related controls: AC-18, IA-3.

(13) INFORMATION SYSTEM MONITORING | ANALYZE TRAFFIC / EVENT PATTERNS

The organization:

(a) Analyzes communications traffic/event patterns for the information system;

(b) Develops profiles representing common traffic patterns and/or events; and

(c) Uses the traffic/event profiles in tuning system-monitoring devices to reduce the number of false positives and the number of false negatives.

(14) INFORMATION SYSTEM MONITORING | WIRELESS INTRUSION DETECTION

The organization employs a wireless intrusion detection system to identify rogue wireless devices and to detect attack attempts and potential compromises/breaches to the information system.

Supplemental Guidance: Wireless signals may radiate beyond the confines of organization-controlled facilities. Organizations proactively search for unauthorized wireless connections including the conduct of thorough scans for unauthorized wireless access points. Scans are not limited to those areas within facilities containing information systems, but also include areas outside of facilities as needed, to verify that unauthorized wireless access points are not connected to the systems. Related controls: AC-18, IA-3.

(15) INFORMATION SYSTEM MONITORING | WIRELESS TO WIRELINE COMMUNICATIONS

The organization employs an intrusion detection system to monitor wireless communications traffic as the traffic passes from wireless to wireline networks.

Supplemental Guidance: Related control: AC-18.

(16) INFORMATION SYSTEM MONITORING | CORRELATE MONITORING INFORMATION

The organization correlates information from monitoring tools employed throughout the information system.

Supplemental Guidance: Correlating information from different monitoring tools can provide a more comprehensive view of information system activity. The correlation of monitoring tools that usually work in isolation (e.g., host monitoring, network monitoring, anti-virus software) can provide an organization-wide view and in so doing, may reveal otherwise unseen attack patterns. Understanding the capabilities/limitations of diverse monitoring tools and how to maximize the utility of information generated by those tools can help organizations to build, operate, and maintain effective monitoring programs. Related control: AU-6.

(17) INFORMATION SYSTEM MONITORING | INTEGRATED SITUATIONAL AWARENESS

The organization correlates information from monitoring physical, cyber, and supply chain activities to achieve integrated, organization-wide situational awareness.

Supplemental Guidance: This control enhancement correlates monitoring information from a more diverse set of information sources to achieve integrated situational awareness. Integrated situational awareness from a combination of physical, cyber, and supply chain monitoring activities enhances the capability of organizations to more quickly detect sophisticated cyber attacks and investigate the methods and techniques employed to carry out such attacks. In contrast to SI-4 (16) which correlates the various cyber monitoring information, this control enhancement correlates monitoring beyond just the cyber domain. Such monitoring may help reveal attacks on organizations that are operating across multiple attack vectors. Related control: SA-12.

(18) INFORMATION SYSTEM MONITORING | ANALYZE TRAFFIC / COVERT EXFILTRATION

The organization analyzes outbound communications traffic at the external boundary of the information system (i.e., system perimeter) and at [*Assignment: organization-defined interior points within the system (e.g., subsystems, subnetworks)*] to detect covert exfiltration of information.

Supplemental Guidance: Covert means that can be used for the unauthorized exfiltration of organizational information include, for example, steganography.

(19) INFORMATION SYSTEM MONITORING | INDIVIDUALS POSING GREATER RISK

The organization implements [*Assignment: organization-defined additional monitoring*] of individuals who have been identified by [*Assignment: organization-defined sources*] as posing an increased level of risk.

Supplemental Guidance: Indications of increased risk from individuals can be obtained from a variety of sources including, for example, human resource records, intelligence agencies, law enforcement organizations, and/or other credible sources. The monitoring of individuals is closely coordinated with management, legal, security, and human resources officials within organizations conducting such monitoring and complies with federal legislation, Executive Orders, policies, directives, regulations, and standards.

(20) INFORMATION SYSTEM MONITORING | PRIVILEGED USERS

The organization implements [*Assignment: organization-defined additional monitoring*] of privileged users.

(21) INFORMATION SYSTEM MONITORING | PROBATIONARY PERIODS

The organization implements [*Assignment: organization-defined additional monitoring*] of individuals during [*Assignment: organization-defined probationary period*].

(22) INFORMATION SYSTEM MONITORING | UNAUTHORIZED NETWORK SERVICES

The information system detects network services that have not been authorized or approved by [*Assignment: organization-defined authorization or approval processes*] and [*Selection (one or more): audits; alerts* [*Assignment: organization-defined personnel or roles*]].

Supplemental Guidance: Unauthorized or unapproved network services include, for example, services in service-oriented architectures that lack organizational verification or validation and therefore may be unreliable or serve as malicious rogues for valid services. Related controls: AC-6, CM-7, SA-5, SA-9.

(23) INFORMATION SYSTEM MONITORING | HOST-BASED DEVICES

The organization implements [*Assignment: organization-defined host-based monitoring mechanisms*] at [*Assignment: organization-defined information system components*].

Supplemental Guidance: Information system components where host-based monitoring can be implemented include, for example, servers, workstations, and mobile devices. Organizations consider employing host-based monitoring mechanisms from multiple information technology product developers.

(24) INFORMATION SYSTEM MONITORING | INDICATORS OF COMPROMISE

The information system discovers, collects, distributes, and uses indicators of compromise.

Supplemental Guidance: Indicators of compromise (IOC) are forensic artifacts from intrusions that are identified on organizational information systems (at the host or network level). IOCs provide organizations with valuable information on objects or information systems that have been compromised. IOCs for the discovery of compromised hosts can include for example, the creation of registry key values. IOCs for network traffic include, for example, Universal Resource Locator (URL) or protocol elements that indicate malware command and control servers. The rapid distribution and adoption of IOCs can improve information security by reducing the time that information systems and organizations are vulnerable to the same exploit or attack.

References: NIST Special Publications 800-61, 800-83, 800-92, 800-94, 800-137.

Priority and Baseline Allocation:

| P1 | LOW SI-4 | MOD SI-4 (2) (4) (5) | HIGH SI-4 (2) (4) (5) |

SI-5   SECURITY ALERTS, ADVISORIES, AND DIRECTIVES

Control: The organization:

a. Receives information system security alerts, advisories, and directives from [*Assignment: organization-defined external organizations*] on an ongoing basis;

b. Generates internal security alerts, advisories, and directives as deemed necessary;

c. Disseminates security alerts, advisories, and directives to: [*Selection (one or more): [Assignment: organization-defined personnel or roles]; [Assignment: organization-defined elements within the organization]; [Assignment: organization-defined external organizations]*]; and

d. Implements security directives in accordance with established time frames, or notifies the issuing organization of the degree of noncompliance.

Supplemental Guidance: The United States Computer Emergency Readiness Team (US-CERT) generates security alerts and advisories to maintain situational awareness across the federal government. Security directives are issued by OMB or other designated organizations with the responsibility and authority to issue such directives. Compliance to security directives is essential due to the critical nature of many of these directives and the potential immediate adverse effects on organizational operations and assets, individuals, other organizations, and the Nation should the directives not be implemented in a timely manner. External organizations include, for example, external mission/business partners, supply chain partners, external service providers, and other peer/supporting organizations. Related control: SI-2.

Control Enhancements:

(1) SECURITY ALERTS, ADVISORIES, AND DIRECTIVES | AUTOMATED ALERTS AND ADVISORIES

The organization employs automated mechanisms to make security alert and advisory information available throughout the organization.

Supplemental Guidance: The significant number of changes to organizational information systems and the environments in which those systems operate requires the dissemination of security-related information to a variety of organizational entities that have a direct interest in the success of organizational missions and business functions. Based on the information provided by the security alerts and advisories, changes may be required at one or more of the three tiers related to the management of information security risk including the governance level, mission/business process/enterprise architecture level, and the information system level.

References: NIST Special Publication 800-40.

Priority and Baseline Allocation:

| P1 | LOW SI-5 | MOD SI-5 | HIGH SI-5 (1) |

SI-6   SECURITY FUNCTION VERIFICATION

Control: The information system:

a. Verifies the correct operation of [*Assignment: organization-defined security functions*];

b. Performs this verification [*Selection (one or more): [Assignment: organization-defined system transitional states]; upon command by user with appropriate privilege; [Assignment: organization-defined frequency]*];

c. Notifies [*Assignment: organization-defined personnel or roles*] of failed security verification tests; and

d. [*Selection (one or more): shuts the information system down; restarts the information system; [Assignment: organization-defined alternative action(s)]*] when anomalies are discovered.

Supplemental Guidance: Transitional states for information systems include, for example, system startup, restart, shutdown, and abort. Notifications provided by information systems include, for example, electronic alerts to system administrators, messages to local computer consoles, and/or hardware indications such as lights. Related controls: CA-7, CM-6.

Control Enhancements:

(1) SECURITY FUNCTION VERIFICATION | NOTIFICATION OF FAILED SECURITY TESTS

[Withdrawn: Incorporated into SI-6].

(2) SECURITY FUNCTION VERIFICATION | AUTOMATION SUPPORT FOR DISTRIBUTED TESTING

The information system implements automated mechanisms to support the management of distributed security testing.

Supplemental Guidance: Related control: SI-2.

(3) SECURITY FUNCTION VERIFICATION | REPORT VERIFICATION RESULTS

The organization reports the results of security function verification to [Assignment: organization-defined personnel or roles].

Supplemental Guidance: Organizational personnel with potential interest in security function verification results include, for example, senior information security officers, information system security managers, and information systems security officers. Related controls: SA-12, SI-4, SI-5.

References: None.

Priority and Baseline Allocation:

| P1 | LOW Not Selected | MOD Not Selected | HIGH SI-6 |

SI-7 SOFTWARE, FIRMWARE, AND INFORMATION INTEGRITY

Control: The organization employs integrity verification tools to detect unauthorized changes to [Assignment: organization-defined software, firmware, and information].

Supplemental Guidance: Unauthorized changes to software, firmware, and information can occur due to errors or malicious activity (e.g., tampering). Software includes, for example, operating systems (with key internal components such as kernels, drivers), middleware, and applications. Firmware includes, for example, the Basic Input Output System (BIOS). Information includes metadata such as security attributes associated with information. State-of-the-practice integrity-checking mechanisms (e.g., parity checks, cyclical redundancy checks, cryptographic hashes) and associated tools can automatically monitor the integrity of information systems and hosted applications. Related controls: SA-12, SC-8, SC-13, SI-3.

Control Enhancements:

(1) SOFTWARE, FIRMWARE, AND INFORMATION INTEGRITY | INTEGRITY CHECKS

The information system performs an integrity check of [Assignment: organization-defined software, firmware, and information] [Selection (one or more): at startup; at [Assignment: organization-defined transitional states or security-relevant events]; [Assignment: organization-defined frequency]].

Supplemental Guidance: Security-relevant events include, for example, the identification of a new threat to which organizational information systems are susceptible, and the installation of new hardware, software, or firmware. Transitional states include, for example, system startup, restart, shutdown, and abort.

(2) SOFTWARE, FIRMWARE, AND INFORMATION INTEGRITY | AUTOMATED NOTIFICATIONS OF INTEGRITY VIOLATIONS

The organization employs automated tools that provide notification to [Assignment: organization-defined personnel or roles] upon discovering discrepancies during integrity verification.

Supplemental Guidance: The use of automated tools to report integrity violations and to notify organizational personnel in a timely matter is an essential precursor to effective risk response.

Personnel having an interest in integrity violations include, for example, mission/business owners, information system owners, systems administrators, software developers, systems integrators, and information security officers.

(3) SOFTWARE, FIRMWARE, AND INFORMATION INTEGRITY | CENTRALLY-MANAGED INTEGRITY TOOLS

The organization employs centrally managed integrity verification tools.

Supplemental Guidance: Related controls: AU-3, SI-2, SI-8.

(4) SOFTWARE, FIRMWARE, AND INFORMATION INTEGRITY | TAMPER-EVIDENT PACKAGING

[Withdrawn: Incorporated into SA-12].

(5) SOFTWARE, FIRMWARE, AND INFORMATION INTEGRITY | AUTOMATED RESPONSE TO INTEGRITY VIOLATIONS

The information system automatically [Selection (one or more): shuts the information system down; restarts the information system; implements [Assignment: organization-defined security safeguards]] when integrity violations are discovered.

Supplemental Guidance: Organizations may define different integrity checking and anomaly responses: (i) by type of information (e.g., firmware, software, user data); (ii) by specific information (e.g., boot firmware, boot firmware for a specific types of machines); or (iii) a combination of both. Automatic implementation of specific safeguards within organizational information systems includes, for example, reversing the changes, halting the information system, or triggering audit alerts when unauthorized modifications to critical security files occur.

(6) SOFTWARE, FIRMWARE, AND INFORMATION INTEGRITY | CRYPTOGRAPHIC PROTECTION

The information system implements cryptographic mechanisms to detect unauthorized changes to software, firmware, and information.

Supplemental Guidance: Cryptographic mechanisms used for the protection of integrity include, for example, digital signatures and the computation and application of signed hashes using asymmetric cryptography, protecting the confidentiality of the key used to generate the hash, and using the public key to verify the hash information. Related control: SC-13.

(7) SOFTWARE, FIRMWARE, AND INFORMATION INTEGRITY | INTEGRATION OF DETECTION AND RESPONSE

The organization incorporates the detection of unauthorized [Assignment: organization-defined security-relevant changes to the information system] into the organizational incident response capability.

Supplemental Guidance: This control enhancement helps to ensure that detected events are tracked, monitored, corrected, and available for historical purposes. Maintaining historical records is important both for being able to identify and discern adversary actions over an extended period of time and for possible legal actions. Security-relevant changes include, for example, unauthorized changes to established configuration settings or unauthorized elevation of information system privileges. Related controls: IR-4, IR-5, SI-4.

(8) SOFTWARE, FIRMWARE, AND INFORMATION INTEGRITY | AUDITING CAPABILITY FOR SIGNIFICANT EVENTS

The information system, upon detection of a potential integrity violation, provides the capability to audit the event and initiates the following actions: [Selection (one or more): generates an audit record; alerts current user; alerts [Assignment: organization-defined personnel or roles]; [Assignment: organization-defined other actions]].

Supplemental Guidance: Organizations select response actions based on types of software, specific software, or information for which there are potential integrity violations. Related controls: AU-2, AU-6, AU-12.

(9) SOFTWARE, FIRMWARE, AND INFORMATION INTEGRITY | VERIFY BOOT PROCESS

The information system verifies the integrity of the boot process of [Assignment: organization-defined devices].

Supplemental Guidance: Ensuring the integrity of boot processes is critical to starting devices in known/trustworthy states. Integrity verification mechanisms provide organizational personnel with assurance that only trusted code is executed during boot processes.

(10) SOFTWARE, FIRMWARE, AND INFORMATION INTEGRITY | PROTECTION OF BOOT FIRMWARE

The information system implements [Assignment: organization-defined security safeguards] to protect the integrity of boot firmware in [Assignment: organization-defined devices].

Supplemental Guidance: Unauthorized modifications to boot firmware may be indicative of a sophisticated, targeted cyber attack. These types of cyber attacks can result in a permanent denial of service (e.g., if the firmware is corrupted) or a persistent malicious code presence (e.g., if code is embedded within the firmware). Devices can protect the integrity of the boot firmware in organizational information systems by: (i) verifying the integrity and authenticity of all updates to the boot firmware prior to applying changes to the boot devices; and (ii) preventing unauthorized processes from modifying the boot firmware.

(11) SOFTWARE, FIRMWARE, AND INFORMATION INTEGRITY | CONFINED ENVIRONMENTS WITH LIMITED PRIVILEGES

The organization requires that [Assignment: organization-defined user-installed software] execute in a confined physical or virtual machine environment with limited privileges.

Supplemental Guidance: Organizations identify software that may be of greater concern with regard to origin or potential for containing malicious code. For this type of software, user installations occur in confined environments of operation to limit or contain damage from malicious code that may be executed.

(12) SOFTWARE, FIRMWARE, AND INFORMATION INTEGRITY | INTEGRITY VERIFICATION

The organization requires that the integrity of [Assignment: organization-defined user-installed software] be verified prior to execution.

Supplemental Guidance: Organizations verify the integrity of user-installed software prior to execution to reduce the likelihood of executing malicious code or code that contains errors from unauthorized modifications. Organizations consider the practicality of approaches to verifying software integrity including, for example, availability of checksums of adequate trustworthiness from software developers or vendors.

(13) SOFTWARE, FIRMWARE, AND INFORMATION INTEGRITY | CODE EXECUTION IN PROTECTED ENVIRONMENTS

The organization allows execution of binary or machine-executable code obtained from sources with limited or no warranty and without the provision of source code only in confined physical or virtual machine environments and with the explicit approval of [Assignment: organization-defined personnel or roles].

Supplemental Guidance: This control enhancement applies to all sources of binary or machine-executable code including, for example, commercial software/firmware and open source software.

(14) SOFTWARE, FIRMWARE, AND INFORMATION INTEGRITY | BINARY OR MACHINE EXECUTABLE CODE

The organization:

(a) Prohibits the use of binary or machine-executable code from sources with limited or no warranty and without the provision of source code; and

(b) Provides exceptions to the source code requirement only for compelling mission/operational requirements and with the approval of the authorizing official.

Supplemental Guidance: This control enhancement applies to all sources of binary or machine-executable code including, for example, commercial software/firmware and open source software. Organizations assess software products without accompanying source code from sources with limited or no warranty for potential security impacts. The assessments address the fact that these types of software products may be very difficult to review, repair, or extend, given that organizations, in most cases, do not have access to the original source code, and there may be no owners who could make such repairs on behalf of organizations. Related control: SA-5.

(15) SOFTWARE, FIRMWARE, AND INFORMATION INTEGRITY | CODE AUTHENTICATION

The information system implements cryptographic mechanisms to authenticate [Assignment: organization-defined software or firmware components] prior to installation.

Supplemental Guidance: Cryptographic authentication includes, for example, verifying that software or firmware components have been digitally signed using certificates recognized and approved by organizations. Code signing is an effective method to protect against malicious code.

(16) *SOFTWARE, FIRMWARE, AND INFORMATION INTEGRITY | TIME LIMIT ON PROCESS EXECUTION W/O SUPERVISION*

The organization does not allow processes to execute without supervision for more than [*Assignment: organization-defined time period*].

Supplemental Guidance: This control enhancement addresses processes for which normal execution periods can be determined and situations in which organizations exceed such periods. Supervision includes, for example, operating system timers, automated responses, or manual oversight and response when information system process anomalies occur.

References: NIST Special Publications 800-147, 800-155.

Priority and Baseline Allocation:

P1	LOW Not Selected	MOD SI-7 (1) (7)	HIGH SI-7 (1) (2) (5) (7) (14)

SI-8 SPAM PROTECTION

Control: The organization:

a. Employs spam protection mechanisms at information system entry and exit points to detect and take action on unsolicited messages; and

b. Updates spam protection mechanisms when new releases are available in accordance with organizational configuration management policy and procedures.

Supplemental Guidance: Information system entry and exit points include, for example, firewalls, electronic mail servers, web servers, proxy servers, remote-access servers, workstations, mobile devices, and notebook/laptop computers. Spam can be transported by different means including, for example, electronic mail, electronic mail attachments, and web accesses. Spam protection mechanisms include, for example, signature definitions. Related controls: AT-2, AT-3, SC-5, SC-7, SI-3.

Control Enhancements:

(1) *SPAM PROTECTION | CENTRAL MANAGEMENT*

The organization centrally manages spam protection mechanisms.

Supplemental Guidance: Central management is the organization-wide management and implementation of spam protection mechanisms. Central management includes planning, implementing, assessing, authorizing, and monitoring the organization-defined, centrally managed spam protection security controls. Related controls: AU-3, SI-2, SI-7.

(2) *SPAM PROTECTION | AUTOMATIC UPDATES*

The information system automatically updates spam protection mechanisms.

(3) *SPAM PROTECTION | CONTINUOUS LEARNING CAPABILITY*

The information system implements spam protection mechanisms with a learning capability to more effectively identify legitimate communications traffic.

Supplemental Guidance: Learning mechanisms include, for example, Bayesian filters that respond to user inputs identifying specific traffic as spam or legitimate by updating algorithm parameters and thereby more accurately separating types of traffic.

References: NIST Special Publication 800-45.

Priority and Baseline Allocation:

P2	LOW Not Selected	MOD SI-8 (1) (2)	HIGH SI-8 (1) (2)

SI-9   INFORMATION INPUT RESTRICTIONS

[Withdrawn: Incorporated into AC-2, AC-3, AC-5, AC-6].

SI-10   INFORMATION INPUT VALIDATION

Control: The information system checks the validity of [*Assignment: organization-defined information inputs*].

Supplemental Guidance: Checking the valid syntax and semantics of information system inputs (e.g., character set, length, numerical range, and acceptable values) verifies that inputs match specified definitions for format and content. Software applications typically follow well-defined protocols that use structured messages (i.e., commands or queries) to communicate between software modules or system components. Structured messages can contain raw or unstructured data interspersed with metadata or control information. If software applications use attacker-supplied inputs to construct structured messages without properly encoding such messages, then the attacker could insert malicious commands or special characters that can cause the data to be interpreted as control information or metadata. Consequently, the module or component that receives the tainted output will perform the wrong operations or otherwise interpret the data incorrectly. Prescreening inputs prior to passing to interpreters prevents the content from being unintentionally interpreted as commands. Input validation helps to ensure accurate and correct inputs and prevent attacks such as cross-site scripting and a variety of injection attacks.

Control Enhancements:

(1) INFORMATION INPUT VALIDATION | MANUAL OVERRIDE CAPABILITY

The information system:

(a) Provides a manual override capability for input validation of [*Assignment: organization-defined inputs*];

(b) Restricts the use of the manual override capability to only [*Assignment: organization-defined authorized individuals*]; and

(c) Audits the use of the manual override capability.

Supplemental Guidance: Related controls: CM-3, CM-5.

(2) INFORMATION INPUT VALIDATION | REVIEW / RESOLUTION OF ERRORS

The organization ensures that input validation errors are reviewed and resolved within [*Assignment: organization-defined time period*].

Supplemental Guidance: Resolution of input validation errors includes, for example, correcting systemic causes of errors and resubmitting transactions with corrected input.

(3) INFORMATION INPUT VALIDATION | PREDICTABLE BEHAVIOR

The information system behaves in a predictable and documented manner that reflects organizational and system objectives when invalid inputs are received.

Supplemental Guidance: A common vulnerability in organizational information systems is unpredictable behavior when invalid inputs are received. This control enhancement ensures that there is predictable behavior in the face of invalid inputs by specifying information system responses that facilitate transitioning the system to known states without adverse, unintended side effects.

(4) INFORMATION INPUT VALIDATION | REVIEW / TIMING INTERACTIONS

The organization accounts for timing interactions among information system components in determining appropriate responses for invalid inputs.

Supplemental Guidance: In addressing invalid information system inputs received across protocol interfaces, timing interactions become relevant, where one protocol needs to consider the impact of the error response on other protocols within the protocol stack. For example, 802.11 standard wireless network protocols do not interact well with Transmission Control Protocols (TCP) when packets are dropped (which could be due to invalid packet input). TCP assumes packet losses are due to congestion, while packets lost over 802.11 links are typically dropped due to collisions or noise on the link. If TCP makes a congestion response, it takes precisely the wrong action in response to a collision event. Adversaries may be able to use apparently acceptable individual behaviors of the protocols in concert to achieve adverse effects through suitable construction of invalid input.

(5) INFORMATION INPUT VALIDATION | RESTRICT INPUTS TO TRUSTED SOURCES AND APPROVED FORMATS

The organization restricts the use of information inputs to [*Assignment: organization-defined trusted sources*] and/or [*Assignment: organization-defined formats*].

Supplemental Guidance: This control enhancement applies the concept of whitelisting to information inputs. Specifying known trusted sources for information inputs and acceptable formats for such inputs can reduce the probability of malicious activity.

References: None.

Priority and Baseline Allocation:

P1	LOW Not Selected	MOD SI-10	HIGH SI-10

SI-11 ERROR HANDLING

Control: The information system:

a. Generates error messages that provide information necessary for corrective actions without revealing information that could be exploited by adversaries; and

b. Reveals error messages only to [*Assignment: organization-defined personnel or roles*].

Supplemental Guidance: Organizations carefully consider the structure/content of error messages. The extent to which information systems are able to identify and handle error conditions is guided by organizational policy and operational requirements. Information that could be exploited by adversaries includes, for example, erroneous logon attempts with passwords entered by mistake as the username, mission/business information that can be derived from (if not stated explicitly by) information recorded, and personal information such as account numbers, social security numbers, and credit card numbers. In addition, error messages may provide a covert channel for transmitting information. Related controls: AU-2, AU-3, SC-31.

Control Enhancements: None.

References: None.

Priority and Baseline Allocation:

P2	LOW Not Selected	MOD SI-11	HIGH SI-11

SI-12 INFORMATION HANDLING AND RETENTION

Control: The organization handles and retains information within the information system and information output from the system in accordance with applicable federal laws, Executive Orders, directives, policies, regulations, standards, and operational requirements.

Supplemental Guidance: Information handling and retention requirements cover the full life cycle of information, in some cases extending beyond the disposal of information systems. The National Archives and Records Administration provides guidance on records retention. Related controls: AC-16, AU-5, AU-11, MP-2, MP-4.

Control Enhancements: None.

References: None.

Priority and Baseline Allocation:

| P2 | LOW SI-12 | MOD SI-12 | HIGH SI-12 |

SI-13 PREDICTABLE FAILURE PREVENTION

Control: The organization:

a. Determines mean time to failure (MTTF) for [*Assignment: organization-defined information system components*] in specific environments of operation; and

b. Provides substitute information system components and a means to exchange active and standby components at [*Assignment: organization-defined MTTF substitution criteria*].

Supplemental Guidance: While MTTF is primarily a reliability issue, this control addresses potential failures of specific information system components that provide security capability. Failure rates reflect installation-specific consideration, not industry-average. Organizations define criteria for substitution of information system components based on MTTF value with consideration for resulting potential harm from component failures. Transfer of responsibilities between active and standby components does not compromise safety, operational readiness, or security capability (e.g., preservation of state variables). Standby components remain available at all times except for maintenance issues or recovery failures in progress. Related controls: CP-2, CP-10, MA-6.

Control Enhancements:

(1) PREDICTABLE FAILURE PREVENTION | TRANSFERRING COMPONENT RESPONSIBILITIES

The organization takes information system components out of service by transferring component responsibilities to substitute components no later than [*Assignment: organization-defined fraction or percentage*] of mean time to failure.

(2) PREDICTABLE FAILURE PREVENTION | TIME LIMIT ON PROCESS EXECUTION WITHOUT SUPERVISION

[Withdrawn: Incorporated into SI-7 (16)].

(3) PREDICTABLE FAILURE PREVENTION | MANUAL TRANSFER BETWEEN COMPONENTS

The organization manually initiates transfers between active and standby information system components [*Assignment: organization-defined frequency*] if the mean time to failure exceeds [*Assignment: organization-defined time period*].

(4) PREDICTABLE FAILURE PREVENTION | STANDBY COMPONENT INSTALLATION / NOTIFICATION

The organization, if information system component failures are detected:

(a) Ensures that the standby components are successfully and transparently installed within [*Assignment: organization-defined time period*]; and

(b) [*Selection (one or more): activates* [*Assignment: organization-defined alarm*]; *automatically shuts down the information system*].

Supplemental Guidance: Automatic or manual transfer of components from standby to active mode can occur, for example, upon detection of component failures.

(5) PREDICTABLE FAILURE PREVENTION | FAILOVER CAPABILITY

The organization provides [*Selection: real-time; near real-time*] [*Assignment: organization-defined failover capability*] for the information system.

Supplemental Guidance: Failover refers to the automatic switchover to an alternate information system upon the failure of the primary information system. Failover capability includes, for example, incorporating mirrored information system operations at alternate processing sites or periodic data mirroring at regular intervals defined by recovery time periods of organizations.

References: None.

Priority and Baseline Allocation:

| P0 | LOW Not Selected | MOD Not Selected | HIGH Not Selected |

SI-14 NON-PERSISTENCE

Control: The organization implements non-persistent [*Assignment: organization-defined information system components and services*] that are initiated in a known state and terminated [*Selection (one or more): upon end of session of use; periodically at [Assignment: organization-defined frequency]*].

Supplemental Guidance: This control mitigates risk from advanced persistent threats (APTs) by significantly reducing the targeting capability of adversaries (i.e., window of opportunity and available attack surface) to initiate and complete cyber attacks. By implementing the concept of non-persistence for selected information system components, organizations can provide a known state computing resource for a specific period of time that does not give adversaries sufficient time on target to exploit vulnerabilities in organizational information systems and the environments in which those systems operate. Since the advanced persistent threat is a high-end threat with regard to capability, intent, and targeting, organizations assume that over an extended period of time, a percentage of cyber attacks will be successful. Non-persistent information system components and services are activated as required using protected information and terminated periodically or upon the end of sessions. Non-persistence increases the work factor of adversaries in attempting to compromise or breach organizational information systems.

Non-persistent system components can be implemented, for example, by periodically re-imaging components or by using a variety of common virtualization techniques. Non-persistent services can be implemented using virtualization techniques as part of virtual machines or as new instances of processes on physical machines (either persistent or non-persistent).The benefit of periodic refreshes of information system components/services is that it does not require organizations to first determine whether compromises of components or services have occurred (something that may often be difficult for organizations to determine). The refresh of selected information system components and services occurs with sufficient frequency to prevent the spread or intended impact of attacks, but not with such frequency that it makes the information system unstable. In some instances, refreshes of critical components and services may be done periodically in order to hinder the ability of adversaries to exploit optimum windows of vulnerabilities. Related controls: SC-30, SC-34.

Control Enhancements:

(1) NON-PERSISTENCE | REFRESH FROM TRUSTED SOURCES

The organization ensures that software and data employed during information system component and service refreshes are obtained from [*Assignment: organization-defined trusted sources*].

Supplemental Guidance: Trusted sources include, for example, software/data from write-once, read-only media or from selected off-line secure storage facilities.

References: None.

Priority and Baseline Allocation:

| P0 | LOW Not Selected | MOD Not Selected | HIGH Not Selected |

SI-15 INFORMATION OUTPUT FILTERING

Control: The information system validates information output from [*Assignment: organization-defined software programs and/or applications*] to ensure that the information is consistent with the expected content.

Supplemental Guidance: Certain types of cyber attacks (e.g., SQL injections) produce output results that are unexpected or inconsistent with the output results that would normally be expected from software programs or applications. This control enhancement focuses on detecting extraneous content, preventing such extraneous content from being displayed, and alerting monitoring tools that anomalous behavior has been discovered. Related controls: SI-3, SI-4.

Control Enhancements: None.

References: None.

Priority and Baseline Allocation:

| P0 | LOW Not Selected | MOD Not Selected | HIGH Not Selected |

SI-16 **MEMORY PROTECTION**

Control: The information system implements [*Assignment: organization-defined security safeguards*] to protect its memory from unauthorized code execution.

Supplemental Guidance: Some adversaries launch attacks with the intent of executing code in non-executable regions of memory or in memory locations that are prohibited. Security safeguards employed to protect memory include, for example, data execution prevention and address space layout randomization. Data execution prevention safeguards can either be hardware-enforced or software-enforced with hardware providing the greater strength of mechanism. Related controls: AC-25, SC-3.

Control Enhancements: None.

References: None.

Priority and Baseline Allocation:

| P1 | LOW Not Selected | MOD SI-16 | HIGH SI-16 |

SI-17 **FAIL-SAFE PROCEDURES**

Control: The information system implements [*Assignment: organization-defined fail-safe procedures*] when [*Assignment: organization-defined failure conditions occur*].

Supplemental Guidance: Failure conditions include, for example, loss of communications among critical system components or between system components and operational facilities. Fail-safe procedures include, for example, alerting operator personnel and providing specific instructions on subsequent steps to take (e.g., do nothing, reestablish system settings, shut down processes, restart the system, or contact designated organizational personnel). Related controls: CP-12, CP-13, SC-24, SI-13.

Control Enhancements: None.

References: None.

Priority and Baseline Allocation:

| P0 | LOW Not Selected | MOD Not Selected | HIGH Not Selected |

APPENDIX G

INFORMATION SECURITY PROGRAMS
ORGANIZATION-WIDE INFORMATION SECURITY PROGRAM MANAGEMENT CONTROLS

The Federal Information Security Management Act (FISMA) requires organizations to develop and implement an organization-wide information security program to address information security for the information and information systems that support the operations and assets of the organization, including those provided or managed by another organization, contractor, or other source. The information security program management (PM) controls described in this appendix are typically implemented at the organization level and not directed at individual organizational information systems. The program management controls have been designed to facilitate compliance with applicable federal laws, Executive Orders, directives, policies, regulations, and standards. The controls are independent of any FIPS Publication 200 impact levels and therefore, are not directly associated with any of the security control baselines described in Appendix D. The program management controls do, however, complement the security controls in Appendix F and focus on the programmatic, organization-wide information security requirements that are independent of any particular information system and are essential for managing information security programs. Tailoring guidance can be applied to the program management controls in a manner similar to how the guidance is applied to security controls in Appendix F. Organizations specify the individual or individuals responsible and accountable for the development, implementation, assessment, authorization, and monitoring of the program management controls. Organizations document program management controls in the *information security program plan*. The organization-wide information security program plan supplements the individual security plans developed for each organizational information system. Together, the security plans for the individual information systems and the information security program cover the totality of security controls employed by the organization.

In addition to documenting the information security program management controls, the security program plan provides a vehicle for the organization, in a central repository, to document all security controls from Appendix F that have been designated as *common controls* (i.e., security controls inheritable by organizational information systems).[111] The information security program management controls and common controls contained in the information security program plan are implemented, assessed for effectiveness,[112] and authorized by a senior organizational official, with the same or similar authority and responsibility for managing risk as the authorization officials for information systems. Plans of action and milestones are developed and maintained for the program management and common controls that are deemed through assessment to be less than effective. Information security program management and common controls are also subject to the same continuous monitoring requirements as security controls employed in individual organizational information systems.

Table G-1 provides a summary of the security controls in the program management family from Appendix G. Organizations can use the recommended *priority code* designation associated with each program management control to assist in making sequencing decisions for implementation

---

[111] Common controls are those security controls that are inheritable by one or more organizational information systems, and thus are separate and distinct from information security program management controls.

[112] Assessment procedures for program management controls and common controls can be found in NIST Special Publication 800-53A.

(i.e., a Priority Code 1 [P1] control has a higher priority for implementation than a Priority Code 2 [P2] control; and a Priority Code 2 [P2] control has a higher priority for implementation than a Priority Code 3 [P3] control.

TABLE G-1: PROGRAM MANAGEMENT CONTROLS

CNTL NO.	CONTROL NAME	PRIORITY	INITIAL CONTROL BASELINES		
			LOW	MOD	HIGH
PM-1	Information Security Program Plan	P1			
PM-2	Senior Information Security Officer	P1			
PM-3	Information Security Resources	P1			
PM-4	Plan of Action and Milestones Process	P1			
PM-5	Information System Inventory	P1	Deployed organization-wide. Supporting information security program. Not associated with security control baselines. Independent of any system impact level.		
PM-6	Information Security Measures of Performance	P1			
PM-7	Enterprise Architecture	P1			
PM-8	Critical Infrastructure Plan	P1			
PM-9	Risk Management Strategy	P1			
PM-10	Security Authorization Process	P1			
PM-11	Mission/Business Process Definition	P1			
PM-12	Insider Threat Program	P1			
PM-13	Information Security Workforce	P1			
PM-14	Testing, Training, and Monitoring	P1			
PM-15	Contacts with Security Groups and Associations	P3			
PM-16	Threat Awareness Program	P1			

Cautionary Note

Organizations are required to implement security program management controls to provide a foundation for the organizational information security program. The successful implementation of security controls for organizational information systems depends on the successful implementation of organization-wide program management controls. However, the manner in which organizations implement the program management controls depends on specific organizational characteristics including, for example, the size, complexity, and mission/business requirements of the respective organizations.

PM-1 INFORMATION SECURITY PROGRAM PLAN

Control: The organization:

a. Develops and disseminates an organization-wide information security program plan that:

  1. Provides an overview of the requirements for the security program and a description of the security program management controls and common controls in place or planned for meeting those requirements;

  2. Includes the identification and assignment of roles, responsibilities, management commitment, coordination among organizational entities, and compliance;

  3. Reflects coordination among organizational entities responsible for the different aspects of information security (i.e., technical, physical, personnel, cyber-physical); and

  4. Is approved by a senior official with responsibility and accountability for the risk being incurred to organizational operations (including mission, functions, image, and reputation), organizational assets, individuals, other organizations, and the Nation;

b. Reviews the organization-wide information security program plan [*Assignment: organization-defined frequency*];

c. Updates the plan to address organizational changes and problems identified during plan implementation or security control assessments; and

d. Protects the information security program plan from unauthorized disclosure and modification.

Supplemental Guidance: Information security program plans can be represented in single documents or compilations of documents at the discretion of organizations. The plans document the program management controls and organization-defined common controls. Information security program plans provide sufficient information about the program management controls/common controls (including specification of parameters for any *assignment* and *selection* statements either explicitly or by reference) to enable implementations that are unambiguously compliant with the intent of the plans and a determination of the risk to be incurred if the plans are implemented as intended.

The security plans for individual information systems and the organization-wide information security program plan together, provide complete coverage for all security controls employed within the organization. Common controls are documented in an appendix to the organization's information security program plan unless the controls are included in a separate security plan for an information system (e.g., security controls employed as part of an intrusion detection system providing organization-wide boundary protection inherited by one or more organizational information systems). The organization-wide information security program plan will indicate which separate security plans contain descriptions of common controls.

Organizations have the flexibility to describe common controls in a single document or in multiple documents. In the case of multiple documents, the documents describing common controls are included as attachments to the information security program plan. If the information security program plan contains multiple documents, the organization specifies in each document the organizational official or officials responsible for the development, implementation, assessment, authorization, and monitoring of the respective common controls. For example, the organization may require that the Facilities Management Office develop, implement, assess, authorize, and continuously monitor common physical and environmental protection controls from the PE family when such controls are not associated with a particular information system but instead, support multiple information systems. Related control: PM-8.

Control Enhancements: None.

References: None.

PM-2 SENIOR INFORMATION SECURITY OFFICER

Control: The organization appoints a senior information security officer with the mission and resources to coordinate, develop, implement, and maintain an organization-wide information security program.

Supplemental Guidance: The security officer described in this control is an organizational official. For a federal agency (as defined in applicable federal laws, Executive Orders, directives, policies, or regulations) this official is the Senior Agency Information Security Officer. Organizations may also refer to this official as the Senior Information Security Officer or Chief Information Security Officer.

Control Enhancements: None.

References: None.

PM-3 INFORMATION SECURITY RESOURCES

Control: The organization:

a. Ensures that all capital planning and investment requests include the resources needed to implement the information security program and documents all exceptions to this requirement;

b. Employs a business case/Exhibit 300/Exhibit 53 to record the resources required; and

c. Ensures that information security resources are available for expenditure as planned.

Supplemental Guidance: Organizations consider establishing champions for information security efforts and as part of including the necessary resources, assign specialized expertise and resources as needed. Organizations may designate and empower an Investment Review Board (or similar group) to manage and provide oversight for the information security-related aspects of the capital planning and investment control process. Related controls: PM-4, SA-2.

Control Enhancements: None.

References: NIST Special Publication 800-65.

PM-4 PLAN OF ACTION AND MILESTONES PROCESS

Control: The organization:

a. Implements a process for ensuring that plans of action and milestones for the security program and associated organizational information systems:

　1. Are developed and maintained;

　2. Document the remedial information security actions to adequately respond to risk to organizational operations and assets, individuals, other organizations, and the Nation; and

　3. Are reported in accordance with OMB FISMA reporting requirements.

b. Reviews plans of action and milestones for consistency with the organizational risk management strategy and organization-wide priorities for risk response actions.

Supplemental Guidance: The plan of action and milestones is a key document in the information security program and is subject to federal reporting requirements established by OMB. With the increasing emphasis on organization-wide risk management across all three tiers in the risk management hierarchy (i.e., organization, mission/business process, and information system), organizations view plans of action and milestones from an organizational perspective, prioritizing risk response actions and ensuring consistency with the goals and objectives of the organization. Plan of action and milestones updates are based on findings from security control assessments and continuous monitoring activities. OMB FISMA reporting guidance contains instructions regarding organizational plans of action and milestones. Related control: CA-5.

Control Enhancements: None.

References: OMB Memorandum 02-01; NIST Special Publication 800-37.

PM-5 INFORMATION SYSTEM INVENTORY

Control: The organization develops and maintains an inventory of its information systems.

Supplemental Guidance: This control addresses the inventory requirements in FISMA. OMB provides guidance on developing information systems inventories and associated reporting requirements. For specific information system inventory reporting requirements, organizations consult OMB annual FISMA reporting guidance.

Control Enhancements: None.

References: Web: http://www.omb.gov.

PM-6 INFORMATION SECURITY MEASURES OF PERFORMANCE

Control: The organization develops, monitors, and reports on the results of information security measures of performance.

Supplemental Guidance: Measures of performance are outcome-based metrics used by an organization to measure the effectiveness or efficiency of the information security program and the security controls employed in support of the program.

Control Enhancements: None.

References: NIST Special Publication 800-55.

PM-7 ENTERPRISE ARCHITECTURE

Control: The organization develops an enterprise architecture with consideration for information security and the resulting risk to organizational operations, organizational assets, individuals, other organizations, and the Nation.

Supplemental Guidance: The enterprise architecture developed by the organization is aligned with the Federal Enterprise Architecture. The integration of information security requirements and associated security controls into the organization's enterprise architecture helps to ensure that security considerations are addressed by organizations early in the system development life cycle and are directly and explicitly related to the organization's mission/business processes. This process of security requirements integration also embeds into the enterprise architecture, an integral *information security architecture* consistent with organizational risk management and information security strategies. For PM-7, the information security architecture is developed at a system-of-systems level (organization-wide), representing all of the organizational information systems. For PL-8, the information security architecture is developed at a level representing an individual information system but at the same time, is consistent with the information security architecture defined for the organization. Security requirements and security control integration are most effectively accomplished through the application of the Risk Management Framework and supporting security standards and guidelines. The Federal Segment Architecture Methodology provides guidance on integrating information security requirements and security controls into enterprise architectures. Related controls: PL-2, PL-8, PM-11, RA-2, SA-3.

Control Enhancements: None.

References: NIST Special Publication 800-39.

PM-8 CRITICAL INFRASTRUCTURE PLAN

Control: The organization addresses information security issues in the development, documentation, and updating of a critical infrastructure and key resources protection plan.

Supplemental Guidance: Protection strategies are based on the prioritization of critical assets and resources. The requirement and guidance for defining critical infrastructure and key resources and for preparing an associated critical infrastructure protection plan are found in applicable federal laws, Executive Orders, directives, policies, regulations, standards, and guidance. Related controls: PM-1, PM-9, PM-11, RA-3.

Control Enhancements: None.

References: HSPD 7; National Infrastructure Protection Plan.

PM-9 RISK MANAGEMENT STRATEGY

Control: The organization:

a. Develops a comprehensive strategy to manage risk to organizational operations and assets, individuals, other organizations, and the Nation associated with the operation and use of information systems;

b. Implements the risk management strategy consistently across the organization; and

c. Reviews and updates the risk management strategy [*Assignment: organization-defined frequency*] or as required, to address organizational changes.

Supplemental Guidance: An organization-wide risk management strategy includes, for example, an unambiguous expression of the risk tolerance for the organization, acceptable risk assessment methodologies, risk mitigation strategies, a process for consistently evaluating risk across the organization with respect to the organization's risk tolerance, and approaches for monitoring risk over time. The use of a risk executive function can facilitate consistent, organization-wide application of the risk management strategy. The organization-wide risk management strategy can be informed by risk-related inputs from other sources both internal and external to the organization to ensure the strategy is both broad-based and comprehensive. Related control: RA-3.

Control Enhancements: None.

References: NIST Special Publications 800-30, 800-39.

PM-10 SECURITY AUTHORIZATION PROCESS

Control: The organization:

a. Manages (i.e., documents, tracks, and reports) the security state of organizational information systems and the environments in which those systems operate through security authorization processes;

b. Designates individuals to fulfill specific roles and responsibilities within the organizational risk management process; and

c. Fully integrates the security authorization processes into an organization-wide risk management program.

Supplemental Guidance: Security authorization processes for information systems and environments of operation require the implementation of an organization-wide risk management process, a Risk Management Framework, and associated security standards and guidelines. Specific roles within the risk management process include an organizational risk executive (function) and designated authorizing officials for each organizational information system and common control provider. Security authorization processes are integrated with organizational continuous monitoring processes to facilitate ongoing understanding and acceptance of risk to organizational operations and assets, individuals, other organizations, and the Nation. Related control: CA-6.

Control Enhancements: None.

References: NIST Special Publications 800-37, 800-39.

PM-11 MISSION/BUSINESS PROCESS DEFINITION

Control: The organization:

a. Defines mission/business processes with consideration for information security and the resulting risk to organizational operations, organizational assets, individuals, other organizations, and the Nation; and

b. Determines information protection needs arising from the defined mission/business processes and revises the processes as necessary, until achievable protection needs are obtained.

Supplemental Guidance: Information protection needs are technology-independent, required capabilities to counter threats to organizations, individuals, or the Nation through the compromise of information (i.e., loss of confidentiality, integrity, or availability). Information protection needs are derived from the mission/business needs defined by the organization, the mission/business processes selected to meet the stated needs, and the organizational risk management strategy. Information protection needs determine the required security controls for the organization and the associated information systems supporting the mission/business processes. Inherent in defining an organization's information protection needs is an understanding of the level of adverse impact that could result if a compromise of information occurs. The security categorization process is used to make such potential impact determinations. Mission/business process definitions and associated information protection requirements are documented by the organization in accordance with organizational policy and procedure. Related controls: PM-7, PM-8, RA-2.

Control Enhancements: None.

References: FIPS Publication 199; NIST Special Publication 800-60.

PM-12 INSIDER THREAT PROGRAM

Control: The organization implements an insider threat program that includes a cross-discipline insider threat incident handling team.

Supplemental Guidance: Organizations handling classified information are required, under Executive Order 13587 and the National Policy on Insider Threat, to establish insider threat programs. The standards and guidelines that apply to insider threat programs in classified environments can also be employed effectively to improve the security of Controlled Unclassified Information in non-national security systems. Insider threat programs include security controls to detect and prevent malicious insider activity through the centralized integration and analysis of both technical and non-technical information to identify potential insider threat concerns. A senior organizational official is designated by the department/agency head as the responsible individual to implement and provide oversight for the program. In addition to the centralized integration and analysis capability, insider threat programs as a minimum, prepare department/agency insider threat policies and implementation plans, conduct host-based user monitoring of individual employee activities on government-owned classified computers, provide insider threat awareness training to employees, receive access to information from all offices within the department/agency (e.g., human resources, legal, physical security, personnel security, information technology, information system security, and law enforcement) for insider threat analysis, and conduct self-assessments of department/agency insider threat posture.

Insider threat programs can leverage the existence of incident handling teams organizations may already have in place, such as computer security incident response teams. Human resources records are especially important in this effort, as there is compelling evidence to show that some types of insider crimes are often preceded by nontechnical behaviors in the workplace (e.g., ongoing patterns of disgruntled behavior and conflicts with coworkers and other colleagues). These precursors can better inform and guide organizational officials in more focused, targeted monitoring efforts. The participation of a legal team is important to ensure that all monitoring activities are performed in accordance with appropriate legislation, directives, regulations, policies, standards, and guidelines. Related controls: AC-6, AT-2, AU-6, AU-7, AU-10, AU-12, AU-13, CA-7, IA-4, IR-4, MP-7, PE-2, PS-3, PS-4, PS-5, PS-8, SC-7, SC-38, SI-4, PM-1, PM-14.

Control Enhancements: None.

References: Executive Order 13587.

PM-13 INFORMATION SECURITY WORKFORCE

Control: The organization establishes an information security workforce development and improvement program.

Supplemental Guidance: Information security workforce development and improvement programs include, for example: (i) defining the knowledge and skill levels needed to perform information security duties and tasks; (ii) developing role-based training programs for individuals assigned information security roles and responsibilities; and (iii) providing standards for measuring and building individual qualifications for incumbents and applicants for information security-related positions. Such workforce programs can also include associated information security career paths to encourage: (i) information security professionals to advance in the field and fill positions with greater responsibility; and (ii) organizations to fill information security-related positions with qualified personnel. Information security workforce development and improvement programs are complementary to organizational security awareness and training programs. Information security workforce development and improvement programs focus on developing and institutionalizing core information security capabilities of selected personnel needed to protect organizational operations, assets, and individuals. Related controls: AT-2, AT-3.

Control Enhancements: None.

References: None.

PM-14 TESTING, TRAINING, AND MONITORING

Control: The organization:

a. Implements a process for ensuring that organizational plans for conducting security testing, training, and monitoring activities associated with organizational information systems:

   1. Are developed and maintained; and
   2. Continue to be executed in a timely manner;

b. Reviews testing, training, and monitoring plans for consistency with the organizational risk management strategy and organization-wide priorities for risk response actions.

Supplemental Guidance: This control ensures that organizations provide oversight for the security testing, training, and monitoring activities conducted organization-wide and that those activities are coordinated. With the importance of continuous monitoring programs, the implementation of information security across the three tiers of the risk management hierarchy, and the widespread use of common controls, organizations coordinate and consolidate the testing and monitoring activities that are routinely conducted as part of ongoing organizational assessments supporting a variety of security controls. Security training activities, while typically focused on individual information systems and specific roles, also necessitate coordination across all organizational elements. Testing, training, and monitoring plans and activities are informed by current threat and vulnerability assessments. Related controls: AT-3, CA-7, CP-4, IR-3, SI-4.

Control Enhancements: None.

References: NIST Special Publications 800-16, 800-37, 800-53A, 800-137.

PM-15 CONTACTS WITH SECURITY GROUPS AND ASSOCIATIONS

Control: The organization establishes and institutionalizes contact with selected groups and associations within the security community:

a. To facilitate ongoing security education and training for organizational personnel;

b. To maintain currency with recommended security practices, techniques, and technologies; and

c. To share current security-related information including threats, vulnerabilities, and incidents.

Supplemental Guidance: Ongoing contact with security groups and associations is of paramount importance in an environment of rapidly changing technologies and threats. Security groups and associations include, for example, special interest groups, forums, professional associations, news groups, and/or peer groups of security professionals in similar organizations. Organizations select groups and associations based on organizational missions/business functions. Organizations share threat, vulnerability, and incident information consistent with applicable federal laws, Executive Orders, directives, policies, regulations, standards, and guidance. Related control: SI-5.

Control Enhancements: None.

References: None.

PM-16 THREAT AWARENESS PROGRAM

Control: The organization implements a threat awareness program that includes a cross-organization information-sharing capability.

Supplemental Guidance: Because of the constantly changing and increasing sophistication of adversaries, especially the advanced persistent threat (APT), it is becoming more likely that adversaries may successfully breach or compromise organizational information systems. One of the best techniques to address this concern is for organizations to share threat information. This can include, for example, sharing threat events (i.e., tactics, techniques, and procedures) that organizations have experienced, mitigations that organizations have found are effective against certain types of threats, threat intelligence (i.e., indications and warnings about threats that are likely to occur). Threat information sharing may be bilateral (e.g., government-commercial cooperatives, government-government cooperatives), or multilateral (e.g., organizations taking part in threat-sharing consortia). Threat information may be highly sensitive requiring special agreements and protection, or less sensitive and freely shared. Related controls: PM-12, PM-16.

Control Enhancements: None.

References: None.

APPENDIX H

INTERNATIONAL INFORMATION SECURITY STANDARDS
SECURITY CONTROL MAPPINGS FOR ISO/IEC 27001 AND 15408

The mapping tables in this appendix provide organizations with a *general* indication of security control coverage with respect to ISO/IEC 27001, *Information technology–Security techniques–Information security management systems–Requirements*[113] and ISO/IEC 15408, *Information technology -- Security techniques -- Evaluation criteria for IT security.*[114] ISO/IEC 27001 may be applied to all types of organizations and specifies requirements for establishing, implementing, operating, monitoring, reviewing, maintaining, and improving a documented information security management system (ISMS) within the context of business risks. NIST Special Publication 800-39 includes guidance on managing risk at the organizational level, mission/business process level, and information system level, is consistent with ISO/IEC 27001, and provides additional implementation detail for the federal government and its contractors. ISO/IEC 15408 (also known as the Common Criteria) provides functionality and assurance requirements for developers of information systems and information system components (i.e., information technology products). Since many of the technical security controls defined in Appendix F are implemented in hardware, software, and firmware components of information systems, organizations can obtain significant benefit from the acquisition and employment of information technology products evaluated against the requirements of ISO/IEC 15408. The use of such products can provide evidence that certain security controls are implemented correctly, operating as intended, and producing the desired effect in satisfying stated security requirements.

Previously, the ISO/IEC 27001 mappings were created by relating the primary security topic identified in each of the Special Publication 800-53 base controls to a similar security topic in the ISO/IEC standard. This methodology resulted in a mapping of security control relationships rather than a mapping of equivalent security control requirements. The ISO/IEC 27001:2013 update provided an opportunity to reassess whether the implementation of a security control from Special Publication 800-53 satisfied the intent of the mapped control from ISO/IEC 27001 and conversely, whether the implementation of a security control from ISO/IEC 27001 satisfied the intent of the mapped control from Special Publication 800-53. To successfully meet the mapping criteria, the implementation of the mapped controls should result in an equivalent information security posture. However, this does not mean that security control equivalency based solely on the mapping tables herein should be assumed by organizations. While the revised security control mappings are more accurate, there is still some degree of subjectivity in the mapping analysis because the mappings are not always one-to-one and may not be completely equivalent. The following examples illustrate some of the mapping issues:

- **Example 1:** Special Publication 800-53 contingency planning and ISO/IEC 27001 business continuity management were deemed to have similar, but not the same, functionality.

- **Example 2:** In some cases, similar topics are addressed in the two security control sets but provide a different context, perspective, or scope. Special Publication 800-53 addresses

---

[113] ISO/IEC 27001 was published in October 2013 by the International Organization for Standardization (ISO) and the International Electrotechnical Commission (IEC).

[114] ISO/IEC 15408 was published in September 2012 by the International Organization for Standardization (ISO) and the International Electrotechnical Commission (IEC).

information flow control broadly in terms of approved authorizations for controlling access between source and destination objects, whereas ISO/IEC 27001 addresses information flow more narrowly as it applies to interconnected network domains.

- **Example 3:** Security control A.6.1.1, Information Security Roles and Responsibilities, in ISO/IEC 27001 states that "all information security responsibilities shall be defined and allocated" while security control PM-10, Security Authorization Process, in Special Publication 800-53 that is mapped to A.6.1.1, has three distinct parts. The first part states that the organization "designates individuals to fulfill specific roles and responsibilities…" If A.6.1.1 is mapped to PM-10 without providing any additional information, organizations might assume that if they implement A.6.1.1 (i.e., all responsibilities are defined and allocated), then the intent of PM-10 would also be fully satisfied. However, this would not be the case since the other two parts of PM-10 would not have been addressed. To resolve and clarify the security control mappings, when a security control in the right column of Tables H-1 and H-2 does not fully satisfy the intent of the security control in the left column of the tables, the control in the right column is designated with an asterisk (*).

In a few cases, an ISO/IEC 27001 security control could only be directly mapped to a Special Publication 800-53 control enhancement. In such cases, the relevant enhancement is specified in Table H-2 indicating that the corresponding ISO/IEC 27001 control satisfies only the intent of the specified enhancement and does not address the associated base control from Special Publication 800-53 or any other enhancements under that base control. Where no enhancement is specified, the ISO/IEC 27001 control is relevant only to the Special Publication 800-53 base control.

And finally, the security controls from ISO/IEC 27002 were not considered in the mapping analysis since the standard is informative rather than normative.

Table H-1 provides a mapping from the security controls in NIST Special Publication 800-53 to the security controls in ISO/IEC 27001. Please review the introductory text at the beginning of Appendix H before employing the mappings in Table H-1.

TABLE H-1: MAPPING NIST SP 800-53 TO ISO/IEC 27001

NIST SP 800-53 CONTROLS		ISO/IEC 27001 CONTROLS Note: An asterisk (*) indicates that the ISO/IEC control does not fully satisfy the intent of the NIST control.
AC-1	Access Control Policy and Procedures	A.5.1.1, A.5.1.2, A.6.1.1, A.9.1.1, A.12.1.1, A.18.1.1, A.18.2.2
AC-2	Account Management	A.9.2.1, A.9.2.2, A.9.2.3, A.9.2.5, A.9.2.6
AC-3	Access Enforcement	A.6.2.2, A.9.1.2, A.9.4.1, A.9.4.4, A.9.4.5, A.13.1.1, A.14.1.2, A.14.1.3, A.18.1.3
AC-4	Information Flow Enforcement	A.13.1.3, A.13.2.1, A.14.1.2, A.14.1.3
AC-5	Separation of Duties	A.6.1.2
AC-6	Least Privilege	A.9.1.2, A.9.2.3, A.9.4.4, A.9.4.5
AC-7	Unsuccessful Logon Attempts	A.9.4.2
AC-8	System Use Notification	A.9.4.2
AC-9	Previous Logon (Access) Notification	A.9.4.2
AC-10	Concurrent Session Control	None
AC-11	Session Lock	A.11.2.8, A.11.2.9
AC-12	Session Termination	None
AC-13	**Withdrawn**	---
AC-14	Permitted Actions without Identification or Authentication	None
AC-15	**Withdrawn**	---
AC-16	Security Attributes	None
AC-17	Remote Access	A.6.2.1, A.6.2.2, A.13.1.1, A.13.2.1, A.14.1.2
AC-18	Wireless Access	A.6.2.1, A.13.1.1, A.13.2.1
AC-19	Access Control for Mobile Devices	A.6.2.1, A.11.2.6, A.13.2.1
AC-20	Use of External Information Systems	A.11.2.6, A.13.1.1, A.13.2.1
AC-21	Information Sharing	None
AC-22	Publicly Accessible Content	None
AC-23	Data Mining Protection	None
AC-24	Access Control Decisions	A.9.4.1*
AC-25	Reference Monitor	None
AT-1	Security Awareness and Training Policy and Procedures	A.5.1.1, A.5.1.2, A.6.1.1, A.12.1.1, A.18.1.1, A.18.2.2
AT-2	Security Awareness Training	A.7.2.2, A.12.2.1
AT-3	Role-Based Security Training	A.7.2.2*
AT-4	Security Training Records	None
AT-5	**Withdrawn**	---
AU-1	Audit and Accountability Policy and Procedures	A.5.1.1, A.5.1.2, A.6.1.1, A.12.1.1, A.18.1.1, A.18.2.2
AU-2	Audit Events	None
AU-3	Content of Audit Records	A.12.4.1*
AU-4	Audit Storage Capacity	A.12.1.3
AU-5	Response to Audit Processing Failures	None
AU-6	Audit Review, Analysis, and Reporting	A.12.4.1, A.16.1.2, A.16.1.4
AU-7	Audit Reduction and Report Generation	None
AU-8	Time Stamps	A.12.4.4
AU-9	Protection of Audit Information	A.12.4.2, A.12.4.3, A.18.1.3
AU-10	Non-repudiation	None
AU-11	Audit Record Retention	A.12.4.1, A.16.1.7
AU-12	Audit Generation	A.12.4.1, A.12.4.3

NIST SP 800-53 CONTROLS		ISO/IEC 27001 CONTROLS Note: An asterisk (*) indicates that the ISO/IEC control does not fully satisfy the intent of the NIST control.
AU-13	Monitoring for Information Disclosure	None
AU-14	Session Audit	A.12.4.1*
AU-15	Alternate Audit Capability	None
AU-16	Cross-Organizational Auditing	None
CA-1	Security Assessment and Authorization Policies and Procedures	A.5.1.1, A.5.1.2, A.6.1.1, A.12.1.1, A.18.1.1, A.18.2.2
CA-2	Security Assessments	A.14.2.8, A.18.2.2, A.18.2.3
CA-3	System Interconnections	A.13.1.2, A.13.2.1, A.13.2.2
CA-4	**Withdrawn**	---
CA-5	Plan of Action and Milestones	None
CA-6	Security Authorization	None
CA-7	Continuous Monitoring	None
CA-8	Penetration Testing	None
CA-9	Internal System Connections	None
CM-1	Configuration Management Policy and Procedures	A.5.1.1, A.5.1.2, A.6.1.1, A.12.1.1, A.18.1.1, A.18.2.2
CM-2	Baseline Configuration	None
CM-3	Configuration Change Control	A.12.1.2, A.14.2.2, A.14.2.3, A.14.2.4
CM-4	Security Impact Analysis	A.14.2.3
CM-5	Access Restrictions for Change	A.9.2.3, A.9.4.5, A.12.1.2, A.12.1.4, A.12.5.1
CM-6	Configuration Settings	None
CM-7	Least Functionality	A.12.5.1*
CM-8	Information System Component Inventory	A.8.1.1, A.8.1.2
CM-9	Configuration Management Plan	A.6.1.1*
CM-10	Software Usage Restrictions	A.18.1.2
CM-11	User-Installed Software	A.12.5.1, A.12.6.2
CP-1	Contingency Planning Policy and Procedures	A.5.1.1, A.5.1.2, A.6.1.1, A.12.1.1, A.18.1.1, A.18.2.2
CP-2	Contingency Plan	A.6.1.1, A.17.1.1, A.17.2.1
CP-3	Contingency Training	A.7.2.2*
CP-4	Contingency Plan Testing	A.17.1.3
CP-5	**Withdrawn**	---
CP-6	Alternate Storage Site	A.11.1.4, A.17.1.2, A.17.2.1
CP-7	Alternate Processing Site	A.11.1.4, A.17.1.2, A.17.2.1
CP-8	Telecommunications Services	A.11.2.2, A.17.1.2
CP-9	Information System Backup	A.12.3.1, A.17.1.2, A.18.1.3
CP-10	Information System Recovery and Reconstitution	A.17.1.2
CP-11	Alternate Communications Protocols	A.17.1.2*
CP-12	Safe Mode	None
CP-13	Alternative Security Mechanisms	A.17.1.2*
IA-1	Identification and Authentication Policy and Procedures	A.5.1.1, A.5.1.2, A.6.1.1, A.12.1.1, A.18.1.1, A.18.2.2
IA-2	Identification and Authentication (Organizational Users)	A.9.2.1
IA-3	Device Identification and Authentication	None
IA-4	Identifier Management	A.9.2.1
IA-5	Authenticator Management	A.9.2.1, A.9.2.4, A.9.3.1, A.9.4.3
IA-6	Authenticator Feedback	A.9.4.2
IA-7	Cryptographic Module Authentication	A.18.1.5
IA-8	Identification and Authentication (Non-Organizational Users)	A.9.2.1
IA-9	Service Identification and Authentication	None

NIST SP 800-53 CONTROLS		ISO/IEC 27001 CONTROLS *Note: An asterisk (*) indicates that the ISO/IEC control does not fully satisfy the intent of the NIST control.*
IA-10	Adaptive Identification and Authentication	None
IA-11	Re-authentication	None
IR-1	Incident Response Policy and Procedures	A.5.1.1, A.5.1.2, A.6.1.1, A.12.1.1 A.18.1.1, A.18.2.2
IR-2	Incident Response Training	A.7.2.2*
IR-3	Incident Response Testing	None
IR-4	Incident Handling	A.16.1.4, A.16.1.5, A.16.1.6
IR-5	Incident Monitoring	None
IR-6	Incident Reporting	A.6.1.3, A.16.1.2
IR-7	Incident Response Assistance	None
IR-8	Incident Response Plan	A.16.1.1
IR-9	Information Spillage Response	None
IR-10	Integrated Information Security Analysis Team	None
MA-1	System Maintenance Policy and Procedures	A.5.1.1, A.5.1.2, A.6.1.1, A.12.1.1, A.18.1.1, A.18.2.2
MA-2	Controlled Maintenance	A.11.2.4*, A.11.2.5*
MA-3	Maintenance Tools	None
MA-4	Nonlocal Maintenance	None
MA-5	Maintenance Personnel	None
MA-6	Timely Maintenance	A.11.2.4
MP-1	Media Protection Policy and Procedures	A.5.1.1, A.5.1.2, A.6.1.1, A.12.1.1, A.18.1.1, A.18.2.2
MP-2	Media Access	A.8.2.3, A.8.3.1, A.11.2.9
MP-3	Media Marking	A.8.2.2
MP-4	Media Storage	A.8.2.3, A.8.3.1, A.11.2.9
MP-5	Media Transport	A.8.2.3, A.8.3.1, A.8.3.3, A.11.2.5, A.11.2.6
MP-6	Media Sanitization	A.8.2.3, A.8.3.1, A.8.3.2, A.11.2.7
MP-7	Media Use	A.8.2.3, A.8.3.1
MP-8	Media Downgrading	None
PE-1	Physical and Environmental Protection Policy and Procedures	A.5.1.1, A.5.1.2, A.6.1.1, A.12.1.1, A.18.1.1, A.18.2.2
PE-2	Physical Access Authorizations	A.11.1.2*
PE-3	Physical Access Control	A.11.1.1, A.11.1.2, A.11.1.3
PE-4	Access Control for Transmission Medium	A.11.1.2, A.11.2.3
PE-5	Access Control for Output Devices	A.11.1.2, A.11.1.3
PE-6	Monitoring Physical Access	None
PE-7	**Withdrawn**	---
PE-8	Visitor Access Records	None
PE-9	Power Equipment and Cabling	A.11.1.4, A.11.2.1, A.11.2.2, A.11.2.3
PE-10	Emergency Shutoff	A.11.2.2*
PE-11	Emergency Power	A.11.2.2
PE-12	Emergency Lighting	A.11.2.2*
PE-13	Fire Protection	A.11.1.4, A.11.2.1
PE-14	Temperature and Humidity Controls	A.11.1.4, A.11.2.1, A.11.2.2
PE-15	Water Damage Protection	A.11.1.4, A.11.2.1, A.11.2.2
PE-16	Delivery and Removal	A.8.2.3, A.11.1.6, A.11.2.5
PE-17	Alternate Work Site	A.6.2.2, A.11.2.6, A.13.2.1
PE-18	Location of Information System Components	A.8.2.3, A.11.1.4, A.11.2.1
PE-19	Information Leakage	A.11.1.4, A.11.2.1
PE-20	Asset Monitoring and Tracking	A.8.2.3*
PL-1	Security Planning Policy and Procedures	A.5.1.1, A.5.1.2, A.6.1.1, A.12.1.1, A.18.1.1, A.18.2.2
PL-2	System Security Plan	A.14.1.1
PL-3	**Withdrawn**	---
PL-4	Rules of Behavior	A.7.1.2, A.7.2.1, A.8.1.3

NIST SP 800-53 CONTROLS		ISO/IEC 27001 CONTROLS *Note: An asterisk (*) indicates that the ISO/IEC control does not fully satisfy the intent of the NIST control.*
PL-5	**Withdrawn**	---
PL-6	**Withdrawn**	---
PL-7	Security Concept of Operations	A.14.1.1*
PL-8	Information Security Architecture	A.14.1.1*
PL-9	Central Management	None
PS-1	Personnel Security Policy and Procedures	A.5.1.1, A.5.1.2, A.6.1.1, A.12.1.1, A.18.1.1, A.18.2.2
PS-2	Position Risk Designation	None
PS-3	Personnel Screening	A.7.1.1
PS-4	Personnel Termination	A.7.3.1, A.8.1.4
PS-5	Personnel Transfer	A.7.3.1, A.8.1.4
PS-6	Access Agreements	A.7.1.2, A.7.2.1, A.13.2.4
PS-7	Third-Party Personnel Security	A.6.1.1*, A.7.2.1*
PS-8	Personnel Sanctions	A.7.2.3
RA-1	Risk Assessment Policy and Procedures	A.5.1.1, A.5.1.2, A.6.1.1, A.12.1.1, A.18.1.1, A.18.2.2
RA-2	Security Categorization	A.8.2.1
RA-3	Risk Assessment	A.12.6.1*
RA-4	**Withdrawn**	---
RA-5	Vulnerability Scanning	A.12.6.1*
RA-6	Technical Surveillance Countermeasures Survey	None
SA-1	System and Services Acquisition Policy and Procedures	A.5.1.1, A.5.1.2, A.6.1.1, A.12.1.1, A.18.1.1, A.18.2.2
SA-2	Allocation of Resources	None
SA-3	System Development Life Cycle	A.6.1.1, A.6.1.5, A.14.1.1, A.14.2.1, A.14.2.6
SA-4	Acquisition Process	A.14.1.1, A.14.2.7, A.14.2.9, A.15.1.2
SA-5	Information System Documentation	A.12.1.1*
SA-6	**Withdrawn**	---
SA-7	**Withdrawn**	---
SA-8	Security Engineering Principles	A.14.2.5
SA-9	External Information System Services	A.6.1.1, A.6.1.5, A.7.2.1, A.13.1.2, A.13.2.2, A.15.2.1, A.15.2.2
SA-10	Developer Configuration Management	A.12.1.2, A.14.2.2, A.14.2.4, A.14.2.7
SA-11	Developer Security Testing and Evaluation	A.14.2.7, A.14.2.8
SA-12	Supply Chain Protections	A.14.2.7, A.15.1.1, A.15.1.2, A.15.1.3
SA-13	Trustworthiness	None
SA-14	Criticality Analysis	None
SA-15	Development Process, Standards, and Tools	A.6.1.5, A.14.2.1,
SA-16	Developer-Provided Training	None
SA-17	Developer Security Architecture and Design	A.14.2.1, A.14.2.5
SA-18	Tamper Resistance and Detection	None
SA-19	Component Authenticity	None
SA-20	Customized Development of Critical Components	None
SA-21	Developer Screening	A.7.1.1
SA-22	Unsupported System Components	None
SC-1	System and Communications Protection Policy and Procedures	A.5.1.1, A.5.1.2, A.6.1.1, A.12.1.1, A.18.1.1, A.18.2.2
SC-2	Application Partitioning	None
SC-3	Security Function Isolation	None
SC-4	Information In Shared Resources	None
SC-5	Denial of Service Protection	None
SC-6	Resource Availability	None

NIST SP 800-53 CONTROLS		ISO/IEC 27001 CONTROLS *Note: An asterisk (*) indicates that the ISO/IEC control does not fully satisfy the intent of the NIST control.*
SC-7	Boundary Protection	A.13.1.1, A.13.1.3, A.13.2.1, A.14.1.3
SC-8	Transmission Confidentiality and Integrity	A.8.2.3, A.13.1.1, A.13.2.1, A.13.2.3, A.14.1.2, A.14.1.3
SC-9	**Withdrawn**	---
SC-10	Network Disconnect	A.13.1.1
SC-11	Trusted Path	None
SC-12	Cryptographic Key Establishment and Management	A.10.1.2
SC-13	Cryptographic Protection	A.10.1.1, A.14.1.2, A.14.1.3, A.18.1.5
SC-14	**Withdrawn**	---
SC-15	Collaborative Computing Devices	A.13.2.1*
SC-16	Transmission of Security Attributes	None
SC-17	Public Key Infrastructure Certificates	A.10.1.2
SC-18	Mobile Code	None
SC-19	Voice Over Internet Protocol	None
SC-20	Secure Name/Address Resolution Service (Authoritative Source)	None
SC-21	Secure Name/Address Resolution Service (Recursive or Caching Resolver)	None
SC-22	Architecture and Provisioning for Name/Address Resolution Service	None
SC-23	Session Authenticity	None
SC-24	Fail in Known State	None
SC-25	Thin Nodes	None
SC-26	Honeypots	None
SC-27	Platform-Independent Applications	None
SC-28	Protection of Information at Rest	A.8.2.3*
SC-29	Heterogeneity	None
SC-30	Concealment and Misdirection	None
SC-31	Covert Channel Analysis	None
SC-32	Information System Partitioning	None
SC-33	**Withdrawn**	---
SC-34	Non-Modifiable Executable Programs	None
SC-35	Honeyclients	None
SC-36	Distributed Processing and Storage	None
SC-37	Out-of-Band Channels	None
SC-38	Operations Security	A.12.x
SC-39	Process Isolation	None
SC-40	Wireless Link Protection	None
SC-41	Port and I/O Device Access	None
SC-42	Sensor Capability and Data	None
SC-43	Usage Restrictions	None
SC-44	Detonation Chambers	None
SI-1	System and Information Integrity Policy and Procedures	A.5.1.1, A.5.1.2, A.6.1.1, A.12.1.1, A.18.1.1, A.18.2.2
SI-2	Flaw Remediation	A.12.6.1, A.14.2.2, A.14.2.3, A.16.1.3
SI-3	Malicious Code Protection	A.12.2.1
SI-4	Information System Monitoring	None
SI-5	Security Alerts, Advisories, and Directives	A.6.1.4*
SI-6	Security Function Verification	None
SI-7	Software, Firmware, and Information Integrity	None
SI-8	Spam Protection	None
SI-9	**Withdrawn**	---

NIST SP 800-53 CONTROLS		ISO/IEC 27001 CONTROLS Note: An asterisk (*) indicates that the ISO/IEC control does not fully satisfy the intent of the NIST control.
SI-10	Information Input Validation	None
SI-11	Error Handling	None
SI-12	Information Handling and Retention	None
SI-13	Predictable Failure Prevention	None
SI-14	Non-Persistence	None
SI-15	Information Output Filtering	None
SI-16	Memory Protection	None
SI-17	Fail-Safe Procedures	None
PM-1	Information Security Program Plan	A.5.1.1, A.5.1.2, A.6.1.1, A.18.1.1, A.18.2.2
PM-2	Senior Information Security Officer	A.6.1.1*
PM-3	Information Security Resources	None
PM-4	Plan of Action and Milestones Process	None
PM-5	Information System Inventory	None
PM-6	Information Security Measures of Performance	None
PM-7	Enterprise Architecture	None
PM-8	Critical Infrastructure Plan	None
PM-9	Risk Management Strategy	None
PM-10	Security Authorization Process	A.6.1.1*
PM-11	Mission/Business Process Definition	None
PM-12	Insider Threat Program	None
PM-13	Information Security Workforce	A.7.2.2*
PM-14	Testing, Training, and Monitoring	None
PM-15	Contacts with Security Groups and Associations	A.6.1.4
PM-16	Threat Awareness Program	None

Table H-2 provides a mapping from the security controls in ISO/IEC 27001 to the security controls in Special Publication 800-53.[115] Please review the introductory text at the beginning of Appendix H before employing the mappings in Table H-2.

TABLE H-2: MAPPING ISO/IEC 27001 TO NIST SP 800-53

ISO/IEC 27001 CONTROLS	NIST SP 800-53 CONTROLS Note: An asterisk (*) indicates that the ISO/IEC control does not fully satisfy the intent of the NIST control.
A.5 Information Security Policies	
A.5.1 Management direction for information security	
A.5.1.1 Policies for information security	All XX-1 controls
A.5.1.2 Review of the policies for information security	All XX-1 controls
A.6 Organization of information security	
A.6.1 Internal organization	
A.6.1.1 Information security roles and responsibilities	All XX-1 controls, CM-9, CP-2, PS-7, SA-3, SA-9, PM-2, PM-10
A.6.1.2 Segregation of duties	AC-5
A.6.1.3 Contact with authorities	IR-6
A.6.1.4 Contact with special interest groups	SI-5, PM-15
A.6.1.5 Information security in project management	SA-3, SA-9, SA-15
A.6.2 Mobile devices and teleworking	
A.6.2.1 Mobile device policy	AC-17, AC-18, AC-19
A.6.2.2 Teleworking	AC-3, AC-17, PE-17
A.7 Human Resources Security	
A.7.1 Prior to Employment	
A.7.1.1 Screening	PS-3, SA-21
A.7.1.2 Terms and conditions of employment	PL-4, PS-6
A.7.2 During employment	
A.7.2.1 Management responsibilities	PL-4, PS-6, PS-7, SA-9
A.7.2.2 Information security awareness, education, and training	AT-2, AT-3, CP-3, IR-2, PM-13
A.7.2.3 Disciplinary process	PS-8
A.7.3 Termination and change of employment	
A.7.3.1 Termination or change of employment responsibilities	PS-4, PS-5
A.8 Asset Management	
A.8.1 Responsibility for assets	
A.8.1.1 Inventory of assets	CM-8
A.8.1.2 Ownership of assets	CM-8
A.8.1.3 Acceptable use of assets	PL-4
A.8.1.4 Return of assets	PS-4, PS-5
A.8.2 Information Classification	
A.8.2.1 Classification of information	RA-2
A.8.2.2 Labelling of Information	MP-3
A.8.2.3 Handling of Assets	MP-2, MP-4, MP-5, MP-6, MP-7, PE-16, PE-18, PE-20, SC-8, SC-28
A.8.3 Media Handling	
A.8.3.1 Management of removable media	MP-2, MP-4, MP-5, MP-6, MP-7
A.8.3.2 Disposal of media	MP-6
A.8.3.3 Physical media transfer	MP-5
A.9 Access Control	

---

[115] The use of the term *XX-1 controls* in mapping Table H-2 refers to the set of security controls represented by the first control in each family in Appendix F, where *XX* is a placeholder for the two-letter family identifier.

ISO/IEC 27001 CONTROLS	NIST SP 800-53 CONTROLS Note: An asterisk (*) indicates that the ISO/IEC control does not fully satisfy the intent of the NIST control.
A.9.1 Business requirement of access control	
A.9.1.1 Access control policy	AC-1
A.9.1.2 Access to networks and network services	AC-3, AC-6
A.9.2 User access management	
A.9.2.1 User registration and de-registration	AC-2, IA-2, IA-4, IA-5, IA-8
A.9.2.2 User access provisioning	AC-2
A.9.2.3 Management of privileged access rights	AC-2, AC-3, AC-6, CM-5
A.9.2.4 Management of secret authentication information of users	IA-5
A.9.2.5 Review of user access rights	AC-2
A.9.2.6 Removal or adjustment of access rights	AC-2
A.9.3 User responsibilities	
A.9.3.1 Use of secret authentication information	IA-5
A.9.4 System and application access control	
A.9.4.1 Information access restriction	AC-3, AC-24
A.9.4.2 Secure logon procedures	AC-7, AC-8, AC-9, IA-6
A.9.4.3 Password management system	IA-5
A.9.4.4 Use of privileged utility programs	AC-3, AC-6
A.9.4.5 Access control to program source code	AC-3, AC-6, CM-5
A.10 Cryptography	
A.10.1 Cryptographic controls	
A.10.1.1 Policy on the use of cryptographic controls	SC-13
A.10.1.2 Key Management	SC-12, SC-17
A.11 Physical and environmental security	
A.11.1 Secure areas	
A.11.1.1 Physical security perimeter	PE-3*
A.11.1.2 Physical entry controls	PE-2, PE-3, PE-4, PE-5
A.11.1.3 Securing offices, rooms and facilities	PE-3, PE-5
A.11.1.4 Protecting against external and environmental threats	CP-6, CP-7, PE-9, PE-13, PE-14, PE-15, PE-18, PE-19
A.11.1.5 Working in secure areas	SC-42(3)*
A.11.1.6 Delivery and loading areas	PE-16
A.11.2 Equipment	
A.11.2.1 Equipment siting and protection	PE-9, PE-13, PE-14, PE-15, PE-18, PE-19
A.11.2.2 Supporting utilities	CP-8, PE-9, PE-10, PE-11, PE-12, PE-14, PE-15
A.11.2.3 Cabling security	PE-4, PE-9
A.11.2.4 Equipment maintenance	MA-2, MA-6
A.11.2.5 Removal of assets	MA-2, MP-5, PE-16
A.11.2.6 Security of equipment and assets off-premises	AC-19, AC-20, MP-5, PE-17
A.11.2.7 Secure disposal or reuse of equipment	MP-6
A.11.2.8 Unattended user equipment	AC-11
A.11.2.9 Clear desk and clear screen policy	AC-11, MP-2, MP-4
A.12 Operations security	
A.12.1 Operational procedures and responsibilities	
A.12.1.1 Documented operating procedures	All XX-1 controls, SA-5
A.12.1.2 Change management	CM-3, CM-5, SA-10
A.12.1.3 Capacity management	AU-4, CP-2(2), SC-5(2)
A.12.1.4 Separation of development, testing, and operational environments	CM-4(1)*, CM-5*
A.12.2 Protection from malware	
A.12.2.1 Controls against malware	AT-2, SI-3

ISO/IEC 27001 CONTROLS	NIST SP 800-53 CONTROLS Note: An asterisk (*) indicates that the ISO/IEC control does not fully satisfy the intent of the NIST control.
A.12.3 Backup	
A.12.3.1 Information backup	CP-9
A.12.4 Logging and monitoring	
A.12.4.1 Event logging	AU-3, AU-6, AU-11, AU-12, AU-14
A.12.4.2 Protection of log information	AU-9
A.12.4.3 Administrator and operator logs	AU-9, AU-12
A.12.4.4 Clock synchronization	AU-8
A.12.5 Control of operational software	
A.12.5.1 Installation of software on operational systems	CM-5, CM-7(4), CM-7(5), CM-11
A.12.6 Technical vulnerability management	
A.12.6.1 Management of technical vulnerabilities	RA-3, RA-5, SI-2, SI-5
A.12.6.2 Restrictions on software installation	CM-11
A.12.7 Information systems audit considerations	
A.12.7.1 Information systems audit controls	AU-5*
A.13 Communications security	
A.13.1 Network security management	
A.13.1.1 Network controls	AC-3, AC-17, AC-18, AC-20, SC-7, SC-8, SC-10
A.13.1.2 Security of network services	CA-3, SA-9
A.13.1.3 Segregation in networks	AC-4, SC-7
A.13.2 Information transfer	
A.13.2.1 Information transfer policies and procedures	AC-4, AC-17, AC-18, AC-19, AC-20, CA-3, PE-17, SC-7, SC-8, SC-15
A.13.2.2 Agreements on information transfer	CA-3, PS-6, SA-9
A.13.2.3 Electronic messaging	SC-8
A.13.2.4 Confidentiality or nondisclosure agreements	PS-6
A.14 System acquisition, development and maintenance	
A.14.1 Security requirements of information systems	
A.14.1.1 Information security requirements analysis and specification	PL-2, PL-7, PL-8, SA-3, SA-4
A.14.1.2 Securing application services on public networks	AC-3, AC-4, AC-17, SC-8, SC-13
A.14.1.3 Protecting application services transactions	AC-3, AC-4, SC-7, SC-8, SC-13
A.14.2 Security in development and support processes	
A.14.2.1 Secure development policy	SA-3, SA-15, SA-17
A.14.2.2 System change control procedures	CM-3, SA-10, SI-2
A.14.2.3 Technical review of applications after operating platform changes	CM-3, CM-4, SI-2
A.14.2.4 Restrictions on changes to software packages	CM-3, SA-10
A.14.2.5 Secure system engineering principles	SA-8
A.14.2.6 Secure development environment	SA-3*
A.14.2.7 Outsourced development	SA-4, SA-10, SA-11, SA-12, SA-15
A.14.2.8 System security testing	CA-2, SA-11
A.14.2.9 System acceptance testing	SA-4, SA-12(7)
A.14.3 Test data	
A.14.3.1 Protection of test data	SA-15(9)*
A.15 Supplier Relationships	
A.15.1 Information security in supplier relationships	
A.15.1.1 Information security policy for supplier relationships	SA-12
A.15.1.2 Address security within supplier agreements	SA-4, SA-12

ISO/IEC 27001 CONTROLS	NIST SP 800-53 CONTROLS Note: An asterisk (*) indicates that the ISO/IEC control does not fully satisfy the intent of the NIST control.
A.15.1.3 Information and communication technology supply chain	SA-12
A.15.2 Supplier service delivery management	
A.15.2.1 Monitoring and review of supplier services	SA-9
A.15.2.2 Managing changes to supplier services	SA-9
A.16 Information security incident management	
A.16.1 Managing of information security incidents and improvements	
A.16.1.1 Responsibilities and procedures	IR-8
A.16.1.2 Reporting information security events	AU-6, IR-6
A.16.1.3 Reporting information security weaknesses	SI-2
A.16.1.4 Assessment of and decision on information security events	AU-6, IR-4
A.16.1.5 Response to information security incidents	IR-4
A.16.1.6 Learning from information security incidents	IR-4
A.16.1.7 Collection of evidence	AU-4*, AU-9*, AU-10(3)*, AU-11*
A.17 Information security aspects of business continuity management	
A.17.1 Information security continuity	
A.17.1.1 Planning information security continuity	CP-2
A.17.1.2 Implementing information security continuity	CP-6, CP-7, CP-8, CP-9, CP-10, CP-11, CP-13
A.17.1.3 Verify, review, and evaluate information security continuity	CP-4
A.17.2 Redundancies	
A.17.2.1 Availability of information processing facilities	CP-2, CP-6, CP-7
A.18 Compliance	
A.18.1 Compliance with legal and contractual requirements	
A.18.1.1 Identification of applicable legislation and contractual requirements	All XX-1 controls
A.18.1.2 Intellectual property rights	CM-10
A.18.1.3 Protection of records	AC-3, AC-23, AU-9, AU-10, CP-9, SC-8, SC-8(1), SC-13, SC-28, SC-28(1)
A.18.1.4 Privacy and protection of personal information	Appendix J Privacy controls
A.18.1.5 Regulation of cryptographic controls	IA-7, SC-12, SC-13, SC-17
A.18.2 Information security reviews	
A.18.2.1 Independent review of information security	CA-2(1), SA-11(3)
A.18.2.2 Compliance with security policies and standards	All XX-1 controls, CA-2
A.18.2.3 Technical compliance review	CA-2

Note: The content of Table H-3, the mapping from the functional and assurance requirements in ISO/IEC 15408 (Common Criteria) to the security controls in Special Publication 800-53, is unaffected by the changes above.

Table H-3 provides a generalized mapping from the functional and assurance requirements in ISO/IEC 15408 (Common Criteria) to the security controls in Special Publication 800-53. The table represents an *informal* correspondence between security requirements and security controls (i.e., the table is not intended to determine whether the ISO/IEC 15408 security requirements are fully, partially, or not satisfied by the associated security controls). However, the table can serve as a beneficial starting point for further correspondence analysis. Organizations are cautioned that satisfying ISO/IEC 15408 security requirements for an particular evaluated and validated information technology product as represented by the presence of certain security controls from Appendix F, does not imply that such requirements have been satisfied throughout the entire information system (which may consist of multiple, integrated individual component products). Additional information explaining the specific mappings that appear in Table H-3 is available at the National Information Assurance Partnership (NIAP) website at: http://www.niap-ccevs.org.

TABLE H-3: MAPPING ISO/IEC 15408 TO NIST SP 800-53

ISO/IEC 15408 REQUIREMENTS		NIST SP 800-53 CONTROLS	
Functional Requirements			
FAU_ARP.1	Security Audit Automatic Response Security Alarms	AU-5	Response to Audit Processing Failures
		AU-5(1)	Response to Audit Processing Failures *Audit Storage Capacity*
		AU-5(2)	Response to Audit Processing Failures *Real-Time Alerts*
		AU-5(3)	Response to Audit Processing Failures *Configurable Traffic Volume Thresholds*
		AU-5(4)	Response to Audit Processing Failures *Shutdown on Failure*
		PE-6(2)	Monitoring Physical Access *Automated Intrusion Recognition / Responses*
		SI-3	Malicious Code Protection
		SI-3(8)	Malicious Code Protection *Detect Unauthorized Commands*
		SI-4(5)	Information System Monitoring *System-Generated Alerts*
		SI-4(7)	Information Systems Monitoring *Automated Response to Suspicious Events*
		SI-4(22)	Information Systems Monitoring *Unauthorized Network Services*
		SI-7(2)	Software, Firmware, and Information Integrity *Automated Notifications of Integrity Violations*
		SI-7(5)	Software, Firmware, and Information Integrity *Automated Response to Integrity Violations*
		SI-7(8)	Software, Firmware, and Information Integrity *Auditing Capability for Significant Events*
FAU_GEN.1	Security Audit Data Generation Audit Data Generation	AU-2	Audit Events
		AU-3	Content of Audit Records
		AU-3(1)	Content of Audit Records *Additional Audit Information*
		AU-12	Audit Generation

ISO/IEC 15408 REQUIREMENTS		NIST SP 800-53 CONTROLS	
FAU_GEN.2	Security Audit Data Generation User Identity Association	AU-3	Content of Audit Records
FAU_SAA.1	Security Audit Analysis Potential Violation Analysis	SI-4	Information System Monitoring
FAU_SAA.2	Security Audit Analysis Profile-Based Anomaly Detection	AC-2(12)	Account Management *Account Monitoring / Atypical Usage*
		SI-4	Information System Monitoring
FAU_SAA.3	Security Audit Analysis Simple Attack Heuristics	SI-3(7)	Malicious Code Protection *Non Signature-Based Protection*
		SI-4	Information System Monitoring
FAU_SAA.4	Security Audit Analysis Complex Attack Heuristics	SI-3(7)	Malicious Code Protection *Non Signature-Based Protection*
		SI-4	Information System Monitoring
FAU_SAR.1	Security Audit Review Audit Review	AU-7	Audit Reduction and Report Generation
FAU_SAR.2	Security Audit Review Restricted Audit Review	AU-9(6)	Protection of Audit Information *Read Only Access*
FAU_SAR.3	Security Audit Review Selectable Audit Review	AU-7	Audit Reduction and Report Generation
		AU-7(1)	Audit Reduction and Report Generation *Automatic Processing*
		AU-7(2)	Audit Reduction and Report Generation *Automatic Sort and Search*
FAU_SEL.1	Security Audit Event Selection Selective Audit	AU-12	Audit Generation
FAU_STG.1	Security Audit Event Storage Protected Audit Trail Storage	AU-9	Protection of Audit Information
FAU_STG.2	Security Audit Event Storage Guarantees of Audit Data Availability	AU-9	Protection of Audit Information *Alternate audit capability*
FAU_STG.3	Security Audit Event Storage Action In Case of Possible Audit Data Loss	AU-5	Response to Audit Processing Failures
		AU-5(1)	Response to Audit Processing Failures *Audit Storage Capacity*
		AU-5(2)	Response To Audit Processing Failures *Real-Time Alerts*
		AU-5(4)	Response To Audit Processing Failures *Shutdown on Failure*
FAU_STG.4	Security Audit Event Storage Prevention of Audit Data Loss	AU-4	Audit Storage Capacity
		AU-5	Response to Audit Processing Failures
		AU-5(2)	Response To Audit Processing Failures *Real-Time Alerts*
		AU-5(4)	Response To Audit Processing Failures *Shutdown on Failure*
FCO_NRO.1	Non-Repudiation of Origin Selective Proof of Origin	AU-10	Non-Repudiation
		AU-10(1)	Non-Repudiation *Association Of Identities*
		AU-10(2)	Non-Repudiation *Validate Binding of Information Producer Identity*

ISO/IEC 15408 REQUIREMENTS		NIST SP 800-53 CONTROLS	
FCO_NRO.2	**Non-Repudiation of Origin** Enforced Proof of Origin	AU-10	**Non-Repudiation**
		AU-10(1)	**Non-Repudiation** *Association Of Identities*
		AU-10(2)	**Non-Repudiation** *Validate Binding of Information Producer Identity*
FCO_NRR.1	**Non-Repudiation of Receipt** Selective Proof of Receipt	AU-10	**Non-Repudiation**
		AU-10(1)	**Non-Repudiation** *Association Of Identities*
		AU-10(2)	**Non-Repudiation** *Validate Binding of Information Producer Identity*
FCO_NRR.2	**Non-Repudiation of Receipt** Enforced Proof of Receipt	AU-10	**Non-Repudiation**
		AU-10(1)	**Non-Repudiation** *Association Of Identities*
		AU-10(2)	**Non-Repudiation** *Validate Binding of Information Producer Identity*
FCS_CKM.1	**Cryptographic Key Management** Cryptographic Key Generation	SC-12	**Cryptographic Key Establishment and Management**
FCS_CKM.2	**Cryptographic Key Management** Cryptographic Key Distribution	SC-12	**Cryptographic Key Establishment and Management**
FCS_CKM.3	**Cryptographic Key Management** Cryptographic Key Access	SC-12	**Cryptographic Key Establishment and Management**
FCS_CKM.4	**Cryptographic Key Management** Cryptographic Key Destruction	SC-12	**Cryptographic Key Establishment and Management**
FCS_COP.1	**Cryptographic Operation** Cryptographic Operation	SC-13	**Cryptographic Protection**
FDP_ACC.1	**Access Control Policy** Subset Access Control	AC-3	**Access Enforcement**
		AC-3(3)	**Access Enforcement** *Mandatory Access Control*
		AC-3(4)	**Access Enforcement** *Discretionary Access Control*
		AC-3(7)	**Access Enforcement** *Role-Based Access Control*
FDP_ACC.2	**Access Control Policy** Complete Access Control	AC-3	**Access Enforcement**
		AC-3(3)	**Access Enforcement** *Mandatory Access Control*
		AC-3(4)	**Access Enforcement** *Discretionary Access Control*
		AC-3(7)	**Access Enforcement** *Role-Based Access Control*
FDP_ACF.1	**Access Control Functions** Security Attribute Based Access Control	AC-3	**Access Enforcement**
		AC-3(3)	**Access Enforcement** *Mandatory Access Control*
		AC-3(4)	**Access Enforcement** *Discretionary Access Control*
		AC-3(7)	**Access Enforcement** *Role-Based Access Control*
		AC-16	**Security Attributes**

ISO/IEC 15408 REQUIREMENTS		NIST SP 800-53 CONTROLS	
		SC-16	Transmission of Security Attributes
FDP_DAU.1	Data Authentication Basic Data Authentication	SI-7	Software, Firmware, and Information Integrity
		SI-7(1)	Software, Firmware, and Information Integrity *Integrity Checks*
		SI-7(6)	Software, Firmware, And Information Integrity *Cryptographic Protection*
		SI-10	Information Input Validation
FDP_DAU.2	Data Authentication Data Authentication With Identity of Guarantor	SI-7	Software, Firmware, and Information Integrity
		SI-7(1)	Software, Firmware, and Information Integrity *Integrity Checks*
		SI-7(6)	Software, Firmware, And Information Integrity *Cryptographic Protection*
		SI-10	Information Input Validation
FDP_ETC.1	Export from the TOE Export of User Data without Security Attributes	No Mapping.	
FDP_ETC.2	Export from the TOE Export of User Data with Security Attributes	AC-4(18)	Information Flow Enforcement *Security Attribute Binding*
		AC-16	Security Attributes
		AC-16(5)	Security Attributes *Attribute Displays for Output Devices*
		SC-16	Transmission of Security Attributes
FDP_IFC.1	Information Flow Control Policy Subset Information Flow Control	AC-3	Access Enforcement
		AC-3(3)	Access Enforcement *Mandatory Access Control*
		AC-4	Information Flow Enforcement
		AC-4(1)	Information Flow Enforcement *Object Security Attributes*
FDP_IFC.2	Information Flow Control Policy Complete Information Flow Control	AC-3	Access Enforcement
		AC-3(3)	Access Enforcement *Mandatory Access Control*
		AC-4	Information Flow Enforcement
FDP_IFF.1	Information Flow Control Functions Simple Security Attributes	AC-3	Access Enforcement
		AC-3(3)	Access Enforcement *Mandatory Access Control*
		AC-4	Information Flow Enforcement
		AC-4(1)	Information Flow Enforcement *Object Security Attributes*
		AC-4(2)	Information Flow Enforcement *Processing Domains*
		AC-4(7)	Information Flow Enforcement *One-Way Flow Mechanisms*
		AC-16	Security Attributes
		SC-7	Boundary Protection

ISO/IEC 15408 REQUIREMENTS		NIST SP 800-53 CONTROLS	
FDP_IFF.2	Information Flow Control Functions Hierarchical Security Attributes	AC-3	Access Enforcement
		AC-3(3)	Access Enforcement *Mandatory Access Control*
		AC-4(1)	Information Flow Enforcement *Object Security Attributes*
		AC-16	Security Attributes
FDP_IFF.3	Information Flow Control Functions Limited Illicit Information Flows	SC-31	Covert Channel Analysis
		SC-31(2)	Covert Channel Analysis *Maximum Bandwidth*
FDP_IFF.4	Information Flow Control Functions Partial Elimination of Illicit Information Flows	SC-31	Covert Channel Analysis
		SC-31(2)	Covert Channel Analysis *Maximum Bandwidth*
FDP_IFF.5	Information Flow Control Functions No Illicit Information Flows	SC-31	Covert Channel Analysis
		SC-31(2)	Covert Channel Analysis *Maximum Bandwidth*
FDP_IFF.6	Information Flow Control Functions Illicit Information Flow Monitoring	SC-31	Covert Channel Analysis
		SI-4(18)	Information System Monitoring *Analyze Traffic / Covert Exfiltration*
FDP_ITC.1	Import from Outside of the TOE Import of User Data without Security Attributes	AC-4(9)	Information Flow Enforcement *Human Reviews*
		AC-4(12)	Information Flow Enforcement *Data Type Identifiers*
FDP_ITC.2	Import from Outside of the TOE Import of User Data with Security Attributes	AC-4(18)	Information Flow Enforcement *Security Attribute Binding*
		AC-16	Security Attributes
		SC-16	Transmission of Security Attributes
FDP_ITT.1	Internal TOE Transfer Basic Internal Transfer Protection	SC-8	Transmission Confidentiality and Integrity
		SC-8(1)	Transmission Confidentiality and Integrity *Cryptographic or Alternate Physical Protection*
		SC-5	Denial of Service Protection
FDP_ITT.2	Internal TOE Transfer Transmission Separation by Attribute	SC-8	Transmission Confidentiality and Integrity
		SC-8(1)	Transmission Confidentiality and Integrity *Cryptographic or Alternate Physical Protection*
		SC-5	Denial of Service Protection
		AC-4(21)	Information Flow Enforcement *Physical / Logical Separation of Information Flows*
FDP_ITT.3	Internal TOE Transfer Integrity Monitoring	SI-7	Software, Firmware, and Information Integrity
		SI-7(1)	Software, Firmware, and Information Integrity *Integrity Checks*
		SC-8(1)	Transmission Integrity *Cryptographic or Alternate Physical Protection*
		SI-7(5)	Software, Firmware, and Information Integrity *Automated Response to Integrity Violations*

ISO/IEC 15408 REQUIREMENTS		NIST SP 800-53 CONTROLS	
FDP_ITT.4	Internal TOE Transfer Attribute-Based Integrity Monitoring	SI-7	Software, Firmware, and Information Integrity
		SI-7(1)	Software, Firmware, and Information Integrity *Integrity Checks*
		SC-8(1)	Transmission Integrity *Cryptographic or Alternate Physical Protection*
		AC-4(21)	Information Flow Enforcement *Physical / Logical Separation of Information Flows*
		SI-7(5)	Software, Firmware, and Information Integrity *Automated Response to Integrity Violations*
FDP_RIP.1	Residual Information Protection Subset Residual Information Protection	SC-4	Information in Shared Resources
FDP_RIP.2	Residual Information Protection Full Residual Information Protection	SC-4	Information in Shared Resources
FDP_ROL.1	Rollback Basic Rollback	CP-10(2)	Information System Recovery and Reconstitution *Transaction Recovery*
FDP_ROL.2	Rollback Advanced Rollback	CP-10(2)	Information System Recovery and Reconstitution *Transaction Recovery*
FDP_SDI.1	Stored Data Integrity Stored Data Integrity Monitoring	SI-7	Software, Firmware, and Information Integrity
		SI-7(1)	Software, Firmware, and Information Integrity *Integrity Scans*
FDP_SDI.2	Stored Data Integrity Stored Data Integrity Monitoring and Action	SI-7	Software, Firmware, and Information Integrity
		SI-7(1)	Software, Firmware, and Information Integrity *Integrity Scans*
		SI-7(5)	Software, Firmware, and Information Integrity *Automated Response to Integrity Violations*
FDP_UCT.1	Inter-TSF User Data Confidentiality Transfer Protection Basic Data Exchange Confidentiality	SC-8	Transmission Confidentiality and Integrity
		SC-8(1)	Transmission Confidentiality and Integrity *Cryptographic or Alternate Physical Protection*
FDP_UIT.1	Inter-TSF User Data Integrity Transfer Protection Data Exchange Integrity	SC-8	Transmission Confidentiality and Integrity
		SC-8(1)	Transmission Confidentiality and Integrity *Cryptographic or Alternate Physical Protection*
		SI-7	Software, Firmware, and Information Integrity
		SI-7(6)	Software, Firmware, and Information Integrity *Cryptographic Protection*
FDP_UIT.2	Inter-TSF User Data Integrity Transfer Protection Source Data Exchange Recovery	No Mapping.	

ISO/IEC 15408 REQUIREMENTS		NIST SP 800-53 CONTROLS	
FDP_UIT.3	Inter-TSF User Data Integrity Transfer Protection Destination Data Exchange Recovery	No Mapping.	
FIA_AFL.1	Authentication Failure Authentication Failure Handling	AC-7	Unsuccessful Logon Attempts
FIA_ATD.1	User Attribute Definition User Attribute Definition	AC-2	Account Management
		IA-2	Identification and Authentication (Organizational Users)
FIA_SOS.1	Specification of Secrets Verification of Secrets	IA-5	Authenticator Management
		IA-5(1)	Authenticator Management Password-Based Authentication
		IA-5(12)	Authenticator Management Biometric Authentication
FIA_SOS.2	Specification of Secrets TSF Generation of Secrets	IA-5	Authenticator Management
		IA-5(1)	Authenticator Management Password-Based Authentication
		IA-5(12)	Authenticator Management Biometric Authentication
FIA_UAU.1	User Authentication Timing of Authentication	AC-14	Permitted Actions without Identification or Authentication
		IA-2	Identification and Authentication (Organizational Users)
		IA-8	Identification and Authentication (Non-Organizational Users)
FIA_UAU.2	User Authentication User Authentication Before Any Action	AC-14	Permitted Actions without Identification or Authentication
		IA-2	Identification and Authentication (Organizational Users)
		IA-8	Identification and Authentication (Non-Organizational Users)
FIA_UAU.3	User Authentication Unforgeable Authentication	IA-2(8)	Identification and Authentication (Organizational Users) Network Access To Privileged Accounts - Replay Resistant
		IA-2(9)	Identification and Authentication (Organizational Users) Network Access To Non-Privileged Accounts - Replay Resistant
FIA_UAU.4	User Authentication Single-Use Authentication Mechanisms	IA-2(8)	Identification and Authentication (Organizational Users) Network Access To Privileged Accounts - Replay Resistant
		IA-2(9)	Identification and Authentication (Organizational Users) Network Access To Non-Privileged Accounts - Replay Resistant
FIA_UAU.5	User Authentication Multiple Authentication Mechanisms	IA-2(1)	Identification and Authentication (Organizational Users) Network Access To Privileged Accounts
		IA-2(2)	Identification and Authentication (Organizational Users) Network Access To Non-Privileged Accounts

ISO/IEC 15408 REQUIREMENTS		NIST SP 800-53 CONTROLS	
		IA-2(3)	**Identification and Authentication (Organizational Users)** Local Access To Privileged Accounts
		IA-2(4)	**Identification and Authentication (Organizational Users)** Local Access To Non-Privileged Accounts
		IA-2(6)	**Identification and Authentication (Organizational Users)** Network Access To Privileged Accounts - Separate Device
		IA-2(7)	**Identification and Authentication (Organizational Users)** Network Access To Non-Privileged Accounts - Separate Device
		IA-2(11)	**Identification and Authentication (Organizational Users)** Remote Access - Separate Device
FIA_UAU.6	**User Authentication** Re-Authenticating	IA-11	**Re-authentication**
FIA_UAU.7	**User Authentication** Protected Authentication Feedback	IA-6	**Authenticator Feedback**
FIA_UID.1	**User Identification** Timing of Identification	AC-14	**Permitted Actions without Identification or Authentication**
		IA-2	**Identification and Authentication (Organizational Users)**
		IA-8	**Identification and Authentication (Non-Organizational Users)**
FIA_UID.2	**User Identification** User Identification Before Any Action	AC-14	**Permitted Actions without Identification or Authentication**
		IA-2	**Identification and Authentication (Organizational Users)**
		IA-8	**Identification and Authentication (Non-Organizational Users)**
FIA_USB.1	**User-Subject Binding** User-Subject Binding	AC-16(3)	**Security Attributes** Maintenance Of Attribute Associations By Information System
FMT_MOF.1	**Management of Functions in TSF** Management of Security Functions Behavior	AC-3(7)	**Access Enforcement** Role-Based Access Control
		AC-6	**Least Privilege**
		AC-6(1)	**Least Privilege** Authorize Access To Security Functions
FMT_MSA.1	**Management of Security Attributes** Management of Security Attributes	AC-6	**Least Privilege**
		AC-6(1)	**Least Privilege** Authorize Access To Security Functions
		AC-16(2)	**Security Attributes** Attribute Value Changes By Authorized Individuals
		AC-16(4)	**Security Attributes** Association of Attributes By Authorized Individuals
		AC-16(10)	**Security Attributes** Attribute Configuration By Authorized Individuals

ISO/IEC 15408 REQUIREMENTS		NIST SP 800-53 CONTROLS	
FMT_MSA.2	Management of Security Attributes Secure Security Attributes	AC-16	Security Attributes
		CM-6	Configuration Settings
		SI-10	Information Input Validation
FMT_MSA.3	Management of Security Attributes Static Attribute Initialization	No Mapping.	
FMT_MSA.4	Management of Security Attributes Security Attribute Value Inheritance	No Mapping.	
FMT_MTD.1	Management of TSF Data Management of TSF Data	AC-3(7)	Access Enforcement Role-Based Access Control
		AC-6	Least Privilege
		AC-6(1)	Least Privilege Authorize Access To Security Functions
		AU-6(7)	Audit Review, Analysis, and Reporting Permitted Actions
		AU-9(4)	Protection of Audit Information Access By Subset of Privileged Users
FMT_MTD.2	Management of TSF Data Management of Limits on TSF Data	AC-3(7)	Access Enforcement Role-based Access Control
		AC-6	Least Privilege
		AC-6(1)	Least Privilege Authorize Access To Security Functions
FMT_MTD.3	Management of TSF Data Secure TSF Data	SI-10	Information Input Validation
FMT_REV.1	Revocation Revocation	AC-3(7)	Access Enforcement Rose-based Access Control
		AC-3(8)	Access Enforcement Revocation Of Access Authorizations
		AC-6	Least Privilege
		AC-6(1)	Least Privilege Authorize Access To Security Functions
FMT_SAE.1	Security Attribute Expiration Time-Limited Authorization	AC-3(7)	Access Enforcement Role-based Access Control
		AC-6	Least Privilege
		AC-6(1)	Least Privilege Authorize Access To Security Functions
FMT_SMF.1	Specification of Management Functions Specification of Management Functions	No Mapping.	
FMT_SMR.1	Security Management Roles Security Roles	AC-2(7)	Account Management Role-based schemes
		AC-3(7)	Access Enforcement Role-Based Access Control
		AC-5	Separation of Duties
		AC-6	Least Privilege
FMT_SMR.2	Security Management Roles Restrictions on Security Roles	AC-2(7)	Account Management Role-based schemes
		AC-3(7)	Access Enforcement Role-Based Access Control
		AC-5	Separation of Duties

ISO/IEC 15408 REQUIREMENTS		NIST SP 800-53 CONTROLS	
		AC-6	Least Privilege
FMT_SMR.3	**Security Management Roles** Assuming Roles	AC-6(1)	**Least Privilege** Authorized Access to Security Functions
		AC-6(2)	**Least Privilege** Non-Privileged Access For Nonsecurity Functions
FPR_ANO.1	**Anonymity** Anonymity	No Mapping.	
FPR_ANO.2	**Anonymity** Anonymity Without Soliciting Information	No Mapping.	
FPR_PSE.1	**Pseudonymity** Pseudonymity	No Mapping.	
FPR_PSE.2	**Pseudonymity** Reversible Pseudonymity	No Mapping.	
FPR_PSE.3	**Pseudonymity** Alias Pseudonymity	No Mapping.	
FPR_UNL.1	**Unlinkability** Unlinkability	No Mapping.	
FPR_UNO.1	**Unobservability** Unobservability	No Mapping.	
FPR_UNO.2	**Unobservability** Allocation of Information Impacting Unobservability	No Mapping.	
FPR_UNO.3	**Unobservability** Unobservability Without Soliciting Information	No Mapping.	
FPR_UNO.4	**Unobservability** Authorized User Observability	No Mapping.	
FPT_FLS.1	**Fail Secure** Failure with Preservation of Secure State	SC-7(18)	**Boundary Protection** Fail Secure
		SC-24	**Fail in Known State**
FPT_ITA.1	**Availability of Exported TSF Data** Inter-TSF Availability within a Defined Availability Metric	CP-10	**Information System Recovery And Reconstitution** Restore Within Time Period
		SC-5	**Denial of Service Protection**
		SC-5(2)	**Denial of Service Protection** Excess Capacity/Bandwidth/Redundancy
		SC-5(3)	**Denial of Service Protection** Detection/Monitoring
FPT_ITC.1	**Confidentiality of Exported TSF Data** Inter-TSF Confidentiality During Transmission	SC-8	**Transmission Confidentiality and Integrity**
		SC-8(1)	**Transmission Confidentiality and Integrity** Cryptographic Or Alternate Physical Protection
FPT_ITI.1	**Integrity of Exported TSF Data** Inter-TSF Detection of Modification	SC-8	**Transmission Confidentiality and Integrity**
		SC-8(1)	**Transmission Confidentiality and Integrity** Cryptographic Or Alternate Physical Protection
		SI-7	**Software, Firmware, and Information Integrity**
		SI-7(1)	**Software, Firmware, and Information Integrity** Integrity Scans

ISO/IEC 15408 REQUIREMENTS		NIST SP 800-53 CONTROLS	
		SI-7(5)	**Software, Firmware, and Information Integrity** Automated Response to Integrity Violations
		SI-7(6)	**Software, Firmware, and Information Integrity** Cryptographic Protection
FPT_ITI.2	**Integrity of Exported TSF Data** Inter-TSF Detection and Correction of Modification	SC-8	**Transmission Confidentiality and Integrity**
		SC-8(1)	**Transmission Confidentiality and Integrity** Cryptographic Or Alternate Physical Protection
		SI-7	**Software, Firmware, and Information Integrity**
		SI-7(1)	**Software, Firmware, and Information Integrity** Integrity Scans
		SI-7(5)	**Software, Firmware, and Information Integrity** Automated Response to Integrity Violations
		SI-7(6)	**Software, Firmware, and Information Integrity** Cryptographic Protection
FPT_ITT.1	**Internal TOE TSF Data Transfer** Basic Internal TSF Data Transfer Protection	SC-8	**Transmission Confidentiality and Integrity**
		SC-8(1)	**Transmission Confidentiality and Integrity** Cryptographic Or Alternate Physical Protection
FPT_ITT.2	**Internal TOE TSF Data Transfer** TSF Data Transfer Separation	AC-4(21)	**Information Flow Enforcement** Physical / Logical Separation Of Information Flows
		SC-8	**Transmission Confidentiality and Integrity**
		SC-8(1)	**Transmission Confidentiality and Integrity** Cryptographic Or Alternate Physical Protection
FPT_ITT.3	**Internal TOE TSF Data Transfer** TSF Data Integrity Monitoring	SI-7	**Software, Firmware, and Information Integrity**
		SI-7(1)	**Software, Firmware, and Information Integrity** Integrity Scans
		SI-7(5)	**Software, Firmware, and Information Integrity** Automated Response to Integrity Violations
		SI-7(6)	**Software, Firmware, and Information Integrity** Cryptographic Protection
FPT_PHP.1	**TSF Physical Protection** Passive Detection of Physical Attack	PE-3(5)	**Physical Access Control** Tamper Protection
		PE-6(2)	**Monitoring Physical Access** Automated Intrusion Recognition / Responses
		SA-18	**Tamper Resistance and Detection**
FPT_PHP.2	**TSF Physical Protection** Notification of Physical Attack	PE-3(5)	**Physical Access Control** Tamper Protection
		PE-6(2)	**Monitoring Physical Access** Automated Intrusion Recognition / Responses
		SA-18	**Tamper Resistance and Detection**
FPT_PHP.3	**TSF Physical Protection** Resistance to Physical Attack	PE-3(5)	**Physical Access Control** Tamper Protection

ISO/IEC 15408 REQUIREMENTS		NIST SP 800-53 CONTROLS	
		SA-18	Tamper Resistance and Detection
FPT_RCV.1	Trusted Recovery Manual Recovery	CP-10	Information System Recovery and Reconstitution
		CP-12	Safe Mode
FPT_RCV.2	Trusted Recovery Automated Recovery	CP-10	Information System Recovery and Reconstitution
		CP-12	Safe Mode
FPT_RCV.3	Trusted Recovery Automated Recovery Without Undue Loss	CP-10	Information System Recovery and Reconstitution
		CP-12	Safe Mode
FPT_RCV.4	Trusted Recovery Function Recovery	SI-6	Security Function Verification
		SI-10(3)	Information Input Validation Predictable Behavior
		SC-24	Fail in Known State
FPT_RPL.1	Replay Detection Replay Detection	IA-2(8)	Identification and Authentication (Organizational Users) Network Access To Privileged Accounts - Replay Resistant
		IA-2(9)	Identification and Authentication (Organizational Users) Network Access To Non-Privileged Accounts - Replay Resistant
		SC-23	Session Authenticity
		SI-3(9)	Malicious Code Protection Authenticate Remote Commands
FPT_SSP.1	State Synchrony Protocol Simple Trusted Acknowledgement	No Mapping.	
FPT_SSP.2	State Synchrony Protocol Mutual Trusted Acknowledgement	No Mapping.	
FPT_STM.1	Time Stamps Reliable Time Stamps	AU-8	Time Stamps
FPT_TDC.1	Inter-TSF TSF Data Consistency Inter-TSF Basic Data Consistency	AC-16(7)	Security Attributes	Consistent Attribute Interpretation
		AC-16(8)	Security Attributes Association Techniques/Technologies
FPT_TEE.1	Testing of External Entities Testing of External Entities	SI-6	Security Functionality Verification
FPT_TRC.1	Internal TOE TSF Data Replication Consistency Internal TSF Consistency	SI-7	Software, Firmware, and Information Integrity
FPT_TST.1	TSF Self-Test TSF Testing	SI-6	Security Functionality Verification
		SI-7	Software, Firmware, and Information Integrity
FRU_FLT.1	Fault Tolerance Degraded Fault Tolerance	AU-15	Alternate Audit Capability
		CP-11	Alternate Communications Protocols
		SC-24	Fail in Known State
		SI-13	Predictable Failure Prevention
		SI-13(1)	Predictable Failure Prevention Transferring Component Responsibilities

ISO/IEC 15408 REQUIREMENTS		NIST SP 800-53 CONTROLS	
		SI-13(2)	Predictable Failure Prevention Time Limit on Process Execution Without Supervision
		SI-13(3)	Predictable Failure Prevention Manual Transfer Between Components
		SI-13(4)	Predictable Failure Prevention Standby Component Installation/Notification
		SI-13(5)	Predictable Failure Prevention Failover Capability
FRU_FLT.2	Fault Tolerance Limited Fault Tolerance	AU-15	Alternate Audit Capability
		CP-11	Alternate Communications Protocols
		SC-24	Fail in Known State
		SI-13	Predictable Failure Prevention
		SI-13(1)	Predictable Failure Prevention Transferring Component Responsibilities
		SI-13(2)	Predictable Failure Prevention Time Limit on Process Execution Without Supervision
		SI-13(3)	Predictable Failure Prevention Manual Transfer Between Components
		SI-13(4)	Predictable Failure Prevention Standby Component Installation/Notification
		SI-13(5)	Predictable Failure Prevention Failover Capability
FRU_PRS.1	Priority of Service Limited Priority of Service	SC-6	Resource Availability
FRU_PRS.2	Priority of Service Full Priority of Service	SC-6	Resource Availability
FRU_RSA.1	Resource Allocation Maximum Quotas	SC-6	Resource Availability
FRU_RSA.2	Resource Allocation Minimum and Maximum Quotas	SC-6	Resource Availability
FTA_LSA.1	Limitation on Scope of Selectable Attributes Limitation on Scope of Selectable Attributes	AC-2(6)	Account Management Dynamic Privilege Management
		AC-2(11)	Account Management Usage Conditions
FTA_MCS.1	Limitation on Multiple Concurrent Sessions Basic Limitation on Multiple Concurrent Sessions	AC-10	Concurrent Session Control
FTA_MCS.2	Limitation on Multiple Concurrent Sessions Per-User Limitation on Multiple Concurrent Sessions	AC-10	Concurrent Session Control
FTA_SSL.1	Session Locking and Termination TSF-Initiated Session Locking	AC-11	Session Lock
		AC-11(1)	Session Lock Pattern-Hiding Displays
FTA_SSL.2	Session Locking and Termination User-Initiated Locking	AC-11	Session Lock
		AC-11(1)	Session Lock Pattern-Hiding Displays

ISO/IEC 15408 REQUIREMENTS		NIST SP 800-53 CONTROLS	
FTA_SSL.3	Session Locking and Termination TSF-Initiated Termination	AC-12	Session Termination
		SC-10	Network Disconnect
FTA_SSL.4	Session Locking and Termination User-Initiated Termination	AC-12(1)	Session Termination User-Initiated Logouts / Message Displays
FTA_TAB.1	TOE Access Banners Default TOE Access Banners	AC-8	System Use Notification
FTA_TAH.1	TOE Access History TOE Access History	AC-9	Previous Login (Access) Notification
		AC-9(1)	Previous Login (Access) Notification Unsuccessful Logons
FTA_TSE.1	TOE Session Establishment TOE Session Establishment	AC-2(11)	Account Management Usage Conditions
FTP_ITC.1	Inter-TSF Trusted Channel Inter-TSF Trusted Channel	IA-3(1)	Device Identification and Authentication Cryptographic Bidirectional Authentication
		SC-8	Transmission Confidentiality and Integrity
		SC-8(1)	Transmission Confidentiality and Integrity Cryptographic or Alternate Physical Protection
FTP_TRP.1	Trusted Path Trusted Path	SC-11	Trusted Path
Assurance Requirements			
ASE_INT.1 EAL1 EAL2 EAL3 EAL4 EAL5 EAL6 EAL7	ST Introduction ST Introduction	SA-4	Acquisition Process
ASE_CCL.1 EAL1 EAL2 EAL3 EAL4 EAL5 EAL6 EAL7	Conformance Claims Conformance Claims	PL-2	System Security Plan
		SA-4(7)	Acquisition Process NIAP-Approved Protection Profiles
ASE_SPD.1 EAL1 EAL2 EAL3 EAL4 EAL5 EAL6 EAL7	Security Problem Definition Security Problem Definition	PL-2	System Security Plan
		SA-4	Acquisition Process
ASE_OBJ.1 EAL1	Security Objectives Security Objectives for the Operational Environment	PL-2	System Security Plan
		SA-4	Acquisition Process
ASE_OBJ.2 EAL2 EAL3 EAL4 EAL5 EAL6 EAL7	Security Objectives Security Objectives	PL-2	System Security Plan
		SA-4	Acquisition Process

ISO/IEC 15408 REQUIREMENTS		NIST SP 800-53 CONTROLS	
ASE_ECD.1 EAL1 EAL2 EAL3 EAL4 EAL5 EAL6 EAL7	**Extended Components Definition** Extended Components Definition	No Mapping.	
ASE_REQ.1 EAL1	**Security Requirements** Stated Security Requirements	PL-2	**System Security Plan**
		SA-4	**Acquisition Process**
ASE_REQ.2 EAL2 EAL3 EAL4 EAL5 EAL6 EAL7	**Security Requirements** Derived Security Requirements	PL-2	**System Security Plan**
		SA-4	**Acquisition Process**
ASE_TSS.1 EAL1 EAL2 EAL3 EAL4 EAL5 EAL6 EAL7	**TOE Summary Specification** TOE Summary Specification	PL-2	**System Security Plan**
		SA-4(1)	**Acquisition Process** Functional Properties of Security Controls
ASE_TSS.2	**TOE Summary Specification** TOE Summary Specification with Architectural Design Summary	PL-2	**System Security Plan**
		SA-4(1)	**Acquisition Process** Functional Properties of Security Controls
		SA-4(2)	**Acquisition Process** Design / Implementation Information For Security Controls
		SA-17	**Developer Security Architecture and Design**
ADV_ARC.1 EAL2 EAL3 EAL4 EAL5 EAL6 EAL7	**Security Architecture** Security Architecture Description	AC-25	**Reference Monitor**
		SA-17	**Developer Security Architecture and Design**
		SA-18	**Tamper Resistance and Detection**
		SC-3	**Security Function Isolation**
		SC-3(1)	**Security Function Isolation** Hardware Separation
		SC-3(2)	**Security Function Isolation** Minimize Nonsecurity Functionality
		SC-41	**Process Isolation**
ADV_FSP.1 EAL1	**Functional Specification** Basic Functional Specification	SA-4(1)	**Acquisition Process** Functional Properties of Security Controls
		SA-4(2)	**Acquisition Process** Design / Implementation Information for Security Controls
ADV_FSP.2 EAL2	**Functional Specification** Security-Enforcing Functional Specification	SA-4(1)	**Acquisition Process** Functional Properties of Security Controls
		SA-4(2)	**Acquisition Process** Design / Implementation Information for Security Controls

ISO/IEC 15408 REQUIREMENTS		NIST SP 800-53 CONTROLS	
		SA-17(4)	Developer Security Architecture and Design Informal Correspondence
ADV_FSP.3 EAL3	Functional Specification Functional Specification With Complete Summary	SA-4(1)	Acquisition Process Functional Properties of Security Controls
		SA-4(2)	Acquisition Process Design / Implementation Information for Security Controls
		SA-17(4)	Developer Security Architecture and Design Informal Correspondence
ADV_FSP.4 EAL4	Functional Specification Complete Functional Specification	SA-4(1)	Acquisition Process Functional Properties of Security Controls
		SA-4(2)	Acquisition Process Design / Implementation Information for Security Controls
		SA-17(4)	Developer Security Architecture and Design Informal Correspondence
ADV_FSP.5 EAL5 EAL6	Functional Specification Complete Semi-Formal Functional Specification with Additional Error Information	SA-4(1)	Acquisition Process Functional Properties of Security Controls
		SA-4(2)	Acquisition Process Design / Implementation Information for Security Controls
		SA-17(4)	Developer Security Architecture and Design Informal Correspondence
ADV_FSP.6 EAL7	Functional Specification Complete Semi-Formal Functional Specification with Additional Formal Specification	SA-4(1)	Acquisition Process Functional Properties of Security Controls
		SA-4(2)	Acquisition Process Design / Implementation Information for Security Controls
		SA-17(3)	Developer Security Architecture and Design Formal Correspondence
		SA-17(4)	Developer Security Architecture and Design Informal Correspondence
ADV_IMP.1 EAL4 EAL5	Implementation Representation Implementation Representation of the TSF	SA-4(2)	Acquisition Process Design / Implementation Information for Security Controls
ADV_IMP.2 EAL6 EAL7	Implementation Representation Complete Mapping of the Implementation Representation of the TSF	SA-4(2)	Acquisition Process Design / Implementation Information for Security Controls
		SA-17(3)	Developer Security Architecture and Design Formal Correspondence
ADV_INT.1	TSF Internals Well-Structured Subset of TSF Internals	SA-8	Security Engineering Principles
		SC-3(3)	Security Function Isolation Minimize Nonsecurity Functionality
		SC-3(4)	Security Function Isolation Module Coupling and Cohesiveness
		SC-3(5)	Security Function Isolation Layered Structures

ISO/IEC 15408 REQUIREMENTS		NIST SP 800-53 CONTROLS	
ADV_INT.2 EAL5	**TSF Internals** Well-Structured Internals	SA-8	**Security Engineering Principles**
		SC-3(3)	**Security Function Isolation** Minimize Nonsecurity Functionality
		SC-3(4)	**Security Function Isolation** Module Coupling and Cohesiveness
		SC-3(5)	**Security Function Isolation** Layered Structures
ADV_INT.3 EAL6 EAL7	**TSF Internals** Minimally Complex Internals	SA-8	**Security Engineering Principles**
		SA-17(5)	**Developer Security Architecture and Design** Conceptually Simple Design
		SC-3(3)	**Security Function Isolation** Minimize Nonsecurity Functionality
		SC-3(4)	**Security Function Isolation** Module Coupling and Cohesiveness
		SC-3(5)	**Security Function Isolation** Layered Structures
		AC-25	**Reference Monitor**
ADV_SPM.1 EAL6 EAL7	**Security Policy Modeling** Formal TOE Security Policy Model	SA-17(1)	**Developer Security Architecture and Design** Formal Policy Model
		SA-17(3)	**Developer Security Architecture and Design** Formal Correspondence
ADV_TDS.1 EAL2	**TOE Design** Basic Design	SA-4(2)	**Acquisition Process** Design / Implementation Information for Security Controls
		SA-17	**Developer Security Architecture and Design**
ADV_TDS.2 EAL3	**TOE Design** Architectural Design	SA-4(2)	**Acquisition Process** Design / Implementation Information for Security Controls
		SA-17	**Developer Security Architecture and Design**
ADV_TDS.3 EAL4	**TOE Design** Basic Modular Design	SA-4(2)	**Acquisition Process** Design / Implementation Information for Security Controls
		SA-17	**Developer Security Architecture and Design**
ADV_TDS.4 EAL5	**TOE Design** Semiformal Modular Design	SA-4(2)	**Acquisition Process** Design / Implementation Information for Security Controls
		SA-17	**Developer Security Architecture and Design**
		SA-17(2)	**Developer Security Architecture and Design** Security Relevant Components
		SA-17(4)	**Developer Security Architecture and Design** Informal Correspondence

ISO/IEC 15408 REQUIREMENTS		NIST SP 800-53 CONTROLS	
ADV_TDS.5 EAL6	**TOE Design** Complete Semiformal Modular Design	SA-4(2)	**Acquisition Process** Design / Implementation Information for Security Controls
		SA-17	**Developer Security Architecture and Design**
		SA-17(2)	**Developer Security Architecture and Design** Security Relevant Components
		SA-17(4)	**Developer Security Architecture and Design** Informal Correspondence
ADV_TDS.6 EAL7	**TOE Design** Complete Semiformal Modular Design with Formal High-Level Design Presentation	SA-4(2)	**Acquisition Process** Design / Implementation Information for Security Controls
		SA-17	**Developer Security Architecture and Design**
		SA-17(2)	**Developer Security Architecture and Design** Security Relevant Components
		SA-17(3)	**Developer Security Architecture and Design** Formal Correspondence
		SA-17(4)	**Developer Security Architecture and Design** Informal Correspondence
AGD_OPE.1 EAL1 EAL2 EAL3 EAL4 EAL5 EAL6 EAL7	**Operational User Guidance** Operational User Guidance	SA-5	**Information System Documentation**
AGD_PRE.1 EAL1 EAL2 EAL3 EAL4 EAL5 EAL6 EAL7	**Preparative Procedures** Preparative Procedures	SA-5	**Information System Documentation**
ALC_CMC.1 EAL1	**CM Capabilities** Labeling of the TOE	CM-9	**Configuration Management Plan**
		SA-10	**Developer Configuration Management**
ALC_CMC.2 EAL2	**CM Capabilities** Use of a CM System	CM-9	**Configuration Management Plan**
		SA-10	**Developer Configuration Management**
ALC_CMC.3 EAL3	**CM Capabilities** Authorization Controls	CM-3	**Configuration Change Control**
		CM-9	**Configuration Management Plan**
		SA-10	**Developer Configuration Management**
ALC_CMC.4 EAL4 EAL5	**CM Capabilities** Production Support, Acceptance Procedures, and Automation	CM-3	**Configuration Change Control**
		CM-3(1)	**Configuration Change Control** Automated Document / Notification / Prohibition of Changes
		CM-3(3)	**Configuration Change Control** Automated Change Implementation
		CM-9	**Configuration Management Plan**

ISO/IEC 15408 REQUIREMENTS		NIST SP 800-53 CONTROLS	
		SA-10	Developer Configuration Management
ALC_CMC.5 EAL6 EAL7	CM Capabilities Advanced Support	CM-3	Configuration Change Control
		CM-3(1)	Configuration Change Control Automated Document / Notification / Prohibition of Changes
		CM-3(2)	Configuration Change Control Test / Validate / Document Changes
		CM-3(3)	Configuration Change Control Automated mechanisms to field and deploy
		CM-9	Configuration Management Plan
		SA-10	Developer Configuration Management
ALC_CMS.1 EAL1	CM Scope TOE CM Coverage	CM-9	Configuration Management Plan
		SA-10	Developer Configuration Management
ALC_CMS.2 EAL2	CM Scope Parts of the TOE CM Coverage	CM-9	Configuration Management Plan
		SA-10	Developer Configuration Management
ALC_CMS.3 EAL3	CM Scope Implementation Representation CM Coverage	CM-9	Configuration Management Plan
		SA-10	Developer Configuration Management
ALC_CMS.4 EAL4	CM Scope Problem Tracking CM Coverage	CM-9	Configuration Management Plan
		SA-10	Developer Configuration Management
ALC_CMS.5 EAL5 EAL6 EAL7	CM Scope Development Tools CM Coverage	CM-9	Configuration Management Plan
		SA-10	Developer Configuration Management
ALC_DEL.1 EAL2 EAL3 EAL4 EAL5 EAL6 EAL7	Delivery Delivery Procedures	MP-5	Media Transport
		SA-10(1)	Developer Configuration Management Software / Firmware Integrity Verification
		SA-10(6)	Developer Configuration Management Trusted Distribution
		SA-18	Tamper Resistance and Detection
		SA-19	Component Authenticity
ALC_DVS.1 EAL3 EAL4 EAL5	Development Security Identification of Security Measures	SA-1	System and Services Acquisition Policy and Procedures
		SA-3	System Development Lifecycle
		SA-12	Supply Chain Protection
ALC_DVS.2 EAL6 EAL7	Development Security Sufficiency of Security Measures	CM-5	Access Restrictions for Change
		SA-3	System Development Lifecycle
		SA-12	Supply Chain Protection
ALC_FLR.1	Flaw Remediation Basic Flaw Remediation	SA-10	Developer Configuration Management
		SA-11	Developer Security Testing / Evaluation
		SI-2	Flaw Remediation
ALC_FLR.2	Flaw Remediation Flaw Reporting Procedures	SA-10	Developer Configuration Management
		SA-11	Developer Security Testing / Evaluation
		SI-2	Flaw Remediation
ALC_FLR.3	Flaw Remediation Systematic Flaw Remediation	SA-10	Developer Configuration Management
		SA-11	Developer Security Testing / Evaluation
		SI-2	Flaw Remediation

ISO/IEC 15408 REQUIREMENTS		NIST SP 800-53 CONTROLS	
ALC_LCD.1 EAL3 EAL4 EAL5 EAL6	**Life-Cycle Definition** Developer Defined Life-Cycle Model	SA-3 SA-15	**System Development Life Cycle** **Development Process, Standards, and Tools**
ALC_LCD.2 EAL7	**Life-Cycle Definition** Measurable Life-Cycle Model	SA-3 SA-15	**System Development Life Cycle** **Development Process, Standards, and Tools**
ALC_TAT.1 EAL4	**Tools and Techniques** Well-Defined Development Tools	SA-15	**Development Process, Standards, and Tools**
ALC_TAT.2 EAL5	**Tools and Techniques** Compliance with Implementation Standards	SA-15	**Development Process, Standards, and Tools**
ALC_TAT.3 EAL6 EAL7	**Tools and Techniques** Compliance with Implementation Standards – All Parts	SA-15	**Development Process, Standards, and Tools**
ATE_COV.1 EAL2	**Coverage** Evidence of Coverage	SA-11 SA-11(7)	**Developer Security Testing and Evaluation** **Developer Security Testing and Evaluation** *Verify Scope of Testing / Evaluation*
ATE_COV.2 EAL3 EAL4 EAL5	**Coverage** Analysis of Coverage	SA-11 SA-11(7)	**Developer Security Testing and Evaluation** **Developer Security Testing and Evaluation** *Verify Scope of Testing / Evaluation*
ATE_COV.3 EAL6 EAL7	**Coverage** Rigorous Analysis of Coverage	SA-11 SA-11(7)	**Developer Security Testing and Evaluation** **Developer Security Testing and Evaluation** *Verify Scope of Testing / Evaluation*
ATE_DPT.1 EAL3	**Depth** Testing: Basic Design	SA-11 SA-11(7)	**Developer Security Testing and Evaluation** **Developer Security Testing and Evaluation** *Verify Scope of Testing / Evaluation*
ATE_DPT.2 EAL4	**Depth** Testing: Security Enforcing Modules	SA-11 SA-11(7)	**Developer Security Testing and Evaluation** **Developer Security Testing and Evaluation** *Verify Scope of Testing / Evaluation*
ATE_DPT.3 EAL5 EAL6	**Depth** Testing: Modular Design	SA-11 SA-11(7)	**Developer Security Testing and Evaluation** **Developer Security Testing and Evaluation** *Verify Scope of Testing / Evaluation*
ATE_DPT.4 EAL7	**Depth** Testing: Implementation Representation	SA-11 SA-11(7)	**Developer Security Testing and Evaluation** **Developer Security Testing and Evaluation** *Verify Scope of Testing / Evaluation*
ATE_FUN.1 EAL2 EAL3 EAL4 EAL5	**Functional Tests** Functional Testing	SA-11	**Developer Security Testing and Evaluation**
ATE_FUN.2 EAL6 EAL7	**Functional Tests** Ordered Functional Testing	SA-11	**Developer Security Testing and Evaluation**
ATE_IND.1 EAL1	**Independent Testing** Independent Testing – Conformance	CA-2 CA-2(1) SA-11(3)	**Security Assessments** **Security Assessments** *Independent Assessors* **Developer Security Testing and Evaluation** *Independent Verification of Assessment Plans / Evidence*

ISO/IEC 15408 REQUIREMENTS		NIST SP 800-53 CONTROLS	
ATE_IND.2 EAL2 EAL3 EAL4 EAL5 EAL6	**Independent Testing** Independent Testing – Sample	CA-2	**Security Assessments**
		CA-2(1)	**Security Assessments** *Independent Assessors*
		SA-11(3)	**Developer Security Testing and Evaluation** *Independent Verification of Assessment Plans / Evidence*
ATE_IND.3 EAL7	**Independent Testing** Independent Testing – Complete	CA-2	**Security Assessments**
		CA-2(1)	**Security Assessments** *Independent Assessors*
		SA-11(3)	**Developer Security Testing and Evaluation** *Independent Verification of Assessment Plans / Evidence*
AVA_VAN.1 EAL1	**Vulnerability Analysis** Vulnerability Survey	CA-2(2)	**Security Assessments** *Specialized Assessments*
		CA-8	**Penetration Testing**
		RA-3	**Risk Assessment**
		SA-11(2)	**Developer Security Testing and Evaluation** *Threat And Vulnerability Analyses / Flaw Remediation*
		SA-11(5)	**Developer Security Testing and Evaluation** *Penetration Testing*
AVA_VAN.2 EAL2 EAL3	**Vulnerability Analysis** Vulnerability Analysis	CA-2(2)	**Security Assessments** *Specialized Assessments*
		CA-8	**Penetration Testing**
		RA-3	**Risk Assessment**
		SA-11(2)	**Developer Security Testing and Evaluation** *Threat And Vulnerability Analyses / Flaw Remediation*
		SA-11(5)	**Developer Security Testing and Evaluation** *Penetration Testing*
AVA_VAN.3 EAL4	**Vulnerability Analysis** Focused Vulnerability Analysis	CA-2(2)	**Security Assessments** *Specialized Assessments*
		CA-8	**Penetration Testing**
		RA-3	**Risk Assessment**
		SA-11(2)	**Developer Security Testing and Evaluation** *Threat And Vulnerability Analyses / Flaw Remediation*
		SA-11(5)	**Developer Security Testing and Evaluation** *Penetration Testing*
AVA_VAN.4 EAL5	**Vulnerability Analysis** Methodical Vulnerability Analysis	CA-2(2)	**Security Assessments** *Types of Assessments*
		CA-8	**Penetration Testing**
		RA-3	**Risk Assessment**
		SA-11(2)	**Developer Security Testing and Evaluation** *Threat And Vulnerability Analyses / Flaw Remediation*
		SA-11(5)	**Developer Security Testing and Evaluation** *Penetration Testing*
AVA_VAN.5 EAL6 EAL7	**Vulnerability Analysis** Advanced Methodical Vulnerability Analysis	CA-2(2)	**Security Assessments** *Types of Assessments*
		CA-8	**Penetration Testing**
		RA-3	**Risk Assessment**

ISO/IEC 15408 REQUIREMENTS		NIST SP 800-53 CONTROLS	
		SA-11(2)	**Developer Security Testing and Evaluation** *Threat And Vulnerability Analyses / Flaw Remediation*
		SA-11(5)	**Developer Security Testing and Evaluation** *Penetration Testing*
ACO_COR.1	**Composition Rationale** Composition Rationale	SA-17	**Developer Security Architecture and Design**
ACO_DEV.1	**Development Evidence** Functional Description	SA-17	**Developer Security Architecture and Design**
ACO_DEV.2	**Development Evidence** Basic Evidence of Design	SA-17	**Developer Security Architecture and Design**
ACO_DEV.3	**Development Evidence** Detailed Evidence of Design	SA-17	**Developer Security Architecture and Design**
ACO_REL.1	**Reliance on Dependent Component** Basic Reliance Information	SA-17	**Developer Security Architecture and Design**
ACO_REL.2	**Reliance on Dependent Component** Reliance Information	SA-17	**Developer Security Architecture and Design**
ACO_CTT.1	**Composed TOE Testing** Interface Testing	SA-11	**Developer Security Testing and Evaluation**
ACO_CTT.2	**Composed TOE Testing** Rigorous Interface Testing	SA-11	**Developer Security Testing and Evaluation**
ACO_VUL.1	**Composition Vulnerability Analysis** Composition Vulnerability Review	CA-2	**Security Assessments**
		CA-8	**Penetration Testing**
		RA-3	**Risk Assessment**
		SA-11	**Developer Security Testing and Evaluation**
ACO_VUL.2	**Composition Vulnerability Analysis** Composition Vulnerability Analysis	CA-2	**Security Assessments**
		CA-8	**Penetration Testing**
		RA-3	**Risk Assessment**
		SA-11	**Developer Security Testing and Evaluation**
ACO_VUL.3	**Composition Vulnerability Analysis** Enhanced-Basic Composition Vulnerability Review	CA-2	**Security Assessments**
		CA-8	**Penetration Testing**
		RA-3	**Risk Assessment**
		SA-11	**Developer Security Testing and Evaluation**

APPENDIX I

OVERLAY TEMPLATE
APPLYING TAILORING GUIDANCE FOR SPECIAL CONDITIONS OR COMMUNITY-WIDE USE[116]

Organizations may use the following template when developing tailored baselines using the concept of overlays.[117] The template is provided as an example only—organizations may choose to use other formats or modify the format in this appendix based on organizational needs and the type of overlay being developed. The level of detail included in the overlay is at the discretion of the organization initiating the overlay but should be of sufficient breadth and depth to provide an appropriate rationale and justification for the resulting tailored baseline developed, including any risk-based decisions made during the overlay development process. Security control baseline tailoring using the concept of overlays results in security plans that are subject to approval by authorizing officials. The example template consists of eight sections:

- Identification;
- Overlay Characteristics;
- Applicability;
- Overlay Summary;
- Detailed Overlay Control Specifications;
- Tailoring Considerations;
- Definitions; and
- Additional Information or Instructions.

How Overlays Can Be Used

Within the Risk Management Framework (RMF), overlays are implemented as part of the tailoring process after the completion of an initial security categorization process described in Section 3.1 and any organization-specific guidance. The security categorization process results in the determination of an *impact level* of the information system, and is subsequently used to select an initial set of security controls from one of the security control baselines in Appendix D.[118] After the initial set of security controls is identified, organizations initiate the tailoring process to modify and align the controls more closely with the specific conditions within the organizations. Overlays provide tailoring guidance from a community-wide perspective to address specialized requirements, missions/business functions, technologies, or environments of operation. Overlays provide uniformity and efficiency of security control selection by presenting tailoring options

---

[116] Tailored baselines produced using the concept of *overlays* can be published independently in a variety of venues and publications including, for example, OMB policies, CNSS Instructions, NIST Special Publications, industry standards, and sector-specific guidance. As part of the overlay initiative, the previous guidance in Appendix I regarding industrial and process control system security will be transferred to NIST Special Publication 800-82.

[117] While organizations are encouraged to use the overlay concept to tailor security control baselines, generating widely divergent overlays on the same topic may prove to be counterproductive. The overlay concept is most effective when communities of interest work together to create consensus-based overlays that are not duplicative.

[118] CNSS Instruction 1253 provides security categorization guidance and security control baselines for national security systems.

developed by security experts and other subject matter experts to information system owners responsible for implementing and maintaining such systems.

There is a considerable range of options that can be used to construct overlays, depending on the specificity desired by the overlay developers. Some overlays may be very specific with respect to the hardware, firmware, and software that form the key components the information system and the environment in which the system operates. Other overlays may be more abstract in order to be applicable to a large class of information systems that may be deployed in different environments. The example template described below can be used for any level of specificity on this continuum of potential options for overlays.

Overlays that provide *greater specificity* are typically developed by organizations with authority over the information system owners and environments of operation. Organizations decide on the appropriate tailoring actions for the selected baseline security controls as described in Section 3.2. Many of the variables and conditions that qualify the overlay for use on a specific information system are made explicit to ensure consistency when applying the overlay. Overlays that provide *less specificity* can also be developed by security and subject matter experts for application to large classes of information systems or in situations where there is less than full knowledge about the specific implementation details related to the system. Less specific overlays may require additional tailoring to customize the set of security controls for the specific information system. These overlays leave many of the assignment and selection statements in the security controls (i.e., the variable portion of the controls) to be completed by the organization that owns and operates the information system. The eight sections comprising the overlay are described below.

Identification

Organizations identify the overlay by providing: (i) a unique name for the overlay; (ii) a version number and date; (iii) the version of NIST Special Publication 800-53 used to create the overlay; (iv) other documentation used to create the overlay; (v) author or authoring group and point of contact; and (vi) type of organizational approval received. Organizations define how long the overlay is to be in effect and any events that may trigger an update to the overlay other than changes to NIST Special Publication 800-53 or organization-specific security guidance. If there are no unique events that can trigger an update for the overlay, this section provides that notation.

Overlay Characteristics

Organizations describe the characteristics that define the intended use of the overlay in order to help potential users select the most appropriate overlay for their missions/business functions. This may include, for example, a description of: (i) the environment in which the information system will be used (e.g., inside a guarded building within the continental United States, in an unmanned space vehicle, while traveling for business to a foreign country that is known for attempting to gain access to sensitive or classified information, or in a mobile vehicle that is in close proximity to hostile entities); (ii) the type of information that will be processed, stored, or transmitted (e.g., personal identity and authentication information, financial management information, facilities, fleet, and equipment management information, defense and national security information, system development information); (iii) the functionality within the information system or the type of system (e.g., standalone system, industrial/process control system, or cross-domain system); and (iv) other characteristics related to the overlay that help protect organizational missions/business functions, information systems, information, or individuals from a specific set of threats that may not be addressed by the assumptions described in Chapter Three.

Applicability

Organizations provide criteria to assist potential users of the overlay in determining whether or not the overlay applies to a particular information system or environment of operation. Typical formats include, for example, a list of questions or a decision tree based on the description of the characteristics of the information system (including associated applications) and its environment of operation at the level of specificity appropriate to the overlay.

Overlay Summary

Organizations provide a brief summary of the salient characteristics of the overlay. This summary may include, for example: (i) the security controls and control enhancements that are affected by the overlay; (ii) an indication of which controls/enhancements are selected or not selected based on the characteristics and assumptions in the overlay, the tailoring guidance provided in Section 3.2, or any organization-specific guidance; (iii) the selected controls/enhancements including an overview of new supplemental guidance and parameter values; and (iv) references to applicable laws, Executive Orders, directives, instructions, regulations, policies, or standards.

Detailed Overlay Control Specifications

Organizations provide a comprehensive expression of the security controls/control enhancements in the overlay as part of the tailoring process. This may include, for example: (i) justification for selecting or not selecting a specific security control/control enhancement; (ii) modifications to the supplemental guidance or the addition of new supplemental guidance for the security controls and control enhancements to address the characteristics of the overlay and the environments in which the overlay is intended to operate; (iii) unique parameter values for security control selection or assignment statements; (iv) specific statutory and/or regulatory requirements (above and beyond FISMA) that are met by a security control or control enhancement; (v) recommendations for compensating controls, as appropriate; and (vi) guidance that extends the basic capability of the control/enhancement by specifying additional functionality, altering the strength of mechanism, or adding or limiting implementation options.

Tailoring Considerations

Organizations provide information to information system owners and authorizing officials to consider during the tailoring process when determining the set of security controls applicable to their specific information systems. This is especially important for overlays that are used in an environment of operation different from the one assumed by the security control baselines (as defined in Section 3.1). In addition, organizations can provide guidance on the use of multiple overlays applied to a security control baseline and address any potential conflicts that may arise between overlay specifications and baseline controls.

Definitions

Organizations provide any terms and associated definitions that are unique and relevant to the overlay. The terms and definitions are listed in alphabetical order. If there are no unique terms or definitions for the overlay, this is stated in this section.

Additional Information or Instructions

Organizations provide any additional information or instructions relevant to the overlay not covered in the previous sections.

APPENDIX J

PRIVACY CONTROL CATALOG
PRIVACY CONTROLS, ENHANCEMENTS, AND SUPPLEMENTAL GUIDANCE

The need to protect an individual's privacy is as important today as it was in 1974 when the Privacy Act first sought to balance the government's need to collect information from an individual with a citizen's right to be notified as to how that information was being used, collected, maintained, and disposed of after the requisite period of use. These concerns are also shared in the private sector, where healthcare, financial, and other services continue to be delivered via the web with increasingly higher levels of personalization. The proliferation of social media, Smart Grid, mobile, and cloud computing, as well as the transition from structured to unstructured data and metadata environments, have added significant complexities and challenges for federal organizations in safeguarding privacy. These challenges extend well beyond the traditional information technology security view of protecting privacy which focused primarily on ensuring confidentiality. Now there are greater implications with respect to controlling the integrity of an individual's information, and with ensuring that an individual's information is available on demand. The challenging landscape requires federal organizations to expand their view of privacy, in order to meet citizen expectations of privacy that go beyond information security.

Privacy, with respect to personally identifiable information (PII),[119] is a core value that can be obtained only with appropriate legislation, policies, procedures, and associated controls to ensure compliance with requirements. Protecting the privacy of individuals and their PII that is collected, used, maintained, shared, and disposed of by programs and information systems, is a fundamental responsibility of federal organizations. Privacy also involves each individual's right to decide when and whether to share personal information, how much information to share, and the particular circumstances under which that information can be shared. In today's digital world, effective privacy for individuals depends on the safeguards employed within the information systems that are processing, storing, and transmitting PII and the environments in which those systems operate. Organizations cannot have effective privacy without a basic foundation of information security. Privacy is more than security, however, and includes, for example, the principles of transparency, notice, and choice.

This appendix provides a structured set of controls for protecting privacy and serves as a roadmap for organizations to use in identifying and implementing privacy controls concerning the entire life cycle of PII, whether in paper or electronic form. The controls focus on information privacy as a value distinct from, but highly interrelated with, information security. Privacy controls are

---

[119] OMB Memorandum 07-16 defines PII as information which can be used to distinguish or trace an individual's identity such as their name, social security number, biometric records, etc., alone, or when combined with other personal or identifying information which is linked or linkable to a specific individual, such as date and place of birth, mother's maiden name, etc. OMB Memorandum 10-22 further states that "the definition of PII is not anchored to any single category of information or technology. Rather, it requires a case-by-case assessment of the specific risk that an individual can be identified by examining the context of use and combination of data elements. In performing this assessment, it is important for agencies to recognize that non-PII can become PII, whenever additional information is made publicly available, in any medium and from any source that, when combined with other available information, could be used to identify an individual." NIST Special Publication 800-122 also includes a definition of PII that differs from this appendix because it was focused on the security objective of confidentiality and not privacy in the broad sense. Organizational definitions of PII may vary based on the consideration of additional regulatory requirements. The privacy controls in this appendix apply regardless of the definition of PII by organizations.

the administrative, technical, and physical safeguards employed within organizations to protect and ensure the proper handling of PII.[120] Organizations may also engage in activities that do not involve the collection and use of PII, but may nevertheless raise privacy concerns and associated risk. The privacy controls are equally applicable to those activities and can be used to analyze the privacy risk and mitigate such risk when necessary.

The privacy controls in this appendix are based on the Fair Information Practice Principles (FIPPs)[121] embodied in the Privacy Act of 1974, Section 208 of the E-Government Act of 2002, and Office of Management and Budget (OMB) policies. The FIPPs are designed to build public trust in the privacy practices of organizations and to help organizations avoid tangible costs and intangible damages from privacy incidents. There are eight privacy control families, each aligning with one of the FIPPs. The privacy families can be implemented at the organization, department, agency, component, office, program, or information system level, under the leadership and oversight of the Senior Agency Official for Privacy (SAOP)/Chief Privacy Officer (CPO)[122] and in coordination with the Chief Information Security Officer, Chief Information Officer, program officials, legal counsel, and others as appropriate. Table J-1 provides a summary of the privacy controls by family in the privacy control catalog.

TABLE J-1: SUMMARY OF PRIVACY CONTROLS BY FAMILY

ID	PRIVACY CONTROLS
AP	**Authority and Purpose**
AP-1	Authority to Collect
AP-2	Purpose Specification
AR	**Accountability, Audit, and Risk Management**
AR-1	Governance and Privacy Program
AR-2	Privacy Impact and Risk Assessment
AR-3	Privacy Requirements for Contractors and Service Providers
AR-4	Privacy Monitoring and Auditing
AR-5	Privacy Awareness and Training
AR-6	Privacy Reporting
AR-7	Privacy-Enhanced System Design and Development
AR-8	Accounting of Disclosures
DI	**Data Quality and Integrity**
DI-1	Data Quality
DI-2	Data Integrity and Data Integrity Board
DM	**Data Minimization and Retention**
DM-1	Minimization of Personally Identifiable Information
DM-2	Data Retention and Disposal

---

[120] In 2010, the Federal CIO Council Privacy Committee issued a framework for designing and implementing a privacy program entitled *Best Practices: Elements of a Federal Privacy Program (Elements White Paper)*. The privacy controls in this appendix mirror a number of the elements included in the paper. Organizations can use the privacy controls and the guidance in the paper to develop an organization-wide privacy program or enhance an already existing program.

[121] The FIPPs are widely accepted in the United States and internationally as a general framework for privacy and are reflected in other federal and international laws and policies. In a number of organizations, FIPPs serve as the basis for analyzing privacy risks and determining appropriate mitigation strategies. The Federal Enterprise Architecture Security and Privacy Profile (FEA-SPP) also provided information and materials in development of the privacy controls.

[122] All federal agencies and departments designate an SAOP/CPO as the senior organizational official with the overall organization-wide responsibility for information privacy issues. OMB Memorandum 05-08 provides guidance for the designation of SAOPs/CPOs. The term SAOP/CPO as used in this appendix means an organization's senior privacy leader, whose job title may vary from organization to organization.

ID	PRIVACY CONTROLS
DM-3	Minimization of PII Used in Testing, Training, and Research
IP	**Individual Participation and Redress**
IP-1	Consent
IP-2	Individual Access
IP-3	Redress
IP-4	Complaint Management
SE	**Security**
SE-1	Inventory of Personally Identifiable Information
SE-2	Privacy Incident Response
TR	**Transparency**
TR-1	Privacy Notice
TR-2	System of Records Notices and Privacy Act Statements
TR-3	Dissemination of Privacy Program Information
UL	**Use Limitation**
UL-1	Internal Use
UL-2	Information Sharing with Third Parties

There is a strong similarity between the structure of the privacy controls in this appendix and the structure of the security controls in Appendices F and G. For example, the control AR-1 (Governance and Privacy Program) requires organizations to develop privacy plans that can be implemented at the organizational or program level. These plans can also be used in conjunction with security plans to provide an opportunity for organizations to select the appropriate set of security and privacy controls in accordance with organizational mission/business requirements and the environments in which the organizations operate. Incorporating the fundamental concepts associated with managing information security risk helps to ensure that the employment of privacy controls is carried out in a cost-effective and risk-based manner while simultaneously meeting compliance requirements. Standardized privacy controls and assessment procedures (developed to evaluate the effectiveness of the controls) will provide a more disciplined and structured approach for satisfying federal privacy requirements and demonstrating compliance with those requirements.

In summary, the Privacy Appendix achieves several important objectives. The appendix:

- Provides a structured set of privacy controls, based on best practices, that helps organizations comply with applicable federal laws, Executive Orders, directives, instructions, regulations, policies, standards, guidance, and organization-specific issuances;

- Establishes a linkage and relationship between privacy and security controls for purposes of enforcing respective privacy and security requirements that may overlap in concept and in implementation within federal information systems, programs, and organizations;

- Demonstrates the applicability of the NIST Risk Management Framework in the selection, implementation, assessment, and ongoing monitoring of privacy controls deployed in federal information systems, programs, and organizations; and

- Promotes closer cooperation between privacy and security officials within the federal government to help achieve the objectives of senior leaders/executives in enforcing the requirements in federal privacy legislation, policies, regulations, directives, standards, and guidance.

HOW TO USE THIS APPENDIX

The privacy controls outlined in this publication are primarily for use by an organization's Senior Agency Official for Privacy (SAOP)/Chief Privacy Officer (CPO) when working with program managers, mission/business owners, information owners/stewards, Chief Information Officers, Chief Information Security Officers, information system developers/integrators, and risk executives to determine how best to incorporate effective privacy protections and practices (i.e., privacy controls) within organizational programs and information systems and the environments in which they operate. The privacy controls facilitate the organization's efforts to comply with privacy requirements affecting those organizational programs and/or systems that collect, use, maintain, share, or dispose of personally identifiable information (PII) or other activities that raise privacy risks. While the security controls in Appendix F are allocated to the low, moderate, and high baselines in Appendix D, the privacy controls are selected and implemented based on the privacy requirements of organizations and the need to protect the PII of individuals collected and maintained by organizational information systems and programs, in accordance with federal privacy legislation, policies, directives, regulations, guidelines, and best practices.

Organizations analyze and apply each privacy control with respect to their distinct mission/business and operational needs based on their legal authorities and obligations. Implementation of the privacy controls may vary based upon this analysis (e.g., organizations that are defined as *covered entities* pursuant to the Health Insurance Portability and Accountability Act [HIPAA] may have additional requirements that are not specifically enumerated in this publication). This enables organizations to determine the information practices that are compliant with law and policy and those that may need review. It also enables organizations to tailor the privacy controls to meet their defined and specific needs at the organization level, mission/business process level, and information system level. Organizations with national security or law enforcement authorities take those authorities as well as privacy interests into account in determining how to apply the privacy controls in their operational environments. Similarly, organizations subject to the Confidential Information Protection and Statistical Efficiency Act (CIPSEA), implement the privacy controls consistent with that Act. All organizations implement the privacy controls consistent with the Privacy Act of 1974, 5 U.S.C. § 552a, subject to any exceptions and/or exemptions.

Privacy control enhancements described in Appendix J reflect best practices which organizations should strive to achieve, but are not mandatory. Organizations should decide when to apply control enhancements to support their particular missions/business functions. Specific *overlays* for privacy, developed in accordance with the guidance in Section 3.2 and Appendix I, can also be considered to facilitate the tailoring of the security control baselines in Appendix D with the requisite privacy controls to ensure that both security and privacy requirements can be satisfied by organizations. Many of the security controls in Appendix F provide the fundamental information protection for confidentiality, integrity, and availability within organizational information systems and the environments in which those systems operate—protection that is essential for strong and effective privacy.

Organizations document the agreed upon privacy controls to be implemented in organizational programs and information systems and the environments in which they operate. At the discretion of the implementing organization, privacy controls may be documented in a distinct privacy plan or incorporated into other risk management documents (e.g., system security plans). Organizations also establish appropriate assessment methodologies to determine the extent to which the privacy controls are implemented correctly, operating as intended, and producing the desired outcome with respect to meeting designated privacy requirements. Organizational assessments of privacy controls can be conducted either by the SAOP/CPO alone or jointly with the other organizational risk management offices including the information security office.

Implementation Tip

- Select and implement privacy controls based on the privacy requirements of organizations and the need to protect the personally identifiable information (PII) of individuals collected and maintained by systems and programs.

- Coordinate privacy control selection and implementation with the organizational Risk Executive Function, mission/business owners, enterprise architects, Chief Information Officer, SAOP/CPO, and Chief Information Security Officer.

- View the privacy controls in Appendix J from the same perspective as the Program Management controls in Appendix G—that is, the controls are implemented for each organizational information system irrespective of the FIPS 199 categorization for that system.

- Select and implement the optional privacy control enhancements when there is a demonstrated need for additional privacy protection for individuals and PII.

- Apply the privacy controls consistent with any specific exceptions and exemptions included in legislation, Executive Orders, directives, policies, and regulations (e.g., law enforcement or national security considerations).

FAMILY: AUTHORITY AND PURPOSE

> This family ensures that organizations: (i) identify the legal bases that authorize a particular personally identifiable information (PII) collection or activity that impacts privacy; and (ii) specify in their notices the purpose(s) for which PII is collected.

AP-1 AUTHORITY TO COLLECT

Control: The organization determines and documents the legal authority that permits the collection, use, maintenance, and sharing of personally identifiable information (PII), either generally or in support of a specific program or information system need.

Supplemental Guidance: Before collecting PII, the organization determines whether the contemplated collection of PII is legally authorized. Program officials consult with the Senior Agency Official for Privacy (SAOP)/Chief Privacy Officer (CPO) and legal counsel regarding the authority of any program or activity to collect PII. The authority to collect PII is documented in the System of Records Notice (SORN) and/or Privacy Impact Assessment (PIA) or other applicable documentation such as Privacy Act Statements or Computer Matching Agreements. Related controls: AR-2, DM-1, TR-1, TR-2.

Control Enhancements: None.

References: The Privacy Act of 1974, 5 U.S.C. § 552a (e); Section 208(c), E-Government Act of 2002 (P.L. 107-347); OMB Circular A-130, Appendix I.

AP-2 PURPOSE SPECIFICATION

Control: The organization describes the purpose(s) for which personally identifiable information (PII) is collected, used, maintained, and shared in its privacy notices.

Supplemental Guidance: Often, statutory language expressly authorizes specific collections and uses of PII. When statutory language is written broadly and thus subject to interpretation, organizations ensure, in consultation with the Senior Agency Official for Privacy (SAOP)/Chief Privacy Officer (CPO) and legal counsel, that there is a close nexus between the general authorization and any specific collection of PII. Once the specific purposes have been identified, the purposes are clearly described in the related privacy compliance documentation, including but not limited to Privacy Impact Assessments (PIAs), System of Records Notices (SORNs), and Privacy Act Statements provided at the time of collection (e.g., on forms organizations use to collect PII). Further, in order to avoid unauthorized collections or uses of PII, personnel who handle PII receive training on the organizational authorities for collecting PII, authorized uses of PII, and on the contents of the notice. Related controls: AR-2, AR-4, AR-5, DM-1, DM-2, TR-1, TR-2, UL-1, UL-2.

Control Enhancements: None.

References: The Privacy Act of 1974, 5 U.S.C. § 552a (e)(3)(A)-(B); Sections 208(b), (c), E-Government Act of 2002 (P.L. 107-347).

FAMILY: ACCOUNTABILITY, AUDIT, AND RISK MANAGEMENT

> This family enhances public confidence through effective controls for governance, monitoring, risk management, and assessment to demonstrate that organizations are complying with applicable privacy protection requirements and minimizing overall privacy risk.

AR-1   GOVERNANCE AND PRIVACY PROGRAM

Control: The organization:

a. Appoints a Senior Agency Official for Privacy (SAOP)/Chief Privacy Officer (CPO) accountable for developing, implementing, and maintaining an organization-wide governance and privacy program to ensure compliance with all applicable laws and regulations regarding the collection, use, maintenance, sharing, and disposal of personally identifiable information (PII) by programs and information systems;

b. Monitors federal privacy laws and policy for changes that affect the privacy program;

c. Allocates [*Assignment: organization-defined allocation of budget and staffing*] sufficient resources to implement and operate the organization-wide privacy program;

d. Develops a strategic organizational privacy plan for implementing applicable privacy controls, policies, and procedures;

e. Develops, disseminates, and implements operational privacy policies and procedures that govern the appropriate privacy and security controls for programs, information systems, or technologies involving PII; and

f. Updates privacy plan, policies, and procedures [*Assignment: organization-defined frequency, at least biennially*].

Supplemental Guidance: The development and implementation of a comprehensive governance and privacy program demonstrates organizational accountability for and commitment to the protection of individual privacy. Accountability begins with the appointment of an SAOP/CPO with the authority, mission, resources, and responsibility to develop and implement a multifaceted privacy program. The SAOP/CPO, in consultation with legal counsel, information security officials, and others as appropriate: (i) ensures the development, implementation, and enforcement of privacy policies and procedures; (ii) defines roles and responsibilities for protecting PII; (iii) determines the level of information sensitivity with regard to PII holdings; (iv) identifies the laws, regulations, and internal policies that apply to the PII; (v) monitors privacy best practices; and (vi) monitors/audits compliance with identified privacy controls.

To further accountability, the SAOP/CPO develops privacy plans to document the privacy requirements of organizations and the privacy and security controls in place or planned for meeting those requirements. The plan serves as evidence of organizational privacy operations and supports resource requests by the SAOP/CPO. A single plan or multiple plans may be necessary depending upon the organizational structures, requirements, and resources, and the plan(s) may vary in comprehensiveness. For example, a one-page privacy plan may cover privacy policies, documentation, and controls already in place, such as Privacy Impact Assessments (PIA) and System of Records Notices (SORN). A comprehensive plan may include a baseline of privacy controls selected from this appendix and include: (i) processes for conducting privacy risk assessments; (ii) templates and guidance for completing PIAs and SORNs; (iii) privacy training and awareness requirements; (iv) requirements for contractors processing PII; (v) plans for eliminating unnecessary PII holdings; and (vi) a framework for measuring annual performance goals and objectives for implementing identified privacy controls.

Control Enhancements: None.

References: The Privacy Act of 1974, 5 U.S.C. § 552a; E-Government Act of 2002 (P.L. 107-347); Federal Information Security Management Act (FISMA) of 2002, 44 U.S.C. § 3541; OMB Memoranda 03-22, 05-08, 07-16; OMB Circular A-130; Federal Enterprise Architecture Security and Privacy Profile.

AR-2 PRIVACY IMPACT AND RISK ASSESSMENT

Control: The organization:

a. Documents and implements a privacy risk management process that assesses privacy risk to individuals resulting from the collection, sharing, storing, transmitting, use, and disposal of personally identifiable information (PII); and

b. Conducts Privacy Impact Assessments (PIAs) for information systems, programs, or other activities that pose a privacy risk in accordance with applicable law, OMB policy, or any existing organizational policies and procedures.

Supplemental Guidance: Organizational privacy risk management processes operate across the life cycles of all mission/business processes that collect, use, maintain, share, or dispose of PII. The tools and processes for managing risk are specific to organizational missions and resources. They include, but are not limited to, the conduct of PIAs. The PIA is both a process and the document that is the outcome of that process. OMB Memorandum 03-22 provides guidance to organizations for implementing the privacy provisions of the E-Government Act of 2002, including guidance on when PIAs are required for information systems. Some organizations may be required by law or policy to extend the PIA requirement to other activities involving PII or otherwise impacting privacy (e.g., programs, projects, or regulations). PIAs are conducted to identify privacy risks and identify methods to mitigate those risks. PIAs are also conducted to ensure that programs or information systems comply with legal, regulatory, and policy requirements. PIAs also serve as notice to the public of privacy practices. PIAs are performed before developing or procuring information systems, or initiating programs or projects, that collect, use, maintain, or share PII and are updated when changes create new privacy risks.

Control Enhancements: None.

References: Section 208, E-Government Act of 2002 (P.L. 107-347); Federal Information Security Management Act (FISMA) of 2002, 44 U.S.C. § 3541; OMB Memoranda 03-22, 05-08, 10-23.

AR-3 PRIVACY REQUIREMENTS FOR CONTRACTORS AND SERVICE PROVIDERS

Control: The organization:

a. Establishes privacy roles, responsibilities, and access requirements for contractors and service providers; and

b. Includes privacy requirements in contracts and other acquisition-related documents.

Supplemental Guidance: Contractors and service providers include, but are not limited to, information providers, information processors, and other organizations providing information system development, information technology services, and other outsourced applications. Organizations consult with legal counsel, the Senior Agency Official for Privacy (SAOP)/Chief Privacy Officer (CPO), and contracting officers about applicable laws, directives, policies, or regulations that may impact implementation of this control. Related control: AR-1, AR-5, SA-4.

Control Enhancements: None.

References: The Privacy Act of 1974, 5 U.S.C. § 552a(m); Federal Acquisition Regulation, 48 C.F.R. Part 24; OMB Circular A-130.

AR-4 PRIVACY MONITORING AND AUDITING

Control: The organization monitors and audits privacy controls and internal privacy policy [*Assignment: organization-defined frequency*] to ensure effective implementation.

Supplemental Guidance: To promote accountability, organizations identify and address gaps in privacy compliance, management, operational, and technical controls by conducting regular assessments (e.g., internal risk assessments). These assessments can be self-assessments or third-party audits that result in reports on compliance gaps identified in programs, projects, and information systems. In addition to auditing for effective implementation of all privacy controls identified in this appendix, organizations assess whether they: (i) implement a process to embed privacy considerations into the life cycle of personally identifiable information (PII), programs, information systems, mission/business processes, and technology; (ii) monitor for changes to applicable privacy laws, regulations, and policies; (iii) track programs, information systems, and applications that collect and maintain PII to ensure compliance; (iv) ensure that access to PII is only on a *need-to-know* basis; and (v) ensure that PII is being maintained and used only for the legally authorized purposes identified in the public notice(s).

Organizations also: (i) implement technology to audit for the security, appropriate use, and loss of PII; (ii) perform reviews to ensure physical security of documents containing PII; (iii) assess contractor compliance with privacy requirements; and (iv) ensure that corrective actions identified as part of the assessment process are tracked and monitored until audit findings are corrected. The organization Senior Agency Official for Privacy (SAOP)/Chief Privacy Officer (CPO) coordinates monitoring and auditing efforts with information security officials and ensures that the results are provided to senior managers and oversight officials. Related controls: AR-6, AR-7, AU-1, AU-2, AU-3, AU-6, AU-12, CA-7, TR-1, UL-2.

Control Enhancements: None.

References: The Privacy Act of 1974, 5 U.S.C. § 552a; Federal Information Security Management Act (FISMA) of 2002, 44 U.S.C. § 3541; Section 208, E-Government Act of 2002 (P.L. 107-347); OMB Memoranda 03-22, 05-08, 06-16, 07-16; OMB Circular A-130.

AR-5 PRIVACY AWARENESS AND TRAINING

Control: The organization:

a. Develops, implements, and updates a comprehensive training and awareness strategy aimed at ensuring that personnel understand privacy responsibilities and procedures;

b. Administers basic privacy training [*Assignment: organization-defined frequency, at least annually*] and targeted, role-based privacy training for personnel having responsibility for personally identifiable information (PII) or for activities that involve PII [*Assignment: organization-defined frequency, at least annually*]; and

c. Ensures that personnel certify (manually or electronically) acceptance of responsibilities for privacy requirements [*Assignment: organization-defined frequency, at least annually*].

Supplemental Guidance: Through implementation of a privacy training and awareness strategy, the organization promotes a culture of privacy. Privacy training and awareness programs typically focus on broad topics, such as responsibilities under the Privacy Act of 1974 and E-Government Act of 2002 and the consequences of failing to carry out those responsibilities, how to identify new privacy risks, how to mitigate privacy risks, and how and when to report privacy incidents. Privacy training may also target data collection and use requirements identified in public notices, such as Privacy Impact Assessments (PIAs) or System of Records Notices (SORNs) for a program or information system. Specific training methods may include: (i) mandatory annual privacy awareness training; (ii) targeted, role-based training; (iii) internal privacy program websites; (iv) manuals, guides, and handbooks; (v) slide presentations; (vi) events (e.g., privacy awareness week, privacy clean-up day); (vii) posters and brochures; and (viii) email messages to all employees and contractors. Organizations update training based on changing statutory, regulatory, mission, program, business process, and information system requirements, or on the results of compliance monitoring and auditing. Where appropriate, organizations may provide privacy training as part of existing information security training. Related controls: AR-3, AT-2, AT-3, TR-1.

Control Enhancements: None.

References: The Privacy Act of 1974, 5 U.S.C. § 552a(e); Section 208, E-Government Act of 2002 (P.L. 107-347); OMB Memoranda 03-22, 07-16.

AR-6 PRIVACY REPORTING

Control: The organization develops, disseminates, and updates reports to the Office of Management and Budget (OMB), Congress, and other oversight bodies, as appropriate, to demonstrate accountability with specific statutory and regulatory privacy program mandates, and to senior management and other personnel with responsibility for monitoring privacy program progress and compliance.

Supplemental Guidance: Through internal and external privacy reporting, organizations promote accountability and transparency in organizational privacy operations. Reporting also helps organizations to determine progress in meeting privacy compliance requirements and privacy controls, compare performance across the federal government, identify vulnerabilities and gaps in policy and implementation, and identify success models. Types of privacy reports include: (i) annual Senior Agency Official for Privacy (SAOP) reports to OMB; (ii) reports to Congress required by the *Implementing Regulations of the 9/11 Commission Act*; and (iii) other public reports required by specific statutory mandates or internal policies of organizations. The organization Senior Agency Official for Privacy (SAOP)/Chief Privacy Officer (CPO) consults with legal counsel, where appropriate, to ensure that organizations meet all applicable privacy reporting requirements.

Control Enhancements: None.

References: The Privacy Act of 1974, 5 U.S.C. § 552a; Section 208, E-Government Act of 2002 (P.L. 107-347); Federal Information Security Management Act (FISMA) of 2002, 44 U.S.C. § 3541; Section 803, 9/11 Commission Act, 42 U.S.C. § 2000ee-1; Section 804, 9/11 Commission Act, 42 U.S.C. § 2000ee-3; Section 522, Consolidated Appropriations Act of 2005 (P.L. 108-447); OMB Memoranda 03-22; OMB Circular A-130.

AR-7 PRIVACY-ENHANCED SYSTEM DESIGN AND DEVELOPMENT

Control: The organization designs information systems to support privacy by automating privacy controls.

Supplemental Guidance: To the extent feasible, when designing organizational information systems, organizations employ technologies and system capabilities that automate privacy controls on the collection, use, retention, and disclosure of personally identifiable information (PII). By building privacy controls into system design and development, organizations mitigate privacy risks to PII, thereby reducing the likelihood of information system breaches and other privacy-related incidents. Organizations also conduct periodic reviews of systems to determine the need for updates to maintain compliance with the Privacy Act and the organization's privacy policy. Regardless of whether automated privacy controls are employed, organizations regularly monitor information system use and sharing of PII to ensure that the use/sharing is consistent with the authorized purposes identified in the Privacy Act and/or in the public notice of organizations, or in a manner compatible with those purposes. Related controls: AC-6, AR-4, AR-5, DM-2, TR-1.

Control Enhancements: None.

References: The Privacy Act of 1974, 5 U.S.C. § 552a(e)(10); Sections 208(b) and(c), E-Government Act of 2002 (P.L. 107-347); OMB Memorandum 03-22.

AR-8 ACCOUNTING OF DISCLOSURES

Control: The organization:

a. Keeps an accurate accounting of disclosures of information held in each system of records under its control, including:

  (1) Date, nature, and purpose of each disclosure of a record; and

  (2) Name and address of the person or agency to which the disclosure was made;

b. Retains the accounting of disclosures for the life of the record or five years after the disclosure is made, whichever is longer; and

c. Makes the accounting of disclosures available to the person named in the record upon request.

Supplemental Guidance: The Senior Agency Official for Privacy (SAOP)/Chief Privacy Officer (CPO) periodically consults with managers of organization systems of record to ensure that the required accountings of disclosures of records are being properly maintained and provided to persons named in those records consistent with the dictates of the Privacy Act. Organizations are not required to keep an accounting of disclosures when the disclosures are made to individuals with a need to know, are made pursuant to the Freedom of Information Act, or are made to a law enforcement agency pursuant to 5 U.S.C. § 552a(c)(3). Heads of agencies can promulgate rules to exempt certain systems of records from the requirement to provide the accounting of disclosures to individuals. Related control: IP-2.

Control Enhancements: None.

References: The Privacy Act of 1974, 5 U.S.C. § 552a (c)(1), (c)(3), (j), (k).

FAMILY: DATA QUALITY AND INTEGRITY

> This family enhances public confidence that any personally identifiable information (PII) collected and maintained by organizations is accurate, relevant, timely, and complete for the purpose for which it is to be used, as specified in public notices.

DI-1   DATA QUALITY

Control: The organization:

a. Confirms to the greatest extent practicable upon collection or creation of personally identifiable information (PII), the accuracy, relevance, timeliness, and completeness of that information;

b. Collects PII directly from the individual to the greatest extent practicable;

c. Checks for, and corrects as necessary, any inaccurate or outdated PII used by its programs or systems [*Assignment: organization-defined frequency*]; and

d. Issues guidelines ensuring and maximizing the quality, utility, objectivity, and integrity of disseminated information.

Supplemental Guidance: Organizations take reasonable steps to confirm the accuracy and relevance of PII. Such steps may include, for example, editing and validating addresses as they are collected or entered into information systems using automated address verification look-up application programming interfaces (API). The types of measures taken to protect data quality are based on the nature and context of the PII, how it is to be used, and how it was obtained. Measures taken to validate the accuracy of PII that is used to make determinations about the rights, benefits, or privileges of individuals under federal programs may be more comprehensive than those used to validate less sensitive PII. Additional steps may be necessary to validate PII that is obtained from sources other than individuals or the authorized representatives of individuals.

When PII is of a sufficiently sensitive nature (e.g., when it is used for annual reconfirmation of a taxpayer's income for a recurring benefit), organizations incorporate mechanisms into information systems and develop corresponding procedures for how frequently, and by what method, the information is to be updated. Related controls: AP-2, DI-2, DM-1, IP-3, SI-10.

Control Enhancements:

(1) DATA QUALITY | VALIDATE PII

The organization requests that the individual or individual's authorized representative validate PII during the collection process.

(2) DATA QUALITY | RE-VALIDATE PII

The organization requests that the individual or individual's authorized representative revalidate that PII collected is still accurate [*Assignment: organization-defined frequency*].

References: The Privacy Act of 1974, 5 U.S.C. § 552a (c) and (e); Treasury and General Government Appropriations Act for Fiscal Year 2001 (P.L. 106-554), app C § 515, 114 Stat. 2763A-153-4; Paperwork Reduction Act, 44 U.S.C. § 3501; OMB Guidelines for Ensuring and Maximizing the Quality, Objectivity, Utility, and Integrity of Information Disseminated by Federal Agencies (October 2001); OMB Memorandum 07-16.

DI-2   DATA INTEGRITY AND DATA INTEGRITY BOARD

Control: The organization:

a. Documents processes to ensure the integrity of personally identifiable information (PII) through existing security controls; and

b. Establishes a Data Integrity Board when appropriate to oversee organizational Computer Matching Agreements[123] and to ensure that those agreements comply with the computer matching provisions of the Privacy Act.

Supplemental Guidance: Organizations conducting or participating in Computer Matching Agreements with other organizations regarding applicants for and recipients of financial assistance or payments under federal benefit programs or regarding certain computerized comparisons involving federal personnel or payroll records establish a Data Integrity Board to oversee and coordinate their implementation of such matching agreements. In many organizations, the Data Integrity Board is led by the Senior Agency Official for Privacy (SAOP)/Chief Privacy Officer (CPO). The Data Integrity Board ensures that controls are in place to maintain both the quality and the integrity of data shared under Computer Matching Agreements. Related controls: AC-1, AC-3, AC-4, AC-6, AC-17, AC-22, AU-2, AU-3, AU-6, AU-10, AU-11, DI-1, SC-8, SC-28, UL-2.

Control Enhancements:

(1) *DATA INTEGRITY AND DATA INTEGRITY BOARD | PUBLISH AGREEMENTS ON WEBSITE*
The organization publishes Computer Matching Agreements on its public website.

References: The Privacy Act of 1974, 5 U.S.C. §§ 552a (a)(8)(A), (o), (p), (u); OMB Circular A-130, Appendix I.

---

[123] Organizations enter into Computer Matching Agreements in connection with computer matching programs to which they are a party. With certain exceptions, a computer matching program is any computerized comparison of two or more automated systems of records or a system of records with nonfederal records for the purpose of establishing or verifying the eligibility of, or continuing compliance with, statutory and regulatory requirements by, applicants for, recipients or beneficiaries of, participants in, or providers of services with respect to cash or in-kind assistance or payments under federal benefit programs or computerized comparisons of two or more automated federal personnel or payroll systems of records or a system of federal personnel or payroll records with nonfederal records. See Computer Matching and Privacy Protection Act of 1988, 5 U.S.C. § 552a (a)(8)(A).

FAMILY: DATA MINIMIZATION AND RETENTION

> This family helps organizations implement the data minimization and retention requirements to collect, use, and retain only personally identifiable information (PII) that is relevant and necessary for the purpose for which it was originally collected. Organizations retain PII for only as long as necessary to fulfill the purpose(s) specified in public notices and in accordance with a National Archives and Records Administration (NARA)-approved record retention schedule.

DM-1 MINIMIZATION OF PERSONALLY IDENTIFIABLE INFORMATION

Control: The organization:

a. Identifies the minimum personally identifiable information (PII) elements that are relevant and necessary to accomplish the legally authorized purpose of collection;

b. Limits the collection and retention of PII to the minimum elements identified for the purposes described in the notice and for which the individual has provided consent; and

c. Conducts an initial evaluation of PII holdings and establishes and follows a schedule for regularly reviewing those holdings [*Assignment: organization-defined frequency, at least annually*] to ensure that only PII identified in the notice is collected and retained, and that the PII continues to be necessary to accomplish the legally authorized purpose.

Supplemental Guidance: Organizations take appropriate steps to ensure that the collection of PII is consistent with a purpose authorized by law or regulation. The minimum set of PII elements required to support a specific organization business process may be a subset of the PII the organization is authorized to collect. Program officials consult with the Senior Agency Official for Privacy (SAOP)/Chief Privacy Officer (CPO) and legal counsel to identify the minimum PII elements required by the information system or activity to accomplish the legally authorized purpose.

Organizations can further reduce their privacy and security risks by also reducing their inventory of PII, where appropriate. OMB Memorandum 07-16 requires organizations to conduct both an initial review and subsequent reviews of their holdings of all PII and ensure, to the maximum extent practicable, that such holdings are accurate, relevant, timely, and complete. Organizations are also directed by OMB to reduce their holdings to the minimum necessary for the proper performance of a documented organizational business purpose. OMB Memorandum 07-16 requires organizations to develop and publicize, either through a notice in the Federal Register or on their websites, a schedule for periodic reviews of their holdings to supplement the initial review. Organizations coordinate with their federal records officers to ensure that reductions in organizational holdings of PII are consistent with NARA retention schedules.

By performing periodic evaluations, organizations reduce risk, ensure that they are collecting only the data specified in the notice, and ensure that the data collected is still relevant and necessary for the purpose(s) specified in the notice. Related controls: AP-1, AP-2, AR-4, IP-1, SE-1, SI-12, TR-1.

Control Enhancements:

(1) *MINIMIZATION OF PERSONALLY IDENTIFIABLE INFORMATION | LOCATE / REMOVE / REDACT / ANONYMIZE PII*

The organization, where feasible and within the limits of technology, locates and removes/redacts specified PII and/or uses anonymization and de-identification techniques to permit use of the retained information while reducing its sensitivity and reducing the risk resulting from disclosure.

Supplemental Guidance: NIST Special Publication 800-122 provides guidance on anonymization.

References: The Privacy Act of 1974, 5 U.S.C. §552a (e); Section 208(b), E-Government Act of 2002 (P.L. 107-347); OMB Memoranda 03-22, 07-16.

DM-2 DATA RETENTION AND DISPOSAL

Control: The organization:

a. Retains each collection of personally identifiable information (PII) for [*Assignment: organization-defined time period*] to fulfill the purpose(s) identified in the notice or as required by law;

b. Disposes of, destroys, erases, and/or anonymizes the PII, regardless of the method of storage, in accordance with a NARA-approved record retention schedule and in a manner that prevents loss, theft, misuse, or unauthorized access; and

c. Uses [*Assignment: organization-defined techniques or methods*] to ensure secure deletion or destruction of PII (including originals, copies, and archived records).

Supplemental Guidance: NARA provides retention schedules that govern the disposition of federal records. Program officials coordinate with records officers and with NARA to identify appropriate retention periods and disposal methods. NARA may require organizations to retain PII longer than is operationally needed. In those situations, organizations describe such requirements in the notice. Methods of storage include, for example, electronic, optical media, or paper.

Examples of ways organizations may reduce holdings include reducing the types of PII held (e.g., delete Social Security numbers if their use is no longer needed) or shortening the retention period for PII that is maintained if it is no longer necessary to keep PII for long periods of time (this effort is undertaken in consultation with an organization's records officer to receive NARA approval). In both examples, organizations provide notice (e.g., an updated System of Records Notice) to inform the public of any changes in holdings of PII.

Certain read-only archiving techniques, such as DVDs, CDs, microfilm, or microfiche, may not permit the removal of individual records without the destruction of the entire database contained on such media. Related controls: AR-4, AU-11, DM-1, MP-1, MP-2, MP-3, MP-4, MP-5, MP-6, MP-7, MP-8, SI-12, TR-1.

Control Enhancements:

(1) DATA RETENTION AND DISPOSAL | SYSTEM CONFIGURATION

The organization, where feasible, configures its information systems to record the date PII is collected, created, or updated and when PII is to be deleted or archived under an approved record retention schedule.

References: The Privacy Act of 1974, 5 U.S.C. § 552a (e)(1), (c)(2); Section 208 (e), E-Government Act of 2002 (P.L. 107-347); 44 U.S.C. Chapters 29, 31, 33; OMB Memorandum 07-16; OMB Circular A-130; NIST Special Publication 800-88.

DM-3 MINIMIZATION OF PII USED IN TESTING, TRAINING, AND RESEARCH

Control: The organization:

a. Develops policies and procedures that minimize the use of personally identifiable information (PII) for testing, training, and research; and

b. Implements controls to protect PII used for testing, training, and research.

Supplemental Guidance: Organizations often use PII for testing new applications or information systems prior to deployment. Organizations also use PII for research purposes and for training. The use of PII in testing, research, and training increases risk of unauthorized disclosure or misuse of the information. If PII must be used, organizations take measures to minimize any associated risks and to authorize the use of and limit the amount of PII for these purposes. Organizations consult with the SAOP/CPO and legal counsel to ensure that the use of PII in testing, training, and research is compatible with the original purpose for which it was collected.

Control Enhancements:

(1) *MINIMIZATION OF PII USED IN TESTING, TRAINING, AND RESEARCH | RISK MINIMIZATION TECHNIQUES*

The organization, where feasible, uses techniques to minimize the risk to privacy of using PII for research, testing, or training.

Supplemental Guidance: Organizations can minimize risk to privacy of PII by using techniques such as de-identification.

References: NIST Special Publication 800-122.

FAMILY: INDIVIDUAL PARTICIPATION AND REDRESS

> This family addresses the need to make individuals active participants in the decision-making process regarding the collection and use of their personally identifiable information (PII). By providing individuals with access to PII and the ability to have their PII corrected or amended, as appropriate, the controls in this family enhance public confidence in organizational decisions made based on the PII.

IP-1 CONSENT

Control: The organization:

a. Provides means, where feasible and appropriate, for individuals to authorize the collection, use, maintaining, and sharing of personally identifiable information (PII) prior to its collection;

b. Provides appropriate means for individuals to understand the consequences of decisions to approve or decline the authorization of the collection, use, dissemination, and retention of PII;

c. Obtains consent, where feasible and appropriate, from individuals prior to any new uses or disclosure of previously collected PII; and

d. Ensures that individuals are aware of and, where feasible, consent to all uses of PII not initially described in the public notice that was in effect at the time the organization collected the PII.

Supplemental Guidance: Consent is fundamental to the participation of individuals in the decision-making process regarding the collection and use of their PII and the use of technologies that may increase risk to personal privacy. To obtain consent, organizations provide individuals appropriate notice of the purposes of the PII collection or technology use and a means for individuals to consent to the activity. Organizations tailor the public notice and consent mechanisms to meet operational needs. Organizations achieve awareness and consent, for example, through updated public notices.

Organizations may obtain consent through opt-in, opt-out, or implied consent. Opt-in consent is the preferred method, but it is not always feasible. Opt-in requires that individuals take affirmative action to *allow* organizations to collect or use PII. For example, opt-in consent may require an individual to click a radio button on a website, or sign a document providing consent. In contrast, opt-out requires individuals to take action to *prevent* the new or continued collection or use of such PII. For example, the Federal Trade Commission's Do-Not-Call Registry allows individuals to opt-out of receiving unsolicited telemarketing calls by requesting to be added to a list. Implied consent is the least preferred method and should be used in limited circumstances. Implied consent occurs where individuals' behavior or failure to object indicates agreement with the collection or use of PII (e.g., by entering and remaining in a building where notice has been posted that security cameras are in use, the individual implies consent to the video recording). Depending upon the nature of the program or information system, it may be appropriate to allow individuals to limit the types of PII they provide and subsequent uses of that PII. Organizational consent mechanisms include a discussion of the consequences to individuals of failure to provide PII. Consequences can vary from organization to organization. Related controls: AC-2, AP-1, TR-1, TR-2.

Control Enhancements:

(1) CONSENT | MECHANISMS SUPPORTING ITEMIZED OR TIERED CONSENT

The organization implements mechanisms to support itemized or tiered consent for specific uses of data.

Supplemental Guidance: Organizations can provide, for example, individuals' itemized choices as to whether they wish to be contacted for any of a variety of purposes. In this situation, organizations construct consent mechanisms to ensure that organizational operations comply with individual choices.

References: The Privacy Act of 1974, 5 U.S.C. § 552a (b), (e)(3); Section 208(c), E-Government Act of 2002 (P.L. 107-347); OMB Memoranda 03-22, 10-22.

IP-2 **INDIVIDUAL ACCESS**

Control: The organization:

a. Provides individuals the ability to have access to their personally identifiable information (PII) maintained in its system(s) of records;

b. Publishes rules and regulations governing how individuals may request access to records maintained in a Privacy Act system of records;

c. Publishes access procedures in System of Records Notices (SORNs); and

d. Adheres to Privacy Act requirements and OMB policies and guidance for the proper processing of Privacy Act requests.

Supplemental Guidance: Access affords individuals the ability to review PII about them held within organizational systems of records. Access includes timely, simplified, and inexpensive access to data. Organizational processes for allowing access to records may differ based on resources, legal requirements, or other factors. The organization Senior Agency Official for Privacy (SAOP)/Chief Privacy Officer (CPO) is responsible for the content of Privacy Act regulations and record request processing, in consultation with legal counsel. Access to certain types of records may not be appropriate, however, and heads of agencies may promulgate rules exempting particular systems from the access provision of the Privacy Act. In addition, individuals are not entitled to access to information compiled in reasonable anticipation of a civil action or proceeding. Related controls: AR-8, IP-3, TR-1, TR-2.

Control Enhancements: None.

References: The Privacy Act of 1974, 5 U.S.C. §§ 552a (c)(3), (d)(5), (e) (4); (j), (k), (t); OMB Circular A-130.

IP-3 **REDRESS**

Control: The organization:

a. Provides a process for individuals to have inaccurate personally identifiable information (PII) maintained by the organization corrected or amended, as appropriate; and

b. Establishes a process for disseminating corrections or amendments of the PII to other authorized users of the PII, such as external information-sharing partners and, where feasible and appropriate, notifies affected individuals that their information has been corrected or amended.

Supplemental Guidance: Redress supports the ability of individuals to ensure the accuracy of PII held by organizations. Effective redress processes demonstrate organizational commitment to data quality especially in those business functions where inaccurate data may result in inappropriate decisions or denial of benefits and services to individuals. Organizations use discretion in determining if records are to be corrected or amended, based on the scope of redress requests, the changes sought, and the impact of the changes. Individuals may appeal an adverse decision and have incorrect information amended, where appropriate.

To provide effective redress, organizations: (i) provide effective notice of the existence of a PII collection; (ii) provide plain language explanations of the processes and mechanisms for requesting access to records; (iii) establish criteria for submitting requests for correction or amendment; (iv) implement resources to analyze and adjudicate requests; (v) implement means of correcting or amending data collections; and (vi) review any decisions that may have been the result of inaccurate information.

Organizational redress processes provide responses to individuals of decisions to deny requests for correction or amendment, including the reasons for those decisions, a means to record individual objections to the organizational decisions, and a means of requesting organizational reviews of the initial determinations. Where PII is corrected or amended, organizations take steps to ensure that all authorized recipients of that PII are informed of the corrected or amended information. In instances where redress involves information obtained from other organizations, redress processes include coordination with organizations that originally collected the information. Related controls: IP-2, TR-1, TR-2, UL-2.

Control Enhancements: None.

References: The Privacy Act of 1974, 5 U.S.C. § 552a (d), (c)(4); OMB Circular A-130.

IP-4 **COMPLAINT MANAGEMENT**

Control: The organization implements a process for receiving and responding to complaints, concerns, or questions from individuals about the organizational privacy practices.

Supplemental Guidance: Complaints, concerns, and questions from individuals can serve as a valuable source of external input that ultimately improves operational models, uses of technology, data collection practices, and privacy and security safeguards. Organizations provide complaint mechanisms that are readily accessible by the public, include all information necessary for successfully filing complaints (including contact information for the Senior Agency Official for Privacy (SAOP)/Chief Privacy Officer (CPO) or other official designated to receive complaints), and are easy to use. Organizational complaint management processes include tracking mechanisms to ensure that all complaints received are reviewed and appropriately addressed in a timely manner. Related controls: AR-6, IP-3.

Control Enhancements:

(1) *COMPLAINT MANAGEMENT | RESPONSE TIMES*

The organization responds to complaints, concerns, or questions from individuals within [*Assignment: organization-defined time period*].

References: OMB Circular A-130; OMB Memoranda 07-16, 08-09.

Special Publication 800-53 Revision 4   Security and Privacy Controls for Federal Information Systems and Organizations

---

FAMILY: SECURITY

> This family supplements the security controls in Appendix F to ensure that technical, physical, and administrative safeguards are in place to protect personally identifiable information (PII) collected or maintained by organizations against loss, unauthorized access, or disclosure, and to ensure that planning and responses to privacy incidents comply with OMB policies and guidance. The controls in this family are implemented in coordination with information security personnel and in accordance with the existing NIST Risk Management Framework.

SE-1   INVENTORY OF PERSONALLY IDENTIFIABLE INFORMATION

Control: The organization:

a. Establishes, maintains, and updates [*Assignment: organization-defined frequency*] an inventory that contains a listing of all programs and information systems identified as collecting, using, maintaining, or sharing personally identifiable information (PII); and

b. Provides each update of the PII inventory to the CIO or information security official [*Assignment: organization-defined frequency*] to support the establishment of information security requirements for all new or modified information systems containing PII.

Supplemental Guidance: The PII inventory enables organizations to implement effective administrative, technical, and physical security policies and procedures to protect PII consistent with Appendix F, and to mitigate risks of PII exposure. As one method of gathering information for their PII inventories, organizations may extract the following information elements from Privacy Impact Assessments (PIA) for information systems containing PII: (i) the name and acronym for each system identified; (ii) the types of PII contained in that system; (iii) classification of level of sensitivity of all types of PII, as combined in that information system; and (iv) classification of level of potential risk of substantial harm, embarrassment, inconvenience, or unfairness to affected individuals, as well as the financial or reputational risks to organizations, if PII is exposed. Organizations take due care in updating the inventories by identifying linkable data that could create PII. Related controls: AR-1, AR-4, AR-5, AT-1, DM-1, PM-5.

Control Enhancements: None.

References: The Privacy Act of 1974, 5 U.S.C. § 552a (e) (10); Section 208(b)(2), E-Government Act of 2002 (P.L. 107-347); OMB Memorandum 03-22; OMB Circular A-130, Appendix I; FIPS Publication 199; NIST Special Publications 800-37, 800-122.

SE-2   PRIVACY INCIDENT RESPONSE

Control: The organization:

a. Develops and implements a Privacy Incident Response Plan; and

b. Provides an organized and effective response to privacy incidents in accordance with the organizational Privacy Incident Response Plan.

Supplemental Guidance: In contrast to the Incident Response (IR) family in Appendix F, which concerns a broader range of incidents affecting information security, this control uses the term Privacy Incident to describe only those incidents that relate to personally identifiable information (PII). The organization Privacy Incident Response Plan is developed under the leadership of the SAOP/CPO. The plan includes: (i) the establishment of a cross-functional Privacy Incident Response Team that reviews, approves, and participates in the execution of the Privacy Incident Response Plan; (ii) a process to determine whether notice to oversight organizations or affected individuals is appropriate and to provide that notice accordingly; (iii) a privacy risk assessment process to determine the extent of harm, embarrassment, inconvenience, or unfairness to affected individuals and, where appropriate, to take steps to mitigate any such risks; (iv) internal procedures to ensure prompt reporting by employees and contractors of any privacy incident to information security officials and the Senior Agency Official for Privacy (SAOP)/Chief Privacy Officer (CPO), consistent with organizational incident management structures; and (v) internal procedures for reporting noncompliance with organizational privacy policy by employees or contractors to appropriate management or oversight officials. Some organizations may be required by law or policy to provide notice to oversight organizations in the event of a breach. Organizations may also choose to integrate Privacy Incident Response Plans with Security Incident Response Plans, or keep the plans separate. Related controls: AR-1, AR-4, AR-5, AR-6, AU-1 through 14, IR-1 through IR-8, RA-1.

Control Enhancements: None.

References: The Privacy Act of 1974, 5 U.S.C. § 552a (e), (i)(1), and (m); Federal Information Security Management Act (FISMA) of 2002, 44 U.S.C. § 3541; OMB Memoranda 06-19, 07-16; NIST Special Publication 800-37.

FAMILY: TRANSPARENCY

> This family ensures that organizations provide public notice of their information practices and the privacy impact of their programs and activities.

TR-1   PRIVACY NOTICE

Control: The organization:

a. Provides effective notice to the public and to individuals regarding: (i) its activities that impact privacy, including its collection, use, sharing, safeguarding, maintenance, and disposal of personally identifiable information (PII); (ii) authority for collecting PII; (iii) the choices, if any, individuals may have regarding how the organization uses PII and the consequences of exercising or not exercising those choices; and (iv) the ability to access and have PII amended or corrected if necessary;

b. Describes: (i) the PII the organization collects and the purpose(s) for which it collects that information; (ii) how the organization uses PII internally; (iii) whether the organization shares PII with external entities, the categories of those entities, and the purposes for such sharing; (iv) whether individuals have the ability to consent to specific uses or sharing of PII and how to exercise any such consent; (v) how individuals may obtain access to PII; and (vi) how the PII will be protected; and

c. Revises its public notices to reflect changes in practice or policy that affect PII or changes in its activities that impact privacy, before or as soon as practicable after the change.

Supplemental Guidance: Effective notice, by virtue of its clarity, readability, and comprehensiveness, enables individuals to understand how an organization uses PII generally and, where appropriate, to make an informed decision prior to providing PII to an organization. Effective notice also demonstrates the privacy considerations that the organization has addressed in implementing its information practices. The organization may provide general public notice through a variety of means, as required by law or policy, including System of Records Notices (SORNs), Privacy Impact Assessments (PIAs), or in a website privacy policy. As required by the Privacy Act, the organization also provides direct notice to individuals via Privacy Act Statements on the paper and electronic forms it uses to collect PII, or on separate forms that can be retained by the individuals.

The organization Senior Agency Official for Privacy (SAOP)/Chief Privacy Officer (CPO) is responsible for the content of the organization's public notices, in consultation with legal counsel and relevant program managers. The public notice requirement in this control is satisfied by an organization's compliance with the public notice provisions of the Privacy Act, the E-Government Act's PIA requirement, with OMB guidance related to federal agency privacy notices, and, where applicable, with policy pertaining to participation in the Information Sharing Environment (ISE).[124] Changing PII practice or policy without prior notice is disfavored and should only be undertaken in consultation with the SAOP/CPO and counsel. Related controls: AP-1, AP-2, AR-1, AR-2, IP-1, IP-2, IP-3, UL-1, UL-2.

Control Enhancements:

(1) *PRIVACY NOTICE | REAL-TIME OR LAYERED NOTICE*
    The organization provides real-time and/or layered notice when it collects PII.

    Supplemental Guidance: Real-time notice is defined as notice at the point of collection. A layered notice approach involves providing individuals with a summary of key points in the organization's privacy policy. A second notice provides more detailed/specific information.

---

[124] The Information Sharing Environment is an approach that facilitates the sharing of terrorism and homeland security information. The ISE was established by the Intelligence Reform and Terrorism Prevention Act of 2004, Public Law 108-458, 118 Stat. 3638. See the ISE website at: http://www.ise.gov.

References: The Privacy Act of 1974, 5 U.S.C. § 552a (e)(3), (e)(4); Section 208(b), E-Government Act of 2002 (P.L. 107-347); OMB Memoranda 03-22, 07-16, 10-22, 10-23; ISE Privacy Guidelines.

TR-2 SYSTEM OF RECORDS NOTICES AND PRIVACY ACT STATEMENTS

Control: The organization:

a. Publishes System of Records Notices (SORNs) in the Federal Register, subject to required oversight processes, for systems containing personally identifiable information (PII);

b. Keeps SORNs current; and

c. Includes Privacy Act Statements on its forms that collect PII, or on separate forms that can be retained by individuals, to provide additional formal notice to individuals from whom the information is being collected.

Supplemental Guidance: Organizations issue SORNs to provide the public notice regarding PII collected in a system of records, which the Privacy Act defines as "a group of any records under the control of any agency from which information is retrieved by the name of an individual or by some identifying number, symbol, or other identifier." SORNs explain how the information is used, retained, and may be corrected, and whether certain portions of the system are subject to Privacy Act exemptions for law enforcement or national security reasons. Privacy Act Statements provide notice of: (i) the authority of organizations to collect PII; (ii) whether providing PII is mandatory or optional; (iii) the principal purpose(s) for which the PII is to be used; (iv) the intended disclosures (routine uses) of the information; and (v) the consequences of not providing all or some portion of the information requested. When information is collected verbally, organizations read a Privacy Act Statement prior to initiating the collection of PII (for example, when conducting telephone interviews or surveys). Related control: DI-2.

Control Enhancements:

(1) SYSTEM OF RECORDS NOTICES AND PRIVACY ACT STATEMENTS | PUBLIC WEBSITE PUBLICATION
The organization publishes SORNs on its public website.

References: The Privacy Act of 1974, 5 U.S.C. § 552a (e)(3); OMB Circular A-130.

TR-3 DISSEMINATION OF PRIVACY PROGRAM INFORMATION

Control: The organization:

a. Ensures that the public has access to information about its privacy activities and is able to communicate with its Senior Agency Official for Privacy (SAOP)/Chief Privacy Officer (CPO); and

b. Ensures that its privacy practices are publicly available through organizational websites or otherwise.

Supplemental Guidance: Organizations employ different mechanisms for informing the public about their privacy practices including, but not limited to, Privacy Impact Assessments (PIAs), System of Records Notices (SORNs), privacy reports, publicly available web pages, email distributions, blogs, and periodic publications (e.g., quarterly newsletters). Organizations also employ publicly facing email addresses and/or phone lines that enable the public to provide feedback and/or direct questions to privacy offices regarding privacy practices. Related control: AR-6.

Control Enhancements: None.

References: The Privacy Act of 1974, 5 U.S.C. § 552a; Section 208, E-Government Act of 2002 (P.L. 107-347); OMB Memoranda 03-22, 10-23.

FAMILY: USE LIMITATION

> This family ensures that organizations only use personally identifiable information (PII) either as specified in their public notices, in a manner compatible with those specified purposes, or as otherwise permitted by law. Implementation of the controls in this family will ensure that the scope of PII use is limited accordingly.

UL-1   INTERNAL USE

Control: The organization uses personally identifiable information (PII) internally only for the authorized purpose(s) identified in the Privacy Act and/or in public notices.

Supplemental Guidance: Organizations take steps to ensure that they use PII only for legally authorized purposes and in a manner compatible with uses identified in the Privacy Act and/or in public notices. These steps include monitoring and auditing organizational use of PII and training organizational personnel on the authorized uses of PII. With guidance from the Senior Agency Official for Privacy (SAOP)/Chief Privacy Officer (CPO) and where appropriate, legal counsel, organizations document processes and procedures for evaluating any proposed new uses of PII to assess whether they fall within the scope of the organizational authorities. Where appropriate, organizations obtain consent from individuals for the new use(s) of PII. Related controls: AP-2, AR-2, AR-3, AR-4, AR-5, IP-1, TR-1, TR-2.

Control Enhancements: None.

References: The Privacy Act of 1974, 5 U.S.C. § 552a (b)(1).

UL-2   INFORMATION SHARING WITH THIRD PARTIES

Control: The organization:

a. Shares personally identifiable information (PII) externally, only for the authorized purposes identified in the Privacy Act and/or described in its notice(s) or for a purpose that is compatible with those purposes;

b. Where appropriate, enters into Memoranda of Understanding, Memoranda of Agreement, Letters of Intent, Computer Matching Agreements, or similar agreements, with third parties that specifically describe the PII covered and specifically enumerate the purposes for which the PII may be used;

c. Monitors, audits, and trains its staff on the authorized sharing of PII with third parties and on the consequences of unauthorized use or sharing of PII; and

d. Evaluates any proposed new instances of sharing PII with third parties to assess whether the sharing is authorized and whether additional or new public notice is required.

Supplemental Guidance: The organization Senior Agency Official for Privacy (SAOP)/Chief Privacy Officer (CPO) and, where appropriate, legal counsel review and approve any proposed external sharing of PII, including with other public, international, or private sector entities, for consistency with uses described in the existing organizational public notice(s). When a proposed new instance of external sharing of PII is not currently authorized by the Privacy Act and/or specified in a notice, organizations evaluate whether the proposed external sharing is compatible with the purpose(s) specified in the notice. If the proposed sharing is compatible, organizations review, update, and republish their Privacy Impact Assessments (PIAs), System of Records Notices (SORNs), website privacy policies, and other public notices, if any, to include specific descriptions of the new uses(s) and obtain consent where appropriate and feasible. Information-sharing agreements also include security protections consistent with the sensitivity of the information being shared. Related controls: AR-3, AR-4, AR-5, AR-8, AP-2, DI-1, DI-2, IP-1, TR-1.

Control Enhancements: None.

References: The Privacy Act of 1974, 5 U.S.C. § 552a (a)(7), (b), (c), (e)(3)(C), (o); ISE Privacy Guidelines.

Acknowledgements

This appendix was developed by the National Institute of Standards and Technology and the Privacy Committee of the Federal Chief Information Officer (CIO) Council. In particular, we wish to thank the members of the Privacy Committee's Best Practices Subcommittee and its Privacy Controls Appendix Working Group—Claire Barrett, Chris Brannigan, Pamela Carcirieri, Debra Diener, Deborah Kendall, Martha Landesberg, Steven Lott, Lewis Oleinick, and Roanne Shaddox—for their valuable insights, subject matter expertise, and overall contributions in helping to develop the content for this appendix to Special Publication 800-53. We also wish to recognize and thank Erika McCallister, Toby Levin, James McKenzie, Julie McEwen, and Richard Graubart for their significant contributions to this project. A special note of thanks goes to Peggy Himes and Elizabeth Lennon for their superb administrative support. The authors also gratefully acknowledge and appreciate the significant contributions from individuals, groups, and organizations in the public and private sectors, whose thoughtful and constructive comments improved the overall quality, thoroughness, and usefulness of this publication.

Made in the USA
Columbia, SC
16 October 2020